Peter Harclerode was commissioned into the Irish Guards in 1967, thereafter serving in the UK, Middle East and Far East. In 1973, he transferred to the 2nd King Edward VII's Own Goorkhas (The Sirmoor Rifles) and served with the 1st Battalion in Brunei and Hong Kong. As a Territorial Army officer, he also saw service with the Special Air Service and The Parachute Regiment. He is now established as one of our leading writers on international terrorism and special warfare.

WINGS OF WAR
Airborne Warfare 1918–1945

PETER HARCLERODE

CASSELL

This book is dedicated to
all those who went to war by air

'Where is the prince who can afford so to cover his country with
troops for its defence, as that ten thousand men descending from the
clouds might not, in many places, do an infinite deal of mischief
before force could be brought together to repel them?'

BENJAMIN FRANKLIN, 1784

Cassell Military Paperbacks

Cassell
Wellington House, 125 Strand
London WC2R 0BB

1 3 5 7 9 10 8 6 4 2

Copyright © Peter Harclerode 2005

First published in 2005
by Weidenfeld & Nicolson
This Cassell Military Paperbacks edition 2006

British Library Cataloguing-in-Publication Data.
A catalogue record for this book is available from the British Library.

ISBN-13 978-0-3043-6730-6
ISBN-10 0-3043-6730-3

Printed and bound in Great Britain by
Cox & Wyman Ltd, Reading, Berkshire

The Orion Publishing Group's policy is to use papers that are natural,
renewable and recyclable products and made from wood grown in
sustainable forests. The logging and manufacturing processes are expected
to conform to the environmental regulations of the country of origin.

www.orionbooks.co.uk

CONTENTS

LIST OF MAPS

INTRODUCTION

Two of Leonardo da Vinci's distinctions are his inventions of the parachute and the glider. On 9 August 1918, almost 400 years after his death, one of his fellow countrymen was dropped behind enemy lines in what is believed to have been the first ever insertion of a parachutist on an operational mission.

Italy formed a number of airborne units in the 1930s, closely followed by Russia and Germany, who devoted considerable effort to the development of airborne forces, both parachute and gliderborne troops. These first saw operational service when the Luftwaffe's fallschirmjäger of 7th Air Division spearheaded the German invasions of Denmark, Norway and the Low Countries in 1940 and the invasion of Crete the following year. The Germans invaded Russia in 1941 and during the following four years Russian airborne forces played their part in the defence of their country.

Britain's newly formed airborne forces carried out their first operation early in 1941. Subsequently, 1st Parachute Brigade, by then part of 1st Airborne Division, deployed to North Africa. In mid-1942 the US Army formed the 82nd and 101st Airborne Divisions and by the end of 1943 the British Army had added another formation, 6th Airborne Division, to its order of battle. From 1942 to 1945, during the campaigns in North Africa, Sicily, Italy and Europe, Allied airborne forces won undying fame during the invasion of Normandy, the epic battle at Arnhem, the Ardennes campaign, and the crossing of the Rhine.

Airborne operations also featured in the war in the Pacific, the first being conducted in the Dutch East Indies in early 1942 by paratroops of the Imperial Japanese Navy. The US 503rd Parachute Infantry Regiment was deployed in the Pacific in December 1942, its first operation being mounted nine months later in New Guinea. The US 11th Airborne Division arrived in mid-1943and subsequently conducted a number of airborne operations in the Philippines. Among the final operations in the Pacific were an airborne assault by a battalion of the 503rd Parachute Regimental Combat Team on the island of Corregidor and a raid by a battalion of the 11th Airborne Division on a Japanese prisoner-of-war camp on Leyte.

The Indian Army had meanwhile created its own airborne forces in the form of 50th Indian Parachute Brigade, subsequently expanded to become 44th Indian Airborne Division. In March 1944, the British landed four brigades and three smaller detachments of Chindits by glider and transport aircraft behind Japanese lines in Burma where they operated for almost six months before being withdrawn. The following year witnessed the only major parachute operation in Burma when at the beginning of May 1945 a battalion of 44th Indian Airborne Division was dropped near Rangoon prior to an amphibious assault on the Burmese capital.

Throughout the Second World War airborne forces played important roles in the majority of campaigns, and by the end of the conflict techniques for the aerial delivery of troops and equipment were well developed. At the crossing of the Rhine, 1,545 aircraft and 1,305 gliders delivered 17,000 paratroops and gliderborne troops, along with their heavy weapons and equipment, within the space of two hours. Nevertheless, in almost every operation, losses were high, notably in Crete, where the Germans suffered heavy casualties, and at Arnhem where the British 1st Airborne Division was decimated. Despite their successes during the crossing of the Rhine, in just a few hours the British 6th and US 17th Airborne Divisions also sustained heavy losses totalling over 2,500 men.

In writing this book, I had occasion to call on the expertise of a number of individuals. General Sir Anthony Farrar-Hockley and Mr Doug Markham, who served with 6th Parachute Battalion, helped me with details of 2nd Independent Parachute Brigade Group's part in Operation Rugby in Southern France in August 1944, as did Major Dick Hargreaves, of 4th Parachute Battalion, and Colonels Bill Corby and George Christie who served with 5th Parachute Battalion. Colonel David M. Glanz, US Army (Retired), the highly respected military historian, former director of the US Army's Foreign Military Studies Office and author of *A History of Soviet Airborne Forces*, the first detailed and authoritative study of Soviet airborne operations in the Second World War, was kind enough to allow me extensive use of material from his book. Alan Brown, Assistant Curator and Archivist at the Airborne Forces Museum, was most generous with his help, as was Major Bob Bragg, whose knowledge of and personal archive on airborne forces worldwide is unmatched. Last but by no means least, my old friend Major Jack Watson, who served with 13th Parachute Battalion, as always was unfailingly generous with his extensive knowledge and memories of 6th Airborne Division's operations in Normandy and the Ardennes, and on the crossing of the Rhine.

I am most grateful to them all and offer my sincerest thanks for their assistance.

Peter Harclerode 2005

CHAPTER ONE

EARLY DAYS

The first use of parachutists on military missions took place during the last months of the First World War when the Italians, who were fighting alongside the British, despatched a number of individuals on reconnaissance and sabotage missions. Four parachutes of the 'Guardian Angel' type, invented by Everard Calthrop, had been supplied by the British to the Italian Eighth Army, based in the area of Resana in the northern Italian province of Treviso. Members of a Royal Flying Corps unit, No. 139 Squadron, commanded by Major William Barker, provided training in the use and maintenance of the parachutes, as well as in the techniques of parachuting from an aircraft. Instruction was given by Barker and his adjutant Captain William Wedgwood Benn at an air base at Villaverla, near Vicenza.

A small group of officers was selected and trained for the reconnaissance and sabotage missions which were carried out under the auspices of the Eighth Army's intelligence branch headed by a Colonel Dupont. The group of four comprised Lieutenants Alessandro Tandura, Ferruccio Nicoloso, Antonio Pavan and Arrigo Barnaba. The first mission was carried out by Lieutenant Tandura who, on the night of 9 August 1918, took off from Villaverla in a Savoia-Pomilio S.P.4 twin-engined reconnaissance aircraft flown by Major Barker, with Captain Wedgwood Benn acting as navigator and observer. In addition to a pistol and fighting knife, Tandura was equipped with civilian clothing, cash in the form of 2,000 Austrian crowns and 500 Italian lire, food and homing pigeons. Seated on a trapdoor in the rear of the aircraft behind the pilot, he faced the tail. The rigging lines of his Guardian Angel parachute led from his harness to the canopy in a cone-shaped container mounted under the S.P.4's fuselage behind the undercarriage.

En route to the target area of Vittorio Veneto, the aircraft encountered a violent thunderstorm over Conegliano and Barker had difficulty in keeping control. Nevertheless, he succeeded in reaching the target area and in reducing his altitude and speed. On arriving at the release point over the intended dropping zone (DZ) Wedgwood Benn, positioned in an open cockpit in the nose, operated the trapdoor and Tandura dropped away, his rigging lines extracting the canopy from its container. After a successful descent, he landed near Vittorio Veneto. The aircraft meanwhile dropped three bombs on its return journey to disguise its true mission and to provide Barker and Wedgwood Benn with a cover story in the event of their being shot down.

During the ensuing three months Tandura provided information on Austrian troop movements and dispositions, twice narrowly avoiding capture before eventually being caught. En route to a prison camp in Serbia, however, he managed to jump from a moving train and made good his escape, subsequently carrying out several sabotage tasks. He survived the war to be decorated with Italy's highest award, the Gold Medal for Valour.

Following the success of Tandura's mission, a number of other Italians were also dropped behind Austrian lines to carry out similar tasks, among them Lieutenants Nicoloso, Barnaba, de Carlo and Corporal de Carli.

The idea of airborne delivery of troops and weapons on a large scale, however, was conceived in October 1918, just a month before the armistice. On 17 October, Brigadier General William 'Billy' Mitchell, in charge of the United States Army Air Corps element within the US

First Army, commanded by General John J. 'Black Jack' Pershing, proposed the delivery by air of the entire 12,000-strong 1st Infantry Division behind German lines into the area of the city of Metz, the landing to take place in conjunction with a large Allied thrust on the ground.

The US First Army had just scored a significant victory in a major battle at Saint-Mihiel lasting thirty–six hours, during which it had taken prisoner 15,000 German troops and captured 250 artillery pieces. On the morning of the 17th, Pershing was anxious to visit his front, some five miles to the north of Verdun, and his initial reaction was to disregard Mitchell's proposal, insisting that the primary task of the latter's squadrons was to achieve air superiority and thus prevent enemy aircraft from conducting attacks on his troops. Thereafter, they were to focus on attacking any German troop concentrations threatening the US First Army, after which they were to carry out reconnaissance missions to gather information on enemy troop movements.

Mitchell agreed with Pershing's priority of tasks for the provision of air support for his divisions. He himself was looking beyond these, however, envisaging a situation in which his aircraft could play a strategic role by providing air mobility for a large number of troops. His plan called for the entire 1st Infantry Division to be dropped by parachute from sixty squadrons of bombers, albeit the latter were in short supply at that time. As Mitchell explained to Pershing, however, by the spring of the following year production of bombers would be such that there would be sufficient to provide the number required to drop the entire division behind the German lines defending Metz. Protection for an armada of such aircraft would be ensured by a large number of fighters accompanying it, with others giving close air support for the division after the landing had taken place.

Although initially sceptical, Pershing gave his approval in principle and agreed that Mitchell should duly produce a plan showing clearly the considerable resources required for the operation. The officer tasked with drawing up the detailed plan was Mitchell's newly appointed operations officer, Major Lewis Brereton, whose first problem was acquiring the number of aircraft necessary to lift the division. From the start, it was clear that virtually every bomber in the Allied inventory would need to be pressed into service. The majority of the aircraft would be Handley Page 0/400s, a twin-engined aircraft capable of carrying ten parachutists and two machine guns; at that time, the Royal Air Force (RAF) possessed 258 of this type and had placed an order for a further 1,500. The remainder would be Handley Page V/1500s, a four-engined bomber with sufficient capacity for approximately twenty parachutists. However, there were only a small number in service in late 1918, with 255 on order. Assuming that enough aircraft could be delivered in time, suitable airfields within range of Metz would have to be found at which they could be assembled beforehand.

Brereton's next consideration was the parachutists. In addition to the problem of acquiring 12,000 parachutes, there was the question of training each man in exit, flight and landing drills. Neither the 0/400 nor the V/1500 had been designed with the dropping of parachutists in mind; each man would have to clamber out of the aircraft before launching himself over the side – a difficult process almost certain to result in 'sticks' being scattered over wide areas. There was also the matter of the two machine guns to be dropped with each ten-man squad and how they would be located after landing. Once on the ground, the division would need to be resupplied by air, requiring more parachutes and further sorties.

The task facing Brereton was nothing less than Herculean. Quite apart from the fact that the US First Army did not possess the resources required to train so many parachutists, it lacked the facilities to organise and control such a large fleet of aircraft; and its radio communications systems were inadequate to command and control the division once it had been deployed on the ground. Moreover, there was the question of security. Given the assembly of such a large number of aircraft and the concentration of the 1st Infantry Division to carry out the necessary training and preparations, it would not be long before the Germans became aware of the impending operation and took the necessary countermeasures.

Although he considered it to be feasible, General Pershing decided to abandon Mitchell's plan on the grounds that it would have been too costly in terms of resources and that the risks of proceeding with it were too high at that stage in the conflict. In any event, the following month saw the armistice and cessation of hostilities on 11 November, rendering any further planning unnecessary.

During the years following the war, however, Mitchell persisted in advocating the concept of parachute-trained infantry. This was carried out at a facility, established at McCook Field at Dayton, Ohio, in the summer of 1918, where development initially had been concentrated on two types of automatic parachute. In the autumn of 1928, the first demonstration of dropping men and weapons took place when six parachutists were dropped successfully from a Martin bomber on to Kelly Field, Texas. But this aroused no interest and for the time being the US Army devoted no further effort to the development of airborne forces, although in the second half of the 1920s and early 1930s there was a limited use of aircraft in the transport role. During the period 1925–9, in a campaign in Nicaragua, the United States Marine Corps' aviation arm evacuated casualties by air and deployed troops to remote outposts, while in 1931 a US Army field artillery battery was flown from the Atlantic to the Pacific end of the Panama Canal.

A similar lack of interest in parachuting was displayed by the British Army and the RAF. In 1922, however, the latter received its first transport aircraft, the Vickers Vernon, a derivative of the Vickers Vimy bomber. This plane was capable of long-range operations, as had been demonstrated three years earlier in 1919 when a Vimy flown by Sir John Alcock and Sir John Whitten made the first crossing of the Atlantic by air.

The Vernon, which could also be used as a bomber, was flown by a crew of two and could accommodate up to twelve fully equipped troops. The first RAF units to be equipped with it were Nos 45 and 70

Squadrons, based in Iraq, which at that time was ruled by Britain under a League of Nations mandate. Early in 1920 unrest, whipped up by nationalists, broke out in the north of the country. By July it had spread south down the Euphrates Valley, the situation continuing to deteriorate as violence erupted throughout the country, which was in a state of anarchy for three months. Local British forces were unable to cope with the crisis and reinforcements were sent from India. The British response to the insurrection was to deploy RAF bombers and fighter-bombers supported by ground operations. Troops were airlifted in the Vernons to areas suitable as landing grounds from which they deployed to deal with the insurgents in that zone. On completion of their task, they were withdrawn and lifted out. Eventually, the country was pacified and returned to a state of uneasy peace.

In 1932 trouble broke out once again and it became necessary for reinforcements to be sent as a matter of urgency. The 1st Battalion The Northamptonshire Regiment was airlifted from Egypt to Iraq over a period of six days by Nos 70 and 216 Squadrons RAF, which were equipped with a total of twenty-one Vickers Victoria transport aircraft.

Unlike its allies during the First World War, Italy had recognised the possibilities of parachute troops. Following their successful deployments of individual parachutists behind Austrian lines, the Italians formed a parachute company equipped with the Salvator D.30, a parachute based on the Guardian Angel design. In 1927 the company took part in a series of exercises, the first drop of a body of troops being carried out at Cinisell, near Milan, on 6 November from CA-73 transport aircraft of the Regis Aeronautica (National Air Force).

This success led the Italians to form a parachute training establishment in Libya in January 1938. Based at an airfield at Castel Benito, near Tripoli, and commanded by Lieutenant Colonel Prospero Freri of the Air Force, its staff comprised officers and NCOs drawn from the Italian Army and Air Force. An initial draft of 300 men was established as the 1st Libyan Parachute Battalion, under the command of Lieutenant Colonel Goffredo Tonini, and began its training on 22 March.

Three weeks later, the entire battalion carried out a mass drop on the airfield. Shortly afterwards, the 2nd Libyan Parachute Battalion was formed, both units subsequently being incorporated into the 1st Air Infantry Regiment which was comprised totally of Libyans commanded by approximately fifty Italian officers and NCOs.

By this time, the Italians had introduced into service the Salvator D.37 parachute, which was soon superseded by the D.39. Like the D.30, however, both models were operated by the parachutist pulling a ripcord release, being designed for emergency use by aircrew and thus being unsuitable for use by airborne troops carrying out mass drops. During the first two months, over a hundred accidents took place with more than twenty men being killed. This caused a drastic reduction in the number of parachute descents undertaken while the losses in manpower led to the two battalions being amalgamated into a single unit.

On 3 October 1939, the Italians established the Regia Scuola Paracudisti dell' Aeronautica (National Air Force Parachute School) in Tarquinia under the command of Colonel Giuseppe Baudouin. This unit comprised: a headquarters; transport aircraft unit; training battalion; service unit, technical maintenance unit, logistical support unit; research and development unit; and medical unit. Early 1940 saw the introduction of the Salvator D.40 parachute which, while still featuring a ripcord-operated release, incorporated modifications designed to overcome the problems experienced with the D.37 and D.39. Following its arrival, parachute training was resumed.

The first three-month-long course for potential instructors began in Tarquinia on 28 March 1940 and covered not only parachute training but also instruction in physical fitness; close-quarter battle and unarmed combat; weapon training; radio communications; signals interception; intelligence gathering; first aid; loading of aircraft; air resupply; parachute descents in small and large numbers; and airborne assault and capture of an enemy airfield. When the course finished at the end of June, thirty-six out of a total of fifty-seven trainees had completed it successfully and qualified as parachute instructors.

The first training course for the Italian Army's new parachute units began on 10 July, with trainees comprising volunteers from all arms. In addition to the skills already mentioned, they received instruction in: use of foreign weapons including artillery; driving and maintenance of vehicles; and the use of explosives and demolitions. Lasting fifty days, the course culminated in an exercise in which trainees carried out three mass descents followed by a live firing exercise.

Unfortunately, three deaths occurred due to parachute malfunctions and once again training was suspended. Fortunately, the research and development unit at Tarquinia had been working on the development of a new parachute for airborne troops. Designated the IF.41/SP, (Infantry Harness Model 1941 – Parachute School), it was a static-line-operated model equipped with a harness comprising two shoulder straps, two leg straps and a belt. The canopy had a surface area of 538 square feet, giving a rate of descent of just over sixteen feet per second.

The IF.41/SP did, however, suffer from one major limitation in that it was non-steerable, the rigging lines being secured to the harness without lift webs. Parachutists launched themselves from the aircraft door in the 'angel' position, with arms and legs spreadeagled. Despite this disadvantage, the parachute proved very reliable and the rate of fatalities caused by malfunctions fell almost to zero. After successful trials of the IF.41/SP, parachute training was resumed at Tarquinia in early October 1940.

Three months before, in July, the Italian Army had formed its first parachute units, distinct from the colonial paratroops of the 1st and 2nd Libyan Parachute Battalions of the 1st Air Infantry Regiment. Another unit, composed entirely of Italians and designated the 1st National Parachute Battalion, was formed in Libya and trained at the parachute school at Castel Benito. Meanwhile, the 1st and 2nd Parachute Battalions were formed in Italy from volunteers from throughout the Army while a third unit was raised from members of the Carabinieri, being designated the 3rd Carabinieri Parachute Battalion. The Carabinieri, however, is the senior arm of the Italian armed forces and thus, in September, the unit was redesignated as the 1st Carabinieri Parachute Battalion with the 1st and 2nd Battalions being renumbered 2nd and 3rd respectively.

In 1941 the 4th, 5th and 6th Parachute Battalions were formed, this being followed by the formation of parachute artillery, engineers and other supporting arm units. On 1 September, the six battalions and supporting arm units were grouped together into the 1st and 2nd Parachute Regiments and the 1st Parachute Artillery Regiment, these being placed under the overall command of another new formation, the 1st Parachute Division, whose first commander was Brigadier General Francesco Sapienza. During the period 1941–2 a third parachute regiment, incorporating the 6th, 7th and 8th Parachute Battalions, along with the 8th Guastatori Assault Battalion, was established and added to the division's order of battle. At this stage, each parachute battalion and the assault battalion comprised three companies, while each of the parachute artillery regiment's battalions consisted of two batteries of four 32mm guns.

In July 1942, the 1st Parachute Division (less the 1st Parachute Regiment) was sent to North Africa where it served in the infantry role alongside Field Marshal Erwin Rommel's Afrika Korps. During that year, in an apparent attempt to confuse Allied intelligence, the division, by this time commanded by Major General Enrico Frattani and subsequently by Brigadier General Riccardo Bignami, was redesignated as the 185th Folgore Division, its four components being the 185th, 186th and 187th Folgore Infantry Regiments and the 185th FolgoreArtillery Regiment. In November 1942 the division was largely destroyed during the battle of El Alamein and was reduced to the strength of one small battalion, the remainder having been killed or taken prisoner.

Late 1942 saw the formation of a new parachute formation, the Nembo Division, this being created from the 185th Folgore Regiment which had remained in Italy. Designated the Nembo Division, it comprised the 183rd, 184th and 185th Nembo Infantry Regiments. Like the 185th Folgore Division, however, it was destined never to serve in the parachute role during the Second World War. In the spring of 1943, it was deployed on operations against Yugoslav partisans in the northern province of Gorizia, on the Italian-Yugoslav border. In June, the 183rd and 184th Nembo Infantry Regiments were sent to Sardinia, where a major Allied landing was expected, while the 185th was deployed to Calabria.

Italy was not alone in the development of airborne forces. The late 1920s had seen the Soviet Union carrying out trials, beginning in 1928 with a study by Mikhail Tukhachevsky, the commander of the Leningrad Military District, of the offensive use of 'air assault forces' and culminating in an exercise in which a reinforced company was landed by air. The following year saw the first operational deployment of troops by air when a small detachment of fifteen men was landed successfully in three aircraft at the town of Garm, in Tadzhikistan, to reinforce a Soviet garrison under siege from a force of Basmachi tribesmen. Tukhachevsky continued with his trials and experiments during 1930 and that year submitted a detailed plan for the organisation and equipment requirements for a motorised division trained and designed for air-landing operations.

Working in parallel with Tukhachevsky was A. N. Lapchinsky, the Chief of Staff of the Red Army Air Force. Together with another officer, N. P. Ivanov, he carried out a detailed study of the aviation aspects of airborne operations up to regimental/brigade level. In the meantime, production of equipment for airborne troops began in 1930, with the manufacture of parachutes commencing in April of that year. In August, a trial took place in which two twelve-man detachments of paratroops, armed with rifles and light machine guns (LMG), were dropped by three R-1 aircraft from altitudes of 975 and 1,625 feet. The next month, in a similar experiment, eleven paratroops were dropped from an ANT-9 aircraft, subsequently mounting a *coup de main* raid on an 'enemy' headquarters.

Further trials followed during 1931 which also saw the formation in the Leningrad Military District March of an experimental 'aviation motorised landing detachment' comprising: a rifle company; engineer signals and light motor transport platoons. In addition to light vehicles and small arms, the detachment was armed with two T-27 tankettes, two 76mm guns and four heavy machine guns (HMG). A heavy bomber squadron and a corps aviation detachment, equipped with twelve TB-1 bombers and ten R-5 light aircraft, provided aviation support. The role of the unit was the conduct of airborne operations with tactical aims, specifically the assault and capture by a parachute element of airfields in the enemy's rear, prior to the landing of a main force. During the initial period of its existence, however, the unit concentrated on airlanding operations rather than delivering personnel by parachute. In June 1931, a parachute detachment was formed within the Red Army's 1st Aviation Brigade and during August and September took part in a number of exercises outside Leningrad and in the Ukraine.

By the end of 1931, when more than 550 airborne exercises had taken place, I. P. Belov, who had succeeded Mikhail Tukhachevsky as commander of the Leningrad Military District, was calling for the formation of a number of airborne divisions, each to comprise an airlanding brigade, an aviation brigade, a parachute detachment and supporting units. The Red Army Air Force, however, while supportive of the concept, was critical of the limitations and shortcomings of the fledgling airborne forces. It pointed out that the majority of parachute drops had been conducted in good weather and during daylight, with few being carried out at night. Moreover, the size of the forces involved had been small, with paratroops being dropped over wide areas. The Air Force also stressed that greater effort should be devoted to the development and manufacture of parachutes.

In early January 1932, authority was given for the formation of four aviation motorised detachments to be based in the Moscow, Leningrad, Belorussian and Ukrainian Military Districts. In the event, only the Leningrad unit, the 3rd Motorised Airborne Landing Detachment, was raised to full strength. One hundred and forty–four strong, it was organised in two parachute companies, an airlanding company and an artillery battery equipped with six 76mm guns. Three aviation squadrons provided support, being equipped with six ANT-9 transports, three TB-1 bombers, three U-2 and six R-5 light aircraft. Lack of equipment and trained troops, however, prevented the three other detachments being formed although a thirty-strong parachute platoon was raised in the Ukraine.

Early 1932 also saw the production of the Red Army's first strategic doctrine on the use of airborne forces in a document titled *Regulation on the Operational-Tactical Employment of Air-Motorised Landing Detachments* in tandem with another larger document, *Temporary Regulation on the Organisation of Deep Battle*, which emphasised the role of mechanised forces. The former stated that motorised airborne landing detachments would operate in close coordination with ground forces while identifying their roles as: the conduct of 'diversionary missions' in support of ground offensive operations, namely attacks on enemy lines of communications and supply in rear areas; and blocking enemy reinforcement or withdrawal routes. During Soviet defensive operations, they would attack enemy command and control elements, disrupt troop movements, and seize airfields in enemy rear areas.

These documents were supplemented by a number of directives from the Red Army Training Directorate, covering the training of airborne forces. Divided into four categories, these covered parachute, glider, airlanding and combined operations. In April 1932 a directive with the title *Regulations Governing the Special Design Bureau of the Red Army Air Force* laid down the equipment requirements for Soviet airborne forces and tasked the Special Design Bureau (OKB) with designing and developing all air assault equipment, including gliders, parachutes and heavy-drop platforms for the delivery of guns and vehicles. The OKB's responsibilities also included the necessary modifications to the TB-1 and TB-3 bombers which would provide support for the airborne forces; each would accommodate thirty-two fully equipped parachutists or fifty airlanding troops.

Such a rapid expansion of airborne units was possible because of the existence of sport parachuting in the Soviet Union at that time. Fostered by organisations such as the Communist Union of Youth (Komosol) and the Society for the Promotion of Defence and the Furthering of Aviation and of the Chemical Industry of the USSR (OSOAVIAKHIM), it had become popular and the large number of trained parachutists supplied thousands of recruits for the Red Army's airborne forces. Similarly, some 2,000 glider schools had been established by OSOAVIAKHIM, providing large numbers of qualified glider pilots.

On 11 December 1932 the 3rd Motorised Airborne Landing Detachment became the nucleus of the Red Army's first airborne formation, being redesignated the 3rd Airlanding Brigade (Special Purpose) under the command of M. V. Boitsov. The new brigade was a combined arms formation comprising a parachute battalion, a motorised/mechanised battalion, an artillery battalion and organic aviation assets consisting of two squadrons of modified TB-3 bombers and a squadron of R-5 light aircraft. During the following year twenty-nine further airborne battalions, with a total of 8,000 men, were formed, and by the beginning of 1934 the Red Army's airborne forces comprised one airlanding brigade, four motorised airborne landing detachments and twenty-nine airborne battalions. All troops in these units underwent an airborne combat training course including parachute training and instruction in all the tactics and roles laid down in the Red Army's doctrine for such forces.

The Soviets continued their development of airborne forces throughout 1935 with large airborne assaults by parachute and gliderborne troops featuring in all major exercises. Western military attachés were observers at these manoeuvres and subsequently reported in detail to their respective governments. Among them was Major Philip R. Faymonville of the US Army whose description to his superiors of an exercise conducted in the area of Kiev during September 1935 included the following passage:

The most important feature of the manoeuvres was undoubtedly the mass parachute jump executed from bombing planes in the space of three minutes by 500 infantrymen and machine gunners. The mass parachute jump took place at dawn approximately 20 kilometres behind the 'enemy' lines. The parachute jumpers entrenched themselves in a strongpoint and were ready for defence within a few minutes. Supplies of ammunition were launched from parachutes shortly after the machine gunners jumped.

The defending forces immediately assembled and despatched to the strongpoint established by the parachutists a strong detachment of fast tanks. The tanks, according to the umpires, put out of commission all the machine guns in the strongpoint and completely cleaned the rear areas of hostile parachutists.

Under the plan of manoeuvre, it was the defending side which rushed a force of tanks to the strongpoint and destroyed it. There is reason to believe, however, that under Soviet tactics a strong tank detachment would be combined with the air attack and would attempt a break-through simultaneously with the launching of a mass parachute jump. Deep penetration by such a tank detachment would permit it to arrive at a rendezvous in the enemy's rear areas and act as a security detachment while the strongpoint established by parachute jumpers is being reinforced by additional flights of parachutists.

It seems evident that the tactics of the Red Army seriously contemplate mass parachute jumps combined with deep tank attacks in order to create strongpoints in enemy rear areas.

In December, Faymonville followed up with another report which provided further details on the exercises around Kiev:

1 Further information has just become available with reference to the manoeuvres of the air units which participated in the general manoeuvres at Kiev on September 14–17 1935.

2 The numbers of parachutists landed behind enemy lines (reported

in Report No. 333, Sept 18 1935) now appear to have been understated by observers. The Commissar for Defence states that 1,200 parachutists leaped simultaneously at one stage of the manoeuvres and that in the course of 40 minutes 2,500 men were landed from airplanes.

3 The Commissar has also stated in public that in another military district, 1,800 parachutists have jumped simultaneously and that a force of 5,700 men were landed from airplanes within a brief period of time.

4 At the Kiev manoeuvres, armoured cars and two different types of light tanks were carried by bombers and successfully landed behind enemy lines, moving off under their own power a few seconds after being released from the racks which secured them to the bombers.

5 Complete batteries of artillery were also landed by bombers behind enemy lines.

6 Machine guns with assembled carts and wheels, made up into tarpaulin bundles, cigar-shaped and about ten feet long, were parachuted down from planes in flight.

By 1939, Soviet airborne forces comprised six formations, each of 3,000 men, namely the 201st, 202nd, 204th, 211th, 212th and 214th Airborne Brigades, and three regiments: the 1st Rostov, 2nd Gorokhovets and 3rd Voronezh. Elements of these received their baptism of fire in 1939 when conflict broke out between the Soviet Union and Japan, culminating in July in a major battle at Khalkin-Gol on the border of Mongolia and Manchuria. The 212th Airborne Brigade, commanded by Colonel I. I. Zatevakhin, was deployed from its base in the Far East to eastern Mongolia where it operated in the ground role as part of a corps commanded by General Georgi Zhukov, distinguishing itself in a series of attacks against Japanese forces on Mount Fuji.

During the Russo-Finnish war in the winter of 1939–40, the 210th and 204th Airborne Brigades formed part of the Soviet Fifteenth Army which was engaged in the conflict, the 204th being held in reserve until the latter stage of the war. Each of the brigades comprised two parachute battalions and a headquarters company. Each battalion, numbering some 500 men in all, consisted of two rifle companies, a reconnaissance and engineer platoon, and an artillery battery. Groups of up to fifteen men, equipped with small arms and explosives, were dropped in Finnish rear areas, their missions being reconnaissance and sabotage. A number of groups were captured and two were wiped out.

The Soviet occupation of Romanian Bessarabia in June 1940 saw the first proper use of Soviet airborne troops. On 28 June, while ground forces commenced their advance, the 201st, 204th and 214th Airborne Brigades moved by rail to their mounting airfields and on the following day emplaned aboard 170 TB-3 heavy bombers. The 204th was dropped eight miles north of the city of Bolgrad, which it took that evening. On 30 July, the brigade's 1st Battalion seized the city of Kagul at the mouth of the River Danube. That same day saw the 201st Airborne Brigade dropped in the area of the city of Izmail which it occupied that evening without meeting any resistance.

Following these operational deployments, a major reappraisal of airborne forces took place, resulting in a list of specific roles being allocated to them, namely: disruption of enemy command and control infrastructures and lines of supply; cutting of enemy lines of communication; interdiction of enemy reinforcement and resupply routes; capture and destruction of airfields and air bases; seizing and holding coastal areas prior to amphibious landings by Soviet forces; reinforcement of encircled Soviet forces and those operating deep in enemy-held areas; and countering landings by enemy airborne forces in Soviet rear areas.

Late 1940 saw further enhancement of Soviet airborne forces with the introduction in November of a new airborne brigade organisation. The new formation incorporated parachute, glider and airlanding troops as follows:

PARACHUTE GROUP

Two parachute battalions – each of 546 men, comprising:

    Headquarters element

    Three parachute rifle companies – each of 141 men

    Light mortar platoon (50mm mors)

    Signal platoon

    Reconnaissance platoon

    Engineer platoon

    Logistics platoon

    Medical section

Reconnaissance company – on motorcycles

Signals company

GLIDER GROUP

Two glider battalions – each of 546 men, comprising:

    Headquarters element

    Three parachute rifle companies – each of 141 men

    Light mortar platoon (50mm mors)

    Signal platoon

    Reconnaissance platoon

    Engineer platoon

    Logistics platoon

    Medical section

Reconnaissance company – on motorcycles

Signals company

AIRLANDING GROUP

Two airlanding battalions – each of 546 men, comprising:

    Headquarters element

    Three parachute rifle companies – each of 141 men

    Light mortar platoon (50mm mors)

    Signal platoon

    Reconnaissance platoon

Engineer platoon
Logistics platoon
Medical section
Reconnaissance company – on motorcycles
Signals company
Medium mortar company (9 x 82mm mors)
Air defence company (12 x HMG)
Tank company (11 x T-38 or T-40)
Artillery battalion:
Artillery battery (4 x 45mm)
Artillery battery (4 x 76mm)

Although enhanced, the number of brigades remained at six until March 1941 when the Red Army expanded its airborne forces to five corps which were formed around the 201st, 204th, 211th, 212th and 214th Airborne Brigades. Each corps was 10,400 strong and organised as follows:

AIRBORNE CORPS
Three airborne brigades – each comprising:
Headquarters element
Four parachute battalions (458 men each) – each of three
    rifle companies
Artillery battalion (6 x 76mm, 12 x 45mm, 6 x 82mm)
Reconnaissance company
Air defence machine gun company (6mm, 7mm and
    12mm MG)
Signals company
Tank battalion (50 x T32) – 3 tank companies and a
    long-range recce platoon
Mobile equipment platoon
Light aircraft flight

Each of the five corps were stationed in a military district: I Airborne Corps (1st, 204th and 211th Airborne Brigades) in Kiev Special; II Airborne Corps (2nd, 3rd and 4th Airborne Brigades) in Kharkov; III Airborne Corps (5th, 6th and 212th Airborne Brigades) in Odessa; IV Airborne Corps (7th, 8th and 214th Airborne Brigades) in the Western Special; and V Airborne Corps (9th, 10th and 201st Airborne Brigades) in the Pre-Baltic Special. Thus, by June 1941, the Soviet Union's airborne forces comprised five corps, the 202nd Airborne Brigade and a number of smaller units, all of which were up to full strength.

In Europe, meanwhile, the swift development of the Red Army's airborne arm had caused other countries to begin to follow suit. Close relations between Russia and France during the 1930s had resulted in the French Air Force, the Armée de l'Air, sending a group of officers to Russia to study the use of airborne troops. Some of these underwent several months of training at the Soviet Air Force's Advanced School of Parachuting at Moscow where they qualified as instructors. Returning to France at the end of 1936, they established a training school at an airfield at Avignon-Pujaut. Courses commenced at the beginning of 1937 and by the end of that year 250 parachutists had been trained. These were formed into two units, the 601er and 602e Compagnies de l'Infanterie de l'Air, deemed to be operational by the end of 1938.

It was Germany, however, which observed the developments in the Soviet Union with keenest interest. Under the terms of a secret treaty signed with the Soviet Union in 1922, the Germans had attached officers to the Red Army and Air Force, some of whom thus became familiar with Soviet developments in the field of airborne forces. At the same time, under the pretext of producing a passenger aircraft for civil use, the Germans developed the three-engined Junkers Ju-52 transport which was capable of carrying troops, dropping parachutists and towing gliders.

From 1936 onwards, Germany began secretly forming her own

airborne forces. The first German parachute unit was established by the Air Force, the Luftwaffe, in early 1936, following an order published on 29 January by Reichsmarschall Hermann Göring in his capacities as Commander-in-Chief of the Luftwaffe and Air Transport Minister. Göring ordered that a parachute unit, subsequently designated the 1st Parachute Regiment (Fallschirmjägerregiment 1 – FJR-1), should be formed without delay, its nucleus comprising volunteers from the Hermann Göring Regiment, a Luftwaffe unit raised from the Prussian state police. Its headquarters, 1st Battalion and training school were to be based at a Luftwaffe base at Stendhal in north-west Germany, and command was vested in Major (later Colonel) Bruno Brauer. His immediate superior was Lieutenant Colonel Gerhard Bassenge, the station commander of Stendhal. That same year also saw the formation of an Army parachute company which underwent training at Stendal, being expanded shortly afterwards to become the Parachute Infantry Battalion under the command of Major Richard Heidrich. In due course, a platoon of the Waffen-SS also underwent training as the nucleus for an SS parachute unit to be formed at some point in the future.

The airborne training school was initially commanded by Major F. W. Immanns who, supported by a staff of fifteen officers and some seventy other ranks, was tasked with training and development of airborne forces. Trials were carried out on different types of parachute, these soon showing that a static-line operated type with a rapidly opening canopy was essential to meet the operational requirement for a dropping altitude of 300 feet. In due course, the parachute initially selected for use was the RZ-I (Rückenpackung Zwangauslösung I), fitted with a canopy of twenty-eight gores, which was developed by the Luftwaffe's experimental research establishment at Rechlin. This, however, proved unsatisfactory due to the severe jolt experienced by the user as the canopy opened; in order to lessen the shock, parachutists dived headfirst and spreadeagled from the delivering aircraft. Moreover, the RZ-I did not always open fully, due to the static line hindering the release of the canopy, and a large number of landings took place at speeds well above the accepted norm. Nevertheless, it would remain in service until the spring of 1940 when it was replaced by the RZ-16, which featured an improved method of packing the static line. Further improvements resulted in the RZ-20 appearing that same year. All three types featured a harness which suspended the parachutist from a single point high up on his back, resulting in him hanging forwards and allowing him no facility to steer the parachute.

Trainee fallschirmjäger were required to undergo three months of initial training, which included instruction on all infantry weapons and equipment (including those of the enemy) and close-quarter battle. Thereafter, they underwent the sixteen-day parachute course which covered aircraft drills, exit techniques, parachute flight control and landing drills. The last six days of the course were devoted to six jumps made from a Ju-52/3m, including a company jump.

Each fallschirmjäger was required to pack his own parachute and much attention was paid to this aspect of his training. The altitude at which training descents were made was the same as operational jumps, 300-400 feet, in order to minimise the time parachutists spent in the air and their dispersal on the ground. A stick of twelve could be dropped from a Ju-52 within approximately seven seconds, so that the men landed some 60 feet apart. The maximum ground wind speed acceptable to the Luftwaffe was twelve knots, anything greater considered likely to result in an unacceptable level of injuries and lengthy delays in troops rallying after landing.

The fallschirmjäger was distinguishable by his combat dress, comprising a narrow-brimmed lightweight steel helmet normally worn with a camouflage cloth cover, being heavily padded inside with rubber and a harness comprising chin and neckstraps. A weatherproof, knee-length, loose-fitting smock (originally plain olive drab but of camouflage pattern cloth from 1940 onwards) was worn over the uniform and equipment during a jump, the equipment being worn over it following a landing. Grey, loose-fitting trousers, with pockets on each thigh, were worn tucked into high leather boots which were laced up the sides and featured thick rubber soles. Rubber knee protectors and padded leather gauntlets were worn during a jump to provide protection for the knees and hands during landing.

The only weapon with which a fallschirmjäger jumped was a 9mm pistol and two magazines. His principal weapon, be it machine carbine, rifle, light machine gun or mortar, was dropped in one of four containers which carried the weapons of the other eleven members of his stick. A parachute was attached to one end of each container which was fitted with shock absorbers to reduce the impact of landing, and with handles and small wheels to facilitate manhandling and removal from the DZ to a point where it could be unpacked.

The fallschirmjäger was equipped with standard small arms as issued throughout the Wehrmacht, these including the MP-38 and MP-40 9mm machine pistols, Mauser 98K 7.92mm rifle, MG-34 7.92mm light machine gun (later replaced by the faster-firing MG-42), light anti-tank weapons and 81mm and 105mm medium mortars. Of these, the 81mm mortar was adapted by having its barrel reduced in length to increase manageability. Further support weapons included the 37mm anti-tank gun, mounted on a two-wheeled carriage and towed by a motorcycle combination, and the Gebirgskanon 36 75mm mountain gun which became the principal artillery piece for airborne troops.

The one exception was the Fallschirmgewehr-42 (FG-42) which was developed specifically for use by airborne troops. Of 7.92mm calibre, it was a gas-operated weapon capable of semi and fully automatic fire. Equipped with a 20-round magazine mounted on the left side of the receiver, it was fitted with a telescopic sight, an extending bayonet and a bipod. With an overall length of 37 inches, it weighed 9.92 lbs and had a cyclic rate of fire of 750 rounds per minute.

In 1937, Lieutenant Colonel Gerhard Bassenge took over responsibility for airborne training and operational command of all airborne units and began putting into practice the requirements dictated by the

Wehrmacht's General Staff. This resulted in an exercise, observed by the German Chancellor Adolf Hitler, and senior officers, in which fourteen teams of paratroops were dropped to carry out dummy attacks on railway installations and other targets. The exercise was a success and the observers considerably impressed.

By this time, the responsibilities for training and operational command of airborne units had expanded to the point where it was no longer feasible for them to be held by one individual. Accordingly, authority for airborne units was handed over by Lieutenant Colonel Gerhard Bassenge on 1 July 1938 to Major General Kurt Student, who hitherto had held the appointment of Inspector General of Luftwaffe training establishments and had been one of those who had observed the Red Army's airborne forces taking part in the exercises of 1935.

Commissioned into the Reichswehr in 1911 as an infantry officer, Student had volunteered in 1913 for flying training and subsequently served on the Eastern and Western fronts, being credited with five kills and reaching the rank of captain by the time the war ended. In 1920, he was posted as a staff officer to the Fleigerzentrale (Central Flying Office), a government body ostensibly established to develop commercial aviation in Germany but in reality acting as a cover for the establishment of a future Luftwaffe. Student assisted in drawing up plans for such a force, although it was prohibited under the terms of the Versailles Treaty. During this period, German officers were despatched to the Soviet Union as 'liaison officers', ostensibly to assist in the formation of a Soviet air force but actually to undergo training as fighter and bomber pilots. Meanwhile, a German flying school was established there in great secrecy at Lipetsk, in the area of Voronezh. At the same time, flying schools and gliding clubs were established throughout Germany and young men and women were encouraged to take up these pastimes as sporting activities. In 1929, Student left the Fliegerzentrale and returned to the infantry as a major, being given command of a battalion of the 2nd Infantry Regiment. Three years later, as a lieutenant colonel, he returned to military aviation as Director of Air

Technical Training Schools, establishments which would be responsible for training technicians for the future Luftwaffe.

By September 1938, Student had formed the 7th Air Division, a formation comprising: the 1st Battalion FJR-1; the Army's Parachute Infantry Battalion; a battalion of the Hermann Göring Regiment; the 16th Infantry Regiment (borrowed from the 22nd Infantry Division); a contingent of parachutists formed from the Sturm Abteilung (SA), a Nazi paramilitary political organisation known popularly as the 'Brown-shirts' because of the colour of its uniform; and supporting artillery, medical and logistics units. Providing aviation support for the newly formed division was a formation of 250 Junkers Ju-52 transports and a small unit equipped with DFS-230 assault gliders.

That same month saw the invasion and annexation by Germany of the Czechoslovakian border region of the Sudetenland. The 7th Air Division was placed on stand-by to provide follow-up support by carrying out airlanding operations at Freudenthal, in the Czech province of Moravia. In the event the Czechs surrendered and the division was not deployed. Elements of two other formations, the 7th and 22nd Infantry Divisions were landed at Freudenthal as part of an exercise before being withdrawn. Shortly afterwards, the 16th Infantry Regiment returned to 22nd Infantry Division, the Hermann Göring Regiment battalion was sent back to its parent formation and the SA contingent returned to its political activities.

Student, who at this juncture was given the additional appointment of Inspector of Parachute Troops, was left with only the 1st Battalion FJR-1 and the nucleii of supporting arm units. He nevertheless set to work, creating 7th Air Division as a fully independent airborne formation possessing its own artillery, engineer and signals supporting arms. Colonel Gerhard Bassenge, who by this time was Student's Chief-of-Staff, was of the opinion that all airborne units should be drawn from the Army in view of the fact that they would be carrying out tasks as part of a ground battle. Student, however, was well aware that the Commander-in-Chief of the Army, Field Marshal Walther von

Brauchitsch, was sceptical of the entire concept of airborne forces whereas Göring was an ardent supporter. The latter agreed readily to Student's suggestion that all airborne troops should form part of the Luftwaffe, which should exercise control over their operations.

By the end of 1938, command of all airborne forces was invested in the Luftwaffe. The Army handed over its Parachute Infantry Battalion which became a Luftwaffe unit and was redesignated the 2nd Battalion FJR-1, command being assumed on 1 January 1939 by Major Fritz Prager. It retained 22nd Infantry Division which was, nevertheless, placed under Luftwaffe command as an airlanding formation to make an airborne corps with 7th Air Division. Within 22nd Infantry Division, however, only the 16th Infantry Regiment initially received intensive training in airlanding operations, its other two components, the 47th and 65th Infantry Regiments, not beginning theirs until early 1940.

The 7th Air Division had meantime acquired its own organic aviation support assets in the form of Luftwaffe tactical transport squadrons equipped with the Ju-52. In 1936 Group IV of Bomber Group Hindenburg, based at Fürstenwalde, had been allotted the role of providing transport for the Luftwaffe's fledgling airborne forces, being redesignated Special Purpose Battle Group 1 in 1937 when it was transferred to the command of 7th Air Division. Shortly afterwards, a second unit, Special Purpose Battle Group 2, was formed from a nucleus of personnel and aircraft from Special Purpose Battle Group 1. Each of the two groups was subsequently expanded to a strength of four squadrons, each with twelve Ju-52s and a further flight of five aircraft, bringing the total number of aircraft in each group to fifty-three. Subsequent expansion saw the formation of a complete wing, comprising four groups with a total of 220 aircraft. In the autumn of 1939 a second wing was formed, together with a special group allotted the role of transporting heavy weapons.

The workhorse of these units was the Ju-52/3m, a tri-motor transport aircraft featuring a tubular steel frame and corrugated aluminium skin and powered by three 725hp BMW radial engines.

With a maximum cruising speed of 152mph (131knots) at 2,950 feet, the Ju-52/3m had a maximum tactical radius of 621 miles. Known to the fallschirmjäger as *'Tante Ju'*, the aircraft was flown by a crew of three and could accommodate twelve paratroops while carrying four weapon and equipment containers in a bomb bay. As an alternative to dropping paratroops, the Ju-52 could also undertake airlanding operations, being capable of accommodating up to seventeen fully equipped troops.

In addition, the aircraft was able to tow the DFS 230 assault glider, a high-winged aircraft based on a sailplane originally intended for meteorological purposes and designed during the early 1930s by the German Institute for Glider Research, the Deutsches Forschungsinstitut für Segelflugzeug. Entering service in 1940, the DFS-230 could carry ten fully equipped troops, including two pilots who fought in the ground role after landing. With a payload of almost a ton, it comprised a fuselage of tubular steel covered with a canvas skin and wooden wings, the latter featuring flaps on the upper surfaces which, when raised, permitted the glider to make its approach at a steep angle of descent. Wheels were normally jettisoned after take-off, the aircraft landing on a skid fitted under the forward half of the fuselage and coming to a halt within a few yards. The principal advantage of the DFS-230 was its virtually silent approach, thus achieving the element of surprise, coupled with its capability of delivering heavy weapons and light vehicles.

The summer of 1939 found 7th Air Division based in western Germany, in the towns of Tangermünde, Hildesheim, Gardelegen and Braunschweig. It was at this time that the decision was taken to form two more parachute regiments, designated the 2nd and 3rd Parachute Rifle Regiments (Fallschirmjägerregiments 2 and 3 – FJR-2 & FJR-3), each comprising three battalions, each of which consisted of three rifle companies and a support company with mortars and machine guns. Artillery support, in the form of anti-tank and light mountain guns, would be provided by separate companies allotted to battalions as required. Other new units to be formed would consist of divisional troops comprising signals, reconnaissance, anti-tank and medical units.

Measures were still being put in hand for the expansion of the division when on 1 September Germany invaded Poland. The 7th Air Division, reinforced by the 16th Infantry Regiment in the airlanding role, was deployed to Lower Silesia, under direct command of the Oberkommando Wehrmacht (OKW), the German High Command, ready to take advantage of any opportunities for parachute or airlanding operations. On three occasions the division was stood by for action: initially, to carry out landings over the River Vistula, in the area of Pulawy, in order to deny crossing points to Polish forces and to cut off the latter's reserves; secondly, to seize and hold the bridge across the River San at Jaroslaw ahead of advancing German armour; and thirdly to capture the Polish government and military high command which had established themselves in Krzemieniewice, in south-eastern Poland.

In the event, the speed of the German advance through Poland rendered the use of 7th Air Division unnecessary for the first two tasks, although the 16th Infantry Regiment was airlifted forward to take part in fighting north of Lodz in the conventional infantry role. It was not long, however, before Student and his men would see action, as the division was earmarked to play a leading role in Germany's planned occupation of Denmark and Norway and her forthcoming invasion of western Europe in the following year.

CHAPTER TWO

INTO BATTLE: DENMARK, NORWAY AND THE LOW COUNTRIES, 1940

Planning for the invasion of Denmark and Norway, codenamed Operation Weserübung, took place during the winter of 1939–40. Overall command was vested in General Nikolaus von Falkenhorst, the commander of XXI Corps, whose initial plan called for two of his divisions to invade Denmark while a further six were launched against Norway.

In addition to his own corps, Falkenhorst was allocated the 1st Battalion FJR-1, the airborne phase of the operation being the responsibility of Lieutenant General Hans Geisler, commander of the Luftwaffe's 10th Air Fleet, a large formation comprising fighter, bomber, reconnaissance and transport squadrons. Denmark was the initial target, with two airfields in North Jutland being among the objectives to be seized on the first day along with Norwegian airfields. The task of taking them was allotted to the 1st Battalion FJR-1, commanded by Major Erich Walther. A platoon of the battalion's No. 4 Company would seize the airfields at Aalborg, in North Jutland, the remainder of the company, commanded by Captain Walther Gericke, being assigned to capture another key objective: the two-mile-long Vordingborg Bridge connecting the Danish island of Falster with Zealand, on which is located the Danish capital of Copenhagen. Its capture would give the

Germans control of the Gedser ferry terminal to the south, and Copenhagen itself. In support of No. 4 Company would be three battalions
of the 305th Infantry Regiment.

Nos 1 and 2 Companies, led by Lieutenant Herbert Schmidt and
Captain Kurt Gröschke respectively, and under the overall command
of Major Walther himself, would meanwhile drop on the Norwegian
airfield at Fornebu, being followed by two battalions of the 324th
Infantry Regiment, together with elements of Headquarters XXI Corps
and Luftwaffe ground crews, who would be landed in Ju-52s after the
airfield had been secured. In the meantime, No. 3 Company, commanded by Lieutenant Baron Cordt von Brandis, would drop on the airfield
at Sola, near Stavanger; once it had been captured, two battalions of
the 193rd Infantry Regiment would be landed by air.

Operation Weserübung began in the early hours of 9 April 1940
when the No. 4 Company platoon seized and secured the two airfields
at Aalborg. In the meantime, heavy cloud and deteriorating visibility
had forced the transport aircraft carrying Nos 1 and 2 Companies to
Fornebu to divert to Aalborg where they landed shortly after the airfields
had been secured. Meanwhile, the aircraft carrying the two infantry
battalions of the 324th Infantry Regiment were still heading for
Fornebu, which they believed to have been secured, only to find it still
in Norwegian hands. The leading formation, commanded by Captain
Wagner, received a radio message ordering it to turn back and land at
Aalborg, but Wagner, believing it to be a Norwegian hoax, decided to
ignore it and press on. In fact, the message was genuine as the decision
had been taken to abort the airlanding since the airfield was still in
Norwegian hands.

As it made its approach, Wagner's aircraft came under anti-aircraft
fire and was hit; Wagner himself and some of the infantrymen aboard
the aircraft were killed but the co-pilot took evasive action and followed
the remainder of the formation, which by then was heading for Aalborg.
Meanwhile, six Messerschmitt Me-110s, under the command of Lieutenant Werner Hansen, had been circling the area, to provide support

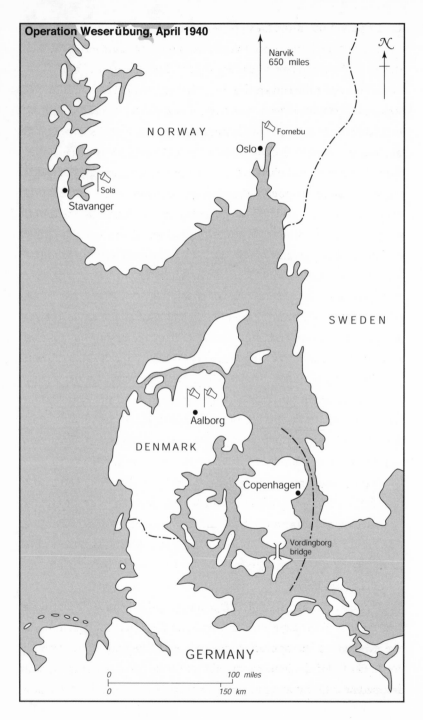

Operation Weserübung, April 1940

Narvik
650 miles

N

NORWAY

Fornebu
Oslo●

Sola
Stavanger●

SWEDEN

Aalborg●

DENMARK

Copenhagen●

Vordingborg
bridge

0   100 miles
0   150 km

GERMANY

for the parachute drop. Despite being very low on fuel as they were operating at the limit of their range from their base in Germany, they attacked the airfield before landing with their tanks almost empty. One aircraft overshot the runway but the other five landed successfully and taxied to positions from which their rear gunners could engage the airfield's anti-aircraft gun positions. At this point, all resistance by the Norwegian defenders collapsed and at 9.15 a.m., having been summoned back by a radio message from Lieutenant Hansen, the Ju-52s reappeared and dropped Nos 1 and 2 Companies. The airfield was swiftly secured and held by Major Walther and his men until the arrival of the leading elements of the two battalions of the 324th Infantry Regiment. By early afternoon, six companies of the regiment had landed at Fornebu and by 4.00 p.m. were heading for the Norwegian capital of Oslo.

At Sola, near Stavanger, Lieutenant von Brandis' No. 3 Company dropped at 9.00 a.m. and came under fire from machine-gun positions around the airfield. As the paratroops landed, two Messerschmitt Me-110 fighter bombers attacked the airfield and provided supporting fire as von Brandis' men attacked and overran the defenders' positions. Having done so, they cleared the runway of obstacles and ten minutes later the first of the Ju-52s carrying the leading elements of the two battalions of the 193rd Infantry Regiment touched down.

In the meantime, the Vordingborg Bridge had been seized by the rest of No. 4 Company who took the Danish defenders completely by surprise, swiftly disarming them and capturing the bridge without a shot being fired. Shortly afterwards, Captain Gericke and his men were joined by troops of the 305th Infantry Regiment, who pushed on towards Copenhagen.

Thus the initial phase of Weserübung had been carried out with total success. Four days later, the 1st Battalion FJR-1 took part in the second stage of the operation: the capture of key objectives farther north. On 15 April, Lieutenant Herbert Schmidt's No. 1 Company was dropped near Dombas, ninety miles north-west of Oslo, its task being to block a narrow pass through which ran the railway linking the Norwegian capital with Trondheim, and block the line of withdrawal of Norwegian troops pulling back from Oslo to join up with British forces which had landed at Andalsnes. The operation was not a success: the company was scattered during the drop which, carried out at too low an altitude, resulted in some men being killed as there was insufficient time for their parachutes to deploy. Most of the survivors landed among Norwegian defensive positions and suffered heavy casualties, Lieutenant Schmidt among them. The remainder fought on for four days before their ammunition was exhausted and they were forced to surrender. Nevertheless, news of the drop caused dismay among the Norwegians who thereafter displayed caution at a time when decisive action would have been more appropriate.

The final airborne operation in Norway involved the 1st Battalion FJR-1 being deployed to Narvik, in northern Norway, to reinforce German forces under Lieutenant General Eduard Dietl being besieged by the British and Norwegians. Taking off on 26 May from Trondheim, the battalion was dropped on the Björnfeld Heights along the Swedish border. Such was the extended range over which the aircraft were required to fly that the Ju-52s had to be fitted with additional fuel tanks in order to be able to return to Trondheim. This, however, reduced their carrying capacity by two men per aircraft. Following the drop, the battalion moved along the railway line into Narvik where they linked up with Dietl's forces. Meantime, sorely needed light artillery, in the form of 75mm mountain guns, was flown in by a small number of Ju-52s which landed on a frozen lake at Bardufoss. But there was no way the aircraft could take off again and they had to be sacrificed.

A few days later, two companies of the 3rd Mountain Division's 137th Mountain Rifle Regiment, having undergone a crash course in parachuting, were also dropped. Despite being scattered during the drop and a number suffering injuries, most of the mountain infantrymen linked up with Dietl's hard-pressed forces which subsequently withdrew by sea from Narvik at the end of May and were transported to Oslo. A week later, on 7 June, the Allies retreated from Norway and two days later all organised resistance to the German invasion collapsed.

Shortly afterwards, the 1st Battalion FJR-1 returned by sea to Germany where Lieutenant General Kurt Student, who had been promoted to that rank on 1 June, expressed his satisfaction at its performance. Apart from the loss of No. 1 Company at Dombas, the battalion had suffered relatively light casualties. The 10th Air Fleet, however, had suffered severely during the campaign in Norway, losing over 100 Ju-52s, which were considered far from expendable, largely through enemy action, the weather or coming down on insufficiently prepared landing strips.

Hitler was now turning his attention to Belgium and Holland, which would be the first countries in Western Europe to be invaded by Germany. The British and French were well aware that an attack was in the offing and had made their dispositions accordingly, the French putting their faith in the seemingly impregnable Maginot Line. Constructed during the period 1930–35 and named after André Maginot, the Defence Minister at the time, the line comprised three interdependent belts of fortifications stretching from Luxembourg to Switzerland, along the French border with Germany. The key elements of these were 108 large forts, constructed of eleven-feet-thick steel-reinforced concrete and positioned within nine miles of one another, each housing over 1,000 troops. They were equipped with steel cupolas from which artillery pieces could bring mutually supporting fire to bear. Other smaller fortified bases, each accommodating between 500 and 200 troops, were situated between their larger brethren. The network of forts formed the backbone for a large number of additional fortifications, each positioned less than half a mile from one another and accommodating platoons or companies of troops. All positions were heavily protected by minefields, anti-tank defences, barbed wire fences, with observation posts positioned well forward to give early warning of any attack.

The combined manpower of Britain, France, Holland and Belgium outnumbered that of Germany by a factor of 2:1 and they possessed a greater number of tanks. The three allies thus felt confident of being able to block any German thrust through the Low Countries. During the previous year, however, the German OKW had produced a plan to invade the Low Countries by outflanking the Maginot Line to the north and, thrusting through southern Belgium and northern France, head straight for the Channel ports with the aims of cutting off the British Expeditionary Force and forcing the French government to surrender. The scheme was initially rejected by Hitler but, after modifications, was approved in February 1940 and adopted as the 'Manstein Plan'.

The modified plan envisaged the advance into Belgium as a secondary move designed to draw off British and Belgian forces from the main German thrust through the semi-mountainous forests of the Ardennes – which the French mistakenly deemed to be impassable to armoured and motorised formations – heading past Sedan and on to the estuary of the River Somme.

The original plan had envisaged a key role for 7th Air Division, which was tasked with seizing bridges, airfields and other key objectives whose capture was vital for the advance of the Wehrmacht's Army Groups A and B into Belgium and Holland. Approximately 4,500 paratroops would take part, the majority of them being dropped in Holland in battalion- and company-sized groups and supported by 12,000 airlanding troops of Lieutenant General Count Hans von Sponeck's 22nd Airlanding Division which, like 7th Air Division, was allocated to the Eighteenth Army of General Georg von Küchler. The two airborne formations would be part of a temporarily formed air corps also commanded by Lieutenant General Student.

Holland's defences comprised three lines. The first, stretching along the Rivers Maas and Ijssel, was only lightly fortified and designed to act as a delaying position. Extending from the southern shore of the Zuider Zee south-east to the Belgian border in the area of Weert, the second and main line, known as the 'Grebbe-Peel Line', was eighty miles long and comprised extensive fortifications interspersed with natural obstacles. The latter included the Geld Valley, which could be flooded easily, the Peel and Maas marshes and, in the southern-most sector of the line, the Noorder Canal. The third line, known as 'Fortress Holland' and stretching from Den Helder to the Holland Deep, was a prepared defensive area embracing Rotterdam, Amsterdam, The Hague and Utrecht. It was protected by the Rhine-Maas estuary to the south, while to the east lay the Ijsselmeer and the area between the estuary and Nuiden, which could be flooded as a defensive measure if necessary.

The Belgian defences meanwhile included a delaying position on the Albert Canal and a main defensive line along the Dyle, the latter covering the port of Antwerp and the capital, Brussels. The delaying position was protected along its entire length by a series of forward positions except in one location where the canal ran close to the Dutch border in an area known as the 'Maastricht Appendix'. The canal in this sector ran through a deep cutting over 100 yards in width and was spanned by three bridges at Veldvezelt, Vreoenhofen and Canne. Deployment of outposts was impossible due to the proximity of the Dutch border and thus the Belgians deployed their 7th Infantry Division into this area, a brigade being allocated to the defence of each bridge. Defensive emplacements included blockhouses, equipped with machine guns, lining the canal bank for 600 yards on either side of each bridge. Furthermore, all three bridges were fitted with demolition charges and two firing circuits, one electrical and the other initiated by a conventional two-minute fuse.

Artillery support for the garrison at each bridge was provided by the guns of the seemingly impregnable fortress of Eben Emael. In external appearance a huge grassy mound with a flat top measuring some 200 by 400 yards, the fortress had been built in the mid-1930s by being blasted out of granite and possessed walls and roofs made of five-feet-thick reinforced concrete. Manned by a 1,185 strong garrison, it was equipped with artillery comprising: six 120mm guns, each with a range of ten miles and two of which possessed a traverse of 360°; sixteen 75mm quick-firing guns; twelve 60mm high velocity anti-tank guns; twenty-five twin-mounted machine guns for close-in defence; and a number of anti-aircraft machine guns mounted on the roof which also featured four casemates which could be retracted into the ground when so required.

One side of the fortress towered 120 feet over the Albert Canal while the other sides were heavily defended by minefields, deep ditches, a twenty-feet-high wall, concrete pillboxes containing light and heavy machine guns, 60mm anti-tank guns and searchlights.

The entire defensive system was based on a plan which called for the Belgians to hold the delaying position on the Albert Canal long enough for British and French forces to come to their aid, after which all would withdraw to the main defensive line along the Dyle. The Germans, however, were well aware of this and had laid their own plans accordingly. The initial phase would be carried out by 7th Air Division and 22nd Airlanding Division. The former, comprising three parachute regiments and the 16th Infantry Regiment, was tasked with carrying out a series of drops to seize and secure bridges over the rivers and canals leading from the south to Fortress Holland. Among these were the bridges spanning the Holland Deep at Moerdijk and the Oude Maas near Dordrecht. Other objectives included an airfield at Waalhaven and two bridges crossing the Nieuwe Maas at Rotterdam.

The 22nd Airlanding Division, comprising the 47th and 65th Infantry Regiments, and a reinforced parachute unit, the 1st Battalion FJR-2, meanwhile would seize a number of airfields in the area of The Hague, at Valkenburg, Ockenburg and Ypenburg, by parachute assault. The remainder of the division would land thereafter and advance on the Dutch capital with the purpose of capturing the entire government along with the High Command and, hopefully, the Royal Family. In addition, the division was also to interdict all railway lines and roads in the area to prevent the movement of Dutch reserves.

Overall, the intention was to lay a 'carpet' of airborne troops in order to secure a corridor along which formations of the Eighteenth Army would cross the water obstacles and advance into Fortress

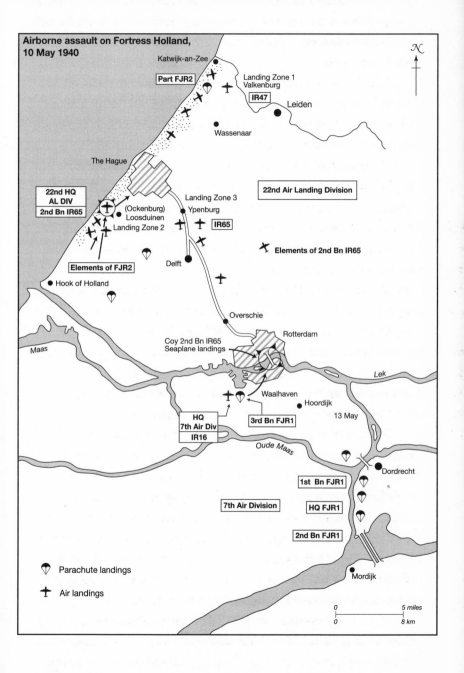

Airborne assault on Fortress Holland, 10 May 1940

N

Katwijk-an-Zee

Part FJR2

Landing Zone 1
Valkenburg

IR47

Leiden

Wassenaar

The Hague

22nd HQ
AL DIV

2nd Bn IR65

(Ockenburg)
Loosduinen

Landing Zone 3
Ypenburg

IR65

Landing Zone 2

22nd Air Landing Division

Elements of 2nd Bn IR65

Elements of FJR2

Delft

Hook of Holland

Maas

Overschie

Rotterdam

Coy 2nd Bn IR65
Seaplane landings

Lek

Waalhaven

Hoordijk

13 May

HQ
7th Air Div

IR16

3rd Bn FJR1

Oude Maas

Dordrecht

1st Bn FJR1

7th Air Division

HQ FJR1

2nd Bn FJR1

Parachute landings

Air landings

Mordijk

| 0 | | 5 miles |
| 0 | | 8 km |

49

Holland. These would comprise the 9th Panzer Division, an SS motorised regiment, a division of cavalry and six infantry divisions.

During the days prior to the operation, codenamed Yellow, some 400 Ju-52 transports were concentrated at mounting airfields at Gütersloh, Paderborn, Munster, Lippspringe, Werl and Loddenheide. Following nightfall on the evening of 9 May, 4,500 fallschirmjäger of 7th Air Division moved to the airfields and carried out their final preparations.

At 4.00 a.m. on 10 May, 22nd Airlanding Division's leading element, the 1st Battalion FJR-2, commanded by Captain Noster, took off in sixty-five Ju-52s and headed west for the area of The Hague. An hour later another 100 aircraft followed, carrying the airlanding troops who were accompanied by Lieutenant General Hans Graf von Sponeck and his tactical headquarters.

Flying at low level, the transports crossed into Holland and shortly afterwards ran into anti-aircraft fire. This proved ineffective, however, and at 6.30 a.m. companies of the 1st Battalion FJR-2 were dropped on the airfields at Valkenburg, Ockenburg and Ypenburg. The defenders' resistance was fierce at all three locations, the paratroops encountering three battalions of Dutch infantry who drove them off. Furthermore, anti-aircraft artillery at all three airfields inflicted casualties on the transport squadrons; at Ypenburg, eleven out of twelve aircraft, carrying the leading companies of the 65th Infantry Regiment, were shot down.

By the time the second wave of 22nd Airlanding Division's aircraft arrived, it was apparent that further landings were impossible. The order was given for the transports to divert to Katwijk where they landed on the beach, roads and any other areas of open ground large enough to accommodate a Ju-52. The Dutch, however, had foreseen such an eventuality and had erected obstacles which caused heavy casualties among aircraft and airlanding troops alike. Those of the latter who survived were killed or captured shortly afterwards by Dutch troops.

The division's situation continued to deteriorate throughout the day, the Dutch recapturing the airfields at Ockenburg and Ypenburg. Meanwhile, the 1st Battalion FJR-2 company at Valkenburg came under heavy artillery fire and was subjected to a number of strong counter-attacks by the Dutch. By this time, with the division having failed to take any of its objectives, the third wave of its aircraft had been diverted to Waalhaven airfield, in the area of Rotterdam, where it landed virtually unopposed.

The 7th Air Division was enjoying more success. The task of attacking and knocking out the fortress of Eben Emael, and capturing the three bridges at Veldvezelt, Vroenhoven and Canne which spanned the Albert Canal opposite Maastricht, had been allocated to an assault force designated Sturm Abteilung Koch (Storm Group Koch), comprising troops of the 1st Battalion FJR-1 and Lieutenant Rudolf Witzig's company of 7th Air Division's engineer battalion.

The entire force, under the command of Captain Walter Koch of the 1st Battalion FJR-1, numbered eleven officers and 427 men including Witzig's company and forty-two glider pilots. Koch divided his force into four assault groups: Group Granite – commanded by Lieutenant Witzig, comprising eighty-five men in eleven gliders whose objective was the fortress; Group Steel, under Lieutenant Gustav Altmann, consisting of ninety-two men in nine gliders who would take the Veld-vezeldt bridge; Group Concrete, commanded by Lieutenant Gerhard Schacht, ninety-six men men in eleven gliders, tasked with capturing the Vroenhoven bridge; and Group Iron under Lieutenant Martin Schächter, comprising ninety men in ten gliders, whose objective was the Kannes bridge.

Just prior to the landings by the 1st Battalion FJR-2 and 22nd Air-landing Division, Groups Steel, Concrete and Iron would be landed by glider at their respective objectives on the western bank of the canal. Their orders were to overwhelm the defenders at each location, remove the demolition charges placed by the Dutch and defend the bridges against any counter-attack. Forty minutes later, three transports would

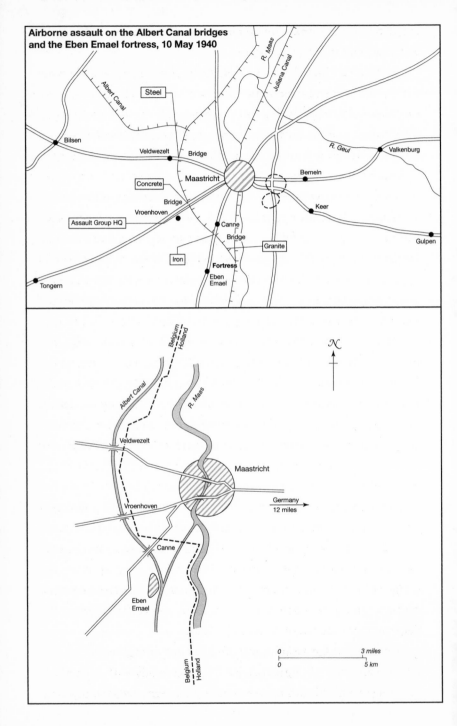

Airborne assault on the Albert Canal bridges and the Eben Emael fortress, 10 May 1940

R. Maas

Juliana Canal

Albert Canal

Steel

Bilsen

Veldwezelt

Bridge

Maastricht

R. Geul

Valkenburg

Bemeln

Concrete

Bridge

Vroenhoven

Keer

Assault Group HQ

Canne

Bridge

Granite

Gulpen

Iron

Fortress

Eben
Emael

Tongern

Belgium
Holland

Albert Canal

R. Maas

N

Veldwezelt

Maastricht

Germany
12 miles

Vroenhoven

Canne

Eben
Emael

Belgium
Holland

| 0 | | 3 miles |
| 0 | | 5 km |

drop a platoon of twenty-four reinforcements, additional machine guns and ammunition at each location.

In the meantime, Witzig's Group Granite would be landed on the flat top of the fortress. Equipped with 50kg shaped-charge explosives capable of blowing a twelve-inch diameter hole through the six-feet-thick concrete of the fortress's casemates, Witzig and his men were to knock out its guns. During the previous months of training for the operation, they had practised on a full-size replica of the fortress constructed at Grafenwohr, near the border with Czechoslovakia.

The success of the operation depended heavily on successful navigation by the pilots of the Ju-52 transports towing the gliders carrying the Storm Group Koch. The approach flight to the Dutch border would be carried out in darkness to preserve secrecy and thus two lines of beacons were set up, providing clear indication of the route from the mounting airfields in the area of Cologne to a point near the border.

At 4.15 a.m. on 10 May, the four groups of Koch's force took off in forty-one DFS-230 gliders towed by Ju-52 'tugs' which, during the following thirty minutes, climbed steadily to an altitude of 8,000 feet. All went well until suddenly the tow rope of the glider carrying Lieutenant Witzig and some of his engineers broke and the aircraft was forced to land in a field inside Germany. On approaching the border, the pilot of another glider carrying men of Group Granite released his tow rope prematurely and was unable to reach Eben Emael.

Groups Steel and Iron, however, successfully cast off their two ropes at the predetermined point and altitude some twenty miles inside Germany and flew on in silence as the tugs peeled away and headed back towards Cologne. Group Concrete, tasked with capturing the bridge at Vroenhoven, meanwhile was towed over the Dutch border. Anti-aircraft artillery detected the tugs and opened fire, alerting the defences in the area to the imminent threat.

All three bridge assault groups, each comprising five sections of infantry and four of engineers, landed successfully with each glider touching down and coming to rest at its predetermined landing point.

Disembarking swiftly at each location, the fallschirmjäger launched their assaults on the bridge defences, the engineers using flamethrowers and explosive charges to knock out pillboxes and emplacements before turning their attention to the demolition charges set into the bridges and cutting the firing circuits.

The bridges at Veldwezelt and Vroenhoven were captured intact but Lieutenant Schachter's Group Iron failed to seize the third and southernmost bridge at Kannes. He and his men landed late, the element of surprise having been lost, and then had to cover several hundred yards from the landing zone to reach their objective, where the defenders brought heavy fire to bear and prevented the paratroops from approaching the bridge and its defences. Shortly afterwards, the bridge was blown.

In the meantime, the nine remaining gliders carrying Group Granite had landed successfully on the roof of Eben Emael. Using arrester parachutes, they came to a halt within some 20 yards of touching down and their passengers lost little time in attacking the twelve gun emplacements which were capable of bringing fire to bear on the three bridges and on the roof of the fortress itself. First, they blew their way into six casemates, blasting holes in the roofs with their 50kg shaped charges before dropping grenades and small explosive charges into the chambers below, killing or incapacitating the occupants. They then blew entrances, thus gaining access to the casemates from which they could dominate the entire area of the fortress roof. Attempts by the garrison to dislodge them would have proved futile as any counter-attacks from inside the fortress would have had to be launched up sixty-feet-high spiral staircases, a nigh impossible feat.

At 6.10 a.m., formations of Ju-52s appeared over each of the three bridges and dropped the reinforcements, machine guns and explosives. Casualties were heavy among the reinforcements who came under determined fire from the defenders. At the Kannes bridge, Group Iron eventually overcame all resistance and secured its objective.

At 8.30 a.m., a solitary Ju-52 towing a DFS-230 glider was seen approaching Eben Emael. Having cast off, the glider flew towards the fortress and landed in an area near by. It carried Lieutenant Witzig who had succeeded in calling by radio for a relief Ju-52 to land by his glider and therafter take off again, towing him and his men to their objective. The glider landed safely and Witzig lost little time in rejoining his men and resuming command.

Forward elements of the Eighteenth Army were meanwhile advancing into Holland and at 10.15 a.m. began providing artillery support for Storm Group Koch. By 1.00 p.m., the leading units had linked up with the fallschirmjäger companies at the bridges. Sappers of the 51st Engineer Battalion were supposed to relieve Group Granite on the fortress but had been delayed by the Dutch blowing the bridges crossing the River Maas in Maastricht. It was not until 7.00 a.m. on 11 May, having thrown bridges across the Maas and the Albert Canal, that the battalion was able to reach Witzig, whose men had continued throughout 10 May and the following night to blast their way into other parts of the fortress where the Belgian garrison could do little but take shelter in its underground quarters.

Shortly after the arrival of the 51st Engineer Battalion, a regiment of infantry appeared and the entire combined force mounted an attack on the main entrance to the fortress. At 12.30 p.m. the garrison surrendered, having lost sixty men killed and forty wounded during the battle, over 1,000 being marched away into captivity. At 4.00 p.m. Witzig and his men withdrew, having suffered only six killed and nineteen wounded.

While Storm Group Koch had been securing its objectives, other elements of 7th Air Division were engaged elsewhere. The 2nd Battalion FJR-1, commanded by Captain Fritz Prager, dropped in the area of the three bridges over the Holland Deep, its companies landing to the north and south of its objective. At the bridge at Moerdijk, a brief but fierce action ensued, during which Captain Prager was badly wounded, but the defenders were swiftly overrun and the bridge secured. At Dordrecht, however, the 1st Battalion FJR-1 managed to seize only part of its objective, the commander of No. 3 Company, Lieutenant Baron Cordt von Brandis, being killed during the action. The Dutch then counter-attacked and recaptured the bridge.

On the outskirts of Rotterdam, meanwhile, the 120-strong 11th Company of the 16th Infantry Regiment, which was under command of 7th Air Division, had landed in twelve Heinkel 59 seaplanes on the Nieuwe Maas close to two bridges. Having gained the shore unob-served, the company, led by Captain Schrader, cut the demolition firing circuits and seized both bridges before the defenders could react. The Dutch counter-attacked, bringing effective fire to bear on the company. Meanwhile, a force of fifty fallschirmjäger of the 3rd Battalion FJR-1, commanded by Lieutenant Horst Kerfin, was dropped on to a sports stadium just south of the two bridges. Commandeering some trams, they headed north to support Schrader and his men who by this time were being subjected to heavy fire by Dutch artillery.

At Waalhaven airfield to the south-west the 3rd Battalion FJR-1, commanded by Captain Karl-Lothar Schulz, had been dropped to the east of the airfield itself. The Dutch defending forces immediately engaged this threat, only to find troops of the 3rd Battalion 16th Infantry Regiment landing to their rear in Ju-52s. A brief battle ensued before the airfield fell to the Germans, the latter setting off for the bridges shortly afterwards.

Throughout that first day of the operation, although the airfield was under constant artillery fire from Dutch forces and bombing by RAF aircraft, a total of 250 landings were carried out at Waalhaven. During the afternoon, two more battalions of the 16th Infantry Regiment were landed. Meantime, a force comprising the 3rd Battalion FJR-1 and elements of the 16th Infantry Regiment, under the overall command of Colonel Bruno Bräuer, FJR-1's commander, set off in captured vehicles for Dordrecht to reinforce the beleaguered fallschir-mjäger company there.

By this time, it had become apparent that 22nd Airlanding Division had failed to achieve its primary objective of carrying out a *coup de main* action in The Hague. Despite failing to gain control of the airfields, however, it had rendered their use by RAF aircraft impossible. At this juncture, Lieutenant General von Sponeck, whose tactical headquarters was co-located with a small element of his division, received orders from the commander of the Luftwaffe's 2nd Air Fleet, General Albert Kesselring, to head for the northern edge of Rotterdam where he was to form a block between Dutch reserve forces and the elements of 7th Air Division manning the bridgehead to the north of the Maas.

Fierce fighting continued, 11 May seeing the appearance of elements of the French Seventh Army, a mechanised group of which advanced on Moerdijk but was beaten back by swarms of Stuka dive-bombers. On 12 May, the leading regiments of 9th Panzer Division, under Major General Ritter von Hubicki, arrived at the Moerdijk bridges where they linked up with the fallschirmjäger holding them.

The 7th Air Division now came under control of the ground forces, commanded by Lieutenant General Rudolf Schmidt, which by this time comprised 9th Panzer Division, 254th Infantry Division and an SS mechanised regiment. The task facing Schmidt was to finish the attack on Fortress Holland and seize The Hague. Dutch resistance, however, was strong and the urban areas did not favour armour. By 14 May, their advance had been halted for forty-eight hours and thus the Germans resorted to air power to crush all resistance in Rotterdam, to the north of which the surviving elements of 22nd Airlanding Division were still holding their own.

On the afternoon of 14 May, large formations of Heinkel bombers attacked the city and reduced broad areas of it to ruins. At 6.00 p.m. that evening, Rotterdam surrendered. Two and a half hours later the Dutch government capitulated.

By nightfall on the 14th Lieutenant General Kurt Student had established his divisional command post in the headquarters of the Dutch High Command. Shortly after he did so, however, he was wounded in the head by a stray bullet fired during a brief skirmish outside the headquarters between surrendering Dutch forces and leading elements of the SS mechanised regiment who appeared on the scene. Student was evacuated, command of 7th Air Division being assumed by Major General Richard Pütziger, the commander of the Luftwaffe formations which had provided air support during the entire operation.

On 15 May, the surviving sections of 22nd Airlanding Division linked up with the ground forces. Among the 2,000 men of the division who had been landed on 10 May, casualties had been particularly heavy among the leading elements of the 47th and 65th Infantry Regiments. Losses had also been high among the Luftwaffe transport squadrons, with 170 Ju-52s destroyed and almost the same number badly damaged. A large number of aircrew had also been lost.

After its return to Germany, 7th Air Division was expanded to three parachute regiments, each of three battalions, with the Storm Group Koch becoming the 1st Battalion of the 1st Airlanding Assault Regiment (Luftlande-Sturmregiment I – LSR-1), a new formation comprising four battalions of fallschirmjäger trained as a gliderborne assault force. Command of the new regiment was given to Colonel Eugen Meindl, with the newly promoted Major Walter Koch assuming command of the 1st Battalion. Together with 22nd Airlanding Division, 7th Air Division was incorporated into a new formation, XI Air Corps, which was established in the summer.

June 1940 saw the invasion of France by Germany. During the following months, buoyed by his successes so far, Hitler ordered the Army High Command (Oberkommando der Heeres – OKH) to draw up plans for the invasion of Britain, codenamed Operation Sealion. These were produced in August and proposed landings by the Ninth and Sixteenth Armies along the south-eastern coast of southern England between Dover and Brighton. The 7th Air Division would be dropped and landed on the left and right wings of the landings, the main element being deployed near Brighton. The Luftwaffe, however, objected to these plans, insisting that the division should be concentrated on the right, near Folkestone. The OKH's planners eventually agreed to this but ordered 7th Air Division to take up positions to the north and north-west of Dover to block any attacks on the Sixteenth Army's right flank.

Field Marshal Kesselring (who was promoted to that rank on 19 July 1940), the overall commander of the Luftwaffe formations taking part in Sealion, nevertheless ignored the tasks set out for 7th Air Division and ordered Major General Putziger to select DZs and LZs for use by the division's three parachute regiments and the 1st Airlanding Assault Regiment. The latter by this time comprised four battalions, each of 600 men, which would be transported in 300 DFS-230 gliders towed by Ju-52s carrying paratroops.

Air reconnaissance of southern England soon revealed, however, that the threat of airborne landings had been well recognised by the British who were busy laying minefields and installing anti-landing obstacles, including telephone poles and large ditches, on all areas of open ground suitable for use by gliders and parachutists. Nearly all the DZs and LZs selected by Major General Putziger were among these areas and thus the feasibility of airborne landings began to be cast into doubt.

The success of Sealion, however, depended above all on the Germans achieving air superiority and control of the English Channel. Despite the extravagant boasts of Reichsmarschall Hermann Göring that his squadrons would drive the RAF from the skies, the Luftwaffe was defeated during the Battle of Britain which was waged in the skies over southern England during the summer of 1940. Likewise, the Kriegsmarine (Navy) did not reign supreme in the Channel and without air superiority would have been unable to prevent the Royal Navy inflicting massive damage on the invasion fleet of flat-bottomed barges, assembled by the Germans at ports along the French coast, and on the troops to be carried by them. By the end of August, it had become apparent to Hitler and the OKW that the factors vital to the success of Sealion were lacking and on 17 September the decision was taken to postpone the invasion of Britain indefinitely.

CHAPTER THREE

CRETE, MAY 1941

By late 1940 Hitler's attention had switched away from Britain, although on 12 October he gave orders that preparations for Sealion were to continue until the spring of 1941 in order to maintain political and military pressure on Britain. He was increasingly preoccupied with the east where the Nazi-Soviet non-aggression pact, under which Russia remained neutral while Germany invaded Poland, Norway, the Low Countries and France, was becoming increasingly strained as the Soviets strengthened their influence in north-west and south-east Europe – areas that supplied raw materials vital to Germany. Hitler's main fear was that the Soviet dictator, Josef Stalin, would either make increasing demands in return for maintaining Russian neutrality or side with Britain which was beginning to receive support from the United States. Hitler was thus faced with the choice of forcing Britain into negotiating terms with Germany, before such US assistance became effective, or invading and overwhelming Russia and so removing the risk of Germany having to fight simultaneously on two fronts. Once Russia had been neutralised as a threat, Britain would be forced to negotiate with Hitler or face the consequences.

The view of Hitler's senior military advisers, namely the Army's Chief of Staff, General Franz Halder, and his naval counterpart, Grand Admiral Erich Raeder, was that Britain should remain the principal target and that Germany should concentrate on its efforts against British and Allied interests in the Mediterranean where Britain's position was already under threat following Italy's entry into the war on the German side in June 1940. August had seen the seizing of British Somaliland by Italian forces numbering 250,000 and during the following month an Italian army, under Marshal Rodolfo Graziani, had entered Libya from Egypt.

In July, Hitler had vetoed Italian dictator Benito Mussolini's plans to invade Yugoslavia which would, in Hitler's view, have provided further avenues for Russian and British interference by bringing war to the Balkans. The next month, Germany had interceded to prevent hostilities breaking out between Hungary and Romania over the province of Transylvania. Hitler was anxious that the Russians, who in June had confiscated Bessarabia and northern Bukovina from Romania, would seize the Ploesti region and its vital oilfields which annually supplied Germany with 1.2 million barrels of oil. He despatched a large military 'training mission' to the Romanian capital of Bucharest, its real and secret role being the protection of the oilfields.

On 23 October, much to Hitler's fury, Italy invaded Greece. Mussolini had envisaged that the Greek forces would collapse and that the country would fall like a ripe plum into his hands. In this he was mistaken, as the Greeks put up a stout resistance, driving back the Italians who then found themselves bogged down in a mountain war.

General Ioannis Metaxas, the Greek right-wing dictator, appealed to Britain for assistance and the latter responded by sending several RAF squadrons from Egypt to airfields in southern Greece from where they were in striking range of the Ploesti oilfields. At the same time, the British commander-in-chief in the Middle East, General Sir Archibald Wavell, despatched the 6th Australian Division, 2nd New Zealand Division and the British 1st Armoured Brigade to Greece. On 31 October the British occupied the island of Crete.

Faced with this new threat, Hitler issued preparatory orders for Operation Marita, the occupation of Bulgaria and the invasion of the

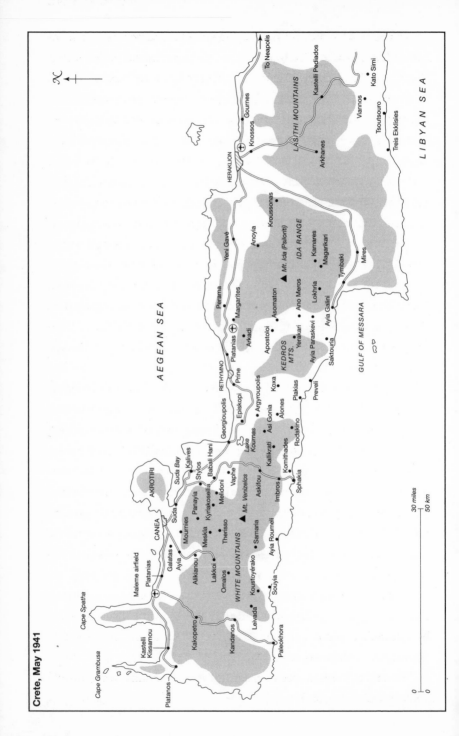

Crete, May 1941

Cape Grambusa
Cape Spatha
Platanos
Kastelli Kissamou
Kakopetro
Kandanos
Leivada
Koustoyérako
Souyia
Paleokhora
Omalos
Lakkoi
Alikianou
Ayia
Galatas
Platanias
Maleme airfield
Meskla
Mournies
Kyriakoselia
Panayia
Therisso
Melidoni
Vaphe
Samaria
Ayia Roumeli
Askifou
Mt. Venizelos ▲
WHITE MOUNTAINS
Imbros
AKROTIRI
CANEA
Suda
Suda Bay
Kalives
Stylos
Babali Hani
Lake Kournas
Kallikrati
Komithades
Sphakia
Asi Gonia
Alones
Rodakino
Plakias
Koxa
Argyroupolis
Episkopi
Georgioupolis
Prine
RETHYMNO
Platanias
Arkadi
Apostoloi
Ayia Paraskevi
Yerakari
KEDROS MTS.
Saktouria
Preveli
Margarites
Perama
Yeni Gavé
Asomaton
Ano Meros
Lokhria
Ayia Galini
Tymbaki
Mires
GULF OF MESSARA
Mt. Ida (Psiloriti) ▲
IDA RANGE
Kamares
Magarikari
Anoyia
Kroussonas
HERAKLION
Knossos
Gournes
To Neapolis
Arkhanes
LASITHI MOUNTAINS
Kastelli Pediados
Viannos
Kato Simi
Tsoutsouro
Treis Ekklisies

LIBYAN SEA

AEGEAN SEA

N

0   30 miles
0   50 km

Greek mainland to the north of the Aegean. At the same time, Germany formed an alliance with Bulgaria and also attempted to do so with Yugoslavia, but was foiled at the last minute by an anti-fascist coup in Belgrade which saw the pro-Axis regent, Prince Paul, ousted by a military junta unsympathetic to Germany. Hitler immediately resorted to force and invaded Yugoslavia on 6 April 1941. The German Second Army, under General Maximilian von Weich, overran the Yugoslav army which suffered heavy casualties, including 344,000 men taken prisoner. Within a week, von Weich's troops had reached the capital, Belgrade, and on 17 April Germany and Yugoslavia signed an armistice.

In Greece, meanwhile, the German Twelfth Army, commanded by Field Marshal Wilhelm List, had made short work of the Allied forces facing it, the Greek Second Army surrendering shortly after the fall of Salonika. List's forces headed south, driving back the Allies. On 20 April the Greeks capitulated, allowing List to concentrate on the British, Australian and New Zealand forces and prevent their evacuation and escape by sea to Crete.

The Allied withdrawal route was across the Corinth Canal via a single bridge. XI Air Corps was given the task of seizing it, in turn allocating it to FJR-2, commanded by Colonel Albert Sturm, which was reinforced with parachute engineer, signals and medical detachments.

The attack was scheduled for 26 April. The bridge itself was defended by four companies of Australian infantry, ten 3.7 inch anti-aircraft guns, a troop of armoured cars, and the regimental headquarters of the 4th Queen's Own Hussars comprising five tanks, under the commanding officer, Lieutenant Colonel Lillington, who was in overall command.

Colonel Sturm decided to attack the bridge with a group of sappers from his fifty-four-strong parachute engineer detachment, commanded by Lieutenant Häffner. In support was his 1st Battalion, under Captain Hans Kroh, which would drop to the north of the objective, and his 2nd Battalion, commanded by Captain Erich Pietzonka, which would be dropped to the south.

The *coup de main* party, consisting of Lieutenant Häffner and thirty of his sappers, was to be carried in six DFS-230 gliders. Three of these, flown by Lieutenants Fulda, Breckenbeck and Mende, would land to the north of the bridge while the remaining three, piloted by Lieutenants Phenn, Lassen and Raschke, would land to the south.

At 4.30 a.m. on 25 April, six Ju-52 tugs took off from an airfield at Larissa to which 7th Air Division had moved from its previous forward base at Plovdiv, in Bulgaria. Each towing a glider, they headed for the Corinth Canal. Thirty minutes later, they were followed by the Ju-52s carrying the 1st and 2nd Battalions FJR-2.

At 6.58 a.m. Luftwaffe aircraft began strafing the bridge and its defences. Two minutes later, the six gliders cast off their tow ropes. The landing to the north of the bridge took place without mishap and the northern end of the bridge was seized quickly, eighty prisoners being taken in the process. Meanwhile, to the south, Lieutenant Häffner and his men landed successfully, swiftly overrunning the defenders before getting to work disconnecting the firing circuits that linked the demolition charges installed on the bridge. By this time, the 1st and 2nd Battalions FJR-2 were dropping and shortly afterwards established a defensive perimeter.

The bridge thus fell intact to the Germans but not for long. Having disconnected the firing circuits, Lieutenant Häffner and his sappers left the explosives in place for use in the event of an enemy counter-attack. Shortly afterwards, however, the bridge came under heavy fire from a 40mm Bofors gun and small arms to the south of the canal. From photographs taken at the time, it appears that a 40mm shell hit one of the demolition charges which exploded, causing sympathetic detonations of the remainder that resulted in the bridge being dropped into the canal. Several fallschirmjäger, including one of the glider pilots, Lieutenant Phenn, were killed in the blast. By the time the battle was over, the Germans had suffered sixty-three killed and 174 wounded.

Despite the loss of the bridge, the operation was deemed a success in that the Allied withdrawal route had been cut, with some 2,000 British and Commonwealth troops, along with 3,500 Yugoslavs and 5,000 Greeks, being cut off. After bridging the canal, the Germans continued their advance south and by 30 April had occupied the entire Corinth isthmus.

Having withdrawn from Greece, the Allied forces regrouped on Crete whence RAF aircraft could still strike at the Ploesti oilfields which were so vital to Germany, while also threatening the latter's now-extended flank in south-east Europe.

As commander of XI Air Corps, General Kurt Student, promoted to the rank of full general on 1 August 1940, was keen for his formation to take a further part in the campaign in Greece. At his headquarters in Berlin, however, he waited in vain for the order to attack Crete. Eventually, he decided that he had to initiate matters himself, and on 20 April flew to Semmering, in Austria, where Hitler had established his headquarters for Operation Marita. There he met Reichsmarschall Hermann Göring and General Hans Jeschonnek, the Chief of Staff of the Luftwaffe.

Student explained his case for an attack on Crete, emphasising that the entire Marita operation could be jeopardised by allowing the island to remain in the hands of Allied forces which might threaten German interests in south-east Europe. Göring was well aware of the threat, having already been warned of it by General Alexander Lohr, the commander of 4th Air Fleet and the senior Luftwaffe officer in the Balkans. It appeared, however, that he felt the Allied presence could jeopardise an undertaking of far greater significance than Marita, namely Operation Barbarossa – the invasion of Russia.

Göring agreed to raise the matter with Hitler and indeed did so without delay. On the following day, Jeschonnek and Student were summoned to Hitler's personal train, parked near a tunnel some fifteen miles from Semmering as a precaution against Allied air attack. Initially, the two Luftwaffe generals met General Alfred Jodl and Field Marshal Wilhelm Keitel of the OKW who rejected out of hand the idea of an airborne assault on Crete, suggesting instead that XI Air Corps should be tasked with capturing the island of Malta in support of General (later Field Marshal) Erwin Rommel's Afrika Korps in the Western Desert.

Student, however, had previously studied the feasibility of an airborne assault on Malta and had concluded that the island possessed insufficient areas suitable for use as DZs while the small size of its fields, enclosed by stone walls, made the use of gliders impossible.

At this point, Hitler appeared and immediately dismissed the idea of an attack on Malta. Thereafter, he listened to Student as the latter proposed that Crete could only be taken from the air and that its capture would be followed by that of Cyprus, and ultimately by an attack on Suez and the seizing of the canal.

Hitler, however, was only interested in the bearing Crete had on Operation Barbarossa which was of overriding importance to him. He insisted, therefore, that the attack on Crete should be launched as soon as possible.

On 25 April Directive No. 28, covering 'an operation to occupy the island of Crete to be prepared with the object of using Crete as an air base against Britain in the Eastern Mediterranean', was issued. Giving Göring overall responsibility, it allotted to the operation all Luftwaffe assets in the Mediterranean, including XI Air Corps, and declared that the Army was to allocate 'suitable reinforcements', including an armoured element. It also laid down that the deadline for the attack was 17 May. Executive command of the operation, codenamed Mercury, was given to the commander of 4th Air Fleet, General Löhr.

Student returned to Berlin where he began work immediately on the planning and preparations for Mercury. Time was of the essence as some of the resources allotted to the operation would be required subsequently for Barbarossa and thus would have to be transferred to Poland and Romania by no later than the end of May.

The immediate problem facing Student was that XI Air Corps was widely dispersed with half of 7th Air Division, now commanded by Lieutenant General Wilhelm Süssmann, distributed among eleven bases in Germany and the remainder in the Balkans and Greece. Furthermore, the major part of the division's weapons and equipment were packed and pre-positioned in northern France for use in Operation Sealion. Arrangements had to be made for them to be moved by rail to the Black Sea port of Constanza for shipment to XI Air Corps' assembly area near Athens. Meanwhile, the entire division was moved in an operation codenamed Flying Dutchman coordinated by the divisional chief quartermaster, Major General Conrad Seibt. The entire operation was conducted under great secrecy, with all orders being Enigma-encrypted and no one other than members of the divisional staff knowing the destination to which the division was being despatched. Furthermore, the troops were ordered to remove all insignia distinguishing them as fallschirmjäger. Units travelled by rail from Germany via Czechoslovakia and Hungary to Romania, from where they continued their journey to Greece by road.

The 22nd Airlanding Division, meanwhile, was in Romania where it had been deployed to protect the Ploesti oilfields. Inadequate roads, many of which were already in use for forces being prepared for Barbarossa, meant that it was impossible for the division to be moved sufficiently quickly to southern Greece. The 5th Mountain Division, commanded by Lieutenant General Julius Ringel, had earlier taken part in the invasion of Greece and was still located in the mountains in the northern part of the country. It was thus selected to replace 22nd Airlanding Division in XI Air Corps and moved south with all speed to join 7th Air Division near Athens.

By the time all its formations and units had been concentrated near Athens, XI Air Corps' strength was 22,750 men comprising: the 10,750-strong 7th Air Division; the 5,000 Gebirgsjäger of 5th Mountain Division; and a 7,000-strong seaborne element.

Air support for Operation Mercury would be provided by General Alexander Löhr's 4th Air Fleet which comprised two elements. VIII Air Corps, commanded by Lieutenant General Baron Wolfram von Richthofen, would provide tactical air support with its Dornier Do-17 and Junkers Ju-88 bombers, Ju-87 Stuka dive-bombers and six groups of Messchersmitt Me-109 and Me-110 fighters. Transports, in the form of 493 Ju-52s, would be supplied by six wings of the 1st and 2nd Transport Battle Groups, with a wing of 1st Airlanding Group providing 80 DFS-230 gliders and tugs. In reserve would be four squadrons of Ju-52s.

All the Ju-52s taking part in the operation were concentrated at bases in northern Germany, Austria and Czechoslovakia where they underwent a thorough overhaul before being flown to Greece. Meanwhile, mounting airfields and fuel dumps were established at Tanágra, Dadion, Corinth, Topolis, Mégara, Elevsis and Phaleron, all in a radius of some eighty miles from Athens where Student had positioned XI Air Corps' forward headquarters in the Hôtel Grande Bretagne. The divisional staff in the meantime had established supply dumps of ammunition, water, rations, medical stores and all other nature of combat supplies to be carried during the attack and for resupply thereafter. It was a massive undertaking requiring a high level of efficiency and dedication on the part of the corps' ten Fliegerhorstkommandanten – officers specialising in the mounting and support of airborne operations.

While XI Air Corps made its preparations for Mercury, the senior Kriegsmarine officer in the region, Admiral Karlgeorg Schüster, the Flag Officer South East, was assembling two flotillas of light vessels, comprising seven small freighters and sixty-three motor-assisted Greek caiques (schooners), to carry the seaborne element consisting of the 2nd Battalion 85th Mountain Rifle Regiment and the 3rd Battalion 100th Mountain Rifle Regiment, together with detachments of 7th Air Division's engineer and anti-tank units, supplies, artillery pieces and light tanks of the 2nd Battalion 31st Panzer Regiment. Protection against air attack was to be provided by the major part of 7th Air Division's anti-aircraft artillery battalion whose guns would be installed aboard the vessels. Naval escorts for the two light flotillas would be provided by the Italian Navy but would consist merely of two obsolete light destroyers, the *Lupo* and *Sagittario*.

Student's plan was for XI Air Corps to carry out four airborne landings along the 160-mile-long northern coast of Crete. He divided his force into three elements: Group West, Group Centre and Group East.

Group West, under the command of Major General Eugen Meindl, commander of the 1st Airlanding Assault Regiment (LSR-1), was to seize the airfield at Máleme, thereafter clearing and securing it for subsequent airlanding operations. His force comprised his regiment less Nos 1 and 2 Companies of the 1st Battalion, a parachute anti-aircraft machine-gun company and a parachute medical platoon. The leading element would comprise a 750-strong force consisting of the battalion headquarters and Nos 3 and 4 Companies of the 1st Battalion, under the commanding officer, Major Walter Koch, transported in fifty-three DFS-230 gliders. The remainder of Group West would be dropped by parachute.

Group Centre, commanded by Lieutenant General Wilhelm Süssmann, was to capture the Cretan capital of Canea, to the west of the port of Suda. It would also seize the main Allied headquarters, believed to be located in the capital, and deal with any enemy reserves in the area. Süssmann was allocated FJR-3, commanded by Colonel Richard Heidrich, reinforced with Nos 1 and 2 Companies of LSR-1 in gliders and 7th Air Division's parachute engineer battalion, the last being allotted a flank protection task at Alikianou a few miles south of Máleme. In addition, he was given FJR-2, less its 2nd Battalion, which would be dropped eight hours later, with the object of seizing the airfield at Rethymnon, to the east of Canea.

The second wave would also see the leading element of Group East dropped on the airfield at Heraklion, forty miles east of Rethymnon. This would comprise FJR-1, reinforced by the 2nd Battalion FJR-2, under the overall command of Colonel Bruno Bräuer, the commander of FJR-1. The remainder of Group East, comprising Gebirgsjäger of 5th Mountain Division, including the 100th Mountain Rifle Regiment (less the 3rd Battalion) and the 95th Mountain Motorcycle Battalion, would be airlanded at Heraklion on the second day. The remainder of the division, comprising the 85th Mountain Rifle Regiment, the 3rd Battalion 100th Mountain Rifle Regiment, the 95th Mountain Artillery Regiment and the division's reconnaissance, anti-tank and engineer battalions, would be landed by sea together with the seaborne elements of 7th Air Division. The light tanks of the 2nd Battalion 31st Panzer Regiment would follow by sea.

German intelligence on the Allied forces on Crete estimated their strength as being no more than 5,000, comprising only British units as all the Australian and New Zealand forces evacuated from Greece reportedly had been transported directly to Egypt. Moreover, intelligence indicated there were no Greek troops on the island.

This information was grossly inaccurate, as the garrison on the island totalled 42,460 men, of whom half were fully trained British, Australian and New Zealand infantry. Of that total, however, 9,000 were poorly armed and equipped Greek troops. Cretan forces on the island provided a further 4,200 men, in the form of a local gendarmerie, and 3,000 scantily armed irregulars.

The entire Allied force was under the command of Major General Bernard Freyberg, a New Zealander who had won the Victoria Cross and the DSO with two bars during the First World War. Until his arrival in Crete on 29 April 1941, he had been in command of the 2nd New Zealand Division, handing over to Brigadier Edward Puttick, his deputy, on assuming command of the island's forces, designated Creforce. Freyberg's headquarters were located in a quarry overlooking Canea, on the western side of the peninsula forming the bay and sheltered harbour at Suda. From there, he and his small staff could observe westwards towards Máleme.

Defence of the area of coast between Canea and Máleme was the responsibility of 2nd New Zealand Division, consisting of the 4th, 5th and New Zealand Brigades. The 4th New Zealand Brigade, commanded by Brigadier Lindsay Inglis and comprising the 18th and 19th New Zealand Infantry Battalions and the 1st Light Troop RA, was positioned in a reserve role near Canea together with a British unit, the 1st Battalion

The Welch Regiment. The divisional reserve, the 20th New Zealand Infantry Battalion, part of 10th New Zealand Brigade, was also located close to the capital.

The defence of Máleme was allotted to 5th New Zealand Brigade, under Brigadier James Hargest, which comprised: the 21st, 22nd and 23rd New Zealand Infantry Battalions, 28th (Maori) New Zealand Infantry Battalion, 1st Greek Regiment, two Matilda tanks of the 7th Royal Tank Regiment and a detachment of engineers.

The 10th New Zealand Brigade, commanded by Lieutenant Colonel Howard Kippenberger, occupied the eastern sector of 2nd New Zealand Division's tactical area of responsibilty (TAOR). An ad hoc formation largely consisting of men from supporting armed units fighting in the infantry role, it comprised: Kippenberger's 20th New Zealand Infantry Battalion, the New Zealand Composite Battalion, and the 6th and 8th Greek Regiments.

The airfield at Rethymnon was defended by the 2nd/1st and 2nd/11th Australian Infantry Battalions, the 4th and 5th Greek Regiments and two Matilda tanks of 7th Royal Tank Regiment, while the town itself was held by the 1,200-strong Cretan Gendarmerie. The entire force was under the command of Lieutenant Colonel Ian Campbell.

Heraklion, meanwhile, was held by the British 14th Infantry Brigade, commanded by Brigadier B. H. Chappell. This comprised: the 2nd Battalion The Black Watch; 2nd Battalion The York & Lancaster Regiment; 2nd Battalion The Leicestershire Regiment; 2nd/4th Australian Infantry Battalion; 3rd and 7th Greek Regiments; six Whippet light tanks of the 3rd King's Own Hussars; two Matilda tanks of 7th Royal Tank Regiment; and the 7th Medium Regiment RA deployed in the infantry role. In due course, the brigade was to be joined by the 2nd Battalion The Argyll & Sutherland Highlanders who would be landed at Tymbaki, on the south coast of the island.

In addition to 4th New Zealand Brigade and the 1st Battalion The Welch Regiment near Canea, Freyberg's reserves consisted of the

2nd/7th and 2nd/8th Australian Infantry Battalions under command of Brigadier George Vasey's Headquarters 19th Australian Infantry Brigade, located halfway between Suda and Rethymnon at Georgioupolis, which featured a sandy beach suitable for a seaborne landing.

Suda Bay itself was defended by a formation called the Mobile Naval Base Defence Organisation (MNBDO), commanded by Major General E. C. Weston of the Royal Marines. This comprised a mixture of units which included: the 15th Coastal Regiment RA; 106th Regiment Royal Horse Artillery (RHA), in the infantry role; 151st and 234 Heavy Anti-Aircraft Batteries RA; 129th and 156th Light Batteries RA; 102nd (Northumberland Hussars) Anti-Tank Regiment RA; 304th Searchlight Battery RA; 2nd Heavy Anti-Aircraft Regiment RM; 23rd Light Anti-Aircraft Battery RM; 9th Battalion The King's Royal Rifle Corps (The Rangers); 16th (2/2nd and 2/3rd) and 17th (2/5th and 2/6th) Australian Brigades' Composite Battalions; the '1st Royal Perivolians', a composite unit formed from British personnel; and a number of medical and logistic support units.

Despite the relatively large size of the Allied force on Crete, it was mostly armed with little more than small arms, its heavier weapons having been lost during the withdrawal through Greece and the subsequent evacuation. The men of the 4th and 5th NZ Brigades, and those of the 19th Australian Infantry Brigade, had arrived with their rifles, Bren LMGs and a few 3-inch mortars, but little else in the way of arms and equipment. Likewise, the Greek units were poorly armed, being equipped largely with rifles of different calibres. The 1,200-strong Cretan Gendarmerie, though considered an effective fighting force, possessed only small arms while the 3,000 Cretan irregulars were for the most part unarmed.

Following his arrival on Crete on 29 April, Freyberg had sent a signal to General Sir Archibald Wavell in Cairo, requesting the despatch of RAF aircraft to reinforce the six Hurricanes and seventeen other obsolete aircraft based on Crete, as well as Royal Navy support without which any defence of the island would be impossible. He pointed out that his forces lacked essential equipment such as digging tools and transport, and possessed only slender reserves of ammunition.

Wavell responded by stating that the Navy would provide support against any attempt by the Germans to launch a seaborne invasion of Crete, which appeared to be Freyberg's main concern despite indications that pointed to the threat of an airborne assault. Indeed, intelligence provided by ULTRA suggested a proposed invasion date of 17 May by an enemy force of two divisions plus corps troops and additional forces. Unfortunately, however, subsequent ULTRA estimates gave rise to confusion in London which was led to believe that 7th Air Division, 22nd Airlanding Division and 5th Mountain Division would all be taking part in the invasion, the entire force comprising 30,000 to 35,000 troops, of which 12,000 were the airborne element with some 10,000 being transported by sea. This information was transmitted to Freyberg and it was on the basis of such that he planned his defence of Crete accordingly.

As mentioned earlier, the attack on Crete had originally been scheduled for 17 May but the 5,000 tons of aviation fuel required for the operation, being transported from the Adriatic aboard a tanker, could not arrive in Greece in time and thus Lieutenant General Student was forced to postpone Mercury until Tuesday 20 May.

At 5.03 a.m. on that day, Major Walter Koch and Nos 3 and 4 Companies of the 1st Battalion LSR-1 took off in forty-eight gliders from the airfield at Tanaga. This force was divided into three detachments: the first, comprising 108 fallschirmjäger in fourteen gliders under Lieutenant Wulf von Plessen, was tasked with landing at the mouth of the River Tavronitis and knocking out an anti-aircraft battery located there; the second, consisting of seventy-two men in nine gliders under Major Franz Braun, was to seize the iron bridge spanning the dried-up bed of the Tavronitis; while the third, 120 men in fifteen gliders under Major Walter Koch himself, was to land on the south-eastern and south-western slopes of Hill 107, a feature dominating Máleme airfield from the south, thereafter capturing the RAF camp there and preventing any counter-attack by Allied forces as the remainder of Group West was dropped.

Nos 1 and 2 Companies, meantime, under command of Lieutenant Alfred Genz and Captain Gustav Altmann respectively, took off in twenty-six gliders from airfields at Megara and Eleusis and headed for their objectives near Canea. Altmann's company was to knock out a number of anti-aircraft artillery positions on the Akrotiri Peninsula behind Suda Bay while Genz was to attack a radio station and some anti-aircraft guns at Mounies, to the south of Canea.

The gliderborne detachments were followed almost immediately by the main force of LSR-1 which numbered some 2,000 fallschirmjäger. At just after 6.00 a.m., as the airborne armada of Ju-52 transports and gliders flew low over the Aegean towards Crete, Messerschmitt 109 and 110 fighters and Ju-87 Stuka divebombers of VIII Air Corps began a series of concentrated attacks on the anti-aircraft defences at Máleme. These were followed by waves of Dornier Do-17s and Junkers Ju-66s who concentrated on the Royal Marine 3.7 inch batteries positioned on Hill 107 just south of the coastal road, and on the 40mm Bofors guns sited around the airfield itself.

No sooner had the strafing and bombing finished than the leading DFS-230 gliders made their appearance. Lieutenant Wulf von Plessen's detachment landed successfully at the mouth of the River Tavronitis, swiftly completing its task of capturing the anti-aircraft battery there. As von Plessen and his men then approached the western perimeter of Máleme airfield, however, they came under fire from troops of C Company 22nd New Zealand Infantry Battalion. Von Plessen and his two immediate subordinates were killed and command of the detachment was assumed by Captain Weinzl, a medical officer. Meantime, Major Franz Braun's detachment had captured the Tavronitis bridge before turning its attention on the New Zealanders' D Company, forcing it to withdraw behind an irrigation canal at the bottom of Hill 107. The New Zealanders recovered swiftly, however, and fought back, bringing heavy fire to bear and pinning down the fallschirmjäger, Braun being killed during this engagement.

Meanwhile, all but one of the gliders carrying Major Walter Koch's detachment had landed on the bed of the Tavronitis and on Hill 107 in the area of the tented camp occupied by RAF personnel. The exception was a DFS-230 which flew on, landing on the beach near Platanias where its occupants were summarily despatched by troops of the 28th (Maori) New Zealand Infantry Battalion. Casualties were high among Koch's men, some being killed or injured as their gliders hit rocks or trees on landing. Others died as they emerged from their aircraft, coming under fire from the defenders of Hill 107, Major Koch being wounded by a bullet passing through his neck.

The main force of LSR-1 was at the same time carrying out its drop. At around 8.30 a.m. Major General Meindl and his tactical headquarters dropped with the 4th Battalion, commanded by Captain Walter Gericke, on to the open ground to the west of the Tavronitis while Major Edgar Stentzler's 2nd Battalion landed farther west. Casualties from the drop were light in both battalions although there was considerable damage to support weapons and motorcycles caused by containers hitting rocks or parachutes malfunctioning.

Having regrouped, both battalions headed for the Tavronitis bridge where they found the surviving members of Major Franz Braun's detachment still under heavy fire. The 4th Battalion LSR-1, reinforced with a company of the 2nd Battalion, was despatched by Major General Meindl to Hill 107 with orders to make contact with Major Koch and his detachment. Captain Gericke performed this task, linking up with elements of Koch's men in the area of the RAF tented camp. The remainder of Koch's detachment had regrouped near the Tavronitis bridge under Senior Medical Officer Heinrich Neumann, who took command. During a search of the camp, Gericke's men came across the RAF operations tent and a search of it revealed a full set of codes which subsequently enabled the Germans to obtain full information on the strength of the island's garrison.

Meindl also ordered Major Edgar Stentzler to attack Hill 107 from the west, thereby driving a wedge between A and B Companies of 22nd New Zealand Infantry Battalion. Shortly afterwards, however, Meindl was wounded twice in the chest. Stentzler's first two attempts to cross the dry bed of the Tavronitis, however, were stalled by the New Zealanders and it was not until the afternoon that he could do so.

The 4th Battalion LSR-1 began to probe the New Zealanders' defences while awaiting the arrival of Major Otto Scherber's 3rd Battalion from its DZ along the coastal road to the east. However, the battalion's departure from Megara had been delayed due to dust clouds, raised by the aircraft carrying other elements of LSR-1 taking off beforehand, which reduced visibility and prevented its own transports from taking off.

By the time the battalion was airborne, it was forty minutes behind schedule and it was not until 10.30 a.m. that it arrived over Máleme, its task being to attack the airfield from the east. Because the supporting air attacks had long ceased, the decision was taken to drop the battalion in the hills to the south of the coastal road, instead of along the road itself, in an area believed to be unoccupied. It had not been reconnoitred from the air, however, and for that the Germans paid dearly. As Major Scherber and his battalion jumped from their Ju-52s, they came under heavy fire from the 21st and 23rd New Zealand Infantry Battalions dug in on the slopes of the hills. Casualties among the 3rd Battalion LSR-1 were heavy, many men being shot dead in mid-air or before they could reach their weapon containers after landing. A total of 400 men, including Major Scherber, died, command of the battalion being assumed by the battalion's staff captain, Lieutenant Horst Trebes. All the other officers were killed or wounded, the latter including Captain Rudolf Witzig whose company was leading the drop. Those who survived eventually succeeded in making their way to Hill 107 where they linked up with the 4th Battalion LSR-1 and the remnants of Major Koch's detachment.

A seventy-two-strong detachment of the 2nd Battalion LSR-1, under Lieutenant Peter Mürbe, had meantime been dropped with three 37mm anti-tank guns beyond the Rodopos Peninsula with the aim of seizing the village of Kastelli Kissamos and a nearby airfield which was under construction. No sooner had Mürbe and his men jumped from their aircraft than they came under fire from the 1st Greek Regiment supported by the local population, who attacked the fallschirmjäger as they landed. The survivors sought refuge in a farmhouse and a fierce battle ensued, by the end of which only seventeen of Mürbe's men were still alive. They were taken prisoner and transported to the police station at Kastelli Kissamou, where they were locked up.

Major Edgar Schentzler had by now despatched a company towards Kolimbari to make contact with Lieutenant Peter Mürbe's detachment and to provide cover for the landings at Máleme; but it encountered strong armed resistance from local people and it took the entire day for it to cover a distance of five miles. The 4th Battalion's No. 16 Company, commanded by Lieutenant Hoefeld, tasked with guarding the road leading from Paleochora across the mountains, also found itself under attack in its positions some eight miles from Tavronitis.

Lieutenant General Süssmann's Group Centre was also experiencing major problems. As described earlier, the leading element comprised Nos 1 and 2 Companies of the 1st Battalion LSR-1, under Lieutenant Alfred Genz and Captain Gustav Altmann, transported in twenty-four gliders. While the two companies were approaching their objective – a troop of guns of 234th Heavy Anti-Aircraft Battery RA – the towropes of two of No. 2 Company's gliders broke and both aircraft crash-landed on the outskirts of Canea. Shortly afterwards a third glider was hit as it landed, almost all aboard being killed. The company was thus reduced to some fifty men but nevertheless managed to overrun the gun positions after some heavy fighting. By the time the action was over, Genz's men numbered only thirty-four.

No. 1 Company had fared even worse. As they approached the northern coast of Crete, the tug pilots mistook Akrotiri for Rodopoas and did not realise their error until over Rethymnon. On approaching the LZ, the fifteen gliders encountered heavy anti-aircraft artillery fire.

Some released their towropes too early and were unable to reach the zone, while others landed too fast and broke up on impact. As they disembarked, the surviving members of the company were engaged by the Northumberland Hussars who swiftly overran the remainder of Altmann's force.

Disaster had also overtaken Lieutenant General Süssmann and part of his headquarters staff travelling with him in a DFS-230 glider. While flying over the island of Aegina, the towrope snapped and the aircraft subsequently crashed, killing the commander of 7th Air Division and all others aboard.

Next to land after the two gliderborne companies of LSR-1 was Colonel Richard Heidrich's FJR-3. The 1st Battalion, commanded by Captain Baron Friedrich von der Heydte, was ordered to advance on Suda Bay via Perivolia, linking up with Captain Gustav Altmann's company of the 1st Battalion LSR-1 en route. It was dropped accurately, landing to the south and east of the prison and incurring few casualties. Von der Heydte himself almost ended up in the reservoir at Alikianos, landing instead in some trees on the edge of it. Thereafter, while hurrying down a road to his battalion's RV, he was strafed by a Messerschmitt and forced to take cover in a ditch. Having regrouped, his battalion headed east into the hills towards Mounies to rendezvous with Altmann and his company.

The 2nd Battalion FJR-3, commanded by Major Helmut Derpa, ran into fire from the anti-aircraft guns on the Akrotiri Peninsula which should have been knocked out by Lieutenant Alfred Genz's company of the 1st Battalion LSR-1. This caused the formation of Ju-52s carrying the battalion to break up and as Heidrich's fallschirmjäger jumped, they encountered heavy small-arms fire from the ground. Only 350 survived the drop and regrouped near the prison, many being killed on the DZ while others fell into the Alikianos reservoir and were drowned. No. 7 Company, under Lieutenant Neuhoff, was dropped south-west of Galatas and attempted unsuccessfully to attack Pink Hill, a feature held by a scratch force made up of troops of 2nd New Zealand Division's petrol company fighting as infantry, a role to which they were singularly unaccustomed.

Major Ludwig Heilmann's 3rd Battalion FJR-3 was dropped well away from its intended DZ in the area of Daratsos. The battalion headquarters and No. 9 Company were dropped south-east of Galatas, an area held by the 6th Greek Regiment, eventually capturing Cemetery Hill after some heavy fighting. No. 10 Company, under Lieutenant Nagele, however, landed on its intended DZ and advanced on a tented camp, on the coast to the rear of Galatas, which proved to contain two British medical units: 16th Field Ambulance and No. 7 General Hospital RAMC. Taking both units and some 500 patients prisoner, Nagele and his men led them off towards the 3rd Battalion's RV but en route were ambushed near the village of Efthymi by troops of the 19th New Zealand Infantry Battalion who killed Nagele and a number of his men, capturing the remainder.

A few members of No. 11 Company, commanded by Lieutenant Kersten, landed on their intended DZ north of Galatas but were swiftly annihilated by the New Zealand Composite Battalion. The rest of the company was dropped several miles away in the area of Perivolia, some forty men landing near a villa in which, unbeknown to them, King George of Greece, who had been evacuated to Crete by the Allies, was in residence with a small entourage and his prime minister. Spirited away by a platoon of New Zealanders detailed to protect them, the king and his companions managed to escape. Some of No. 11 Company were subsequently dealt with by troops hastily despatched from a nearby transit camp, while others fell victim to the 2nd Greek Regiment. The surviving members of the company regrouped in the area of Perivolia and eventually made contact with the 1st Battalion. No. 12 Company meantime found itself dropping on to the same DZ as the 1st Battalion.

The 7th Air Division's engineer battalion came down between the Alikianos reservoir and Alikianos itself, an area defended by the 8th Greek Regiment, and its men immediately found themselves under fire as they searched for their weapon containers. As they headed for Alikianos, they were attacked by members of the local population armed only with shotguns and scythes, and soon afterwards encountered fire from weapons looted from their containers by troops of the 8th Greek Regiment. That afternoon, the Greeks captured more weapons delivered by the Luftwaffe during a resupply drop. The engineers subsequently captured a power station but achieved little else that day.

The commander of FJR-3, Colonel Richard Heidrich, and his regimental headquarters dropped near the prison at 9.00 a.m. He quickly realised that he and the surviving elements of his regiment were in a tight corner, being in a bowl dominated by the heights of Galatas; these would have to be captured or his regiment would remain trapped and unable to break through to its objective, Canea. Gathering a force of three companies under Major Ludwig Heilmann, he despatched it to attack Pink Hill, where No. 7 Company was still heavily engaged, its commander, Lieutenant Neuhoff, having been killed. Meanwhile the 3rd Battalion's headquarters and No. 6 Company, under the commanding officer of the 2nd Battalion, Major Helmut Derpa, took up positions south of the prison to protect Heilmann's right flank while the 1st Battalion, still advancing on Perivolia, covered the left.

Heidrich's first attack on Pink Hill at 10.00 a.m. met with fierce resistance from the drivers, storemen and fuel technicians of the 2nd New Zealand Division's Petrol Company who, despite being forced to fall back, prevented the fallschirmjäger from breaking through. Heavy casualties were inflicted on the Germans and during the afternoon Heidrich launched another assault, using his only reserve: the 3rd Battalion's headquarters and No. 6 Company. Once again, however, the attack failed as Heidrich's men suffered half their number either killed or wounded.

The fallschirmjäger were also taking heavy casualties elsewhere, the 19th New Zealand Infantry Battalion killing 155 and capturing nine while the 23rd New Zealand Infantry Battalion killed a further twenty-nine and took three prisoner.

By late afternoon on 20 May, Group Centre had failed to take any of its objectives. At his headquarters at the Hôtel Grande Bretagne in Athens, however, General Kurt Student had been led to believe that the operation was proceeding completely as planned. Lieutenant General von Richthofen, commander of VIII Air Corps, had reported that the anti-aircraft guns at Máleme and Galatas had been destroyed by the heavy bombing and strafing and that the gliders and paratroops had landed and dropped in the correct locations. He also stated that casualties among the transport squadrons had been light, with only seven aircraft destroyed. The seemingly good news was relayed to Germany where it was greeted with relief.

As a result of these reports, Student decided to proceed with the next stage of his plan, the airlanding at Máleme by troops of Lieutenant General Julius Ringel's 5th Mountain Division. Two Ju-52s, carrying a Luftwaffe airfield control party under Captain Albert Snowadzki, was despatched to Máleme. On their approach to the airfield, the pilots could see a Nazi flag laid out on the runway and, taking this to mean the airfield had been captured, Snowadzki ordered his pilot to land. No sooner had it touched down, however, than the leading Ju-52 came under very heavy fire but, despite being seriously damaged, succeeded in taking off again. Snowadzki lost little time in reporting to Student that the airfield was still in enemy hands.

It was at this juncture that Student began to receive other reports that indicated all was far from well with the progress of the operation. Group Centre reported the failure of its attack on Canea with heavy casualties and the death of Lieutenant General Süssmann. Shortly afterwards, Student received a signal from Colonel Richard Heidrich, requesting that FJR-2, which was part of the second wave due to arrive during the afternoon, be dropped on Prison Valley instead of Rethymnon. Student refused, on the grounds that changing the plan at such a late stage would only result in chaos.

There were insufficient aircraft to lift the entire second wave, comprising Colonel Alfred Sturm's FJR-2 and the whole of Group East, from Megara. A number of those returning from delivering the first wave were unserviceable or crashed on landing, rendering runways unusable until the wreckage was cleared. The plan had called for the transports to be turned round swiftly in order that the second wave should be landed before nightfall, but this proved impossible, the problem being exacerbated by the process of refuelling which took considerably longer than anticipated. This had major ramifications for the operation as the timings for close air support by VIII Air Corps had been coordinated with those governing the arrival of FJR-2 and Group East over their respective objectives. Frantic attempts to inform Headquarters XI Air Corps of the delay in the take-off of the second wave were thwarted by the inadequate Greek telephone system and it was not until after Richthofen's fighters and bombers were already heading for Crete once more that XI Air Corps learned of the problems at Megara.

At 4.00 p.m. the preliminary bombing and strafing began at Rethymnon; fifty minutes later, by which time the attacking aircraft had departed, the leading transports could be seen approaching at an altitude of 400 feet. German intelligence had stated that Rethymnon was only lightly defended and, indeed, the town itself was occupied only by the 800-strong Cretan Gendarmerie, a well-trained and highly disciplined unit under the command of Major Christos Tsiphakis. To the east of the town, however, was an ad hoc brigade formation comprising the 2nd/1st and 2nd/11th Australian Infantry Battalions and the 4th and 5th Greek Regiments (each of battalion strength and poorly equipped) supported by an artillery battery and two Matilda tanks. The entire force, some 3,600 strong, was led by Lieutenant Colonel Ian Campbell, the commanding officer of the 2nd /1st, who had deployed it on a ridgeline running parallel to the coast and dominating the airfield and the coastal road. His own battalion and his battery of six field guns were positioned at the eastern end of the ridge, on a feature known as Hill A, overlooking the airfield, while the 2nd/11th, commanded by

Major Ray Sandover, was located approximately two miles to the west on another feature dubbed Hill B. The area between the two Australian units was defended by the 4th Greek Regiment and an Australian company held in reserve, while the 5th Greek Regiment was positioned in a valley to the rear, concealed in olive groves. Campbell's headquarters was located on a hill feature named Hill D and his two tanks were concealed in a gully to the west of the airfield's runway.

As the 160 transports carrying FJR-2 flew along the coast on their approach to Rethymnon from the east, they unwittingly aproached the Australian positions which, hidden in vineyards and olive groves, had suffered little from the preliminary bombing and strafing. The slow-flying Ju-52s were an easy target for the battalions' machine guns which shot down seven aircraft and severely damaged several others, setting them ablaze.

Due to the German belief that Rethymnon was only lightly defended, FJR-2 was only two battalions strong, the 2nd Battalion having been allotted to FJR-1 for its operation at Heraklion. Captain Hans Kroh's 1st Battalion, together with a machine-gun company, was to drop to the east of Rethymnon airfield and seize it. At the same time, the 3rd Battalion, under Captain Wiedemann, along with two troops of 7th Air Division's artillery regiment, would drop between the village of Perivolia and the River Platanes and seize Rethymnon itself. Meanwhile, Colonel Sturm and his regimental headquarters, accompanied by a reinforced company, would drop to the west of the airfield and remain there as a reserve.

In the event, things did not go to plan for FJR-2. In the confusion caused among the transports by the heavy fire from the ground, some elements of the 1st Battalion were dropped into the sea and drowned while others were killed in mid-air or landed among the Australian positions where they were killed immediately.

The 3rd Battalion, meanwhile, was faring little better, having failed to take its objectives. Colonel Sturm, his regimental headquarters and two companies were in front of the 2nd/11th Australian Infantry

Battalion which proceeded to inflict heavy casualties. Sturm and his staff survived as they landed in an area of dead ground but shortly after last light the Australians carried out a sweep, capturing eighty-eight fallschirmjäger and a large quantity of weapons and ammunition. Colonel Sturm was taken prisoner on the following morning. The rest of the 3rd Battalion had meantime been dropped correctly to the west of the Platanes and, having regrouped, advanced on Rethymnon where, at 6.00 p.m. it encountered stiff resistance from the Cretan Gendarmerie and armed civilians. Having been repulsed, Captain Wiedemann and his men took up defensive positions in the area of the village of Perivolia (not to be confused with the town) and dug in.

The main force of the 1st Battalion had landed a mile or so to the east of Hill A, in the area of an olive-oil factory at Stavromenos. Quickly rallying and regrouping his men, who succeeded in locating their containers from which they recovered their weapons, Captain Hans Kroh advanced west towards Hill A and began to fight his way up through the terraced vineyards held by the Australians. Eventually, after some bitter fighting, the battalion captured the feature but in the process suffered over 400 casualties. It failed, however, to take the airfield which remained in Australian hands.

As last light approached, Lieutenant Colonel Ian Campbell launched a counter-attack with half of his reserve company and the two Matilda tanks, but the latter proved ineffective, as one became immobilised after striking a drain and the other fell into a gully at the bottom of Hill A. He decided therefore to wait for first light on the following day to mount another counter-attack to recapture the feature.

At dawn on 21 May, Campbell launched his attack, the 4th and 5th Greek Regiments providing support on the flanks. The ferocity of the Australian assault was such that Captain Kroh and his men were forced off the feature and driven back to Stavromenos where they took refuge in the olive-oil factory. Both Australian battalions then carried out a mopping-up operation throughout the entire area during which they captured most of the surviving members of the 1st and 3rd Battalions

FJR-2, apart from the detachment with Captain Wiedemann at Perivolia.

Group East had begun its operation at Heraklion during the afternoon of 20 May. The leading element comprised FJR-1 reinforced by the 2nd Battalion FJR-2, 7th Air Division's anti-aircraft machine gun battalion and two troops of parachute artillery. The plan was for the 2nd Battalion FJR-1 to attack and seize the airfield while the 3rd Battalion captured Heraklion itself. The 1st Battalion FJR-1 would seize the Ames Ridge (named after an RAF radar unit, known as the Air Ministry Experimental Station, AMES, located on it) and protect the eastern flank of the main attack, while the 2nd Battalion FJR-2 was dropped to the west of Heraklion where it would cut the coastal road and protect the western flank.

Heraklion was held by 14th Infantry Brigade under Brigadier B. H. Chappell. The airfield itself was defended by ten Bofors 40mm guns, manned by Australian and British gunners, and a battery of Royal Marine Artillery equipped with 3.7-inch anti-aircraft guns and Oerlikon 20mm 'pom-poms'.

As with the forces at Rethymnon, German intelligence had seriously underestimated the forces defending Heraklion, putting their strength at 400 men. Like Lieutenant Colonel Campbell, Brigadier Chappell had allocated the defence of the town and harbour to his Greek units while deploying the rest of his brigade around the airfield to the east of the town. The defences were U-shaped, with the eastern arm held by the 2nd Battalion The Black Watch on a feature known as East Hill which dominated the airfield. In the centre of the 'U' was the 2nd/4th Australian Infantry Battalion positioned on two hills known as the 'Charlies', which had good fields of fire over the airfield's two runways. On the left of the Australians was the 2nd Battalion The Leicestershire Regiment on whose left was the 2nd Battalion The York & Lancaster Regiment. Forward of the latter was the 7th Medium Regiment RA whose positions formed the western arm of the 'U'. To the east of the main defended area was Ames Ridge and its RAF radar station guarded by a platoon of The Black Watch.

Poor communications between Headquarters Creforce and 14th Infantry Brigade resulted in the latter knowing nothing of the airborne landings until 2.30 p.m. when news of the drops around Máleme and Suda reached Brigadier Chappell. At 4.00 p.m. the leading German bombers were sighted and twelve minutes later Ju-87 Stukas began the attack, followed twenty minutes later by Messerschmitt 110 fighter-bombers which proceeded to carry out strafing runs. Clever camou-flage and concealment of all positions throughout the brigade, combined with strict fire discipline which forbade troops to open fire at the aircraft with small arms, led to very few casualties. The same orders had been issued to the crews of the anti-aircraft guns which thus held their fire and escaped any damage. After less than thirty minutes, the Stukas withdrew as they could no longer wait for the delayed trans-ports and, followed by the Messerschmitts, flew back east to their base on the island of Skarpanto.

At 5.30 p.m. the first wave of Ju-52s appeared, flying low in V-for-mations of three as they headed for the airfield. Heavy fire was opened on them from throughout the entire brigade area, the troops of the 2nd/4th Australian Infantry Battalion on the 'Charlies' finding them-selves at almost the same height as the transports and thus firing almost horizontally at them as they flew past.

Fifteen transports were hit, some bursting into flames as their sticks of paratroops jumped, others exploding. A large number of fallschir-mjäger were killed in mid-air while others were mown down as they landed and struggled to rid themselves of their harnesses. The 2nd Battalion FJR-1, commanded by Captain Burckhardt, was dropped over the entire area from the airfield westwards to the positions of the 7th Medium Regiment RA. The western element, comprising Nos 6 and 7 Companies and a machine- gun company, under the overall command of Captain Duntz, suffered heavy casualties, losing over 300 killed, more than 100 wounded and a large number captured. One group of five fallschirmjäger survived by discarding their weapons and equipment before diving into the sea and swimming eastwards down the coast where they managed to join up with elements of the 1st Battalion FJR-1, under Major Erich Walther, which had been dropped at Gournes, eight kilometres to the east of Heraklion.

Several members of Nos 6 and 7 Companies landed on an area of open ground called Buttercup Field which offered little or no cover for the fallschirmjäger who were prevented by heavy fire from reaching their weapon containers. Shortly afterwards, the Leicesters, supported by the six Whippet light tanks of the 3rd King's Own Hussars and the two 7th Royal Tank Regiment Matildas, carried out a sweep of Buttercup Field, accounting for a number still hiding in it. Some fallschirmjäger escaped, however, and took refuge in nearby abandoned barracks and a slaughterhouse from which they put up a stiff resistance before being overrun by the tanks, some being shot and others run over and crushed.

The eastern element of the 2nd Battalion FJR-1, comprising Nos 5 and 8 Companies, also suffered heavy casualties. Those who survived the drop, and succeeded in escaping from the DZ alive, took part in an assault on East Hill led by Lieutenants Hermann and Platow. This encountered a heavy crossfire from the Black Watch positions on the feature which stopped the fallschirmjäger in their tracks and forced them back. By nightfall, the two companies had been reduced to sixty to seventy men.

Less than half an hour after landing, the 2nd Battalion FJR-1 had lost over 300 killed, 100 wounded and a large number captured, the survivors regrouping under Captain Burckmann at the foot of Ames Ridge, about one mile to the south-east.

Farther east, at Gournes, the commander of Group East, Colonel Bruno Bräuer, had dropped to join Major Erich Walther's 1st Battalion FJR-1. He found that only No. 3 Company had been dropped at the correct time, Nos. 1 and 2 Companies, together with the battalion headquarters, being dropped three hours late with No. 2 Company landing too far to the east. For some unknown reason, No. 4 Company had not taken off at all.

Radio communications were poor and Bräuer was unable to obtain any news as to the progress of the rest of his group's operations. Consequently, at last light, he decided to head west to make contact with the 2nd Battalion FJR-1 and thereafter find out for himself the situation regarding the attack on Heraklion. Escorted by a platoon commanded by Lieutenant Count Wolfgang von Blücher, Bräuer set off and headed west. At midnight, however, von Blücher's leading troops encountered standing patrols of the Black Watch who opened fire, forcing the fallschirmjäger to take cover.

To the west, the operation to capture the city of Heraklion was also in trouble. The 2nd Battalion FJR-2 less two companies, under Captain Gerhart Schirmer, had dropped west of Heraklion and, encountering no opposition, had succeeded in carrying out its task of blocking the coastal road. Major Karl-Lothar Schulz's 3rd Battalion FJR-1, however, had been dropped late and very close to the south and west of the city, landing in fields and vineyards close to its walls. During the drop the battalion suffered heavy casualties from anti-aircraft fire; Schulz had a lucky escape, his Ju-52 transport receiving a direct hit in a fuel tank and exploding a split second after he had jumped. On landing, his companies came under attack from the 3rd and 7th Greek Regiments, and from Cretan civilians who attacked the fallschirmjäger as they hung from trees, killing them as they struggled to extract themselves from their harnesses.

Schulz eventually succeeded in rallying two groups of his men. Taking one, he headed for the city's Canea Gate where a furious battle took place between the fallschirmjäger and a motley force of defenders, under Captain Kalaphotakis of the Cretan Gendarmerie, comprising Greek troops, gendarmes and armed civilians who manned the ramparts around the gate. The other group, meanwhile, under Captain Count Wolf von der Schulenberg, moved round to the left to find another point of entry into the city.

Eventually, both Schulz's and von der Schulenberg's groups gained entry to the city. After bitter fighting through the streets, Heraklion capitulated, the city's mayor and a Greek officer formally surrendering the city to Major Schulz. No sooner had they done so, however, than troops of the Leicesters and the York & Lancasters appeared, and Schulz and his men found themselves under attack. Short of ammunition, they were forced to carry out a fighting withdrawal from the town to an area to the south-west, where they regrouped.

On hearing that the attack on the city had failed, Colonel Bräuer ordered Lieutenant von Blücher to seize the high ground east of the airfield. Lacking support from the rest of the battalion, which was having difficulty in regrouping, this inevitably failed and von Blücher and his men became cut off.

By the evening of 20 May, it was all too apparent to General Student and his staff in Athens that Operation Mercury was in deep trouble. None of its objectives, including the capture of the airfields at Máleme, Rethymnon and Heraklion, had been achieved despite the commitment of all XI Air Corps' gliderborne and parachute assets with the exception of a few companies held at Megara due to the lack of aircraft to carry them in the second wave.

Student decided to concentrate his efforts on Máleme. His plan was to drop reinforcements in the form of 7th Air Division's remaining parachute companies whose task would be the seizure of Máleme airfield. Nos 5 and 6 Companies of the 2nd Battalion FJR-2 would drop and attack from the east while the surviving elements of LSR-1 did likewise from the west. The latter would be reinforced by one and a half companies of 7th Air Division's anti-tank battalion and a company of the 1st Battalion FJR-2 which would be dropped west of the airfield under the command of Colonel Hermann Ramcke, who thereafter would assume command of the LSR-1 and Group West from the wounded Major General Eugen Meindl. Once the airfield had been taken, the headquarters of Colonel Willibald Utz's 102nd Mountain Rifle Regiment and his 2nd Battalion would be airlanded at Máleme. As a prelude to the operation, close air support would again be provided by bombers and fighters of VIII Air Corps.

Student needed to know, however, whether the western end of the airfield was defended or covered by enemy direct fire. To find out, he despatched a Ju-52, flown by Captain Kleye and laden with ammunition, detailed to carry out a touch-down and take-off on the runway. Despite coming under sporadic machine-gun fire from the west during his approach, Kleye managed to land and unload his cargo before taking off unscathed. Meanwhile, another Ju-52, flown by Lieutenant Koenitz, landed on the beach west of Tavronitis with a resupply of ammunition for the LSR-1. Shortly afterwards, Koenitz took off again, taking with him the badly injured Major General Meindl and seven other seriously wounded men.

At approximately 3.00 p.m. on 21 May, aircraft of VIII Air Corps began their attacks. No sooner had these ceased than elements of LSR-1 advanced eastwards towards Pirgos but were driven off by heavy fire from the three battalions of 5th New Zealand Brigade. Shortly afterwards, a formation of 24 Ju-52s dropped Nos 5 and 6 Companies of the 2nd Battalion FJR-2 east of Máleme four miles behind the brigade's lines but unknowingly in an area occupied by 28th (Maori) New Zealand Infantry Battalion and 19 Army Troops, the latter an administrative unit which nevertheless gave a very good account of itself. Many fallschirmjäger were shot in mid-air while others were killed on the DZ as the Maoris fixed bayonets and charged. Out of some 240 dropped, approximately eighty survived this onslaught and managed to escape before eventually, under cover of darkness, making their way westwards along the beaches to the area held by the LSR-1.

The companies led by Colonel Ramcke fared better, being dropped an hour later and landing unopposed to the west of the Tavronitis. Forty men, however, were blown by the wind out to sea where they drowned. Assuming command of LSR-1 and Group West, Ramcke pushed forward to the airfield where at 7.00 p.m. he found that the air-landing of the leading elements of 5th Mountain Division had already begun.

Although the earlier attacks had failed to knock out the New

Zealand artillery bringing fire to bear on the airfield, the decision had been taken to proceed with the airlanding operation which began at around 5.00 p.m., albeit under artillery fire from 5th NZ Brigade. One of the first Ju-52s carrying men of the 2nd Battalion 100th Mountain Rifle Regiment received a direct hit as it touched down, exploding in a ball of flame. Some of those following behind were also hit, careering down the runway on their bellies as the mountain troops leapt from the disintegrating fuselages. Soon the runway was piled with heaps of wreckage, forcing pilots to land on nearby beaches or wherever they could find suitable places to touch down, coming under fire from New Zealand artillery and infantry as they did so.

Some twenty aircraft were destroyed at Máleme on 21 May but the landings continued in spite of the casualties, the Germans using captured Bren carriers to tow the wrecked aircraft clear of the runway. By nightfall, Colonel Ramcke had assembled a force of about 650 fallschirmjäger and mountain troops. At 9.00 p.m. he issued his orders: the 900-strong remnants of the 2nd and 4th Battalions LSR-1, reinforced by the one and half companies of other fallschirmjäger who had accompanied him, together with a company of mountain troops, would reorganise and maintain their forward positions. A half-company of mountain troops was to reinforce a fallschirmjäger section in action against Cretan guerrillas on the Paleochora road, while the remainder of the 2nd Battalion 100th Mountain Rifle Regiment would take up positions defending the airfield from the south and west. Further units of 5th Mountain Division were expected to arrive on the following day and these would be used in an attack round to the south, its objective being the major hill feature of Monodhendri which lay three miles to the south of Ay Marina.

Ramcke was also anticipating the arrival of further reinforcements that night in the form of the first of the two flotillas which would cross from a point off the island of Milos, lying halfway between the Greek mainland and Crete. Comprising two tramp steamers and nineteen caiques escorted by the light destroyer *Lupo*, it would carry the 3rd

Battalion 100th Mountain Rifle Regiment, elements of 7 Air Division's anti-aircraft battalion and a large quantities of stores, in particular much-needed ammunition. The second flotilla, escorted by the *Sagittario*, would ferry the 2nd Battalion 85th Mountain Rifle Regiment, the 95th Mountain Artillery Regiment and 5th Mountain Division's reconnaissance, anti-tank and engineer battalions to Heraklion. The Germans' intention was that the crossing should be carried out in daylight during 21 May with air cover provided by VIII Air Corps, the flotillas reaching Crete under cover of darkness. Accordingly, preparations were made for the landing that night with a special detachment of Kriegsmarine personnel setting up lights to guide the vessels to the beach.

Ramcke, however, was to be disappointed. Through signals intelligence, the British were aware of the existence of the two flotillas assembled to transport the seaborne landing element of Operation Mercury to Crete. No sooner had news of the attack on Crete reached the headquarters of the Royal Navy's Mediterranean Fleet in Alexandria than the Commander-in-Chief Mediterranean, Admiral Sir Andrew Cunningham, despatched three task forces into the Aegean on the night of 20 May to seek out and destroy both flotillas. Another task force comprising three destroyers, HMS *Ilex*, *Jervis* and *Nizam*, sailed for a point east of Crete from which they would shell the airfield on the island of Skarpanto, the base of VIII Air Corps' Dorniers and Stukas.

Dawn on 21 May brought Luftwaffe attacks on Cunningham's ships which were by then withdrawing to safer waters. One element, Force D, commanded by Rear Admiral I. G. Glennie and comprising the cruisers HMS *Ajax*, *Dido*, and *Orion* and four destroyers, HMS *Imperial*, *Isis*, *Janus* and *Kimberley*, suffered a particularly heavy attack but escaped any serious damage. To the east, Rear Admiral E. L. S. King's Force C, consisting of the cruisers HMS *Naiad* and HMAS *Perth* and the destroyers HMS *Juno*, *Kandahar*, *Kingston* and *Nubian*, suffered the loss of the *Juno* which received three direct hits and sank almost immediately afterwards.

Despite the air attacks, Forces C and D returned to the Aegean at last light and resumed the hunt for their prey. That night, Force D, now comprising the cruisers HMS *Dido, Orion* and *Ajax* and the destroyers HMS *Janus, Kimberley, Hasty* and *Hereward*, picked up the first flotilla on radar and at 11.30 p.m. came upon it some eighteen miles north of Canea. Illuminated by 20-inch searchlights, the *Lupo* immediately attacked, firing a salvo of torpedoes at Rear Admiral Glennie's three cruisers which took immediate evasive action before opening fire on the little destroyer.

At the same time, Force D's four destroyers launched themselves at the flotilla itself, the two steamers and caiques being easy prey. By the end of the action, which lasted two and a half hours, 327 Germans had been killed. The remainder were picked up by German vessels on the morning of 22 May, by which time Glennie and his ships had withdrawn from the area. Only one caique, carrying 113 men, made landfall at in Crete at Cape Spathia, to the west of Máleme. A small group in a cutter likewise reached Crete, landing on the Akrotiri Peninsula, where soon afterwards it encountered a fighting patrol of the Northumberland Hussars and was captured.

Dawn on 22 May found the second flotilla being hunted by Force C, now comprising the cruisers HMS *Naiad* and HMAS *Perth*, the anti-aircraft cruisers HMS *Calcutta* and *Carlisle* and the three destroyers HMS *Kandahar, Kingston* and *Nubian*. Force C was sweeping north-westwards from Heraklion when, shortly after 8.30 a.m., a lone caique carrying German troops was sighted. This was subsequently engaged and sunk by HMAS *Perth*, but at the same time Force C came under attack by a large formation of Junkers 88 bombers. Rear Admiral King nevertheless continued his pursuit of the second flotilla and shortly afterwards, a small cargo vessel was located and sunk by his destroyers.

At 10.10 a.m., the flotilla of caiques and its escort, the Italian light destroyer *Sagittario*, were sighted some twenty-five miles south east of Milos. The latter immediately began laying a smokescreen under cover of which the caiques scattered in different directions. Some were sunk but the rest escaped as King's ships were unable to pursue them as by this time they were running low on ammunition. Receiving orders from Admiral Cunningham to return to Alexandria, King called off the pursuit and withdrew his force towards the Kithera Channel. Throughout this time, Force C was still being attacked by enemy bombers. HMS *Carlisle* was damaged by a direct hit while another cruiser, *Naiad*, had two turrets put out of action and her maximum speed reduced to sixteen knots.

Three hours later, in response to a call for assistance from Rear Admiral Glennie, Rear Admiral Sir Bernard Rawlings's Force A1, comprising the battleships HMS *Warspite* and *Valiant*, the cruisers *Gloucester* and *Fiji*, and five destroyers entered the Kithera Channel to reinforce Task Force C and cover its withdrawal. Shortly afterwards, however, *Warspite* received a direct hit from a bomb which put its 4- and 6-inch batteries out of action, and fifty minutes later the destroyer HMS *Greyhound* was sunk. At 3.50 p.m. the cruiser HMS *Gloucester* was set ablaze and lost all power following a direct hit.

During the subsequent withdrawal to the south-west by both task forces, *Valiant* was hit and the destroyer *Fiji* sunk. Later that afternoon, Force A1 was joined by the 5th Destroyer Flotilla commanded by Captain The Lord Mountbatten and comprising the destroyers HMS *Kashmir, Kelly* and *Kipling*. By the end of 22 May, Admiral Cunningham's Mediterranean Fleet had suffered losses totalling two cruisers and a destroyer sunk, and two battleships, two cruisers and several destroyers having sustained damage. It had, however, achieved its task of preventing the seaborne element of XI Air Corps from reaching Crete.

On Crete, meanwhile, command of the German forces on the ground had been assumed by Lieutenant General Julius Ringel, commander of 5th Mountain Division. General Kurt Student had intended to transfer himself and the forward element of Headquarters XI Air Corps from Athens to Crete once all his forces had landed, but on the evening of 21 May he had been ordered by General Hans Jeschonnek to remain in Athens. The order had originated from Göring who, like Hitler, was horrified at the heavy losses suffered by 7th Air Division. Hitler, moreover, was infuriated at the possible consequences for Operation Barbarossa through the delay in the redeployment of VIII Air Corps' squadrons to the east. Student had thus fallen from grace, a fact welcomed by those in the OKW and the Luftwaffe, including General Alexander Lohr, commander of 4th Air Fleet, whom he had antagonised previously when pleading the cause of airborne forces.

Orders issued on 22 May stated that XI Air Corps was to continue landing elements of 5th Mountain Division at Máleme airfield along with supplies of weapons, ammunition, rations and other stores. The main attempt to win control of Crete was to be concentrated on Group West, with Groups Centre and East being left to hold their ground at Rethymnon and Heraklion, pinning down the Allied forces there and denying them use of the airfields.

Colonel Richard Heidrich's FJR-3 had established defensive positions along Prison Valley where it had subsequently received a resupply drop of some 300 containers. Heidrich had expected a major counter-attack at any time but this had not materialised. On 21 May, troops of the 19th New Zealand Infantry Battalion, supported by a troop of Whippet light tanks of the 3rd King's Own Hussars, had attacked Cemetery Hill to dislodge one of Heidrich's forward outposts. Although the Germans were driven off the feature and a number of machine gunners were killed, the New Zealanders in turn came under mortar and machine-gun fire from FJR-3 positions in the Ayia Valley which prevented them from occupying the feature.

On the morning of 22 May, Heidrich reinforced his much-weakened 3rd Battalion with parachute engineers. He then sent fighting patrols north to penetrate to the rear of 5th New Zealand Brigade at Platanias. Major Helmut Derpa's 2nd Battalion was assigned the task of attacking the Galatas Heights and at 7.00 p.m. that evening it launched an assault on Pink Hill, driving back the 2nd New Zealand Division Petroleum Company holding the feature. No sooner had they occupied it, however, than Derpa and his men were subjected to a fierce counter-attack by

200 members of the 6th Greek Regiment reinforced by a large number of armed Cretan civilians led by a British officer, Captain Michael Forrester, a member of a British military mission attached to the Greek Army. In the face of such an onslaught, the 2nd Battalion FJR-3 turned and fled. That night, Major Derpa was killed in fierce fighting in the area of positions held by the 2nd New Zealand Divisional Cavalry.

Further to the east at Rethymnon, meantime, FJR-2 had achieved nothing. One battle group, commanded by Captain Hans Kroh, was still occupying the olive-oil factory at Stavromenos while the other, under Captain Wiedemann, was holding positions at Perivolia. Both were short of food and neither was in possession of radio communications, all sets having been lost during the drop. Attempts to remedy the situation by landing one in a Fiesler Storch failed.

On 21 May Kroh's battle group came under attack from the 2nd/1st Australian Infantry Battalion and the 4th Greek Regiment while Captain Wiedemann was assailed by the 2nd/11th Australian Infantry Battalion and the 5th Greek Regiment. The commanding officer of the 2nd/11th, Major R. L. Sandover, possessed a copy of FJR-2's orders for the operation which had been found on the person of a staff member of the captured commander of FJR-2, Colonel Albert Sturm. Also captured was a set of ground-to-air signal panels and flags and the instructions for their use. Sandover spoke German and was able to translate the operational orders and signal instructions, his men putting the flags and panels to good use by directing strikes by German aircraft on to the fallschirmjäger positions and requesting resupply by parachute.

The attack by the 4th Greek Regiment and 2nd/1st Australian Infantry Battalion failed due to lack of coordination between the two units. The night of 21 May saw the start of the attack on Perivolia by the 2nd/11th Australian Infantry Battalion and 5th Greek Regiment. Confusion reigned at one point when the latter changed direction to the south and began harassing the flank of Captain Wiedemann's group. Fierce fighting ensued as the 2nd/11th subsequently closed with the enemy, capturing some buildings on the periphery of the village before coming under fire from light anti-tank weapons which knocked out two Matilda tanks.

For the following five days a stalemate ensued at Perivolia and at Stavromenos until 25 May, when the 2nd/1st Australian Infantry Battalion succeeded finally in capturing the olive-oil factory. On entering the buildings, however, the leading elements found it occupied only by wounded fallschirmjäger, Captain Kroh and the rest of his men having slipped away beforehand.

At Heraklion, Colonel Bruno Bräuer's FJR-1 was in a similarly parlous situation. Thirst was a major problem for the fallschirmjäger, some of whom had resorted to drinking foul water from ditches and subsequently fell prey to dysentery. Others who went seeking water were killed in the process by Allied troops or Cretan guerrillas, while many of the wounded lay where they had fallen, dying of thirst.

Lieutenant Count Wolfgang von Blücher's platoon of the 1st Battalion FJR-1 was trapped in a small bowl to the south of Heraklion airfield, surrounded by the positions of the 2nd Battalion the Black Watch. Von Blücher and his men had dug shell scrapes with their helmets but these afforded poor protection against the constant machine-gun fire and desultory mortaring to which they were subjected. By 21 May, most members of the platoon were wounded and very short of ammunition. Late that afternoon, a horseman was observed galloping towards the platoon, several boxes of ammunition fastened to his saddle. Recovering from their initial amazement, the troops of the Black Watch opened fire but did not succeed in hitting horse and rider until they had reached the fallschirmjäger position, killing them both. Von Blücher later learned that the rider was none other than his younger brother, Corporal Leberecht von Blücher. He did not have long to grieve, however, as he too, together with his youngest brother, Rifleman Hans-Joachim von Blücher, was killed on the following morning along with the remaining members of his platoon.

The Máleme sector in the early hours of the morning of 22 May saw a counter-attack mounted by 5th New Zealand Brigade. At 3.30

a.m., the 20th and 28th (Maori) New Zealand Infantry Battalions, supported by a troop of three Whippets of the 3rd King's Own Hussars under Lieutenant Roy Farran, led the advance westwards astride the coastal road. The 20th New Zealand Infantry Battalion was to clear the enemy from the area of the airfield while the 28th (Maori) was to capture Hill 107, thereafter handing it over to the 20th Battalion before returning to Platanias. The 21st New Zealand Infantry Battalion was to move up from Vineyard Ridge, to the south-west of Kondomari, via Vlacheronitiss and advance round behind Hill 107.

As it advanced on the right and northern side of the coastal road, the 20th New Zealand Infantry Battalion encountered detachments of fallschirmjäger with machine guns, with D Company at one point being confronted by a strongpoint – a fortified house which they attacked with grenades. Resistance grew stronger as the battalion approached Pirgos, a mile or so from the airfield, fallschirmjäger having to be flushed out of their positions in ditches, buildings, fields and gardens, with much of the fighting conducted at close quarters. Eventually, one of the battalion's companies reached the eastern corner of the airfield but, on coming under heavy fire from mortars and machine guns, withdrew to take up a position in some tall bamboo which provided a limited amount of cover.

On the left of the brigade's axis and south of the road, the 28th (Maori) New Zealand Infantry Battalion encountered less opposition, which manifested itself mainly in the form of snipers who inflicted some casualties. As it neared Pirgos, however, resistance stiffened dramatically and the battalion suffered much heavier losses as it was halted in its tracks. Two of the 3rd King's Own Hussars' tanks were put out of action, one by enemy fire and the other from mechanical breakdown; Lieutenant Roy Farran naturally refused to allow the third to advance on its own as it would have been picked off very quickly.

To the south, meanwhile, the 21st New Zealand Infantry Battalion, numbering only 350 all ranks, had advanced from Vineyard Ridge and was fighting its way round to the south of Hill 107 against stiff opposition from enemy mountain troops. During the early part of counter-attack the battalion made good progress, driving the enemy out of the village of Xamadohori and back into Vlacheronitissa. One of its companies, a composite sub-unit comprising New Zealanders, Royal Marines and RAF ground crew, succeeded in reaching a point above the Tavronitis. The battalion's advance slowed during the morning, however, and by midday had ground to a halt. Under fire from enemy on the southern slopes of Hill 107 and exposed to risk of a counter-attack, it withdrew during the afternoon to its former positions on Vineyard Ridge.

With all three battalions blocked, the counter-attack on Máleme had failed. In the early hours of 23 May, Major General Freyberg gave orders for 5th New Zealand Brigade to withdraw to Galatas. Covered by a company of the 28th (Maori) New Zealand Infantry Battalion, the brigade began to draw back under cover of darkness towards a ridgeline west of Platanias where it would take up positions.

During 22 May, despite losing a total of fifty-one transport aircraft, the Germans had succeeded in landing the 1st and 2nd Battalions 102nd Mountain Rifle Regiment and the 2nd Battalion 85th Mountain Rifle Regiment to reinforce the few hundred exhausted surviving members of 1st Airlanding Assault Regiment holding the airfield. Another arrival at Máleme that day was Major General Alfred Schlemm, Chief of Staff of XI Air Corps, who was accompanied by the corps' advanced head-quarters. His own presence on Crete was brief, however, as later that day he was recalled to Athens.

The evening of 22 May saw the arrival at Máleme of Lieutenant General Julius Ringel, commander of 5th Mountain Division, who assumed overall command of all German troops on Crete. He swiftly reorganised Group West's forces into three battle groups, the first comprising the 1st and 2nd Battalions 100th Mountain Rifle Regiment and the 2nd Battalion 85th Mountain Rifle Regiment, under the 100th's commander, Colonel Willibald Utz. The second consisted of the 95th Mountain Engineer Battalion, commanded by Major Schätte, and an understrength fallschirmjäger company; and the third the surviving elements of LSR-1 under Colonel Ramcke. Utz's two battalions of 100th Mountain Rifle Regiment were to advance down the centre over the hills between the Ayia Valley and the sea. The 2nd Battalion 85th Mountain Rifle Regiment, commanded by Major Treck, was to carry out an encircling movement to the south, via the foothills of the White Mountains, in a move designed to outflank 5th New Zealand Brigade's positions on Vineyard Ridge and force the withdrawal of the Allied artillery firing on the airfield. Meanwhile, Schätte's battle group was to advance to the west and south in the direction of the port of Kastelli Kissamou and Paleochora, clear the area of partisans, secure Kastelli Kissamou for the landing of the light tanks of the 2nd Battalion 31st Panzer Regiment, and prevent any surprise attack by Allied troops landing at Paleochora and heading north. Finally, Ramcke's fallschirmjäger were to protect the airfield at Máleme while advancing eastwards along the coastal road.

Dawn on 23 May found the three battle groups on the march. LSR-1, by this time reduced to the strength of one battalion, headed eastwards in hot pursuit of the withdrawing New Zealanders. By midday, Ramcke's men were in close contact with the rearguard company of the 28th (Maori) New Zealand Infantry Battalion which managed to hold them off as the last elements of 5th New Zealand Brigade crossed over the steep heights of the Platanias ridge. Meanwhile, Major Schätte's group of mountain engineers and fallschirmjäger had discovered the bodies of the seventy-two-strong force of the 2nd Battalion LSR-1, commanded by Lieutenant Peter Mürbe, which had been wiped out after being dropped on the morning of 20 May beyond the Rodopos Peninsula with the mission of capturing the airfield at Kastelli Kissamou. Schätte's men reported that the bodies of the fallschirmjäger had been mutilated, this information being passed by radio to Lieutenant General Ringel who was enraged and ordered that severe reprisals be taken against the partisans.

On the morning of 24 May, Ju-87 Stuka divebombers attacked

Kastelli Kissamou, being followed by Major Schätte's battle group which fought its way into the town in the face of fierce resistance from the 1st Greek Regiment and partisans. During the bombing, the jail was hit and the survivors of Lieutenant Mürbe's group managed to escape and enter a nearby building that housed the headquarters of the town's garrison, where they captured two New Zealand liaison officers attached to the 1st Greek Regiment. By midday, the town centre had fallen to the Germans and that afternoon Major Schätte gave orders for 200 male Cretans to be shot in reprisal for the apparent massacre and mutilation of Lieutenant Mürbe's men. This was carried out in spite of protests from the survivors of Mürbe's force who swore that they had been treated correctly as prisoners.

Shortly after 5th New Zealand Brigade had taken up its positions west of Platanias, it came under fire from the guns of 95th Mountain Artillery Regiment. At the same time, LSR-1 began probing attacks north of the coastal road and around the Platanias bridge, several fierce contacts taking place, and by that evening had established contact with the mountain infantry battalions to the south. The latter had meanwhile linked up with Colonel Richard Heidrich's FJR-3 in the area of Prison Valley. The three companies of FJR-3 under Major Ludwig Heilmann headed north from Prison Valley towards the coastal road and 5th New Zealand Brigade's rear area ran into patrols from 10th New Zealand Brigade, positioned west of Galatas, which held them up. At the same time, above Alikianou, the 2nd Battalion 85th Mountain Rifle Regiment encountered the 8th Greek Regiment and a force of Cretan irregulars who succeeded in blocking it.

By now it was apparent that 5th New Zealand Brigade was in danger of being cut off and so, on the night of 23 May, it withdrew eastwards once again, moving into reserve behind 4th and 10th New Zealand Brigades drawn up in positions to the west of Galatas. On the afternoon of 24 May, 100th Mountain Rifle Regiment, supported by LSR-1 advancing from Ay Marina and Stilos, carried out a reconnaissance in force on the Galatas heights while Colonel Krakau's 85th Mountain

Rifle Regiment was tasked with capturing Alikianos, situated at the bottom of Prison Valley; it would then advance towards Stilos and Suda Bay, cutting the coastal road to the rear of the New Zealand forces before moving on to Rethymnon.

In the early hours of 25 May, before Ringel launched his attack on 4th NZ Brigade, General Kurt Student and the advance headquarters of XI Air Corps landed at Máleme, albeit command of German forces on the island still rested with Ringel.

At dawn 18th New Zealand Infantry Battalion, the right-hand forward unit of the brigade, came under a heavy volume of fire from 95th Mountain Artillery Regiment, mortars and a number of captured Bofors guns. During the morning it was also attacked from the air by Stuka divebombers and Messerschmitt fighters of VIII Air Corps. In the early afternoon, LSR-1 and the 2nd Battalion 100th Mountain Rifle Regiment launched an attack on the 18th New Zealand Infantry Battalion, two hours later overrunning D Company, its right-hand forward company. The commanding officer, Lieutenant Colonel Gray, led a counter-attack but this failed. On the battalion's left, meanwhile, A Company was driven back from its positions on Wheat Hill and shortly afterwards the remainder of the battalion was forced to pull back, allowing the Germans to capture Galatas, linking up with the surviving elements of Colonel Richard Heidrich's FJR-3. Thus, after four days of bitter fighting, Group West had finally managed to make contact with Group Centre. Having achieved his initial aim, Lieutenant General Ringel then set about redeploying his forces to continue the advance eastwards to link up with Group East.

The New Zealanders, however, led by the commander of 10th New Zealand Brigade, Colonel Howard Kippenberger, formed a new line of defence along the Daratsos Ridge and that night launched a counter-attack which drove the Germans out of Galatas. Despite this success, 4th New Zealand Brigade was ordered to withdraw behind a new line, running along the Daratsos Ridge to the lower end of Prison Valley, which was to be held by 5th New Zealand Brigade while the 4th regrouped.

The morning of 26 May found LSR-1 advancing eastwards along the coast while 100th Mountain Rifle Regiment moved through Karatsos and headed for the junction of the road linking Canea and Alikianos. On the right of the German advance was FJR-3 which made for Suda via Platanias and Perivolia. It was supported by the 141st Mountain Rifle Regiment, commanded by Colonel Jais, which advanced along a route intended to outflank Australian units holding the bottom of Prison Valley and to cut the coastal road east of Canea. The 85th Mountain Rifle Regiment meantime advanced from Alikianos but made slow progress, only reaching the village of Varipetro, to the south-west of Perivolia, by the evening.

That night, the commander of 2nd New Zealand Division, Brigadier Edward Puttick, ordered a further withdrawal to a new defensive line along 42nd Street, a road leading up into the hills to the east of Canea. Unfortunately the order never reached the Creforce reserve which comprised the 1st Battalion The Welch Regiment, the 102nd (Northumberland Hussars) Anti-Tank Regiment RA and the 9th Battalion The King's Royal Rifle Corps. Commanded by Lieutenant Colonel A. Duncan, the Welch Regiment's commanding officer, it was deployed along the original 5th New Zealand Brigade defensive line.

Around 8.00 a.m. on the morning of 27 May, LSR-1 and the two battalions of 100th Mountain Rifle Regiment launched an attack on the Creforce reserve while Colonel Richard Heidrich and his FJR-3 battle group attacked from the flank and rear via the floor of Prison Valley. Assailed on all sides, Duncan and his men had no option but to carry out a fighting withdrawal, pulling back across the River Kladiso after which some 400 of them made their way back to the 42nd Street defensive line while the remainder withdrew through Canea to the Akrotiri Peninsula where they prepared to make a stand.

The first German troops to appear in front of the 42nd Street line were Gebirgsjäger of 141st Mountain Rifle Regiment. The 1st Battalion was in the van and soon encountered the 5th NZ Brigade and in particular the 28th (Maori) New Zealand Infantry Battalion which led a fierce counter-attack that resulted in the virtual annihilation of the German mountain battalion which lost over 300 men killed and an unknown number wounded and captured.

The 141st Mountain Rifle Regiment thereafter regrouped and took up defensive positions around Katsifarana. Meantime, the FJR-3 battle group under Colonel Heidrich, with Captain Baron Friedrich von der Heydte's 1st Battalion in the lead, had fought its way through to Suda Bay and cut the coastal road on the eastern edge of Canea. Von der Heydte had been tasked with clearing Allied troops from the Akrotiri Peninsula but disregarded his orders and advanced into Canea itself, which he found to be seemingly deserted. Shortly afterwards, the mayor appeared and formally surrendered the capital to von der Heydte and his men.

With Canea and Suda Bay in German hands, Lieutenant General Ringel now ordered his forces to continue their advance eastwards. A mobile force, under Lieutenant Colonel Wittmann, set off on the evening of 27 May for Heraklion, heading along the main road via Rethymnon, while the 141st Mountain Rifle Regiment proceeded via Vamos and Goergioupoli. At the same time, the 85th Mountain Rifle Regiment advanced through Episkopi towards Rethymnon. The 100th Mountain Rifle Regiment meanwhile covered the flanks of the German advance, clearing the terrain on both sides of the road leading to Sfakion.

On the morning of 29 May, the leading elements of Wittmann's mobile force encountered New Zealand troops who had taken up a blocking position at Megala Chorafakia. The latter held firm until the following morning when, with enemy troops infiltrating on either flank and in the rear, they were forced to retreat. Meanwhile, the 2nd Battalion 85th Mountain Rifle Regiment had encountered the 5th New Zealand Brigade, which withdrew. Thereafter, Wittmann's force and the mountain battalion headed inland in pursuit of the Creforce rearguard while the 1st Battalion 85th Mountain Rifle Regiment made for the coast. The Creforce rearguard, however, escaped up the mountain road to Sfakion and it was not until the following morning that elements of the 100th Mountain Rifle Regiment took up its pursuit. Wittmann, meanwhile, together with the mountain battalion, was continuing his advance on Rethymnon. On the evening of 29 May, he linked up with the surviving elements of Captain Wiedemann's 3rd Battalion FJR-2 at Perivolia.

On 30 May Witmann's force, reinforced by two light tanks of the 2nd Battalion 31st Panzer Regiment, which had recently been landed at Kastelli Kissamou, advanced on the positions at Rethymnon held by Lieutenant Colonel Ian Campbell's 3,600-strong ad hoc brigade of the 2nd/1st and 2nd/11th Australian Infantry Battalions and 4th and 5th Greek Regiments deployed on the ridgeline running parallel to the coast and dominating the airfield and coastal road. Wittmann headed for Hill B, held by the 2nd/11th Battalion, subsequently outflanking the Australians.

The ensuing battle was brief. Faced with a strong force supported by artillery and armour, albeit the latter only comprised two tanks, the Australians surrendered and were marched away into captivity. Wittmann then continued his advance east to Heraklion, where the town and airfield by this time were in the hands Colonel Bruno Bräuer's FJR-1 and the 2nd Battalion FJR-2, Brigadier B. H. Chappell's 14th Infantry Brigade having been evacuated by the Royal Navy to Alexandria, in Egypt, on the night of 28–29 May.

Meanwhile, the remainder of Creforce, together with Layforce, a 400-strong commando formation under Colonel Robert Laycock which had landed as reinforcements on the night of 24–25 May, had drawn back to Sphakia, a tiny port on the south coast of Crete. The withdrawal had begun on 27 May when Major General Freyberg had received authority to evacuate his forces from the island. By that stage, however, it was too late to save several units, among them the 1st Battalion The Welch Regiment. Freyberg moved his headquarters to some caves near Sphakia while those elements of Creforce which had escaped being cut off and surrounded by the advancing German forces began the long, exhausting trek over the White Mountains to Sphakia, travelling by night and lying up by day to avoid detection by enemy aircraft.

On the night of 28 May the Royal Navy evacuated 1,000 men, a further 6,000 being taken off the following evening. The Germans meanwhile had begun launching air attacks on Sphakia in an attempt to prevent the escape of the surviving elements of Freyberg's forces. The 100th Mountain Rifle Regiment, which had pursued them over the mountains, began to advance on the port but found its way barred by a force of Royal Marines and Australian troops manning a blocking position established above Sphakia.

The final evacuation of Creforce took place on the night of 31 May, 3,710 men being taken off by the Royal Navy. Left behind, however, were over 6,500 British, Australian, New Zealand and Greek troops. The majority were taken prisoner and by the end of the summer of 1941 all but 800 had been transported by way of Greece to prisoner-of-war camps in Poland. Several hundred avoided capture by taking to the mountains and dispersing throughout the island, being hidden by Cretans who risked immediate execution by the Germans if found doing so; of these, some 300 were subsequently removed by submarine and taken to Egypt.

Both sides suffered dearly during the battle of Crete. The Allied casualties numbered 1,742 killed, 1,737 wounded and 11,835 taken prisoner, with a further 800 casualties incurred at sea after being evacuated from Heraklion. The Royal Navy's losses were also high: three cruisers and six destroyers sunk, with two battleships, one cruiser and two destroyers severely damaged. Casualties among its crews numbered 1,828 killed and some 200 wounded or missing. The RAF lost forty-seven aircraft during the battle.

As for XI Air Corps, its regiments and battalions returned to their bases in Germany having suffered 1,653 dead out of a total of 3,352 Germans killed during the battle. Total German casualties numbered 6,698. Some 200 Ju-52 transports had been lost in what was to be the final major German airborne operation of the Second World War. Hitler was appalled at the losses incurred and on 19 July 1941 informed XI Air Corps' commander, General Kurt Student, that the day of the fallschirmjäger was over, declaring: 'The parachute weapon depends on surprise – the surprise factor has now gone.'

Student himself, whose men would henceforth be employed in the infantry role throughout the rest of the Second World War, later summed up the battle with the words: 'For me the battle of Crete carries bitter memories. I miscalculated when I suggested this attack which resulted in the loss of so many valuable parachutists that it meant the end of the German airborne forces which I had created.'

CHAPTER FOUR

SOVIET OPERATIONS, 1941–2

As recounted in Chapter 1, the Soviets had in March 1941 expanded five of their airborne brigades to corps, each comprising some 10,000 men organised in three brigades, a tank battalion and supporting arms. June of that year also saw the formation of a directorate of airborne forces which were divorced from the Red Army Air Force, becoming a separate arm of the Soviet armed forces and designated the Vozdushno Desantnye Voiska (VDV).

On 22 June 1941 Germany attacked Russia and all five airborne corps were committed as motorised rifle troops in an attempt to block the eastwards thrust of German forces. The first to see action was Major General Ivan Bezugly's V Airborne Corps which was committed initially with XXI Mechanised Corps and subsequently with the Twenty-Seventh Army in a series of actions to try to stem the Germans' advance. On 15 August, having suffered heavy casualties during operations south of Daugavpils, the corps was withdrawn to the Moscow Military District.

Meantime, IV Airborne Corps was engaged in a six-day-long battle along the River Berezina, attempting to stem the advance of the armoured columns of the Wehrmacht's Army Group Centre heading for Bobruisk. The newly appointed corps commander, Major General Aleksei Zhadov, was en route from the Central Asian Military District to take up his new command and thus the corps was led in his absence by the Chief of Staff, Col Aleksandr Kazankin.

On 28 June, IV Airborne Corps received orders from the headquarters of the Red Army's Western Front, commanded by General Georgi Zhukov, to detach one of its brigades for an airborne operation. The 214th Airborne Brigade, under Colonel Aleksei Levashev, was assigned to carry out the operation in support of a counter-attack by XX Mechanised Corps against enemy lines of communication to the west of Bobruisk. Working in cooperation with the 210th Motorised Division, the brigade was to cause maximum disruption in enemy rear areas.

Insufficient aircraft were available to lift the brigade, however, and on the following day the parachute insertion was cancelled. Instead, the brigade, less one battalion and all its artillery, was deployed by road to the regions of Grusha, Slutsk and Staraia Doroga. There its principal mission was to disrupt the Germans' advance on Bobruisk, harassing their lines of communication by blowing up bridges, attacking convoys and destroying armour. At the same time, it was to link up with elements of 204th Airborne Brigade operating in the region of Parichi to the south.

In the event, 214th Airborne Brigade failed in its principal task of hampering the enemy advance, and was also unsuccessful in linking up with the 210th Motorised Division. Nevertheless, it conducted operations in enemy rear areas for over three months, by the end of which it had been reduced in strength to one battalion.

Following the Germans' crossing of the Rivers Berezina and Dnepr, IV Airborne Corps was placed under command of the Thirteenth Army in its operations to defend the approaches to Smolensk. As part of these, it was ordered on 13 July to mount a small airborne operation against a force of some 300 enemy tanks and other vehicles which, having run out of fuel, were stranded in the town of Gorki, to the north-west of Mogilev. The task was allocated to the surviving element of 214th Airborne Brigade, the 4th Composite Parachute Battalion, which detailed its 10th Company, commanded by Lieutenant N. Romanenko, for the mission.

On the afternoon of 14 July, Romanenko and his sixty-three men took off from Klimovichi in four TB-3 bombers. Heavy anti-aircraft fire greeted them on the approach to the DZ and caused casualties but two of the company's three groups succeeded in their tasks of destroying tanks with 'Molotov cocktail' petrol bombs. The third group landed thirty miles from the DZ and, coming under heavy fire, was forced to take refuge in the forests near by. Having regrouped that evening at a predetermined rendezvous (RV) but numbering only thirty-six in total, the company carried out guerrilla actions during which it destroyed an enemy train at a station at Temnyi Les. This operation, which ended later that month, is the first recorded Soviet airborne operation of the Second World War.

The beginning of August saw the 4th Composite Parachute Battalion placed under direct command of Headquarters Western Front, being located at Sukhinichi close to the headquarters and an airfield where supporting aircraft were based.

On 22 August, the battalion was tasked with an airborne operation to seize and destroy two bridges spanning the River Khmost near the city of Dukhovschina, thus blocking the roads leading west from Demidov. Lieutenant P. Tereschenko's 11th Company was allotted the mission. That night, the seventy-two-strong company took off in six TB-3 bombers, subsequently being dropped over the DZ from an altitude of just over 1,600 feet. Ten men were missing when the company rallied and regrouped at its RV but nevertheless, at 4.00 a.m. on the following morning, the task of destroying both bridges was accomplished successfully. Thereafter, Romanenko and his men conducted guerrilla operations in the area before exfiltrating through the German lines and linking up with troops of the 50th Cavalry Division. The company was then transferred by rail to Engels, near Moscow, where it rejoined IV Airborne Corps.

Another airborne operation was carried out on 22 August by the

4th Composite Parachute Battalion's 12th Company, commanded by Lieutenant Kulitsky. Dropped that night, one platoon became lost and was separated from the remainder of the company, which attacked several enemy columns and held up the advance of German reserves for six hours. Thereafter, Kulitsky and his men disengaged and withdrew, subsequently linking up with a large body of 1,000 Soviet troops cut off during earlier operations. Having broken through to Soviet positions near Rzhev, they were despatched to join a newly formed airborne unit, the Western Front Parachute Assault Detachment, commanded by Captain I. G. Starchak, which was operating in the area of Iukhnov.

On 25 August the 10th Company was in action again. On this occasion, its mission was to interdict road and rail routes in the area of Torop and to impede the movement of enemy reinforcements to the front for two weeks.

The company was dropped over three nights, one platoon at a time. Its commander, Lieutenant Romanenko, failed to appear at the RV but his second-in-command took over and the operation proceeded as planned until 14 December when the company exfiltrated across Lake Seliger and made contact with Soviet troops of the Kalinin Front.

On 28 September, the 4th Composite Parachute Battalion rejoined IV Airborne Corps at Engels. The rest of 214th Airborne Brigade meanwhile had been involved in operations which on 25 July saw it linking up with the Central Front's Third Army in the area of Kalinkovichi where it regrouped. In the latter half of September it was nearly cut off during the defence of Kiev but succeeded in withdrawing eastwards to avoid being trapped. On 24 September the remaining elements of the brigade, by this time numbering only some 200 men, made contact with Soviet troops near Lebedin. After nearly three months of continual combat, the brigade was moved by rail to Engels to rejoin the rest of IV Airborne Corps.

The 214th Airborne Brigade was not the only VDV formation to be heavily mauled during the defence of the city of Kiev, which lay in the Kiev Special Military District of the Red Army's South Western

Front. I Airborne Corps, commanded by Major General Matvei Usenko, fought alongside troops of the Soviet Fifth and Sixth Armies attempting to stem the advance of the Wehrmacht's Army Group South. Together with II Airborne Corps, it was surrounded by the Germans during August and September 1941. Both formations suffered such heavy losses that they were temporarily disbanded. III Airborne Corps meanwhile was encircled at Konotop but fought its way out, in November being redesignated the 87th Rifle Division.

October 1941 saw the reorganisation and re-equipping of IV Airborne Corps at Engels. Colonel Aleksei Levashev was appointed as its commander while Lieutenant Colonel N. E. Kolobovnikov took over command of 214th Airborne Brigade. The corps' structure was changed and the establishment of each brigade increased to include a company of assault engineers while every battalion received anti-tank and heavy machine-gun companies.

Reorganisation and training continued throughout October and November and into December in preparation for the coming Soviet counter-offensive. On 21 December IV Airborne Corps left Engels, being moved by rail from Apisovka to an airfield at Ramenskoe south-east of Moscow. There the 4th Composite Parachute Battalion was rejoined by Lieutenant Romanenko's 10th Company following its return from its operation in the area of Torop.

Early September had meantime seen the reforming of I Airborne Corps which began training in the area of Saratov, in the Volga Military District. Comprising the 1st, 204th and 211th Airborne Brigades, it trained hard for three months until, on 24 November, it received orders placing it under command of Headquarters Western Front. Following a move by rail, the corps arrived at Gorbachevo from which it marched to its new base area near Moscow, its headquarters being located at a farm at Ukhtomsky while the three brigades were dispersed around the villages of Dzerzhinsky, Kapotna, Liubertsy and Malakhovki. Close to the last was an airfield from which a number of airborne operations would be mounted.

V Airborne Corps, meanwhile, had been transferred on 15 August from the Baltic Military District to the Moscow region where it would play a major role in the battle against the columns of General Heinz Guderian's 2nd Panzer Group, which were advancing towards Moscow. By 3 October 1941, Guderian had captured the city of Orel and was heading for his next objective, Mtensk, with XXIV Panzer Corps in the lead.

Attempting to block the German thrust was I Guards Rifle Corps, commanded by Major General Dmitri Leliushenko, which took up its positions around Mtensk. In the early hours of 3 October, the commander of V Airborne Corps, Colonel Sergei Gurev, was ordered to carry out a tactical airlanding operation at Orel. At 6.30 a.m. the corps' leading element, 201st Airborne Brigade, under Lieutenant Colonel S. M. Kovalov, took off from Engels in a formation of eighty aircraft comprising PS-84 transports and TB-3 bombers.

The distance flown was just over 300 miles and the brigade landed at Orel under fire from enemy artillery. The leading units immediately went into action, providing covering fire for the landing of the rest of the brigade, whose 1st and 2nd Parachute Battalions cleared the area of the airfield. The 3rd Parachute Battalion meanwhile landed at Optukha, eight miles to the north-east of Orel, and moved swiftly to interdict the Orel–Mtensk highway between Optukha and Ivanovskaia.

Throughout 3 October and the following day, 10th Airborne Brigade and corps troops landed at Orel. By nightfall on 4 October, some 5,000 troops, heavy weapons and equipment of V Airborne Corps had been assembled and were joined later in the day by 4th Tank Brigade.

After two weeks of heavy fighting, V Airborne Corps was withdrawn and moved by road and rail to the region of Podol'sk where by 20 October it had taken over a sector along the River Nara to the west of Moscow. During the next two months, the corps was involved in defensive operations to the north of Mmaloiaroslavets and on the approaches to Moscow itself.

December 1941 witnessed a series of airborne operations mounted as part of the Soviet counter-offensive in the Moscow region. The first of these took place on 14–15 December on the Kalinin Front when a 415-strong force of 214th Airborne Brigade, comprising Captain I. G. Starchak's Western Front Parachute Assault Detachment and elements of the 4th Composite Parachute Battalion, was dropped in the area of the town of Lotoschino with the task of cutting a road along which German forces were withdrawing from Klin through Teriaeva Sloboda to establish a defensive line along the Rivers Lama and Ruza, in the area of Volokolamsk.

The operation, which was in support of efforts by the Soviet Thirtieth Army and First Shock Army to drive back the German 3rd and 4th Panzer Groups from the northern areas of Moscow, was successful. Starchak's force not only succeeded in interdicting the road near Teriaeva Sloboda but also caused disruption throughout the region from Lotoschino east to Teriaeva, which was occupied by elements of 7th Panzer Division and 14th Motorised Division. During the first nine days, Starchak succeeded in preventing all movement at night by the enemy who were forced to provide armoured escorts for convoys by day. In addition, he and his men cut the railway line between Shakhovskaia to Novo Petrovskoe which was being used by the Germans as a base from which to provide logistic support for their troops. On 19 December Starchak's force headed west, continuing its operations in the enemy rear before being withdrawn.

Other airborne operations were carried out by I Airborne Corps' 1st Airborne Brigade, all of them comprising 'diversionary' raids carried out by company-sized groups with the aim of causing maximum disruption in enemy rear areas.

January 1942 saw the Soviets go on the offensive with the Red Army's Kalinin and Western Fronts in a combined effort to surround and destroy the German Army Group Centre. The initial phase would include an airborne operation in which troops were to be dropped in the rear of the city of Medyn to facilitate the advance of Western Front forces from the Kaluga region to Iukhnov and Viaz'ma. Subsequently, another larger drop would be carried out in the area of Viaz'ma to coincide with the arrival of ground forces.

The force for the initial airborne operation comprised: the now promoted Major Starchak's Western Front Parachute Assault Detachment; the 1st Parachute Battalion of V Airborne Corps' 201st Airborne Brigade, commanded by Captain I. A. Surzhik; a battalion of the 250th Independent Airborne Regiment and an airlanding force comprising the rest of the regiment under its commanding officer, Major Nikolai Soldatov who was in overall charge of the operation. Consisting of three airborne infantry battalions, an artillery battery, mortar company and an anti-tank platoon, the 250th numbered 1,425 all ranks and was specially trained to fight in urban areas at night.

The operation was to take place in the rear area of the German Fourth Army's XX and LVII Corps which had been split from one another by a thrust on 29 December by the Soviet Thirty-Third and Forty-Third Armies advancing along an axis of Maloiaroslavets–Borovsk–Medyn. XX Corps had fallen back to the west and north-west while LVII Corps had carried out a fighting withdrawal from Maloiaroslavets towards Medyn.

On 1 January 1942, Major Soldatov received orders for his force to drop and land in the area of Medyn. On the night of 2–3 January, Surzhik's 384-strong 1st Parachute Battalion dropped some nine miles north-west of Medyn in the area of Gusevo. Its tasks were to capture and secure a bridge spanning the River Shanya, take and hold Shansky Zavod and Kremenskoye, and interdict the Iukhnov–Medyn highway at a point where it bridged the Shanya.

Having regrouped following the drop, the battalion attacked Gusevo itself, driving out an enemy force occupying it and the neighbouring villages of Gribovo and Maslova. Having taken the bridge across the Shanya, Surzhik and his men destroyed it before regrouping and taking up defensive positions.

At 9.00 p.m. on the night of 3–4 January, the leading troops of Major Starchak's Western Front Parachute Assault Detachment, reinforced

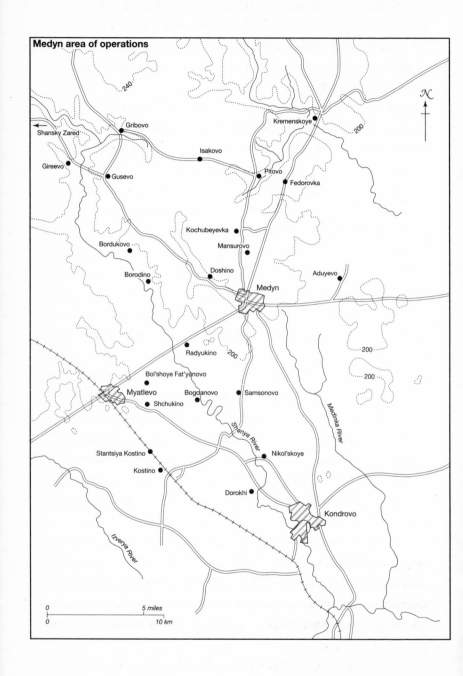

Medyn area of operations

Shansky Zared
Gribovo
Kremenskoye
Gireevo
Isakovo
Pitovo
Gusevo
Fedorovka
Kochubeyevka
Mansurovo
Bordukovo
Aduyevo
Borodino
Doshino
Medyn
Radyukino
Bol'shoye Fat'yanovo
Myatlevo
Bogdanovo
Samsonovo
Shchukino
Shanya River
Medinka River
Stantsiya Kostino
Nikol'skoye
Kostino
Dorokhi
Kondrovo
Izver'ya River

240
200
200
200
200

0   5 miles
0   10 km

by elements of the 250th Independent Airborne Regiment, dropped at Bol'shoe Fat'ianovo from 21 TB-3 bombers and ten PS-84 transports. The number of aircraft available for the operation was insufficient for Starchak's 416-strong force to be transported in one lift and thus it had to be delivered in three.

Starchak's initial task was to secure the airfield for use by the air-landing element of the 250th Independent Airborne Regiment. Thereafter, he was detailed to: cut the highway linking Medyn with Gzhatsk and Kremenskoye; seize the railway station at Miatlevo and sever the railway line there; interdict enemy withdrawal routes from Medyn to Iukhnov and from Polotnianyi Zavod to Detchina; and impede the movement of enemy reinforcements to Medyn.

Air strikes had been carried out on the Bol'shoe Fat'ianovo airfield prior to the drop but the aircraft carrying Starchak and his men encountered heavy anti-aircraft fire as they approached the drop and landing zones. Some took evasive action, scattering their sticks of parachutists during the drop, while others failed to drop their sticks and returned to base.

Despite such problems, eighty-five per cent of Starchak's force succeeded in regrouping and immediately mounted an attack on the enemy defensive positions around the airfield, these consisting of twelve well-sited strongpoints. The Germans put up a stout resistance and the battle for the airfield was protracted and hard. It was not until dusk on 4 January that Starchak's force secured the airfield and the nearby villages of Maloe Fat'ianovo and Shchukino, taking up defensive positions throughout the area.

Starchak, however, was without radio communications with Headquarters Western Front which despatched two aircraft to make contact with him. Both were prevented from doing so by bad weather and thus, unable to ascertain whether or not the airfield had been secured, the operation's controllers cancelled the airlanding by Maj Soldatov and the rest of his force.

On the following day, having received orders to operate independently, Starchak and his men left the airfield and set off to cause maximum disruption to the German forces in the area. Having destroyed a bridge at Kostino, they seized the railway station at Miatlevo on the night of 7–8 January and destroyed two enemy trains and twenty-eight tanks. Thereafter, they headed south from Medyn towards the area of Kondrovo, ambushing convoys and harassing enemy forces which were in the process of withdrawing. They also destroyed three bridges across the Shanya at Bodganov, Samsonovo and Iabukovsky, all of which were vital to the success of the German withdrawal.

On 20 January Starchak withdrew to link up with the leading elements of the Soviet Forty-Third Army near Nikol'shoe on the Shanya. By this time, his force had been reduced in strength from 416 to eighty-seven after seventeen days of fighting during which Starchak himself had been wounded. Nevertheless, he had carried out the tasks given to him: the seizure of the airfield at Bol'shoe Fat'ianovo; the cutting of the railway line at Miatlevo; and the interdiction of enemy withdrawal routes. The success of the entire operation, however, had been marred by inadequate reconnaissance, which had failed to detect the true numbers of the enemy holding the airfield, and poor radio communications which resulted in the cancellation of the airlanding of the rest of the airborne force. Moreover, those responsible for the planning of the operation had failed to allocate sufficient aircraft for the operation and to take into account adverse weather conditions.

No sooner had the Medyn operation taken place than planning began for another, which was to form part of the growing Soviet offensive in January against the flanks of the German Army Group Centre.

Mid-January 1942 found the Soviet Tenth and Fiftieth Armies, forming the left wing of the Western Front, having penetrated the enemy defences, striking the left flank of the German Fourth Army and opening a large gap between it and the Second Panzer Army. On the Fourth Army's right flank, meanwhile, XL Motorised Corps fought hard to beat off Soviet attacks in the German rear on XLIII Corps' right flank.

At the same time, while the Soviet Forty-Third and Forty-Ninth Armies drove elements of the German Fourth Army back towards Iukhnov from the east, the Thirty-Third Army posed a major threat from the north. To the north and east of Iukhnov, a gap of some twelve miles opened up between Fourth Panzer Army's XX Corps and Fourth Army's LVII Corps whose divisions, along with those of XII and XIII Corps, were pulling back to positions along the Shanya covering the northern, eastern and southern approaches to Iukhnov.

On the left flank of Fourth Army, the Soviet Thirty-Third Army thrust past the left flank of the German 98th Infantry Division north of Miatlevo, in the area of Domashnevo. Headquarters Western Front and the Red Army's High Command intended that the Thirty-Third Army should advance as far as Viaz'ma where it would link up with I Guards Cavalry Corps moving up from the south, thus encircling and trapping a large part of the German Army Group Centre. Before that could happen however, I Guards Cavalry Corps would have to thrust through newly established German positions located along the Moscow–Warsaw highway to the south-west of Iukhnov.

It was therefore decided to mount an airborne operation north of the highway to assist I Guards Cavalry Corps to penetrate the German line and cross the route. The 250th Independent Airborne Regiment, along with the 1st and 2nd Parachute Battalions of 201st Airborne Brigade, would be dropped some twenty-five miles to the south-east of Viaz'ma, near the villages of Znamenka, Zhelan'e and Lugi, an area approximately twenty-five miles behind German lines. The 652-strong airborne force's task was to deny use of the Viaz'ma–Iukhnov and Lugi–Temkino highways and the Viaz'ma–Briansk railway line to the Germans, thus hindering logistic support for their forces in Iukhnov. At the same time, it was also to attack the Germans in Iukhnov from the rear.

Preparations carried out at an airfield at Vnukovo were complete by

17 January. Twenty-one PS-84 transports were allocated to the operation, along with a number of TB-3 bombers which would drop the paratroops' 45mm anti-tank guns.

The operation was to comprise three phases. In the first, the 1st and 2nd Parachute Battalions would drop on an airfield at Znamenka and secure it. Two and a half hours later, they would be followed by an advance group of the 250th Independent Airborne Group tasked with preparing the airfield for the landing of the main force. Thirty minutes later, the latter would begin to land in flights of three aircraft to avoid congestion on the runway.

At 3.35 a.m. on 18 January the first sixteen aircraft took off from Vnukovo. By 9.00 a.m. a total of 452 men of the two parachute battalions had been dropped between Znamenka and Zhelan'e. The sixty-five-strong advance group of the 250th Independent Airborne Regiment was airlanded under cover of darkness at 5.30 p.m. that evening, its four PS-84 transports being guided in by partisans to a location a mile and a half south of Znamenka. Without skis, however, the aircraft subsequently found it difficult to take off again in the snow and only one succeeded in doing so.

Having rendezvoused successfully, the 1st Parachute Battalion, commanded by Captain Surzhik, and the advance group mounted an attack on the German force defending the Znamenka airfield but this was beaten off. Thereafter, they withdrew and headed for Zhelan'e.

At 1.20 a.m. on 19 January, ten PS-84 transports, carrying more members of the two parachute battalions, arrived over the area but bad weather forced some to abandon the drop and return to base. Only 200 men were successfully dropped, bringing the force on the ground to a total of 642.

During that day, Surzhik and his men constructed an alternative airstrip to the north-west of Plesnovo for the landing of Major Soldatov's 250th Independent Airborne Regiment. Despite heavy enemy fire and adverse weather conditions, the regiment carried out a series of night landings during 20–22 January, bringing the airborne force strength on the ground to 1,643. Losses during the landings were relatively light, amounting to three aircraft shot down with twenty-seven men killed and nine wounded.

Soldatov's force was in action within nine hours of landing. Orders received from Headquarters Western Front directed him to interdict enemy withdrawal routes from Iukhnov by capturing and occupying the villages of Bogatyri, Znamenka and Zarech'e. At the same time, he was to prevent the advance of enemy reinforcements from the area of Temkino.

On the nights of 22 and 23 January, the 250th Independent Airborne Regiment, supported by a partisan group, attacked Znamenka but failed to take it. Meanwhile, the regiment's 3rd Battalion and a company of the 1st Parachute Battalion fought a fierce engagement with enemy forces on the Viaz'ma–Iukhnov highway, also the scene of a battle in which a company of the 2nd Parachute Battalion captured a convoy of fifty-four enemy supply trucks near Zamosh'e and Murashovka. Two days of savage fighting saw the troops subjected to a counter-attack by two companies of infantry supported by artillery.

On 25 January, elements of the 250th Independent Airborne Regiment captured Gorodianka and prepared to attack Bogatyri and Lipniki along the Viaz'ma–Iukhnov highway. During the following four days, the regiment extended its area of operations eastwards along the highway. On the night of 29–30 January, it mounted a major assault on Znamenka but again failed to take it.

On 31 January I Guards Cavalry Corps reached the south-eastern outskirts of Viaz'ma where on 2 February its leading units encountered paratroops of 8th Airborne Brigade, recently arrived in the area. Thereafter, the 250th Independent Airborne Regiment headed north-westwards to link up with the leading elements of the Soviet Thirty-Third Army, subsequently joining forces with the 329th Rifle Division during heavy fighting along the approaches to Viaz'ma.

The operation had been a success, the 250th Independent Airborne Regiment and 201st Airborne Brigade's 1st and 2nd Parachute Battalions having achieved all their objectives. They had established a base in the rear area of the enemy, disrupted his lines of communication and supply and helped to pave the way for the advance of I Guards Cavalry Corps. There were, however, certain shortcomings in operational planning. Although the parachute insertion and airlanding had been successful, the latter took place over five days, which was too long and cost the element of surprise. Furthermore, the entire operation itself lasted too long with the airborne troops being too lightly equipped and lacking both armour and artillery support during the fifteen days required prior to linking up with the Soviet ground forces. Other shortcomings in planning included a lack of training for winter warfare, the troops experiencing difficulties using the skis with which they were issued.

While the Zhelan'e operation was under way, planning had already started on an operation to be carried out in the area of Ozerechnia, approximately twenty miles to the south-west of the city of Viaz'ma. It would consist of a number of parachute drops carried out at night in arctic weather conditions with temperatures considerably below zero. On 17 January the operation was assigned to Major General Aleksei Levashev's IV Airborne Corps whose task would be, in cooperation with the Western and Kalinin Fronts, to complete the encirclement and destruction of the German Army Group Centre. The main element of the corps would be dropped south-west of Viaz'ma, with the initial task of cutting enemy lines of communication between Viaz'ma and Smolensk, while a detached task force would intercept enemy troops withdrawing from Viaz'ma to the west. At the same time a deception plan, involving the dropping of several reconnaissance groups and the use of dummy drops, would be put into effect to confuse the enemy as to the location of the main drop.

The forces opposing IV Airborne Corps comprised predominantly 11th Panzer Division, which was responsible for the security of the main highway west of Viaz'ma beyond the crossing point over the River Depr, and 3rd Motorised Division which patrolled the highways to the east and south of Viaz'ma. Populated areas along the highways were defended by garrisons of approximately battalion strength, while companies and platoons were deployed in villages up to twelve miles or so from the highways. The latter part of January saw the 309th Infantry Regiment, an element of the 208th Infantry Division, take over responsibility of the highway west of Viaz'ma from 11th Panzer Division while on 30 January 5th Panzer Division occupied Viaz'ma itself and the area to the south-west.

Initially scheduled to commence on 21 January, IV Airborne Corps' operation was postponed until the 26–27 January due to the slow movement of the corps into its staging areas at Kaluga. Travelling by rail, it was hampered by lines cut by the enemy who had also blown the main bridge over the Oka, forcing the corps to detrain and ford the frozen river on foot, carrying all their supplies across which took several days. Due to poor operational security, the Germans were well aware that an airborne operation was in the offing: the troops were wearing newly issued winter clothing, with which no other Soviet formations had been provided at that time, and supply dumps were left unconcealed. Moreover, the concentration of aircraft at the mounting airfields at Grabtsevo, Zhashkovo, Rzhavets and Peremsyshl, Newar Kaluga and some nineteen to twenty-five miles behind the Soviet front lines, also gave clear indications to German agents that an airborne operation was in the process of being mounted.

On 23 January 8th Airborne Brigade, commanded by Lieutenant Colonel Aleksandr Onufriev, arrived in the area of Kaluga, the 1st Parachute Battalion moving to its mounting airfield at Grabtsevo, while the 2nd and 3rd Battalions moved to Zhashkovo and the 4th Battalion to Peremsyshl. The 9th Airborne Brigade, under Colonel Ivan Kuryshev, also concentrated at Zhashkovo while Lieutenant Colonel N. E. Kolobovnikov's 214th Airborne Brigade, did likewise at Rzhavets. All formations and units were in their assembly areas in time for the operation's new start date of the night of 26–27 January.

By this time the Kalinin Front's Thirty-Ninth Army had punched through the German positions to the west of Rzhev and thrust forward to the south-west of Sycheka with XI Cavalry Corps in the lead. Meanwhile, the Thirty-Third Army was advancing from the east towards Viaz'ma. As already recounted, on 27 January farther south I Guards Cavalry Corps had crossed the Moscow–Warsaw highway to the west of Iukhnov and on the following day had linked up with the 250th Independent Airborne Regiment. Some units of the corps, together with elements of the Fiftieth Army, however, had been held up short of the highway due to stiff resistance by German forces predominantly comprising units of the 10th Motorised Division. It was at this juncture that the Soviets decided to mount a large airborne operation in the enemy rear.

IV Airborne Corps' principal task was to carry out a landing to the south-west of Viaz'ma in the area of Ozorechnia, Kurdiumovo and Komovo. Thereafter, it was to advance to the area of forest to the west of Viaz'ma; capture and hold the villages of Iamkovo, Mosolovo, Pleshkovo and Azarovo; interdict enemy main lines of communications; and prevent the Germans from withdrawing from, or reinforcing, Viazma. Finally, it was to take part in the encirclement and destruction of German Army Group Centre.

Diversionary and reconnaissance missions in the area of the corps' DZs and LZs meanwhile would be carried out by seven platoon-sized groups from 214th Airborne Brigade, their task being to block any approach by German forces. At the same time, four smaller groups from the brigade would link up with XI Cavalry Corps and the 250th Independent Airborne Regiment operating in the Zhelan'e area.

The 8th Airborne Brigade, spearheaded by its 2nd Parachute Battalion dropped ahead of the main force, would land in the area of Ozorechnia and secure a line from Rebrovo through Gradino to Berezniki, its task being to block any enemy movement along the roads linking Viaz'ma with Smolensk and Dorogobuzh. The 2nd Parachute Battalion would secure Ozorechnia and the DZ prior to the drop of the rest of the brigade which would then proceed to secure its other objectives.

The 9th Airborne Brigade meanwhile would be dropped near Gorainovo, thereafter securing a line from there through Ivaniki to Popovo, blocking German reinforcements for Viaz'ma from the west. The 214th Airborne Brigade, reinforced by IV Airborne Corps' artillery and anti-tank battalions, was to be dropped in the area of Vekhotskoe, Plshkovo and Uvarovo where it would remain in reserve.

The principal problem facing the commander of IV Airborne Corps was the acute shortage of aircraft. Only forty PS-84 transports and twenty-five TB-3 light bombers were allocated to the operation, these being totally inadequate for the swift deployment of the entire corps as it would take two to three sorties per night over three or four days to deliver it to the operational area. Furthermore, the planners once again neglected to take into account such vital factors as adverse weather conditions and mechanical breakdowns.

At 2.30 p.m. on 27 January 1942, 8th Airborne Brigade's 2nd Parachute Battalion, commanded by Captain M. I. Karnaukhov, took off from Zhashkovo in thirty-nine PS-84 transports. Due to the pilots becoming disorientated over the DZ area by a severe snowstorm, the force was dropped at 4.00 p.m. from a higher altitude than intended and some thirteen miles to the south of the planned DZ at Ozorech-nia. These problems were compounded by Karnaukhov and his men being scattered over a radius of between thirteen and sixteen miles around the village of Tabory. Immediately on landing, Karnaukhov despatched a patrol to reconnoitre Tabory, which was found to be unoc-cupied by the Germans. In the meantime, 214th Airborne Brigade's seven reconnaissance-diversionary groups were dropped along with the four others tasked with establishing contact with XI Cavalry Corps and the 250th Independent Airborne Regiment.

The 8th Airborne Brigade's drop encountered problems. The 2nd Parachute Battalion took a considerable amount of time to rally and regroup, with only 476 men, out of a total strength of 618, appearing at its RV by the morning of 28 January. Moreover, almost all of the unit's weapons and equipment had been lost in the drop. Radio communications were poor and Karnaukhov only had time to report to the brigade headquarters that his battalion had landed before contact was lost. That morning, he despatched a detachment to Tabory to establish a landing zone (LZ) while he and the remainder of his men headed for Ozerechnia, which they found to be occupied by a small German force.

That night, he was joined there by elements of 8th Airborne Brigade's 3rd Parachute Battalion, commanded by Major A. G. Kobets, which had been dropped on the night of 27–28 January. The absence of radio contact with Karnaukhov, and thus a lack of information about the problems he was encountering, had resulted in 8th Airborne Brigade's main drop beginning as planned that night with the drop of Kobets' battalion. Like the 2nd Battalion, however, he and his men had been dropped inaccurately; half the unit landed near Tabory and the remainder in the area of Ozerechnia. Those dropping in and around the latter met enemy fire and frantically tried to steer themselves away into the nearby forests, most succeeding in doing so. Major Kobets found himself on his own as he made his way to the battalion regrouping area, some four miles from Ozerechnia, where to his amazement he encountered Karnaukhov with 300 men of the 2nd Parachute Battalion and eighty of the 3rd. As a result of a navigational error, the rest of the 3rd Battalion had meanwhile been dropped at different locations in the Smolensk district, the 7th and 9th Companies finding themselves north of Viaz'ma among the forward positions of the Thirty-Ninth Army of the Kalinin Front.

The two much-depleted battalions joined ranks and, as the senior officer present, Kobets assumed command. At 11.00 p.m. on the night of 28 January the combined force launched a night attack on Ozerechnia, achieving total surprise over the Germans who, having seen the Soviet airborne troops scattered over a wide area during the drop earlier that day, did not expect such an assault at night by almost 400 men. The attack was successful and the paratroops inflicted heavy losses on the enemy logistical support unit occupying the village, while also capturing six vehicles and an anti-aircraft gun. Having taken Ozerechnia, Kobets and the small element of the 3rd Parachute Battalion then parted from the 2nd Battalion and headed east for the railway line running west from Viaz'ma.

Further complications arose for IV Airborne Corps when the Germans, already aware of the airborne operation, bombed the mounting airfield at Zhashkovo and subsequently those at Grabtsevo and Rzhavets, destroying seven TB-3 bombers and seven vital fuel dumps. Moreover, the presence of only a few Soviet fighters meant that the aircraft transporting the paratroops would have to fly over enemy-controlled territory without escorts. This placed severe limitations on the number of aircraft despatched on each flight and consequently the leading elements of Major V. P. Drobyshevsky's 1st Parachute Battalion took off in only fifteen aircraft on the night of 27 January. At the same time, however, the weather deteriorated sharply into a blizzard and Drobyshevsky and his men found themselves scattered over the area of Belomir, some five miles to the south-east of Ozerechnia.

Despite the lack of aircraft, 8th Airborne Brigade continued with its dropping of troops and equipment. The night of 28–29 January saw supplies, including ammunition, skis and other stores, dropped at Ozerechnia even though only ten PS-84 transports and two TB-3 bombers were serviceable. More aircraft were allocated to the operation on the 29th and that night a further 540 men were dropped. Heavy snows, freezing temperatures and enemy air activity on the following day were such that only 120 men could be dropped.

The brigade commander, Lieutenant Colonel Aleksandr Onufriev and his tactical headquarters staff, were dropped just after midnight on the night of 28–29 January after two earlier unsuccessful attempts, landing approximately nine miles from Ozerechnia where they encountered some enemy. An action ensued during which the Russians suffered casualties before making their way to the village of Ivanovka, where they met a patrol from the 2nd Parachute Battalion. Radio contact with Captain Karnaukhov was established on the morning of 30 January and on the following day, Onufriev and his men rendezvoused with him.

Karnaukhov briefed the brigade commander on the situation and later that day the latter transmitted a detailed report to Headquarters IV Airborne Corps in which he stated that an enemy battalion, supported by armour, was in possession of the Ermolino–Bessonovo road junction while smaller units held the villages of Ermolino, Alferovo and Borovoi. The force occupying Izdeshkovo, comprising units of 11th Panzer Division and administrative and support elements of Fourth Panzer Army, was approximately 400 strong. Onufriev also reported that his brigade had been widely dispersed over the Ozerechnia–Androsovo–Komovo area during the drop and that the locations of a large number of his sub-units was unknown. Some of his troops, however, were in action along the Viaz'ma-Smolensk highway.

Major Kobets' 3rd Parachute Battalion, by this time numbering 131 men, was meantime heading for its objective: the railway line and road to the west of Viaz'ma. On 30 January Kobets occupied Evdokimovo, from where he sent forward reconnaissance patrols. Two days later, following an engagement with a small enemy force, he and his men pushed on towards the stretch of railway line between Alferovo and Rebrovo which they subsequently cut in four places, mining the immediate area of each location as they went. Thereafter, they took up a defensive position to the west of Es'kovo, overlooking the railway.

The Germans soon became aware of the presence of Kobets' force and despatched troops, supported by an armoured train, to eject him from the area. An attack on 2 February failed to do so and the Germans withdrew to Alferovo. On the following day, one of Kobets' patrols attacked and annihilated a German railway repair detachment. By this time Kobets had moved his men into Es'kovo itself and on 4 February the Germans mounted a battalion attack on the village, which was beaten off. Three days later, they tried again but met with a similar lack of success.

During one of these actions, Kobets himself was seriously wounded and Lieutenant Checherin assumed command of the force, moving it out of the village, which by this time was ablaze, into the nearby forest. He and his men were short of ammunition and burdened by a large number of wounded; furthermore, they were faced by German forces on three sides. Nevertheless the remnants of the 3rd Parachute Battalion continued to harass the enemy. On 18 February, Checherin sent out a patrol to establish contact with the brigade's main body, but this failed to return. Thereafter, he decided to head south-east to Pustoshka where he believed the brigade to be operating from the area from Izborovo in the direction of Bekasovo which lay some five miles to the east of Es'kovo.

Major Kobets and the other eighty-five wounded, escorted by a thirty-man platoon under Lieutenant Fomenkov, headed the column, followed by the approximately one hundred strong main body. On about 20 February, Fomenkov's group linked up with the 41st Cavalry Division of I Guards Cavalry Corps and, following the evacuation of the wounded by air to Glukhovo, on 22 February rejoined 8th Airborne Brigade which was about to launch an attack on Bekasovo, where it subsequently saw some very heavy fighting. Meantime, Lieutenant Checherin and the main body had fought their way through and linked up with 1st Guards Cavalry Division, thereafter rejoining 8th Airborne Brigade where he and his men were absorbed into the 2nd Parachute Battalion.

Although the 3rd Parachute Battalion's operation, which lasted just over three weeks, had failed to achieve any major objectives, along with missions mounted by other airborne units and elements of I Guards Cavalry Corps, it had proved to be of considerable diversionary value. The Viaz'ma–Smolensk rail link between Alferovo and Rebrovo had been cut eight times and its use denied to the enemy, while the highway could only be used by convoys accompanied by armour, being closed from 28 to 31 January. Moreover, the operation had forced Fourth Panzer Army to commit valuable resources in attempts to reopen both lines of communication and supply.

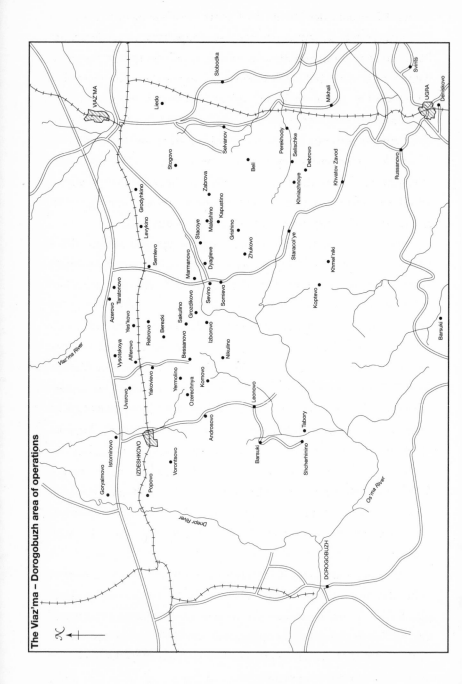

The Viaz'ma – Dorogobuzh area of operations

VIAZ'MA

Liado

Slobodka

Svirts

UGRA

Deniskovo

Stogovo

Selvanov

Perekhody

Mikhali

Beli

Selischke

Debrovo

Khvatov Zavod

Russanovo

Grodynkino

Zabrova

Kapustino

Khniazhnoye

Levykino

Stacoye

Maleshino

Grishino

Staracol'ye

Semievo

Marmanovo

Dyagleve

Zhukovo

Koptevo

Khmel'niki

Azerovo

Taratonovo

Grozdikovo

Sevino

Somievo

Barsuki

Yes'kovo

Sakulino

Vysotskoya

Berezki

Izborovo

Alferovo

Bessanovo

Nikulino

Uverovo

Yakovievo

Yermolino

Komovo

Leonovo

Ozerechnya

Tabony

Goryalinovo

Androsovo

Istominovo

IZDESHKOVO

Barsuki

Shcherhinino

Popovo

Vorontsovo

Viaz'ma River

Dnepr River

Os'ma River

DOROGOBUZH

130

On 8 February, despite much of its strength having been scattered during its drop on 27 January, Major V. P. Drobyshevsky's 1st Parachute Battalion had launched attacks on the small enemy garrisons in Astashevo, Belomir and Gvozdenkovo, destroying them all. Thereafter, it turned its attention on the villages of Diagilevo and Savino, where reconnaissance operations had revealed German formation headquarters elements and large concentrations of vehicles based there. It seized Savino, forcing the hasty evacuation of the headquarters of 5th Panzer Division and a battalion of the 116th Artillery Regiment which withdrew to Semlevo, taking 1,500 prisoners (among them a general) and capturing large quantities of vehicles and equiment.

The 2nd Parachute Battalion had by now captured Semenovskoe and Gvozdenkovo, and then advanced on Marmonovo, which was held by the 8th Artillery Regiment. On the evening of 9 February it launched its attack and drove the Germans from the village, the latter suffering 330 killed. On the following day, 8th Airborne Brigade, in cooperation with partisan units, attacked the headquarters of 5th Panzer Division, capturing a large quantity of equipment, and occupied Morshanovo and Diagilevo, where Lieutenant Colonel Onufriev established his own headquarters. Part of the brigade headquarters, including the Chief of Staff, Major N. I. Sagaidachnyi, was located at Kurdiumovo. Sagaidachnyi, with a small group, had been dropped on 28 January, landing north-east of Alferovo from where they had headed north, assembling four platoons of paratroops with whom they had seized Kurdiumovo in a night attack on 9 February. Two days later, however, a strong enemy force attacked the village and wiped out Sagaidachnyi and his entire group.

On 12 February, Onufriev received orders from the commander of I Guards Cavalry Corps, Lieutenant General Pavel Belov, outlining his plan for an advance northwards in conjunction with Onufriev's brigade and XI Cavalry Corps prior to an attack on Viaz'ma from the west. Initially, 8th Airborne Brigade would be relieved at Diagilevo and Marmanovo by two regiments of the 41st Cavalry Division. The 250th

Independent Airborne Regiment, along with two battalions of 201st Airborne Brigade and the 329th Rifle Division of I Guards Cavalry Corps, would meantime take up positions along a front to the south of Viaz'ma. The 8th Airborne Brigade and the rest of I Guards Cavalry Corps would regroup and concentrate for a night attack on Semlevo. Onufriev's paratroops were to attack the north-eastern area of the town while I Guards Cavalry Corps assaulted the eastern and south-eastern sectors. Due to the losses sustained by his corps in the recent fighting, Belov was reinforced by partisan units from the Dorogobuzh region to the west.

The attack began at 6.00 a.m. on 13 February with a heavy mortar barrage on the German positions in Semlevo. Shortly afterwards, 8th Airborne Brigade began its assault but once in the town was halted by fierce resistance from the Germans, who brought heavy fire to bear from artillery, armour, mortars and machine guns, and then counterattacks by infantry. Meanwhile, Belov's 1st Guards and 41st Cavalry Divisions had been delayed by deep snow in reaching their start lines but subsequently joined the fray which saw fierce street fighting throughout that day, causing heavy casualties among 8th Airborne Brigade and Belov's troops.

Marmanovo and Diagilevo, meanwhile, were the scenes of counterattacks by the Germans. In Marmanovo, a German force of one battalion supported by five tanks and other armoured vehicles drove Belov's 188th Cavalry Regiment from the town before turning its attention to Diagilevo. There it expelled the 170th Cavalry Regiment and elements of the two battalions of 201st Airborne Brigade which lost 200 men killed or taken prisoner. Farther to the east along I Guards Cavalry Corps' front south of Viaz'ma, the situation became equally grim as the forward elements of 329th Rifle Division were driven from Troshino by two battalions with armour and air support which then began advancing on Semlevo before being halted at Belomir.

The fighting in Semlevo continued throughout 13 February and the next day, neither side achieving an advantage. On 15 February, however, the Germans gained the upper hand following their rein-forcement by two battalions and eight tanks. Shortly afterwards, they launched a counter-attack which drove 8th Airborne Brigade out of the town to the north and the 75th Cavalry Division to the west. Onufriev and his men then found themselves surrounded by the German forces from Semlevo and Diagilevo and attempted to break out to the east towards Belov's 41st Cavalry Division to the south of Diagilevo. This failed, but a second attempt on 16 February was successful and the paratroops made their way through the forests to regroup in the area of Alferovo and Bolsh'shoe Petrovo.

In the face of such reverses, and under pressure from the Germans in all sectors along I Guards Cavalry Corps' front, Belov abandoned his efforts to secure Semlevo as a base from which to mount an attack on Viaz'ma. On 17 February, 8th Airborne Brigade regrouped with Captain Surzlak's and Captain Kalashnikov's 1st and 2nd Parachute Battalions of 201st Airborne Brigade being placed under command.

Headquarters Western Front was determined to continue with its efforts to capture Viaz'ma, and Belov had received orders on the evening of 17 February, instructing him to continue to surround Viaz'ma from the west and interdict the Viaz'ma–Smolensk highway, thereafter linking up with XI Cavalry Corps.

Regrouping continued on 18 February but that day also saw the Germans attacking on I Guards Cavalry Corps' right flank, pushing the 250th Independent Airborne Regiment out of the town of Stogovo. Pressure was also increased on Belov's left and a growing threat was posed to Dorogobuzh, forcing Belov to send a regiment of the 1st Guards Cavalry Division to reinforce the partisan units there and block any German adance southwards.

Belov launched his new assault at 7.00 p.m. on the evening of 18 February and by nightfall his forces, with 8th Airborne Brigade following up, had captured Izborovo. Simultaneously, Lieutenant Petr Pobortsev's 300-strong Composite Parachute Battalion of 214th Airborne Brigade was dropped near Izborovo as reinforcement. Half of the battalion landed in 8th Airborne Brigade's area, the remainder being scattered across the region, most of whom succeeded in reaching the brigade.

On the following day 8th Airborne Brigade, now on the left flank of 2nd Guards Cavalry Division, captured Sakulino. The Soviet offensive continued as the cavalry advanced to seize Gvozdikovo but the para-troops, while still concentrated in Sakulino, were suddenly subjected to a ferocious counter-attack from the rear by German infantry supported by artillery and aircraft. Although the enemy was halted near Izborovo, the 1st Parachute Battalion suffered severe casualties. Nevertheless, the brigade continued its progress through Bolotovo, being reinforced by a platoon of twenty-five men of its 4th Parachute Battalion, and by 22 February had captured Bekasovo, which lay approx-imately three miles to the west of Semlevo.

Lieutenant Colonel Onufriev sent forward the 2nd Parachute Battalion of 201st Airborne Brigade and reconnaissance patrols which crossed the railway line a mile and a half north of Bekasovo to link up with elements of XI Cavalry Corps. These could not be found, however, and two days later the battalion returned to discover that Bekasovo was under heavy attack by the Germans, who had launched their assault on the afternoon of 22 February. A combination of heavy counter-attacks and highly effective air strikes was launched against the eastern sector of the town, driving back 8th Airborne Brigade's 2nd Parachute Battalion and Captain Surzhik's 1st Parachute Battalion of 201st Airborne Brigade.

Further attacks with heavy air support were launched by the Germans on 24 and 25 February, 8th Airborne Brigade being attacked on all sides. Eventually, the brigade was cut off from the rest of I Guards Cavalry Corps and, along with the 41st Cavalry Division, was forced to withdraw to Izborovo. Reinforced by three divisions sent to their aid by Belov, 8th Airborne Brigade and the 41st Cavalry Division managed to disengage and withdraw to take up positions in the area of Kaledino and Vysokoe while the remainder of I Guards Cavalry Corps concen-trated on the paratroops' left flank around Zabolot'e and Byshkovo.

By this time, 8th Airborne Brigade was much reduced in numbers, having suffered very heavy losses in this latest round of fighting. Its 1st Parachute Battalion, along with the 1st Parachute Battalion of 201st Airborne Brigade, was virtually non-existent and thus their surviving members were absorbed into the remaining units which left Onufriev with his 2nd Parachute Battalion, the 2nd Parachute Battalion of 201st Airborne Brigade and the 2nd Parachute Battalion of 214th Airborne Brigade.

The 8th Airborne Brigade remained under command of I Guards Cavalry Corps for over another month. Operating behind enemy lines, it initially mounted an attack on the railway line in the area of Izdeshkovo, west of Viaz'ma, before heading south-east on 7 March in support of Major Nikolai Soldatov's 250th Independent Airborne Regiment and the 329th Rifle Division which had been encircled by enemy forces at Perekhody, east of Debrevo and Kniazhnoe. During the following six days, several attempts were made to break through the surrounding German forces but to no avail. By 14 March, only seventy-five of Soldatov's men and some 250–300 of the 329th Rifle Division had broken out.

During the next two weeks, 8th Airborne Brigade continued operations in the area west of the railway line between Viaz'ma and Ugra. On 7 April, however, it returned to IV Airborne Corps which by this time had been committed to operations in the German rear as it had become apparent that additional forces were required if the Soviets were to achieve their objectives on the Western and Kalinin Fronts. The Supreme Commander Western Direction, General Georgi Zhukov, had decided to expand operations in the enemy rear by inserting IV Airborne Corps into the Viaz'ma region.

Zhukov's task was to coordinate more closely the operations of the Western and Kalinin Fronts. With this principally in mind, he concentrated on the Viaz'ma salient and in particular on the German Iukhnov Group comprising the Fourth Army's XII, XIII, XLIII and LVII Corps. Fourth Army's left wing, formed by XII Corps, had by this time linked up with the right of Fourth Panzer Army and the German front was an unbroken line east of the Ugra river. XII, XIII and XLIII Corps held the northern, eastern and southern approaches to Iukhnov while LVII Corps and the 10th Motorised Division were hard at work establishing a line south-west of Iukhnov to defend the main Moscow–Warsaw highway. The Germans were well aware that control of this main route and the Moscow–Minsk highway would enable them to contain the Soviet Western Front's left wing, consisting of the Tenth, Fiftieth and Forty-Ninth Armies. Moreover, it would ensure the annihilation of those Soviet forces surrounded near Viaz'ma and release formations and units to reinforce their main front.

Zhukov decided to mount an operation aimed at breaking the German grip on Iukhnov, seizing control of the Moscow–Warsaw highway and ultimately capturing Viaz'ma. This would initially take the form of a thrust by the Soviet Fiftieth Army which would drive between sixteen and twenty miles across the Moscow–Minsk highway deep into a German sector south-west of Iukhnov. The remainder of IV Airborne Corps, comprising 9th and 214th Airborne Brigades and the 4th Parachute Battalion of 8th Airborne Brigade, would be dropped in the German rear to the west of Iukhnov. The orders received by the corps commander, Major General Aleksei Levashev, stated that he was to carry out an airborne operation in the region of Velikopol'e, Shhushmin and Zhelan'e, after which he was to advance and attack German defensive positions in the area of Kliuchi, thereafter occupying a line through Kurakino, Borodino and Podsosonski and reaching the line Pesochnia, Kliuchi, Tynovka and Leonovo some sixteen to twenty miles south-west of Iukhnov. Having secured much of the enemy rear area, Levashov was to link up with units of the Fiftieth Army, the combined force thereafter surrounding the German forces in Iukhnov and opening the way for an advance into the region south-west of Viaz'ma where the surviving elements of 8th Airborne Brigade, I Guards Cavalry Corps and the Thirty-Third Army were still surrounded.

IV Airborne Corps mounted its operation from airfields at Liubertsy,

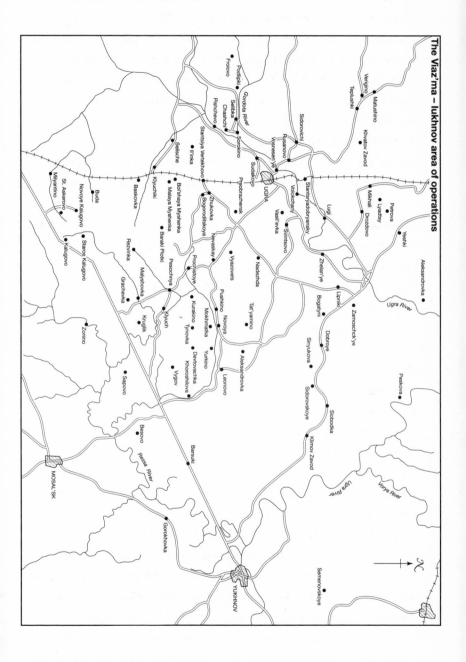

The Viaz'ma – Iukhnov area of operations

Verigino
Teplushki
Matushino
Khvatov Zavod
Froovo
Podlipki
Gordota River
Seliba
Pishchevo
Chashchi
Sorokino
Sidorovichi
Rusanovo
Vosnesen'ye
Mikhali
Petrova
Lyadtsy
Drozdovo
Startsya Vertelkhovo
Il'inka
Selische
Klyuchiki
Sudakovo
UGRA
Volokhayny
Startsyasobryansky
Vasil'evka
Svintsovo
Lugi
Zhelan'ye
Yeshki
Aleksandrovka
Milyantino
St. Askkerovo
Novoye Kalugovo
Buda
Baskovka
Bol'shaya Myshenka
Malaya Myshenka
Zhukovka
Bogorodiskoya
Nevaskay
Preobrazhensk
Nadezhda
Tat'yanino
Lipniki
Bogatyni
Zamoschek'ye
Ugra River
Kalugovo
Stanoe Kalugovo
Rezvinka
Baraki Plotki
Pesochnya
Prochistoye
Vyazovets
Pushkino
Novoya
Aleksandrovka
Dobroye
Zonino
Grachevka
Malyshovka
Kruglik
Klyuch
Kurakino
Tynovka
Mokhmatka
Yurkino
Leonovo
Shiryukova
Siidorovskoye
Klimov Zavod
Slobodka
Peskova
Sapovo
Besovo
Devtovachka
Khorosthlova
Vygov
Gorokhovka
Raessa River
Barsuki
Ugra River
Vorya River
MOSAL'SK
YUKHNOV
Semenovskoye

Vnukovo and Ramenskoe. It was to be dropped over three nights, being transported in two flights of aircraft on each. Aviation support comprised a transport group of 41 PS-84 transports and 23 TB-3 bombers which would fly unescorted. Initially, it was planned that pathfinders with radios would be dropped to guide in the aircraft but this idea was dropped and the task of marking the DZs was given to partisans using bonfires.

First to be inserted was the 4th Parachute Battalion of 8th Airborne Brigade which was dropped on the night of 17–18 February. The drop was not a success as the leading PS-84 transport, carrying eighteen para-troops, failed to find the designated DZ and returned to Liubertsy. The second dropped its stick some nine miles from Zhelan'e and of the eighteen men, only nine succeeded in reaching the RV and assembly point. Bad weather conditions, including fog, were much to blame and forced the aircraft to drop their sticks from altitudes of between 3,000 and 4,000 feet, so that men and equipment were scattered over wide areas of terrain, some of it heavily forested and covered in deep snow which made movement across country to RV points very difficult. Other aircraft, unable to find DZs, returned to base with their sticks. By the following morning, half of the 4th Parachute Battalion had reached the designated assembly point.

A similar fate befell the 2nd Parachute Battalion of 214th Airborne Brigade which dropped in the early hours of 18 February, many of its number landing far from the DZ in the operational area of 8th Airborne Brigade. Some 150 members of the battalion landed on or around the DZ, however, and regrouped near Griada, just east of Zhelan'e. Shortly afterwards, they suffered heavy casualties from enemy air attack and were forced to take cover in the forests near by.

The brigade's 1st Parachute Battalion meanwhile had aborted its drop as it had been unable to detect the correct signal lights from the area of its designated DZ near Zhelan'e. It was dropped that same night but found itself well away from its DZ due to an error on the part of the leading aircraft's navigator.

The 9th Airborne Brigade fared little better during its drop on the night of 18–19 February. The leading aircraft met heavy anti-aircraft fire, the first two being shot down. Some of the paratroops aboard them succeeded in jumping clear but, silhouetted in the sky, themselves came under fire as they descended. The others, trapped aboard the doomed aircraft, died when they crashed. Other aircraft fell prey to German fighters whose presence forced the transports to drop their paratroops from an altitude of 6,500 feet, so that once again sticks were scattered over wide areas. Some 300 men of 9th Airborne Brigade landed in the area of I Guards Cavalry Corps and the Thirty-Third Army, while 110 men of both 9th and 214th Airborne Brigades landed near Dmitrovka. These latter were formed into a sub-unit and thereafter fought under the Thirty-Third Army.

Four days later on 22 February, 3,000 men, comprising the last elements of 214th Airborne Brigade, commanded by Colonel N. E. Kolobovnikov, landed among the positions of the surrounded units of the Soviet Thirty-Third Army to the south-east of Viaz'ma. By early the following morning it had reached its designated location but 1,200 men were missing.

Headquarters IV Airborne Corps took off from Liubertsy on the evening of 22 February. The first aircraft carried half of the headquarters while aboard the second, a TB-3 bomber, was Major General Levashev himself and the remainder of his staff. The leading aircraft arrived at Zhelan'e, landing unscathed. Levashev's plane, however, was not so fortunate and encountered enemy night fighters, which engaged it. The TB-3 managed to land and all but three of those aboard escaped with their lives; Levashev and his personal aide were both killed. His Chief of Staff, Colonel Aleksandr Kazankin, duly assumed command of IV Airborne Corps in his place.

The night of 24 February saw IV Airborne Corps' airborne operation completed with 7,373 men and 1,525 loads of equipment dropped in 612 sorties. Of those dropped, however, over 2,000 men failed to regroup with their units, some 1,800 linking up instead with units of I Guards Cavalry Corps, Thirty-Third Army or partisan formations.

The night of 23–24 February saw 9th and 214th Airborne Brigades advancing south. The 9th, commanded by Colonel Ivan Kuryshev, initially achieved some success when its 1st Parachute Battalion, under Captain A. Plotnikov, ousted an enemy platoon from the village of Tynovka. Thereafter, its 3rd Company captured Khan'kova while the 1st Company and Reconnaissance Platoon cleared an enemy company from Gorbachi without loss. Shortly after midnight, the brigade's 2nd Parachute Battalion seized Prechistoe and by dawn on 24 February had begun attacking Kliuchi, being joined by the 4th Parachute Battalion which had earlier captured Kurakino. Here, however, the enemy were well prepared and both battalions suffered losses from machine-gun and artillery fire before withdrawing into the forests approximately half a mile to the north of Kliuchi. In the meantime, the 3rd Parachute Battalion, together with a partisan unit, had trapped a battalion of 800 enemy in Ugra Station. As it did so, it despatched a company south to Verterkhovo station which was captured and found to contain considerable quantities of ammunition, food and other stores.

Meanwhile, 214th Airborne Brigade, under Colonel N. E. Kolobovnikov, had made good progress in its advance south during the night of 23–24 February, its 1st Parachute Battalion in the lead, followed by the 2nd and 4th. The 3rd remained at Zhelan'e, carrying out reconnaissance tasks around Prechistoe, Kurakino, Kliuchi and Pesochnia. On the morning of 24 February, however, the brigade came under heavy air attack which hindered its progress and caused casualties. Nevertheless, the three battalions launched attacks on Ivantseva, Kostinki and Zherdovka, but encountered heavy resistance. Moreover, the deep snow hampered the transportation forward of the brigade's heavy weapons, resulting in inadequate artillery and mortar support. The attacks were thus unsuccessful and the brigade was forced to withdraw to its start lines and regroup.

The Germans were well prepared. Their garrison at Ivantseva had detected the presence of a 214th Airborne Brigade reconnaissance patrol on the night of 23–24 February and had lost little time in passing warnings to Kostinki and Zherdovka. The three villages formed part of a network of mutually supporting strongpoints, each defended by a company of infantry in all-round defence, backed by artillery, and thus the entire area posed a formidable obstacle to IV Airborne Corps.

The 214th Airborne Brigade launched an attack on enemy positions near Ivantseva on 24 February, but this was beaten off. That night, however, a successful company attack was made on Tat'ianinol' which was captured. The brigade was weak in numbers and Colonel Kolobovnikov had already been forced to distribute his 2nd Parachute Battalion as reinforcements among his other units each of which were only some 120 strong.

The 9th Airborne Brigade meanwhile had failed to capture Pesochnia and had moved on towards Kliuchi, leaving Pesochnia to 214th Airborne Brigade instead. On 25 February, a reconnaissance patrol of the latter's 1st Parachute Battalion was ambushed and annihilated. Colonel Kolobovnikov therefore decided to surround the village and the nearby one of Ekaterinovka, and to wait until 9th Airborne Brigade launched its assault on Kliuchi after last light on 26 February.

The town of Kliuchi was a key objective, being situated at a vital road junction on a ridge and dominating the surrounding area of flat terrain. Together with other strongpoints, it also overlooked the Moscow–Warsaw highway two miles to the south. Manned by infantry and tanks, its defences included fortified buildings, trenches and strongpoints. Its capture was essential if IV Airborne Corps was to achieve its task of thrusting through the German line along the Moscow–Warsaw highway.

The 9th Airborne Brigade began its attack on Kliuchi on 26 February. In the initial phase, its 1st Parachute Battalion occupied the villages of Dertovaia, Han'kova and Tynovka and secured IV Airborne Corps' left flank. Thereafter it reinforced Gorbachi before advancing on Kliuchi from the south-east. Meanwhile, the 2nd and 4th Parachute Battalions, commanded by Captains Smirnov and Bibikov respectively, advanced from the north and west and took up blocking positions.

By this time, 214th Airborne Brigade had begun its attack on Pesochnia but this had been unsuccessful. Thereafter, its 1st Parachute Battalion, commanded by Captain Polozkov, was despatched to join the assault on Kliuchi from the west. After last light, further reinforcements for 9th Airborne Brigade arrived in the form of 8th Airborne Brigade's 4th Parachute Battalion, under Captain Gor'kov, which brought with it IV Airborne Corps' artillery battalion. These were followed soon afterwards by 9th Airborne Brigade's 3rd Parachute Battalion, commanded by Major Sharov, which hitherto had remained in reserve.

Preparations for the attack on Kliuchi continued throughout 26 February, with a platoon of 214th Airborne Brigade's assault engineer company cutting communications between the town and the neighbouring strongpoints at Malyshevska and Kruglik, and mining the roads approaching Kliuchi.

IV Airborne Corps began its assault after last light. The 9th Airborne Brigade's 2nd Parachute Battalion led the way, followed by the 1st and 4th Battalions, all three units succeeding in penetrating the outer defences and capturing a number of buildings in the north and north-western sectors of the town. Subsequently, elements of the 1st and 2nd Battalions circled the town and fought their way in from the south. The fighting was fierce but after three hours 9th Airborne Brigade reached the town centre at which point Colonel Ivan Kuryshev sent in his reserve, the 4th Parachute Battalion of 8th Airborne Brigade.

By dawn the following morning, Kliuchi had been captured and cleared of the enemy who were identified as being two battalions and headquarters of the 12th Infantry Regiment. German casualties were later estimated as 600 dead, with a large quantity of equipment, including 200 vehicles, captured.

The morning of 27 February found 9th Airborne Brigade's 2nd and 4th Parachute Battalions, followed by the two battalions of 8th and

214th Airborne Brigades on their flanks, advancing through thick snow towards the enemy-held village of Malyshevka and the Moscow–Warsaw highway. All four battalions, however, were soon subjected to very heavy fire from German artillery and air strikes, followed by attacks by infantry with armour in support. Such were their losses that they were eventually forced to pull back to Kliuchi where they regrouped, the 8th and 214th Airborne Brigade battalions being withdrawn into reserve. Meantime, the Germans followed up, launching attacks throughout 28 February, all of which were beaten off.

Such strong opposition, which inflicted losses amounting to 1,200 men, prevented IV Airborne Corps from achieving its objectives of linking up with the Soviet Fiftieth Army and interdicting the Moscow–Warsaw highway, while lack of mobility and logistical support were also critical factors that hampered it greatly.

On 1 March, the corps established a defensive line running twenty miles to the east and west of Kliuchi and running through the villages of Novaia, Andronovo, Iurkino, Tynovka, Petrischevo, Gorbach, Dubrovnia and Verterkhovo Station, all of which became defensive redoubts. The most pressing problem facing the corps commander, Colonel Aleksandr Kazankin, was the fast-dwindling stock of ammunition and rations. His chief quartermaster, Colonel Ivan Morozov, set up a centralised logistical support formation which drew on the resources of I Guards Cavalry Corps and captured enemy stocks as well as seeking support from local inhabitants and partisan groups. At the same time, he improved the landing strip at Zhelan'e and established a number of supply dumps between Zhelan'e and the corps' forward positions in the area of Kliuchi.

The Germans, however, continued the pressure on IV Airborne Corps, launching two major assaults on the morning of 1 March. The first, by a battalion of infantry supported by armour and artillery, took place south of Kliuchi but was beaten off after several tanks had been destroyed. The second, heavier attack was mounted against 9th Airborne Brigade whose 2nd Parachute Battalion came under severe pressure before the Germans eventually withdrew. The brigade was subjected to two further assaults that day, also beating them off but suffering heavy casualties in the process. All these attacks were carried out by the 131st Infantry Division which, based at Podsosonski, had the task of clearing any Soviet forces to the north of the Moscow–Warsaw highway.

On 3 March IV Airborne Corps, by this time only some 3,000 in strength, began to receive a resupply of ammunition and rations and was able to evacuate its ever-increasing numbers of wounded to the rear. This was completed on 5 March, by which time the Germans had been forced to abandon the city of Iukhnov, XLIII Corps withdrawing to the south-west where it linked up with the 137th Infantry Division and other units of the German Fourth Army south of the Moscow–Warsaw highway. The German line faced south-east towards the Soviet Fiftieth Army, each division taking up positions of all-round defence within its own sector, with battalion battle groups occupying a line of villages linked by the highway.

On 3 March, Colonel Kazankin received instructions from the commander of the Fiftieth Army, Colonel General Ivan Boldin, to reconnoitre a route along which IV Airborne Corps units were to link up with the latter's units. Thereafter Kazankin issued his own orders whereby 9th Airborne Brigade, along with elements of 214th Airborne Brigade and the corps' artillery battalion, was to seize Malyshevka and thereafter capture Babykino, situated some 900 yards north of the Moscow–Warsaw highway, where it was to rendezvous with Fiftieth Army units. The remainder of 214th Airborne Brigade would provide flank protection on 9th Airborne Brigade's right.

The commander of 9th Airborne Brigade, Colonel Kuryschev, allocated the task of capturing Malshevka and Babykino to his 2nd, 3rd and 4th Parachute Battalions, the 1st remaining in defence at Kliuchi. On the night of 5 March, the three battalions set off for their start lines but at 9.00 p.m. Major Smirnov's 2nd Parachute Battalion encountered a strong German force and came under heavy fire which forced it to pull back. The other two battalions continued to move up and at 1.00 a.m. on 6 February the 3rd Parachute Battalion, commanded by Major Sharov, attacked Malyshevka from the north-east, but was subsequently forced to withdraw by heavy opposition and a counter-attack from the flank by a German ski battalion. The 4th Parachute Battalion, under Captain Bibikov, meanwhile, had been delayed by deep snow in arriving at its start line but nevertheless mounted an attack. Having briefly gained footholds in the north-eastern and north-western outskirts of the village, however, the battalion was subsequently driven out by a strong counter-attack.

The operation had failed due to poor coordination and lack of impetus, the latter largely due to the thick snow which made movement slow and laborious. An additional major factor was poor reconnaissance which had resulted in an inaccurate estimate of the enemy force holding Malyshevka, whose garrison comprised two infantry battalions, supported by mortars and anti-tank guns, and a ski battalion.

The three battalions were then forced to carry out a slow and lengthy withdrawal through thick snow to their original assembly areas. The Germans were quick to follow up with attacks of their own, two companies mounting an assault at Dertvchka but being beaten off after suffering some fifty casualties. The 214th Airborne Brigade's 1st Parachute Battalion, in its positions near Tynovka, was also subjected to an attack but repelled it, inflicting thirty-five dead on the enemy.

On 11 March, following a heavy artillery bombardment, the Germans attacked Iurkino and Andronovo from three sides, driving back 214th Airborne Brigade's 4th Parachute Battalion into the forest to the west where it regrouped and stood firm. At the same time, attacks were launched on IV Airborne Corps at Tynovka, Novaia Mokhnata and Tat'ianin, while a particularly fierce battle took place on the corps' southern perimeter at Gorbachi. Fighting continued through to the following day, by the end of which V Airborne Corps had beaten off all attacks. By then, 214th Airborne Brigade held Dubrovnia, Prechistoe and Kurakino, thereby blocking the enemy's 12th Infantry Regiment at Ekaterina and Pesochnia, while also holding Mohnatka and Novaia in the face of opposition from the 33rd and 434th Infantry Regiments. Meanwhile, 9th Airborne Brigade was in possession of Kliuchi, Gorbachi and Tynovka, being opposed by the 143rd and 442th Infantry Regiments.

The Germans, meantime, were bringing up reinforcements, among them the 107th Infantry Regiment which moved from Iukhnov expressly to engage 4th Airborne Corps which by 13 March was further reduced in numbers, to a total strength of 2,000 all ranks. That same day saw another major assault by the Germans with two infantry battalions of the 31st and 34th Infantry Divisions which had recently been transferred to Russia from France. Supported by armour, they attacked Gorbachi from the north-east, west and south and eventually gained a foothold in the south-eastern sector. The 9th Airborne Brigade's 1st Parachute Battalion took the brunt of these attacks and was unable to dislodge the Germans but that afternoon the brigade threw in its 2nd Parachute Battalion which attacked the Germans' left flank and forced them to pull back to Astapovo, having suffered 200 casualties.

Despite this reverse, further German reinforcements continued to arrive, through deteriorating weather conditions, thus increasing the pressure on IV Airborne Corps. In order to pre-empt another attack, Colonel Kazankin decided to launch his own on Pesochnia, using 9th and 214th Airborne Brigades and the 4th Parachute Battalion of the 8th Brigade. This took place on the night of 17 March but failed, the entire paratroop force being driven out of the town.

The Germans responded on the following morning as the 131st Infantry Division attacked Novaia and Mokhnatka, wresting Pushkino from 214th Airborne Brigade's 4th Parachute Battalion which suffered heavy casualties that reduced it to a strength of no more than thirty men. That afternoon, they attacked Kliuchi, Gorbachi, Tynovka and Borodino and forced back IV Airborne Corps' defensive line east of Kurakino. Colonel Kazankin sought and received permission to withdraw to a new line stretching from Verterkhovo Station through Zhukovka, Akulovo, Prechistoe and Kurakino to Novinskaia Dacha. This took place on 18 March with 214th Airborne Brigade pulling back to the area of Akulovo while 9th Airborne Brigade withdrew at the same time with the 1st Parachute Battalion taking up positions at Novinskaia Dacha, the 2nd at Prechistoe and the 3rd at Kurakino.

The withdrawal was completed by the evening of 20 March, by which time the Germans had become aware of it and lost little time in following up. On 25 March, units of the 131st Infantry Division attacked 9th Airborne Brigade's 4th Parachute Battalion at Kurakino. Despite suffering thirty-eight killed and ninety-one wounded, and being reduced to a total strength of eighty-eight all ranks, the battalion held on and succeeded in beating off the attack. There followed, however, a series of minor raids which culminated on 31 March in a major assault by three infantry battalions supported by armour, artillery and air strikes. This was launched at the point on IV Airborne Corps' southern perimeter where 9th Airborne Brigade's positions met those of the 214th at Prechistoe, Dubrovnia and Kurakino. IV Airborne Corps suffered very heavy losses in this attack and 9th Airborne Brigade was forced to pull back from Dubrovnia, Prechistoe and Kurakino and take up new defensive positions in the forests to the north-west.

While IV Airborne Corps attempted vainly to link up with the Fiftieth Army, the 250th Independent Airborne Regiment, still commanded by Major Nikolai Soldatov, had extricated itself from the surrounded Thirty-Third Army, which had been virtually annihilated, and had linked up with I Guards Cavalry Corps which, following its failure to capture Viaz'ma, had withdrawn to the west towards Dorogobuzh where it had regrouped and refitted. At this juncture, the 329th Rifle Division was reformed from the 250th Independent Airborne Regiment and various corps units, with Major Soldatov placed in command.

On 14 March the commander of I Guards Cavalry Corps, Lieutenant General Belov, having ceased all efforts to capture Viaz'ma or cut the Smolensk–Viazma highway, moved his forces south to link up with IV Airborne Corps prior to launching a series of attacks to seize a number of stations along the Viaz'ma–Kirov railway line. Spearheading these was Lieutenant Colonel Onufriev's 8th Airborne Brigade, under command of I Guards Cavalry Corps The operation commenced in the early hours of 21 March when the 2nd Parachute Battalion, under Captain Karnaukhov, successfully negotiated its way through enemy minefields to take Deniskovo station. Next evening the battalion, together with Captain Petr Pobortsev's composite parachute battalion and elements of the 2nd Guards Cavalry Division, attacked Ugra station which was defended by an 800-strong enemy force. Despite three days of heavy fighting, the Soviets failed to take the station.

By the end of March 1942, IV Airborne Corps had been reduced to a total strength of just over 1,480 men, and was virtually surrounded. Its weakened state meant that, like the other Soviet forces trapped in the German rear, namely the Thirty-Third and Thirty-Ninth Armies and I Guards Cavalry Corps, it was incapable of breaking out on its own. At the beginning of April, the Soviet High Command ordered these troops to link up and break out in strength

I Guards Cavalry Corps moved east in an attempt to rescue the remnants of the beleaguered Soviet Thirty-Third Army. As it did so, however, the Germans increased the pressure on IV Airborne Corps, on 3 April mounting an attack with infantry supported by armour and artillery on 214th Airborne Brigade at Akulovo. While sustaining some 300 casualties and losing four tanks, they wrested the town from the Soviets, who suffered 150 casualties. That same night 9th Airborne Brigade attacked the town of Prechistoe, capturing it and killing thirty-four Germans.

Onufriev's 8th Airborne Brigade, meanwhile, linked up with elements of IV Airborne Corps on 3 April at Preobrazhensk, a short distance south-east of Ugra station. Its 1st, 2nd and 3rd Parachute Battalions numbered some 800 men while a fourth composite unit, under Colonel Shmelev, comprised 400 men who had escaped when their units were surrounded. The brigade was in poor shape as it possessed only ten mortars, one anti-tank gun and sixteen anti-tank rifles, while its supplies of food, ammunition and other materials were almost exhausted.

Shortly afterwards, the 2nd Guards Cavalry Division arrived at Ugra station. By this time, I Guards Cavalry Corps had failed in its attempt to break through to the Thirty-Third Army and Belov had subsequently despatched the division south to join IV Airborne Corps. Having secured Ugra station, 2nd Guards Cavalry Division took up positions stretching from Selische through the area of Baskakova to Malaia Myshenka and Verterkhovo station. From 7 April onwards, it operated in conjunction with 8th Airborne Brigade in beating off German attacks probing northwards along the railway line from Buda.

On 9 April, the Germans launched a major attack at the point where 2nd Guards Cavalry Division's positions met those of IV Airborne Corps, thereafter seizing Verterkhovo station and Zhukovka and pushing IV Airborne Corps and 2nd Guards Cavalry Division east and westwards respectively. By the night of 10 April, they had captured Ugra station and Kombain, and had relieved their besieged garrison at Voznesen'e. The following day saw them attacking Preobrazhensk and Marinovka, while other German forces advanced from the north-east.

I Guards Cavalry Corps launched a counter-attack on 12 April. Having regrouped, IV Airborne Corps' role was to advance southwards, to the east of the railway line to Miliatino, with Belov's corps. Some fifteen miles to the south was the Fiftieth Army which meanwhile moved north to meet Belov. Between the two Soviet formations, however, were German forces in strongly held positions in all-round defence.

The 214th Airborne Brigade remained in IV Airborne Corps' firm base area, securing a defensive line extending from Akulovo to Plotki and covering the corps' left flank. Meanwhile, 8th and 9th Airborne Brigades headed south towards Buda, Novoe Askerovo, Staroe Askerovo and Miliatino with the aim of linking up with Fiftieth Army units and helping to interdict the Moscow–Warsaw highway. The 8th Airborne

Brigade advanced along an axis of Bol'shaia Myshenka–Malaia Myshenka–western Buda–Staroe Askerovo, while 9th Airborne Brigade headed through eastern Buda and Novoe Askerovo. Meantime, IV Airborne Corps' rear was protected by Major Soldatov's 329th Rifle Division and a partisan unit.

IV Airborne Corps' counter-offensive commenced on the night of 13–14 April and by last light on the following day 8th and 9th Airborne Brigades had taken Terekhovka, Bol'shaia Myshenka and Bogorodit-skoe. Following news that the Fiftieth Army had advanced to within only four miles of Miliatino, IV Airborne Corps took Platonovka, Baraki and Plotki on the night of 14–15 April. The 214th Airborne Brigade captured Akulovo but thereafter its advance was stemmed by stiff resist-ance from the Germans. Meanwhile, 2nd Guards Cavalry Division advanced to within a mile or so of Baskakovka station.

The following day saw the Soviets suffer severe reverses when German counter-attacks, supported strongly from the air, pushed the Fiftieth Army back from Zaitseva and the Moscow–Warsaw highway. IV and I Guards Cavalry Corps continued their advance in an attempt to punch through the German lines to the Fiftieth Army but on 15 April IV Airborne Corps was halted two miles north of Miliatino and was soon subjected to a series of counter-attacks. Two days later, after heavy fighting, 8th Airborne Brigade's 1st and 2nd Parachute Battalions succeeded in entering north-eastern Buda and captured the railway station there. Meanwhile, 9th Airborne Brigade attacked south-eastern Buda; by last light, the whole of Buda had been taken by IV Airborne Corps.

By this time, Fiftieth Army was only five miles away but failed to take two German strongpoints at Zaitseva Gora and Fomino 2. IV Airborne Corps meanwhile received orders from Headquarters Western Front to take Askerovo by 19 April at the latest. The task was given to the 1st and 2nd Parachute Battalions of 8th Airborne Brigade (less one company of the 2nd Battalion). In the meantime, 9th Airborne Brigade dispatched its 1st and 2nd Parachute Battalions to attack Kalugovo.

Neither attack succeeded, however, having been anticipated by the Germans who strengthened their forces in both areas.

On 18 April, the Germans attacked Buda which was defended by a weak force comprising 9th Airborne Brigade's 4th Parachute Battalion and a company of 8th Airborne Brigade's 2nd Parachute Battalion. Although the Germans paid dearly, incurring 400 dead and 600 wounded, they nevertheless took Buda by that afternoon. Most of the 4th Parachute Battalion, commanded by Captain D. I. Bibikov, was annihilated along with many of the 8th Airborne Brigade company, the survivors retreating to the north before eventually circling round to the south to rejoin their respective brigades.

The following day saw the welcome arrival of reinforcements for IV Airborne Corps. Three days earlier, the 645-strong 4th Parachute Battalion of 23rd Airborne Brigade, under Lieutenant S. D. Kreuts, had been dropped west of Svintsovo. With its strength increased, if only slightly so, IV Airborne Corps regrouped and launched another attack on Novoe Askerovo. On the night of 20–21 April, 8th Airborne Brigade mounted an assault during which the commanding officer of the 1st Parachute Battalion, Captain Pobortsev, was killed. The attack failed and at 2.00 a.m. on 21 April, the brigade withdrew to the edge of the forest north of the objective.

On the night of 21 April the Fiftieth Army, spearheaded by the 58th and 60th Rifle Divisions, renewed its assault on the strongpoint at Fomino 2 but again failed to take it, the impending spring and thaw bringing with them waterlogged ground and flooded valleys that hindered the use of armour and made roads impassable to transport, resulting in inadequate supplies of ammunition reaching forward units.

On the night of 23–24 April, IV Airborne Corps made one final desperate attempt to wrest control of the Moscow–Warsaw highway from the Germans. Three separate assaults were mounted against Novoe Askerovo but on each occasion were beaten off by heavy machine-gun and mortar fire.

The following day saw the Germans launch counter-attacks against

I Guards Cavalry Corps and IV Airborne Corps, mounting them at Buda, Staroe, Novoe Askerovo and Kalugovo. Supported strongly from the air, they pushed IV Airborne Corps back to new lines of defence.

By this time, the situation facing IV Airborne Corps and I Guards Cavalry Corps was dire. The Soviet Thirty-Third Army had virtually been eliminated while the Western and Kalinin Fronts had been driven on to the defensive, forced to cease all offensive operations. The arrival of spring and the accompanying thawing of the hitherto frozen landscape brought further problems as roads became virtually impassable, making resupply and casualty evacuation extremely difficult. Consequently, Colonel Kazankin withdrew his corps to the north, with 8th Airborne Brigade taking up new positions from Verterkhovo station to Terekhova, while 9th and 23rd Airborne Brigades did likewise at Bogoroditskoe and Zhukovka respectively. 214th Airborne Brigade meanwhile took up positions covering IV Airborne Corps' eastern flank from Prechistoe to Novinskaia Dacha.

The first two weeks of May were quiet, bringing a welcome respite to Kalinin's battle-weary troops. Resupply missions brought in muchneeded weapons and equipment while casualties were evacuated by air. By this time, IV Airborne Corps numbered some 2,300 men, along with 2,000 wounded and the 1,700-strong 1st Partisan Regiment; its heavy weapons consisted of only seven artillery pieces, thirty-four medium mortars and thirty-seven anti-tank rifles.

At 4.00 a.m. on 24 May the Germans launched a major assault on IV Airborne Corps to wipe out the Soviet forces in their rear. Two German corps, comprising seven divisions, mounted an assault from Znamenka, Miliatino and Dorogobuzh in an operation designed to separate I Guards Cavalry Corps from IV Airborne Corps and thereafter to destroy both Soviet formations. The attack began with a heavy artillery bombardment, following which troops of the 23rd, 31st and 131st Infantry Divisions, along with others of the 19th and 197th Panzer Divisions, all supported by air strikes and armour, attacked along a front from Mikhali and Znamenka to Miliatino. The 1st Partisan Regiment came under particularly heavy pressure and was forced to withdraw, leaving a six-mile-wide gap in IV Airborne Corps' twenty-mile-long perimeter.

The Germans also launched a further heavy attack with a 3,000-strong force, supported by twenty tanks, against the 8th Airborne Brigade at Bol'shaia Myshenka, forcing it northwards and inflicting heavy casualties on the paratroops as they withdrew. At the same time, a third attack was launched on 2nd Guards Cavalry Division which was holding Vskhody and also Selische, Pishchevo, Chashchi and Selibka to the north, and on the River Ugra's west bank in the rear of IV Airborne Corps, which was now at risk of being totally surrounded.

The paratroops had no choice but to withdraw. On the night of 24–25 May, they headed west towards the Ugra river and Selibka where Colonel Kazankin intended to carry out a crossing and link up once more with elements of I Guards Cavalry Corps. Leading the withdrawal was 8th Airborne Brigade whose 2nd Parachute Battalion, on reaching the river on the morning of 25 May, found that Selibka, along with Pishchevo and Sorokino, was occupied by the Germans. Lacking proper equipment to carry out a river crossing, the paratroops were forced to improvise, using six small boats to ferry across the leading elements of 8th Airborne Brigade, which then reconnoitred and secured a bridge-head. The remainder of the brigade, followed by 9th and 214th Airborne Brigades, then crossed the river without incident until the last stage when the 4th Parachute Battalion of 214th Airborne Brigade came under heavy fire which caused heavy casualties, among them the battalion's commanding officer, Captain A. Khoteenkov. One of the battalion's companies was unable to cross and withdrew to the south-east, eventually reaching the lines of the Soviet Fiftieth Army on 15 July, by which time it numbered only forty-two men.

After the crossing of the Ugra, IV Airborne Corps regrouped in the forests between Selibka and Chashchi. Meanwhile, I Guards Cavalry Corps had mounted a series of counter-attacks designed to divert the Germans from pursuing the paratroops. One of these was carried out by the 6th Guards Cavalry Regiment which attacked German forces crossing the Ugra at Vskhody, forcing them to withdraw. At the same time, 2nd Guards Cavalry Division's 3rd and 7th Guards Cavalry Regiments had joined 8th Airborne Brigade in its bridgehead at Sorokino and assisted the remainder of IV Airborne Corps in crossing the river on the night of 26–27 May.

Colonel Kazankin decided to continue heading west to link up with the main body of I Guards Cavalry Corps. Screened by elements of 214th Airborne Brigade deployed to the north, the corps began to move in the early hours of 28 May. Under cover of darkness, 8th and 9th Airborne Brigades infiltrated their way around German defences as they made their way towards Podlipki. Such was the stealth and secrecy with which this was carried out that at 6.00 a.m. German artillery opened fire on the corps' abandoned positions at Selibka and Chashchi which were also subjected to air attacks. Daylight and an improvement in the weather, however, enabled the enemy to make contact with 214th Airborne Brigade's covering force which withdrew south into the forests. Under fire from artillery and harried by German infantry, it suffered heavy casualties including the capture of a fifty-strong group led by the brigade's Chief of Staff, Major V. I. Spirin. The rest escaped and, having crossed the River Gordota, rejoined IV Airborne Corps in the area of Fursovo on 29 May.

That same day saw Soviet air strikes against German forces at Pustoshka and north of Vskhody in response to a request for air support from Colonel Kazankin as his corps crossed the Vskhody–Pustoshka road. The night of 29–30 May found IV Airborne Corps continuing its withdrawal westwards through Shchadrino, eventually reaching an area west of Aleksino where it regrouped.

By the early hours of 30 May, IV Airborne Corps had linked up with I Guards Cavalry Corps, bringing Lieutenant General Belov's forces to a total strength of some 17,000 men. Belov had planned to launch a counter-attack in concert with a new offensive planned for June and had earmarked IV Airborne Corps, along with the 1st Guards Cavalry Division and a partisan regiment, to take part in an advance by the

Fiftieth Army. His plans were frustrated, however, by a major reverse suffered by the Soviets when an offensive in the southern Russian area of Khar'kov was heavily defeated by the Germans, aborting any hopes of another Soviet offensive in the Moscow region.

By this time, the Germans were once again increasing the pressure on I Guards Cavalry Corps and IV Airborne Corps from the north and east. With the agreement of Headquarters Western Front, both corps set off south-eastwards with the aim of linking up with the Soviet Tenth Army. While Belov's corps headed south through the forests to the south of El'nia and then into those west of Kirov, IV Airborne Corps moved through the German lines to the west of El'nia and then, with the 2nd Guards Cavalry and 329th Rifle Divisions advancing on its left flank, headed along an axis of Khlysty–Glinka–Bel'yi Kholm–Filimony.

At this point, two more Soviet airborne formations joined the fray as reinforcements in the form of 23rd and 211th Airborne Brigades, commanded by Lieutenant Colonels A. G. Mil'sky and M. I. Shilin respectively and numbering in all some 4,000 men. 23rd Airborne Brigade was dropped in the area of the village of Starintsa, some six miles to the south of Dorogobuzh and by 2 June had taken up positions in the area of Kriakovo, Afonino and Gavrikovo where it blocked the advance of a German force heading for the airstrip at Volochek. Shortly afterwards, 211th Airborne Brigade landed and immediately joined its sister formation in fighting a delaying action against the 5th Panzer Division which was hell-bent on seizing the Volochek airstrip.

On 5 June the two brigades carried out a fighting withdrawal under heavy fire as the rearguard for IV Airborne Corps, enabling the latter to retreat to the area of Khlysty, to the north of of El"nia. Thereafter, I Guards Cavalry Corps and IV Airborne Corps headed west towards Glinka station, on the railway line west of El'nia which was guarded and patrolled by troops of a German security division and two battalions of panzergrenadiers of the 19th Panzer Division.

Heavy fighting followed the initial contact between Belov's forces and the railway line's defenders. The latter were overrun after a battle lasting several hours and the Soviets then crossed the railway and regrouped in the forests a mile and a half to the south. On the night of 6–7 June IV Airborne Corps resumed its march with 23rd and 211th Airborne Brigades in the van. Heading south, it marched all night and all next day, towards Filimony. As they approached the El'nia-Roslavl' road, on which the town was situated, the paratroops were subjected to heavy artillery fire but nevertheless pressed on and succeeded in taking Filimony. Thereafter, until the evening of 8 June, they beat off a number of counter-attacks by German units, supported by aircraft, advancing from both the north-east and south-west along the El'nia–Roslavl' road.

In the early hours of 9 June, IV Airborne and I Guards Cavalry Corps resumed their march and headed for the village of Byki, the cavalry approaching it from the north and the paratroops from the south-west via Berniki. At dawn, they reached the village, which was defended by a company-sized German garrison. The 23rd Airborne Brigade's 2nd Parachute Battalion, commanded by Captain Deriugin, attacked the village, overrunning the garrison by midday, while the 1st Parachute Battalion, under Major S. Gurin, moved round to the south and forced a gap through the German defences on the road through which the brigade's 3rd Parachute Battalion and 1st Guards Cavalry Division passed.

The night of 10–11 June found the two corps heading south-east again before taking shelter in an area of forest occupied by partisan units. There they replenished their supplies of food and ammunition, and rested for three days before resuming their march. Late on 13 June, moving in two columns, they reached the Moscow–Warsaw highway. IV Airborne Corps, with 1st Guards Cavalry Division under command, comprised the right-hand column which arrived at the highway at a point near Lazino, approximately two and a half miles south of the I Guards Cavalry Corps column at Krutoi Kholm.

The area of highway facing IV Airborne Corps some twelve miles away to its front was defended by the German 211th Security Division whose defences comprised a network of strongpoints, minefields, pillboxes, barbed wire, field works and other obstacles. All trees had been cleared on either side of the road to a depth of 100 yards, giving good fields of fire to the company of tanks which patrolled the highway continuously. Such was the strength and depth of the German defences that any attempt to envelop them was out of the question. The only option was a surprise attack.

During the night of 14 June, the two corps moved up. IV Airborne Corps reached Lazino before dawn on 15 June and deployed on to its start lines near Denisovka. The leading element consisted of 23rd Airborne Brigade and 1st Guards Cavalry Division, with 211th Airborne Brigade in support. Behind came 8th Airborne Brigade, incorporating the surviving remnants of 9th and 214th Airborne Brigades, bringing with it the corps' wounded. Several miles away to the north-west, I Guards Cavalry Corps moved on to its start lines with 2nd Guards Cavalry Division in the van.

Just prior to dawn, 23rd Airborne Brigade and 1st Guards Cavalry Division launched their combined assault. The leading elements of the latter succeeded in crossing the highway despite coming under heavy machine-gun and mortar fire. The second wave of cavalry units, however, ran into enemy tanks, which appeared as dawn broke, and appeared reluctant to face the heavy fire being directed down the highway. They were rallied by their divisional commander, Major General Viktor Baranov, and, together with a large number of para-troops, stormed south across the highway in a large body, incurring heavy casualties.

The 23rd Airborne Brigade meanwhile punched a corridor across the highway, its two flank battalions holding it as 211th Airborne Brigade and Headquarters IV Airborne Corps moved across and headed south. Heavy fighting then took place as German strongpoints were cleared along the southern side of the highway. By noon on 15 June, IV Airborne Corps had regrouped in the forests to the east of Bukovo, but it was without 8th Airborne Brigade, which had been unable to cross the highway.

Wasting no time, Colonel Kazankin soon had his depleted force on the move again, heading south-east into the partisan-occupied forests east of Podgerb where it rested for the four days 17–21 June, replenishing its supplies of food and ammunition and evacuating its wounded.

On 22 June IV Airborne Corps, which had been joined by a large group of partisans, set off northwards on the final leg of its journey, taking up positions the next day in the forest to the north-west of Zhilino only some six miles to the rear of the German lines facing the Soviet Tenth Army. Kazankin had already established radio contact with Headquarters Tenth Army and advised it of his plan to break through the German lines. Shortly afterwards, he had received instructions as to the exact sector where he was to make his breakthough.

Following last light on 23 June, IV Airborne Corps took up its positions. At 11.00 p.m., the Tenth Army's 326th Rifle Division opened fire with its artillery on German positions in the breakthrough sector. Immediately, 23rd Airborne Brigade's 1st and 2nd Parachute Battalions launched their assault, being followed by the rest of the corps and the partisans. The Germans responded by bringing heavy fire to bear with small arms, machine guns, mortars and ultimately artillery. This grew heavier as the attack progressed and casualties in the corps grew, among them Colonel Kazankin and the commander of 23rd Airborne Brigade, Lieutenant Colonel Milsky. Eventually, though, the 1st Parachute Battalion pushed through to link up with the forward elements of the Tenth Army, being followed by the remainder of the brigade and 211th Airborne Brigade. Four hours later, having suffered 120 casualties, the rest of IV Airborne Corps managed to reach the Tenth Army lines.

The 8th Airborne Brigade had meantime linked up with General Belov and I Guards Cavalry Corps as it withdrew north of the Moscow–Warsaw highway following its unsuccessful attempt to break through the German lines. The combined force then headed south-westwards to a point where it was deemed safer to attempt to cross the highway. On the night of 20–21 June, Belov's force crossed the highway to the north of Pobeda and by the morning of 22 June reached the forests to the east of Kopol' where they made contact with partisans. Two days later Belov, together with a number of wounded, was evacuated by air from an airstrip at Kopol'.

Command of the entire combined force of cavalry and paratroops now fell on Major N. I. Karnaukhov, commander of 8th Airborne Brigade's 2nd Parachute Battalion. On the night of 28–29 June, he and his men broke through the German lines and reached those of the Tenth Army at Zhilino, being reunited with the rest of IV Airborne Corps shortly afterwards. A few days later, the 4,000 surviving members of the corps set off by rail for their base at Ramenskoe.

Thus one of the longest and largest operations in the history of airborne warfare drew to a close, having lasted over six months. During that period, while operating in the German Fourth Army rear areas, IV Airborne Corps, along with I Guards Cavalry Corps and partisan units, had posed a serious threat, compelling the Germans to devote a force that eventually numbered seven divisions to counter it.

The operation, however, had failed to achieve its primary mission. A German assessment later pinpointed the reasons for this, notably the failure of IV Airborne Corps to achieve surprise, and its lack of artillery and heavy weapons. Added to these were the problems posed by the weather and difficult terrain, with deep snow hampering the mobility of the airborne troops inadequately equipped with skis and other items of winter warfare equipment. Problems of resupply and the heavy casualties suffered throughout the operation were also significant.

A major factor, also recognised in a subsequent Soviet report on the operation, was the lack of coordination between the airborne force and the main front forces. The report also criticised the planning of the several airborne operations during this period as being hasty and incomplete, resulting in badly planned movement of aircraft and troops which had an adverse effect on the overall operation. Moreover, there was inadequate aviation support, both transport and ground support,

allocated to the operation. Lack of transports capable of dropping paratroops prolonged the insertion phase of the operation, while lack of
suitable navigational equipment resulted in inaccurate delivery of
troops, landing over an area of some thirty square miles; over 800 men
were dropped in the vicinity of the surrounded Soviet Thirty-Third
Army and thus were unable to rejoin IV Airborne Corps.

The report also underlined the unreliability of parachuting as a
method of accurate delivery and suggested that only the initial element
of a force should be inserted by parachute with the task of securing
airstrips or suitable areas for the airlanding of the main body.

IV Airborne Corps paid a heavy price for these shortcomings,
suffering a total of some 10,000 casualties out of a total strength of
14,000 men who were dropped into the battle for Viaz'ma.

CHAPTER FIVE

SOVIET OPERATIONS, 1942–5

While IV Airborne Corps took part in the long and bitter battles around Viaz'ma, I Airborne Corps – reformed following its near decimation during the fighting around Kiev in September 1941 – was involved in a three-month-long operation in the area of Rzhev and Demiansk in support of North-Western Front forces.

On 8 January 1942 the Kalinin Front's Thirty-Ninth Army had smashed its way through the German lines to the west of Rzhev and advanced southwards through German rear areas towards Viaz'ma with the intention of linking up with Western Front forces to the west of Mosal'sk. The following day saw the left flank of the North-Western Front, comprising the Third and Fourth Shock Armies, on the right of the Kalinin Front, penetrating German lines in the area of Lake Seliger and advancing through the enemy rear in the direction of Toropets.

By the end of that month Kalinin Front forces were nearing the approaches to Vitebsk, Smolensk and Iartsevo, posing a major danger to the German Army Group Centre, threatening to envelop it from the north-west and cut its lines of communication. At the same time, a force of seven German divisions risked being surrounded by the front's Twenty-Second and Twenty-Ninth Armies in the region of Olenino, west of Rzhev. The Germans responded to this threat by mounting a relief operation and surrounding seven divisions of the Twenty-Ninth

Army around Olenino. These were ordered to break out and IV Airborne Corps was tasked with assisting them to do so.

The leading element of the corps was the 500-strong 4th Parachute Battalion of 204th Airborne Brigade which was dropped from TB-3 bombers on the night of 16–17 February. Heavy anti-aircraft fire was encountered over the area of the DZ but no aircraft were hit. Some 400 members of the battalion dropped from an altitude of around 1,200 feet, but 100 failed to do so. Those who survived the drop found themselves landing in the middle of heavy fighting and under fire from enemy machine guns, and thus had difficulty in locating their equipment and weapon containers.

The battalion's 1st Company, under Lieutenant Kovalevsky, and part of the 2nd Company led by Lieutenant Brusintsy, were involved in fierce street fighting in the town of Everzovo while the remainder of the 2nd Company was likewise engaged in defending Monchalovo against counter-attacks by enemy infantry supported by armour. Meanwhile the 3rd Company, commanded by Lieutenant Borismansky, had been dropped at Okorokovo and took up positions covering the approaches to the town from the north-east. The commanding officer of the 4th Parachute Battalion, Lieutenant P. L. Belotserkovsky, together with sixty members of the 3rd Company who had landed south of the town, joined the company later that day. By last light on 17 January, he had established radio communications with Headquarters Twenty-Ninth Army.

During the following week, 4th Parachute Battalion covered the flanks and rear of the Twenty-Ninth Army as it broke out to the southwest, beating off a number of attacks by the Germans. During the fighting, however, it suffered very heavy casualties and by the time it withdrew on 22 February it numbered only 100 all ranks.

Farther north, the Third Shock and Thirty-Fourth Armies of the North-Western Front, whose objectives were Staraia Russa and Kholm, had reached Kholm, cutting off the German Sixteenth Army's II Corps and elements of X Corps, in the region of Demiansk, which lay between the two main axes of the front's advance. In January, the commander of

North-Western Front, Colonel General Pavel Kurochkin, began operations to surround and destroy the German forces in the 'Demiansk Pocket'. His First Shock Army would attack southwards from east of Staraia Russa towards Kholm while, on its left flank, the Thirty-Fourth Army encircled the Demiansk Pocket from the north. Meanwhile, the Kalinin Front's Third and Fourth Shock Armies would attack towards. Kholm. The task of surrounding and destroying the Demiansk Pocket itself was given to I and II Guards Rifle Corps.

On 29 January I Guards Rifle Corps began its attack to the east of Staraia Russa, being joined on 3 February by II Guards Rifle Corps. By 15 February, the two formations had thrust through the German defences and had linked up with elements of the Third Shock Army at Kholm. A few days later the First Shock Army completed the encirclement of the Demiansk Pocket, although still faced by large enemy forces defending Staraia Russa.

The German forces in the Demiansk Pocket comprised II Corps and part of X Corps, consisting of the 12th, 30th, 32nd, 123rd and 290th Infantry Divisions, the SS Division Totenkopf and a number of supporting arm units. No sooner were they surrounded than the Germans launched an operation, codenamed Bridging, which entailed the forcing through of a corridor by five divisions of Sixteenth Army attacking eastwards from south of Staraia Russa to the Demiansk Pocket. It was now a race between Sixteenth Army and the Soviets' North-Western Front as to who reached Demiansk first.

General Kurochkin's plan also called for an airborne force to take part in the operation. A leading element would be dropped into the Demiansk Pocket to prepare airstrips and assembly areas while the main body entered it from the north, linked up with the leading element and thereafter headed south with the aim of disrupting enemy lines of communication and supply. The brigades' primary objectives were a number of key airfields near Demiansk which were to be seized and destroyed, their loss being certain to expedite the collapse of the enemy forces in the pocket.

The 1st, 2nd and 204th Airborne Brigades of I Airborne Corps, plus the 54th Ski Battalion, were to take part in the operation. The 1st and 204th Brigades would advance at night into the pocket from the north through the region of Beglevo and head south via Putyynia, Solov'evo and Maloe Opuevo to attack Demiansk and destroy the airfields. Meanwhile, 2nd Airborne Brigade and the 54th Ski Battalion would follow up behind and pass through Pustynia to a point before the River Polomet where it would swing north-east and attack the rear of the German 30th Division defending Lychkovo.

The leading element, comprising 204th Airborne Brigade's 4th Parachute Battalion and part of the 1st Parachute Battalion, was dropped in mid-February into the regions of Demiansk and Iasski to carry out reconnaissance missions, linking up with partisan units and preparing base camps for the main body. One hundred TB-3 bombers were used to lift the entire force which was dropped over the four nights of 15–18 February, elements of the 4th Parachute Battalion being dropped near Olenino. The first lift carried men of the battalion's 11th Company who jumped at low level and thereafter headed south-east in the direction of Maloe Opuevo, subsequently reconnoitring and establishing a number of base camps to the west.

The rest of the battalion, along with elements of the 1st Parachute Battalion, followed on the night of 16 February, being dropped to the south-east of Iasski, to the west of the Russa–Velikie Luki road. The purpose of this force was to link up with a partisan group and interdict enemy lines of communications and supply in the area of Dedovitchi to the north, in particular the railway line linking Kholm and Loknia, which was the main means of resupply for the German forces defending Kholm.

On 7 March the remainder of 204th Airborne Brigade, commanded by Major A. V. Grinev, left its base at Liubertsy airfield, near Moscow, and moved by rail and road to an assembly area at Vereteika where on 11 March it was joined by 2nd Airborne Brigade, under Lieutenant Colonel Vasilenko.

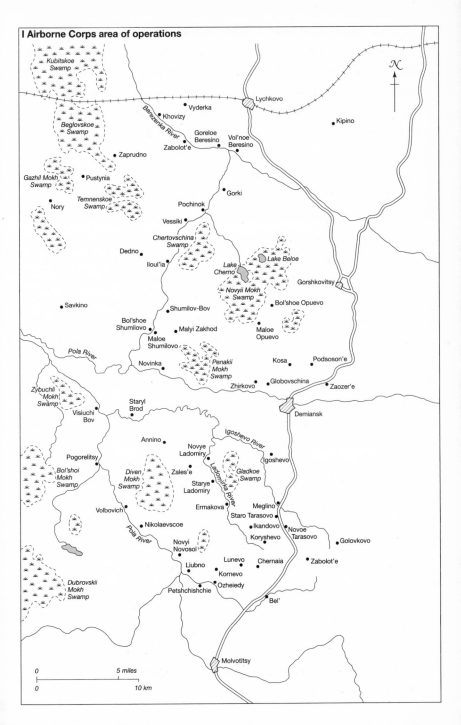

I Airborne Corps area of operations

Kubitskoe Swamp

Beglovskoe Swamp

Berezenka River

Khovizy

Vyderka

Lychkovo

Kipino

Goreloe Beresino

Vol'noe Beresino

Zabolot'e

Zaprudno

Gazhil Mokh Swamp

Pustynia

Temnenskoe Swamp

Nory

Gorki

Pochinok

Vessiki

Chertovschina Swamp

Dedno

Iloul'ia

Lake Cherno

Lake Beloe

Gorshkovitsy

Novyii Mokh Swamp

Savkino

Shumilov-Bov

Bol'shoe Opuevo

Bol'shoe Shumilovo

Malyi Zakhod

Maloe Shumilovo

Maloe Opuevo

Pola River

Novinka

Penakii Mokh Swamp

Kosa

Podsoson'e

Zhirkovo

Globovschina

Zaozer'e

Zybuchli Mokh Swamp

Visiuchi Bov

Staryl Brod

Demiansk

Igoshevo River

Annino

Novye Ladomiry

Igoshevo

Pogorelitsy

Bol'shoi Mokh Swamp

Diven Mokh Swamp

Zales'e

Gladkoe Swamp

Ladomirka River

Volbovich

Starye Ladomiry

Ermakova

Meglino

Staro Tarasovo

Nikolaevscoe

Ikandovo

Novoe Tarasovo

Golovkovo

Koryshevo

Pola River

Novyi Novosol

Lunevo

Chernaia

Zabolot'e

Liubno

Kornevo

Dubrovskii Mokh Swamp

Ozheiedy

Petshchishchie

Bel'

Molvotitsy

0	5 miles
0	10 km

N

165

The 1st Airborne Brigade, commanded by Lieutenant Colonel N. E. Tarasov, had arrived at Vereteika on 4 March. Two days later, it began deploying to a forward assembly area and by the evening of 8 March had infiltrated south of the German lines at Pustnyia, heading south of the Temnenskoe Swamp. By the following morning the brigade had crossed the River Polomet and midday on 10 March found it heading south through swampland towards Maloe Opuevo. That day, however, saw its first encounter with an enemy patrol during which its 2nd Parachute Battalion suffered five men wounded. Other engagements took place on the brigade's flanks but by last light it was securely ensconced in its base camps west of Maloe Opuevo. Over the following days it received a number of resupply drops.

The 204th Airborne Brigade carried out its infiltration during 11–15 March but found the Germans on the alert, bringing down harassing fire once the brigade's presence had been detected. This intensified as the brigade headed south and forced its commander, Major A. V. Grinev, to split his force with the 1st Parachute Battalion heading off to the north while the 4th swung off to the south, subsequently suffering heavy casualties from artillery fire in the area of Pustynia. The 2nd and 3rd Parachute Battalions followed the same axis and on the night of 14–15 March reached the Polomet, where they came under heavy fire from artillery and bombers. The leading elements of the brigade reached the base camp area of 1st Airborne Brigade late on 14 March but there was little respite for them as that night 1st Airborne Brigade's 4th Parachute Battalion, along with 204th Brigade's 2nd Parachute Battalion and part of the 3rd, mounted an attack on the German garrison at Maloe Opuevo. Fierce fighting took place, during which the paratroops suffered some 200 killed, before the surviving elements of the garrison withdrew west to Bol'shoe Opuevo. The remainder of 1st Airborne Brigade advanced towards Demiansk via Kosa and Pod-soson'e.

The 2nd Airborne Brigade had begun its infiltration on the evening of 13 March. The night of 16 March found its two leading units, the

1st and 2nd Parachute Battalions, under harassing fire, which subsequently caused a number of casualties among the battalions following behind. By altering course to the north-east just as it was approaching the Polomet, however, the brigade avoided further losses and by the later hours of 17 March had concentrated to the south of Zabolot'e in the rear area of the German 30th Infantry Division. Leaving the 4th Parachute Battalion to establish a firm base and administer the wounded, the remainder of the brigade began preparing to mount an attack on German forces at Zabolot'e and Goreloe Berezno.

On the night of 19 March, 1st and 204th Airborne Brigades launched attacks on the German defences at Demiansk. 1st Airborne Brigade's 2nd and 4th Parachute Battalions assaulted the Globovschchina airfield while its 1st and 3rd Battalions, together with elements of 204th Airborne Brigade's 1st and 3rd Parachute Battalions, attacked Dobrosli. Both attacks, however, were beaten off with 600 paratroops being killed at Dobrosli alone, the 7th Company of 204th Airborne Brigade's 3rd Parachute Battalion losing fifty out of its total strength of 140.

On the evening of 18 March, 2nd Airborne Brigade had meanwhile begun its attacks on the rear area of the German 30th Infantry Division to the south-west of Lychkovo. In conjunction with an attack by forces of the Soviet Thirty-Fourth Army to the east of Lychkovo, the 1st, 2nd and 3rd Parachute Battalions mounted assaults on garrisons at Goreloe Berezino and Zabolot'e, and attacked west into the Berezena Valley. Once again, however, these attacks were repulsed with 2nd Airborne Brigade losing 230 killed during the assault on Zabolot'e.

On 23 March the entire brigade, reinforced by two ski battalions which had arrived some nights beforehand, attacked Lychkovo and during heavy fighting succeeded in reaching the railway station before being forced back. Again it suffered heavily, the 2nd Parachute Battalion losing over 400 of its total strength of 580. Despite these losses, the brigade mounted another attack on the night of 26–27 March, once more incurring heavy casualties. By now it was no longer a viable fighting formation and Lieutenant Colonel Vasilenko split his surviving men into small groups and ordered them to exfiltrate from the German 30th Infantry Division rear area.

On the night of 24 March, 204th Airborne Brigade launched an assault on the German garrison at Igoshevo, attacking just before midnight. The battle lasted until around 7.00 a.m. on the following morning at which point the brigade withdrew, having lost 181 men killed, including the commanding officer of its 1st Parachute Battalion, and a number taken prisoner. Thereafter, it set off for a prearranged rendezvous with 1st Airborne Brigade at a location to the west of Staroe Tarasovo.

The 1st Airborne Brigade, having regrouped to the east of the Gladkoe Swamp where it received a resupply by air, attacked the German garrison at Staroe Tarasovo after last light on 26 March. Elements of its 1st Parachute Battalion interdicted the roads leading from Starye Ladomiry to the west and Meglino in the east while the other three battalions attacked Staroe Tarasovo itself. This operation was carried out in coordination with other Soviet forces attacking from the south but it failed, with the paratroops incurring heavy losses: some 200 killed in the 1st Parachute Battalion already reduced to a total strength of 300; eighty-six killed and 100 wounded in the 3rd Parachute Battalion; and 150 killed in the 500-strong 4th Parachute Battalion. The brigade commander, Lieutenant Colonel Tarasov, was wounded.

After this action the brigade withdrew, encumbered by some 400 wounded, and headed west for its rendezvous with the surviving elements of 204th Airborne Brigade. On 28 March a number of the wounded were evacuated by aircraft, which landed on an airstrip constructed by 1st and 204th Airborne Brigades' sappers in the Gladskoe Swamp, the remainder being left to exfiltrate from the Demiansk Pocket with the surviving elements of the brigade.

By this time, it had been decided that both 1st and 204th Airborne Brigades would now withdraw from the Gladkoe Swamp area and break their respective ways out of the Demiansk Pocket. The 1st Airborne Brigade would move south and regroup in the forests a short distance to the north-east of Kornevo. It would then head southwards in three columns, on separate axes via Kornevo, Lunevo and Chernaia respectively, exfiltrate through the German lines and link up with Group Ksenefontov – an element of Fourth Shock Army detached to cooperate with Thirty-Fourth Army in destroying the Demiansk Pocket. The 204th Airborne Brigade, meanwhile, would march south-westwards via Novye and Starye Ladomiry to the area of Nikolaevskoe where it would attempt to make its breakthrough.

The 1st Airborne Brigade set off before dawn on 28 March but one column soon encountered a motorised battle group of the SS Division Totenkopf, the action lasting until some time after first light. A second column was meanwhile engaged in an action south of Masloe with troops of the 123rd Infantry Division. The third column also met German forces west of Chenaia and suffered 120 men killed.

Group Ksenefontov continued to fight its way towards Chernaya to link up with the 1st Airborne Brigade columns as they struggled south, two of its formations, the 23rd and 130th Rifle Divisions, advancing to within a few hundred yards of the town. By this stage, however, the paratroops were too weak in number to break through and were forced to withdraw and regroup in the Gladkoe Swamp. On 29 March, they attempted another breakout, heading south-east towards Kornevo but ran into a battle group of the German 12th Infantry Division, losing some 60 men killed. Another breakout attempt near Lunevo by 200 men of the brigade resulted in forty more being killed. At the same time, survivors of 204th Airborne Brigade regrouped in the area of Starye Ladomiry and made for Nikolaevskoe, but soon found themselves being pursued by the enemy.

The early hours of 29 March saw the Germans strike when troops of the SS Division Totenkopf attacked the paratroops' base camps in the area of Maloe Opuevo. In an action lasting two hours, the SS overran the camps, killing 180 paratroops and capturing twenty-seven, along with a large quantity of arms and ammunition. Three other camps to the north-east were shelled by German artillery, one of them being destroyed.

The remnants of 1st Airborne Brigade headed west from Chenaia ad Lunevo in the direction of the Ladomirka Valley, to the south of Novoe Maslovo, where they regrouped on 30 March prior to attempting to find their way out of a fast-closing trap. At the same time, groups of 204th Airborne Brigade survivors made their way south-westwards from Zales'e towards Nikolaevskoe to link up with them. Throughout 31 March and 1 April, groups of paratroops made repeated but unsuccessful attempts to break through the German lines between Chaernaia, Lunevo and Novyi Novosel, an increasing number being taken prisoner.

During the following days and nights, the surviving members of both brigades continued to attempt to break out, being harried all the time by German forces closing in on them. One such attempt was made to the south of Volbovichi by a 600-strong group but again was thwarted by the Germans; among those captured was the commander of 1st Airborne Brigade, Lieutenant Colonel N. E. Tarasov. Little more is known of the movements of 1st Airborne Brigade thereafter. A German report of 9 April recorded that 400 members of the brigade attempted to break out on 8 April to the south-west of Demiansk but suffered heavy casualties. Of 204th Airborne Brigade there was no mention at all.

By the end of this operation 1st, 2nd and 204th Airborne Brigades ceased to exist, but not for long. By the end of April 1942, all three had been reformed with the 1st and 2nd being redesignated the 5th and 6th Independent Rifle Brigades respectively, and 204th Airborne Brigade being deployed to the Gridino region.

The operation to destroy the Demiansk Pocket had failed completely. Once again, the Soviets had lost the element of surprise, the drop of 204th Airborne Brigade's 4th Parachute Battalion to establish the base camps alerting the Germans, who were swift to anticipate the Soviets' intentions and reacted accordingly, inflicting heavy casualties on the three brigades as they infiltrated south into the pocket. Signals intelligence, largely gleaned from poor radio security on the part of the Soviets, provided the Germans with further information, enabling them to thwart the paratroops' plans at every turn and inflict heavy casualties. Losses among the 7,000-strong airborne force were little short of appalling: of the 5,000 men of 1st and 204th Airborne Brigades, it is estimated that a maximum of only 400 survived the operation, with 2nd Airborne Brigade sustaining similar losses.

In September 1943, the Soviets mounted an airborne operation as part of their counter to a major enemy thrust at Kursk in July, this being the last major offensive mounted by the Germans on the Eastern Front. The Soviet counter-offensive began in mid-July and continued through into August, by which time the whole of the front, from Smolensk to the Black Sea, was witness to very heavy fighting. Early September saw the Soviets' Central Front penetrating the enemy defences to the north of Sumy and thrusting deep towards Chernigov and the German rear areas. The Germans had no alternative but to withdraw to the River Dnepr where they intended to establish a defensive line. Aware that the river itself was a formidable obstacle, the Soviets realised that they had to establish bridgeheads across it before the Germans could establish their new defences. Thus the last two weeks of September saw a race for the Dnepr, as the German Army Group South frantically attempted to stem a headlong dash by the Soviet Voronezh Front's Third Guards Tank Army which, led by Lieutenant General P. S. Rybalko and with I Guards Cavalry Corps under command, advanced on a front of four corps.

The leading elements of I Guards Cavalry Corps reached the river on the night of 21-22 September 1943 and during the following day small bridgeheads were secured on the south bank at Velikyi Bukrin and Rzhischev. That same day saw the arrival of the Soviet Fortieth Army which also established a small bridgehead, infantry units swimming the river and subsequently floating across their anti-tank guns and light artillery pieces. The Soviets, however, were unable to ferry across any armour or heavy artillery and thus the infantry manning the bridgeheads had to remain within range of supporting fire from the north bank of the river.

Lack of armour and continuous heavy air and ground counter-

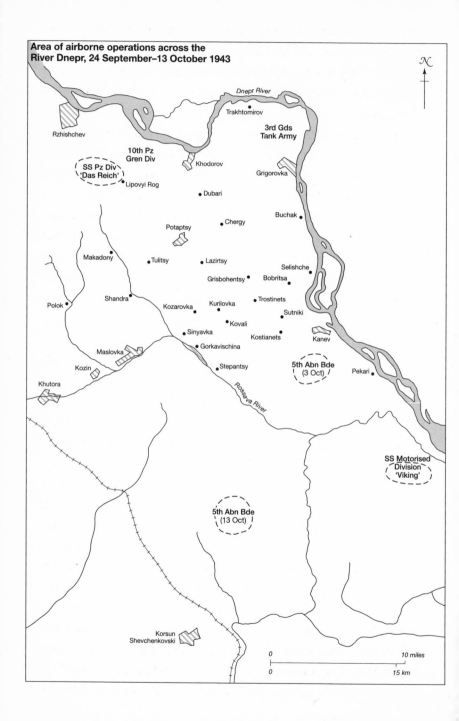

Area of airborne operations across the
River Dnepr, 24 September–13 October 1943

N

Dnepr River

Trakhtomirov

Rzhishchev

3rd Gds
Tank Army

10th Pz
Gren Div

SS Pz Div
'Das Reich'

Khodorov

Grigorovka

Lipovyi Rog

Dubari

Buchak

Potaptsy

Chergy

Makadony

Tulitsy

Lazirtsy

Selishche

Grisbohentsy

Bobritsa

Shandra

Kozarovka

Kurilovka

Trostinets

Polok

Kovali

Sutniki

Sinyavka

Kostianets

Kanev

Maslovka

Gorkavischina

5th Abn Bde
(3 Oct)

Pekari

Kozin

Stepantsy

Khutora

Rossava River

SS Motorised
Division
'Viking'

5th Abn Bde
(13 Oct)

Korsun
Shevchenkovski

0   10 miles

0   15 km

attacks soon resulted in the bridgeheads coming under severe pressure from the Germans. The only way in which the Soviets could reinforce them effectively was through the use of airborne troops and the decision was taken to mount an operation to enlarge the bridgehead at Velikyi Bukrin.

The likelihood of the use of airborne forces had been foreseen earlier and thus the 1st, 3rd and 5th Guards Airborne Brigades had been formed into a 10,000-strong temporary airborne corps. Under the command of Major General Ivan Zatevakhin, hitherto Deputy Commander of Airborne Forces, it was assigned to the Voronezh Front and immediately began training for likely missions. By 16 September, Zatevakhin and his staff had finalised their detailed plans in cooperation with an aviation operational group and the forward command element of the 2nd Air Army which provided aerial support for the Voronezh Front.

The task given to the corps by the commander of the Voronezh Front, General Nikolai Vatutin, was to assist the ground forces in establishing and securing bridgeheads on the south bank of the Dnepr in the area of Velikyi Bukrin, and thereafter expand and strengthen them sufficiently for additional forces to deploy into them prior to launching another major offensive. The corps' specific objectives were the capture of Lipovyi Rog, Makedony and Stepantsy, while at the same time preventing enemy counter-attacks from reaching the south bank in the area from Kanev to Trakomirov. Its entire area of responsibility would be between nine and twelve miles wide and nineteen miles in depth.

1st Guards Airborne Brigade, commanded by Colonel P. I. Krasovsky, would drop in the area of Lazurtsy, Beresniagi and Grishentsy with the task of blocking any enemy counter-attacks in the direction of Kurilovka and Bobritsa. Meantime, Colonel P. A. Goncharov's 3rd Guards Airborne Brigade would be dropped near Grushevo, Makedony and Tulitsy in order to establish a defensive line stretching from Lipovyi Rog to Makedony, thereafter holding it until relieved by units of the Fortieth Army advancing from Traktomirov and Zarubentsy. Finally,

5th Guards Airborne Brigade, under Lieutenant Colonel P. M. Sidorchuk, would drop in the area of Trostinets, Kovali and Kostianets to set up a defensive line extending from Gorkavshchina through Stepantsy to Kostianets, thereafter blocking any attempt by the enemy to advance on the Dnepr from the south and south-west.

The landings would be carried out over two nights with 1st and 5th Guards Airborne Brigades being deployed on the first night and 3rd Guards Airborne Brigade on the second. The number of aircraft assigned to the operation, comprising 50 PS-84 transports, 150 IL-4 and B-25 bombers, and forty-five gliders, was insufficient for a single lift on either night; therefore each would be required to carry out two or three sorties on both nights, the distance from the mounting airfields at Smorodino and Bogodukhov, near Lebedin, to the DZs and LZs being between 110 and 140 miles. The gliders, carrying the brigades' artillery, would land in between the parachute drops.

Prior to the drops, air attacks would be launched against enemy forces in the areas of each DZ, with bombers carrying out strikes immediately beforehand. The initial phase of the airborne operation would see small groups of paratroops dropped with the task of clearing and securing the brigades' DZs and LZs , and then making contact with partisan units. The main drops would then take place, after which close air support would be on hand for the three brigades with artillery forward observers in light aircraft providing fire support from guns on the northern bank of the Dnepr.

The operation was scheduled to commence on 23 September but problems arose with regard to lack of rail transport which resulted in a delay in the concentration of the three brigades, their supplies and equipment at the two mounting airfields. Furthermore, adverse weather delayed the arrival of the aircraft, with only eight at the airfields by the given deadline. The commander of the Voronezh Front, General Vatutin, had no choice but to postpone the operation for twenty-four hours to the night of 24–25 September. At the same time, he altered the plan so that 3rd and 5th Guards Airborne Brigades, both of whom would be complete at their mounting airfields by the new deadline, were to be deployed first. 3rd Guards Airborne Brigade would now be dropped to the south-east of Rzhishchev in the area of Tulitsy, Beresniagi, Lazurtsy and Potaptsy where it would establish a defensive line from Kipovyi Rog through Makedony and Siniavka to Kozarovka, holding it until the arrival of the leading elements of Fortieth Army. 5th Guards Airborne Brigade meanwhile was to be dropped to the west of Kanev, in the area of Kovali, Kostianets and Trostinets, where it would establish and hold a line from Gorkovschina through Stepantsy to Sutniki, pending the arrival of Soviet ground forces advancing from Buchak, Selische and Kanev, and block any attempt by the Germans to advance from the south and south-west. 1st Guards Airborne Brigade would be held in reserve until such time as it was fully assembled at its mounting airfield, thereafter being dropped on the night of 25–26 or 26–27 September.

The changes to the original plan and the very tight time schedule caused considerable difficulties in 3rd and 5th Guards Airborne Brigades, particularly in the parachute battalions where company commanders had only fifteen minutes or so before take-off to brief their platoon commanders, the latter having to give new orders to their men during the flight. These were limited in the main to briefings about the DZs, assembly areas and immediate objectives. The paratroops themselves were very lightly equipped, the assumption being that ground forces would link up with them swiftly, and thus were not even carrying entrenching tools and light anti-tank weapons with which to establish basic defences.

On 22 September, when Soviet leading elements crossed the river, German forces at Bukrin, on the south bank at a bend in the Dnepr, comprised only a thin defensive screen consisting of the reconnaissance unit of 19th Panzer Division and 120 officer cadets of an anti-aircraft school. The 19th Panzer Division itself was forty miles to the north, crossing the river at Kiev. During the previous evening, XXIV Panzer Corps had been ordered by the German Eighth Army to cross from the north bank to the south without delay and occupy the undefended sector. Immediately disengaging themselves from battle, the corps' leading elements arrived on the south bank during the afternoon of 23 September.

By this time, however, Soviet infantry had begun attacking the defensive screen at Bukrin. Fourth Panzer Army, whose right flank was now dangerously exposed, requested Eighth Army to send some of its forces to reinforce the reconnaissance unit screen at Bukrin. The latter responded immediately, ordering 19th Panzer Division and the 72nd Infantry Division to head for Bukrin with all haste.

By the evening of 23 September, XXIV Panzer Corps had moved most of its strength across the Dnepr farther to the south at Kanev and by that night the 57th Infantry Division was taking up positions to the east and west of the town. The 112th Infantry Division meanwhile was crossing the river to reinforce the defensive screen at Bukrin and by late afternoon on 24 September arrived just in time to counter the attacks by Soviet infantry who had secured Traktomirov, Zarubentsy and Grig-orovka. XXIV Panzer Corps had completed its crossing of the Dnepr by early morning of 24 September, destroying the bridge at Kanev as it did so. The 10th Motorised Division and 19th Panzer Division headed south, the latter joining its reconnaissance unit at Bukrin, to take up their new positions which, unknown to the Soviets, straddled the areas in which lay the planned DZs and LZs for the impending airborne operation.

By 24 September the three airborne brigades and their aircraft were still assembling at the two mounting airfields. Despite the twenty-four-hour postponement, the entire transport fleet never materialised. Of the sixty-five LI-2 transports required to lift 5th Guards Airborne Brigade, only forty-eight appeared, as bad weather prevented the arrival of the remainder. Further problems for the brigades arose when pilots, concerned with safety and anxious about overloading their aircraft, insisted that the size of paratroop sticks should be decreased from twenty to eighteen or fifteen and the number of equipment containers reduced. This resulted in men and containers having to be reallocated to other aircraft, with inevitably chaotic consequences.

At 6.30 p.m. that evening, 3rd Guards Airborne Brigade began taking off from the airfields. 5th Guards Airborne Brigade was scheduled to follow two hours later but almost immediately plans went awry due to the lack of fuel bowsers, so that aircraft were not being refuelled in time. The first two waves of aircraft became intermingled as individual aircraft took off the moment they had been refuelled. The confusion worsened as fuel supplies ran short, causing the lift of 5th Guards Airborne Brigade to be halted in the early hours of 25 September.

Despite these problems, 298 sorties were flown and 4,575 paratroops dropped along with 660 small containers of supplies and ammunition. By dawn on 25 September, all elements of 3rd Guards Airborne Brigade flown from the mounting airfield at Lebedin had been dropped; but just over 2,000 men, representing some thirty per cent of the combat strength of the two brigades, still remained at the mounting airfields along with 3rd Guards Airborne Brigade's 45mm light anti-tank guns whose aircraft had been prevented by bad weather from dropping them.

Adverse weather had also prevented the marking in advance of the DZs and LZs with coloured panels and fires. This led to inaccurate dropping, with sticks being scattered over large areas. One was dropped into the Dnepr, another landed on the Soviet-held northern bank of the river, and two others found themselves deep in the German rear. Other aircraft failed to drop their sticks at all and returned to base.

The first thirteen aircraft reaching the DZs encountered heavy enemy anti-aircraft fire and were forced to take evasive action, dropping their sticks at varying altitudes up to 6,500 feet. On landing, the paratroops found themselves scattered over a wide area very heavily defended by the Germans. As the leading elements landed around Dubari-Grushevo, they were immediately engaged by the main body of 19th Panzer Division, comprising the 73rd and 74th Panzer Grenadier Regiments and the 19th Panzer Regiment, which had just arrived in the area. The paratroops came under fire in mid-air from small arms and 20mm anti-aircraft guns. Subsequent aircraft, on seeing the hostile reception awaiting them, turned north and dropped their sticks around Romashki, where they were engaged immediately by the logistic support elements of 19th Panzer Division.

During the night of 24 September, large numbers of paratroops were captured or hunted down and destroyed; in the first twenty-four hours of the operation, 209 were taken prisoner and 692 killed out of a total of some 1,500 dropped in the area between Dubari and Rossava. In the area of Grushevo, a 150-strong paratroop company was destroyed by the 3rd Company of the 73rd Panzer Grenadier Regiment, albeit the latter suffered severe casualties in the process.

The fighting continued into the following day, with further casualties being sustained by the surviving elements of 3rd Guards Airborne Brigade who formed themselves into ad hoc units as they fought back against overwhelming odds.

Those elements of 5th Guards Airborne Brigade which had been dropped were attempting meantime to regroup but finding their efforts hampered by the lack of radio communications. Twenty-six signallers were dispersed over a wide area, and only five radio sets were operational, the rest having been either destroyed or buried to avoid their falling into enemy hands. The brigade commander, Lieutenant Colonel P. M. Sidorchuk, was able to pass a message requesting further operators and radios and a number of sets were despatched to him across the Dnepr. Three groups of signallers with radios were dropped on the night of 27–28 September but there was no trace of them thereafter.

The brigade regrouped slowly, hindered by the enemy who deployed mobile units throughout the area of the drop; in II Panzer Corps' area, the SS Division Viking carried out mopping-up operations to the south and south-west of Pekari. By 26 September, the Germans had completed this task and no longer regarded the paratroops – the remaining elements of whom by then had taken refuge in the forests to the south of Kanev and Dubari, and to the north of Buchak – as a threat. By this time, the Germans were focusing their main attention on the bridgeheads, with XXIV Panzer Corps receiving reinforcements in the form of the 7th and 20th Panzer Divisions from Army Group South to assist it in its attack on the bridgehead at Bukrin.

The Soviets, meanwhile, were attempting to salvage what they could from the debacle that had befallen 3rd and 5th Guards Airborne Brigades. Of the 4,575 men who had been dropped, 2,300 succeeded in regrouping in the area between Rzhischev and Cherkassy, while others joined the nine partisan units operating in the region. One 230-strong group, comprising men who had been dropped into the Dnepr or on to the northern bank, joined Voronezh Front forces. The largest group numbered six hundred men in the forests of Kanev and Cherkassy, while another two hundred regrouped in the area of Chernyshi. Four further groups, with a total strength of three hundred, assembled near Iablonovo.

Despite their limited supplies of ammunition and supplies, these groups soon set to work harassing the Germans in their respective areas. One such group of 150 men, commanded by Lieutenant S. Petrosian, attacked a German headquarters in Potok and subsequently mounted a successful ambush on a convoy south of the village. It then headed south via Maslovka to Kanev where, on 5 October, it joined up with a larger group commanded by Lieutenant Colonel Sidorchuk.

By early October, the surviving elements of 3rd and 5th Guards Airborne Brigades dropped on the night of 24–25 September were operating either in the north of the operational area, extending from Rzhischev to Kanev, or farther south between Kanev and Cherkassy. In the northern area, consisting mainly of open terrain heavily defended by the enemy, the paratroops were forced to operate in small groups and thus were confined to small hit-and-run raids. The terrain in the south, however, largely thick forest, was only lightly defended and lent itself to attacks on the enemy by larger groups. During October, five groups with a total strength of over 1,200 men conducted harassing operations against the Germans.

One of these groups was commanded by Major A. Bluvshtein, second-in-command of 3rd Guards Airborne Brigade's 2nd Parachute Battalion, who had landed to the north-west of Tulitsy. Accompanied by nine men, he had made his way to the battalion's predesignated rally point where there was no sign of the commanding officer and the remainder of the unit. During the following days, he headed south, the size of his group reaching almost battalion-size as men from other units joined him.

In early October, having established radio contact with Headquarters 5th Guards Airborne Brigade, Bluvshtein was ordered to attack a German battalion providing the garrison in the town of Bovany, close to the northern edge of the Kanev Forest. Carried out on the night of 8–9 October, the assault was successful, routing the enemy battalion and capturing a quantity of weapons, ammunition, supplies and documents. But the Germans counter-attacked soon afterwards, and by last light on 11 October were threatening Bluvshtein's base in the forest. That night, he and his men withdrew to the south-west to the Tagancha Forest where they met Lieutenant Colonel P. M. Sidorchuk's force.

Another group was led by Major V. F. Fofanov, the Chief of Staff of 3rd Guards Airborne Brigade. On the night of 25 September, he had been dropped west of Rzhishchev and, having formed a twenty-nine-strong group, subsequently sent out reconnaissance patrols. Next night he mounted a successful attack on an enemy position at Medvedovka. Two nights later, having failed to establish contact with the rest of the brigade or any other units, he and his men headed for the area of Veselaia Dubrava, the planned location for 3rd Guards Airborne Brigade's defensive perimeter, which they reached at last light on 28 September. There Fofanov was joined by other groups and during the following days attacked a number of enemy positions at Tulitsy and Shandra before heading south, reaching the forest just to the north-east of Potashnia on 1 October. Three weeks later, he and his men linked up with Lieutenant Colonel Sidorchuk's force in the Tagancha Forest.

By this time, Sidorchuk's force numbered 1,000 men and was organised as a brigade of three battalions and a support element, the latter comprising reconnaissance, anti-tank, signals and engineer platoons. At the end of the first week of October, it had established radio communications with the headquarters of the Soviet Fortieth Army through which it had made contact with the headquarters of the Voronezh Front which during the following week had organised resupply drops of supplies and ammunition. Sidorchuk's 600-strong force had then come under heavy attack by the Germans and had been forced to move its base on 19 October from the Kanev Forest south to a new sanctuary in the Tagancha Forest. There it was subsequently joined by groups that brought its total strength to more than a thousand men.

Thereafter, Sidorchuk's force operated as 5th Guards Airborne Brigade, and on 22 October attacked the railway line between Tagancha and Korsun, destroying a train. During the evening, the brigade also attacked the village of Buda-Vorobievska, putting to flight the head-quarters element of the German 157th Infantry Battalion, and nearby Potashnia where it set a number of warehouses ablaze. These actions drew severe reprisals from the enemy who launched a series of heavy attacks on Sidorchuk's base, causing a number of casualties and forcing the brigade to withdraw and head south through the woods to the Cherkassy Forest, north-east of Bol'shoe Starosel'e. As it did so, however, its ranks were swelled by a large number of lost paratroops, bringing its strength to approximately 1,700 and enabling Sidorchuk to form a fourth battalion.

On 28 November, having established a new base in the Cherkassy Forest, 5th Guards Airborne Brigade mounted a series of raids on enemy positions and installations. In addition, it passed intelligence to the headquarters of the 2nd Ukrainian Front, under Marshal Ivan Konev, in whose area of responsibility it was now operating. Across the Dnepr was the Fifty-Second Army but Sidorchuk was only able to establish sporadic radio contact with its headquarters.

On 11 November, by which time he and his men had been in action for forty days, Sidorchuk was ordered to take part in an operation to facilitate the crossing of the Dnepr by 2nd Ukrainian Front forces. This would take place 12–14 November with the Front's main force heading for Krivoi Rog while the Fifty-Second Army, on the Front's right flank, crossed the Dnepr to the north of Cherkassy which it was to capture after establishing a bridgehead. 5th Guards Airborne Brigade was to capture the villages of Lozovok, Sekirna and Svidovok on the south bank of the Dnepr and thus facilitate the crossing of the river by Fifty-Second Army units. The task would not be easy as the enemy forces defending the brigade's objectives comprised: an infantry battalion and engineer units defending Lozovik; two companies of infantry of the 72nd Infantry Division in the nearby village of Elizavetovka; and an infantry battalion and five tanks at Svidovok.

The assault took place in the early hours of 13 November. The plan, drawn up by Major Bluvshtein, was for a silent attack with no preliminary artillery bombardment, in order to achieve maximum surprise. The 1st Parachute Battalion's objective was Sekirna while the 3rd Parachute Battalion attacked Lozovok. The most difficult task, of attacking Svidovok with its garrison of a battalion supported by armour, was allocated to Major Bluvshtein's 2nd Parachute Battalion.

The assault began at 4.00 a.m. with the 4th and 5th Companies of the 2nd Parachute Battalion reaching the centre of Svidovok before the alarm was raised. There they encountered fire from machine guns and tanks which halted their advance. The 6th Company, meanwhile, also encountered stiff resistance as it attacked its objective, a hill feature, and was eventually forced to withdraw.

The 4th Parachute Battalion, advancing on the 2nd Battalion's left flank, also came under heavy fire. Having detached a platoon to cover the 2nd Battalion's advance, it pushed forward into Svidovok from the west in order to outflank a number of enemy strongpoints in the centre of the town. At the same time, the 2nd Parachute Battalion moved its reserve around to the east to carry out a right flanking attack on the strongpoints. At this stage, its 4th and 5th Companies were joined by a company of the 4th Parachute Battalion to reinforce them in their final efforts to overcome all enemy resistance.

The Germans, having lost three of the five tanks in the town, however, withdrew from Svidovok to the north-east. The 2nd Parachute Battalion had little opportunity to enjoy its success then as the Germans counter-attacked from the south and east with a battalion supported by seven tanks. Unfortunately, the 2nd Ukrainian Front's 254th Rifle Division failed to come to 5th Guards Airborne Brigade's assistance as it had been unable to cross the Dnepr that night. Consequently, the 2nd and 4th Parachute Battalions were forced to withdraw from Svidovok to avoid being surrounded and head for the forest south-west of the town. Next night, however, the leading elements of the 254th Rifle Division succeeded in crossing the Dnepr. On 15 November, followed by the rest of the Soviet Fifty Second Army, the division cleared the towns along the river and linked up with 5th Guards Airborne Brigade. Thirteen days later, during which it was involved in further heavy fighting, the brigade was withdrawn to the rear, by which time it had been in action for two months.

There were a number of lessons to be learned from the Dnepr debacle, predominantly that it was a classic case of how not to carry out an airborne operation. There was criticism of the decision to launch it at night but its errors and deficiencies were such that it would still have been doomed to failure even if it had been conducted in daylight. Initially, it was launched without sufficient time for preparation by the participants. Coordination between the airborne troops and the aviation units supporting the operation was poor, as was the allocation of logistic support and provision of equipment by those responsible for the planning. Finally, intelligence on the enemy forces in the target area was virtually non-existent.

One critic of the Dnepr operation subsequently pointed out that the Commander of Airborne Forces should have been reprimanded, as he had failed to heed the lessons to be drawn from the IV Airborne

Corps operation at Viaz'ma in the winter of 1942. That had at least achieved some results of a tactical and diversionary nature; the airborne forces deployed had survived for some four months before being withdrawn. The Dnepr mission, on the other hand, accomplished very little and its results certainly did not justify the severe losses suffered by those committed to it. Ironically, in early 1944, when the Soviets crossed the Dnepr almost along its entire length, the only stretch of the river still held by the Germans was that in the area of Kanev – the objective of the operation mounted in September 1943.

By 1944, following the three operations at Viaz'ma, the Demiansk Pocket and the Dnepr, the Soviet High Command viewed major airborne activity with serious misgivings and decided that the elite units of the VDV should be deployed as infantry on conventional operations. During the remaining months of the Second World War there were only two further occasions when the Soviets committed their airborne forces to battle on a large scale.

In September 1943, the Soviets began planning operations to free the Ukraine and Belorussia from German occupation. These would take the form of combined offensives by the Kalinin and Baltic Fronts along an axis leading through Vitebsk and Gomel with the aim of enveloping the German Army Group Centre from the north. At the same time, the Western and Central Fronts would attack Mogilov and Bobruisk from the east and south respectively.

The Kalinin Front launched its attack on 2 October with assaults by its Third and Fourth Shock Armies on Nevel, which fell five days later, resulting in the collapse of the German triangular network of defences based on Nevel, Novosokol'niki and Velikie Luiki which covered the railway line connecting Dno, Novosokol'niki and Nevel. This line linked the enemy's Army Groups North and Centre, permitting the rapid movement of troops along the left flank of the entire Soviet–German front.

After the capture of Nevel, the Soviets began planning an even larger offensive. At this juncture, the Kalinin Front was redesignated the 1st Baltic Front and the Baltic Front the 2nd, the Central Front becoming the Belorussian Front.

In early November 1943, the Soviets decided to deploy an airborne corps under command of the 1st Baltic Front to assist in an advance by the 1st and 2nd Baltic Fronts. The latter's Third Shock Army was to push forward westwards from Nevel to interdict the Nevel–Polotsk railway line, thereafter thrusting deep into German-held territory and surrounding the enemy forces in the area west of Nevel. Meanwhile, the 1st Baltic Front's Fourth Shock Army would also advance westwards before moving south-westwards along the railway line via Dretun', heading for Polotsk. The operation got off to a good start and by 10 November, aided by unseasonally good weather conditions which resulted in forest tracks remaining passable to vehicles, the Soviets had reached Putoshka and Dretun', much to the mounting alarm of the Germans.

The airborne formation assembled for this operation was a composite 11,680-strong corps comprising 1st, 2nd and 11th Guards Airborne Brigades, all of which were based in the area around Moscow. It would be dropped and landed over three nights on six DZs and landing strips in the Begomi'-Ushiachi region which covered an area of 460 square miles to the south and south-west of Polotsk. It was then to link up with a force of over 19,000 partisans operating in the area, which was relatively free of German forces, and mount an attack on Polotsk from the south-east and south-west. Meanwhile, partisan forces would secure a number of bridges and crossing places along the Western Dvina River, and cover the airborne corps' flanks and rear.

The 4th Parachute Battalion of 2nd Guards Airborne Brigade would be dropped to the south-west of Novosel'e on the first night, along with specialist sub-units, to help partisan units secure and prepare the DZs and landing strips (LS). On the following two nights, 1st and 11th Guards Airborne Brigades would be dropped to the west and south of Starniki with heavy weapons and equipment being flown into a number of LSs.

The Partisan movement featured prominently in the planning of this operation. The recommendations of its Central Staff were formally approved in a *Plan of Cooperation of Partisan Formations Operating in the Northern Regions of Belorussia with Airborne Forces of the Red Army*. Once the landings had taken place, elements of the Central and Belorussian Partisan Staffs would deploy into the field to coordinate partisan operations. Brigades in the region were tasked with securing the entire operational area, blocking any advance into it by enemy forces, establishing, securing and defending the DZs and LZs, gathering intelligence, and disrupting enemy communications. In addition, they were to supply guides for the paratroops down to platoon level, manpower to replace casualties within airborne units, and labour gangs to maintain and repair roads and tracks along the paratroops' axes of advance. Furthermore, they were to provide horses and sleighs, and supply food for the entire airborne force.

As the scheduled date for the airborne operation approached, with the Fourth Shock Army continuing its advance, the partisans stepped up the tempo of their activities. One brigade, operating in the area of Polotsk, destroyed seventeen enemy trains, while another north of Vitebsk seized a number of bridges and crossing places and established bridgeheads over the Dvina. Other brigades meanwhile carried out reconnaissance tasks during which their patrols linked up with leading elements of the Fourth Shock Army.

At this juncture, however, the weather took a hand in the proceedings, and conditions deteriorated sharply. From 15 November onwards heavy rain fell; a thaw made roads and tracks impassable and obstructed the movement of troops and supplies, dashing all hopes of reaching Polotsk by 15 November. Consequently, the airborne operation was cancelled.

Ten months later, in September 1944, the last substantial Soviet airborne operation of the Second World War took place. A month earlier, in Slovakia, the Slovak Army and elements of the Slovak National Council had led an uprising against Slovakia's German-backed government, seizing control of a number of cities in eastern Slovakia. A key element was the Army's Eastern Corps, comprising the 1st and 2nd Divisions, which was to seize the Dukla and Lupkow Passes and facilitate the advance into Slovakia of Soviet forces already assembled to the east of the Carpathian Mountains.

Since July, the Soviets had been providing support for Slovak partisans, dropping Soviet-trained personnel, weapons and supplies. On 31 August 1944 the deputy commander of the Eastern Corps and a number of Slovak officers arrived at Marshal Ivan Konev's Headquarters 1st Ukrainian Front to request Soviet assistance. This was swiftly forthcoming and four days later Soviet aircraft began to deliver partisan units and large consignments of weapons, ammunition and explosives to a rebel-held airfield at Tri Duba.

The Germans reacted swiftly and aggressively to the uprising. On 1–2 September they disarmed both divisions of the Eastern Corps and regained control of some of the areas seized by the insurgents. On 10 September German forces were transferred from Poland and Hungary to the Dukla Pass, blocking the advance of the Soviet Thirty-Eighth Army and the three brigades of the Czech I Corps. One of these was the 2nd Czech Airborne Brigade, commanded by Colonel Prokryl; this had been formed on 1 February 1944, at Efremov, near Tula on the River Upa in western Russia, as the Czechoslovak Independent Airborne Brigade. Comprising Czechs who had fled to the Soviet Union after the German invasion of Czechoslovakia in 1939, it numbered 4,280 and consisted of: a brigade headquarters; four parachute battalions; artillery, anti-tank, anti-aircraft and armoured battalions; and reconnaissance, signals and engineer companies.

Along with the Soviet 242nd Tank Brigade, the Czech paratroops were on the right flank of the 1st Ukrainian Front's Thirty-Eighth Army and by mid-September had captured a pass through the mountains near Roztoki and seized the town of Pulavy. At this point, though, the 2nd Czech Airborne Brigade was withdrawn to mount an operation in support of partisan units assisting the advance of the Thirty-Eighth

Army. On 17 September, an advance party of twelve men was dropped on to the airfield at Tri-Duba. Ten days later, the leading elements of the brigade followed with the main body and heavy weapons and equipment arriving in early October. By the 25th, 1,855 members of the brigade had been landed and deployed in the Banska Stiavnica region to the west and south-west where they joined the partisan forces numbering over 15,800 men.

On 18 October the Germans launched a major counter-attack designed to crush the Slovak rebellion, seizing Brezno and Zvolen. On 27 October, they captured Banska Bystrica, the capital of the insurgent-held part of Slovakia, forcing the remnants of the Slovak Army and the 2nd Czech Airborne Brigade to flee to the mountains, the latter taking heavy casualties.

By late 1944, the Soviet High Command had decided that large-scale airborne operations were too costly and decided that airborne forces should thereafter be used only for reinforcement of partisan formations, and reconnaissance and so-called 'diversionary' activities.

Such diversionary operations featured prominently in airborne warfare as waged by the Soviets during the Second World War. In the main, they were carried out by special forces, known familiarly in the West as Spetsnaz (an acronym of spetsial'noe naznachenie) which operated under the command of the NKVD (forerunner of the KGB), GRU (Soviet military intelligence), front or army control. Others were conducted by elements of the VDV but such was the number mounted by the Soviets that it is only possible to outline a few examples.

During July 1941, during a German advance into the Ukraine, the 204th Airborne Brigade of I Airborne Corps carried out over ten operations, dropping troops into the enemy rear to interdict lines of communications and supply. In September of that year, a detachment of twenty-three paratroops was deployed as part of a diversionary action during the defence of Odessa which was under siege by German and Romanian forces. A counter-offensive was launched on 22 September, the leading element being a twenty-three-strong detachment of paratroops dropped in the enemy rear at 1.30 a.m., thereafter attacking lines of communication and destroying an enemy command post before linking up at 5.00 a.m. with the 3rd Naval Infantry Regiment which meanwhile had carried out an amphibious assault east of Odessa, driving Romanian forces from Grigor'evka. This combined airborne and seaborne assault had the desired effect, clearing the enemy from the area of Chebanka. Meanwhile, the 157th and 421st Rifle Divisions had joined the fray and drove the Romanians back north and north-westwards, inflicting some 1,000 casualties and taking two hundred prisoners. The counter-offensive was entirely successful and resulted in the safe evacuation of the Odessa garrison to Sevastopol early the following month.

December 1941 saw another airborne operation mounted as part of an attempt to recapture the Kerch Peninsula, situated at the east-ernmost end of the Crimea, which had been seized by forces of the German Eleventh Army under General Erich von Manstein two months earlier. The Transcaucasus Front was to recapture the peninsula and relieve Sevastopol, which was under siege by von Manstein, in an operation to be carried out by ground, airborne and amphibious forces of the Forty-Fourth and Fifty-First Armies, and the Black Fleet. The plan called for the Fifty-First Army and amphibious elements of the Black Fleet to force the Kerch Straits, occupy Kerch and thereafter advance on Ak Monai at the base of the peninsula. The Forty-Fourth Army, meanwhile, was to attack Marfovka and thereafter, with the Fifty-First Army, clear all enemy forces from the peninsula before preparing to raise the siege of Sevastopol.

The airborne element of the operation would comprise two elements. First, a parachute company would be dropped in the area of Baragova station, to the west of Kerch, where it would establish a firm base from which it would support the amphibious landing. Secondly, a parachute battalion of II Airborne Corps would capture the airfield at Vladislavovka for subsequent use by Soviet aircraft. On completion of their missions, the paratroops would come under command of Forty-

Fourth Army. At the eleventh hour, however, high seas and floating ice forced the cancellation of the landing at Ak Monai and the airborne units were given a new mission: they were to drop in the area of Arabat and thereafter block any enemy advance from Genischesk down the Arabat spit or any withdrawal along it.

The initial stage of the operation saw a small force of Red Navy parachutists equipped with radio sets dropped in the enemy rear from which they were to gather intelligence on enemy dispositions. On 31 December a parachute battalion, commanded by Major Niashin, took off in TB-3 bombers but adverse weather forced the aircraft to fly at a very low altitude of some 250 feet before climbing to a height of 1,350 feet from where the paratroops found themselves jumping into thick cloud and high winds. Scattered by the wind, they also came under fire from enemy machine guns.

Despite these grave difficulties, small groups of paratroops succeeded in infiltrating German defences and moving on Ak Monai. Once he had assembled sufficient men, Niashin mounted an attack on an enemy artillery position on the northern side of the Ak Monai defences. By the early hours of 1 January 1942, the battalion had occupied these defences and those lining the base of the Arabat spit.

By this time, the Forty-Fourth Army had taken Feodosiia and advanced inland some ten miles towards Sevastopol before encountering stiff resistance from the Germans, who were fighting hard to prevent their forces being surrounded as they withdrew westwards. At this juncture, Niashin's battalion split up into small groups to conduct diversionary operations, harassing the German units during their withdrawal. Subsequently, the battalion was replaced by a naval infantry unit.

This operation suffered from the same problems that had plagued earlier, far larger ones. Those responsible for planning it failed to determine the exact objectives and thus the force employed was too small. Moreover, lack of effective reconnaissance resulted in inaccurate intelligence on enemy strengths and dispositions. Once again, problems had been caused by bad weather so that many members of the airborne force were scattered during the drop. That Major Niashin's battalion had performed creditably thereafter was entirely to the credit of him and his men.

In October 1942, the Transcaucasus Front mounted another airborne operation. On this occasion, the objective was a German airfield at Maikop from which Luftwaffe aircraft were attacking Soviet installations along the Black Sea coast with great effect. A special forty-two-strong detachment, commanded by Major M. Orlov, was formed and trained for the operation which was under the direct control of the front headquarters. On the night of 24 October, Orlov and his men were dropped on Maikop, half of them landing on the airfield itself and the remainder a short distance away to the west. A fierce action ensued, lasting approximately an hour, during which twenty-two out of fifty-four aircraft were destroyed and a further twenty damaged before the paratroops were eventually forced to withdraw, leaving behind fourteen dead.

The winter of 1943 found Soviet forces surrounding the German Sixth Army at Stalingrad and forcing back the Army Group Don westwards in the direction of Khar'kov and the Dnepr. Meanwhile, other forces were attempting to clear the Germans from the region of the Northern Caucasus where by early February their defences were to the east of the Taman Peninsula and on the eastern edges of the Black Sea port of Novorossisk.

The Soviets decided to mount a major combined land and sea operation to expedite the liberation of Novorossisk and the peninsula, the task being allotted to the Black Sea Group of Forces.

An initial frontal assault on the German defences to the north-east of the port failed, as did an attack launched by the Soviet Fifty Sixth Army in the Krasnodor area. It was therefore decided to mount a major amphibious operation against Novorossisk itself, the main force landing in the area of Iuzhnaia Ozereika and a smaller element going ashore near Stanichka.

An airborne operation would meanwhile act as a diversionary measure as well as disrupting enemy command and control. This would be carried out by an eighty-strong detachment of the 31st Parachute Regiment, comprising elements of the now-defunct II Airborne Corps, which was to drop in the area of Vasil'evka and Glebovka near the reported location of the headquarters of the German 10th Infantry Division. The detachment was to attack and destroy the headquarters, thereafter blowing up a number of bridges in the area to prevent the move forward of enemy reinforcements or the withdrawal of forces from Iuzhnaia Ozereika.

The operation began at 1.00 a.m. on 4 February, the detachment being dropped from PS-84 transports in four twenty-strong groups. Air strikes were carried out by supporting Soviet aircraft as the drop was made and the detachment mounted an attack on Vasil'evka and annihilated the garrison. Of the enemy divisional headquarters, however, there was no sign. During the following three days, the detachment operated in the enemy rear, killing over one hundred Germans and disrupting lines of communication, itself losing fifteen men.

The main amphibious landing had meanwhile failed due to the late arrival of the ships and strong enemy resistance; but the landing at Stanichka proved successful. overcoming strong resistance. On completion of its mission, the parachute detachment made its way to Stanichka where it linked up with the landing force. It had been entirely successful in carrying out its task, pinning down a large number of enemy in the area of Iuzhnaia Ozereika and thus indirectly assisting the amphibious landing.

In August 1945 the Soviets also carried out more than fifteen airborne operations in the Far East, albeit by ground troops who were airlanded deep inside Manchuria, after the Japanese decision to surrender, with the aim of expediting the capitulation of enemy units in the region.

The first of these actions took place following the Soviet capture of Mutanchiang on 16 August and the subsequent advance by the Soviet

1st Far Eastern Front's First Red Banner and Fifth Armies on Harbin and Kirin, the locations of the headquarters of the Japanese First Area Army and Kwantung Army respectively. On 14 August, the Japanese had issued orders for their forces to surrender and lay down their arms but these had either not reached all units or were being ignored. On 17 August the commander of the Soviet Far Eastern Theatre of Military Operations, Marshal Alexander Vasilevsky, had sent a message by radio to the commander of the Kwantung Army, General Otozo Yamada, requiring the latter to cease all military action at 12.00 midday on 20 August and declaring that Soviet forces would do likewise as soon as Japanese forces began to surrender.

To reinforce his proposal, Vasilevsky ordered all fronts under his command to despatch specially trained and equipped detachments of troops to seize key objectives so as to put pressure on Japanese forces to surrender as quickly as possible.

The 1st Far Eastern Front formed two 150-strong assault companies from the 20th Motorised Assault Engineer Brigade, these comprising specially picked and highly experienced men who had seen earlier action against the Japanese in eastern Manchuria. Each company was heavily armed with automatic weapons, flame throwers, grenades and explosives, and each sapper, equipped with a map marked with routes and objectives, had been specially trained and thoroughly rehearsed in his own individual tasks.

The first company, commanded by Lieutenant Colonel I. N. Zabelin, took off for Harbin at 5.00 p.m. on 18 August. Accompanying it was Major General Georgii Shelakov, Military Commissar 1st Far Eastern Front, who had been instructed to negotiate the surrender with the Japanese. The company landed at Harbin and secured the airfield within minutes. The Japanese offered no resistance and shortly afterwards the Chief of Staff of the Kwantung Army, Lieutenant General Hata, and a group of officers arrived. On being taken to the Soviet Consulate by Major General Shelakov, he was presented with the Soviet terms for surrender. By that night, Zabelin and his company had seized

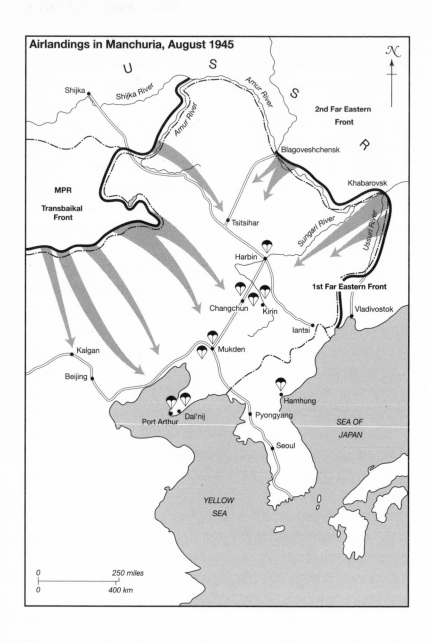

Airlandings in Manchuria, August 1945

their objectives: the bridges over the River Sungari, the railway station, telegraph office, police station and other key installations. Thereafter, the Japanese surrender proceeded smoothly and Soviet ground forces reached Harbin on 20 August.

The second company, commanded by Lieutenant Colonel D. A. Krutskikh and accompanied by Colonel V. I. Lebedev, had departed for Kirin on 19 August, where it landed at 7.00 p.m. Once again, no opposition was encountered and the airfield and key installations were secured by Krutskikh and his company who subsequently linked up with leading elements of the Soviet X Mechanised Corps, which arrived on the following day.

Farther south, similar operations were carried out by the Soviet Twenty-Fifth Army which received the surrender of the Japanese Third Army and other forces, two landings taking place at Wongson and Kanko on the east coast of Korea.

The Transbaikal Front, meantime, was conducting similar operations with landings taking place at Changchun, Mukden and Tuplaio, and subsequently at Darien and Port Arthur. The Changchun force comprised a 200-strong company of IX Guards Mechanised Corps' 30th Guards Mechanised Brigade under Colonel P. N. Avremenko, the landing itself being under the command of Lieutenant Colonel M. I. Mel'nichenko, Assistant Chief of Intelligence at Headquarters Sixth Guards Tank Army.

First to land at dawn on 19 August was the special representative of the Commander of the Transbaikal Front, Colonel I. T. Artemenko, accompanied by a small group of officers. On landing, he signalled his safe arrival and instructed Colonel Avremenko and his company to follow suit before heading for the Japanese headquarters where he subsequently presented the terms of surrender. Shortly after 11.00 a.m., Mel'nichenko and a detachment of eighteen men landed in an aircraft, followed shortly afterwards by Colonel Avremenko and his company, part of which was flown to Tupliao, the location of another Japanese headquarters. By 1.15 p.m. that afternoon, all key objectives had been secured and by the end of the day some 40,000 Japanese troops had laid down their arms. Next morning, the leading elements of the Sixth Guards Tank Army reached Changchun.

A 225-strong assault company of the 2nd Battalion of 6th Guards Motorised Rifle Brigade, part of V Guards Tank Corps, landed at Mukden on 19 August. Commanded by Major P. E. Chelyshev, it was accompanied by Major General Aleksandr Pritula, representative of the commander of the Transbaikal Front. Once again, the landing was unopposed and Mukden was seized and secured without resistance. Later that same day, the commander of V Guards Tank Corps, General Andrei Kravchenko, landed at Mukden to receive the surrender of the Japanese Third Army. On the following day, the leading units of V Guards Tank Corps entered the city.

Airlanding operations continued during the following days. On 22 August, a 200-strong company under Major N. K. Beloded, Assistant Chief of Operations at Headquarters IX Guards Mechanised Corps, landed at Port Arthur. On this occasion, the aircraft had come under fire as they approached the airfield but this was swiftly suppressed by escorting Soviet fighters and the landing took place without mishap. Shortly afterwards, a 250-strong force, commanded by Lieutenant Colonel B. S. Likhachev, landed at Dairen and seized the city, subsequently linking up with elements of Sixth Guards Tank Army.

All these operations proved successful in that they served to speed up the surrender and disarmament of Japanese forces at each location where key objectives were secured and a Soviet presence swiftly established throughout Manchuria. Moreover, they were carried out by small, well-trained and equipped forces who achieved results out of all proportion to their numbers. Classed as diversionary actions, they would set a pattern for Soviet airborne operations in the post-war era to come.

CHAPTER SIX

BRITISH AIRBORNE FORCES: EARLY OPERATIONS

The development of airborne forces in Germany had been watched with keen interest in Britain by a number of observers, among them the Prime Minister, Winston Churchill, who on 22 June 1940 wrote the following minute to General Sir Hastings Ismay, head of the Military Wing of the War Cabinet Secretariat:

> We ought to have a corps of at least 5,000 parachute troops, including a proportion of Australians, New Zealanders and Canadians, together with some trustworthy people from Norway and France... advantage of the summer must be taken to train these troops, who can nonetheless play their part meanwhile as shock troops in home defence. Pray let me have a note from the War Office on the subject.

In fact, creation of a fledgling airborne capability had already occurred with the formation by the Royal Air Force of the Central Landing School (CLS) at Ringway, near Manchester, under the command of Squadron Leader Louis Strange. His second-in-command was Major John Rock of the Royal Engineers who had been tasked with 'the military organisation of British airborne forces'. The school's staff comprised nine parachute jumping instructors (PJI) from the Army under Regimental Sergeant Major Mansie and fourteen from the RAF under Flight Sergeant (later Wing Commander) Bill Brereton.

The initial parachute training aircraft and equipment consisted of little more than six ageing Whitley bombers and a thousand parachutes. Despite Churchill's enthusiastic support, the Air Ministry adopted a somewhat obstructive attitude towards providing any further facilities and thus the staff at Ringway swiftly had to become experts in the art of improvisation in designing and building apparatus for 'synthetic' parachute training. In addition, the Whitleys had to be adapted with apertures cut in the floors of the rear of their fuselages and their rear gun turrets removed. The parachute developed for military use during this time was the GQ X-Type Statichute which, equipped with a 28-foot diameter canopy, provided limited steerability, and would remain in service until the early 1960s.

While the CLS was being formed, the search was on throughout the army for volunteers to become parachutists. At the same time, the decision was taken to convert one of the newly formed commando units to the parachute role and accordingly No. 2 Commando was selected, shortly afterwards being moved to a new base location at Knutsford, not far from Ringway.

On 3 July 1940, Lieutenant Colonel C. I. A. Jackson of the Royal Tank Regiment assumed command of No. 2 Commando and six days later B and C Troops reported to Ringway to begin training. On 13 July, RAF PJIs gave a demonstration of jumping from a Whitley and on the 22nd the trainee parachutists carried out their first descent. Tragically, three days later, a member of the unit, Driver Evans of the Royal Army Service Corps, was killed when his parachute failed to open properly. Despite such initial setbacks, by August a further 500 troops had been selected for parachute training from a total of 3,500 volunteers. By the end of the following month, a total of 961 descents had been carried out by 290 trainees. Casualties were very low: two deaths, thirteen injured, thirty refusals and thirteen men returned to their parent units as unsuitable.

During its period of conversion to the parachute role, No. 2 Commando comprised a headquarters and a number of troops, each of fifty men, with an overall strength of 500 all ranks. In November 1940, it was redesignated 11th Special Air Service (SAS) Battalion and reorganised into a headquarters, a parachute wing and a gliderborne wing. By the end of the year, the unit consisted of twenty-two sub-sections, each of ten men.

On 19 September 1940, the CLS was expanded to become the Central Landing Establishment (CLE), incorporating both a parachute training school and a glider training squadron, the latter under command of Squadron Leader H. E. Hervey. Wing Commander Sir Nigel Norman took over command of the CLE while Group Captain L. G. Harvey was appointed station commander. Squadron Leader Strange remained in charge of No. 1 Parachute Training School (No. 1 PTS), as the school was now designated, while Major Rock was promoted to lieutenant colonel. In July of the following year, Wing Commander Maurice Newnham DFC assumed command of No. 1 PTS, a post he held throughout the rest of the war.

The glider training squadron was equipped initially with Tiger Moth aircraft, used as tugs, and Kirby Kite civil-pattern gliders. There were no military gliders in existence in Britain at that time and so an appeal was made to all owners of gliders to lend or donate them to the squadron. On 26 October, the first tug and glider demonstration took place. On 28 December 1940 the glider training squadron moved to RAF Thame, in Oxfordshire, where it was re-equipped in February 1941 with Hawker Hector tugs. By this time, designs had been produced for a military glider and that same month saw the maiden flight of the GAL 48 Hotspur Mk. I which was flown by two pilots seated in tandem and carried eight troops. The first Hotspurs were delivered to the training squadron in April 1941. Although 1,012 were built, the aircraft's limited payload capability resulted in its soon being relegated to a training role.

Early 1941 saw the British Army's fledgling airborne forces receive their baptism of fire, albeit on a small scale, when it was decided to carry out an operation in southern Italy. Its aim was to disrupt water supplies to the ports of Taranto, Bari and Brindisi, all of which were embarkation points for Italian forces engaged in North Africa and Albania. Such an operation, it was believed, would demonstrate to the rest of the world that Britain was still very much a force to be reckoned with. While this was the reason given for mounting the operation, the real justification for it was that the War Office was anxious to test the fighting ability of its new airborne unit, and thus the standards of training and equipment, as well as the RAF's ability to deliver para-troops at predetermined locations at the right time.

The objective was an aqueduct crossing the Tragino, a small water-course, at a point about thirty miles north-east of the small town of Salverno in the province of Campania, which provided the main water supply route for the province of Apulia and its population of two million.

A raiding force of thirty-eight men – seven officers and thirty-one other ranks – was selected from 11th SAS Battalion. Designated X Troop, it was commanded by Major T. A. G. Pritchard of the Royal Welch Fusiliers. Attached to it for the operation were three Italian-speaking interpreters: Squadron Leader Lucky MC, Rifleman Nasri of the Rifle Brigade and a civilian named Fortunato Picchi.

Preparations for what was codenamed Operation Colossus began in January 1941. Eight Whitleys of No. 91 Squadron RAF, under the command of Wing Commander J. B. Tate, were allotted to fly X Troop to the target area, while a further two Whitleys were to carry out a diversionary bombing raid against some railway yards at Foggia, some sixty miles to the north. Training was intense, including attacks on a full-scale mock-up of the aqueduct, and lasted until the end of the first week in February,

The plan was for X Troop, which included a party of seven sappers under Captain G. F. K. Daly of the Royal Engineers, to fly on 7 February from England to Malta whence the operation would be launched.

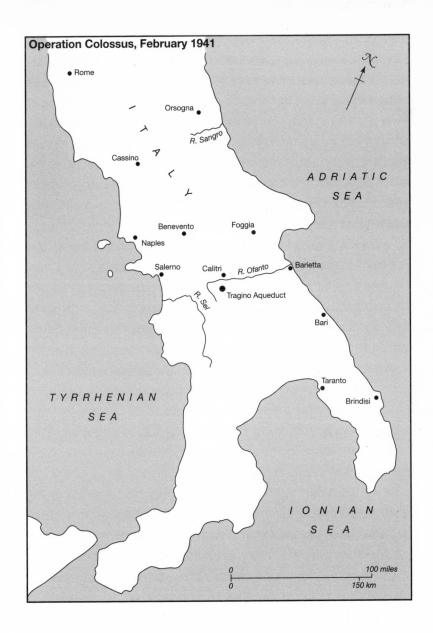

Operation Colossus, February 1941

Rome

Orsogna

R. Sangro

Cassino

ADRIATIC
SEA

Benevento Foggia

Naples

Salerno Calitri *R. Ofanto* Barietta

Tragino Aqueduct

R. Sel

Bari

TYRRHENIAN
SEA

Taranto

Brindisi

IONIAN
SEA

0   100 miles
0   150 km

ITALY

This initial stage would involve a night flight of some 1,600 miles, part of it over enemy-occupied France. Three days later, at 9.30 p.m. on 10 February, the entire force would be dropped in the area of its objective. Once the attack had been completed, X Troop would withdraw and make its way over fifty miles of mountainous terrain to the coast and the mouth of the River Sele where a submarine, HMS *Triumph*, would be waiting to take them off on the night of 15/16 February.

The flight to Malta went as planned, with X Troop emplaning at Mildenhall, in Suffolk, and flying through the night without mishap. It had been preceded on 24 January by Lieutenant Anthony Deane-Drummond of the Royal Signals who had gone ahead to ensure that preparations were in hand for its arrival.

At 6.30 p.m. on the evening of 10 February, the six Whitleys took off from Malta, each carrying an officer and five other ranks of X troop. The flight was uneventful, the weather being perfect and visibility excellent. The DZ was approximately half a mile to the north of the aqueduct and the leading Whitley, flying at a height of 400 feet, reached it at 9.42 p.m., dropping its six-man stick and its equipment within 250 yards. The next four aircraft then arrived and dropped their sticks, including two sappers, within 400 yards of the DZ. Two, however, failed to drop their containers of weapons and explosives due to icing-up of the container release mechanisms. Unfortunately the sixth Whitley, carrying Captain Daly and the other five sappers, was unable to locate the DZ and eventually dropped its stick and equipment two hours later in a valley two miles to the north-east of the objective.

The remainder of X Troop was meantime attempting to retrieve the weapons and explosives containers but was hampered by the fact that the lights on the containers had proved inoperable. One container, holding 800 lbs of explosive, sufficient for at least part of the mission, was eventually found and, in the absence of Captain Daly, Second Lieutenant A. Paterson RE took charge of the demolition task on the main viaduct with the assistance of another sapper, Sergeant Drury. They soon discovered, however, that the central pier was constructed of reinforced concrete, which the limited amount of explosive in their possession was insufficient to destroy. Paterson and Drury thus switched their attention to another pier and a small bridge spanning the River Ginestra near by. At 12.30 a.m. on 11 February, the charges were blown and the pier destroyed, taking half the aqueduct with it as it crumbled. As X Troop watched, water poured through the breach and down the Tragino Valley. Almost immediately afterwards, the charges on the small wooden bridge exploded and destroyed it totally. X Troop had successfully completed its mission.

At 1.00 a.m. the raiders withdrew and headed towards the coast, moving in three groups commanded by Major Pritchard, Captain C. G. Lea of The Lancashire Fusiliers and 2nd Lieutenant G. Jowett of the Highland Light Infantry. Moving by night, they laid up during the day to avoid any contact with local inhabitants or enemy forces.

Unfortunately, all three groups were captured on 12 February. Major Pritchard's group, resting in a cave, was spotted by a farmer and the alarm raised; the inhabitants of a nearby village, followed by Italian troops and *carabinieri*, appeared soon afterwards. Pritchard, however, realised that his small, lightly armed group could hold out for only a limited time and that there was a risk of women and children being killed or wounded in any engagement. He thus felt that he had no choice but to surrender. Luck had also deserted Captain Lea's group which had been captured already, as had 2nd Lieutenant Jowett and his men, who had been ambushed.

The missing group of five sappers and Captain Daly had travelled for three nights and covered over thirty miles in their journey towards the coast. Exhausted and suffering from lack of food, they still had some eighteen miles ahead of them when they encountered a group of Italian troops and police. Using Fortunato Picchi, the interpreter attached to their group, they attempted to bluff their way out by claiming they were German troops on a special operation and demanding transport to take them to Naples. This ploy was almost successful but failed when the Italians demanded identification papers. Daly and his men were taken away as prisoners – all except for Fortunato Picchi who was handed over to the fascist militia. In spite of being tortured while undergoing interrogation, he remained silent and was subsequently court-martialled and executed by firing squad.

Had Captain Daly and his sappers reached the coast, they would not have found HMS *Triumph* waiting for them. While the operation was under way, one of the two Whitleys carrying out the diversionary bombing raid on the railway yards at Foggia had suffered engine trouble. The pilot had radioed the operational base on Malta, reporting that he was heading for the mouth of the River Sele where he planned to ditch his aircraft, being completely unaware that this was the rendezvous location for the evacuation of X Troop. In view of the risk of his message having been monitored, thus exposing the submarine to possible detection by enemy naval forces, the decision was taken not to send HMS *Triumph*.

While Operation Colussus was of little value in terms of the effect of the disruption of water supplies to the three Italian ports, and thus on Italian operations in Albania and North Africa, it gave a valuable boost to morale in Britain as well as providing experience which was subsequently put to good use.

In May 1941 the Chiefs of Staff directed that a parachute brigade was to be raised at the earliest opportunity, with 11th SAS Battalion being used as the nucleus. In July, authority was given for the formation of a brigade headquarters, four parachute battalions and a troop of sappers. A request for volunteers was sent throughout the British Army although a limitation of ten men per unit was introduced to avoid undue depletion. Recruitment teams visited units and, despite the understandable reluctance on the part of commanding officers to release their best men, received a good response.

In early September 1941, Headquarters 1st Parachute Brigade was formed at Hardwick Hall under the command of Brigadier Richard Gale, comprising a small staff with Major P. E. Bromley-Martin of the Grenadier Guards as brigade major and Captain J.G. Squirrel as staff captain. Attached to the new headquarters was a signals section and No. 1 Air Troop Royal Engineers.

It had been decided to disband 11th SAS Battalion and distribute its strength among the four new parachute battalions. After meeting its new commanding officer, Lieutenant Colonel Eric Down, however, Brigadier Gale decided that it should be retained and redesignated 1st Parachute Battalion. The decision was also taken to form only two more battalions initially with the fourth being raised at a later date. Consequently, 2nd and 3rd Parachute Battalions were formed in September under Lieutenant Colonels Edward Flavell and Gerald Lathbury respectively, both comprising a headquarters and three rifle companies. In January 1942, 4th Parachute Battalion was formed under Lieutenant Colonel M. R. J. 'Tim' Hope Thomson.

The task of forming the new brigade was not easy. The lack of good warrant officers and NCOs caused problems, and officers had to make their presence felt on several occasions when discipline needed to be enforced. Moreover, many of the volunteers were unsuitable, either due to the fact that they were physically unable to meet the exacting demands of the parachute selection course or because their disciplinary records left much to be desired; in several instances, commanding officers had relieved themselves of unwanted individuals. Despite such problems, however, the enthusiasm among the volunteers for Airborne Forces helped to overcome these difficulties and the fledgling units began to take shape.

During the second half of 1941, the decision was taken to form a brigade of gliderborne troops and on 10 October 31st Independent Infantry Brigade Group was redesignated 1st Airlanding Brigade. Commanded from 31 October by Brigadier G. F. Hopkinson, it incorporated four battalions: the 1st Battalion Royal Ulster Rifles; 2nd Battalion Oxfordshire & Buckinghamshire Light Infantry; 2nd Battalion The South Staffordshire Regiment; and the 1st Battalion The Border Regiment.

At this juncture, it was decided to group 1st Parachute Brigade and

1st Airlanding Brigade into a divisional formation and consequently Headquarters 1st Airborne Division was formed at the end of October under the command of Major General Frederick 'Boy' Browning who was also appointed Commander Paratroops & Airborne Troops.

21 December 1941 saw the formation of The Glider Pilot Regiment which initially comprised one battalion commanded by Lieutenant Colonel John Rock, with a second to be formed in due course. Each battalion was to comprise six companies of pilots who would be trained to fight as infantry once on the ground. Flying training for glider first pilots, all of whom were staff sergeants, would begin with an initial eight weeks spent at an RAF Elementary Flying Training School (EFTS) flying Tiger Moths, followed by a further eight weeks at a glider training school (GTS) on Hotspurs. On completion of these sixteen weeks, first pilots then would spend four weeks converting to the Airspeed Horsa, which entered service during the latter part of 1941. Flown by two pilots, this aircraft could carry a platoon of fully equipped infantry or alternatively a jeep and trailer or 6-pounder anti-tank gun, or an M8 75mm pack howitzer; it was normally towed by a Halifax or Stirling bomber, or a C-47 Dakota.

Second pilots, holding the rank of sergeant, would receive a shorter training, spending four weeks at an EFTS and three to four weeks on gliders. Distinction between first and second pilots was to be denoted by their respective wings awarded on qualification and worn on the uniform above the left breast pocket: a first pilot would wear a brevet comprising a lion surmounting a crown between two blue wings, and a second pilot a brevet comprising the letter 'G' between two wings.

By the end of 1941 Airborne Forces were well and truly established as a new element of the British Army's order of battle. They did not, however, possess a corporate identity in the shape of a parent regiment and thus it was decided by the War Office that all parachute battalions and The Glider Pilot Regiment would become part of a new formation to be designated the Army Air Corps, which came into being on 24 February 1942.

The end of 1941 also saw the expansion of the RAF training organ-isation for Airborne Forces. On 15 February 1942, No. 1 PTS was estab-lished as a unit in its own right, while elementary and flying training schools were formed for the training of glider pilots. The Airborne Forces Experimental Establishment, comprising a technical develop-ment unit and an experimental flight, was also set up on the same date. The principal problem facing the RAF, however, was the lack of suitable aircraft for dropping parachutists. Unlike its German counterpart, the RAF possessed virtually no transport aircraft and was forced initially to convert a number of obsolete Whitley bombers for dropping para-chutists. Such was the priority given to the creation of airborne forces, however, that ultimately it was obliged to convert a number of its bomber squadrons to the troop-carrying and glider-towing roles, grouping them together under No. 38 Wing (subsequently 38 Group). Bombers used in these roles included four-engined Stirlings and Halifaxes, and twin-engined Albemarles.

February 1942 witnessed the second action ever carried out by British Airborne Forces. At 10.30 p.m. on the night of 27 February twelve Whitley bombers of No. 51 Squadron RAF, under the command of Wing Commander Charles Pickard, took off from an airfield at Thruxton, in Hampshire, carrying a force of 120 paratroops. This comprised C Company 2nd Parachute Battalion, commanded by Major Johnny Frost of The Cameronians (Scottish Rifles), nine sappers of 1st Parachute Squadron Royal Engineers, four signallers and an RAF radar specialist, Flight Sergeant E. W. F. Cox. Each aircraft carried ten men sitting on the floor of the fuselage, the noise and vibration making con-versation difficult. Nevertheless, spirits throughout the force were high and songs were sung with great gusto as the bombers headed through the night. Little did they know it, but the men of C Company and those attached to them were about to make history as they headed for the coast of northern France and their objective.

Towards the end of 1941, the RAF had suffered increasing losses of bombers carrying out raids over Europe due to the efficiency of

German radar, which enabled the Luftwaffe to track incoming aircraft and guide its night fighters in to intercept them. A chain of radar posts had been established along the French coast for this purpose, one of them having been located by RAF aerial reconnaissance north of the village of Bruneval, twelve miles to the north of Le Havre.

British experts at the Telecommunications Research Establishment already possessed a considerable amount of technical data on the German acquisition radar, codenamed *Freya*. They were anxious, however, to acquire information on the *Würzburg* narrow-beam radar which the Luftwaffe employed to vector its night fighters for interception. The radar at Bruneval was one of this type and the decision was taken to mount an operation to seize key components for examination. Initially, consideration was given to the use of commandos but examination of aerial photographs revealed that the site was well defended against seaborne assault. As surprise would be a factor essential to the success of the operation, it was decided that paratroops should be used instead. 2nd Parachute Battalion was allotted the task and the commanding officer, Lieutenant Colonel Edward Flavell, selected Major Johnny Frost and his company to carry it out.

C Company itself had only recently been formed and some of its number had not completed their parachute training. When briefed initially by a liaison officer from Headquarters 1st Airborne Division, Frost was informed that he and his men were to provide a demonstration to the War Cabinet, and that training for it would be carried out in an area near Alton Priors, in Wiltshire, where the terrain was very similar to that over which the display would take place. He was also told that his company would have to be split into four groups, each to be specially trained and equipped for specific tasks. Frost was not happy about the reorganisation of his company and intended to make his objections very clear to Major General 'Boy' Browning during a forthcoming visit to divisional headquarters. Browning was away, however, and Frost had to confine himself to an interview with the GSO 1 during which his objections fell on stony ground. He returned to 2nd Parachute Battalion's base puzzled by the attitude shown towards his own plan, which retained the company's normal order of battle of three platoons. On the following day, however, the 1st Airborne Division liaison officer appeared and, having sworn Frost to secrecy, revealed that he and his company would in fact be carrying out an operation in enemy-occupied France. On hearing this, Frost dropped his objections and immediately turned his attention fully to preparing his men for the task ahead.

After a period spent training on Salisbury Plain in Wiltshire, where it was based at Tilshead, C Company and its attached section of sappers travelled to Inveraray in Scotland. On completion of their mission, Frost and his men would be evacuated by sea and over the following days and nights, therefore, they underwent training on the banks of Loch Fyne, rehearsing night embarkations on the landing craft that would take them off. During this period, they were visited by the Chief of Combined Operations, Admiral The Lord Louis Mountbatten, who addressed the company and the crews of the landing craft. His speech gave those listening the first hints of the operation for which they were training – until then, Frost had kept the entire details to himself.

On returning to Tilshead, C Company carried out its first practice drop with No. 51 Squadron. Despite the fact that the aircrews had no previous experience of dropping parachutists, the exercise proved successful. Further training in landing craft was carried out with the Royal Navy off the Dorset coast, but this proved to be fraught with problems. A full moon was required for the operation and a rising tide necessary for the landing craft to carry out the evacuation from the beach at Bruneval. The four-day period scheduled for the operation was 24–27 February. On 23 February, a final rehearsal was carried out, and proved disastrous: despite perfect weather conditions, the landing craft became grounded sixty yards offshore with the subsequent best efforts of C Company failing to shift them.

Frost's force was organised into five groups, all named after famous Royal Navy admirals: Nelson, Jellicoe, Hardy, Drake and Rodney.

Nelson, forty-strong and commanded by Captain John Ross, had the task of clearing and securing the enemy positions defending the evacuation beach. Jellicoe, Hardy and Drake, under Frost himself, would capture the radar site and a nearby villa occupied by Luftwaffe radar technicians and guards. Captain Dennis Vernon and his sappers, together with Flight Sergeant Cox, would accompany Frost. It would be Cox's task to supervise the dismantling of the *Würzburg* radar by the sappers. In the meantime, Rodney, the reserve element under Lieutenant John Timothy, would take up positions between the radar site and the main likely enemy approach to block any counter-attack.

The enemy at Bruneval were divided into three groups. The radar site was manned by Luftwaffe technicians protected by a detachment of guards, the total number at that location being some thirty men. About 300 yards to the north lay *Le Presbytère*, a group of buildings surrounded by woods and occupied by more technicians and troops whose total strength was estimated at over one hundred. In Bruneval itself there was a small garrison of forty men. Finally, the evacuation beach, linked to the village by a narrow road, was defended by emplacements and positions on the cliff tops and down below.

As the Whitleys crossed the French coast, they came under fire from enemy anti-aircraft fire and were forced to take violent evasive action. None were hit, however, and they continued heading for the dropping zone. 'Action Stations!' The No. 1 in each stick swung his legs into the aperture, watching intently the red light glowing above him. The green light suddenly came on and above the noise of the engines came the despatcher's shouted command of 'Go!' Tumbling into the bright, moonlit sky went the men of C Company. As Frost floated earthwards beneath his canopy, he recognised the layout of the snow-covered terrain below him from the highly detailed maps, air photographs and models which he and his men had studied at length during their preparations for the mission. There was no wind and the only sound was the receding noise of the departing aircraft. The snow provided a soft landing and within ten minutes Frost and his men had rallied and were

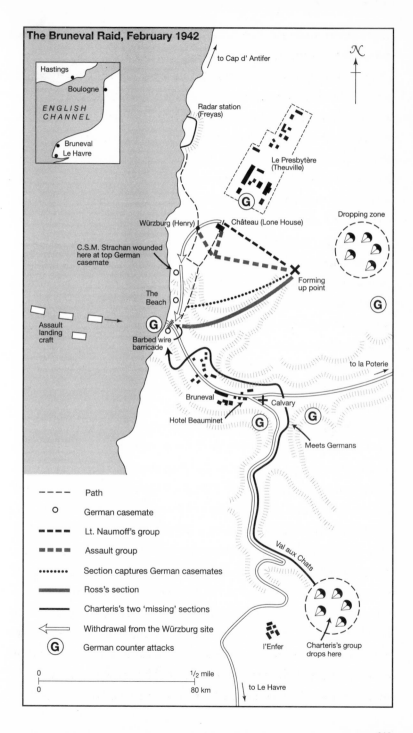

The Bruneval Raid, February 1942

Hastings

Boulogne

ENGLISH CHANNEL

Bruneval
Le Havre

to Cap d' Antifer

Radar station (Freyas)

Le Presbytère (Theuville)

Ⓖ

Dropping zone

Würzburg (Henry)

Château (Lone House)

C.S.M. Strachan wounded here at top German casemate

Ⓖ

Forming up point

The Beach

Assault landing craft

Ⓖ

Barbed wire barricade

to la Poterie

Bruneval

Calvary

Hotel Beauminet

Ⓖ

Ⓖ

Meets Germans

Val aux Chats

- - - - — Path

○ — German casemate

■ ■ ■ ■ — Lt. Naumoff's group

■ ■ ■ ■ — Assault group

•••••••• — Section captures German casemates

━━━━ — Ross's section

——— — Charteris's two 'missing' sections

⟸ — Withdrawal from the Würzburg site

Ⓖ — German counter attacks

l'Enfer

Charteris's group drops here

0 ——— 1/2 mile

0 ——— 80 km

to Le Havre

ready to move off. As they headed for their objective, they observed the men of Nelson landing.

Moving towards the radar site, Jellicoe, Hardy and Drake encountered no opposition nor any indication of alertness on the part of the enemy. Once all his men were in position and the villa was surrounded, Frost gave the signal for the assault to begin. As he did so, the noise of exploding grenades and automatic weapons could be heard from the direction of the radar site. Frost and those with him encountered only one enemy soldier who, on opening fire from an upstairs window of the villa, was swiftly shot dead. Meanwhile, the enemy at the radar site had been overrun and two taken prisoner. It was learned from them that there was only a small number of troops located there, the rest being based further inland. At that point, however, Frost and his men came under fire from enemy in the area of *Le Presbytère* and Private McIntyre was killed as he left the villa. Shortly afterwards, Captain Vernon and his sappers, accompanied by Flight Sergeant Cox, arrived at the radar site and began dismantling the equipment.

The fire from *Le Presbytère* grew heavier and shortly afterwards enemy vehicles could be seen moving up through the woods. Frost grew anxious, particularly as the newly issued No. 38 radio sets, with which his force had been equipped for the operation, failed to work and thus he had no means of communication with his other groups. It was not long, however, before Flight Sergeant Cox and the sappers completed dismantling the radar and loading it on to trolleys. Losing no time, Frost headed for the beach but as he and his men reached the area of the clifftop they came under fire from a machine gun and Company Sergeant Major Strachan was badly wounded in the stomach. It soon became apparent that the men of Nelson had not taken and cleared the enemy defences, this being confirmed almost immediately by Captain John Ross, who shouted up from the beach. Frost began working his way across to Rodney, to order Lieutenant John Timothy to attack the enemy defences. At that point, however, he was told that the enemy had reoccupied the villa and were advancing on the clifftop.

Altering his plan, he led his own group back to deal with this threat, which proved not to be serious and was quickly dispersed.

On returning to the clifftop, Frost met Lieutenant Euen Charteris of Nelson waiting for him by the main enemy machine-gun emplacement which had been cleared. It was only then that he learned that Charteris and two sections of Nelson had been dropped two miles short of the DZ and subsequently had to make their way across country to Bruneval. The going had been difficult and, while skirting around the village towards the clifftop, Charteris and his men had encountered an enemy patrol with which they had fought a sharp action. On arriving at the clifftop, they had attacked the machine-gun emplacement from a flank and taken it, killing all but one of its occupants.

By this time it was 2.15 a.m. and Frost's force was now ready for evacuation. There was no sign of the landing craft, however, and all efforts to establish radio contact with them proved unsuccessful. Attempts were made to call them in, using a signal lamp and, ultimately, red flares, which was the prearranged emergency signal, but all proved to be of no avail. Frost decided to redeploy his men in positions in the clifftop area and at the entrance to Bruneval. He had just completed the manoeuvre when a shout from one of his signallers announced that the landing craft had arrived.

The evacuation plan called for two craft to approach the beach at a time, the withdrawal being conducted in three phases. All six craft, however, moved in simultaneously as C Company began assembling on the beach. As they did so, their crews opened fire with Bren LMGs on the clifftop where some of Frost's men were still in positions covering the withdrawal. They ceased fire only after a chorus of shouts from the beach.

The wounded and the sappers with the dismantled radar equipment were loaded aboard one landing craft without any problems, but thereafter the withdrawal became somewhat chaotic. Matters were made no easier by the enemy who, on realising that their attackers were withdrawing, brought mortar fire to bear on the beach and began throwing grenades from the clifftop. After wading through the waves and scrambling aboard, the men of C Company were eventually embarked on the landing craft which then withdrew out to sea.

At 3.30 a.m., the entire force was transferred to motor gunboats which then took the landing craft in tow. It was only at that point, when a radio message was received from them, that it was realised that two signallers had been left behind; having lost their way, they had reached the beach too late. It was also at this juncture that Major Frost learned the reason for the delayed arrival of the landing craft at the beach. While waiting offshore for the signal to evacuate C Company, they had observed a German destroyer and two E-boats passing less than a mile away and had been forced to remain motionless in the moonlight until the enemy vessels had sailed out of range. At dawn on 28 February, the small flotilla was met by a squadron of Spitfires and a number of destroyers which took up station on either side and escorted the gunboats to Portsmouth.

C Company was rightly accorded a heroes' welcome on its return. Not only had Major Johnny Frost and his men successfully accomplished their mission in capturing the *Würzburg* radar, but they had also provided a great boost for British morale in what were very dark times indeed.

In April 1942, the Airborne Forces Depot & Battle School was formed. Initial selection for parachute training was carried out at Hardwick Hall, near Chesterfield in Derbyshire, where all volunteers regardless of rank underwent a gruelling fortnight of physical aptitude tests. By any standards, the course was a hard one with troops enduring a fortnight of intensive physical tests in the gymnasium, on the assault course and over roads and the surrounding countryside. Organised in small squads, each supervised by an Army Physical Training Corps instructor, they carried out everything at the double while being observed closely for any signs of weakness. The aim of the selection course was to find those men who possessed the high degree of stamina and self-discipline so essential in a paratrooper. The failure rate was high and the fate that all dreaded was to be returned to their units.

Co-located with the depot was the battle school which operated independently. Training, including field firing exercises with live ammunition, was conducted by day and night in the area of the Derwent Valley and the surrounding moors. One exercise comprised an initiative test in which groups of trainees were dropped off individually around Mansfield and Nottingham; from here they had to make their way to a rendezvous (RV) near Chesterfield, to be reached by dawn of the following day. Inevitably, a number made use of the railways but on several occasions were shunted around before being transported in the wrong direction. Usually only a small number succeeded in reaching the RV, the remainder having been apprehended by other troops or police hunting for them and subsequently locked up in the cells of Chesterfield police station.

Battle training was tough and intensive. From the very start it was appreciated that airborne troops would have to be capable of fighting and surviving against larger and more heavily armed formations until they could link up with ground troops. What they lacked in armour and firepower had to be balanced by extremely high standards of physical fitness and personal skills. Each man was expected to possess a very high degree of courage, self-discipline and self-reliance. Training commenced with the individual soldier, thereafter progressing to section, platoon, company and ultimately battalion levels. Exercises were carried out by day and night, frequently culminating in long marches back to the units' barracks. The ability to cover long distances at high speed in full battle order became a matter of pride in the newly formed parachute units – ten miles in two hours, twenty in four and, ultimately, fifty miles in twenty-four hours.

Those who were successful in passing the selection course at Hardwick Hall progressed to Ringway and No. 1 PTS where the parachute course lasted two weeks. In the initial week, troops underwent ground and synthetic training during which they learned to exit from an aircraft, control their parachutes in the air and land correctly. Fuselages of Whitleys, and subsequently of Stirlings, Halifaxes, Albemarles and ultimately Dakotas, were positioned in the hangars at Ringway. The trainee parachutists learned to jump from all of these, using the correct exit position. Other training aids included trapezes, on which trainees swung while learning correct flight drills, and wooden chutes down which they slid before falling and rolling as they landed. There was also the 'Fan', an apparatus comprising a drum around which was wound a steel cable, the end being attached to a parachute harness. When a trainee jumped from a platform twenty feet from the ground, his weight caused the drum to revolve; its speed, however, was controlled by two vanes which acted as air brakes and thus allowed the trainee to land with the same impact as he would when using a parachute. Another training aid, introduced later, was a 100-foot-high tower constructed of steel girders from the top of which protruded a long steel arm. Suspended from this by a cable was a parachute canopy stretched over a large metal hoop. On launching himself from the tower, a trainee found himself hanging in mid-air beneath the parachute. Once he had practised his flight drills and adopted the correct position for landing, the cable was released and he floated to the ground.

Synthetic training was followed at the end of the first week by two descents from a 'cage' suspended underneath a barrage balloon. These were not popular as the slow, swaying and silent ascent of the balloon to the jump height of 700 feet frequently added nausea to the tribula-tions of the nervous trainees who sat in the cage in a 'stick' of four, seated round the aperture in the centre of the floor. On a command from the PJI, the first man to jump swung his legs into the hole and adopted a position of sitting to attention while gripping the rim. On the command 'Go!', he thrust himself forward, bringing his hands to his sides and keeping his feet together. Next followed a stomach-churning drop of 120 feet before the trainee's parachute opened. Needless to say, the sensation of the parachute opening was a thrilling one but any feeling of bliss was soon interrupted by an instructor on the ground shouting orders through a megaphone with regard to correct flight drills and the position for landing.

Balloon descents were soon followed by five from an aircraft, these being conducted initially in 'slow pairs' and then 'quick pairs'. Thereafter, trainees jumped in sticks of five and ultimately ten. Parachuting from a Whitley could be disconcerting if the correct exit position was not maintained, the result being either one or two somewhat dramatic somersaults which usually resulted in the 'twists' – the front and rear sets of rigging lines becoming twisted together, restricting the proper development of the canopy and so increasing the rate of descent as well as preventing control of the parachute. The same problems later faced parachutists jumping from other converted bombers, such as Halifaxes, Stirlings and Albemarles, which had never been designed for such a purpose. It was not until the arrival of the Douglas C-47 Dakota that exits could be made from a door in the side of the fuselage, thus making life for the parachutist safer and relatively more enjoyable.

Other problems that faced parachutists included the 'blown periphery', which happened when part of the periphery of the canopy was blown inwards and subsequently outwards through the rigging lines, thus producing a second inverted canopy. Another type of blown periphery occurred when part of the canopy blew between two rigging lines, after which the canopy tended to roll up at the skirt. Other malfunctions included the 'streamer' or 'roman candle', when a canopy failed to open at all.

On completion of the course at Ringway, trainees received the coveted parachute wings to wear on the right-hand shoulder. Thereafter, they were posted to units as fully qualified parachutists.

Early in 1942 the decision had been taken to form another parachute brigade to bring 1st Airborne Division up to full establishment. On 17 July, Headquarters 2nd Parachute Brigade was formed under the command of Brigadier Eric Down who, prior to his promotion to that rank, had been commanding 1st Parachute Battalion. The nucleus of the new formation was 4th Parachute Battalion which was transferred from 1st Parachute Brigade. At that time, in view of the insufficient number of volunteers successfully qualifying as parachutists, the War Office decided that in future parachute units would be formed by converting infantry battalions to the role. Consequently, the 7th Battalion The Queen's Own Cameron Highlanders and the 10th Battalion The Royal Welch Fusiliers were transferred to 2nd Parachute Brigade. These two units were redesignated as 5th (Scottish) and 6th (Royal Welch) Parachute Battalions and were commanded respectively by Lieutenant Colonels A. Dunlop of the Argyll & Sutherland Highlanders and Lieutenant Colonel Charles Pritchard of the Royal Welch Fusiliers. Officers and men not wishing to become parachutists were transferred to other units, being replaced by men who had successfully passed through Hardwick Hall and Ringway.

In August, another important milestone in the creation of the British Army's airborne forces was reached with the formation of The Parachute Regiment; this became the parent regiment for the new parachute battalions, comprising part of the Army Air Corps along with The Glider Pilot Regiment.

August also witnessed the entry into service of the GAL Hamilcar Heavy Transport Military Glider, designed to transport heavy loads such as a Tetrarch or Locust light tank, two Bren carriers, a 17-pounder anti-tank gun and tractor, or engineer stores. With a payload of up to 19,000 pounds, it was flown by a crew of two pilots in a cockpit on top of the fuselage and towed by a Halifax bomber. Of wooden and fabric construction, the aircraft was designed to be dispensable and to be used only once, its operational airframe life being only ten hours.

During September 1942, it was decided that an airborne unit would be included in the Allied forces to take part in the forthcoming campaign against Italian and German forces in North Africa, the latter comprising Field Marshal Erwin Rommel's Afrika Korps. The unit initially allotted was American, the 2nd Battalion 503rd Parachute Infantry Regiment which had arrived in Britain in mid-June and been placed under command of 1st Airborne Division. Major General 'Boy' Browning, however, successfully argued that one battalion would prove insufficient for the task and consequently 1st Parachute Brigade was detailed in addition to the 2nd/503rd, being placed under command of the Supreme Allied Commander, General Dwight Eisenhower. He in turn allocated the brigade to First British Army under Lieutenant General Sir Kenneth Anderson.

1st Parachute Brigade, however, was not up to full strength nor fully equipped to war scales. Consequently, men and equipment had to be taken from 2nd Parachute Brigade and other units from 1st Airborne Division, depleting them somewhat. Prior to their departure, the men of 1st Parachute Brigade had to learn to jump from the C-47s of the US Army Air Force's (USAAF) No. 60 Troop Carrier Group, which arrived in Britain at the end of September, as the RAF was unable to spare any aircraft for airborne operations in North Africa. Until now, the men of the brigade had been accustomed to jumping from converted bombers, making their exits through apertures in the floors of the aircraft. The C-47, however, was equipped with a door in its port side through which paratroops or containers were despatched.

The first drop from C-47s took place on 9 October, a total of 250 men carrying out a descent. Tragically, four of them were killed. It was subsequently discovered that the static line on the British 'X' Type parachute was too short for use with the C-47, causing two of the canopies to become entangled with the aircraft's tailwheel. It was found that raising the tail of the aircraft during a drop eliminated the risk of this happening.

Towards the end of October, elements of 3rd Parachute Battalion, comprising Battalion Headquarters, B and C Companies and the Mortar Platoon, left their base at Bulford, in Wiltshire, and moved to an airfield near by at Netheravon. Shortly afterwards, the remainder of the battalion, along with the rest of 1st Parachute Brigade, moved to Greenock in Scotland, from which on 29 October it sailed for an undisclosed destination. Meantime, Battalion Headquarters, the two rifle companies and the Motar Platoon were preparing to fly to Gibraltar in readiness for an airborne operation in North Africa. There was a shortage of C-47s, however, and it was for that reason that A Company, commanded by Major Stephen Terrell, had to travel by sea with the rest of the brigade. Additional problems also arose when it was found that the C-47s' payloads had been reduced by approximately 2,000 pounds because extra fuel tanks had been fitted, and therefore the loading manifest for each aircraft had to be changed.

On 5 November the battalion moved to Hurn airfield, near Bournemouth. The aircraft arrived on the following day and at that juncture the commanding officer, Lieutenant Colonel Geoffrey Pine Coffin, briefed his men on the task that lay ahead. News was meanwhile awaited of the Allied seaborne landings in North Africa which were due to take place on Sunday 8 November. Reports of their success soon arrived but the battalion was unable to take off from Hurn because of thick fog. On the following day, the weather forecast indicated that the entire south of England, with the exception of western Cornwall, would remain fog-bound. It was thus decided to transport the battalion by train to Newquay and then by road to an RAF airfield at St Eval. This was completed by 11.00 p.m. that night, by which time the Dakotas and their crews were awaiting the arrival of Pine Coffin and his men. At 11.30 p.m. the leading elements of the battalion took off from St Eval, and headed for Gibraltar.

November also saw an operation mounted by elements of 1st Airborne Division. On 19 November a combined force of thirty sappers from two of the division's engineer units, 9th Airborne Field Company RE and 261st Airborne Field Park Company RE, took off in two Horsa gliders, towed by Halifax bombers, from an RAF airfield at Skitten, in Scotland, and headed for southern Norway. The operation, codenamed Freshman, was mounted by Headquarters Combined Operations and its objective was the Norsk Hydro plant at Vermork, about sixty miles west of Oslo, where the sappers were to destroy the stocks of heavy water held there for the German atomic weapons development programme. On completion of their task, the sappers were to make good their escape and head overland for neutral Sweden, some ninety miles away.

Preparations for the operation had begun in early October, the sappers being organised into two groups commanded by 2nd Lieutenant Michael Green and Lieutenant A. C. Allen respectively. Training initially took place in Wales, was extremely tough, incorporating long and arduous marches over rough terrain in Snowdonia and was designed not only to ensure that all taking part would be at peak physical and mental fitness but also to weed out any individuals unable to cope with the arduous requirements of the operation. Thereafter, the sappers were despatched to Fort William in Scotland, where they were made familiar with a hydro-electric plant similar to the target and received instruction on the placing of explosive charges to cause maximum damage. Similar training took place at Port Sunlight, where they were shown how to demolish large condensers of the type inside the Norsk Hydro plant. Detailed briefings on the layout of the plant were conducted, using large models of the plant and the surrounding terrain, together with mock-ups of the installations to be attacked – all based on information supplied by Norwegian agents of the Special Operations Executive (SOE). Training proceeded smoothly throughout, the only casualty being towards the end when Michael Green was forced to drop out due to a shooting accident, his place being taken by Lieutenant David Methuen.

An advance party of four SOE agents, all Norwegians and former members of the Linge Company, a Norwegian commando unit formed in Britain, was dropped on to the Hardanger Plateau on 18 October, landing near Fjarefit in Songadalen. The four men then made their way 100 miles to Skolandsmyrene and the site of the planned landing zone (LZ) for the two gliders, which lay approximately six miles from the objective, arriving there on 6 November. Their task was to provide intelligence on enemy movements and weather conditions in the area. On the night of the operation, they would use Eureka radio homing beacons to guide in the two tug aircraft which would be fitted with Rebecca receivers.

At 5.45 p.m. on 19 November, the first Halifax-Horsa combination took off from Skitten, carrying Lieutenant Methuen and his fourteen sappers. Fifteen minutes later, the second combination followed with Lieutenant Allen and his men. Neither reached the predesignated LZ, the operation ending in failure and tragedy when both Horsas, and one of the two Halifaxes, crashed into mountainsides. All members of the crew of the Halifax were killed, as were the pilots and co-pilots of both gliders. Twenty-six of the sappers also died, the four survivors being taken prisoner by the Germans. All four were subsequently handed over to the Gestapo, who murdered them.

November also witnessed two further parachute brigades being raised as part of 1st Airborne Division: 3rd Parachute Brigade was raised in Britain, under the command of Brigadier Gerald Lathbury, and incorporated the 7th (Light Infantry), 8th (Midland) and 9th (Eastern & Home Counties) Parachute Battalions. 3rd Parachute Squadron RE and 224th Parachute Field Ambulance were raised at the same time. In the meantime, 4th Parachute Brigade was formed in North Africa under the command of Brigadier John Hackett and incorporated 156th Parachute Battalion (formed in India in 1941 and initially designated 151st Parachute Battalion) together with 10th and 11th Parachute Battalions. The two latter units were established with volunteers from British units serving in the Middle East. In January of the following year, 4th Parachute Squadron RE and 133rd Parachute Field Ambulance were formed as part of the brigade.

The early part of the following year saw 1st Airborne Division departing on operations overseas. On 9 March 1943 the division, less 3rd Parachute Brigade, two battalions of 1st Airlanding Brigade and the Airborne Light Tank Squadron, was ordered to mobilise by 1 May for deployment to North Africa. It sailed from England in two convoys, 2nd Parachute Brigade landing at Oran on 26 April and 1st Airlanding Brigade a month later on 26 May. An account of the division's operations in North Africa, and thereafter in Sicily and Italy, is given in Chapter 7.

Further developments were taking place in Britain. The Airborne Forces Depot, which hitherto had existed on an unofficial basis, was formally established on 11 May as the Airborne Forces Depot & Development Centre. On 5 July, Brigadier Edward Flavell, in the initial process of forming the newly authorised 5th Parachute Brigade, assumed command of the depot and centre in his new capacity as Commander Airborne Establishments. The depot remained at Hardwick Hall while the development centre, whose role was the design and testing of equipment for airborne forces, was located at Amesbury Abbey, in Wiltshire, under the command of Lieutenant Colonel J. G. Squirrell.

On 23 April 1943 the War Office had issued authorisation for the creation of a second airborne division. This would incorporate 3rd Parachute Brigade, and two newly authorised formations: 5th Parachute Brigade and 6th Airlanding Brigade. The new grouping was designated 6th Airborne Division and its commander was Major General Richard Gale who had founded and commanded 1st Parachute Brigade before being appointed Deputy Director of Air at the War Office.

Initially, the nucleus of the new division was provided by 3rd Parachute Brigade now under the command of Brigadier James Hill, the former commanding officer of 1st Parachute Battalion. It was, however, weak in numbers, having supplied reinforcements for 1st Parachute Brigade. In late May, the brigade's strength was decreased further with the transfer of 7th Parachute Battalion to 5th Parachute Brigade. This left Hill with 8th Parachute Battalion, commanded by Lieutenant Colonel Alastair Pearson, and 9th Parachute Battalion under Lieutenant Colonel Terence Otway. In its place he would receive the 1st Canadian Parachute Battalion, which would arrive from Canada within three months.

During May, 6th Airlanding Brigade was formed under the command of Brigadier The Honourable Hugh Kindersley. It incorporated the 2nd Battalion The Oxfordshire & Buckinghamshire Light Infantry, commanded by Lieutenant Colonel Michael Roberts, the 1st

Battalion Royal Ulster Rifles under Lieutenant Colonel Jack Carson, and the 12th Battalion The Devonshire Regiment under the command of Lieutenant Colonel Dick Stephens.

5th Parachute Brigade was formed on 1 July under Brigadier Nigel Poett. In addition to 7th Parachute Battalion under Geoffrey Pine Coffin, formerly commanding officer of 3rd Parachute Battalion, it incorporated two newly raised units: 12th (Yorkshire) Parachute Battalion, formed from the 10th Battalion The Green Howards, and 13th (Lancashire) Parachute Battalion formed from the 2nd/4th Battalion The South Lancashire Regiment. These two units were commanded by Lieutenant Colonels Reggie Parker and Peter Luard respectively.

July witnessed the arrival in England of 1st Canadian Parachute Battalion, commanded by Lieutenant Colonel George Bradbrooke, which proceeded to No. 1 PTS to undergo instruction in British parachuting techniques before joining 6th Airborne Division. On 11 August, the battalion joined 3rd Parachute Brigade.

The formation of divisional units took place during the period from May to September. Among these were the division's pathfinder unit, the 22nd Independent Company, under the command of Major Francis Lennox Boyd. Like 21st Independent Company, its counterpart in 1st Airborne Division, the 22nd consisted of a headquarters and three platoons, each of which comprised one officer and thirty-two other ranks. Each platoon was made up of three sticks commanded by a sergeant or corporal. For pathfinding tasks, sticks were equipped with Eureka ground-to-air radio beacons which transmitted homing signals to Rebecca receivers fitted in aircraft carrying paratroops or towing gliders. In addition, coloured cloth panels, laid out on the ground in the form of a 'T', were used to mark drop zones during daylight. At night, battery-powered holophane lamps were used instead, an orange lamp being placed at the end of each arm of the 'T' and a green one at the base. The latter was operated by a member of the stick who signalled the DZ code letter to the approaching aircraft.

Major General Gale lost little time in raising and training his new division. Those members of parachute units not already qualified as parachutists, in particular those of 12th and 13th Parachute Battalions who had previously been ordinary infantrymen, had to undergo selection and training at Hardwick Hall and No. 1 PTS. Throughout the second half of 1943, all units in 6th Airborne Division concentrated on training at all levels, from the individual soldier through section, platoon, company, battalion, brigade and ultimately divisional levels. Training took place day and night, exercises frequently beginning with parachute drops and glider landings and nearly always ending with a twenty-mile march back to unit bases. Considerable emphasis was placed on physical fitness, with every member of the division, including its commander and his staff, marching, flying, jumping, landing and exercising. The ceaseless and intensive training programme resulted in a tremendous *esprit de corps* being generated throughout the division.

Nor was staff training ignored. Major General Gale initiated a programme of exercises and study days for his officers, all of which included problems concerning administration and air movements to train them to operate under adverse conditions. These were tailored to the types of operation with which the division was likely to be tasked in the future. Gale had studied closely the airborne operations conducted by the Germans in 1940 at Eben Emael and at the Corinth Canal in 1941.

6th Airborne Division's administrative and logistical support echelons and units also trained hard during this period. All divisional exercises included full-scale resupply by RAF and USAAF aircraft, the division's Royal Army Service Corps (RASC) units playing their part in despatching containers from aircraft as well as collecting stores from DZs and setting up supply dumps in the field. The parachute and air-landing field ambulances were also fully exercised, 'wounded' personnel undergoing evacuation, being given first aid or experiencing simulated field surgery.

By the end of 1943, the necessary results had been achieved, but only just in time. On 23 December 1943, less than eight months after its formation, 6th Airborne Division was ordered to mobilise and be prepared for operations by 1 February 1944.

In addition to the British airborne formations, a number of parachute units had also been raised from troops belonging to countries occupied by the Germans, including France, Belgium and Poland. In July 1941, a company of Free French parachutists was formed in Britain, subsequently being absorbed into the Special Air Service (SAS) Brigade with which it subsequently served in the Middle East and the Aegean. In 1943, the 1er Régiment Chasseurs Parachutistes was formed from two Free French parachute battalions in Algeria, along with the 1er Bataillon de Choc. The 2e and 3e Régiments Chasseurs Parachutistes were also formed, in Britain, and absorbed by the SAS Brigade, being designated the 3rd and 4th SAS Regiments respectively.

A Belgian Independent Parachute Company had been formed in January 1943 and incorporated into the British 8th Parachute Battalion. A year later, however, it was redesignated as the Belgian Parachute Squadron and transferred to the SAS Brigade. The largest of the Allied airborne contingents was the 1st Polish Independent Parachute Brigade, which was established in Scotland in the latter part of 1942. It initially comprised three battalions and supporting arm units, with a fourth battalion being added later.

CHAPTER SEVEN

BRITISH OPERATIONS IN NORTH AFRICA, SICILY AND SOUTHERN ITALY, 1942–3

At dawn on 10 November 1942, 3rd Parachute Battalion landed at Gibraltar. There Lieutenant Colonel Geoffrey Pine Coffin was informed that the battalion was to carry out an operation on the next day, its task being to capture an airfield at Bône, a port on the border between Tunisia and Algeria, some 250 miles east of Algiers. It was to fly early on the following morning to an airfield at Maison Blanche, near Algiers, from which the mission would be mounted.

At 4.30 a.m. on 11 November, the battalion took off from Gibraltar and flew to Maison Blanche, which it reached at 9.00 a.m. That same day, Pine Coffin was briefed by the GOC First British Army, Lieutenant General Sir Kenneth Anderson, aboard the latter's headquarters vessel in Algiers harbour. The battalion was to seize the airfield at Bône, subsequently being relieved by No. 6 Commando which would carry out a seaborne landing. Due to the lack of experience of the USAAF crews in dropping paratroops at night, however, take-off would not be until 4.30 a.m. with P–Hour (the time at which the drop would take place) being at 8.30 a.m.

The morning of 12 November found the battalion taking off as planned and arriving over its DZ at exactly 8.30 a.m. Each aircraft delivered its stick of paratroops accurately; both of the battalion's rifle companies, along with Battalion Headquarters and the Mortar Platoon, landed on or around the airfield. Casualties were light, numbering only fourteen, some breaking legs on the very hard, stony ground. There was, however, a fatality during the drop itself when one man accidentally shot himself with his Sten gun during the descent.

Unknown to Pine Coffin and his men, their arrival had been observed by a battalion of their German counterparts, the fallschirmjäger, who themselves were en route to Bône in a formation of Junkers 52 transports. Seeing that the airfield was already in Allied hands, the enemy turned around and headed back to their base at Tunis.

Shortly after 3rd Parachute Battalion seized the airfield, the Germans responded by launching an attack on it with Stuka dive-bombers, but the battalion held firm and was eventually joined by No. 6 Commando, which was followed shortly afterwards by a squadron of Spitfires to provide air support. Three days later, on 15 November, the battalion withdrew from Bône and headed west to the village of St Charles where it subsequently rendezvoused with A Company which, with the rest of 1st Parachute Brigade, had disembarked at Algiers on 13 November.

Lieutenant General Anderson's original intention had been to mount an airborne operation to seize a key road junction at Beja and the El Aouina airfield at Tunis. 1st Parachute Battalion, commanded by Lieutenant Colonel James Hill, had been allotted the task but by the time it had arrived in Algiers there were reports of large numbers of German troops, numbering some 10,000, being flown into Tunis. Anderson decided that the battalion, supported by detachments of 1st Parachute Squadron RE and 16th Parachute Field Ambulance, would be dropped at Souk el Arba to secure the crossroads there, establish contact with French forces stationed at Beja, forty miles to the north-east, and carry out harassing operations to the east.

Not least of 1st Parachute Battalion's problems in preparing for the

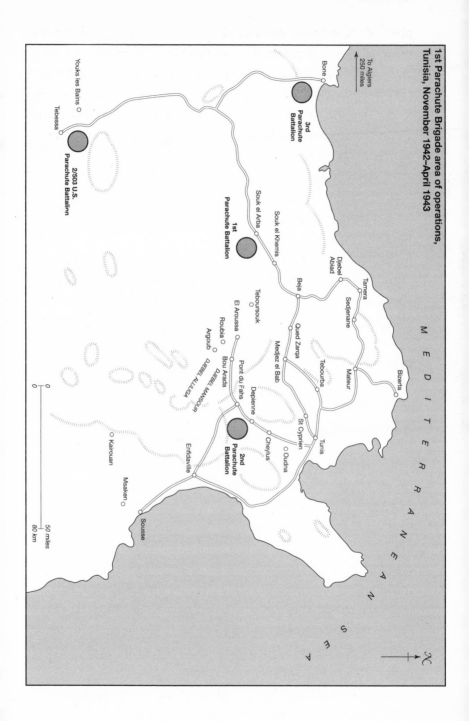

1st Parachute Brigade area of operations,
Tunisia, November 1942–April 1943

To Algiers
250 miles

Bone

3rd
Parachute
Battalion

Youks les Bains

Tebessa

2/503 U.S.
Parachute Battalion

Souk el Arba

1st
Parachute Battalion

Souk el Khemis

Djebel
Abiad

Tamera

Sedjenane

Beja

Oued Zarqa

Teboursouk

El Aroussa

Roubia

Argoub

DJEBEL MANSOUR

DJEBEL ALLILIGA

Bou Arada

Pont du Fahs

Medjez el Bab

Depienne

Tebourba

Mateur

Bizerta

St Cyprien

Cheylus

Oudna

Tunis

2nd
Parachute
Battalion

Kairouan

Enfidaville

Msaken

Sousse

M E D I T E R R A N E A N   S E A

0

0

50 miles

80 km

229

operation was insufficient time. Added to that was lack of transport because 1st Parachute Brigade had not been allowed to bring any of its own vehicles, owing to limited shipping space, this hampering the movement of equipment to the mounting airfield at Maison Blanche after it had been unloaded from the ships in Algiers harbour. Many of the stores required for the operation did not appear at the airfield until 4.30 p.m. on the afternoon of 14 November. These had to be broken down and packed into containers, while parachutes had to be unpacked from the crates used for shipment by sea and inspected by the parachute packing section of the RAF's No. 38 Wing attached to 1st Parachute Brigade.

The battalion was to be transported in C-47 Dakotas of No. 64 Troop Carrier Group of the USAAF's 51st Troop Carrier Wing. There were only thirty-two aircraft, however, and so only one of the rifle companies could be flown in the first lift. Moreover, the aircrews had no previous experience of dropping paratroops, and there were no radio communications between aircraft nor intercom facilities between pilots and despatchers. Added to these shortcomings was the absence of any charts of the area, other than French quarter-inch-to-the-mile maps designed for use by motorists, which made it highly unlikely that the aircrews would locate the dropping zones. Consequently, James Hill decided to travel in the cockpit of the aircraft flown by the commander of the 51st Troop Carrier Wing and with him select the most suitable DZ in the area of the objective. Having done so, Hill would then retire to the rear of the aircraft and jump with the other members of his stick.

1st Parachute Battalion took off for Souk el Arba, but the aircraft encountered heavy cloud and were forced to turn back, landing at Maison Blanche at 11.00 a.m. The operation was then postponed for two days. At 11.00 a.m. on 16 November, the battalion took off once again but by this time its mission had been changed: it was now to seize the town of Beja, persuade the French garrison there to join the Allied cause, and carry out probing and harassing operations. It was also to secure the area of the Souk el-Khemis–Souk el Arba plain for subsequent use as landing strips by the RAF.

The drop took place without mishap, the only fatality being a man who was strangled by one of his parachute's rigging lines which became wound round his neck. Major Sir Richard des Voeux, a liaison officer accompanying the battalion, suffered a broken leg on landing and four men were slightly wounded by an accidental discharge from a Sten gun. The principal problem was caused by local Arabs, who attempted to spirit away some of the equipment containers.

Shortly afterwards, the battalion rallied and formed up before heading off for Beja as quickly as possible. On arrival at the road junction, Hill and his men were confronted by a 3,000-strong French force of two battalions dug in and supported by machine guns. They gave the paratroops a friendly welcome, however, as did the town's mayor and local population who plied Hill and his men with copious quantities of champagne and wine.

During his negotiations with the French commander, Hill learned that the former had been threatened by the Germans with reprisals if he permitted British force to take Beja. He succeeded, however, in bluffing the Frenchman into believing that the paratroops were larger in number than was the case, and informed him that British armoured divisions were already advancing. Fortunately, the French commander believed him and agreed that his units would hand over to Hill and his men during the evening. Throughout the rest of the day, as part of the bluff designed to give the impression of a much larger force, 1st Parachute Battalion marched through Beja twice – first wearing helmets and then its maroon berets. The ruse worked and reports subsequently reached the Germans in Tunis that a large British force had occupied the town. They responded by bombing it.

Soon afterwards, Hill learned from the French that the Germans were in the habit of sending a patrol of eight armoured cars to the railway station at the village of Sidi N'Sir, which lay some twenty miles from Beja and was occupied by a company of French native infantry.

Arriving each day at around 10.00 a.m., the Germans exchanged pleas-antries with the French before returning to their base on the coast at Bizerta. Deciding to demonstrate to the enemy that they were not invincible, and to win over the French even further, Hill decided to ambush the patrol and persuaded the French to permit him to send a company through their lines to Sidi N'Sir.

The following day S Company, commanded by Major Peter Cleasby-Thompson, accompanied by a small party of sappers, was despatched to make contact with the French company commander at Sidi N'Sir and to ambush the German patrol. Having arrived at the village and received a warm welcome from the French, the company lay up for the night before setting up its ambush on the following morning. The enemy patrol, of four large armoured cars and four smaller armoured reconnaissance vehicles, duly appeared on time and drove through the ambush area and on towards Sidi N'Sir. S Company and its sapper party then proceeded to lay a necklace of No. 75 Hawkins anti-tank grenades across the road and settled down to await the Germans' return.

The ground on one side of the road consisted of a steeply rising slope; on the other there was a large bog. Cleasby-Thompson placed a 3-inch mortar on a hill near by and two Bren LMG groups in the bog. The main ambush group was positioned on the hillside some eighty yards from the road. Lieutenants Philip Mellor and Arthur Kellas, equipped with a number of Gammon bombs, were hidden in a ditch at the side of the road.

S Company did not have long to wait. The column of enemy vehicles reappeared, the company holding its fire until the grenades were detonated. As the last vehicle entered the killing area, a second necklace of Hawkins grenades was pulled on to the road behind it to block off any attempt at escape by reversing out of the ambush. The leading armoured car passed over the first necklace without exploding any of the Hawkins grenades, and disappeared from sight round the corner. The second was not so fortunate and detonated a grenade, swerving over to one side and blocking the road. S Company opened fire immediately, two of the armoured reconnaissance vehicles being destroyed and their crews killed by grenades thrown by Mellor and Kellas. Just then, the leading armoured car reappeared but was immediately disabled by a Hawkins grenade. Meanwhile, S Company's 3-inch mortar on the hill was bringing down fire on the tail of the column, forcing the remaining vehicles to move forward into the centre of the killing area. All four armoured cars were destroyed and their crews captured by the time the remainder of the enemy surrendered.

Casualties among S Company were light. Among them were Lieutenant Kellas, who had been wounded in the eye, and Company Sergeant Major Steadman. Loading the wounded on to the two armoured reconnaissance vehicles which were still intact, the company withdrew to Sidi N'Sir and returned to Beja. Keen to demonstrate the fact that the Germans were far from indefatigable, Lieutenant Colonel Hill ordered the two vehicles and the prisoners to be driven around the town. S Company's action did much to convince the French in the area to rally to the Allied cause, not least because it gave rise to the belief that the British possessed a secret anti-tank weapon capable of destroying German armour.

On 20 November, the enemy attacked the French forces at Medjez el Bab. On the previous day, at a meeting with the French divisional commander, the Germans had insisted that they be permitted to take control of the bridge there. The French, who had already been warned by Hill that any German attempt to cross the bridge would meet with strong opposition from 1st Parachute Battalion, had rejected the German demand and announced that any advance would be blocked. R Company, under Major Conron, had been deployed in support of the French and when the Germans attacked at 11.00 a.m. they met stiff resistance. Despite the French suffering heavy casualties, the enemy were beaten off and subsequent aggressive patrolling by 1st Parachute Battalion helped to prevent any attempts by the enemy to advance westwards.

Two days later, on 22 November, Hill received a report that a 300-

strong Italian force, supported by tanks, was harboured up nine miles to the north-east of Sidi N'Sir at the base of a small hill feature called Gue. He decided to attack it, and on the following night 1st Parachute Battalion moved to Sidi N'Sir where it rendezvoused with a company of French Senegalese infantry which was to be attached to it. The company was to help carry ammunition for the battalion's 3-inch mortars which, under the control of the battalion's second-in-command, Major Alastair Pearson, would bring down heavy fire as the battalion advanced on its objective. Meantime, a twenty-seven-strong detachment of sappers of 1st Parachute Squadron RE, under Captain Geary, would move round Gue and mine the road to the rear of the objective with Hawkins grenades to hinder any withdrawal or attempt at reinforcement by the enemy.

R and S Companies, accompanied by the Mortar Platoon, the French company and Battalion Headquarters, moved across country, following a railway line. Reaching its baseline location, the platoon began setting up its mortars while the sapper detachment set off on its flanking move. Just prior to H-Hour, as the two rifle companies were preparing for the assault, there were three loud explosions caused by the accidental detonation of some of the Hawkins grenades being carried by the sappers, all but two of whom were killed in the blasts.

All surprise was lost and the enemy opened fire immediately. R and S Companies put in an immediate assault with two platoons attacking the positions on the hill itself on which they encountered a mixed force of Germans and Italians. Lieutenant Colonel Hill observed that there were only three Italian light tanks on the position and, together with a small group of his men, approached them himself. Inserting the barrel of his revolver into an observation port in the nearest tank, he fired a round into the vehicle. This brought about the rapid surrender of the Italian crew and so Hill approached the second tank, knocking on its turret with his walking stick and achieving similar results. When he attempted the same technique with the third tank, however, a German crew emerged firing their personal weapons and throwing grenades from the turret. Hill was shot in the chest three times while his adjutant, Captain Miles Whitelock, was wounded by shrapnel from the grenades, the tank crew being swiftly despatched by the remainder of Hill's group.

Major Pearson assumed command of the battalion as Hill and Whitelock were evacuated on a captured enemy motorcycle combination driven slowly alongside the railway line to Beja. There they underwent treatment by the forward surgical team of 16th Parachute Field Ambulance.

Two days later, on 26 November, 1st Parachute Battalion moved to a new location ten miles south of Mateur from which it carried out a vigorous programme of patrolling during the next ten days, subsequently withdrawing to Algiers where it went into reserve.

Following its arrival in Algiers on 12 November, 2nd Parachute Battalion had been kept in reserve for a few days at Maison Blanche where it lost some of its equipment from enemy bombing. On 18 November, Headquarters 1st Parachute Brigade was ordered to drop a battalion at Sousse, on the coast sixty miles south-east of Tunis, and detailed 2nd Parachute Battalion for the task. Due to the limited number of aircraft available, however, only two companies would be flown in the first lift on the morning of 19 November, the rest of the battalion being dropped next day. The commanding officer, Lieutenant Colonel Johnny Frost, carried out an aerial reconnaissance of the area, in order to select a suitable DZ, but on his return learned that the operation had been cancelled and that his battalion was to drop instead on Enfidaville, thirty miles north-west of Sousse. Having reconnoitred another DZ, however, Frost returned to find that this operation had also been cancelled.

On 27 November, the brigade headquarters was ordered by Headquarters First British Army to place one of its battalions on standby for another operation. Once again, 2nd Parachute Battalion was tasked and that afternoon Lieutenant Colonel Frost learned that the objective was an enemy airfield at Pont du Fahs, forty miles south of Tunis, which the battalion was to attack and destroy the aircraft there. It was then to move to Depienne, twelve miles from its initial objective, and thereafter a further twenty miles to Oudna, carrying out similar tasks at both locations.

Two days later, 2nd Parachute Battalion, together with a troop of 1st Parachute Squadron RE and a section of 16th Parachute Field Ambulance, emplaned at Maison Blanche aboard Dakotas of Nos. 62 and 64 Troop Carrier Groups USAAF. Shortly before take-off, Frost was informed that the enemy aircraft at Pont de Fahs and Depienne had been removed and the battalion was to drop at Depienne instead and move to Oudna to carry out its designated task. Thereafter, it was to link up with British units at Saint Cyprien. There was no time for further aerial reconnaissance, so Frost had to rely on being able to select a suitable DZ from the lead aircraft in which he was travelling. The flight itself was unpleasant as bad weather caused considerable turbulence and many of the men fell prey to airsickness. Fortunately, as the aircraft approached Depienne, Frost saw a large expanse of open terrain suitable for use as a DZ.

The drop was unopposed but scattered, with seven casualties incurred, one of them fatal. Having rallied, the battalion set about retrieving its parachutes and containers but were hindered by local Arabs intent on stealing as much as possible. A platoon of C Company had to be left behind to guard them and to look after those injured in the drop. At 4.00 p.m. that afternoon, a patrol of three armoured cars of 56th Reconnaissance Regiment appeared on the road, heading north towards Cheylus. An hour later, it returned and reported the presence of a German roadblock four miles along the road.

Just before midnight, 2nd Parachute Battalion set off for Oudna. The going was difficult over hilly and stony terrain with rutted tracks, the troops being weighed down with equipment and ammunition. Fortunately, they were able to commandeer some mules and carts on to which they loaded their 3-inch mortars and other heavy items. By 4.30 a.m. on 30 November, the battalion had covered twelve miles and a halt was called although the bitter cold made rest virtually impossible. The march was resumed three hours later and by 11.00 a.m. the battalion had reached a position from which it could observe its objective.

At 2.30 p.m. A Company, commanded by Major Dick Ashford, advanced down into the valley towards the airfield while C Company and Battalion Headquarters moved to the left along some high ground. Suddenly, the battalion came under fire from the direction of the airfield, a few men being hit. A Company reached the objective and the cover of some nearby buildings but at that point six enemy tanks appeared and attacked the battalion, followed shortly by a number of Messerschmitt fighters and Stuka divebombers. The tanks, however, were beaten off and the air attacks proved largely ineffective owing to the paratroops' good camouflage and concealment on the scrub-covered hillside.

At last light, Frost withdrew his battalion westwards to Prise de l'Eau which offered a favourable location for a defensive position and a good supply of water from a well. There he would wait to link up with the advancing units of First British Army next morning as they headed for Tunis. The battalion, however, was exhausted and severely depleted in strength, as well as being very low on ammunition. Frost was sure that the enemy would follow up on the next day, and so he prepared an ambush on the track at the foot of the battalion's position.

Next morning, 1 December, a column of enemy armoured vehicles approached from the direction of Oudna. After a while, it halted at a range of some 2,000 yards and several vehicles detached themselves and headed rapidly along the track. Unfortunately, they surprised a small group of Frost's men filling water bottles at the well, and thus the ambush group was unable to engage them effectively, merely managing to kill the commander of the leading vehicle, which escaped. The other vehicles withdrew and rejoined the column; this then deployed and opened fire on the battalion, which replied with its 3-inch mortars. Shortly afterwards, a direct hit was scored on a vehicle and the enemy withdrew out of range.

C Company now reported that three armoured vehicles, two tanks and an armoured car, were approaching from a different direction and displaying yellow triangles, the First British Army recognition signal. Frost naturally assumed that these were the leading element of the troops with whom he was to link up, but a few minutes later received a report from C Company's commander, Major John Ross, that the vehicles were German and that three members of his company, who had gone forward to meet them in the belief that they were British, had been captured. The Germans then sent one of the captured men back, informing Frost that he was surrounded and demanding his surrender. The situation became even grimmer when a radio message was received from Headquarters First British Army, informing Frost that the advance on Tunis had been postponed.

Rejecting the German demands, Frost decided to evacuate his position immediately and move to higher ground from which the battalion would exfiltrate after last light and continue its march westwards towards the Allied lines some fifty miles away. After destroying its 3-inch mortars and radio sets, 2nd Parachute Battalion, whose ammunition and batteries were exhausted, moved off, but as it did so the enemy armour opened fire, causing a number of casualties.

The battalion climbed the high ground to the north of Prise de l'Eau but the physical effort took its toll on the heavily laden and exhausted men, who were suffering badly from thirst. Frost thus decided to call a halt and take up positions on the northern face of a hill called the Djebel Sidi Bou Hadjeba which, as luck would have it, possessed a well. The hill had two summits; B Company, commanded by Major Frank Cleaver, was positioned on the right with the remnants of C Company on the left. What remained of A Company was in reserve with Battalion Headquarters to the right and in the rear.

At about 3.00 p.m., the enemy launched an attack with light tanks and infantry mounted in armoured half-tracks. A heavy volume of artillery and mortar fire was brought to bear on the battalion and a fierce battle took place. Casualties mounted in 2nd Parachute Battalion, which had not yet managed to dig in. Among those killed were the commander of B Company, Major Cleaver, and one of C Company's platoon commanders, Lieutenant The Honourable Henry Cecil. The battalion's chaplain, Padre Macdonald, was among those wounded. At the height of the battle, enemy aircraft appeared but mistakenly fired on their own troops and halted the attack, thus providing a very welcome breathing space for Frost and his men.

By this time, it was evident to Frost that his battalion, which by then had suffered some 150 killed and wounded, could not hold on for much longer and would have to make its escape by nightfall. He decided to withdraw by companies, each heading independently for the village of Massicault. The wounded would have to be left behind in the care of Lieutenant Jock McGavin and his section of 16th Parachute Field Ambulance, protected by a platoon of B Company under Lieutenant Pat Playford.

At 6.30 p.m., after last light, the battalion left its positions and moved silently down the steep slopes of the Djebel Sidi Bou Hadjeba, each company following its own route on a compass bearing over the rough terrain. Resting for ten minutes in every hour, it moved through the moonless night until they reached the River Medjerda, where the exhausted paratroops were able to slake their raging thirsts before resuming their march westwards. During the night, elements of the battalion were lost when some men of B Company became separated from the rest and were captured after being surrounded. Others, among them Captain Ronnie Stark, avoided capture and managed to reach the British lines. C Company's commander, Major John Ross, and six of his men also made it to safety. Major Philip Teichman, the battalion's second-in-command, and Captain Jock Short, the adjutant, who were moving with a group from B Company, were ambushed. Teichman was killed while Short was wounded and taken prisoner.

Shortly before dawn on 2 December, Frost and his group, comprising Battalion Headquarters, Support Company and the sapper troop, halted in a wadi. Frost despatched a reconnaissance patrol which returned soon afterwards, having discovered an Arab farm a few minutes' march away. He and his men moved forward to the farm which offered plenty of cover in which to lie up, as well as a good supply of water. The farmer proved amenable, making the weary paratroops welcome and selling them food. Not long afterwards, it was learned that another body of men was resting in another farm near by. This proved to be A Company which immediately joined Frost's group.

Frost had learned from local Arabs that the nearest elements of First British Army were at Furna, farther to the west than he had thought. The battalion was in dire need of ammunition and equipment, and he decided that an attempt had to be made to establish contact with Headquarters First British Army to request resupply. Lieutenant Euen Charteris and two men were despatched to make their way to Furna but unfortunately they were ambushed and killed en route.

By this time Frost's group comprised some 200 men, but there was still no sign of B or C Companies. Suddenly the Arabs, who until then had been friendly and cooperative, departed in haste and it soon became apparent that enemy troops had made an appearance – indeed, they could be observed on a ridgeline a few hundred yards away. Soon, more were seen moving into positions on all sides. Fortunately, Frost and his men were well concealed and held their fire, making it more difficult for the Germans to gauge their strength.

At around 3.00 p.m. the enemy opened fire with mortars and machine guns, but the battalion was well dug in with plenty of cover being afforded by the farm buildings and thick vegetation. Two hours later, a group of enemy approached A Company's positions but were wiped out, causing the Germans to lay down even heavier fire which forced a small picquet, posted by Frost on the high ground above the farm, to withdraw to the main position.

At this juncture, Frost decided that he would make a mass breakout after last light. His entire force would concentrate at Battalion Head-quarters' location before charging the enemy positions blocking the route to the hills, thereafter reforming on the Djebel el Mengoub, a hill feature which lay on the line of march to Furna. At this point, however, the enemy mounted a heavy attack which was beaten off by

A Company, waiting until its adversaries were at close range before opening fire. Just after last light, the Germans put in another assault from the high ground above the farm, but this was also repulsed. Shortly afterwards, Frost blew the signal for the breakout on the hunting horn he always carried and he and his men, carrying their wounded, moved out with all speed. Having reached a prearranged rendezvous point, he used his horn to guide in the stragglers and eventually 110 out of the 200 men who had broken out of the farm made their way in. After waiting a short while to see if any more appeared, Frost led the remnants of his force to the Djebel el Mengoub. At 3.00 p.m. a large body of troops could be seen ahead on the same track, heading in the same direction. These turned out to be the men missing after the breakout, being led by Captain Dennis Vernon, the commander of the sapper troop.

An hour later, Frost and his men reached a farm owned by a French family who provided the exhausted troops with food. It was not long, however, before news came of the approach of enemy armoured vehicles and thus the paratroops were forced to make their escape into the nearby hills. By this time they could see the town of Medjez el Bab which, they learned from an Arab, was in the hands of the Allies. Heading towards it, they observed a troop of enemy armoured cars near a road junction ahead but shortly afterwards these moved off in the direction of Tunis and the march was resumed. Shortly afterwards, more armoured vehicles were seen in the distance but these were soon identified as American.

That afternoon, on 3 December, the remnants of 2nd Parachute Battalion made their way past French positions outside Medjez el Bab. Ten days later, they were withdrawn to Souk el Khemis to rest and reorganise. The battalion was sorely depleted, having lost sixteen officers and 250 other ranks. B and C Companies had been decimated and virtually ceased to exist. Eventually, some 200 men arrived as replacements but many of them were anti-aircraft gunners with no previous infantry experience. The battalion nevertheless took them in hand

and soon made good their deficiencies as far as infantry skills were concerned.

Some members of the battalion who had been captured eventually managed to escape and returned to the unit. One of these, Corporal McConney, was among those injured in the drop and taken prisoner. Although suffering from a dislocated shoulder, he concealed his fighting knife in his sling. Subsequently, he killed a guard before escaping and making his way back to Allied lines. Others who returned included members of B and C Companies who, having been captured, were being escorted to a prisoner-of-war cage in a convoy escorted by Italian armoured cars. They overpowered their guards and escaped, eventually reaching the safety of the Allied lines.

The Oudna operation was a disastrous episode, badly planned and based on faulty intelligence. The blame must be laid squarely on the shoulders of those at Headquarters First British Army who conceived it, including Lieutenant General Sir Kenneth Anderson himself. 2nd Parachute Battalion was committed needlessly against a target which did not exist by the time the battalion had been dropped into the area. Moreover, following the drop, little or no interest was shown by Anderson and his headquarters, nor for that matter by the battalion's parent formation, 1st Parachute Brigade. No effort was made to provide support or maintain communications, or to assist in extracting the battalion once it was evident that its task had been carried out. The fact that any elements at all of 2nd Parachute Battalion survived the operation and the subsequent fighting withdrawal was testimony to the magnificent courage of all who took part, and in particular the determination and leadership of their commanding officer.

While 2nd Parachute Battalion had been fighting its way back from Oudna, Headquarters 1st Parachute Brigade received a warning order from First British Army that it was to be deployed in the infantry role. By 11 December, with 1st and 2nd Parachute Battalions having returned to the fold, the brigade was relocated at Souk el Khemis, with No. 1 Commando and a French unit, the 2e Bataillon 9e Régiment de

Tirailleurs Algériennes, under command and had taken up positions covering Beja under command of V Corps. During this period, weather conditions deteriorated, making any major operations impossible. An attack on Tunis from Medjez, which was held by V Corps, was cancelled due to torrential rain.

On 3 January 1943 A Company 3rd Parachute Battalion, under command of 36th Infantry Brigade, took part in a night attack on an objective named Green Hill. The feature was one of two, the other being dubbed Commando Hill, which dominated the road linking the town of Sedjenane with that of Mateur. The attack itself was unsuccessful although A Company, commanded by Major Stephen Terrell, did reach the top of the hill. On the following day, two companies of 3rd Parachute Battalion were attached to two units of 36th Infantry Brigade for another attack on Green Hill: A Company to the 4th Battalion The Buffs, and B Company to a battalion of the Royal West Kent Regiment. C Company was located to the rear to prevent any attempt at infiltration by the enemy.

The assault took place just after first light, and by 10.00 a.m. the first crest had been gained. The second, however, was heavily fortified with gun emplacements, barbed wire and minefields. A Company, which was in an exposed position on the first crest and under heavy fire, called for artillery support. Unfortunately, some of the shells fell on it owing to its proximity to the objective. That evening, however, B Company succeeded temporarily in seizing the second crest. The Germans then launched two counter-attacks, the first being wiped out by heavy fire. This resulted in B Company nearly exhausting its ammunition and being driven off by the second counter-attack. That same day, 3rd Parachute Battalion was withdrawn to Souk el Khemis and then to St Charles for rest.

On 7/8 January 1st Parachute Brigade, less 2nd Parachute Battalion which was by then under command of 78th Infantry Division, returned to Algiers to prepare for an airborne operation in support of II US Corps in which it was to drop in the area of Sfax and Gabes with the aim of blocking enemy lines of communication between Tunis and Tripolitania. In the event, however, the operation was cancelled and on 14 January the brigade was placed under command of 6th Armoured Division, its headquarters being located at Bou Arada while its two battalions deployed in the area of el Aroussa. On 30 January, the brigade was transferred to the command of XIX French Corps to relieve French units being withdrawn to re-equip. Almost immediately, it was ordered to mount an attack on an important feature, the massifs of Jebel Mansour and Jebel Alliliga, the task in turn being allotted to Lieutenant Colonel Alastair Pearson's 1st Parachute Batttalion which was allocated a company of the French Foreign Legion under command and a battery of 17th Field Regiment RA in support.

The attack was to take place on the night of 2/3 February. On the night of 31 January, a large fighting patrol was despatched to probe the German positions on Djebel Mansour. Commanded by Captain Vic Coxen, it worked its way to within close distance of the summit of the massif before it was challenged. Putting in an immediate assault, Coxen and his men overran some of the enemy positions and captured fourteen Germans and a number of machine guns. Coming under fire from other enemy on the position and on Djebel Alliliga, the patrol withdrew under covering artillery fire.

On 2 February 1st Parachute Battalion, which had been relieved in its positions by the 3rd Battalion Grenadier Guards, mounted a night approach march to the Djebel Mansour. Captain Vic Coxen and a small group went ahead and laid mine-marking tape to guide the battalion to its start line. R and T Companies arrived without mishap but S Company lost its way and headed too far to the left, coming under machine-gun fire and encountering a minefield, which caused several casualties.

The remainder of the battalion crossed the start line at 5.00 a.m. As it did so, it came under heavy mortar and machine-gun fire from a German mountain battalion holding the feature but nevertheless reached its objective before first light. By this time, the enemy had withdrawn but a heavy barrage of mortar fire was brought down on 1st Parachute Battalion, being followed by a counter-attack which was beaten off. The battle continued throughout the day, with S and T companies taking part of the Djebel Alliliga for a while. At that point the battalion's Foreign Legion company and the Grenadier Guards were to have moved up to assist in occupying both features but heavy artillery fire prevented them from doing so. By this time, the battalion had suffered 105 casualties, S Company in particular having lost a large number of men after coming under fire from one particular machine-gun position. After attempting unsuccessfully to attack its second objective, the Djebel Alliliga, 1st Parachute Battalion went firm on the Djebel Mansour, and requested that the Grenadier Guards should assume the task.

At 3.00 p.m. on the following day, 4 February, a company of the Grenadiers attacked the feature and succeeded in reaching the top, by which time all of its officers had been killed or wounded, the company sergeant major assuming command. Shortly afterwards, however, the enemy struck back and drove the guardsmen off the hill, following this up with a series of counter-attacks on 1st Parachute Battalion.

At 7.00 a.m. next morning, 1st Parachute Battalion was attacked in force and came under heavy fire from the Djebel Alliliga. By this time the battalion was very low on ammunition and weak in numbers. It was decided that the Djebel Mansour was no longer tenable, and at 11.00 a.m. the battalion and the Grenadiers withdrew under cover of smokeshells fired by tanks of 26th Armoured Brigade. During the withdrawal, 3rd Parachute Battalion took up covering positions as 1st Parachute Battalion retired into reserve, having lost thirty-five killed, 132 wounded and sixteen missing.

On 4 February 2nd Parachute Battalion had found itself placed under command of 139th Infantry Brigade with the task of taking and holding a crossroads in the Ousselta Valley. On being informed that the enemy threat comprised ten battalions of infantry supported by 100 tanks, Lieutenant Colonel Johnny Frost asked what support was available to him. He was informed that no anti-tank guns could be spared, but that six tanks would be sent, albeit these would be of little use against the more powerful enemy armour. Next day, Frost and his company commanders carried out a reconnaissance of the crossroads and the area where the battalion would site its positions. As they approached in three Bren carriers, Frost suddenly noticed that the surface of the road had been disturbed and realised that it had been mined. His warning shout came too late as one of the other carriers hit a mine and was blown up, two officers in the vehicle, the commanders of A and Headquarter Company, Majors Dick Ashford and 'Dinty' Moore, being killed.

In the event, the enemy threat did not materialise and 2nd Parachute Battalion was relieved at the crossroads on 7 February, returning to 1st Parachute Brigade on the following day. Employed in an area nicknamed 'Happy Valley' where it took over from a French unit, the battalion was spread over a very wide front of three miles and found itself somewhat overstretched. It was, however, supported by several French units which included a number of anti-tank gun detachments, artillery, two squadrons of Spahis and two dismounted squadrons of Chasseurs d'Afrique.

The following two weeks were relatively quiet but on 26 February the battalion, which was well dug in and plentifully stocked with ammunition, was assailed by enemy infantry and by 9.00 a.m. was under artillery fire. C Company was attacked first but beat off the enemy without difficulty. The mixed force of German gebirgsjäger and Italian alpini mountain troops then attempted to carry out a flanking attack but soon found themselves pinned down in a gully by the artillery supporting 2nd Parachute Battalion. Frost dismounted his Spahis and moved them forward to the Djebel Salah, a feature from which the French cavalrymen were able to cover the battalion's left flank. The enemy then attacked B Company, which held the centre of the battalion's sector. Having failed to make any progress, they tried to infiltrate the large areas between the companies. There they encountered fire from the battalion's 3-inch mortars and Vickers medium machine guns (MMG) which covered the areas which the overstretched rifle companies were unable to dominate.

By last light, the battalion had broken up every assault mounted against it, suffering little loss in the process. That night, a force of two platoons under Captain Ronnie Stark swept the battalion's front, flushing out and dealing with any enemy they encountered. Just after dawn on 27 February, they reappeared with eighty prisoners. During this action, the enemy had suffered 150 casualties while 2nd Parachute Battalion had lost one man killed and two wounded. Later that morning, Frost learned that some German armour had breached the brigade's positions to the left of 2nd Parachute Battalion and had penetrated twelve miles, reaching 1st Parachute Brigade's B Echelon, from which it met stiff resistance organised by the quartermasters of the three battalions before being routed by tanks of 6th Armoured Division which appeared in support.

3rd Parachute Battalion, with 1st Parachute Squadron RE in support, had suffered the main brunt of the attack on the morning of 26 February, enemy troops having infiltrated its positions during the previous night. Savage close-quarter fighting took place within A and B Companies' areas and that of Battalion Headquarters, but eventually the enemy were forced to withdraw to a wadi where they took cover. Unfortunately for them, the battalion had registered it among its mortar DF tasks and had set up its Vickers MMGs to cover the area of terrain on the far side of it. Within an hour and a half, a heavy barrage of 3-inch mortar bombs was dropped into the wadi with unerring accuracy, while the machine guns laid down a murderous fire on the slopes on the far side. Caught in a lethal trap, the enemy suffered very heavy casualties, some 400 killed while a further 200 surrendered. 3rd Parachute Battalion, on the other hand, sustained very light losses with only two officers and twelve other ranks killed, and between thirty and forty wounded. 1st Parachute Battalion had also inflicted heavy casualties on the enemy who had found themselves being channelled by cleverly positioned barbed-wire entanglements into killing areas selected by Lieutenant Colonel Alastair Pearson.

On the night of 4 March, 1st Parachute Brigade withdrew from Bou Arada after being relieved by American troops and moved to the Beja sector. It took up positions with 1st Parachute Battalion on the right, south of the road between Tamera and Sedjenane, with 3rd Parachute Battalion on its left. Meantime, 2nd Parachute Battalion had been ordered by Headquarters 46th Infantry Division to clear any enemy from the high ground above Beja itself. Having completed this, the battalion was ordered to carry out an operation to capture a hill feature called Spion Kop. It would be supported by divisional artillery and a small composite force comprising a company of infantry and a troop of tanks. In the event, however, no artillery support was forthcoming, despite repeated calls once the battalion came under fire, and the infantry company and tanks withdrew after making contact with the enemy. As darkness fell, 2nd Parachute Battalion withdrew and next day, 7 March, rejoined 1st Parachute Brigade.

At 8.00 a.m. on the following morning, the enemy launched attacks on 1st and 2nd Parachute Battalions under cover of artillery and mortar fire. The enemy forces comprised four elements: the 7th Parachute Engineer Battalion, the 10th Panzer Grenadier Regiment, The Barenthin Regiment and The Tunisian Regiment. 1st Parachute Battalion was attacked by two companies which approached along the line of the road. S Company, commanded by Major Taffy Lloyd Jones, waited until the enemy were at a range of some 300 yards before opening fire and enfilading them. At the same time, artillery and mortar fire was brought to bear on them, inflicting some forty casualties.

2nd Parachute Battalion had meantime suffered a number of casualties and all its companies were running low on ammunition. At 10.00 a.m. the commander of A Company, Major Johnny Lane, reported over the radio that he and his men were surrounded but were holding out. During the day, enemy troops worked their way to within close range of the battalion's positions and eventually infiltrated themselves between the battalion and 1st Parachute Battalion. The adjutant, Captain Willoughby Radcliffe, was killed while leading a small mule train loaded with ammunition for A Company. The Germans also attempted to outflank 1st Parachute Brigade by moving round to its right along a ridgeline to the south. This tactic was thwarted by 2nd Parachute Battalion's MMGs, sited on a feature named Cork Wood.

By the afternoon, the enemy attack had slackened and the brigade commander decided to mount a counter-attack to drive out those enemy who had infiltrated between 1st and 2nd Parachute Battalions. This was carried out successfully by A Company 3rd Parachute Battalion, commanded by Major Stephen Terrell, which linked up with C Company 2nd Parachute Battalion once it had crossed the road. A number of prisoners were taken, including several parachute engineers. By 4.00 p.m. the enemy had been driven off, but just before dusk a flight of Stuka divebombers attacked A Company 2nd Parachute Battalion, causing a number of casualties.

During the next four days 1st Parachute Brigade, which from 10 March was augmented by a number of additional units, including 139th Infantry Brigade placed under command, was engaged in defensive operations against a powerful German formation of approximately divisional strength. Additional reinforcements, in the form of the 5th Battalion The Sherwood Foresters, also arrived and were soon committed on 12 March to an attack on Djebel Bel, the feature of high ground adjacent to 1st Parachute Battalion's positions. Supported by a company of 1st Parachute Battalion, the Sherwood Foresters were initially successful but were subsequently beaten back by a powerful enemy counter-attack, suffering heavy casualties. That evening, 1st Parachute Battalion was withdrawn into reserve.

On the next day, 14 March, 2nd Parachute Battalion came under heavy artillery fire in its positions in Cork Wood, this being followed by an enemy flanking attack which nearly succeeded before being repulsed. That evening, troops of the 10th Panzer Grenadier Regiment launched another attack on the battalion and again achieved a degree of success before being bombed accidentally by a squadron of Stukas.

The following two days passed relatively quietly, although 1st Parachute Brigade and the units under its command were subjected to bombing and some accurate shellfire. On 17 March the Germans attacked once again in force, penetrating the positions of 139th Infantry Brigade and some French units. 1st and 3rd Parachute Battalions, which by that time were in reserve, moved forward to link up with 2nd Parachute Battalion and establish a line to cover the withdrawal of 139th Infantry Brigade, No. 1 Commando and the French units. Next day, 18 March, the divisional commander ordered a withdrawal to new positions on a line running east to west at Djebel Abiad.

1st Parachute Battalion made its way back over the hills while 2nd Parachute Battalion withdrew along the bed of the Oued el Medene river. The going was difficult, the river being deep and fast-flowing. Periodically, salvoes of shells landed among the battalion and caused casualties, while enemy troops attempted to harry the rearguard. In all, losses during the withdrawal numbered two killed, eleven wounded and five missing. Eventually, the battalion was able to climb out of the river and follow a railway line to the location of its new positions on three hills dubbed 'The Pimples'. There it met the second-in-command, Major John Marshall, who had led the battalion's transport in its move by road during the withdrawal. On the evening of 20 March, the battalion retired for a rest after handing over to the 2nd/5th Battalion The Leicestershire Regiment.

There was little respite for 1st Parachute Brigade, however, as on the following night the 10th Panzer Grenadier Regiment appeared once again and attacked the largest of 'The Pimples', nicknamed 'Bowler Hat', situated on the enemy-held side of the river and overlooked on two flanks. The Leicesters were pushed off the feature and 3rd Parachute Battalion was ordered to recapture it on the next night. It failed to do so, owing to inadequate time for reconnaissance and proper planning, and the task was handed on to 1st Parachute Battalion. Concerned at the exhausted condition of his men, Lieutenant Colonel Alastair Pearson remonstrated with the commander of V Corps, Lieutenant General Sir Charles Allfrey, who was visiting the battalion at the time. A compromise was reached, with Allfrey agreeing that 1st Parachute Battalion would take the feature, thereafter handing over to 3rd Parachute Battalion which would hold it.

Pearson and his men carried out the attack at 10.30 p.m. on the night of 23 March, taking the enemy completely by surprise and catching them asleep with no sentries posted. By 3.00 a.m. on the following morning, Bowler Hat had been retaken and a considerable number of prisoners captured, these being from an infantry unit which had taken over from the 10th Panzer Grenadier Regiment during the night.

That same day, 1st Parachute Brigade received orders for an operation to be undertaken with 36th and 138th Infantry Brigades. This was the capture of the enemy positions at Tamera. 1st Parachute Brigade would be on the left, with a unit of French Goums under command and 70th Field Regiment RA in support. At 11.00 p.m. on 27 March, 1st and 3rd Parachute Battalions and the Goums crossed their start lines under cover of a heavy barrage laid down by the guns of 46th Infantry Division's artillery. 2nd Parachute Battalion meanwhile remained in its positions on Bowler Hat. As was discovered later by Lieutenant Colonel Frost when he inspected them, the enemy's defences on the high ground consisted initially of a screen of observation and machine-gun posts on the forward slopes, concentrated on the most likely approaches. These and alternative positions, sited to meet threats from different directions, were well stocked with stores and ammunition. On top of the feature were more in which there were signs marking routes to positions to the front and rear as well as to the flanks. On the reverse slope of the feature were well-constructed dug-outs equipped with radios and electric lighting, trenches, barbed-wire entanglements and minefields. Overall, the enemy positions at Tamera were formidable.

2nd Parachute Battalion's leading companies, A and B, moved

forward as quickly as possible in order to remain on schedule with the fire plan, the shells from the artillery moving ahead of them as the battalion advanced. Frost followed with a small group laying a white tape marking the axis of advance as they moved through the darkness. The going was difficult, however, and the artillery barrage had passed the crest of the feature and moved on to the reverse slopes before the battalion was ready to launch its assault. The enemy on the forward slope positions recovered as A and B Companies reached them. A Company met stiff resistance on the right while B Company, which had made better progress, encountered a minefield and came under heavy fire as it attempted to make its way round it. The company commander, Major Mickey Wardle, was wounded, together with Captain Victor Dover. Lieutenant Douglas Crawley assumed command but was also wounded shortly afterwards as B Company was making its way to rejoin the rest of the battalion which had regrouped on a false crest which in the dark had been mistaken for the top of the feature.

As dawn broke, Frost realised the situation and the battalion made haste to continue its attack. B Company, now under Captain Simpson, a sapper officer attached to the battalion, carried out a left flanking movement while A Company and the rest of the battalion remained to establish a firm base. C Company, under Major John Ross, had been in reserve and now attacked without delay, encountering stiff opposition from elements of the 7th Parachute Engineer Battalion, commanded by Major Rudolf Witzig, who counter-attacked vigorously. Captain Dicky Spender was killed thwarting an attempt by the enemy to outflank the company, killing four Germans in the process. Eventually, the company's advance was halted and Major Ross, by then the only surviving officer, and his men were forced to withdraw after taking heavy casualties. At that point Brigadier Edward Flavell despatched B Company 3rd Parachute Battalion, commanded by Major David Dobie, to help the sorely pressed 2nd Parachute Battalion. As Dobie and his men arrived, Witzig's parachute engineers launched another fierce counter-attack under cover of a heavy barrage of mortar and artillery fire which, however, proved largely ineffective. The British artillery responded and, together with 2nd Parachute Battalion's own mortars, broke up the counter-attack as it reached A Company.

B Company meanwhile had carried out its left flanking movement and proceeded to attack the 7th Parachute Engineer Battalion from the right and rear. Artillery fire was called down and this proved effective, although unfortunately some shells fell among the company itself, causing casualties. By then, 2nd Parachute Battalion numbered only some 160 all ranks and so Brigadier Flavell sent A Company 3rd Parachute Battalion to reinforce the battalion further. Lieutenant Colonel Frost then reorganised his men, forming a rifle company from the remaining elements of A, B and C Companies under Major John Ross and designating it No. 1 Company. His other two companies, redesignated Nos. 2 and 3, were those from 3rd Parachute Battalion.

At 3.00 a.m. on the following morning, 29 March, 2nd Parachute Battalion resumed its advance with No. 1 Company in the lead. Little opposition was encountered, and by the time the battalion reached its old positions in Cork Wood it had captured fifty members of The Tunisian Regiment, together with a large quantity of equipment. Having secured its objective, it sent out a number of patrols which took more prisoners.

1st Parachute Battalion meanwhile had carried out a very successful attack which went almost as planned. After a long approach march, it crossed the River Oued el Medene just as the artillery barrage started, subsequently taking its objective after a fierce fight. On the following morning, it carried out a dawn attack and almost immediately encountered some Germans who surrendered after a brief fight. Advancing into the woods on the higher part of the feature, the battalion became involved in an engagement with the Italian Bersaglieri Regiment, taking 400 of them prisoner. Moving up on the left of 2nd Parachute Battalion, Lieutenant Colonel Alastair Pearson and his men continued their advance, encountering German troops who were well dug in on the high, rocky and heavily wooded terrain. As the fighting died down at the end of the day, 1st Parachute Brigade had achieved all of its objectives and captured 770 prisoners, including 220 fallschirmjäger.

During the following two weeks, 1-14 April, the brigade encountered little sign of the enemy despite an active programme of patrolling. On the night of 14/15 April, it was relieved by the 39th Regimental Combat Team of the 9th US Infantry Division, and was withdrawn into V Corps reserve. Subsequently, it was moved to Boufarik, near Algiers where on 27 April Brigadier Edward Flavell bade farewell to his men and returned to England to take up a new appointment, being replaced by Brigadier Gerald Lathbury.

During its five months on operations in North Africa, 1st Parachute Brigade suffered losses totalling 1,700 but captured over 3,500 prisoners and inflicted more than 5,000 casualties on the enemy. Such was the standing of the British paratroops in the eyes of their German adversaries that the latter christened them Rote Teufel – Red Devils – in a reference to the maroon beret which had been adopted by all British airborne troops in mid-1942. This esteem manifested itself during the brigade's journey by rail to Boufarik. As the train carrying it slowly passed a prisoner-of-war camp, the German inmates caught sight of the maroon berets and ran from their tents to cheer the paratroops whose fighting ability had so aroused their admiration. As Major General 'Boy' Browning subsequently stated in his message of congratulations to the brigade: 'Such distinctions are seldom given in war, and then only to the finest fighting troops.'

Towards the end of April the leading elements of 1st Airborne Division, less 3rd Parachute Brigade and the Airborne Light Tank Squadron which had been transferred to the newly formed 6th Airborne Division, arrived in North Africa with 2nd Parachute Brigade landing at Oran on 26 April. On 10 May, 1st Parachute Brigade rejoined the division at Mascara where it was carrying out training. 1st Airlanding Brigade, less two of its battalions which had remained in

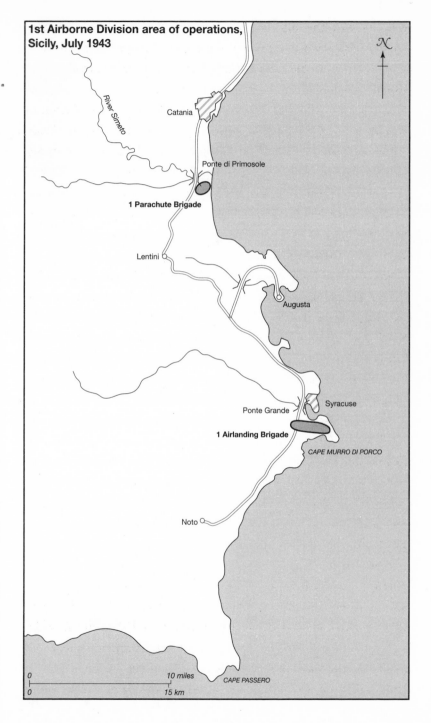

1st Airborne Division area of operations, Sicily, July 1943

N

River Simeto

Catania

Ponte di Primosole

1 Parachute Brigade

Lentini

Augusta

Ponte Grande

Syracuse

1 Airlanding Brigade

CAPE MURRO DI PORCO

Noto

| 0 | 10 miles |
| 0 | 15 km |

CAPE PASSERO

England to form the nucleus of 6th Airlanding Brigade, landed on 26 May.

During the following three weeks or so, the division trained hard with exercises being carried out up to brigade level and parachute-qualified personnel carrying out a total of 8,913 descents. From 19 June to 5 July, it moved from Mascara to Kairouan, near Sousse, where it was joined by 4th Parachute Brigade, less 11th Parachute Battalion which had remained in Palestine to carry out a number of minor airborne operations.

During March 1943, planning had begun for Operation Husky, the forthcoming Allied invasion of Sicily. 1st Airborne Division was to carry out three brigade-level airborne operations in advance of a seaborne landing by XIII Corps. It had been allotted three objectives: the Ponte Grande, a road bridge south of Syracuse, which was to be seized by 1st Airlanding Brigade; the port of Augusta, to be taken and secured by 2nd Parachute Brigade; and the Primosole Bridge, spanning the River Simeto, which was the objective of 1st Parachute Brigade. 4th Parachute Brigade was allotted the role of divisional reserve. 1st Airborne Division was placed under command of General Bernard Montgomery's Eighth Army for the operation.

On the night of 9 July, 1st Airlanding Brigade, commanded by Brigadier Philip 'Pip' Hicks, took off from Syracuse. In order to avoid enemy flak, the USAAF tug pilots had been briefed to release their gliders 3,000 yards from the Sicilian coastline. In the event, however, a combination of inexperienced pilots, adverse weather conditions and anti-aircraft fire resulted in the brigade suffering heavy losses before it had landed, seventy-eight gliders landing in the sea and others being scattered over a distance of some twenty-five miles. Only one glider reached its designated LZ. Nevertheless, a platoon of the 2nd Battalion The South Staffordshire Regiment succeeded in capturing the Ponte Grande intact.

2nd Parachute Brigade had been due to emplane at 6.45 p.m. on 10 July but this timing was put back, the brigade being informed at 9.45 p.m. that its assault on Augusta had been postponed for twenty-four hours. Next day the operation was cancelled as XIII Corps had been able to take the port and a bridge to the south. On the afternoon of 12 July, 1st Parachute Brigade, having emplaned, was ready to carry out its allotted tasks but at 5.45 p.m. the operation was postponed for twenty-four hours.

On the following night, the first aircraft took off at 7.01 p.m. and by 10.00 p.m. a total of 113 paratroop aircraft and sixteen tug-glider combinations were airborne and heading for Sicily. All went well until the aircraft neared the coastline, when anti-aircraft fire from Allied naval vessels was encountered. Some aircraft were hit while others took evasive action or returned to base. Those that reached the DZs met heavy enemy flak and searchlights. In the event only thirty-nine aircraft dropped their sticks on or near the DZs, forty-eight others dropping theirs up to half a mile away. Seventeen returned to base without dropping their troops, while twelve others were unable to find the DZs. Eleven aircraft were shot down, eight of which had dropped their sticks, and several suffered severe damage. Of the sixteen gliders carrying the brigade's heavy equipment, six landed in the sea and a further six crashed on landing. Four reached their LZs while seven others landed safely some distance away. By the time it had rallied and mustered on its DZs, 1st Parachute Brigade numbered only twelve officers and 283 other ranks, out of a total of 1,856 all ranks.

The brigade plan called for two platoons of 1st Parachute Battalion, together with 1st Parachute Squadron RE, to capture the Primosole Bridge. In the meantime, two platoons of 3rd Parachute Battalion would attack and neutralise a nearby enemy anti-aircraft battery while the rest of the battalion deployed to cover the approaches from the north. 2nd Parachute Battalion was to take the high ground to the south of the bridge, this comprising three features nicknamed 'Johnny I', 'Johnny II' and Johnny 'III'.

Lieutenant Colonel Alastair Pearson's 1st Parachute Battalion dropped at 10.30 p.m. By 2.15 a.m. on the following morning a fifty-strong group under Captain Rann had taken the Primosole Bridge and captured about fifty Italian troops. Pearson followed shortly afterwards. By 4.00 a.m., three 6-pounder guns of 1st Airlanding Anti-Tank Battery RA had arrived and the size of the force holding the bridge had increased to some 120 men. The only other support weapons available were one Vickers MMG, two 3-inch mortars and three PIATs (Projector Infantry Anti-Tank). None of the battalion's radio sets had appeared, however, and lack of communications became of increasing concern to Pearson. By first light there were some 200 men holding the bridge, including the sappers of 1st Parachute Squadron RE and two platoons of 3rd Parachute Battalion.

2nd Parachute Battalion meanwhile had been scattered in the drop, and by the time it rallied near the DZ it numbered only 170 all ranks. Among those missing were the second-in-command, Major Johnnie Lane, and the adjutant, Captain Victor Dover. Only Major Dickie Lonsdale's A Company was able to muster most of its strength. At 2.15 a.m., with no sign of the missing men, Frost, who had been injured on landing, led his much-depleted battalion towards its objectives on the high ground south of the bridge. Just over an hour later, at 3.30 a.m., the first objective had been taken and by 5.00 a.m. the battalion had occupied Johnny I, II and III and had taken 100 Italian prisoners.

3rd Parachute Battalion meantime had experienced major problems during the drop. Only one officer and three men succeeded in joining up with 1st Parachute Battalion at the Primosole Bridge at 1.30 a.m. Two and a half hours later, their number had increased to two platoons. Brigadier Lathbury and some members of his headquarters had jumped at 11.30 p.m. and found themselves on the ground after a surprisingly short descent. It transpired that the pilot of their C-47 had turned the aircraft as they were about to jump, and they had been dropped on some high ground about three miles from the DZ. Although the aircraft's altimeter had read 500 feet, Lathbury and his staff had jumped from a height of only 200 feet; fortunately they landed on soft ploughed ground.

Accompanied only by his batman, Lathbury set off towards the

Primosole Bridge, pausing en route on the DZ to collect some weapons and ammunition from a container. While doing so, they met Major David Hunter, the brigade major, and some other members of the brigade headquarters. Heading for the bridge, Lathbury and his companions shortly afterwards met Lieutenant Colonel Frost and 2nd Parachute Battalion heading for their objective.

On reaching the Primosole Bridge, Lathbury and his group started to cross but an Italian soldier threw a number of grenades, one of which wounded Lathbury. After receiving first aid he was able to continue across the bridge and by 6.30 a.m. on 14 July the brigade headquarters was established. Due to the absence of radio sets, however, communications were virtually non-existent. The sole No. 22 set which had arrived was in working order but efforts to establish radio contact with 4th Armoured Brigade, which was due to link up with the paratroops, proved unsuccessful.

The enemy, in the form of fallschirmjäger of the 4th Parachute Regiment, counter-attacked from the west at 6.30 a.m. 2nd Parachute Battalion, which had not had time to dig in, came under machine-gun and mortar fire which caused a number of casualties. A fighting patrol was despatched at 7.30 a.m. in an attempt to neutralise some enemy machine guns sited on Johnny II but was driven back by fire from armoured vehicles. At the same time, the long grass around the southernmost part of the battalion's positions caught fire, causing further problems as it created a smokescreen that concealed the enemy as they advanced to better positions, while at the same time forcing Frost's men to withdraw from their forward locations. At this point, help arrived at 7.00 a.m. in the form of Captain Vere Hodge, a forward observation officer of 1st Airlanding Light Regiment RA, and naval gunfire support. By 9.00 a.m., he had established radio contact with a Royal Navy cruiser lying offshore and shortly afterwards the first salvoes of 6-inch shells burst among the enemy. By 10.00 a.m., the German advance had been halted and 2nd Parachute Battalion was able to push its perimeter forward again. Shortly after doing so, a battery of Italian light howitzers was discovered in a valley beside Johnny I. These were swiftly appropriated by the Mortar Platoon which brought them into action against enemy positions north of the bridge, their effective fire subsequently attracting a counter-battery response from German artillery.

At 9.30 a.m. radio contact with 4th Armoured Brigade was briefly established by the brigade major who passed on the information that the Primosole Ridge had been taken intact. Before contact was lost soon afterwards, he was told that relief for the paratroops was not possible at that stage.

At 1.10 p.m. the enemy counter-attacked again, supported by artillery and aircraft in close support, with infantry advancing under cover of smoke along the axis of the road. 3rd Parachute Battalion, which by this time numbered only five officers and thirty-five other ranks, bore the brunt of this attack but held firm and by 3.00 p.m. had driven off two company attacks. The enemy then increased the pressure and by the middle of the afternoon 1st and 3rd Parachute Battalions had been forced to withdraw to the southern side of the river. Nevertheless, the Germans had been prevented from reaching the bridge.

By last light, 1st Parachute Brigade's position had become increasingly precarious. The Germans had crossed the river farther east under cover of heavy mortar and artillery fire from some self-propelled guns which had been brought up once 1st and 3rd Parachute Battalions had withdrawn to the southern bank. Lathbury and his men were under fire from the north, south and east, and it soon became plain that the situation was rapidly becoming untenable. Consequently, at 7.35 p.m., the order was given for a withdrawal in small groups to 2nd Parachute Battalion's positions. Soon afterwards, however, the leading elements of 4th Armoured Brigade, led by the 9th Battalion The Durham Light Infantry, arrived and were followed by the rest of the brigade at midnight. On the following morning, 15 July, the Durhams attacked the bridge which by then was held and defended by the enemy. The attack, carried out with support from armour and artillery, was unsuccessful and the Durhams suffered heavy casualties. They subsequently withdrew and took over 2nd Parachute Battalion's positions.

The commander of 4th Armoured Brigade announced his intention to mount another frontal assault on the bridge but was prevailed upon by Brigadier Lathbury and Lieutenant Colonel Pearson to carry out a night attack instead. Accordingly, before first light on 16 July, Pearson, accompanied by his batman and 1st Parachute Battalion's provost sergeant, led the Durhams across the river. The latter put in a successful attack and took the bridge with few casualties. At 7.00 a.m., 1st Parachute Brigade withdrew and moved by road to Syracuse. Of the twelve officers and 280 other ranks who had taken part in the Primosole Bridge operation, twenty-seven had been killed, seventy-eight wounded and several were missing.

After its withdrawal from Sicily, 1st Airborne Division was concentrated once again at its base at Sousse by 30 July. During the following month, many of the missing members of 1st Parachute Brigade reappeared, all recounting how they had been dropped up to thirty miles from the DZ. The adjutant of 2nd Parachute Battalion, Captain Victor Dover, and his stick had landed on the slopes of Mount Etna and most of them had been taken prisoner. Dover and another man avoided capture and for almost a month had made their way back to British lines while at the same time attempting to cause as much damage as possible to the enemy.

During August, all elements of 1st Airborne Division trained hard. 1st Parachute Brigade received reinforcements, all three of its battalions being brought up to full strength. At the beginning of September, the division received orders for its part in the forthcoming invasion of Italy. On 8 September, it sailed for Italy in warships of the Royal Navy's 1st Cruiser Squadron and arrived at the port of Taranto during the afternoon of 9 September, in time to see the Italian fleet sailing for Malta to surrender to the Allies. Disaster occurred, however, when HMS *Abdiel*, a fast minelayer carrying troops of 6th Parachute Battalion, struck a mine, the explosion detonating the mines in the ship's magazines and tearing her in half. Aboard the vessel were members of Battalion Headquarters, B and C Companies, the Machine Gun Platoon and the Mortar Platoon. Among the casualties were the commanding officer, Lieutenant Colonel J. A. Goodwin, Major Trefor Evans, Captains J. P. Mathias and E. D. Jones, Lieutenants E. R. Watkins, A. J. Radford and C. W. Egmore, Regimental Sergeant Major E. T. Langford, Company Sergeant Major W. J. Harris and fifty other ranks. Four officers and 150 other ranks were injured and taken to hospital. 2nd Parachute Brigade's two other battalions landed without mishap and after moving through Taranto took up positions beyond the town, 4th Parachute Battalion to the north-west and 5th Parachute Battalion to the east.

1st Parachute Brigade deployed around Taranto itself while 2nd and 4th Parachute Brigades advanced northwards, the latter taking the town of Massafra before moving on to the village of Mottala. During the early part of the advance the commander of 1st Airborne Division, Major General G. F. Hopkinson, was killed by fire from an enemy machine gun while observing 10th Parachute Battalion in action against fallschirmjäger of the 1st Parachute Division at Castellaneta. The commander of 2nd Parachute Brigade, Brigadier Eric Down, immediately assumed charge of the division, being replaced in command of his brigade by Brigadier Charles Pritchard.

By 13 September, 1st Airborne Division had advanced some twenty miles from Taranto. 10th and 156th Parachute Battalions attacked the town of Goia del Colle, which was an important objective because of the airfield there. Some very aggressive patrolling on the part of both battalions and a night attack carried out by 10th Parachute Battalion persuaded the enemy to evacuate the area on the night of 16 September. Two days later the airfield had been taken over by the RAF which flew in six squadrons of Hurricanes to provide close air support.

On 19 September 4th Parachute Brigade, which had been relieved by 1st Airlanding Brigade, withdrew to Taranto after nine days of what was described as 'interesting but not heavy fighting'. During this period,

1st Parachute Brigade had remained in divisional reserve, eventually moving up to Castellaneto and the Altamura from where it withdrew at the end of September.

In the early part of October, a small group of eight men of 2nd Parachute Battalion, under Captain 'Tim' Timothy', was dropped into an area north of Pescara. Its mission was to make contact with escaped Allied prisoners-of-war, many of whom were known to be roaming the countryside. Timothy and his men were then to guide them to RV points on the coast, manned by patrols of the Special Air Service (SAS), from which they would be evacuated by the Royal Navy.

On landing, Timothy became separated from the rest of his stick but moved to his allotted area, carrying out his task alone. Eventually, he encountered a sergeant from 2nd Parachute Battalion who had been captured in North Africa, and between them the pair assembled a group of some 400 prisoners and led them to an RV where they made contact with the SAS patrol manning it. Shortly afterwards, however, as the boats were approaching the shore, firing broke out near by. In the ensuing confusion, only forty men managed to escape, Timothy among them.

In late October, 1st Airborne Division learned that it was to be withdrawn to England, less 2nd Parachute Brigade which was to remain in Italy as an independent brigade group. In November the division sailed from Taranto, its personnel and equipment at its base at Sousse embarking at the same time.

At this point, mention must be made of 11th Parachute Battalion which had remained in Palestine when the rest of 4th Parachute Brigade moved to North Africa to join 1st Airborne Division. Commanded by Lieutenant Colonel R. M. C. Thomas, the battalion was formed in March 1943 at Shallufa, on the Suez Canal, and thereafter accompanied 4th Parachute Brigade to Ramat David in Palestine where it completed its formation and underwent parachute training.

On 15 September 1943 A Company, together with a section of the Machine Gun Platoon and another of the Mortar Platoon, took off from Cyprus and was dropped on the island of Kos, the DZ being marked by men of the Special Boat Squadron, which was operating in the Aegean. At the time, plans already were under way for the invasion of Greece, and it was recognised by the Allies that the capture of the island of Rhodes would be vital for its success. It was also appreciated that the seizure of Kos, with its airfield, would make Rhodes indefensible for the Germans.

After the drop, A Company received a warm welcome from the 4,000-strong Italian garrison. It remained on Kos for ten days during which it came under attack from enemy aircraft operating with virtual impunity because of the inability of the RAF to provide air cover. On 25 September, the company was withdrawn by air and during the following month 11th Parachute Battalion sailed for England to rejoin 4th Parachute Brigade.

CHAPTER EIGHT

US AIRBORNE FORCES: OPERATIONS IN NORTH AFRICA, SICILY AND ITALY, 1942–3

As already recounted in previous chapters, the first three years of the Second World War witnessed the development and use of airborne forces by Germany, the Soviet Union and Britain. The United States, having experimented with parachute troops in 1928, had thereafter showed no further interest for the following ten years until 1938, when the subject of airborne warfare was included in the curriculum of the US Army's Command & General Staff School at Fort Leavenworth, Kansas.

The successful use of airborne troops by Germany in Norway and the Low Countries in 1940 further rekindled interest, albeit limited, in the US Army which on 25 June of that year formed a fifty-strong parachute platoon, commanded by 1st Lieutenant William T. Ryder, as a trials unit at the Infantry School at Fort Benning, Georgia. On 16 August the platoon carried out its first parachute descent, Ryder and Private William N. King becoming the first ever US Army paratroopers to do so.

Three months later the US Army's first airborne unit, the 1st Parachute Battalion, was activated on 16 September 1940 under command of Lieutenant Colonel William M. 'Bud' Miley, subsequently being redesignated the 501st Parachute Battalion. On 10 March 1941, the first airborne formation was activated at Fort Benning as the Provisional Parachute Group under the command of Lieutenant Colonel William C. Lee, in July assuming the functions of a regimental headquarters. A month later, the US Army's Parachute School was activated at Fort Benning, Georgia.

At this time, the standard personnel parachute in service with the US Army was the T-5, a static line-operated 28-foot canopy which had an opening time of approximately three seconds, permitting its use at low level. A major deficiency of the T-5, however, was the design of its harness, which was fastened by three snap-hooks, making it difficult for a parachutist to rid himself of the harness swiftly after landing. It was not until December 1943 that a quick release mechanism was forthcoming, being based on a modified design developed in 1941 by the Irving Parachute Company, and was fitted to the T-5 which was then redesignated the T-7. The latter, however, did not enter service until several months later.

From the very start, a shortage of parachutes was a major problem facing the Parachute School and continued to be so throughout 1941 and most of 1942. Although 3,750 T-5s were ordered for delivery in July 1941 from one supplier, these had not appeared by October. Likewise, another manufacturer had been contracted to supply at the rate of 200 parachutes per week up until September of that year, and 100 per week thereafter, but also failed to deliver. Such was the shortage of parachutes that in late 1941 the stock of T-5s numbered only 208. By May 1942, the Parachute School's requirement was for 8,654 parachutes and this appeared to be met by plans to purchase from June onwards at the rate of 8,500 per month, sufficient to train six parachute infantry regiments. Reality was somewhat different, however, for on 1 July it was revealed that only 3,000 T-5s had been delivered and that others would become available at the rate of only 1,000 per week for the following two months.

July 1941 saw the formation of the US Army's first airlanding unit – the 550th Infantry Airborne Battalion – under Lieutenant Colonel Harris M. Melaskey, in the Panama Canal Zone. Shortly afterwards, it was joined by Company C 501st Parachute Infantry Battalion which had just completed its parachute training at Fort Benning.

Consideration was now given to the question of which element of the US Army would exercise control over the new airborne arm. In the latter part of 1941, the War Department proposed that all airborne forces should come under the Air Support Command of the US Army Air Force (USAAF). Others suggested that a special command be created, incorporating airborne forces and air transport assets. Eventually, the Airborne Command was activated on 21 March 1942 as an element of the Army Ground Forces (AGF), the latter having been created twelve days earlier on 9 March by the Chief of Staff of the US Army, General George C. Marshall, to supervise the formation of 100 divisions as part of the rapid expansion of the army. The Provisional Parachute Group was redesignated Headquarters Airborne Command with the newly promoted Colonel William C. Lee appointed as its commander. The following month, the headquarters moved from Fort Benning to Fort Bragg, North Carolina, and in May the Parachute School at Fort Benning was placed under its command.

During the first six months of 1942, the US Army's fledgling airborne forces grew apace with the activation by Headquarters Airborne Command of the 501st, 502nd and 503rd Parachute Infantry Regiments, the nuclei for which were provided by the 501st Parachute Infantry Battalion, and another airlanding unit in the form of the 88th Infantry Airborne Battalion.

Air transport support for US airborne forces was provided by the USAAF's 1st Troop Carrier Command which was formed in June 1942 with its headquarters located at Stout Field, Indianapolis. Its role was the training of air transport units whose primary mission was to 'provide transportation for parachute troops, airborne infantry and glider units'. Operational training of aircrews was to take place at three USAAF bases at Sedalia in Missouri, Ardmore in Oklahoma, and Alliance in Nebraska. Troop carrier units would also be based at Pope Field, at Fort Bragg, North Carolina, and Lawson Field, at Fort Benning, those at the latter to support the requirements of the Parachute School. In addition, a new airfield, dedicated to the training of airborne forces, was constructed during 1942 at Laurinburg, North Carolina.

The workhorse of such units was the C-47 Skytrain (designated the Dakota in Britain), the military variant of the Douglas DC-3 airliner, which was in service with American airlines. Unlike the converted bombers used by the RAF to drop paratroops and tow gliders, the C-47 featured a door in the port side of the fuselage through which parachutists made their exits or supplies were despatched. The C-47, however, possessed a payload of only 5,000–6,000 pounds, being able to accommodate a stick of eighteen fully equipped paratroops. In June 1942, a larger aircraft appeared in the form of the Curtiss C-46 Commando, which possessed a payload of 10,500 pounds and a range of 1,000 miles. Tests revealed, however, that it did not out-perform the C-47 in many other aspects and therefore the C-47 would remain the principal aircraft used by troop carrier units for the delivery of airborne forces throughout the Second World War. Initially, the 1st Troop Carrier Command's aircraft establishment was laid down as being approximately 600 C-47s and 2,000 gliders, but on formation it possessed only fifty-six C-47s and full ground equipment for four squadrons, with further partial equipment for twenty-seven more. An additional 597 C-47s, however, were scheduled for delivery between April and December 1942.

Like their British counterparts, US airborne forces suffered from problems caused by a serious shortage of aircraft for parachute training and would continue to do so until early 1944. The situation was not helped by the commanding general of Army Ground Forces, Lieutenant General Lesley J. McNair, whose top priority was ground combat training and who was of the opinion that airborne troops needed only one flight in an aircraft or glider prior to commitment on operations. Far from supporting requests for the numbers of aircraft stipulated by the

Airborne Command, he believed that these could be reduced and training requirements still be met. The situation was exacerbated by the despatch of troop carrier formations overseas. In June 1942, the 60th Troop Carrier Group was moved to England as part of the Eighth Air Force, being joined in August by the 64th, the two units taking with them a total of 103 C-47s. By November, the 62nd Troop Carrier Group had been sent to the Twelfth Air Force in North Africa and the 316th to the Ninth Air Force in the Middle East. In addition, in May 1942, the United States supplied 197 C-47s to Britain and thirty-one to China. Such diversion of troop carrier formation and aircraft assets inevitably had an adverse effect on the training of US airborne forces during the critical early stages of their formation.

Similarly, a shortage of gliders also hampered the training of pilots and the US Army's newly formed airlanding units. Only ninety were allocated in August 1942 for instructing pilots and 165 for training troops; this was against a requirement for 500, sufficient for training the gliderborne elements of an airborne division, stated by Army Ground Forces.

The standard glider developed for use by US airborne forces was the CG-4A Waco, whose airframe comprised a tubular steel frame and plywood floor covered with a fabric skin. Flown by a crew of two pilots, it possessed a maximum payload capacity of 3,750 pounds and could accommodate fifteen fully equipped troops or one jeep. Design of the aircraft was such that the entire forward section could be swung upwards to facilitate loading and unloading. Orders were placed with fifteen factories for a total of 5,290 Wacos, with production beginning in June 1942 and delivery scheduled to be complete by June 1943. By April 1942, however, it became apparent that gliders would not be coming off the production lines in sufficient quantities until August or September 1943.

For one particular US airborne unit, baptism of fire was not long in coming. In June 1942, the 2nd Battalion 503rd Parachute Infantry Regiment, commanded by Lieutenant Colonel Edson D. Raff, arrived in England for attachment to the 1st Airborne Division. Shortly after its arrival, the unit was redesignated the 509th Parachute Infantry Battalion. As recounted in Chapter 6, in September 1942 the decision had been taken to include an airborne unit among the Allied forces being despatched from Britain to take part in Operation Torch, the forthcoming campaign in North Africa. Initially, only the 509th was detailed for the task but, following Major General 'Boy' Browning's argument that one battalion would be insufficient, the British 1st Parachute Brigade had also been allotted to the forces in North Africa under the command of the Supreme Allied Commander, General Dwight Eisenhower.

At 9.30 p.m. on the night of 7 November, the 509th Parachute Infantry Battalion took off from two airfields in southern England in thirty-nine C-47s of the 60th Troop Carrier Group. Flying 1,500 miles non-stop to Algeria, it would drop on the airfields at Tafaraoui and La Senia, both situated near Oran, and seize them. In the event that it received a signal from Gibraltar while en route, informing it that the reception would be friendly, the battalion would carry out an airlanding operation instead. It had prepared itself well for the operation, officers and men studying maps, air photographs and scale models of its two objectives, and conducting a number of exercises and rehearsals.

Unfortunately, the same could hardly be said for the air crews who had not taken part in the training, some of the navigators having arrived only just prior to the operation and several of the pilots having no experience of formation flying at night. All went well initially, the thirty-nine aircraft maintaining good formation until they reached Spain and the onset of darkness and deteriorating weather conditions, including fog. The situation was exacerbated by the absence of homing signals from an Allied warship stationed twenty-five miles off the coast of Algeria and from an agent positioned in the area of Tafaraoui – it was subsequently discovered that the vessel had been transmitting on the wrong frequency and the agent had switched off his set at 1.00 a.m. in the belief that the operation had been aborted.

By first light on the following day, 8 November, the aircraft were scattered from Spanish Morocco to east of Oran but six nevertheless succeeded in locating their objective, eventually being followed by others as they found their respective bearings. Three aircraft dropped their sticks on an area of high ground to the north of the Sebkra, a dried-up lake some thirty miles west of Tarafaoui, while others landed on the lake bed itself. Among those dropped was Lieutenant Colonel Raff who suffered a hard landing, cracking three ribs.

By 9.00 a.m. some 300 members of the 509th Parachute Infantry Battalion were assembled in the area of the lake. Three of the aircraft still had sufficient fuel to reach Tarafaoui and took off from the lake, carrying their sticks, while the remainder of the battalion began heading for their objective on foot. Shortly afterwards, however, the three C-47s were attacked by enemy fighters and forced down, suffering two crew members killed. Casualties among their passengers numbered three paratroopers killed and fifteen wounded. The survivors set off for Tarafaoui on foot, arriving there at first light on 9 November to find the airfield in the hands of an American armoured unit. A convoy was despatched immediately to meet those members of the battalion marching from the Sebkra, returning with them later that day, whereupon the 509th took over responsibility for the defence of the airfield.

At La Senia, meanwhile, C-47s arriving to drop their sticks found the airfield being attacked by Allied bombers. Elsewhere, three aircraft landed in Spanish Morocco, their crews and passengers being interned, while another suffered engine trouble and was forced to land at Gibraltar. One landed to the south-east of Oran while two others touched down in French Morocco but were released, arriving at La Senia on the following day.

The 509th Parachute Infantry Battalion was then moved to the airfield at Maison Blanche, Algiers, where on the night of 14 November it received orders to carry out an operation at dawn next day. This was to capture an airfield at Youks-les-Bains which, situated near Tebessa on the border with neighbouring Tunisia, held important stocks of fuel. Such was the haste with which the operation was mounted that there was no time for reconnaissance, no maps or aerial photographs were available and no detailed orders given to Lieutenant Colonel Raff.

The battalion took off in thirty-three C-47s and arrived over the objective at 10.30 a.m., not knowing whether the French forces holding the airport would prove friendly or hostile. The aircraft dropped their sticks directly on to the airfield, the battalion landing among positions held by a French unit, the 3rd Regiment of Zouaves, who fortunately did not open fire and thus enabled Raff and his men to take the airfield unopposed. Company D immediately dug in around the airfield while Company E was despatched by Raff with all haste to secure the airfield at Tebessa, some nine miles away. Soon after it had done so, again meeting no opposition, it shot down a German transport aircraft attempting to land.

A week later, the 509th was reinforced by an American tank destroyer company and a unit of British sappers with whom the battalion began carrying out sorties across the border into Tunisia, attacking German and Italian forces in the area of Gafsa. These actions played a major part in protecting the Allied flank during the advance east towards Tunis.

At the end of December 1942, the battalion was given another, smaller mission to blow up a major railway bridge situated six miles to the north of El Djem, in Tunisia. A detachment of thirty men, commanded by Lieutenant Dan Deleo and including two Free French paratroopers who spoke Arabic, and six demolitions specialists, was dropped from three Dakotas at 10.20 p.m. on the night of 26 December. Unfortunately, the drop was inaccurate and Deleo and his men landed some distance away from their intended DZ. Throughout the rest of that night they searched in vain for their objective but were unable to locate it, albeit they found the railway line. On the following day they observed German patrols searching the area and, having destroyed the line in a number of places, split up into small groups and began heading for the

Allied positions which lay seventy miles to the west. Most were taken prisoner en route, only Lieutenant Deleo, three of his men and the two Free French paratroopers avoiding capture and reaching safety approximately a month later.

During the next six months, from January to June 1943, the 509th Parachute Infantry Battalion remained in North Africa where it trained in preparation for the forthcoming Allied invasion of Sicily.

In the United States, meanwhile, July 1942 saw the creation at Camp Claiborne, near Alexandria in Louisiana, of the US Army's first airborne formation. This was the 82nd Airborne Division, formed from the 82nd Motorised Infantry Division (dubbed the 'All Americans'), commanded by Brigadier General Matthew B. Ridgway. The official establishment for this new type of formation was laid down as being: one parachute infantry regiment of three battalions and two glider infantry regiments of two battalions each; divisional artillery, an engineer battalion, and signals, medical and quartermaster companies, with total divisional strength being 504 officers and 8,321 other ranks. Accordingly, the division incorporated: the 504th Parachute Infantry Regiment under Colonel Theodore L. Dunn (subsequently replaced by Colonel Reuben H. Tucker); the 325th Glider Infantry Regiment, commanded by Colonel Claudius S. Easley (subsequently replaced by Colonel Harry L. Lewis); and the 326th Glider Infantry Regiment under Colonel Stuart Cutler.

Under Brigadier General Joseph M. Swing (subsequently replaced by Brigadier General Maxwell D. Taylor), the divisional artillery comprised three units: the 376th Parachute Field Artillery Battalion, commanded by Lieutenant Colonel Paul E. Wright (later replaced by Lieutenant Wilbur M. Griffith); and the 319th and 320th Glider Field Artillery Battalions under Lieutenant Colonels William H. Bertsch and Francis A. March respectively (the latter subsequently succeeded by Lieutenant Colonel Paul E. Wright). The 376th and 319th were each equipped with twelve 75mm pack howitzers while the 320th was equipped with twelve M-3 105mm howitzers, a short-range version of the US Army's standard M-1 fitted with a shortened barrel and lightweight carriage, enabling it to be flown in a CG-4A Waco glider. The 320th was also equipped with twelve M-1 howitzers which would replace the M-3s once the division's seaborne 'tail' linked up with it after an airborne landing. In addition to these battalions, the divisional artillery also incorporated an anti-aircraft/anti-tank unit in the form of the 80th Airborne Anti-Aircraft Battalion. Commanded by Lieutenant Colonel Whitfield Jack, it comprised three anti-aircraft batteries, each equipped with twelve .50 calibre heavy machine guns, and three anti-tank batteries, each with eight 57mm anti-tank guns.

Activation of the 16,000-strong 82nd Airborne Division took place on 15 August 1942. On that day, however, the newly promoted Major General Ridgway announced that it was to be divided into two, one half to become another airborne formation designated the 101st Airborne Division. Commanded by Brigadier General William C. Lee and also activated on 15 August, the 101st mirrored the 82nd in its establishment and incorporated: the 502nd Parachute Infantry Regiment, commanded by Colonel George P. Howell; the 327th Glider Infantry Regiment under Colonel George Wear; and the 401st Glider Infantry Regiment, commanded by Colonel Joseph H. Harper, this being formed from a battalion each of the 325th and 326th Glider Infantry Regiments.

In September 1942, the 82nd moved to Fort Bragg, North Carolina, being replaced at Camp Claiborne by the 101st. There it continued to train hard during the following months. In early February 1943, Major General Ridgway learned that the division was to receive its baptism of fire by taking part in Operation Husky, the Allied invasion of Sicily. At that time Husky was scheduled to take place on 10 June and thus Ridgway had only 120 days to prepare his division for battle and move it from the United States to North Africa from where the operation would be launched. A major problem now arose when it became apparent that there would be insufficient gliders to transport the division's two glider infantry regiments from North Africa to Sicily. The decision was therefore taken to substitute a second parachute infantry regiment for one of the glider regiments and accordingly, on

12 February, the 326th Glider Infantry Regiment left the division. It was replaced by the 505th Parachute Infantry Regiment, commanded by Colonel James M. Gavin, which brought with it the 456th Parachute Artillery Battalion under Lieutenant Colonel Harrison B. Harden.

On 29 April 1943, the division left the United States and travelled by sea to Casablanca in Morocco from where it moved by train 400 miles east to a camp near Oudja. During the following weeks, it trained intensively in preparation for its role in the forthcoming operation.

The plan for the invasion of Sicily was for General Sir Bernard Montgomery's British Eighth Army and the US Seventh Army, commanded by Lieutenant General George S. Patton, to land on the south-east coast of the island along a 100-mile stretch from Cap Murro di Porco, around the south-eastern end of the island and west to Licata. As already recounted, 1st Airborne Division was to land south of Syracuse and seize various objectives. While it did so, elements of the 82nd Airborne Division were to drop to the rear of Gela and block any movements by enemy reinforcements against the beachheads, thus facilitating the advance of the US 1st Infantry Division following the landings.

With only 250 C-47s available, however, the 82nd's contribution to Husky had to be limited to a parachute regimental combat team comprising a parachute infantry regiment, a battalion of artillery and engineer, signals and medical detachments. The task was given to Colonel James Gavin and his 505th Parachute Regimental Combat Team reinforced by the 3rd Battalion 504th Parachute Infantry Regiment, two batteries of the 456th Parachute Field Artillery Battalion, Company B 307th Airborne Engineer Battalion, signals and medical detachments, and forward air control and naval gunfire support parties. A 2,000-strong force of reinforcements, in the form of the 504th Parachute Regimental Combat Team (less the 3rd Battalion), would be dropped on the following night.

Air transport for the two lifts was to be provided by 250 C-47s of the 52nd Troop Carrier Wing, comprising the 61st, 313th and 314th

Troop Carrier Groups, which would be based on a number of airfields around Oudja. Construction of the fields, however, was behind schedule and they were not completed until 25 May, two weeks after the division landed. Moreover, the arrival of the aircraft, their crews and support personnel was also delayed and it was not until 1 June that the 52nd Troop Carrier Wing was ready to begin intensive training with the division. Even then, high winds of over thirty miles per hour made parachute training very difficult and these, combined with hard rocky DZs, resulted in so many injuries that at one point Major General Ridgway was forced to halt temporarily any further drops, devoting the time instead to rehearsing his men in their respective tasks. This was done with the use of full-size replicas of the 505th Parachute Regimental Combat Team's main objective: a complex of sixteen concrete pillboxes and blockhouses located between Gela and Niscemi controlling the approach road leading into Gela from the north-east. During this period, two drops were carried out at night. The first, by the 505th, resulted in men being scattered and a number of casualties. The second, by the 504th, was conducted with only the first two men in each stick actually jumping from the aircraft; all landed safely on the DZ and the drop was considered a qualified success.

The 52nd Troop Carrier Wing, meanwhile, was training its aircrews in night formation flying and navigation. It soon became apparent that with landmarks invisible in darkness, the pilots would experience difficulty in locating the DZs. This gave rise in the 82nd Airborne Division to the concept of pathfinders equipped with lights and homing beacons, but there was insufficient time to develop and perfect it in time. Prior to the operation, however, Colonel Gavin, accompanied by two of his battalion commanders and three officers of the 52nd Troop Carrier Wing, carried out an aerial reconnaissance of Sicily on the night of 9/10 June. There was sufficient moonlight to enable them to see all the navigational way points and the main features and landmarks on the terrain below, these being clearly recognisable from aerial photographs studied beforehand.

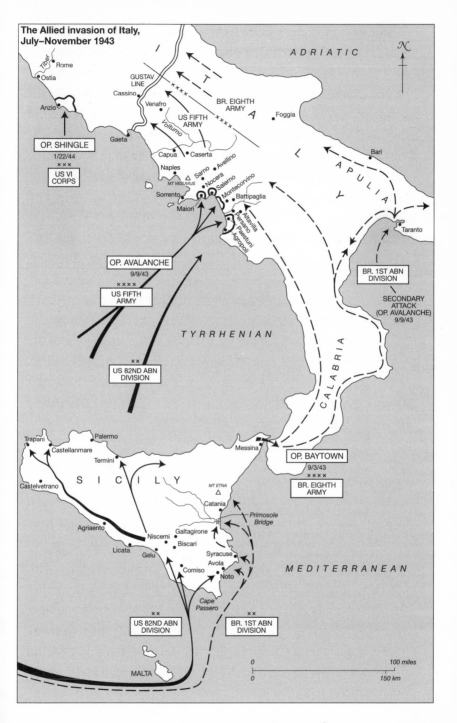

The Allied invasion of Italy, July–November 1943

OP. SHINGLE
1/22/44
×××
US VI CORPS

GUSTAV LINE

OP. AVALANCHE
9/9/43
××××
US FIFTH ARMY

US 82ND ABN DIVISION

BR. EIGHTH ARMY

US FIFTH ARMY

BR. 1ST ABN DIVISION

SECONDARY ATTACK (OP. AVALANCHE)
9/9/43

OP. BAYTOWN
9/3/43
××××
BR. EIGHTH ARMY

US 82ND ABN DIVISION

BR. 1ST ABN DIVISION

ADRIATIC

TYRRHENIAN

MEDITERRANEAN

SICILY

CALABRIA

APULIA

ITALY

MALTA

Rome
Ostia
Tiber
Anzio
Cassino
Venafro
Gaeta
Capua
Caserta
Naples
MT VESUVIUS
Sorrento
Maiori
Sarno
Nocera
Salerno
Avellino
Montecorvino
Battipaglia
Altavilla
Persano
Paestuni
Agropoli
Foggia
Bari
Taranto
Voltuno
Palermo
Castellanmare
Termini
Trapani
Castelvetrano
Agriaento
Licata
Niscemi
Biscari
Gelu
Comiso
Galtagirone
Messina
MT ETNA
Catania
Primosole Bridge
Syracuse
Avola
Noto
Cape Passero

0   100 miles
0   150 km

277

Around 21 June, the 82nd Airborne Division, along with the British 1st Airborne Division, travelled by road and train to a staging area at Kairouan, in Tunisia, arriving three days later. There they remained, living in conditions of great discomfort because of the extreme heat, for the next sixteen days.

On 9 July, D-Day, the Allied seaborne invasion force headed for Sicily and the landing beaches on the island's southern coast. Weather conditions were far from ideal with strong north-westerly winds blowing and the sea becoming increasingly heavy. Aboard the USS *Monrovia*, the attack transport which was the fleet's flagship, Ridgway was growing increasingly concerned about the wind, which soon would be too strong for parachuting.

At 10.00 p.m. that night, before last light, the 505th Parachute Regimental Combat Team started to emplane aboard its 226 aircraft. As dusk began to fall, the leading C-47s began taking off and, forming into Vs, headed for Sicily. Keeping low to avoid detection by enemy radar, at times below 500 feet, they flew east while forming into five serials flying ten minutes apart with the 61st Troop Carrier Group in the lead, followed by the 314th, 313th, 316th and 64th respectively. In all, the column of aircraft stretched over a distance of some 100 miles.

The thirty-nine C-47s comprising the 61st Troop Carrier Group serial, and carrying Lieutenant Colonel Charles Kouns's 3rd Battalion 504th Parachute Regimental Combat Team, located the main waypoint during this 185 mile-long leg over the sea: the island of Malta, from which aerial beacons were flashing. Turning left, it found Sicily and headed west, but by the time it located the DZ to the north of Gela it had lost all but nine of its aircraft. Some 100 men were dropped, the majority landing within two miles of the DZ, but the remainder were scattered by the high wind, a large number suffering injuries. The remaining thirty aircraft dropped their sticks over the southern part of the island, some landing behind enemy lines.

Flying in behind the 61st Troop Carrier Group came the serial of the 314th, bringing in Lieutenant Colonel Edward Krause's 3rd Battalion

505th Parachute Regimental Combat Team. Several aircraft, carrying the battalion's Company I, located the DZ and dropped their sticks accurately, the company landing together and thereafter being able to operate as a cohesive unit. Others failed to drop their sticks, turning south before making another approach, while a few dropped their sticks within three miles of the DZ. The majority, however, delivered theirs fifteen miles away to the east, in the area of Vittoria.

Next came the 313th Troop Carrier Group serial bringing in the 1st Battalion of the 505th, commanded by Lieutenant Colonel Arthur F. Gorham. During the early stage of the flight, several of its aircraft had found themselves being blown off course and one squadron had missed Malta by a distance of twenty miles. Another had realised its error and rectified it, locating Sicily and dropping Gorham and some of his men about two miles from the DZ. Of the fifty-three C-47s in the serial, however, twenty-three found themselves completely lost and dropped their sticks, comprising 400 men of the battalion, fifty miles away to the east in the British Eighth Army's sector.

Flying in the leading C-47 of the 316th Troop Carrier Group was Colonel James Gavin. This serial became hopelessly lost before finally locating Sicily. Even when it did so, it found itself too far to the east, making landfall in the area of Syracuse where three aircraft, believing themselves to be over Gela, dropped their sticks over sixty-five miles from the DZ. The remainder of the serial proceeded to drop their sticks randomly over the south-east of Sicily. Gavin himself landed thirty miles to the south-east of the DZ.

The final serial, of the 64th Troop Carrier Group, was alone in remaining in formation throughout the flight. Despite missing Malta, it managed to locate Sicily but thereafter came under enemy anti-aircraft fire. Nevertheless, it maintained formation and dropped Lieutenant Colonel Mark J. Alexander's 2nd Battalion of the 505th in textbook fashion. Unfortunately, the battalion landed badly scattered twenty-five miles to the south-east of the DZ.

The morning of 10 July therefore found the 505th Parachute Regimental Combat Team scattered far and wide. Many of the 3rd Battalion of the 504th were taken prisoner, among them the commanding officer, Lieutenant Colonel Charles Kouns, but one group of twenty-four men took up a position at Castel Nocera, on a road two miles east of the battalion's DZ, and soon found itself in action against an enemy force advancing south towards Gela. Next day, other members of the battalion appeared, bringing the group's strength to some 100 men and enabling it to hold out against further attacks, thereby denying the Germans the use of the road and blocking their counter-attacks against the landings.

Elsewhere, other elements of the 3rd Battalion of the 504th found themselves two miles to the north-west of Biscari. Lieutenant Peter J. Eaton assembled a force of thirty-six men and set off to the north-west along a road towards Niscemi, picking up other men as he proceeded, so that by the following morning, 10 July, his force was fifty strong. At midday, he and his men encountered two Italian vehicles towing anti-tank guns, and approaching from the direction of Niscemi. These were ambushed, Eaton and his men then digging in both guns and mining the road. When a battalion of German infantry, supported by a single tank, appeared, it was engaged by the paratroops who swiftly destroyed the tank and scattered the infantry.

Elements of the 1st Battalion of the 505th were also in action. Most of the battalion had been dropped sixty-five miles east of its DZ at Noto, in the British Eighth Army's sector. Lieutenant Colonel Arthur Gorham, however, landed only a few miles from the DZ and by first light on 10 July he and the commander of Company A, Captain Edwin M. Sayre, had collected almost 100 men and established a position on a hillside overlooking the main Niscemi–Gela road. At 7.00 a.m., a column of German armour was observed heading south along the road, comprising units of General Paul Conrath's Hermann Göring Division on their way to launch a counter-attack against the Allied beachheads.

Gorham and his men opened fire at close range, using their 'bazooka' shoulder-fired anti-tank rocket launchers to knock out two tanks and seriously damage two others. They then engaged two companies of infantry advancing across open ground, annihilating both, and pushed back the entire force. Gorham then regrouped and set off to take the 505th Parachute Regimental Combat Team's main objective, the complex of pillboxes and blockhouses situated further along the road. Launching their attack, by 10.45 a.m. Gorham and his men had overrun the Italian garrison manning the complex and occupied it just as a second German column of four tanks and infantry appeared. Firing from the shelter of the pillboxes and blockhouses, the paratroops brought heavy fire on the column, which withdrew.

An hour and a half later, patrols of the 16th Infantry Regiment of the US 1st Infantry Division, advancing up the road from the beachhead at Gela, linked up with Gorham and his men. Gorham, having made radio contact with Ridgway in the 1st Infantry Division's command post, reported that the 505th's main objective had been taken and that he was moving north with the 16th Infantry.

The 2nd Battalion of the 505th had meantime been dropped twenty-five miles to the south-east of the DZ, in the area of Santa Croce Camerina, where it encountered a large complex of pillboxes manned by Italian troops. The commanding officer, Lieutenant Colonel Mark Alexander, soon rounded up the majority of his battalion and mounted a series of attacks on the complex, which was taken by first light. He then proceeded to attack Santa Croce Camerina itself, taking the town not long before the arrival of troops of the US 45th Infantry Division.

Soon after landing thirty miles to the south-east of the DZ, Colonel James Gavin encountered two members of his staff, and assembled a group of several of his men. Despite a leg injury, he set off swiftly to the north-west, from where the sound of firing could be heard and the flash of explosions observed on the horizon. Just after first light, however, he and his companions met a force of Italians who opened fire, killing one of Gavin's men and forcing the remainder to take cover in a ditch where they were subjected to a barrage of mortar fire. Pinned down there throughout that day, 10 July, it was not until after last light that Gavin and his group were able to resume their march north-westwards; eventually they made contact with a standing patrol of the 45th Infantry Division from whom they were able to determine their location before moving on without stopping throughout that second night.

During the night of 10/11 July, the Germans launched major counter-attacks. Elements of the Hermann Göring Division advanced anew in two columns on the beachheads at Gela and Scoglitti while in the west of the island the 15th Panzer Division moved eastwards to join the fray. Meantime, the German OKW ordered the immediate transfer from France to Sicily of the 1st Parachute Division and the 29th Panzer Grenadier Division from southern Italy.

On the morning of 11 July Gorham and his 100-strong band of the 1st Battalion of the 505th were confronted by elements of the Hermann Göring Division's left-hand column: a battalion of panzer grenadiers supported by twenty tanks which seemed impervious to the shoulder-fired bazookas which were the paratroopers' only anti-tank weapons, their rockets merely bouncing off the thick frontal armour. Gorham, personally knocked out two tanks with a bazooka from a flank before being killed by fire from a third, this feat of great gallantry subsequently resulting in his being awarded posthumously the Distinguished Service Cross.

The Hermann Göring Division right-hand column's counter-attacks were supported heavily by air strikes on the beachheads and at one point the column advanced as far as the outskirts of Gela. There the leading armoured elements encountered the veterans of the US 1st Infantry Division who halted the enemy tanks and infantry with the assistance of well-aimed supporting fire from the 6-inch guns of Allied warships out to sea.

The left-hand column of the Hermann Göring Division, meanwhile, was advancing on Biscari and the beachhead of the US 45th Infantry Division. As mentioned above, the latter had broken out of its beachhead and, having linked up with the 2nd Battalion 505th Parachute

Regimental Combat Team at Santa Croce Camerina, was advancing on Vittoria. Accompanying the column of tanks and panzer grenadier infantry was General Fridolin von Senger, the senior German commander in Sicily, who realised that by swinging east he could split the 45th Infantry Division in two and destroy it. When his advance elements were only two miles from the coast, he therefore ordered them to turn eastwards and head for a feature named Biazza Ridge.

It was at that point that Colonel James Gavin arrived on the ridge where he found a 250-strong contingent of the 3rd Battalion of the 505th under its commanding officer, Lieutenant Colonel Edward C. Krause. Suspecting that the Germans were heading for the feature, Gavin continued moving west to reconnoitre, taking with him a platoon of B Company 307th Airborne Engineer Battalion under Lieutenant Benjamin L. Wechsler. Shortly afterwards, however, he and his men encountered the leading elements of von Senger's column and came under heavy fire, which wounded Wechsler. Gavin immediately called forward Lieutenant Colonel Krause and his men, and a fierce battle began with the paratroops sustaining a heavy bombardment of artillery and mortar fire as they frantically dug in on the ridge. Gavin's men suffered heavy casualties but nevertheless maintained their tenacious grip on the ridge, only later in the day receiving support from some 75mm pack howitzers of the 456th Parachute Field Artillery Battalion, most of which had also been dropped wide of the designated DZ. Subsequently, reinforcements arrived in the form of a battalion of the 45th Infantry Division, followed by some artillery, but it was naval gunfire support which appeared to break the back of the German assault. Called in by a naval gunfire liaison officer (NGLO), heavy fire from the 6-inch and 5-inch guns of a number of cruisers and destroyers impacted accurately on the German forward positions.

The end eventually came just before last light on 11 July when Gavin launched a counter-attack, leading his men in a headlong charge down from the ridge into the German positions and routing the enemy, capturing a large quantity of heavy weapons and ammunition in the process. This resounding defeat at Biazza Ridge was a major setback for General Conrath who, becoming become anxious about his right-hand column at Gela, ordered it to break off its counter-attacks on the Gela beachhead and withdraw immediately.

In the meantime, Major General Ridgway had received orders from Headquarters US Seventh Army to deploy the 504th Parachute Regi-mental Combat Team which was standing by at its mounting airfield in North Africa, waiting for the order to emplane. At 7.00 p.m. on the evening of 11 July, 144 C-47s of the 52nd Troop Carrier Wing began taking off with the 1st and 2nd Battalions of the 504th, the 376th Parachute Field Artillery Battalion and a company of the 307th Airborne Engineer Battalion aboard. Weather conditions were good and, having formed up into their 'V of Vs', the aircraft headed eastwards for Malta from where they turned in the direction of Sicily, making landfall near Cape Passero. In order to avoid the beachhead at Gela, they flew inland during the last leg of the flight to the designated DZ, an abandoned airfield at Farello three miles to the east of Gela. Strenuous efforts had been made to warn all Allied warships and anti-aircraft units of the time of arrival of the aircraft.

At 10.40 p.m. precisely, the leading C-47s arrived over the DZ and began dropping their sticks. On the DZ below were Ridgway and members of his staff, watching as the leading elements of the 504th floated down in the moonlit sky. All appeared to be going well with the drop until suddenly an anti-aircraft gun opened fire somewhere in the beachhead or offshore. Others followed suit until it appeared that every anti-aircraft weapon in the area was firing at the C-47s. The slow-flying aircraft made easy targets and sixty out of 144 were hit, twenty-three of them going down in flames. Of those, six crashed before their sticks could jump clear. Others took immediate evasive action, dropping their sticks where they could before making good their escape, while eight aircraft aborted the drop and flew home with their sticks. Large numbers of the 504th were wounded when their aircraft came under fire or were injured during the drop, some landing behind German lines while others found themselves in the US 45th Infantry Division's area.

Flying in the leading C-47 of the third serial was the commander of the 504th, Colonel Reuben H. Tucker. The aircraft was hit and, unable to locate the DZ, flew over the beachhead area of the US 1st Infantry Division. Tucker ordered the pilot to head west to find a recognisable landmark before making another run in over Gela. Again the aircraft came under heavy fire as Tucker and the members of his stick made their exit, landing not far from five American tanks engaging the aircraft with their cupola-mounted .50 heavy machine guns; these were only silenced when Tucker ran across and ordered them to cease firing. By that time, the C-47 had sustained over a thousand direct hits but succeeded in returning to North Africa. Another C-47, carrying members of Tucker's headquarters, crashed before its fifteen-strong stick could jump. Miraculously, all survived although eleven of them were injured.

By the early morning of 12 July, only some 400 men of the 1st and 2nd Battalions of the 504th, out of a total of 1,600 men, had reached their objectives, which nevertheless were taken and secured. Casualties from the anti-aircraft fire numbered approximately 229, comprising eighty-one killed, 132 wounded and sixteen missing. The 52nd Troop Carrier Wing aircrews lost sixty killed and thirty wounded. The unit suffering particularly heavy casualties was the 376th Parachute Field Artillery Battalion as half of the aircraft shot down had been carrying its Battery C.

By last light on 13 July, 3,024 of the 5,037 paratroops dropped on Operation Husky had reappeared and reported to their units. The remainder, 1,424 in all, by then had been listed as killed, wounded or missing, a twenty-seven per cent casualty rate for the 82nd Airborne Division in this, its baptism of fire.

On 16 July, the remainder of the 82nd Airborne Division was airlifted from North Africa to Sicily. Three days later, the division headed north-westwards as part of an ad hoc corps formed by the US Seventh Army to clear the enemy from the western part of Sicily, this comprising: the 3rd Infantry Division, 2nd Armoured Division, a regiment of the 9th Infantry Division, the 504th and 505th Parachute Regimental Combat Teams, and two ranger battalions.

The division had been given two objectives: the towns of Castellammare and Trapani, situated on the westernmost end of Sicily. These were allotted to the 504th and 505th respectively. Travelling in trucks, the 505th reached the outskirts of Trapani on the late afternoon of 23 July but found the road blocked and sown with mines. No sooner had the leading vehicles halted than they came under fire from Italian artillery. The pack howitzers of the 456th Parachute Field Artillery Battalion responded and an artillery duel ensued before a truce was called. Ridgway, who had accompanied the 505th during its advance, despatched Captain Alfred W. Ireland, the executive officer of the 1st Battalion of the 505th, in a jeep flying a white flag to the headquarters of Trapani's 5,000-strong garrison to demand its surrender. The Italian commander, Admiral Giuseppe Manfredi, and members of his staff returned with Ireland to Ridgway's headquarters and that night Trapani and its garrison surrendered to the 505th.

On the following day, the 504th Parachute Regimental Combat Team took Castellammare while the Sicilian capital, Palermo, fell unopposed to the 2nd Armoured Division, albeit units of the 82nd Airborne Division and other US troops had arrived some hours beforehand.

Inevitably, in the aftermath of Operation Husky, to which a total of 9,163 airborne troops had been committed, there was severe criticism. Major General Joseph M. Swing, the US airborne adviser on the Allied staff, gave five principal reasons for the unsatisfactory results achieved: insufficient planning beforehand of the coordination of routes with all forces in the weeks preceding the operation; the lack of training of pilots and the complicated routes, both factors resulting in the inability of the troop carrier formations to follow the routes designated; the unfortunate coincidence which led to the enemy carrying out a bombing raid just prior to the arrival of the reinforcements on the night of 11 July; the inflexibility of the policy adopted by Allied naval forces with regard to the engagement of aircraft coming within range at night, irrespective of whether or not they were displaying recognition signals; and the failure of commanders of Allied ground forces to brief properly the commanders of their anti-aircraft units on the expected arrival of the transport aircraft formations.

Additional censure came from General Sir Bernard Montgomery, commander of the British Eighth Army, who wrote at the time that the British glider and parachute operations on Sicily had failed due to the fact that:

> The pilots of the aircraft were completely untrained in navigation, and were frightened off their job by flak. The big lesson is that we must not be dependent on American transport aircraft, with pilots that are inexperienced in operational flying; our airborne troops are too good and too scarce to be wasted.

Following Husky, he issued an order cancelling all further British airborne operations in the Italian theatre.

A similar view was expressed by Major General 'Boy' Browning:

> In spite of the clear weather, suitable moon, the existence of Malta as a checkpoint only 70 miles from Sicily and the latter's very obvious and easily recognisable coastline, the navigation by the troop carrier aircrews was bad.
>
> The troops, comprising both British and American airborne divisions, are of a very high quality and their training takes time and is expensive. They are given important tasks which may acutely affect the operations as a whole. It is essential both from the operational and moral point of view that energetic steps be taken to improve greatly on the aircrews' performance up to date.
>
> Intensive training in low flying navigation by night, especially over coast lines, must be organised and carried on continuously. This must form part of the aircrews' training before they reach a theatre of war and the standard must be set very high.

Major General Ridgway was critical of both his own division and the aircrews, stating in the weeks following the operation:

> Both the 82nd Airborne Division and the North African Air Force Troop Carrier Command are today at airborne training levels below combat requirements and were unprepared to conduct with reasonable chances of success night operations, either glider or parachute, employing forces the size of regimental combat teams.

Ridgway saw, however, that important lessons could be drawn from Operation HUSKY for the future, summing them up as follows:

> Night operations offer greater chance of success but with far greater dispersion upon dropping, and greater loss from fire of own forces, both ground and sea. If employed, training under one commander must be intensified, and no operation attempted unless results of training indicate probability of success.
>
> Routes over enemy territory should be selected based on best obtainable intelligence, so as to pass over or near the minimum of anti-aircraft ground defenses. If these defenses are at all strong, they must be neutralised or that route abandoned.
>
> Daylight operations, without ruinous losses, will be practicable only with adequate air support against both hostile ground and air resistance.
>
> Under limitations as to types and quantities of available aircraft, the employment of airborne divisions in airborne operations is not warranted, since it results in their piecemeal use against minor objectives.
>
> A limited number of these divisions, properly trained, should be available against their need in such time as the strategic situation in the European theater opens up sufficiently to justify their use as divisions in support of other forces against larger objectives, or in the final exploitation stage, as Axis opposition crumbles.
>
> Until that time, the airborne divisions should be organized,

equipped, and trained to operate as light infantry divisions, and should be used in combat for short periods to give them essential battle experience. Following this, except for such brief repetitions as may be necessary, they should be held out of action, awaiting airborne employment as divisions.

The 505th Parachute Regimental Combat Team nevertheless was subsequently credited with achieving much in the face of considerable difficulties. Lieutenant General Patton later stated that the US Seventh Army's successful landings and advance inland could not have been achieved without the assistance of the airborne troops. Furthermore, one individual who considered the airborne operation to have been a success was none other than General Kurt Student, commander of the Luftwaffe's XI Air Corps, who emphasised that the Hermann Göring Division would have repulsed the leading seaborne elements of the landing force had it not been hindered continually by the airborne troops. Indeed, Student went so far as to attribute the entire success of Operation Husky to the delaying of the German reserves until such time as the Allied landing forces were of sufficient strength to resist enemy counter-attacks. Moreover, he was joined in this view by Field Marshal Albrecht Kesselring, commander-in-chief of German forces in the Italian theatre.

Following Husky, Ridgway was keen that his division should undergo a period of intensive training with the troop carrier units supporting it to avoid repetition of the problems encountered during the operation. By late July, however, when plans were being laid for the invasion of Italy itself, there were indications that the 82nd Airborne Division would be committed to action once again. On 29 July, Ridgway learned that the commander of the US Fifth Army, Lieutenant General Mark Clark, was indeed intending to use the division in an operation that would see it being inserted ahead of an amphibious landing at Salerno. The division's tasks would be to capture the towns of Nocera and Sarno, situated a short distance to the north of the Sorrento mountain range, and to prevent the Hermann Göring and 15th Panzer Grenadier Divisions, both of which had been withdrawn from Sicily and were now based in the area of Naples, from using the mountain passes to head for the Allied beachhead at Salerno. At the same time, the division was to assist the breakout towards Naples of the British X Corps, commanded by Lieutenant General Sir Richard McCreery, via those same passes.

Ridgway judged that the operation, scheduled for 9 September, was possible albeit risky, and would require his division to undergo three weeks of intensive training with the troop carrier units involved. The division, whose two parachute regimental combat teams were distributed in six locations throughout Sicily, would have to be rapidly reassembled and returned as soon as possible to Tunisia to rejoin the rest of the division. Moreover, both combat teams urgently needed re-equipping as large amounts of weapons and equipment had been lost or worn out during the fighting in Sicily.

On 12 August, by which time orders had still not been issued for the return of the 504th and 505th Parachute Regimental Combat Teams to Tunisia, Ridgway was informed that the mission had been cancelled. Six days later, however, he received orders for another operation in which the division would seize the city of Capua, situated at a key point on the River Volturno approximately forty miles inland from Salerno and some eighteen miles to the north of Naples. The two parachute regimental combat teams would be dropped, while artillery, heavy weapons and ammunition were to be landed by glider. The 325th Glider Infantry Regiment meanwhile would carry out an amphibious landing at the estuary of the Volturno and advance fifteen miles inland to link up with the two parachute formations.

That same day saw receipt of orders for the 504th and 505th Parachute Regimental Combat Teams to be moved to Tunisia, but by this time less than three weeks were available to carry out the much-needed combined training with the troop carrier units of the 51st and 52nd Troop Carrier Wings. On 20 and 21 August, the 504th and 505th were flown from airfields at Borizzo and Castelvetrano to Tunisia where the following week was spent in preparing for the operation. On 25 August, Colonel Harry L. Lewis's 325th Glider Infantry Regiment moved to Bizerte, on the north-easternmost tip of Tunisia, to begin training with the landing craft which would transport it and Ridgway's tactical headquarters to the mouth of the Volturno. Shortly afterwards, however, it was discovered that the estuary contained a number of obstacles in the form of shoals and reefs, which made a landing there landing difficult if not impossible, and the amphibious element of the operation was thus cancelled. This in turn meant that resupply of the two parachute regimental combat teams would have to be conducted by air. The total daily required quantity of supplies was estimated at being approximately 175 tons, requiring 145 C-47s which would have to fly unescorted at night over hostile territory, locate the marked DZs and drop their cargoes before running the gauntlet once again of enemy aircraft and anti-aircraft defences.

With these factors in mind, Ridgway harboured deep reservations about the operation and voiced them to General Mark Clark. The latter agreed to reduce the size of the airborne force to two battalions which would drop in the area of Capua, carrying sufficient supplies for five days by which time it was expected that the British 46th Infantry Division would have linked up with them. In addition to this airborne operation, another would be mounted by the 509th Parachute Infantry Battalion which would be dropped on the night of 15 September in the area of the town of Avellino, well behind enemy lines. Situated on a main German line of communication and supply, along which enemy reinforcements would be despatched to Salerno, the town was also the location of a major German logistical support centre.

In Italy, meanwhile, the regime of Benito Mussolini had been toppled, the fascist dictator being removed from power on 24 July by King Victor Emmanuel III and subsequently placed under arrest. It was replaced by a government under Marshal Pietro Badoglio, who autho-rised an emissary, Giuseppe Castellano, to conduct negotiations for an armistice with the Allies. During these, Castellano raised the idea of an Allied airborne assault on Rome to occupy the capital and protect it, the king and his new government from German retribution following the announcement of the armistice. On 1 September, as part of these negotiations, the Supreme Allied Commander, General Eisenhower, gave his approval for such an operation, allotted to the 82nd Airborne Division which by this time had returned to its base in Tunisia.

On the following day, Ridgway and key members of his staff were summoned to the headquarters of General Alexander's 15th Army Group situated at Cassibile, to the south of Syracuse on the east coast of Sicily, to be briefed on the forthcoming operation. The plan called for the entire 82nd Airborne Division initially to be airlifted back to Sicily from Tunisia. Thereafter, on the night of 8 September, the 504th and 505th Parachute Regimental Combat Teams would be dropped on three airfields to the north and east of Rome, the 325th Glider Infantry Regiment and the rest of the division being airlanded during the following nights as Rome was beyond glider-towing range from Sicily.

Ridgway's reaction to the plan was to declare it a 'hare-brained scheme'. Not only would it take at least two days to fly his division from North Africa to Sicily, but the very limited timeframe meant that his troops would have to emplane fully equipped for the operation in Tunisia and remain aboard the aircraft while they were refuelled and prepared for the flight to Rome. This would inevitably result in their being exhausted by the time they carried out the drop. Furthermore, Operation Husky had demonstrated only too clearly the deficiencies in aircrew night-navigation capabilities and there had been no opportunity since then to remedy them. In addition, the distance between Sicily and Rome was beyond the range of the majority of fighter aircraft; the C-47s would have to fly unescorted on the approach to Rome itself, over the area occupied by the 2nd Parachute Division, known to be well equipped with 88mm anti-aircraft guns that would find the slow-flying transports easy targets. The airlifts bringing in the rest of the division on the second and successive nights would be extremely hazardous undertakings and could result in the 504th and 505th Parachute Regimental Combat Teams being cut off completely without reinforcement and resupply.

Added to these doubts was the question as to whether the five Italian divisions stationed in the area of Rome could be relied upon to remain loyal to the new government and assist in protecting the city against any German counter-attack, particularly as it was known that the Germans had already relieved them of much of their heavy weapons, ammunition and transport. Lastly, Ridgway raised the possibility of the Germans responding to the Allied landings by withdrawing their six divisions in southern Italy to the River Volturno or Rome and the 82nd Airborne Division thus finding itself trapped behind a powerful force.

Having been assured by Eisenhower's Chief of Staff, Lieutenant General Walter Bedell Smith, that an airborne force would drop on Rome, protecting the king and his government from any German attempt to take over the city, Castellano signed the armistice document on the evening of 3 September. During the following ten hours, he was closeted with Ridgway and his senior staff as they produced detailed plans for the operation. Despite his assurances that Italian divisions would hold the airfields, that Italian anti-aircraft units would not open fire on the approaching aircraft, and that there would be sufficient transport to move the two parachute regimental combat teams from the airfields, Ridgway and his senior officers still harboured serious doubts. These were strengthened when Castellano admitted that large numbers of Italian and German anti-aircraft guns were sited along the proposed approach route, following the south bank of the River Tiber, and in the area of the two best airfields.

This information prompted the planners to select two alternative airfields situated twenty-five miles north-west of Rome, at Furbara and Cerveteri, close to the Mediterranean coast in an area held only by Italian forces. Not only would they be easier for the aircraft to locate, but should the 504th and 505th Parachute Regimental Combat Teams find themselves in trouble, they could withdraw to the coast to be evacuated by sea. Even this alternative plan did not assuage Ridgway's fears and he felt sufficiently strongly to communicate them to General Alexander, who made light of them and insisted that the operation should proceed. He did, however, agree that the initial drop force could be reduced to one parachute regimental combat team, less one battalion.

On 4 September, the plan for the operation was finalized and the task allotted to the 504th Parachute Regimental Combat Team, less its 3rd Battalion, which would drop on to the airfields at Furbara and Cerveteri on the evening of 8 September and thereafter head for Rome. On the following night, the 505th Parachute Regimental Combat Team would drop on to airfields near the capital at Guidonia, Littorio and Centocelle, the 325th Glider Infantry Regiment being airlanded on the night of 10 September. A further modification to the plan came next day when it was agreed that a small amphibious support force, comprising an artillery battalion, three anti-aircraft artillery batteries, two platoons of anti-tank guns and a company of infantry would be landed on the estuary of the Tiber.

On 4 September the 82nd Airborne Division began moving from Tunisia to Sicily in aircraft of the 51st and 52nd Troop Carrier Wings, the entire airlift being scheduled to be complete by 7 September. At the same time, the divisional command post moved from Bizerte, on the north-easternmost tip of Tunisia, to Licata, on the south coast of Sicily.

Such was Ridgway's remaining scepticism about the operation, however, that on 7 September he despatched Brigadier General Maxwell D. Taylor, commander of the 82nd Airborne Division's artillery, in great secrecy to Rome to determine the situation there and to assess the true extent of Italian support for the operation. Accompanied by Colonel William T. Gardiner, intelligence officer of the 51st Troop Carrier Wing, Taylor was landed on the Italian coast and taken to Rome and the home of Marshal Pietro Badoglio; here, during the following twenty-four hours, Taylor and Gardiner attended meetings with Italian senior officers and Badoglio himself. All were pessimistic about the chances of success, pointing to the fact that the Germans were increasing the strength of their forces in the area of Rome which included the 12,000-strong 2nd Parachute Division and the 3rd Panzer Grenadier Division, numbering 24,000 men supported by 200 tanks. Moreover, Badoglio, believing that the Allied landings would not take place for some days, was unwilling to announce the armistice, which at this stage was still being kept secret. Even when told by Taylor that they were imminent, he was unwilling to proceed with the announcement, insisting that the Allies had to carry out amphibious landings in force near Rome before carrying out the airborne operation on the capital itself.

On 8 September, now convinced that the operation was impossible, Taylor transmitted his findings, and the information about Badoglio's unwillingness to announce the armistice, by radio to Eisenhower's headquarters. The latter's response was to suspend the operation but by the time the information reached the 82nd Airborne Division's command post at Licata, the leading sixty-two C-47s were beginning to taxi to their take-off positions. Fortunately, Eisenhower had despatched a member of his staff, Brigadier General Lyman L. Lemnitzer, by air to Licata, and his aircraft landed just in time for him to inform Ridgway of the operation's postponement. Later that evening, it was officially cancelled.

The night of 8/9 September saw Lieutenant General Mark Clark's US Fifth Army, comprising the British X Corps and the US VI Corps, landing at Salerno, with the main beachhead area stretching over a front of twenty miles between Salerno and Paestum. A further five miles was added after a landing carried out at Maiori by a force of British commandos and US rangers tasked with seizing the passes leading through the Sorrento mountains to Nocera.

Among the 170,000-strong landing force the news of the Italian armistice had induced a mood of complacency that was rudely shattered by the hot reception accorded them by the 16th Panzer Division, dug in on the hills dominating the beachhead and strongly supported by the Luftwaffe, which attacked in strength. Despite stiff resistance which pinned down one of its regimental combat teams, the US 36th Infantry

Division succeeded in landing and pushing inland, taking Capaccio and the areas of high ground dominating it. The British X Corps also advanced several miles but stiff opposition from the Germans prevented it from taking three initial objectives: the harbour at Salerno, the town of Battipaglia and an airfield at Montecorvino.

The Germans reacted to the landing by reinforcing the 16th Panzer Division, despatching from Naples the Hermann Göring Division and the 15th Panzer Grenadier Division, and the 3rd Panzer Grenadier Division from Rome. From the south came the 26th Panzer and 29th Panzer Grenadier Divisions, falling back in good order in the face of the British Eighth Army which on 9 September had landed at Taranto and whose advance was being slowed by minefields, blown bridges and demolished roads. These formations were joined by elements of other divisions including the 1st Parachute Division, transferred from the east coast.

In Sicily, meanwhile, the 82nd Airborne Division was preparing for its next task: the drop on Capua by two battalions of Colonel James Gavin's 505th Parachute Regimental Combat Team, this plan having been resurrected after the cancellation of the drop on Rome. The first call came on 12 September when Major General Ridgway received orders to despatch a force to Salerno by sea. The task was given to Colonel Harry L. Lewis's 325th Glider Infantry Regiment which had already undergone amphibious warfare training and whose two battalions would be reinforced by the 3rd Battalion of the 504th Parachute Regimental Combat Team. Lewis and his force embarked aboard nine landing craft infantry (LCI) at Licata on the night of 13 September and sailed for Palermo, from where it would head under escort for Salerno.

The German counter-attacks on the beachhead reached a crescendo on 12 September, being concentrated at the boundary between the British X and US VI Corps where a gap had been plugged earlier with the insertion of two regimental combat teams of the US 45th Division. The Allied units suffered very heavy casualties and the situation was saved only by the relentless and accurate naval gunfire support by US warships offshore. In response to Lieutenant General Mark Clark's request for reinforcements, General Eisenhower allotted him the US 3rd Infantry Division, based in Sicily, and the US 1st Armoured and 34th Infantry Divisions, both in North Africa, but it would take several days for them to be moved by sea to Salerno.

Time was running out. Clark, needing to reinforce his beachhead as a matter of urgency, turned to the 82nd Airborne Division. On the afternoon of 13 September, he sent a member of his staff to Sicily with written orders for the division to carry out a drop into the beachhead area that night. As Gavin's 505th Parachute Regimental Combat Team was already committed to the Capua operation, Colonel Reuben H. Tucker's 504th, less its 3rd Battalion which was with the 325th Glider Infantry Regiment en route by sea to Salerno, was tasked with the beachhead drop.

Seven hours after Ridgway had received Clark's orders, three C-47s, carrying a fifty-strong pathfinder force, took off from Sicily and headed through the night towards Salerno, arriving there minutes after a German air raid. The pathfinders were dropped accurately on the DZ, which had been marked with a 'T' made from tins filled with petrol ignited as the aircraft made their final approach, and lost little time in setting up their Eureka transmitters and other equipment. At 11.26 p.m., the leading elements of the main lift arrived over the DZ with the 2nd Battalion of the 504th, commanded by Lieutenant Colonel Daniel W. Danielson, jumping from thirty-six C-47s of the 313th Troop Carrier group flying at an altitude of 800 feet. The drop went well and the majority of the battalion landed within 200 yards of the DZ, the others within a mile.

Matters had not gone so smoothly for Lieutenant Colonel Warren R. Williams's 1st Battalion, reinforced by Company C 307th Airborne Engineer Battalion. Most of the battalion had emplaned in forty-five aircraft of the 61st Troop Carrier Group, four of which were forced to abort prior to take-off. The remaining forty-one subsequently took off but did not arrive over the DZ until 1.30 a.m. on 14 September. Three of the four flights dropped their sticks on, or within a mile of, the DZ while the fourth, whose leading aircraft was not fitted with a Rebecca receiver and thus could not be guided in by the Eurekas on the DZ, dropped a company some ten miles away to the south-east, fortunately not in an enemy-held area. The remainder of the battalion, meanwhile, was aboard eight aircraft of the 314th Troop Carrier Group. Two aircraft, however, were forced to abort before take-off and their sticks had to be redistributed among the other six, which thus took off behind schedule, reaching the DZ at 2.30 a.m. and dropping their sticks within a mile of it.

Having rallied and assembled at its RV, the missing company having arrived just after first light, the 504th Parachute Regimental Combat Team then headed for Monte Soprano, which lay in the 36th Infantry Division's sector, and later that day played a major role in stemming further counter-attacks launched by the Germans.

That same day, Ridgway received a message from Clark cancelling the Capua operation and ordering him to despatch the 505th Parachute Regimental Combat Team to Salerno instead. At 11.38 p.m. that night the 505th's pathfinders dropped, followed by the 3rd Battalion accompanied by Brigadier General Gavin and his headquarters, dropping from fifty-two C-47s at 1.10 a.m. on 15 September. Next to arrive was the 2nd Battalion, which dropped at 1.30 a.m., with the 1st Battalion, which had been delayed, arriving an hour and half later at 3.00 a.m. Forty-five minutes after its last elements had landed, the 505th, along with Company B 307th Airborne Engineer Battalion, had assembled at its RV and shortly afterwards was heading for the US VI Corps, where it went into reserve and patrolled the corps' right flank at the southern end of the beachhead between Ibanella and Agropoli.

The night of 14 September also saw Lieutenant Colonel Doyle R. Yardley's 509th Parachute Infantry Battalion carry out its drop into the area of Avellino which it was to attack. It would then conduct harassing operations against the Germans for a maximum of five days, by which time it was expected that ground forces would have linked up with the battalion. In the event of no such link-up, the battalion was to exfiltrate back to Allied lines. As mentioned earlier, the town, situated behind enemy lines in a valley surrounded by mountains some twenty miles to the north of Salerno, was a key point on the Germans' lines of communication and supply.

The 640-strong battalion emplaned at an airfield at Comiso, on Sicily, aboard aircraft of the 51st TCW. At 9.25 p.m. a C-47 took off carrying a team of eleven pathfinders and headed for Salerno from where it flew twenty miles northwards over enemy lines to Montecorvino, before turning north-west and flying a further fifteen miles through mountains to the area of the designated DZ, situated on a crossroads near the village of Santa Lucia di Sorino. Following ten minutes behind came the forty C-47s carrying the 509th with Lieutenant Colonel Yardley travelling in the leading aircraft.

Despite the good weather conditions and moonlit sky, the pilot of the pathfinder aircraft was unable to locate Santa Lucia di Sorino, but the team jumped nevertheless, landing a mile to the south of the DZ. With the battalion due to arrive overhead in a matter of only minutes, there was no time for the pathfinders to reach the DZ and so they set up their Aldis lamps and 5G radio beacon where they were.

Due to the fact that the aircraft of the 51st Troop Carrier Wing were not fitted with Rebecca receivers, the team was not equipped with a Eureka and this was the undoing of the drop, the 5G beacon proving useless and the narrow-beamed Aldis lamps little better. Only fifteen aircraft succeeded in dropping their sticks within four to five miles of the DZ. One squadron dropped 175 members of the 509th ten miles away, in the area of Cassano, while another became lost over the mountains and flew back to the coast to reorientate itself before making a second attempt. Twelve more aircraft dropped their sticks over a wide area ranging from eight to twenty-five miles from the DZ.

Yardley was fortunate to land near the DZ. He swiftly rounded up some 160 members of the battalion and headed for Avellino. Shortly afterwards, however, he stumbled upon a German armoured unit in a laager on the outskirts of the town and a fierce battle ensued in which he was wounded and captured together with a number of his men. Elsewhere members of the 509th were also making their presence felt, one group blowing up a bridge just as a German convoy was crossing it, before withdrawing unscathed. Other small groups did likewise, harassing the enemy by laying mines and ambushing convoys or despatch riders before withdrawing, as ordered, after five days. Of the 640 men dropped on the night of 14/15 September, 520 succeeded in making their way back to Allied lines.

Inevitably, there was criticism of the mission, some claiming that it had achieved little, had been a failure and had made little impact on the situation at the Salerno beachhead, where it would have been put to better use. General Clark and Colonel James Gavin, however, disagreed with these detractors, the latter stating later that the 509th Parachute Infantry Battalion had: 'Accomplished what General Mark Clark had in mind. It disrupted German communications and partly blocked German supplies and reserves. It also caused the Germans to keep units on anti-parachute missions that otherwise could have been used at the point of their main effort.'

Back at Salerno, 16 September witnessed the Germans launching another major counter-attack during which the US 45th Infantry Division, supported by naval gunfire and aircraft, inflicted heavy casualties. By this time all three regiments of the 82nd Airborne Division were deployed in the beachhead, the 325th Glider Infantry Regiment and the 3rd Battalion 504th Parachute Regimental Combat Team having landed on Red Beach and gone into reserve. That afternoon the 504th, less the 3rd Battalion, moved out of the beachhead as part of the initial breakout by the US Fifth Army. The 1st Battalion, accompanied by Colonel Reuben H. Tucker and his forward tactical headquarters, led the way towards the initial objective – the town of Altavilla and the high ground dominating it. He and his men soon came under very heavy fire and began fighting their way forward over very rough, rocky terrain punctuated by steep-sided ravines. The battle continued throughout the night and into the following day. At one point Tucker's forward command post was surrounded by the enemy. He therefore radioed a request to Ridgway that the 3rd Battalion be sent forward from reserve, to which Ridgway agreed, at the same time arranging for naval gunfire and artillery support for the beleaguered 504th. The response was a massive bombardment by warships and heavy guns alike, reducing Altaville to rubble and causing heavy casualties among the enemy, who were forced to pull back on 18 September.

That day saw the Germans begin a withdrawal to the line of the Volturno where they would hold firm until mid-October, by which time a line of defensive positions, dubbed the Gustav Line, stretching across Italy's narrowest part halfway between Rome and Naples, would be complete. The commander of 15th Army Group, General Sir Harold Alexander, had every intention of pursuing the Germans and preventing them from completing the line. He directed that the US Fifth Army would advance as swiftly as possible up the western half of Italy while the British Eighth Army did likewise up the eastern, both crossing the Volturno and thereafter overrunning the Gustav Line. The task of the 82nd Airborne Division, reinforced by the British 23rd Armoured Brigade, three battalions of rangers, an infantry battalion from the US 36th Infantry Division and some artillery, was to seize and occupy Naples.

The division and its reinforcements began their advance on 27 September, the 504th and 505th Parachute Regimental Combat Teams, along with the 325th Glider Infantry Regiment and the three ranger battalions, fighting their way through the Chiunzi Pass. The following day found the 504th and 505th, supported by the 23rd Armoured Brigade and the division's artillery, advancing down from the mountains and heading along the coastal road towards Naples, the outskirts of which were reached by the 505th on 1 October. By this time the city had been abandoned by the Germans. Accompanied by Lieutenant General Mark Clark, who came forward for the occasion, the 82nd Airborne Division entered the city that afternoon to find that it had suffered devastating damage from Allied bombing and demolitions carried out by the Germans as they withdrew. During the ensuing weeks, as the war moved farther north, the division's engineers were heavily engaged in rendering the city safe from large numbers of bombs and explosive devices left behind by the enemy as booby traps.

Once the US Fifth Army reached the Volturno, however, the 82nd Airborne Division was called forward. Shortly after its arrival, Clark hatched a plan for the division to carry out an assault river crossing of the Volturno, the line of which was held by the German Tenth Army. Included in the Tenth Army order of battle was none other than the 82nd's old foe, the Hermann Göring Division, dug in on high ground dominating the proposed crossing-point. A reconnaissance of the area soon convinced Ridgway that any such crossing would inevitably result in very heavy casualties among his men. Fortunately, Clark's other senior commanders were of the same opinion and the plan was dropped.

When the river was crossed on the night of 13/14, however, elements of the division were at the forefront. The 1st and 2nd Battalions of the 505th were attached to the British X Corps, with the 2nd Battalion leading and suffering heavy casualties as it secured crossing points over five of the canals that interlaced the entire area. The two battalions cleared the way, enabling the 23rd Armoured Brigade and later the British 46th Infantry Division, to push on through. That evening saw the US Fifth Army across the Volturno but by then the Germans had withdrawn to another temporary defensive line from where they subsequently pulled back again to occupy the Gustav Line. As winter arrived, bringing with it cold weather and heavy rains, they were reinforced by more divisions despatched by Field Marshal Kesselring from the north.

Preparations, meanwhile, were being made for the 82nd Airborne Division to be transferred to Britain, where it was required for Operation Overlord, the invasion of enemy-occupied Europe. Lieutenant General Clark, however, wished to retain the division to give him an airborne force within the Fifth Army and it was only after lengthy negotiations at high level that it was agreed that he would keep the 509th Parachute Infantry Battalion and, for the time being, a parachute regimental combat team that comprised the 504th, the 456th Parachute Artillery Battalion and the 376th Glider Artillery Battalion. The understanding was for the 504th to return to the division in good time to prepare for Overlord. During the next two months, it was deployed in the infantry role in the mountains of central Italy, where it led the US Fifth Army as it headed north towards Venafro and Cassino until the onset of winter and the German withdrawal into the Gustav Line brought Italian operations in 1943 to a close.

In November 1943, the 82nd Airborne Division left Italy and sailed for Northern Ireland, arriving there the following month. It was augmented by two additional parachute infantry regiments, the 507th and 508th commanded by Colonels George V. Millett and Roy E. Lindquist respectively, which were transferred from the United States. The 82nd, however, was not the first US airborne formation to arrive in Britain. In September 1943 its sister formation, the 101st Airborne Division, still commanded by Major General William C. Lee, had been shipped from the United States, arriving after a ten-day voyage in convoy across the Atlantic and shortly afterwards moving to its new base in Wiltshire, in south-west England. Four months earlier, in June, its single parachute formation, the 502nd Parachute Infantry Regiment, and two glider infantry regiments, the 327th and 401st, had been augmented by a second parachute infantry regiment, the 506th.

As 1943 drew to a close, the 82nd and 101st Airborne Divisions found themselves hard at work preparing and training for their roles in the forthcoming invasion of Europe in the coming year.

CHAPTER NINE

BRITISH OPERATIONS IN NORMANDY, JUNE–SEPTEMBER 1944

On the morning of 17 February 1944 Major General 'Boy' Browning, the Commander Airborne Troops, arrived at the headquarters of 6th Airborne Division to brief its commander, Major General Richard Gale, on the division's role in Operation Overlord, the invasion of Normandy.

The overall Allied invasion plan called for a massive seaborne assault on the coast of Normandy in the areas between the Cotentin Peninsula and the mouth of the River Orne, with Lieutenant General Omar Bradley's US First Army, comprising V and VII Corps, on the right and Lieutenant General Sir Miles Dempsey's British Second Army, consisting of I and XXX Corps, on the left. Both armies were under command of General Sir Bernard Montgomery's British 21st Army Group during the assault phase of the operation. Bradley's forces would land on two beaches, codenamed Omaha and Utah, to the west of Caen at the base of the Cotentin, thereafter isolating the peninsula and capturing the key port of Cherbourg. Dempsey's Second Army, meanwhile, would land on three beaches, codenamed Gold, Juno and Sword, in the area between Bayeux and Caen. The initial task given to Bradley and Dempsey was the establishment of two beachheads: one between the

Vire and Orne rivers, to include Isigny, Bayeux and Caen; the other on the coast of the Cotentin Peninsula, north of the Vire, extending to the line of the Carentan Canal and beyond the River Merderet.

By the beginning of 1944, enemy forces in the area where the landings would take place comprised five divisions and a number of independent units whose total strength equated to that of a further division. Two of the divisions, the 709th and 716th, based respectively in the areas of Bayeux and Caen, were static formations whose manpower was largely composed of medically down-graded troops or conscripts from Russia or Eastern Europe. Two more, the 77th and 352nd Infantry Divisions, were deployed to the rear of the 716th and 709th, while the fifth formation, the 243rd Infantry Division, was deployed on the west coast of the Cotentin Peninsula.

It was Montgomery's intention that by D+7 the Allied beachhead would be expanded to the north-west, west and south, and to a lesser degree to the east and south-east. The task of the British I Corps, on the left flank of the British sector, would be to hold Caen and the area immediately south of the city as a pivot and a bastion, while resisting at all costs any counter-attacks by the Germans' main armoured reserves located in the area of Chartres–Paris–Amiens–Rouen. The US V Corps and British XXX Corps would advance southwards with the aim of securing by D+9 the area of high ground along the line of La Haye du Puits–Saint Lô–Caumont–Villers-Bocage in order to gain sufficient depth to place the invasion landing points beyond the range of artillery fire. The US VII Corps would attack to the west to isolate the Cotentin Peninsula, and northwards to attack the city and port of Cherbourg.

Major General Richard Gale had been eagerly anticipating the moment when he would learn of the role 6th Airborne Division was to play in Overlord and thus was dismayed when Browning outlined the plan which called for only one parachute brigade and one airlanding anti-tank battery, his feelings being heightened when he learned that two US airborne divisions, the 82nd and 101st, would be deployed in full on the operation. Under command of 3rd Infantry Division, the

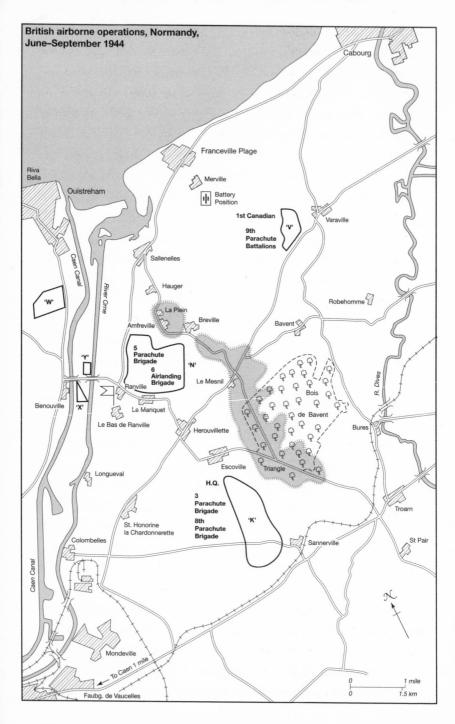

British airborne operations, Normandy, June–September 1944

Cabourg

Franceville Plage

Riva Bella

Ouistreham

Merville

Battery Position

1st Canadian

9th Parachute Battalions

'V'

Varaville

Sallenelles

Hauger

La Plein

Breville

Robehomme

Bavent

Amfreville

Caen Canal

River Orne

'W'

5 Parachute Brigade

6 Airlanding Brigade

'N'

Le Mesnil

Bois de Bavent

R. Dives

'Y'

Ranville

Benouville

'X'

Le Mariquet

Le Bas de Ranville

Herouvillette

Bures

Longueval

Escoville

Triangle

H.Q.

3 Parachute Brigade

8th Parachute Brigade

'K'

Troarn

St. Honorine la Chardonnerette

Colombelles

Sannerville

St Pair

Caen Canal

Mondeville

To Caen 1 mile

N

0   1 mile
0   1.5 km

Faubg. de Vaucelles

latter being part of Lieutenant General Sir John Crocker's I Corps, the brigade's mission would be to seize the bridges over the Caen Canal and the River Orne at Benouville and Ranville. In addition to his disappointment that his entire division was not to be committed to Overlord, Gale's main concern was that a single parachute brigade would be insufficient for the task. He made his feelings sufficiently plain to convince Browning; a few days later the decision was taken to commit the whole of 6th Airborne Division under command of I Corps. Gale and his staff immediately began planning for the operation.

The role of 6th Airborne Division would be to protect the left flank of the British seaborne landings bordered by the Caen Canal and River Orne, taking control of the area to the east of Caen and the features of high ground which dominated it. It was also to carry out two secondary tasks: first, the clearing and securing of the Orne and Dives rivers, including the capture of Sallanelles and Franceville Plage, as well as the clearing of the coastal area between these two towns and Cabourg at the mouth of the Dives; and second, having established a firm base east of the Orne, to block any movement by enemy reserve forces attempting to move towards the covering position from the east and south-east.

The division was also allotted three tasks to be carried out prior to the seaborne landings: first, the capture of the bridges over the Caen Canal and the Orne at Benouville and Ranville and the establishment of a bridgehead to hold them; second, the destruction of the Merville coastal gun battery at Franceville Plage; and third, the blowing of the bridges over the River Dives at Varaville, Robehomme, Bures and Troarn to delay any movement by German forces from the east. Initially, Gale gave the task of capturing the two bridges at Benouville and Ranville to 3rd Parachute Brigade whose commander, Brigadier James Hill, immediately realised that the bridges could only be seized in a *coup de main* operation for which paratroops were not suited. He thus requested that a company of gliderborne troops of 6th Airlanding Brigade be placed under his command for the task. Major General Gale agreed and accordingly D Company 2nd Battalion The Oxfordshire & Buckinghamshire Light Infantry, reinforced by two platoons of B Company, was allotted to Hill.

The division would be delivered by the RAF's 38 and 46 Groups, the former equipped with bombers converted to carry paratroops and tow gliders, and the latter with 175 C-47s. The total number of transport aircraft to be deployed in support of the division was between 400 and 450, together with almost 1,100 Horsa and twenty-five Hamilcar gliders. Owing to the limited numbers of aircraft available, 5th Parachute Brigade would have to be flown in on a second airlift together with the 6th Airborne Armoured Reconnaissance Regiment and other divisional troops. The divisional headquarters, along with elements of 53rd Airlanding Light Regiment RA and the division's three airlanding anti-tank batteries, would land after 6th Airlanding Brigade.

Up to this point, intelligence reports of enemy forces in 6th Airborne Division's area of operations indicated that these comprised two low-category infantry divisions plus two companies of armour and a number of ad hoc infantry units formed from training establishments. A more potent threat was posed by the 12th SS Hitler Jugend Panzer Division based in the Rennes area. Furthermore, it was known that the 352nd Infantry Division was within striking distance.

In April, however, new intelligence reported that the Germans had erected anti-glider defences on the DZs and LZs selected by Gale and his staff. Initially, it was feared that their plans had been compromised but further reports indicated that all areas of open terrain along the coasts of France and Belgium had been similarly obstructed. As a mass glider landing was no longer feasible, Gale altered his plans. The task of capturing the bridges at Benouville and Ranville was now allotted to Brigadier Nigel Poett's 5th Parachute Brigade although the *coup de main* operation would still be carried out by D Company 2nd Battalion The Oxfordshire & Buckinghamshire Light Infantry, which had been undergoing intensive training for the task. The brigade would be dropped shortly after the bridges had been taken and, having cleared and secured the area of Benouville, Ranville and Le Bas de Ranville, would clear the anti-glider defences from 6th Airlanding Brigade's LZs. 3rd Parachute Brigade's tasks of destroying the Merville Battery and the bridges over the Dives remained unchanged. As soon as possible after the seaborne landings, 1st Special Service Brigade, commanded by Brigadier The Lord Lovat, would head for the bridge over the Caen Canal where it would come under command of 6th Airborne Division.

At 10.56 p.m. on the night of 5/6 June, six Halifax bombers took off at one-minute intervals from an airfield in south-west England. In tow behind them were six Horsas carrying men of D Company 2nd Battalion Oxfordshire & Buckinghamshire Light Infantry under the command of Major John Howard, who travelled in the leading glider with No. 1 Platoon, commanded by Lieutenant Den Brotheridge. Howard's company was reinforced by two platoons of B Company and a detachment of thirty sappers of 249th Field Company RE under the command of Captain Jock Neilson. As the aircraft climbed to a maximum altitude of between 4,000 and 5,000 feet, clear moonlight reflected on the Channel below and revealed the dark outline of the French coastline ahead. As stated earlier, D Company's mission was to capture intact the bridges over the Caen Canal and River Orne at Benouville and Ranville, both of which were known to have been prepared for demolition by the Germans.

Just over an hour and a quarter later, the six tug-glider combinations reached their release points over the French coast to the west of Cabourg at an altitude of 5,000 feet. Prior to the gliders being released, the navigator in each Halifax carefully briefed his glider pilot over the intercom on his position and altitude, wind speed, course and airspeed.

Having been released from their tugs, the Horsas flew silently towards their target LZs about six miles away. It was difficult for the pilots to see or recognise any landmarks in the darkness. The leading aircraft, flown by Staff Sergeant Jim Wallwork, reached the Bois de Bavent, one of the largest wooded areas in Normandy, the checkpoint where the first three Horsas were required to make a wide circular turn. Wallwork, however, was unable to see the woods where they should have been – straight ahead on his port bow. Putting his glider through a 90° turn to starboard, he saw below him the two objectives: the bridges over the Caen Canal and River Orne.

Applying half-flap, he descended to an altitude of 1,000 feet before carrying out another 90° turn to starboard, at which point he ordered his co-pilot, Staff Sergeant John Ainsworth, to deploy the Horsa's arrester parachute. The braking effect was immediate and the aircraft steadied down to the correct speed for landing. Just before it touched down, Wallwork instructed Ainsworth to jettison the parachute arrester gear as he flew towards the small triangular LZ south-east of the canal bridge. Landing at a speed of 90 mph, the Horsa careered into a barbed-wire obstacle. As it came to a shattering halt, Wallwork and Ainsworth were both hurled through the perspex windshield of the cockpit into the barbed wire entanglement, being knocked unconscious in the process. They had landed their aircraft to within two feet of the precise spot indicated to them during briefings by John Howard prior to the operation. It was later defined as being one of the most remarkable feats of accurate flying of the Second World War.

Incredibly, there was no response from the enemy. German troops guarding the bridge, some of whom were only fifty yards away, had heard the noise of the first glider landing and assumed it to be caused by debris falling from a crippled Allied bomber.

Major John Howard and the other passengers in Wallwork's glider were very briefly knocked senseless. Howard himself had been thrown against the interior of the aircraft's roof when his seatbelt broke with the force of the landing. Regaining consciousness seconds later, he thought he had been blinded until he realised that his helmet had been forced down over his eyes and ears by the impact. Scrambling out of the wreckage, he looked up to see the bridge only fifty yards away from where he stood, the nose of the glider through the enemy defences. There was no firing, as complete surprise had been achieved. Mean-while, the others in the glider also recovered within a second or two and immediately began quietly breaking their way out of the damaged doors at the front and rear of the aircraft.

Forcing their way out, Lieutenant Den Brotheridge and his platoon extricated themselves from their wrecked Horsa. Taking one section with him, Brotheridge ran straight through the wire and headed for the bridge. As he did so, from the darkness behind him came the sound of the second glider, flown by Staff Sergeants Boland and Hobbs, making its landing. In order to avoid the wreckage of Wallwork's Horsa, Boland was forced to swerve and in so doing broke the back of his own aircraft. The force of the impact was such that the commander of No. 2 Platoon, Lieutenant David Wood, was thrown from the glider but fortunately escaped serious injury. The platoon immediately formed up on him as planned and Wood moved forward to link up with Major Howard, who was waiting for him near the bridge. The latter ordered him to proceed with the platoon's second task, the clearing of the German trenches, machine-gun positions and an anti-tank gun emplacement on the eastern bank.

As Wood and his platoon launched themselves into their task, the third glider, flown by Staff Sergeants Geoff Barkworth and Peter Boyle, hurtled down on to the LZ. Captain John Vaughan of the Royal Army Medical Corps, a medical officer in a parachute unit who had volunteered for this mission, was thrown out of the glider into the mud of a nearby pond, along with Lieutenant Sandy Smith, the commander of No. 3 Platoon. Smith immediately staggered to his feet and headed for the bridge, followed by elements of his platoon, although half a dozen of his men were still trapped in the wreckage of the glider.

Lieutenant Den Brotheridge and his platoon had meantime already run up the embankment on to the bridge. As they did so, an enemy soldier opened fire at Major Howard and his radio operator who were now at the top of the embankment. Brotheridge and his men went running across the bridge, Brotheridge himself shooting a German who had just fired a warning flare. At the same time, the leading section of No. 1 Platoon knocked out a pillbox with grenades. Meanwhile, the sappers were checking the bridge for demolition charges and cutting any wires that they found.

Fully alerted by now, the Germans fought back. As Lieutenant Brotheridge threw a grenade at a machine-gun position, knocking it out seconds later, he was hit in the neck by a bullet. As he fell in the middle of the road at the western end of the bridge, the rest of his platoon came running over the bridge after him, systematically over-whelming all opposition.

Lieutenant David Wood and No. 2 Platoon proceeded to deal with the German positions at the eastern end of the bridge, including a 20mm gun emplacement, and as they did so discovered that many of the enemy had fled. Having completed his task, Wood was returning to report to Major Howard when he came under fire from an enemy machine gun and was hit in the leg. As his platoon sergeant had also been wounded, one of the section commanders assumed command.

As soon as Lieutenant Sandy Smith and No. 3 Platoon reached the bridge, Howard despatched them across it to establish defensive positions on the western side and reinforce No. 1 Platoon. Smith himself, however, was wounded shortly afterwards by a grenade. Although he killed the German who threw it, he was hit by fragments as the grenade exploded, suffering a serious wound to one of his wrists.

The gliders carrying Howard's other three platoons were meanwhile landing for their assault on the Orne bridge at Ranville. Unfortunately, the leading aircraft had been cast off at the wrong location after the two pilots, Staff Sergeants Lawrence and Shorter, had been ordered to make a blind release by the captain of their tug aircraft. Consequently, they had landed Howard's company second-in-command, Captain Brian Priday, and Lieutenant Tony Hooper's No. 4 Platoon five miles to the east near two bridges crossing the River Dives and a canal. Having captured the two bridges, Priday and his men realised that they were in the wrong location and began making their way rapidly back towards their objective.

The crew of the sixth glider, Staff Sergeants Howard and Baacke, had carried out another remarkable feat of flying. They had succeeded in landing their Horsa in the centre of their LZ, a field surrounded by trees north-west of the bridge. After initial opposition from an enemy machine gun had been silenced by a direct hit from its 2-inch mortar, Lieutenant Dennis Fox's No. 6 Platoon was able to take and secure the bridge, which was found to be undefended, within a matter of minutes. The fifth glider, flown by Staff Sergeants Pearson and Guthrie and carrying Lieutenant Tod Sweeney's No. 5 Platoon, had landed 700 yards short of the LZ. By the time Sweeney and his men reached the western end of the bridge, No. 6 Platoon was already deployed on the far side.

Within fifteen minutes of landing, both bridges had been secured and the success codewords 'Ham and Jam' transmitted by radio. At 12.50 a.m. the sound of approaching aircraft engines heralded the arrival of 3rd and 5th Parachute Brigades.

Shortly after Howard and his company had taken off from England, they were followed by 6th Airborne Division's pathfinder unit, the 22nd Independent Parachute Company, under the command of Major Francis Lennox Boyd, whose task it was to mark the DZs and LZs for the division. The company was organised into three platoons, each comprising an officer and thirty-two other ranks, and consisting of three sections or sticks commanded by a sergeant or corporal. For pathfinding tasks, each stick was equipped with the Eureka ground-to-air radio beacon and coloured cloth panels which were laid out in the form of a 'T'. Six-volt battery-powered holophane lamps were used for night drops, an orange lamp being placed at the end of each arm of the 'T' while a green one was positioned at the base. Operated by a member of the stick, this was used to flash the DZ code letter at the approaching aircraft.

The first member of 5th Parachute Brigade to land on DZ 'N' was its commander, Brigadier Nigel Poett, who found himself alone in the darkness. Moving off swiftly, he followed the line of the aircraft, whose exhaust flames he could see in the sky above as they flew away, since he knew that the direction in which they were heading was towards

Ranville. Shortly afterwards he met a member of his headquarters defence platoon and a few seconds later saw the flashes of explosions and heard the noise of gunfire as Major Howard and his company launched their attack on the Caen Canal bridge at Benouville. He immediately headed in the direction of the bridges, where he expected to meet his radio operator, Lieutenant Gordon Royle of 6th Airborne Divisional Signals. Unfortunately, shortly after landing Royle had encountered a number of enemy with a machine gun and had been killed while attacking them single-handed.

On reaching the River Orne bridge, Poett found that all had gone well and the bridges had been secured. As he was being briefed on the situation, he heard the sound of the aircraft bringing in his brigade group which, in addition to 7th, 12th and 13th Parachute Battalions comprised FOO parties from 53rd Airlanding Light Regiment RA, 291st Parachute Squadron RE (less one troop) and 225th Parachute Field Ambulance.

Although the drop went smoothly the three battalions were scattered, mainly due to the fact that each man was very heavily burdened with equipment. This inevitably resulted in slow exits from the aircraft and subsequent dispersal of sticks. In the case of 7th Parachute Battalion, only forty per cent of its number appeared at the battalion's RV by 2.40 a.m. and only a few of the containers with mortars, machine guns and radios had been found. Hearing the whistle blasts signalling the successful capture of the bridges, the commanding officer, Lieutenant Colonel Geoffrey Pine Coffin, decided not to wait for any more members of the battalion to appear and headed for the bridges without further delay. Having relieved Howard and his men, 7th Parachute Battalion established itself in defensive positions in Benouville, B Company engaging a small number of enemy while moving into a wood and hamlet at the northern end of the town.

Meanwhile, among the first members of 12th Parachute Battalion to arrive at its RV was the commanding officer, Lieutenant Colonel Johnny Johnson. Most of the battalion had landed on the eastern side of the DZ and it was some forty-five minutes before more men arrived at the RV. By the time it moved off towards its objective, which was the village of Le Bas de Ranville, the battalion was at no more than sixty per cent of its full strength but by 4.00 a.m. it had secured the village and was digging in.

13th Parachute Battalion, commanded by Lieutenant Colonel Peter Luard, was also at only sixty per cent of its strength when it moved off from its RV. Its objective was to secure Ranville, from which, in conjunction with 12th Parachute Battalion, it was to cover both bridges from the approaches to the south-east. In addition, the battalion had also been tasked with clearing the LZ on which the divisional headquarters and some divisional troops would be landing at 3.30 a.m. A Company, commanded by Major John Cramphorn, had been detailed to carry this out with the assistance of some sappers from 591st Parachute Squadron RE, completing it with half an hour to spare at 3.00 a.m.

By dawn on 6 June, 5th Parachute Brigade was in firm possession of its objectives. 7th Parachute Battalion, which still only numbered some 200 men plus the seventy of Major John Howard's company which was holding the eastern end of the Caen Canal bridge, was deployed in and around Benouville. 13th Parachute Battalion had cleared Ranville by dawn, having encountered small groups of Germans on the northern edge of the town which hitherto had been garrisoned by an enemy company.

The German response came shortly after dawn when at 7.00 a.m. 7th Parachute Battalion was confronted by some light tanks which appeared and halted in full view of one of C Company's platoons positioned as an outpost at the Château de Benouville. To the platoon's surprise, the tank crews dismounted and held a discussion, at which point the platoon opened fire, hitting some of the crewmen and scattering the rest, who remounted their vehicles and sped away. During the morning, the enemy probed A Company's positions in the southern part of Benouville and shortly afterwards self-propelled guns appeared.

Advancing to within close range, they shelled the company and forced one of its platoons to withdraw to the centre of the village. Later that morning enemy infantry, supported by armour, reached the southern outskirts of the village but A Company blocked their advance. At one point a Mk. IV tank reached the village centre but was knocked out with Gammon bombs. During the rest of the morning, 7th Parachute Battalion, hampered by its lack of heavy weapons and radios whose containers had not been found, was subjected to probing attacks by infantry supported by armour. The enemy also attempted to infiltrate the battalion's positions but was prevented from doing so by aggressive patrolling.

At noon on 6 June came the sound of the bagpipes as Private Bill Millin, Brigadier The Lord Lovat's personal piper, heralded the arrival of the leading elements of 1st Special Service Brigade which had bypassed the enemy, pushing on with all haste to link up with 5th Parachute Brigade. The arrival of the commandos, however, brought little respite for 7th Parachute Battalion which continued to be subjected to enemy action while 12th Parachute Battalion was bombarded with heavy mortar and artillery fire. The enemy, in the form of the 125th Panzer Grenadier Regiment, attacked Ranville but was beaten off after losing a tank and a number of men who were taken prisoner. A second attack was mounted but was also repulsed by the battalion with the help of 4th Airlanding Anti-Tank Battery RA which destroyed three self-propelled guns and a tank.

While 5th Parachute Brigade had been securing Benouville and Ranville, 3rd Parachute Brigade had suffered a series of mishaps from the very start of the operation. Almost all the pathfinders' Eurekas and holophane lamps for marking DZ 'V', on which 1st Canadian and 9th Parachute Battalions were due to drop, had been lost. Furthermore, the pathfinders for DZ 'K', on which the brigade headquarters and 8th Parachute Battalion would drop, had landed on one of 5th Parachute Brigade's zones, DZ 'N'. Unaware of this, they had set up their Eureka and lamps and as a result the brigade headquarters and 8th Parachute Battalion found themselves being despatched over DZ 'N' instead of DZ 'K'.

3rd Parachute Brigade's advance party comprised elements of the brigade headquarters and a group from each battalion, together with a company of 1st Canadian Parachute Battalion, tasked with clearing obstructions from DZ 'V'. Their delivery also proved chaotic: of the fourteen converted Albemarle bombers carrying them, two dropped three and nine men respectively, while six men were despatched from a third aircraft as it crossed the coast and only four jumped over the DZ. A fourth Albemarle, while under fire, was forced to make a second approach and thus dropped its stick late. Two more aircraft reported technical problems: one lost time while flying along the coast to locate the correct approach point, while the other was forced to return to base after being hit by flak on its seventh approach to the DZ which it was unable to locate. Major Bill Collingwood, the brigade major, was travelling in this last aircraft and was waiting to jump when it was hit. He was knocked through the aperture by the impact but remained suspended beneath the fuselage, hanging by his static line which had become wound round his leg. Despite there also being a 60-pound kitbag attached to his leg, he was pulled back into the aircraft as it returned to England. He eventually arrived in Normandy during the evening of 6 June, having flown in by glider.

Twenty-six aircraft carried the main body of 3rd Parachute Brigade as well as FOO parties of 53rd Airlanding Light Regiment RA, 3rd Parachute Squadron RE, 224th Parachute Field Ambulance and elements of divisional troops. Of these, nine dropped their sticks some two or three miles away from the DZ, in the marshes lying on both sides of the River Dives, while the remainder were scattered over a wide area. The brigade's commander, Brigadier James Hill, found himself landing approximately half a mile south of Cabourg in four feet of water by the submerged bank of the river. It took him four hours to reach dry land adjacent to the DZ after crossing numerous deep irrigation ditches in which many of his men were drowned. Along the way, however, he encountered several soldiers whom he collected and took with him.

The advance element of 9th Parachute Battalion had meantime been dropped on DZ 'V' and reached the battalion RV without mishap, thereafter setting out the lights that marked the company locations. A small group headed by the battalion's second-in-command, Major George Smith, made their way towards the battalion's objective, the Merville battery, which lay about a mile away. As they did so, however, RAF Lancaster bombers bombed the battery but missed it, most of their bombs falling to the south and narrowly missing Smith's group.

The main body of the battalion was meanwhile approaching the French coast. Unfortunately, due to most of the pathfinding equipment for marking DZ 'V' having been damaged, there were only a few holophane lamps marking the zone when the aircraft arrived overhead. Moreover, visibility had deteriorated because of smoke from the bombing raid billowing across the DZ. Consequently, few of the pilots saw the lights and only a few sticks landed on the zone, others dropping into the Dives marshes or on the high ground between Cabourg and Dozule.

By 2.50 a.m. the commanding officer, Lieutenant Colonel Terence Otway, had assembled 150 of his 550 men. None of the gliders bringing in jeeps, trailers and 6-pounder anti-tank guns had appeared. Furthermore, the battalion's 3-inch mortars, all but one of its Vickers MMGs, a party of sappers, a section of the parachute field ambulance and a naval gunfire forward observation party were all missing. Bearing in mind that the battery had to be knocked out by 5.30 a.m., Otway decided to press on.

Skirting the northern outskirts of the village of Gonneville, Otway and his men made their way to a crossroads where they met Major Smith and his group who had cut their way through a barbed wire fence and, making their way through a minefield to an inner fence, located some enemy positions. A taping party, led by Captain The Honourable Paul Greenway, subsequently cleared and marked four lanes through the minefields, locating and disarming several tripwires attached to mines.

By this time it was 4.30 a.m. and Otway divided his force into four groups. At that juncture, two of the three gliders carrying the fifty-eight-strong assault group, commanded by Captain Robert Gordon-Brown, appeared suddenly, flying in low over the battery. Both aircraft came under fire and were seen to be hit, one flying on into the darkness and eventually landing in a large field two miles away to the east. The other meanwhile headed for a large hedge at the edge of the minefield but the pilot suddenly spotted a minefield warning sign and managed to haul his glider up over the hedge and a lane on the far side before streaming his arrester parachute and crashlanding in an orchard beyond. The platoon inside, commanded by Lieutenant Hugh Pond, made a somewhat dazed exit, only to hear the sound of men approaching. Swiftly deploying into positions on either side of the lane, Pond and his men opened fire on some enemy as they approached.

At that point, Lieutenant Colonel Otway launched his attack which began with the detonating of four Bangalore torpedoes. Four assault groups went in, using two of the cleared lanes through the minefield. Having penetrated the battery's defences, they had to fight their way to the gun casemates, coming under fire from two machine guns, one of which was silenced shortly afterwards. On reaching the casemates, they eventually gained entry, killing twenty-two enemy and capturing a similar number, the rest of the German gunners taking cover in under-ground bunkers where they remained undetected. The guns, which were 100mm light howitzers, and thus of considerably smaller calibre than had been reported, were not destroyed because the sappers accom-panying the battalion had been dropped some distance from the DZ and had not appeared since.

At 5.00 a.m., 9th Parachute Battalion withdrew, having suffered heavy casualties. Of the force of some 150 which had attacked the battery, approximately sixty-five men had been killed, wounded or were missing. On the following day, 7 June, the battery was attacked again by two troops of No. 3 Commando who, attacking in daylight without the use of smoke as cover, also suffered heavy losses. As they withdrew, they were engaged by some of the enemy gunners who brought one of their howitzers out of its casemate and opened fire over open sights, incurring further casualties among the commandos. The guns and their crews remained in the battery position until 17 August when they were withdrawn with other German forces in Normandy.

Lieutenant Colonel Otway now attacked the village of Le Plein, situated on the Bavent Ridge. At 6.00 a.m. he and the remaining members of the battalion moved off and eventually, having been mistakenly bombed by high-flying RAF bombers, reached a crossroads between Le Plein and the neighbouring village of Hauger where B Company, which was in the lead, came under fire. Major George Smith led a company attack on the village, forcing a platoon of enemy back into Le Plein and killing about fifteen of them in the process.

As the battalion was clearing and securing a number of houses at the northern end of the village, another enemy platoon counter-attacked but encountered the battalion's single Vickers MMG which wreaked havoc at close range, killing twelve enemy and forcing the remainder to withdraw. A platoon of B Company, commanded by Lieutenant Halliburton, attacked a large house near the church from the rear. Surrounded by a six-foot-high wall, it appeared to be the main enemy defensive position. As the leading section climbed over the wall, it came under fire and Halliburton, in the lead, was killed and his men forced to withdraw.

9th Parachute Battalion was now very weak in numbers, its strength having been reduced to less than 100 men. Lieutenant Colonel Terence Otway decided to establish defensive positions in the Château d' Amfreville and await the arrival of 1st Special Service Brigade. Moving into its new positions, the battalion found a hoard of German rations, which were shared out, as well as a car and some horses which were commandeered. The early afternoon of 6 June saw the arrival of No. 6 Commando which took up positions within the village.

During the drop, 8th Parachute Battalion, commanded by Lieu-tenant Colonel Alastair Pearson, had also been scattered. Its initial task was to destroy a bridge at Troarn, thereafter securing and holding the town while one of its companies provided cover for sappers of 3rd Parachute Squadron RE who were to blow another two bridges at Bures. At 1.20 a.m., when the commanding officer arrived at the battalion's RV at a track junction near Touffreville, he found only thirty men plus a small group of sappers with a jeep and trailer. By 3.30 a.m. this number had increased to eleven officers and 130 other ranks but there was no sign of any of the other sappers who had dropped with the battalion.

Pearson decided to send a small force to destroy the bridge at Bures while he waited at a crossroads north of Troarn until he had sufficient men to attack the town. At 4.00 a.m. he and his men moved off to the crossroads which was situated in heavily wooded terrain to the east of the main road between Troarn and Le Mesnil. On the way, he set up an ambush comprising two PIAT (Projector Infantry Anti-Tank) detach-ments under the command of a junior NCO to cover his group's rear.

Reaching the crossroads, Pearson despatched a patrol to recon-noitre the bridges at Bures, one of which was a steel girder railway bridge and the other a similar but shorter one carrying a trackway. By 9.15 a.m., however, both had been destroyed by sappers of No. 2 Troop of 3rd Parachute Squadron RE who had reached them at 6.30 a.m. This task completed, No. 2 Troop then joined up with Pearson and his group. More members of 8th Parachute Battalion had meantime made their way to the crossroads, among them Lieutenant Thompson and fifty men of A Company, and the majority of the Mortar and Machine Gun Platoons. Thompson and his men had earlier met the commander of 3rd Parachute Squadron RE, Major Tim Roseveare, and some of his sappers en route to blow the bridge at Troarn. Roseveare had ordered Thompson to establish a firm base at a road junction while he went forward to deal with the bridge. Thompson had complied but shortly afterwards had made contact with Pearson's ambush party and thus learned of the whereabouts of the battalion's main group. Not long afterwards, six enemy vehicles drove into the ambush area and were destroyed. The Germans, subsequently identified as being from the 21st Panzer Division, withdrew on foot towards Troarn.

Pearson despatched patrols to reconnoitre the areas to the north and west of Troarn. He had received no confirmation of the bridge there having been blown, so he sent a group of sappers, escorted by No. 9 Platoon under Lieutenant Brown, to check whether the bridge had been destroyed and, if so, to increase the damage to it if necessary. Brown and his men made their way to the outskirts of the town and headed for the bridge but came under fire from a house near the church. There was a brief skirmish and the platoon captured a small number of Germans who were members of a 21st Panzer Division reconnaissance unit. Shortly afterwards it came under fire again from enemy located in other houses in the area of the church. Once these had been dealt with, the sappers went forward and found that the bridge had already been blown. Placing further charges, they increased the width of the gap to 70 feet. Having completed their task, and been plied with food and wine by the locals, Lieutenant Brown and his men returned to the battalion.

1st Canadian Parachute Battalion, commanded by Lieutenant Colonel George Bradbrooke, had found itself with most of its strength dropped some distance away from DZ 'V'. C Company had flown in as an advance group along with the brigade headquarters and elements of the pathfinder company. One stick, under the company second-in-command, Captain John Hanson, landed about ten miles from the DZ, while another found itself on the opposite side of the River Orne and only 1,200 yards from the invasion beaches. Eventually, those members of C Company who reached the DZ area made their way to Varaville where their task was to neutralise the garrison there. Meanwhile, the pathfinders set up the two remaining serviceable Eurekas to guide in the main body.

By the time the battalion was on the ground, A Company was

scattered over a large area, some of its members subsequently linking up with C Company which was preparing for its attack on Varaville; by then the remainder of A Company were covering the withdrawal of 9th Parachute Battalion. B Company had also been dropped over a wide area, two of its platoons landing in flooded marshes two miles from the DZ. One stick was dropped several miles to the north-east, in the area of Villers-sur-Mer, while five others landed in flooded areas near Robehomme which were crisscrossed with large drainage ditches, many of them up to seven feet deep. Several men were forced to jettison their equipment to avoid being dragged underwater; while others, unable to release themselves from their heavy loads, drowned.

Lieutenant Norman Toseland, commander of No. 5 Platoon in B Company, was fortunate enough to land on firm ground. Having collected a group from the company, he led them towards the Robe-homme bridge, one of the battalion's objectives. As he did so, he encountered ten men from his own platoon together with others from 8th and 9th Parachute Battalions as well as some sappers from 3rd Parachute Squadron RE. On reaching the bridge, Toseland met Major Clayton Fuller who had landed in the river near by. By 3.00 a.m., however, the sappers supposed to blow the bridge had not arrived and so their sergeant, who had joined up with Toseland, collected all the plastic explosive carried by the infantrymen for making Gammon bombs. This amounted to only some thirty pounds in all but nevertheless was sufficient to at least weaken the bridge. At 6.00 a.m. another small group of sappers appeared with 200 pounds of explosive and the bridge was duly destroyed.

The commanding officer, Lieutenant Colonel Bradbrooke, landed in marshes to the west of the River Dives. Having extricated himself from them, he headed for the battalion's RV, situated beside the DZ, where he met his second-in-command, Major Jeff Nicklin, together with his signals officer, Lieutenant John Simpson, and his intelligence officer, Lieutenant R. Weathersbee. Also at the RV were men of 8th and 9th Parachute Battalions, and a detachment of the Anti-Tank

Platoon of the 2nd Battalion Oxfordshire & Buckinghamshire Light Infantry whose glider had landed in the wrong location. Soon afterwards, some members of Headquarter Company and 224th Parachute Field Ambulance also appeared. Lacking information on C Company's progress with its attack on Varaville, Bradbrooke despatched Weathersbee and two men to investigate and report back. Meantime, he led the remainder of his force towards the crossroads at Le Mesnil. He and his men came under fire and had to clear enemy troops out of houses along the road before they could continue. The enemy withdrew after an attack put in by men of Headquarter Company, after which Bradbrooke pushed on. At 11.00 a.m., he reached the crossroads where he established his battalion headquarters.

C Company had been undertaking the four tasks allocated to it but with only a fraction of its normal strength of over 100 men. They were to clear the enemy garrison from Varaville and knock out a 75mm gun position at a road junction near the Château de Varaville just east of the town; demolish a bridge over the River Divette; and destroy a radio transmitter station also located near Varaville. Even for a full-strength company, these were formidable objectives. As it was, when the company commander, Major Murray McLeod, arrived at the company RV at 00.30 a.m., he found only a small number of his men waiting there. He and some of his men had been on the DZ when the RAF Lancasters bombing the Merville Battery had flown over, several dumping their bomb loads on the DZ. McLeod, along with everyone else, had been left badly shocked. His group was only fifteen strong and could muster only one PIAT, three Sten guns, eight rifles and his own pistol. Nevertheless, he led his small force off to attack the enemy at Varaville. On the way, he encountered a small group of No. 9 Platoon who had also survived the bombing of the DZ. Although still badly shocked and concussed, they were otherwise unhurt and in possession of all their weapons and equipment.

With only twenty-five minutes remaining before the arrival of the main body of 3rd Parachute Brigade, Major McLeod and his men made their way through the dark to Varaville. Passing through the village undetected, they reached the gatehouse of the Château de Varaville; this was some distance from the chateau itself and overlooked the enemy positions, which comprised a long trench fortified by concrete and earthworks, with machine-gun positions sited at intervals and a bunker at each end.

McLeod's men searched the deserted gatehouse and discovered that it was being used as accommodation, housing ninety-six men. After positioning his force, McLeod went up to the second floor of the building where, shortly afterwards, he and some others came under fire from a 75mm gun at the rear of the trench. An attempt to knock it out with a PIAT proved unsuccessful and before the operator could fire a second bomb, the gun fired once again at the gatehouse, setting off some PIAT bombs. McLeod was mortally wounded and Lieutenant Chug Walker killed in the explosion.

At that moment the company second-in-command, Captain John Hanson, arrived with two other men carrying a machine gun. They were followed by a corporal and another man with a 2-inch mortar. A massive explosion was then heard away to the south-east, and Hanson and his men guessed that other members of C Company had succeeded in blowing the Varaville bridge.

At 10.00 a.m., having suffered a bombardment of 2-inch mortar bombs, the enemy at the chateau surrendered and the battle for Varaville was over. During the afternoon, having waited for an enemy counter-attack that never materialised, C Company was relieved by commandos of the 1st Special Service Brigade. Captain John Hanson and his men, accompanied by their prisoners, set off for Le Mesnil to rejoin their battalion. They came under fire several times en route but, having dealt with the enemy, pushed on and reached Le Mesnil at 6.00 p.m.

Brigadier James Hill had been making his way meanwhile towards Sallenelles to discover how 9th Parachute Battalion had fared at the Merville Battery. As he did so, he had heard the sound of approaching low-flying aircraft. Shouting to his men to take cover, he had thrown himself to the ground and fallen on top of the mortar platoon commander of 9th Parachute Battalion, Lieutenant Peters. On regaining his feet, he found that somehow Peters had been killed while he had survived, albeit having suffered a painful wound in the buttocks. The only other survivor was his headquarters defence platoon commander, the rest of his group being either badly wounded or dying. After rendering first aid and administering morphine to the wounded, Hill and his companion pressed on and eventually reached the regimental aid post of 9th Parachute Battalion.

His wound dressed, Hill headed on for Headquarters 6th Airborne Division, by then established in Ranville and where, on reporting to Major General Richard Gale, he was informed that 3rd Parachute Brigade had achieved all its objectives. Immediately afterwards, he underwent surgery for his wound. By 4.00 p.m.he had reached his own headquarters, where he found Lieutenant Colonel Alastair Pearson in temporary command of the brigade and discovered that some of his staff were missing, including the brigade major, Bill Collingwood, and the Deputy Assistant Adjutant & Quartermaster General (DAA & QMG), Major Alec Pope. The latter had been dropped fifteen miles to the east of the Dives and, together with his stick and a group of others, had been surrounded by enemy troops. Refusing to surrender, they had died fighting to a man.

As dawn broke, Major General Gale met Brigadier Nigel Poett, who informed him that the bridges had been captured and briefed him on 5th Parachute Brigade's dispositions. The divisional headquarters was meantime being established in the Château de Heaume in Le Bas de Ranville. At 7.00 a.m., the Allied sea and air bombardment of the assault beaches began, this being the signal for radio silence to be broken.

Late that evening, at 9.00 p.m., the noise of hundreds of aircraft could be heard and gradually the sky was filled with 250 aircraft towing the Horsas and Hamilcar gliders bringing in 6th Airlanding Brigade and the divisional troops. It was an awe-inspiring sight as the gliders cast off and swooped down towards the LZs. The enemy reaction was swift, with mortar fire being brought to bear on Ranville and the divisional headquarters. Small arms and mortar fire was directed at the LZs but casualties there were light. An hour and a half later, units were moving off towards their respective RV locations.

By midnight on 6 June, 6th Airborne Division was fully deployed with the exception of part of 6th Airlanding Brigade, namely the 12th Battalion The Devonshire Regiment (less one company which had landed already by glider) and those divisional troops who had not accompanied 6th Airlanding Brigade. They would arrive by sea on the following day. 3rd Parachute Brigade was holding a four-mile front with 9th Parachute Battalion at Le Plein in the north, 1st Canadian Parachute Battalion and the brigade headquarters at Le Mesnil in the centre, and 8th Parachute Battalion in the southern part of the Bois de Bavent. 5th Parachute Brigade meanwhile was occupying Le Bas de Ranville and Ranville with 12th and 13th Parachute Battalions respectively, while 7th Parachute Battalion was in reserve on the western edge of DZ 'N'. 6th Airlanding Brigade had two of its battalions ready to begin operations to extend the bridgehead next morning, while 1st Special Service Brigade was holding the villages of Hauger, Le Plein and Amfreville to the north and north-east of DZ 'N'.

On 7 June 9th Parachute Battalion moved off from the Château d'Amfreville in Hauger and headed across country to the south of the village of Breville to rejoin 3rd Parachute Brigade, arriving by 1.30 p.m. and immediately digging in. Its responsibility was the area of the Château Saint Come, extending from its grounds across a road to a house called the Bois de Mont, located in a woodland clearing. Following a discussion with Brigadier James Hill, however, Lieutenant Colonel Terence Otway altered the battalion's dispositions so that the Bois de Mont became the main defensive position while the area of the chateau was denied to the enemy by patrolling. A Company was located along either side of the chateau drive while B Company was posted along a sunken lane running along the northern edge of the Bois de

Mont woods and overlooking open ground stretching away towards Breville. C Company was in reserve, being deployed on the southern and western flanks of the position, while elements of the Machine Gun Platoon's Vickers MMGs were stationed beside the Breville–Le Mesnil road, near the gates of the chateau, covering both ways along it.

On 8 June a reconnaissance patrol from the battalion was despatched to reconnoitre the Château Saint Come but found it unoccupied, although there were signs that the enemy had made use of it. At midday A Company was attacked by an enemy fighting patrol which was repulsed without difficulty. During the afternoon, further attacks were launched against A and C Companies by elements of the 857th Grenadier Regiment but these were beaten off with the assistance of a counter-attack force, comprising members of the Anti Tank Platoon and a Bren LMG group led by Regimental Sergeant Major Cunningham and supported by a Vickers MMG. That night, the battalion was resupplied with two 3-inch mortars and three Vickers MMGs. All of its mortars had been lost during the drop and most of the Mortar Platoon were still missing. On receiving the new mortars, the platoon's Sergeant Hennessy began training replacements who soon reached a very creditable standard. Meanwhile, Sergeant McGeever formed a new Machine Gun Platoon and mounted one of the Vickers on a jeep for use as a mobile support vehicle.

At dawn on 9 June, the Germans brought down a heavy concentration of mortar fire on 9th Parachute Battalion, following this up with a strong attack on A Company and part of B Company. Both companies, however, waited until the enemy were only at fifty yards' range before opening fire and, with the support of the Mortar Platoon, inflicted very heavy casualties on the enemy infantry who withdrew into the woods surrounding the chateau. An hour later, the Germans mounted another attack but this met a similar fate.

Later that morning, the battalion received a report that the brigade headquarters was under threat. Lieutenant Colonel Otway swiftly assembled a small force of some thirty men from his battalion headquarters and C Company, along with a fire support group under Major George Smith which was equipped with two captured MG-42 machine guns. Moving rapidly through the woods to the south-east, Otway and his men trapped the enemy between themselves and the brigade head-quarters defence platoon, killing nineteen and taking one prisoner.

During the afternoon, two platoons of enemy infantry began infil-trating through the woods to the east and south of A Company's position. A platoon of C Company, led by Major Eddie Charlton and Lieutenant John Parfitt, launched a counter-attack but unfortunately encountered two machine guns. Both Charlton and Parfitt were killed in the ensuing action along with five others, their bodies being recovered by a patrol that night.

The morning of 10 June witnessed the arrival of Captain Robert Gordon-Brown and thirty members of the battalion, increasing its strength to 270 all ranks, although this was still very low. Despite the fact that everyone was tired, morale was extremely high and when the enemy put in an attack on A Company at 11.00 a.m. it was driven off with ease. Shortly afterwards, following the redeployment further forward of a platoon of A Company, a force of some fifty enemy infantry began digging in along the ditch beside the Breville road in full view of two detachments of the Machine Gun Platoon. At a range of 500 yards, they were in perfect enfilade and the two Vickers MMGs, supported by two Bren LMG groups from B Company, virtually wiped out the entire enemy force. Not long afterwards, the A Company platoon ambushed an enemy patrol at close range, almost annihilat-ing it.

By early afternoon, however, the Germans had reoccupied the chateau in force. An infantry company advanced down the drive, supported by two self-propelled guns which concentrated their fire on A and B Companies. By this time, 9th Parachute Battalion's supply of 3-inch mortar ammunition was running very low and PIATs were brought into action as makeshift mortars. Together with the firepower of some of A Company's Bren LMGs, this measure proved very effective in breaking up the enemy attack. Meanwhile, the Machine Gun Platoon's jeep-mounted Vickers engaged one of the self-propelled guns which had appeared unexpectedly to the north of the chateau. To the amazement of those watching, the vehicle suddenly exploded and ground to a halt.

Shortly afterwards, two companies of enemy infantry, heavily supported by mortars, launched a strong attack on B Company from the north. 9th Parachute Battalion's 3-inch mortars responded, driving off the enemy with the assistance of B Company's Bren LMGs. At that point, naval gunfire support was requested from the light cruiser HMS *Arethusa* via a forward observer bombardment (FOB) located at the brigade headquarters. Fifteen minutes later, salvoes of shells from *Arethusa*'s six 6-inch guns rained down 500 yards in front of the battalion's forward positions. Although they suffered heavy casualties, the leading enemy troops succeeded in reaching B Company's positions where they received a further mauling: few survived. Among those taken prisoner was the commanding officer of the 2nd Battalion 857th Grenadier Regiment, who informed his captors that his unit had been destroyed, the remainder of the regiment having suffered a similar fate in fighting around Ranville and Amfreville.

At 11.00 a.m. that night C Company, under Major Ian Dyer, reoccupied the chateau after some skirmishing with small groups of enemy. Throughout the rest of the night, the enemy probed and harassed the company's positions while the remainder of the battalion saw little activity.

On 10 June, meanwhile, the commander of I Corps, Lieutenant General Sir John Crocker, had decided to extend the bridgehead to east of the River Orne. 51st Highland Division was ordered to cross the bridges and take over the southern half of the sector from 6th Airborne Division. That night, the 5th Battalion The Black Watch, detached from 153rd Infantry Brigade and now under command of 3rd Parachute Brigade, arrived at an assembly area a short distance to the south-west of 9th Parachute Battalion. Its task was to attack and capture Breville from the south-west on the following day, dislodging the enemy from their vantage point on the high ground overlooking Ranville. The Château Saint Côme was a vital factor in any attack on Breville from the south, as any assault from that direction would be vulnerable to counter-attack through the area to the north of the chateau. Breville itself was occupied by a strong force of enemy infantry supported by self-propelled guns.

The plan drawn up by The Black Watch's commanding officer called for the main attack to be carried out from the south-west with heavy support from 51st Highland Division's artillery and his own mortars as well as those of 9th Parachute Battalion. Before first light, a company of The Black Watch relieved C Company at the chateau while a patrol under Captain Hugh Smyth made its way along the road towards Breville to reconnoitre the ground over which The Black Watch would approach the town.

The attack began with the leading companies of The Black Watch crossing 250 yards of open terrain. As they did so, the supporting artillery and mortar fire was lifted and the highlanders were subjected to a heavy concentration of mortar and machine-gun fire which inflicted several casualties. At the same time, the enemy brought down a heavy mortar bombardment on the area to the south-west through which The Black Watch reserve companies were moving up. Severe casualties were incurred there as well and the attack soon ground to a halt, The Black Watch withdrawing to 9th Parachute Battalion's positions and subsequently taking up positions around the Château Saint Côme.

8th Parachute Battalion, meanwhile, had been conducting operations from its base in the Bois de Bavent, dominating its area with vigorous and aggressive patrolling by night and day despite being at only fifty per cent of its full strength. The battalion's positions were located in thick forest where visibility and fields of fire were limited to only a few yards and through which it was impossible to move except via the network of tracks and a road running through the woods. The enemy were aware of this and so kept the tracks and road under almost constant mortar fire, in particular the track junctions, which became death traps. A number of casualties were caused by mortar bombs bursting in the trees; overhead cover for trenches had to be constructed to reduce the risk of head wounds being caused by flying shrapnel and wooden splinters.

Conditions in the forest were grim, with everything permanently soaked by rain, the dripping foliage being so dense that the sun was unable to penetrate. Trenches became waterlogged and the mud was slimy and slippery, at times making tracks treacherous. To make matters worse, the forest was infested with large mosquitoes which plagued the battalion, their bites, when scratched, causing skin sores. The commanding officer, Lieutenant Colonel Alastair Pearson, was a sick man, suffering from such sores in addition to a wound and a number of boils. Despite the hardships, however, 8th Parachute Battalion's morale was very high and its confidence undiminished. Patrols were sent out nightly to gather information or harass the enemy, on several occasions making their way into Troarn and Bures, both of which were occupied by the Germans.

1st Canadian Parachute Battalion meanwhile had also been seeing plenty of action. After a resupply of much-needed mortars and ammunition on 7 June, its positions at the Le Mesnil crossroads were attacked in force by enemy infantry of the 857th and 858th Grenadier Regiments, supported by tanks and self-propelled guns. These appeared in a long column along the road from Le Mesnil but before they could deploy were engaged by the battalion's mortars to good effect. Despite heavy casualties, however, the enemy infantry attacked B and C Companies with the support of a Mark IV tank which was driven off by a salvo of PIAT bombs before B Company counter-attacked with a bayonet charge, forcing the enemy to withdraw to a fortified farmhouse some 200 yards down the road. This was heavily defended with machine guns and enabled the Germans to threaten 1st Canadian Parachute Battalion's positions with harassing fire.

At 9.00 a.m., after the enemy attack had been beaten off, B Company was ordered to attack and clear the farmhouse. Two platoons, reinforced by men of Headquarter Company and commanded by Captain Peter Griffin, carried out the task. Griffin deployed two sections as a protection group on his flank before leading his men in a frontal assault through an orchard, catching the enemy by surprise. Lieutenant Norman Toseland and his platoon put in a bayonet charge, coming under fire as they made for a hedgerow. Four men were killed and two were wounded. The flank protection group also took casualties, three men being killed and two wounded by a machine gun which was subsequently knocked out by the assault group as it cleared the farmhouse and neighbouring outbuildings. Spotting some armoured vehicles, Captain Griffin halted the attack. At the same time, enemy mortars brought down fire on the farmhouse and the Germans then counterattacked with the support of a tank. As the assault group withdrew, the flank protection group opened fire on the enemy counter-attack force which was caught in a crossfire. B Company lost eight men killed and thirteen wounded in this action which resulted in the Germans withdrawing from the farmhouse and contenting themselves with sniping at the Canadians from the hedgerows.

On the following day, 9 June, a platoon of C Company under Lieutenant McGowan was sent to the village of Bavent to assess the strength of the enemy as well as to pinpoint the number of guns there. On approaching the village the platoon came under fire from a machine gun at almost point-blank range but fortunately suffered no casualties. McGowan and his men then launched an attack on Bavent which was found to be heavily occupied by enemy troops, many of whom opened fire from the upper storeys of buildings. The platoon responded by bringing its 2-inch mortar into action, dropping a shower of bombs on to the village before withdrawing.

That night, C Company sent a twelve-strong patrol, accompanied by a party of fourteen sappers from 3rd Parachute Squadron RE, into Bavent. Successfully infiltrating the village, the patrol opened fire on the enemy while the sappers placed explosive charges on some heavy mortars and in several houses. This task completed, the patrol withdrew as the enemy responded with machine guns firing wildly in different directions.

The next day saw the Germans attacking in strength, breaking through Breville and advancing on Ranville. Although they were beaten off, they had forced a wedge between 3rd Parachute Brigade and 1st Special Service Brigade. Shortly afterwards, a strong force comprising the 2nd Battalion 857th Grenadier Regiment, elements of the 1st and 2nd Battalions of the 858th and several companies of the 744th, supported by tanks and armoured cars, mounted an attack at a point between 1st Canadian and 9th Parachute Battalions, but this was broken up by heavy artillery and machine-gun fire. Two more attacks, launched to the north of 1st Canadian Parachute Battalion's positions, met a similar fate.

Two days later, on 12 June, the entire length of 3rd Parachute Brigade's front came under heavy shelling and mortar fire. At 3.00 p.m. that afternoon, an enemy battalion attacked 1st Canadian Parachute Battalion while another strong force, supported by six tanks and self-propelled guns, advanced on 9th Parachute Battalion and the 5th Battalion The Black Watch, the latter losing all of its anti-tank guns and nine of its Bren carriers. The battle raged around the Château Saint Côme with the highlanders doggedly resisting attempts by the enemy to seize it but gradually being forced back towards the Bois de Mont.

At the same time, the Germans began to concentrate on 9th Parachute Battalion, with A and C Companies coming under fire from the tanks and self-propelled guns. The Mortar Platoon, however, kept up a steady rate of fire, dropping bombs 300 yards away into the woods while under constant attack itself. More enemy infantry, supported by two tanks, attacked B Company which engaged one of the tanks with a PIAT, scoring two direct hits but failing to knock it out. The tank responded by immobilising two of the company's LMG positions and only withdrew after being hit again by a PIAT, being followed by the infantry which had advanced to within close range of A and B Companies.

By this time, 9th Parachute Battalion was so weak that Lieutenant Colonel Otway realised that it would not be able to hold out for much longer. When Brigadier Hill, in his headquarters only 400 yards away from 9th Parachute Battalion, received a radio message from Otway informing him of this, he himself led a force of forty men from 1st Canadian Parachute Battalion in a counter-attack, driving the enemy from 9th Parachute Battalion's area.

Meanwhile, in 5th Parachute Brigade, 7 June had witnessed 12th Parachute Battalion, in its positions on the high ground south of Le Bas de Ranville, come under attack from seven tanks supported by a company of the 125th Panzer Grenadier Regiment. The enemy advanced on A Company and inflicted a number of casualties, including the crew of the single 6-pounder anti-tank gun supporting the company. The situation was saved by one man, Lance Corporal Hall, who had been an anti-tank gunner prior to volunteering for Airborne Forces. Running over to the gun position, he proceeded to destroy three tanks in rapid succession, forcing the enemy to withdraw. He was subsequently awarded the Military Medal for this act of gallantry.

During that same day in 13th Parachute Battalion's area, a troop of three self-propelled guns attempted to penetrate A Company's positions but were destroyed. On the following day, the battalion knocked out six tanks while repelling another attack.

Two days later, before first light, a strong force of enemy was detected by B Company in the woods to the south-east of Breville. C Company despatched a reconnaissance patrol which reported that the enemy were forming up for an attack. At 9.00 a.m., the Germans began crossing DZ 'N', heading for the Caen Canal and River Orne bridges. Waiting until they were within fifty yards, 13th Parachute Battalion opened fire with deadly effect. C Company then counter-attacked with a bayonet charge, at which point 7th Parachute Battalion brought its Vickers MMGs and 3-inch mortars to bear. The enemy, who by this time had suffered over 400 killed, with 100 taken prisoner following this action, were routed and withdrew into three areas of woods at Le Mariquet, along the road between Ranville and Le Mesnil.

During that morning, reports reached Headquarters 6th Airborne Division of heavy fighting in the areas of both parachute brigades and 1st Special Service Brigade, all of whom were being heavily engaged by enemy forces attacking from the direction of Breville. Major General Gale decided that the enemy was to be cleared out of the wooded areas at Le Mariquet and requested armoured support from I Corps for 5th Parachute Brigade which was to carry out the task. During the early afternoon, B Squadron 13th/18th Royal Hussars arrived and linked up with 7th Parachute Battalion.

Both the squadron leader, Major Anthony Rugge Price, and Lieutenant Colonel Geoffrey Pine Coffin were aware that any form of artillery or mortar support would be impossible because of the risk to 13th Parachute Battalion and the units of 3rd Parachute Brigade. The task of clearing the enemy from the woods would be carried out by A and B Companies who would be preceded by a troop of the Hussars' M-4 Sherman tanks which would move over the open ground of the DZ to the left of the companies' axis of advance. The tanks would bring fire to bear on the woods for two minutes before signalling the companies to move forward by firing smokeshells. A reserve troop would follow the leading tanks while the squadron's reconnaissance troop of four M-5 Stuart light tanks would move along their left flank, covering the Breville ridge.

The tanks encountered problems as they advanced during the attack. One of the reserve troop's tanks was hit and, as the leading troop was laying down fire on the woods, the tracks of the reconnaissance troop leader's Stuart became entangled with the rigging lines of parachutes lying on the DZ. Completely immobilised, it was almost immediately knocked out by a self-propelled gun. Meantime, the leading troop leader's Sherman had also been hit and set ablaze, the rest of the troop coming under fire from a self-propelled gun. Almost at the same moment, Major Rugge Price's tank was also hit and set on fire. The squadron began pulling back but, as it did so, another Sherman and Stuart were hit. A fifth Sherman was knocked out after it became immobilised, its tracks also entangled in rigging lines.

A and B Companies, meanwhile, had been making good progress. B Company had succeeded in clearing the enemy, a battalion of the 857th Grenadier Regiment, out of the first two woods while A Company cleared the third. By the end of the afternoon, twenty Germans had been killed and 100 taken prisoner. The two companies had incurred very light casualties, ten men having been wounded, but the Hussars had suffered badly, losing ten killed and five wounded. They had also lost five Shermans and two Stuarts destroyed.

Since landing in Normandy on the evening of 6 June, 6th Airlanding Brigade had also seen its share of heavy fighting. Brigadier Hugh Kindersley's brigade headquarters and the 1st Battalion The Royal Ulster Rifles, the latter commanded by Lieutenant Colonel Jack Carson, had landed on LZ 'N' while Lieutenant Colonel Michael Roberts's 2nd Battalion The Oxfordshire & Buckinghamshire Light Infantry, less its D Company and two platoons of B Company which had carried out the *coup de main* attack on the bridges, flew into LZ 'W'. With them were A Company 12th Battalion The Devonshire Regiment, 6th Airborne Armoured Reconnaissance Regiment, 211th Airlanding Light Battery RA, 249th Field Company RE and two sections of 195th Airlanding Field Ambulance attached to the two battalions. The 211th Airlanding Light Battery, whose 75mm pack howitzers were in action north of Ranville half an hour after landing at 9.30 p.m., made history that evening when it became the first unit of the Royal Artillery ever to fly into action.

The remainder of 6th Airlanding Brigade, namely the 12th Battalion The Devonshire Regiment (less one company) commanded by Lieutenant Colonel Dick Stephens, would land by sea next day along with the 53rd Airlanding Light Regiment RA (less one battery), 3rd Airlanding Anti-Tank Battery RA (less one troop), 2nd Airlanding Light Anti-Aircraft Battery RA, 195th Airlanding Field Ambulance (less two sections) and other divisional troops.

Following the landing, Brigadier Kindersley assembled his head-quarters in an orchard in Le Bas de Ranville and at 10.30 p.m., only an hour and a half after the leading elements of the brigade had landed, held his first 'O' Group. The 1st Battalion The Royal Ulster Rifles was tasked with capturing the villages of Longueval and Sainte Honorine while the 2nd Battalion The Oxfordshire & Buckinghamshire Light Infantry was to take Escoville.

At 9.00 a.m. on the following morning, the Royal Ulster Rifles set off along the east bank of the River Orne towards Longueval with C Company, under Major Bob Hynds, and the Machine Gun Platoon, commanded by Lieutenant Harry Morgan, remaining dug in on a feature called the Ring Contour to provide fire support for the attack. The battalion's second-in-command, Major John Drummond, remained with C Company which was accompanied by a forward observer bom-bardment in radio contact with the light cruiser HMS *Arethusa* lying offshore.

The battalion carried out a right flanking attack with its 3-inch mortars ready to provide additional fire support from the Mortar Platoon baseline south of Ranville. In the event, however, Longueval proved to be unoccupied by the enemy and was taken and secured without opposition. Lieutenant Colonel Carson decided to push on without delay and attack Sainte Honorine with A and B Companies, commanded by Majors Charles Vickery and Gerald Rickord respec-tively, while leaving Battalion Headquarters and D Company, under Major Tony Dyball, to hold Longueval.

By now, C Company was under very heavy fire from enemy mortars and 88mm self-propelled guns of the 200th Assault Gun Battalion, inflicting severe casualties. Unfortunately, the forward observer had lost radio contact with HMS *Arethusa* and the battalion's mortars were the only source of support. Moreover, H-Hour for the attack on Sainte Honorine had been delayed but neither C Company, the Machine Gun Platoon nor the mortars had been notified of this and therefore the fire support plan for the attack had gone ahead as planned. Consequently, by the time A and B Companies crossed the start line, the machine guns and mortars were running low on ammunition. Meanwhile, C Company observed seven self-propelled guns heading for Sainte Honorine from the north-east; unfortunately, its warning, sent by radio to Battalion Headquarters in Longueval, did not get through.

Under cover of smoke, A and B Companies succeeded in penetrating the German positions to a certain extent but suffered severe casualties from machine guns and self-propelled guns. Contact between them and Battalion Headquarters was lost and eventually they were forced to withdraw to Longueval. Lieutenant Colonel Carson now decided to withdraw C Company and the Machine Gun Platoon from the Ring Contour and concentrate the battalion in defensive positions in Longueval. The attack had cost it dear, with six killed, sixty-five wounded and sixty-eight missing, though twenty of the latter would reappear during the next few days.

The 2nd Battalion The Oxfordshire & Buckinghamshire Light Infantry was also having a tough time. At 4.30 a.m., it had advanced on Herouvillette which was found to be unoccupied by the Germans who had withdrawn in the direction of Escoville. Having taken the village, the battalion was ready by 8.30 a.m. to continue its advance on Escoville. Patrols from A and B Companies were despatched to reconnoitre the village, situated some 1,000 yards south of Herouvillette. The terrain between the two villages consisted of small fields bordered with very dense hedgerows of the type for which the Normandy *bocage* countryside was renowned. No enemy were detected in Escoville itself but the patrols encountered several snipers in its vicinity.

The battalion continued its advance at 10.00 a.m., leaving C Company in Herouvillette to establish a firm base there. It encountered increasingly stiff opposition, but by 11.00 a.m. its three other rifle companies had reached their objectives and were digging in. Major Howard's D Company took up positions in houses on the southern edge of the village with A Company, under Major Gilbert Rahr, on its right. It had been intended to site Battalion Headquarters in the Château d'Escoville but it had been selected as a target by a self-propelled gun and an alternative location had to be chosen.

Escoville was dominated by high ground to the south and east, affording enemy forward observers an excellent viewpoint of which they took full advantage, bringing down heavy and accurate artillery fire which caused casualties among the three rifle companies. At 3.00 p.m. enemy infantry, supported by armour, attacked the village and brought heavy fire to bear on it. The enemy artillery fire had earlier prevented the battalion bringing forward its 6-pounder anti-tank guns and with none of these to support them, and with radio contact with Battalion Headquarters lost, the three companies found themselves under severe pressure. During the next hour, a series of actions took place at close quarters and there was a considerable amount of house-to-house fighting. It became increasingly apparent that with no anti-tank guns to counter the enemy armour, Escoville could not be held without severe casualties being incurred.

At that point, Lieutenant Colonel Roberts ordered his three companies to withdraw under covering fire from C Company which now came forward to a position forward to Herouvillette. Elements of A and D Companies, however, became cut off in Escoville and were saved by a counter-attack led by B Company's commander, Major J. S. R. 'Flaps' Edmunds.

Withdrawing to Herouvillette, the battalion took up defensive positions to deal with any enemy counter-attack, but this failed to materialise. By this time it had suffered eighty-seven casualties. Among these was Lieutenant Colonel Roberts, who was evacuated that evening, having sustained injuries as a result of a collision between his glider and another just before landing. He had insisted on carrying on but by the evening of 7 June was unable to walk. The battalion's second-in-command, Major Mark Darell Brown, then assumed command.

In the afternoon of 7 June, the 12th Battalion The Devonshire Regiment arrived at Le Bas de Ranville and relieved 12th Parachute

Battalion, which was now under command of 6th Airlanding Brigade, and withdrew to the area of the Château de Ranville to rest. The Devons dug in on the southern edge of the village with two companies in reserve. During that night, these were attacked by enemy aircraft dropping anti-personnel bombs, killing three men in B Company and wounding sixteen.

The morning of 8 June initially proved to be a quiet one for 6th Airlanding Brigade. At 11.00 a.m., however, the Devons came under heavy artillery and mortar fire which continued until 6.30 p.m. The day was also marred by an incident when the Reconnaissance Platoon of the Royal Ulster Rifles was shelled by artillery of 3rd Infantry Division. Attempts to halt the shelling by radio proved unsuccessful and so the platoon commander, Captain Robin Rigby, swam across the River Orne to contact the nearest unit. A radio message was flashed to the guns to cease fire, but not before the platoon had suffered three casualties.

At 10.00 a.m. on the following day, 9 June, 6th Airlanding Brigade received a message from Headquarters 6th Airborne Division stating that the Germans were withdrawing from Sainte Honorine. At the same time, an observation post of the Devons, sited on the reverse slope of the Ring Contour feature, confirmed enemy movement out of the village. A reconnaissance patrol was despatched by the Devons to gain further information on the enemy activity but came under heavy mortar and machine-gun fire as it approached the top of the Ring Contour and was forced to withdraw.

On the strength of the reports received from the Devons, Brigadier Hugh Kindersley decided to mount another attack on Sainte Honorine and again detailed the 1st Battalion The Royal Ulster Rifles for the task. 12th Parachute Battalion moved down to Longueval to take over its defence and secure the start line for the attack.

While conducting a preliminary reconnaissance, two platoons of the Royal Ulster Rifles' D Company, led by Major Tony Dyball, successfully ambushed an enemy platoon on the Sainte Honorine–Colombelles road. Another patrol, under Captain Ken Donnelly, observed enemy infantry and armour in the town while the observation post on Ring Contour reported more infantry and armour returning to the town from the east. In view of these reports, and learning that no artillery support would be available, Lieutenant Colonel Jack Carson cancelled the attack. 12th Parachute Battalion returned to its positions in reserve while the Royal Ulster Rifles remained in defence of Longueval.

At 7.00 p.m. that night, the Germans brought down very heavy artillery and mortar fire along the entire southern front from Ranville to Herouvillette. Headquarters 6th Airlanding Brigade suffered shell-bursts among its trenches and the Devons' observation post received a direct hit and was knocked out. At 8.00 p.m., a strong attack was launched against the Devons, the Germans penetrating their positions before being beaten off by a counter-attack. Half an hour later, the enemy put down smoke on the Ring Contour and shortly afterwards three companies of the 125th Panzer Grenadier Regiment, supported by tanks, appeared opposite A Company. Two platoons of C Company and the Machine Gun Platoon's Vickers MMGs opened fire, being joined by artillery of 3rd Infantry Division. Despite suffering heavy casualties, the enemy continued to advance until only some fifty yards from the Devons' positions, at which point they broke and withdrew in disorder.

On 9 June the 2nd Battalion Oxfordshire & Buckinghamshire Light Infantry, which had spent the previous day fortifying Herouvillette, sent C Company back into Escoville to check for any signs of enemy activity. The company reached the Château d'Escoville without incident but on entering the southern part of the village came under mortar and artillery fire. Enemy infantry, supported by armour, advanced into Escoville and made an attempt to outflank the company while a self-propelled gun opened fire on the chateau. At 4.00 p.m. more enemy troops, supported by armoured cars, arrived in the village and half an hour later C Company was ordered to withdraw and return to Herouvillette, leaving behind patrols to monitor the enemy's movements. At 5.30 p.m., these reported a concentration of enemy infantry and armour which was assumed to be in preparation for an attack on Herouvillette.

At 6.30 p.m. the battalion came under intense mortar and artillery fire, this being followed by an air attack by Messchersmitt 109 fighters which strafed the village. Shortly afterwards, infantry of the 192nd Panzer Grenadier Regiment, supported by tanks and self-propelled guns, advanced on Herouvillette. The battalion, however, had laid its defensive plans well and the Vickers MMGs of the Machine Gun Platoon, and the Anti-Tank Platoon's 6-pounder guns, were well sited with good fields of fire. Furthermore, the battalion was supported by the 17-pounder guns of the 3rd and 4th Airlanding Anti-Tank Batteries RA and was able to call on artillery support from field and medium regiments on call to 6th Airborne Division. The enemy advanced to a point some 100 yards from C and D Companies' positions before being driven back by the intense volume of fire brought down on them. At 9.30 p.m. they abandoned their attack and withdrew, leaving behind eight Mark IV tanks, two armoured cars and two self-propelled guns destroyed.

During this period Headquarters 6th Airborne Division, which was located only 500 yards behind the Devons' positions, was also taking its fair share of punishment. The Commander Royal Artillery (CRA), Lieutenant Colonel Jack Norris, had been severely wounded in the throat while observing the landing of 6th Airlanding Brigade on 6 June, while Major Gerry Lacoste, the GSO2 (Intelligence), had also been wounded that same day and had to be evacuated. His post was taken over by Captain Freddie Scholes, who was subsequently killed.

On 12 June, Major General Gale decided that the threat from the enemy forces in Breville had to be removed once and for all. By this time, however, 6th Airborne Division's strength was sorely depleted after the heavy fighting of the previous five days, 3rd Parachute Brigade in particular being exhausted and very low in numbers. He therefore allotted the task of attacking Breville to his reserve, 12th Parachute Battalion, which numbered only some 350 men, reinforced by D

Company 12th Battalion The Devonshire Regiment. In support of the battalion would be a squadron of the 13th/18th Royal Hussars and a formidable amount of artillery: four field regiments and one medium regiment. Gale also decided to use his pathfinder unit, 22nd Independent Parachute Company, in order to deal with any enemy counter-attack.

The attack on Breville was to begin at 10.00 p.m. that night, Gale's intention being to catch the enemy off-guard while recovering from the fighting earlier that day. It would be launched from the west, from the eastern outskirts of Amfreville, No. 6 Commando having secured the start line beforehand. The commanding officer of 12th Parachute Battalion, Lieutenant Colonel Johnny Johnson, thus had little time to draw up his plan. He decided that C Company would capture and secure the initial crossroads while the Devons' D Company was to follow up behind and then deploy to the left on reaching Breville. A company would move through C Company, pushing on to secure the south-eastern part of the village, while B Company brought up the rear in reserve. The approach to Breville consisted of 400 yards of open ground and, to provide cover for the battalion as it advanced, a troop of the 13th/18th Royal Hussars would move along the right flank and destroy a known enemy strongpoint some 200 yards from the village.

At 8.00 p.m. that night, 12th Parachute Battalion prepared for battle while the company commanders attended the commanding officer's 'O' Group and carried out a brief reconnaissance. At 8.35 p.m. the battalion moved off for Amfreville, where it concentrated for the attack. At 9.50 p.m., the supporting artillery opened fire, sending a barrage of shells over the heads of the paratroops as they advanced along the road towards Breville. Soon, however, the battalion came under enemy artillery and mortar fire, and was forced to take cover in the ditches on either side of the road or behind walls of nearby buildings. It was some fifteen minutes before the fire slackened sufficiently to enable the battalion to continue moving up.

On crossing the start line at approximately 10.00 p.m., C Company, commanded by Major 'Steve' Stephens, began to take casualties, losing all of its officers and its company sergeant major. Nevertheless, it continued to advance under command of a senior NCO while still under fire from self-propelled guns. Although enemy mortar and artillery fire continued to rain down, there was no small arms fire from Breville, which by this time was ablaze. Meanwhile, the Sherman tanks of the 13th/18th Royal Hussars were firing tracer from their turret machine guns to guide the assaulting companies to their objective. By the time C Company had reached Breville, however, it was only fifteen strong.

As A Company crossed the start line, it lost its commander, Captain Paul Bernhard, who was wounded, and the whole of No. 2 Platoon, under Lieutenant James Campbell, whose members were either killed or wounded. Company Sergeant Major Marwood assumed command but was killed as the company reached Breville. Captain Bernhard staggered on after his men, passing C Company's commander, Major Stephens, who was lying wounded by the roadside, from where he had urged his men on into the village. On reaching Breville, Bernhard found No. 3 Platoon, which shortly afterwards lost its commander, Lieutenant Brewer. The platoon sergeant took over command of the remaining nine men of the platoon, leading them forward to clear the village's chateau. Meanwhile, the remaining members of No. 1 Platoon took the chateau garden, which was their objective.

As D Company of the Devons, under its second-in-command, Captain John Warwick-Pengelly, was moving past the church in Le Plein on its way to the start line, a number of men were wounded by a shell bursting in the middle of its ranks. Nevertheless, the company continued to head towards Amfreville along a narrow sunken lane, encountering as it did so wounded members of 12th Parachute Battalion coming in the opposite direction. It then met the commander of the Devons' support company, Major Eddie Warren, who had been asked by D Company's commander, Major John Bampfylde, to bring the latter's men to the start line.

As D Company crossed the start line, a salvo of shells, later suspected of having been fired by the supporting artillery of 51st Highland Division, fell short and exploded in the middle of a group of officers gathered near by, among them the commanders of 6th Airlanding and 1st Special Service Brigades, Brigadiers Hugh Kindersley and The Lord Lovat, both of whom were seriously wounded. Among those killed were the commanding officer of 12th Parachute Battalion, Lieutenant Colonel Johnny Johnson, and Major John Bampfylde.

As D Company pushed on, B Company brought up the rear, accompanied by Colonel Reggie Parker, the deputy commander of 6th Airlanding Brigade. The former commanding officer of 12th Parachute Battalion, he had been standing near Lieutenant Colonel Johnson when he was killed and, although wounded himself, was now going forward to take over command of his old battalion.

It was now 10.45 p.m. and dusk was falling. The small remaining element of C Company had secured the crossroads while the eighteen men of A Company had taken up positions on the south-eastern edge of Breville. In the north-eastern corner of the village, the twenty survivors of the Devons' D Company had taken the orchard which had been their objective. At that point Colonel Parker, who was accompanied by an FOO of 53rd Airlanding Light Regiment RA, called for defensive fire from the supporting artillery to prevent an enemy counterattack. Tragically, there was a misunderstanding on the gun line and Breville was subjected to a heavy barrage, causing further casualties among the remnants of 12th Parachute Battalion and the Devons' company. The FOO, Captain Hugh Parker, was killed and it was his signaller who ordered the guns to cease fire. When the shelling stopped, it was found that Major Paul Rogers, commander of B Company, had been mortally wounded and nine more men of 12th Parachute Battalion wounded. A Company's commander, Captain Paul Bernhard, had been wounded again and Captain John Sim of B Company had been hit in the arm.

At 2.00 a.m. on 13 June, the 13th/18th Royal Hussars moved up to the crossroads and linked up with the remnants of C Company. Early that morning, the 22nd Independent Parachute Company, commanded by Major Nigel Stockwell, arrived as reinforcements. Later that day, the 1st Battalion The Royal Ulster Rifles moved up from Ranville to relieve what little remained of 12th Parachute Battalion and the Devons' D Company.

The battle for Breville had exacted a very heavy toll. Casualties in 12th Parachute Battalion and the Devons' company numbered nine officers and 153 men killed during the action. Of the 550 officers and men of the battalion who dropped into Normandy on the night of 5/6 June, only Headquarter Company and fifty-five men of the rifle companies remained. All of the officers, including the commanding officer, and all the warrant officers who had taken part in the attack had been killed or wounded. Enemy casualties during the battle amounted to seventy-seven killed and an unknown number wounded.

During the night of 12 June, 152nd Infantry Brigade of 51st Highland Division crossed the River Orne and at 4.00 a.m. on 13 June the 5th Battalion The Queen's Own Cameron Highlanders attacked and seized Longueval, but at 9.15 a.m. the Germans counter-attacked and recaptured it. At 6.00 p.m. that evening, the 7th Battalion The Argyll & Sutherland Highlanders arrived in 6th Airborne Division's area and occupied Ranville. On the night of 13 June, 6th Airborne Division handed over responsibility for the southern part of the bridgehead to 51st Highland Division.

6th Airborne Division's front now extended over 9,000 yards from a point in the Bois de Bavent due east of Escoville to the sea. To hold that area, Major General Gale had only nine weak battalions and 1st Special Service Brigade, with a total strength of less than 6,000 men, all of whom had been fighting almost ceaselessly for eight days and nights. In order to permit him to withdraw one brigade at a time for rest and to provide him with some form of reserve, Gale was allotted 4th Special Service Brigade, a Royal Marine formation comprising 41, 46, 47 and 48 Commandos RM and commanded by Brigadier B. W. Leicester RM.

First to be withdrawn was 3rd Parachute Brigade as it had suffered particularly heavy casualties. 5th Parachute Brigade took over the southern part of the front, up to and including Le Mesnil, while 6th Airlanding Brigade was stationed along the stretch to Breville, with one of its battalions deployed in depth. 1st and 4th Special Service Brigades meanwhile covered from Breville to the coast.

A few days later, 6th Airborne Division witnessed an armoured battle that began from its bridgehead. During the previous ten days, four enemy infantry divisions had arrived in Normandy, three appearing in the sector opposite Second British Army and relieving three panzer divisions which began moving west to First US Army's front. This westwards movement had to be halted and the decision was taken to mount a thrust which would place British armour on the Bourgebus Ridge, to the south of Caen, thus threatening the Germans with the possibility of an Allied breakout in the direction of Paris.

Codenamed Goodwood, the operation began on 18 July when the British VIII Corps, comprising the 7th, 11th and Guards Armoured Divisions, advanced on a front of 1,000 yards behind a rolling artillery barrage down a corridor which had already been subjected to three hours of concentrated bombing by Allied aircraft. The members of 6th Airborne Division watched in awe from their positions as long columns of tanks advanced while waves of bombers struck at targets further forward. The battle raged for two days, during which the three armoured formations encountered increasingly stiff opposition, finally ending on the afternoon of 20 July when heavy rain turned the ground into a quagmire. Meanwhile, 6th Airborne Division came under some retaliatory fire from mortars and artillery but this failed to cause significant casualties. At the same time, the bridgehead was expanded and 49th Infantry Division moved up between 6th Airborne Division and 51st Highland Division.

Throughout the next two months, 6th Airborne Division was employed in the defensive role, although its battalions continued to patrol aggressively, seeking out the enemy wherever possible and inflicting damage at every opportunity. The Bois de Bavent, previously the hunting ground of 8th Parachute Battalion and now that of the 7th, witnessed much of this type of action with the battalion's snipers proving to be constant thorns in the side of the enemy who had to be on their guard at all times.

In late June the commanding officer, Lieutenant Colonel Pine Coffin, decided to mount an attack on a farm dubbed 'Bob's Farm'. B Company, commanded by Major Bob Keene, was detailed for the task.

Just as the company had moved up to its start line and shaken out into assault formation, one of the platoon commanders, Lieutenant Poole, observed a platoon of enemy forming up a short distance away and obviously preparing to attack in the opposite direction. B Company immediately launched its assault, charging through an orchard into the farm. As they advanced, however, Major Bob Keene and his men came under fire and were forced to take cover in the farm itself, suffering fifteen casualties including two platoon commanders, both of whom were wounded. Among those killed was Company Sergeant Major Durbin, who had been wounded earlier but had continued to man a Bren LMG until hit again, this time fatally. Heavier casualties had been inflicted on the enemy, who suffered thirty killed, an unknown number wounded and nine taken prisoner.

Bob's Farm was subsequently attacked again, this time by a patrol of the 22nd Independent Parachute Company under Lieutenant Bob de Latour. He and his men succeeded in infiltrating the enemy positions and silently taking some prisoners. Unfortunately the alarm was raised as the patrol was withdrawing and Lieutenant de Latour was fatally wounded in the ensuing action.

Pine Coffin then decided to attack Bob's Farm once more. During the early afternoon of 10 July, B Company mounted another assault but this was unsuccessful, the company being forced to withdraw under heavy mortar and machine-gun fire with a senior NCO, Sergeant Lucas, covering the withdrawal by engaging the enemy machine guns with his Bren LMG. Support was forthcoming, however, from the whole of

53rd Airlanding Light Regiment RA which had fired 5,000 rounds from its 75mm pack howitzers by the time the action ended.

On 7 August, Major General Richard Gale received orders from I Corps to prepare 6th Airborne Division for follow-up operations, as there were indications of an impending German withdrawal. The overall plan was for First Canadian Army to break out from the bridge-head, thereafter advancing south-east from Caen towards Falaise and subsequently swinging east towards the River Seine. I Corps, under command of First Canadian Army, would advance along an axis running through Lisieux which lay some fifteen miles inland, and 6th Airborne Division's task would be to maintain pressure on the enemy's right flank to reduce opposition on the Canadians' main axis. In addition to 1st and 4th Special Service Brigades, the division was allotted The Princess Irene Royal Netherlands Brigade Group, commanded by Lieutenant Colonel A. C. de Ruyter van Steveninck, and the 1st Belgian Brigade Group under Lieutenant Colonel Jean-Baptiste Piron.

6th Airborne Division's final objective was the mouth of the River Seine but there were a number of rivers to be crossed en route, the three main ones being the Dives, Touques and Risle, the last two lying in narrow valleys with water meadows. The Dives was the biggest obstacle, lying in a broad and marshy valley with a derelict canal running parallel to it. Between the river and canal was a large island, while to the east of the valley was a dominating line of hills.

Major General Gale was faced by a choice of two routes leading to the Seine. The first led from Troarn through Dozule, Pont l'Éveque and Beuzeville to Pont Audemer, the total distance by road being approximately forty-five miles. The alternative route ran along the coast through Cabourg, Trouville and Honfleur. There was little difference in the terrain on both routes, namely undulating ground with hills covered in scrub and woods, between which was pastureland divided by thick hedgerows.

Gale chose the inland route although it meant crossing an 8,000-yard-wide valley of marshes and streams, as well as the major combined obstacle of the Dives and the canal. His decision was based on the fact that the division was very short of sappers and bridging equipment, which meant that only one route could be maintained. The inland route would pose fewer bridging problems, being farther from the estuaries where the rivers were wider, deeper and tidal.

Gale gave 6th Airlanding Brigade, now led by Brigadier Edward Flavell and with the Dutch and Belgian brigades under command, the task of clearing the coastal areas of enemy while the rest of the division advanced along its main axis via Troarn and Pont Audemer. 3rd Parachute Brigade would lead, advancing to Bures and crossing the Dives there before continuing on to the island in the middle of the valley, being followed by 5th Parachute Brigade. Meantime, 4th Special Service Brigade would remain at Troarn and hold the area to the south, being ready, along with 5th Parachute Brigade, to exploit any gains achieved by 3rd Parachute Brigade. 1st Special Service Brigade would take Bavent and Robehomme, crossing the river at the latter if the opportunity presented itself.

The Germans began their withdrawal on the night of 17 August. At 3.00 a.m. on the following morning, 3rd Parachute Brigade commenced its advance and by 7.00 a.m. 8th and 9th Parachute Battalions had taken Bures without opposition. At 8.00 a.m., 1st Canadian Parachute Battalion started to advance through the Bois de Bavent where it was slowed by mines and booby traps. At the same time, 4th Special Service Brigade was advancing on Troarn and Saint Pair while 1st Special Service Brigade was heading for Bavent and Robehomme.

6th Airlanding Brigade had commenced moving up on the morning of 17 August along two roads with the 12th Battalion The Devonshire Regiment, supported by 210th Airlanding Light Battery RA, on the left, moving along the Breville–Merville road. The 2nd Battalion The Oxfordshire & Buckinghamshire Light Infantry, with 212th Airlanding Light Battery RA in support, was on the right, pushing along the Le Mesnil–Varaville road. Following up in reserve was the 1st Battalion The Royal Ulster Rifles.

At 9.25 a.m. B Company of the Devons came under mortar and machine-gun fire from an enemy delaying position astride the road north of the Longuemare crossroads. The enemy resistance was eventually overcome following some very accurate shelling by 210th Airlanding Light Battery with support from the battalion's mortars and a troop of Belgian armoured cars.

At 1.00 p.m. the Royal Ulster Rifles moved through to take over the lead while the Devons withdrew into reserve in the Breville area. Thereafter, the battalion advanced with a close pursuit force, comprising C Company, the Reconnaissance Platoon, the Pioneer Platoon and a section of 249th Field Company RE, deployed forward. On reaching Le Petit Homme, the Reconnaissance Platoon was within only 800 yards of the enemy when the road in front of it was suddenly blown and cratered. B Company was left in the area to cut off any enemy retreating from La Franceville Plage where the 1st Belgian Brigade Group was operating on the company's left.

The rest of the battalion continued its advance along the coastal road. As speed was of the essence and because the entire area was known to be heavily mined, it remained on the road itself and thus progress was rapid without any resistance being encountered. On the outskirts of Cabourg, however, the battalion met stiff opposition and all attempts to outflank the enemy failed due to the lack of room to manoeuvre. Lieutenant Colonel Jack Carson had been ordered to pursue the enemy without becoming heavily engaged and he decided to concentrate the battalion in the area of Le Homme and Les Panoramas.

Next day, after some skirmishing between the enemy and the Reconnaissance Platoon, the battalion received orders to remain in its location where that evening it was subjected to sporadic and largely ineffective shelling and mortar fire. The following day was relatively quiet but the day after proved very different when, in the early morning, the battalion was subjected to increasingly heavy artillery fire. In the early afternoon, it received orders to move to Le Plein, being relieved by the 1st Belgian Brigade Group. The latter arrived early and the relief-in-line was carried out with difficulty under fire. By midnight, however, the Royal Ulster Rifles were concentrated at Le Plain and in the early morning of 21 August moved in transport to a brigade concentration area east of Troarn where they were joined by the Devons and the 2nd Battalion The Oxfordshire & Buckinghamshire Light Infantry. That night, the battalion moved again to a lying-up area at Lieu Saint Laurent.

The morning of 21 August found the 12th Battalion The Devonshire Regiment continuing the advance with C Company in the lead. No opposition was encountered until the early afternoon when D Company, by then spearheading the battalion, came under machine-gun and mortar fire. Very heavy fighting ensued in and around the hedgerows in A Company's area, with some casualties being suffered. Both companies were too close together for fire support to be used and there was insufficient time before last light for an attack to be mounted against the enemy. The battalion thus remained in its positions at the end of the first bound of 6th Airlanding Brigade's advance while preparing for an attack on the following day.

At 3.00 a.m. on 22 August, C Company carried out a flanking move to Branville with orders to conduct a reconnaissance, prior to an attack at first light, to discover if the enemy had withdrawn and occupied the village. The company arrived at 5.30 a.m., discovering six enemy asleep in their positions and taking them prisoner without any resistance. At the same time, six members of one of the division's parachute units, who had been hidden by local people, were liberated. At 8.00 a.m., Brigadier Flavell ordered the Devons to occupy Branville with two companies, B Company being sent to join C Company.

3rd Parachute Brigade had begun crossing the Dives at Bures during the late afternoon of 18 August, having been delayed while 3rd Parachute Squadron RE replaced a bridge destroyed on 6 June, and by last light all of its units were across the river. By then, 1st Canadian Parachute Battalion had encountered enemy units at Plain-Lugan, and 8th Parachute Battalion had reached the outskirts of Goutranville.

Next morning the brigade advanced on Goutranville, encountering stiff opposition while coming under fire from German artillery on the heights of Putot which dominated the area. As the island was under constant observation by the enemy, it became apparent that any attack would have to be mounted at night. Major General Gale tasked 3rd Parachute Brigade with securing the railway line east of the canal; this was to be the starting point for a second-phase attack by 5th Parachute Brigade which would then push on and attack the heights of Putot.

At 10.00 p.m. that night, 1st Canadian Parachute Battalion led the way as 3rd Parachute Brigade crossed the start line. By 10.35 p.m., C Company had taken the northernmost railway bridge which had been blown by the enemy but was passable to infantry. The next two bridges to the south had also been destroyed but the fourth and southernmost was captured intact by A Company. By 11.59 p.m., the battalion had overrun two positions occupied by troops of the 744th Grenadier Regiment and taken 150 prisoners. 9th Parachute Battalion then advanced through the Canadians towards the railway station at Dozule, and by 1.00 a.m. on 19 August had reached the outskirts of the town. There it came under artillery fire which by mid-morning had caused fifty-four casualties and had hit the regimental aid post.

In the meantime, 5th Parachute Brigade had crossed the canal via the southernmost bridge and had pushed on towards the village of Putôt-en-Auge. 7th Parachute Battalion's task was to take and secure the spur immediately to the east, after which 12th Parachute Battalion would take the village itself. It would not be an easy task as the enemy were well dug in and appeared ready to put up a stiff fight.

13th Parachute Battalion, which was to cross the canal and follow up behind 9th Parachute Battalion, attempted to use the blown railway bridge. By that time, however, the water level rendered a crossing impossible. Lieutenant Colonel Peter Luard therefore led his battalion to a small footbridge which had been discovered earlier by 1st Canadian Parachute Battalion, and there it waited in reserve.

7th Parachute Battalion meanwhile had encountered problems in penetrating the thick hedgerows dividing the fields, forcing it to make detours along its route. Moreover, the Germans had sited machine guns on fixed lines and fired these at frequent intervals while constantly illuminating the surrounding terrain with flares. Another problem was that the area between the canal and railway, the battalion's start line, had not been completely taken and several enemy positions and some anti-tank guns had to be attacked and cleared before the battalion could deploy into assault formation.

B Company, commanded by Major B. R. Braithewaite, led the way and became pinned down by a machine gun as it advanced along a hedgerow. At that point, A and C Companies were crossing the start line and there was a danger that the battalion would become concentrated in a small area. A section was despatched to locate and deal with the machine gun, returning in due course having captured the weapon and its crew.

As the battalion was about to continue its advance, troops were spotted approaching in extended line across a field to the left. Initially, in the half light of dawn, it was thought that these were men of 13th Parachute Battalion but as they drew nearer they were identified as Germans. The battalion swiftly took up ambush positions in the hedgerow and shortly afterwards, at a range of only twenty-five yards, the Germans were ordered to drop their weapons and surrender. But one of them opened fire and the battalion responded likewise, inflicting heavy casualties before the survivors surrendered. Some fifteen minutes later the battalion resumed its advance, subsequently taking its objective, the spur east of Putôt-en-Auge, without further problems.

By this time, 13th Parachute Battalion was advancing on its objective, Hill 13, a prominent feature just beyond Putôt-en-Auge, which it dominated. Having waited in the open for three hours under constant fire, the battalion was now faced with crossing 1,000 yards of open terrain. Lieutenant Colonel Luard recognised that the best chance of minimising casualties lay in the battalion doubling across it in one body, his reasoning being that this tactic was the very last the Germans would expect and would take them by surprise. In this he was correct as, by the time the enemy realised what was happening, the entire battalion had sprinted over three-quarters of a mile of open ground to the safety of cover on the far side.

Shortly afterwards, B Company, under Major Reggie Tarrant, with Major John Cramphorn's A Company, accompanied by Luard, following up behind, stormed Hill 13 with bayonets fixed and reached the top of the feature. At that point an enemy battalion, which had just arrived to reinforce the unit holding the hill, counter-attacked while a well-sited machine gun opened fire, inflicting a number of casualties, seriously wounding Major Tarrant and killing one of the leading platoon commanders, Lieutenant Terry Bibby.

A and B Companies were driven off the top of the feature on to the reverse slope of an intermediate ridgeline, where they lay under heavy fire. As they prepared to face the still-advancing enemy, an artillery FOO accompanying the battalion called for supporting fire. The response was a very accurate salvo of shells which burst among the enemy, halted them in their tracks at a range of only 100 yards from the two companies and broke up the counter-attack. Luard was then ordered by Brigadier Nigel Poett to hold his positions on the ridgeline.

Although Hill 13 had not been taken, the attack on Putôt-en-Auge had been entirely successful. Elsewhere, the enemy had been driven back and 160 prisoners, two 75mm guns, four mortars and a large number of machine guns had been captured.

On the following day, 21 August, 3rd Parachute Brigade advanced on Pont l'Évêque, on the River Touques, encountering stiff opposition around the village of Annabault where enemy infantry were supported by armour. 8th Parachute Battalion was tasked with clearing the village which it captured after some very heavy fighting, having initially been held up by an 88mm gun. During that night, 5th Parachute Brigade advanced through 3rd Parachute Brigade, subsequently pushing on until it reached Pont l'Évêque at noon on 22 August.

Located in a valley dominated by wooded hills on either side, the town is situated on both sides of the river which flows through the town via two channels 200 yards apart. Running along an embankment beside the eastern channel is a railway line. South of the town, which then comprised mainly wooden houses and buildings, are two fords crossing the river, this approach to Pont l'Évêque being dominated by a feature called Saint Julien.

13th Parachute Battalion was detailed to infiltrate the town and establish a bridgehead across both channels. 12th Parachute Battalion, now commanded by Lieutenant Colonel Nigel Stockwell, would meanwhile cross the river via the two fords and secure the railway embankment and Saint Julien.

At 3.00 p.m. A Company, commanded by Captain J. A. S. Baker, led the battalion across open ground towards the fords under cover of smoke laid down by supporting artillery, coming under fire after about 400 yards. Once it appeared that it had reached the river, B Company began to follow up but unfortunately A Company had failed to locate the fords and was unable to inform Battalion Headquarters as its rear link radio set had been hit and was inoperable.

While the rest of his company took cover on the west bank, Captain Baker and nine men swam across the river. On reaching the far side, they succeeded in driving the enemy from the railway embankment but then found themselves running low on ammunition. By now the smoke laid down by the artillery was thinning and B Company, under Major E. J. O'B. 'Rip' Croker, found itself pinned down by machine-gun and artillery fire from Saint Julien and the high ground on the eastern side of the valley. Having called for more smoke, which arrived swiftly, the company advanced to some dykes but became pinned down once more. On the far bank, meanwhile, Captain Baker and his group had exhausted their ammunition and, as A Company was unable to join them, had no choice but to withdraw and swim back to the west bank.

With 12th Parachute Battalion's two leading companies pinned down and the enemy again in possession of the railway embankment which dominated all approaches, Brigadier Nigel Poett realised that there was no possibility of achieving success with a daylight attack and ordered it to be called off. During the next few hours, A and B Companies were forced to remain in their exposed positions, cut off from the remainder of the battalion. It was only after last light that they were able to withdraw, having suffered casualties amounting to sixteen killed and approximately fifty wounded.

Meanwhile, 13th Parachute Battalion had succeeded in working its way into the town and crossing the bridge spanning the western channel. It had encountered stiff resistance, however, and had not managed to clear the town's main street and reach the bridge over the eastern channel. Moreover, the enemy had set several buildings ablaze, adding to the battalion's problems. At this point, a troop of Cromwell tanks of 6th Airborne Armoured Reconnaissance Regiment moved up in support, crossing the western channel via a ford rapidly constructed by sappers using an armoured bulldozer. But after giving covering fire for a while they were forced to withdraw because of their vulnerability to anti-tank guns and the risk of catching fire from the blazing buildings around them.

On the following morning, 22 August, Brigadier Poett and Lieutenant Colonel Luard conducted a reconnaissance. By then a patrol of 13th Parachute Battalion, led by the commander of the Mortar Platoon, Captain Freddie Skeate, had succeeded in crossing the eastern channel by means of the sole remaining girder of one of the bridges blown previously by the enemy. Poett considered there was a better chance of establishing a bridgehead on the eastern bank and ordered Luard to carry out a crossing as rapidly as possible. Shortly afterwards, B Company crossed the river but soon encountered strong resistance. A Company moved forward in support while C Company remained in reserve and established a firm base at the bridge while also keeping a watchful eye on the battalion's left flank.

During the next three hours or so, A and B Companies fought hard against the enemy who were in well-prepared positions. At midday, the second-in-command, Major Gerald Ford, informed Luard that the two companies were held up and that the enemy were attempting to infiltrate their positions. Realising that the bridgehead was too weak and that the attack had little prospect of success, Poett ordered the battalion to withdraw to the west bank through a firm base established by 7th Parachute Battalion. A and B Companies pulled back, wading across the river with the aid of a rope, one seriously wounded man being carried across on a door.

At first light on 24 August, reconnaissance patrols of 7th Parachute Battalion reported that the enemy had withdrawn during the night. It was not long before the battalion was advancing with all haste across the river and climbing the high ground on the eastern side of the valley, followed soon afterwards by the rest of 5th Parachute Brigade, which continued to push forward without encountering any opposition until it reached a point east of the railway line at Bourg where the high ground was taken and secured after a brief action. At this juncture, the brigade was ordered to fall back while 1st Special Service Brigade moved through to take up the lead.

On 22 August, 6th Airlanding Brigade had succeeded in capturing Vauville and Deauville. The 1st Battalion The Royal Ulster Rifles had been relieved outside Cabourg by the 1st Belgian Brigade Group and had pushed on to Troarn via a concentration area at Le Plein. During the night of 21 August, the battalion moved to a lying-up area at Lieu Saint Laurent, continuing its advance on the following morning, moving through the 2nd Battalion The Oxfordshire & Buckinghamshire Light Infantry and the 12th Battalion The Devonshire Regiment to take up a position near Vauville. Shortly afterwards, however, Lieutenant Colonel Carson was ordered to push on and take Deauville and the area of high ground behind it.

On entering the town, where it was to relieve elements of 1st Belgian Brigade Group, the battalion took up positions which subsequently came under fire. C Company's headquarters received a direct hit, killing its commander, Major E. F. Johnston, and wounding several others, while D Company's positions had to be relocated due to being in full view of the enemy. A Company's relief of a Belgian company in the area of the railway station proved difficult because of the exposed nature of the ground.

Next morning a reconnaissance patrol crossed the Touques in a small boat but encountered the enemy on the far side. Carson decided that the battalion would have to cross further upstream, opposite the village of Bonneville sur Touques. Withdrawing from Deauville, with A Company suffering casualties in the process, the battalion moved to the area of La Poterie. During the afternoon, Carson learned that an enemy force of up to 1,200 men was positioned along the railway, the Germans' main line of defence east of the Touques.

In view of the strength of the enemy, a crossing at Bonneville sur Touques was out of the question and the battalion was withdrawn to an area between Glatigny and La Poterie where it was out of range of enemy mortars.

Meanwhile, 22 August found the 2nd Battalion Oxfordshire & Buckinghamshire Light Infantry in the van of 6th Airlanding Brigade when it learned that the enemy had withdrawn to the far banks of the Touques. That night, the battalion was ordered to carry out a crossing and on the morning of 23 August D Company took up positions on the high ground overlooking the river, suffering some casualties while doing so. Major John Howard and his men then swam across the river and established a small bridgehead on the far bank; here they obtained a boat which, with the aid of some local people, was used to ferry the rest of the battalion over the river while its vehicles were transported across using improvised rafts constructed by the pioneers.

Once across the river, the battalion entered the town of Touques and on the following day, 25 August, pressed on towards Saint Philibert, La Correspondence, Petreville and Malhortie. Later that morning it learned that the enemy were holding the bridge at Malhortie and the high ground to the east near the village of Manneville La Raoult. Brigadier Edward Flavell, who was accompanying the battalion, ordered the commanding officer, Lieutenant Colonel Michael Roberts, to take the crossing over the river as soon as possible and at 1.00 p.m. B Company successfully attacked the enemy at the bridge, capturing it intact but encountering opposition from the other enemy positions farther east. C Company meanwhile had been carrying out a right-flanking attack to link up with B Company and if possible advance round Manneville La Raoult up to the line of a road running in a north–south direction to the east. Due to the difficult terrain, this took longer than expected and it was not until 4.00 p.m. that the two companies linked up.

The commander of C Company, Major Johnny Granville, decided to advance on Manneville La Raoult but when he and his men were some 300 yards from the village they came under fire. A platoon attack was mounted, forcing the enemy to withdraw, after which the company continued its advance to its objective, which it took, establishing itself in new positions by last light. Unfortunately, due to all of its radio sets being inoperable, it was unable to inform Battalion Headquarters of its success. Lieutenant Colonel Roberts, meanwhile, on hearing the sounds of action, had ordered A and D Companies to attack the village; it was taken after a fierce battle during which the enemy brought down artillery and mortar fire that caused casualties on both sides. Nevertheless, D Company had occupied the village by last light, capturing a number of prisoners.

On the following day, 26 August, the battalion advanced to Foulbec and by 7.00 p.m. had consolidated in the area of the village, under sporadic mortar fire from the enemy who had withdrawn after blowing the bridge there.

Indeed, the Germans' efficient use of demolitions on roads and bridges during their withdrawal caused delays and problems for 6th Airborne Division's supporting arms following up behind the brigades. The division was now advancing on a ten-mile-wide front with 6th Airlanding Brigade and 1st Belgian Brigade Group moving on a twin axis towards the towns of Honfleur and Foulbec, while the remainder of the division advanced along the road towards Pont Audemer. It was not until its leading elements reached Beuzeville that the division once again encountered stiff resistance from the enemy on its southern axis of advance.

Beuzeville lies at the junction of five roads: one from the north, one from Pont l'Évêque to the west, another from Pont Audemer to the east and two from the south. The town itself is large and sprawling, surrounded by rolling countryside and cider apple orchards.

On the morning of 25 August, 1st Special Service Brigade was held up short of Beuzeville. 3rd Parachute Brigade and 4th Special Service Brigade were ordered to move through and clear the enemy from the town; they sustained initial heavy losses when troops came under heavy mortar fire while approaching the town along a sunken lane from the south as part of a flanking movement.

That evening, Major General Gale received orders from I Corps with regard to operations for the following day. These laid down boundaries for 6th Airborne Division, and excluded Pont Audemer which now would be on the axis of advance of 49th Infantry Division. Gale, however, was convinced that his division was nearer to the town and in a better position to reach it and seize the bridge over the River Risle, a major obstacle, before the Germans could blow it.

Gale gave the task of racing for the bridge to The Princess Irene Royal Netherlands Brigade Group, which was placed under command of 5th Parachute Brigade. On the morning of 26 August, mounted on the Cromwell tanks of A Squadron 6th Airborne Armoured Reconnaissance Regiment, the Dutch brigade headed with all available speed for Pont Audemer but unfortunately arrived too late, the enemy having blown the bridge twenty minutes beforehand. Shortly afterwards, 7th Parachute Battalion arrived and occupied the town while the Dutch brigade took up positions on the high ground overlooking the river.

6th Airlanding Brigade, meanwhile, had been heading rapidly for Berville-sur-Mer, beyond Honfleur. By 8.00 a.m. on 26 August, it became apparent that the Germans had withdrawn and the advance developed into a race between the 1st Belgian Brigade Group and the 12th Battalion The Devonshire Regiment. The Belgians overtook the Devons, only to discover that the 1st Battalion The Royal Ulster Rifles had arrived before them. Following the arrival of the rest of the brigade, the Belgians remained in Berville while the 2nd Battalion Oxfordshire & Buckinghamshire Light Infantry was deployed in Foulbec on the brigade's right. The Royal Ulster Rifles were on the left, in the area of the hamlet of La Judée.

The campaign in Normandy was now over for 6th Airborne Division. Next day, 27 August, the division was ordered to concentrate in the area between Honfleur and Pont Audemer to prepare for its return to England in early September. It had been fighting continuously for almost three months and had suffered 4,457 casualties: 821 killed, 2,709 wounded and 927 missing. In the ten days of combat since 17 August, it had liberated 400 square miles of enemy-occupied territory and captured over 1,000 prisoners.

CHAPTER TEN

US OPERATIONS IN NORMANDY, JUNE–SEPTEMBER 1944

The US airborne formations earmarked to take part in Overlord comprised the 82nd and 101st Airborne Divisions. As recounted in Chapter 8, the 82nd had been transferred from the United States to Northern Ireland in December 1943, moving to England during February 1944 and by mid-March being complete in its new bases in the Midlands, in Nottinghamshire and Leicestershire, where it was located near the headquarters of the 9th Troop Carrier Command and the 52nd Troop Carrier Wing. At this point, the division was augmented further by two more parachute infantry regiments, the 507th and 508th, commanded respectively by Colonels George V. Millett and Roy E. Lindquist. These two regiments came from the US 2nd Parachute Brigade, led by Brigadier General George P. Howell, which recently had been transferred to Britain and now was broken up temporarily, Howell being given command of the 82nd Airborne Division's seaborne 'tail'.

The 101st Airborne Division had arrived in Britain in September 1943, thereafter being based in the south-west of England. In January 1944, it was augmented by a third parachute element, the 501st Parachute Infantry Regiment, which hitherto had been an independent formation. On 8 February, the division suffered a sad blow when its commander, the redoubtable Major General William C. Lee, who had commanded it since its activation on 15 August 1942, suffered a heart attack and was replaced by Brigadier General Maxwell D. Taylor, previously commander of the 82nd Airborne Division's artillery, who was promoted to the rank of major general on assuming command.

The period leading up to June 1944 saw some reorganisation of the gliderborne elements within both divisions. Up to this point, the 101st still possessed two glider infantry regiments, the 327th and 401st, commanded by Colonels George S. Wear and Joseph H. Harper respectively, each with two battalions. The decision was now taken that the 82nd and 101st would henceforth have only one glider infantry regiment, both being increased to three battalions, bringing the strength of each division to a total of approximately 9,000 men. The 401st was thus split up temporarily, its 1st and 2nd Battalions going to the 327th and 325th respectively and being redesignated as their 3rd Battalions.

At this time, the 82nd Airborne Division lacked parachute artillery, the 456th Parachute Field Artillery Battalion having remained in Italy with the 376th Glider Field Artillery Battalion as part of the 504th Parachute Regimental Combat Team. With no other parachute artillery units available, Major General Ridgway resorted to withdrawing a battery of the 456th and transferring it to Britain, where it became the nucleus for a new 456th Parachute Field Artillery Battalion, its former parent unit being redesignated the 463rd.

While 6th Airborne Division was being dropped and landed to protect the eastern flank of the beachhead, the 82nd and 101st would be performing a similar task on the western flank. They were to be dropped and landed behind Utah Beach and across the base of the Cotentin Peninsula, sealing it off. The US VII Corps would land on Utah, behind whose heavily defended dunes was a mile-wide lagoon formed as a result of the deliberate flooding of the area by the Germans and crossed only by five narrow causeways. To the west and south-west of Utah, the river valleys of the Merderet and Douve were also extensively flooded, the latter to the point that it extended almost to the west coast the water barrier formed by the estuary of the River Vire and the Carentan Canal.

There was thus a serious risk that the landings might be restricted and contained, either on the coast or within the pocket formed by the flooded river valleys. Accordingly, the commander of 21st Army Group, General Sir Bernard Montgomery, had directed that the two American airborne formations should be used to seize and secure the beach exits and river crossing points, thus assisting the US VII Corps' spearhead, the 4th Infantry Division, as it came ashore, and thereafter wheeled right, heading northwards towards Cherbourg. The airborne troops were also to link up with the leading elements of the US V Corps, following its landing on Omaha Beach, while forming a defensive line along the northern edge of the flooded areas to block any enemy counter-attacks.

The leading airborne element would be the 101st Airborne Division whose three parachute regimental combat teams would drop behind Utah Beach, between the town of Sainte Mère Église and a large area of marsh, in the early hours of D-day prior to the start of the seaborne landings. They would be followed by fifty-two gliders bringing in anti-tank guns, other heavy weapons, ammunition and essential stores required in the first phase of the operation. The 327th Glider Infantry Regiment, along with the divisional administrative and logistical 'tail', would land from the sea during the day, with dusk seeing the arrival of thirty-two more gliders bringing in further stores for the division. The 101st's initial tasks would be to secure and hold four of the causeways leading from the beach across the marsh, thus ensuring the breakout of 4th Infantry Division. Thereafter, it was to capture Sainte Mère Église itself, set up roadblocks on the road leading to the north and south of the town, and take two bridges spanning the River Merderet to the west. Having completed these tasks, the division was to be ready to move south to attack and take the key city of Carentan.

The 82nd Airborne Division's three parachute regiments, flying in immediately behind those of the 101st, would drop farther to the west in the centre of the Cotentin Peninsula, in the area of the town of St Sauveur-le-Vicomte which the division was to seize before establishing roadblocks on the main road to the north and south. Having taken and secured the bridge over the River Douwe, it was to move south and capture the town of La Haye-du-Puits which dominated the western approach to the Cotentin Peninsula. Meanwhile the division's 'tail' would land on Utah Beach, with the 325th Glider Infantry Regiment landing by glider at dusk. The following day would see further landings by some 200 gliders in support of both divisions.

A large number of aircraft would transport the 82nd and 101st Airborne Divisions. In support of both would be the 9th Troop Carrier Command under Brigadier General Paul L. Williams which incorporated the 52nd Troop Carrier Wing, transferred to Italy from Britain, and two new formations, the 50th and 53rd Troop Carrier Wings, recently arrived from the United States. The experienced 52nd, comprising the 61st, 313th, 314th 315th, 316th and 442nd Troop Carrier Groups, would carry the parachute regiments of both divisions while the eight groups of the 50th and 53rd Troop Carrier Wings would tow gliders. Initially, each group was equipped with fifty-two C-47s but subsequently this figure was increased to seventy-three, nine of which were allocated as reserves. By the beginning of June 1944, 9th Troop Carrier Command had a total of 1,207 aircraft under its command, along with 1,118 Waco CG-4A gliders.

On 25 May new intelligence revealed that the Germans had made considerable changes to their forces in the invasion sector in response to orders from Hitler who, suspecting that the Allied invasion would be launched against Normandy, had issued orders for the strengthening of the so-called Atlantic Wall. Responsibility for the implementation of these had been given to Field Marshal Erwin Rommel, the former commander of the Afrika Korps, who now commanded Army Group B. This comprised LXXXVIII Corps in Holland, the Fifteenth Army whose area of responsibility stretched from the Belgian port of Antwerp to the River Orne in France, and the Seventh Army whose area covered from the Orne to the Loire.

Along the stretch of coast from Calais to Cherbourg, minefields and underwater anti-landing craft obstacles were sown and planted on all beaches, which were dominated by concrete blockhouses, pillboxes and gun emplacements with interlocking arcs of fire. The coastal defence divisions were reinforced, the 352nd Infantry Division being moved forward in line with the 709th Division, and in the area of Caen and Falaise the 21st Panzer Division, hitherto based around Rennes, replaced the 77th Infantry Division which was despatched to Brittany. In addition, the 3,500 paratroops of the 6th Parachute Regiment, part of the 2nd Parachute Division which had been withdrawn from Italy, appeared at Périers-Lessay, in the Cotentin Peninsula, where they were attached to the 91st Infantry Division. The latter had been en route from Germany to Brittany until diverted to Normandy where, along with a number of other formations, it had been tasked with counter-airborne operations in support of 243rd Infantry Division. All German forces in the invasion area were under command of the LXXXIV Corps, commanded by General Erich Marcks, which in turn was under the command of Colonel General Friedrich Dollmann's Seventh Army. To the east, under command of Fifteenth Army, was XLVII Panzer Corps whose two armoured formations, the 12th SS Panzer and the Panzer Lehr Divisions, formed part of Hitler's strategic reserve in the region and would pose a formidable threat to the invasion forces in the event they were moved up to counter the landings.

The most serious element of all this new intelligence, however, was information that the 91st Infantry Division had been deployed around St Sauveur-le-Vicomte, the 82nd Airborne Division's initial objective. This led to immediate modifications in the plan for the deployment of the two American formations. The 101st's DZs and LZs were moved slightly to the east and south so that two of the division's parachute regiments would drop just to the west of the coastal lagoon, silence a battery of heavy guns and seize the western exits of the causeways leading from Utah Beach. The division's third parachute regiment would drop north of Carentan, destroy the main rail and road bridges over the Douve and hold the line of the river and the Carentan canal to protect the southern flank of the US VII Corps.

The 82nd's DZs and LZs were moved some ten miles to the east, the division dropping astride the Merderet to the south and west of Sainte Mère Église which would be taken along with the two bridges over the river. It would then extend its northern flank protection of US VI Corps westwards by destroying two more bridges over the Douve and, by preventing any attempts by the enemy to contain the invasion forces as they advanced, facilitate an early move towards the west coast of the Cotentin Peninsula.

The date for the invasion had been set for the first week of June, the overriding factor being the weather, the minimum requirements for which were that D-Day itself had to be calm, with a further three days of similar conditions to follow. In order to ensure optimum conditions for parachuting and the towing of gliders, it was stipulated that surface winds were to be a maximum of 8–12 mph on shore with the cloud base being above 3,000 feet and visibility being no less than three miles. The final factor for consideration was there should be a late-rising moon to enable the aircraft carrying the airborne divisions to fly to the DZs and LZs before it rose, but to have sufficient moonlight on approach to identify them. Thus it was that Monday 5 June was tentatively selected as the date for D-Day.

The weather throughout May, warm and sunny, proved ideal, but conditions changed dramatically on Thursday 1 June, which dawned dull and overcast with depressions bringing in deteriorating weather over the Channel. The forecast for the period 4–6 June, the only three days in the month when the tides and moon would be suitable, was for high winds, low cloud and some fog over the Normandy coast.

On the morning of Sunday 4 June, the Supreme Allied commander, General Dwight D. Eisenhower, took the decision to postpone the invasion by twenty-four hours to 6 June. If the weather had not improved sufficiently by then, it would be another two weeks before the tide was suitable again. Meanwhile, conditions deteriorated rapidly into a storm which forced the convoys of invasion vessels to seek shelter in Weymouth Bay, many of the hundreds of thousands of troops aboard them suffering from seasickness.

In the early hours of Monday 5 June, following the latest reports from his meteorological experts, Eisenhower took the decision to proceed with the invasion on 6 June. Within two hours, the invasion convoys were leaving the south coast of England and heading out into the Channel where they encountered six-feet-high waves and fierce winds. On either side of them and overhead, Allied warships and aircraft of RAF Coastal Command patrolled ready to engage any enemy submarines or surface warships that posed a threat. Ahead of the convoys went flotillas of minesweepers whose task it was to clear ten channels through which the invasion fleet would approach the French coastline. Meanwhile, Allied aircraft were bombing the Pas de Calais as part of a diversionary operation which had begun four days earlier. By 7.57 p.m. that night, three hours before last light, the leading flotillas of vessels were in sight of Omaha Beach.

In France meanwhile, the bad weather had lulled the Germans into assuming that the Allied invasion was not imminent. Field Marshal Erwin Rommel felt sufficiently confident of the situation to leave his headquarters in Paris and travel to his home near Ulm, in Germany, where he planned to spend Monday 5 June with his family. On the following day, he would travel to Berchtesgaden to make a personal request to Hitler for more troops and obtain permission to move the 12th SS Panzer Division to the area of Carentan and Saint Lô. Dated Monday 5 June and headed *Estimate of Overall Situation*, an extract from Rommel's weekly situation report to his immediate superior, Field Marshal Karl von Runstedt, who held the appointment of Commander-in-Chief West, reads as follows:

Systematic continuation and intensification of enemy air raids and more intensive minelaying in own harbours... indicates an advance in enemy's preparations for invasion. Concentration of air attacks on coastal defences between Dunkirk and Dieppe and on Seine-Oise bridges confirms presumption as to *Schwerpunkt* of large scale landing... Since 1.6.44 increased transmissions on enemy radio of warning messages to French Resistance organisations, [but] judging from experience to date, [this is] not explicable as an indication of invasion being imminent... Air reconnaissance showed no great increase of landing craft in Dover area. Other harbours of England's south coast NOT visited by reconnaissance aircraft. Survey urgently needed of harbour moorings on the entire English south coast by air reconnaissance.

Fortunately, the bad weather prevented the Luftwaffe from carrying out Rommel's request for aerial reconnaissance and forced the Kriegsmarine to abandon its patrols of the Channel and return its warships to harbour.

In Normandy on the afternoon of 5 June, the commander of the 716th Infantry Division, Lieutenant General Wilhelm Richter, held his weekly conference at his headquarters in Caen. He had received a warning that the Allied invasion was expected during the period 3–10 June but there had been many such warnings since April and this latest one was not taken particularly seriously. It was not until later that night that the Germans became aware that an invasion might be imminent. At 9.15 p.m., the BBC broadcast an increased number of coded messages to the French Resistance during which the following announcement was made:

Today the Supreme Commander directs me to say this: In due course instructions of great importance will be given to you through this channel, but it will not be possible always to give you these instructions at a previously announced time. Therefore you must get into the habit of listening at all hours.

At 10.00 p.m. German radar stations at Le Havre and Cherbourg found themselves being jammed while others along the coast from Calais to Fécamp detected movement by large numbers of vessels in the Channel. At the same time, Luftwaffe signals intelligence units picked up transmissions by American meteorological reconnaissance aircraft broadcasting weather data; this resulted in night fighter squadrons being placed on alert as this was the first occasion on which such transmissions had been made at that hour. Despite this increasing evidence, von Runstedt's Chief of Staff, Major General Günther Blumentritt, dismissed any suggestion that an invasion was imminent and no measures were taken by Headquarters Commander-in-Chief West to put German forces in Normandy on the alert. At Headquarters Army Group B, however, action had been taken but only to alert the Fifteenth Army to which a signal was transmitted at 10.00 p.m. Inexplicably, no such alert was sent to the Seventh Army, towards whose stretch of coastline the Allied invasion fleet was heading at that very moment.

In England, the night of 5/6 June found the leading elements of the Allied airborne forces already in the air and heading for Normandy. At 10.00 p.m. the pathfinders of the 82nd and 101st Airborne Divisions took off in twenty C-47s, each aircraft carrying a stick of approximately thirteen men, each equipped with a Eureka radio beacon, lamps and panels to mark the divisions' DZs and LZs. Flying at low level to avoid detection by German radar, the aircraft followed a route marked with vessels equipped with electronic beacons and visual navigation aids designed to avoid the invasion armada being detected in the Channel in order to achieve complete surprise. One C-47, carrying a pathfinder team of the 101st Airborne Division, developed mechanical trouble and was forced to ditch, those aboard subsequently being rescued. The remaining nineteen aircraft continued heading south-east via the Channel Islands before swinging east towards the Cotentin and approaching the peninsula from the opposite side to that of Utah Beach. As they did so, however, they encountered heavy, low-lying cloud and a strong north-westerly wind. Some climbed above the cloud while others

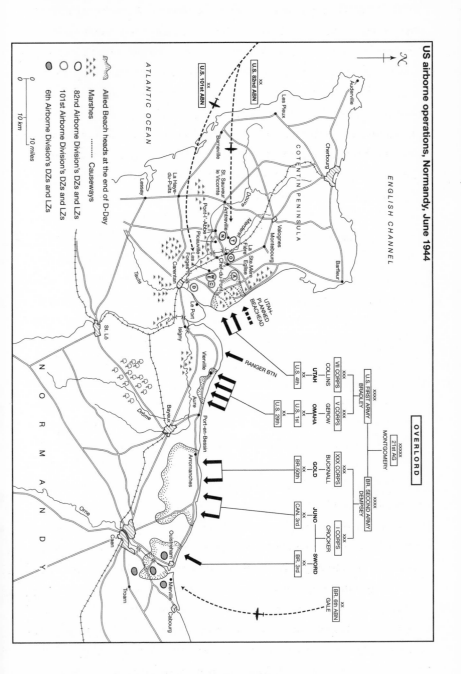

US airborne operations, Normandy, June 1944

Allied Beach heads at the end of D-Day

.... Causeways

82nd Airborne Division's DZs and LZs

101st Airborne Division's DZs and LZs

6th Airborne Division's DZs and LZs

Marshes

0   10 km
0   10 miles

ATLANTIC OCEAN

ENGLISH CHANNEL

N O R M A N D Y

COTENTIN PENINSULA

U.S. 82nd ABN

U.S. 101st ABN

Auderville
Les Pieux
Cherbourg
Barfleur
Valognes
Montebourg
Les Pieux
Barneville
St. Sauveur le Vicomte
Amfreville
St. Mère Eglise
La Ste. Mère Eglise
Picauville
Pont-l'Abbé
Les Forges
Chef-du-Pont
Carentan
Le Port
Isigny
St. Lô
Vierville
Bayeux
Port-en-Bessin
Arromanches
Ouistreham
Caen
Troarn
Merville
Cabourg
La Haye-du-Puits
Lessay
Taute
Drôme
Aure
Orne
Douve
Merderet
St. Mère Eglise

UTAH – PLANNED BEACHEAD

RANGER BTN

OVERLORD

21st AG
MONTGOMERY

U.S. FIRST ARMY
BRADLEY

VII CORPS
COLLINS

UTAH
U.S. 4th

V CORPS
GEROW

OMAHA
U.S. 1st
U.S. 29th

BR. SECOND ARMY
DEMPSEY

XXX CORPS
BUCKNALL

GOLD
BR. 50th

I CORPS
CROCKER

JUNO
CAN. 3rd

SWORD
BR. 3rd

BR. 6th ABN
GALE

373

either flew through it or dived underneath, their hitherto tight formations beginning to break up, with some aircraft straying off-course. Radio silence was being strictly enforced and thus there was no way that a warning about the cloud could be transmitted back to England.

Despite these problems, the leading pathfinders jumped from their aircraft at around 12.15 a.m. on 6 June. Only two of the seven teams were dropped accurately, the remainder finding themselves landing up to two miles away from their intended DZs. Some landed in terrain flooded as a result of the Germans having dammed the River Douve which had resulted, unknown to Allied intelligence, in the Merderet bursting its banks and turning fields into marshes and swamps. This in turn had led to a heavy growth of vegetation which from the air presented an image of flat pasture but in reality consisted of very heavy foliage covering water up to five or six feet in depth.

Some of the pathfinders, weighed down with equipment, drowned while others had to fight their way through deep mud to dry ground. A number were completely disorientated, believing they had been dropped far to the south in the area of Carentan and the flooded Douve. Others managed to pinpoint their locations but were powerless to send a warning to their respective divisions who would soon be arriving overhead.

Approximately half an hour after the pathfinders had landed, 433 aircraft carrying the three parachute regiments of the 101st Airborne Division arrived over its designated DZs and LZ. They had followed the route of the pathfinders' aircraft and had encountered the same fifteen-mile-wide band of thick cloud, lying at between 1,100 and 2,000 feet, as they flew over the west coast of the Cotentin Peninsula. Flying at an altitude of 1,500 feet, the aircraft had flown into the cloud where some pilots, becoming disorientated and fearing collision, had disobeyed orders and broken formation, climbing above or diving below the cloud.

Those aircraft that maintained the set course found, on coming out of the cloud after four or five minutes, that they were west of the River Merderet. Those that had deviated from it when climbing out of the cloud, however, soon realised that they had to dive swiftly to reach the drop height of 600 feet but in doing so were forced to fly at well over the maximum drop speed of 120 mph. Those that had dived out of the cloud found themselves too low to identify known landmarks with the result that a number of pilots soon became lost.

Heading for DZ 'A', the leading four serials of aircraft carried the three battalions of Colonel George Van Horn Moseley's 502nd Parachute Infantry Regiment and the 377th Parachute Field Artillery Battalion commanded by Lieutenant Colonel Benjamin Weisberg. Unfortunately the DZ had not been marked and the result of this was disastrous as the men, 75mm pack howitzers and ammunition of the 377th were dropped between three and twenty miles away from the DZ. Weisberg's gunners came down on rooftops, the squares of small towns, canals, rivers and flooded marshes. The more fortunate landed in open fields and orchards, narrowly missing the poles erected as anti-glider defences. In many instances the aircraft were flying too fast when they despatched their sticks, the paratroops being knocked unconscious by the severe shock of their parachutes opening and a considerable amount of equipment being torn away and raining down on the ground below. A few men were killed and many injured on landing.

The following three serials, comprising 126 aircraft, brought in Colonel Robert F. Sink's 506th Parachute Infantry Regiment accompanied by the divisional commander, Major General Maxwell D. Taylor, and members of his tactical forward headquarters. For Taylor, who had not qualified previously as a parachutist, it was only his second jump and he made history that day by being the first ever general in the US Army to jump into action, he and his headquarters staff landing within one and a half miles of DZ 'C'. Others were not so fortunate, being dropped all over the eastern part of the Cotentin Peninsula. Some found themselves on the 82nd Airborne Division's DZs, while others landed in Sainte Mère Église. Eight sticks, numbering 128 men in total, were dropped on the southern side of the River Douve, eight miles to the south-west of the DZ.

The last three serials, comprising 135 aircraft, brought in Colonel Howard R. Johnson's 501st Parachute Infantry Regiment which was due to drop on DZ 'D' situated to the south of DZ 'C' and only some three miles from the large concentration of enemy troops in the area of Carentan. The aircraft encountered heavy flak and automatic weapons fire as they approached the DZ, five being shot down and a sixth being forced to make a crash-landing. Others suffered damage as they dropped their sticks, which were scattered over a wide area. Only one landed on the DZ: that of the regimental commander himself.

Following behind came the C-47s towing forty-nine Waco gliders carrying 155 men of the 81st Airborne Anti-Aircraft Battalion, sixteen anti-tank guns, twenty-five jeeps, a lightweight bulldozer, ammunition and other stores. Of the fifty-two that had taken off from England, one glider had suffered a broken towrope and been forced to land; the loss of this particular aircraft was serious as it was carrying the main base radio set for the divisional headquarters. A second glider was lost when it and its tug were shot down over the Cotentin, while a third landed south of Carentan after the pilot of its tug became lost and released the glider.

The remaining tug pilots, however, found LZ 'E' and released their gliders accordingly. Six landed accurately on the LZ while eighteen touched down close to it, with fifteen more coming down within half a mile away. The remaining ten landed one and a half miles away at Les Forges. The landings themselves were little short of horrendous, most of the aircraft crashing and being damaged beyond repair. Some hit houses or stone walls while others encountered trees, thick hedges and ditches. Casualties, however, were light with only five men killed, seventeen injured and seven missing. Among those killed was Major General Maxwell Taylor's ADC, Brigadier General Don F. Pratt, who was the first American general to fly into action in a glider. He died when the accompanying jeep and equipment broke loose as the aircraft landed, crushing him instantly.

Half an hour behind the 101st came the 82nd Airborne Division led by the 505th Parachute Infantry Regiment, under Colonel William E. Ekman, which was due to drop on DZ 'O', located between Sainte Mère Église and the Merderet. The leading element of the regiment was its 2nd Battalion, commanded by Lieutenant Colonel Benjamin H. Vandervoort, followed by Lieutenant Colonel Edward C. Krause's 3rd Battalion accompanied by elements of the 456th Parachute Field Artillery Battalion. Bringing up the rear was the 1st Battalion, under Lieutenant Colonel Francis C. Kellam, which was accompanied by Major General Matthew Ridgway, the 505th's regimental headquarters and a platoon of the 307th Airborne Engineer Battalion.

Once again, the aircraft encountered the five-mile wide band of cloud as they crossed the west coast of the Cotentin, several in each serial breaking formation and climbing above it with inevitable consequences. Dropped too high and at speeds over the 120 mph maximum drop speed, all three battalions were scattered with elements of the 2nd Battalion landing in the Merderet marshes while others found themselves in Sainte Mère Église. Of the regiment's 118 sticks, 31 were dropped on or close to DZ 'O' while some 29 landed within one mile of it. The 505th's commander, Colonel Ekman, found himself near Fresville, some two miles north of the DZ 'O'. Twenty sticks were dropped over five miles away, three approximately fourteen miles to the north. In all, 1,100 men, representing approximately half of the regiment's strength, landed on or within one mile of the DZ, with a further 350 within two miles. The remaining 600 were scattered over a wide area.

Following the 505th came the 508th Parachute Infantry Regiment, commanded by Colonel Roy E. Lindquist and transported in 132 aircraft flying in four serials. It was heading for DZ 'N', situated west of the Merderet at a point equidistant between the bridges over the river at La Fière and Chef-du-Pont, and half a mile north of the hamlet of Picauville. Unknown to the Allies, the headquarters of the 91st Infantry Division had recently moved to Picauville along with elements of the division, the presence of which had led to the pathfinders' inabilty to reach the DZ which thus was unmarked.

Thick cloud again resulted in the break-up of the formation as aircraft attempted to fly over or under it. The 508th was badly scattered and its three battalions unable to regroup into companies and platoons. A large number of men were dropped to the north of the DZ while others, including the commanding officers of all three battalions, landed among the elements of the 91st Infantry Division at Picauville. Lieutenant Colonel Herbert F. Batcheller, commanding the 1st Battalion, was among those killed there. Others fell into the flooded marshes of the Merderet or into those of the Douve farther south, some being drowned after being dragged down by their heavy equipment.

Close behind followed the 507th Parachute Infantry Regiment, commanded by Colonel George V. Millett, flying in three serials consisting of 117 aircraft which headed for DZ 'T' to the west of the Merderet, approximately half a mile north of the town of Amfreville. The regiment's pathfinders had reached the DZ but heavy enemy fire had prevented them from marking it. Once again, the drop was a disaster with some aircraft overshooting the DZ by up to 2,000 yards and dropping their sticks into the Merderet marshes, which claimed more victims. Other sticks were dropped on the east bank of the river, to find themselves among units of the 505th PIR.

Colonel Millett was among those who landed accurately on the DZ. He rapidly set about collecting together a force of some 425 men of his regiment before attempting to carry out his regiment's initial task of attacking and capturing Amfreville. The Germans responded in strength, however, and soon Millett and his men were cut off.

Last to arrive was the 82nd Airborne Division's gliderborne element whose fifty-two Wacos were due to land on DZ 'O', bringing in two batteries of the 80th Airborne Anti-Aircraft Battalion with its sixteen 57mm anti-tank guns. Like those of the 101st, the gliders had suffered mishaps from the start when a towrope broke, and seven more parted company with their tugs on entering the cloud over the Cotentin Peninsula. After clearing the cloud, seven more were lost when they were released prematurely and crash-landed to the west of the Merderet.

The remaining thirty-seven gliders succeeded in reaching DZ 'O" and cast off from their tugs, thereafter landing under heavy enemy fire. Of those, twenty-three touched down close to the DZ while nine others did so in locations up to two miles away, two of them crashing in Sainte Mère Église. The majority of the landings ended in disaster, with gliders careering into stone walls, trees and anti-glider defences which accounted for approximately fifty per cent of the aircraft as they landed. Twenty-two Wacos were destroyed with the rest barely considered suitable for salvage. Similarly, eight of the sixteen anti-tank guns and eleven out of twenty-five jeeps were destroyed in the landing. Three men were killed and twenty-three injured.

By the time both the 82nd and 101st Airborne Divisions had completed their landings on 6 June, 13,100 paratroops and 375 glider-borne troops had been dropped and landed by 816 aircraft and approximately 100 gliders. On the whole, however, airborne delivery had been unimpressive. Out of the six parachute regiments, only the 505th Parachute Infantry Regiment had been dropped with any degree of accuracy and thus by first light was alone in being capable of operating as a cohesive formation, albeit with fifty per cent of its strength missing. The drops of the 507th and 508th west of the River Merderet had been nothing short of disastrous, with only one third of their total strengths being landed in their respective operational areas. Neither regiment was able to operate as planned to the west of the Merderet, with most of the 508th's missions, notably the destruction of the bridges over the Douve, having to be abandoned.

The finger of blame was pointed at the 9th Troop Carrier Command and the lack of training of its aircrews. There was a strong feeling at senior levels in both airborne divisions that there had been a lack of urgency in the way that the build-up of aircraft and gliders had been conducted. Headquarters 9th Troop Carrier Command later cited bad weather and the short daylight of Britain in March and April as being a major factor limiting the training of aircrew, but this was dismissed by both divisions who were of the opinion that the bad-weather factor should have been built into such training. They also pointed out that not only should an aircraft have been sent in advance to report back on the weather but that advance serials or pathfinders should have been authorised to break radio silence to warn the aircraft following behind. Other vital factors were the lack of navigators, as not every aircraft carried one as a member of its crew, and the insufficient number of planes equipped with electronic navigational aids and the Rebecca to receive signals from the pathfinders' Eurekas. As a result, pilots became disorientated and lost, subsequently being unable to recover their bearings and ultimately to locate the DZs and LZs.

Once it had regrouped, the 101st Airborne Division's priority task was to secure the western exits of the four causeways that led across the flooded area immediately to the rear of the dunes of Utah Beach. At the head of a ninety-strong group which included several senior members of his staff and the commanding officer of the 3rd Battalion of the 501st Parachute Infantry Regiment, Major General Maxwell Taylor headed for the exit point of the southernmost of these, situated at Pouppeville. At the same time a group of the 506th, under the commanding officer of the 1st Battalion, Lieutenant Colonel William L. Turner, was despatched to the same exit by the 506th's commander, Colonel Robert F. Sink, who had gathered together a force of those men who had landed in the same vicinity as him. Meantime, the commanding officer of the 2nd Battalion, Lieutenant Colonel Robert L. Strayer, was leading a 200-strong group towards the second exit.

Farther to the north were the third and fourth exits which, together with a coastal artillery battery, were the objectives of the 502nd Parachute Infantry Regiment. Lieutenant Colonel Robert G. Cole, the commanding officer of the 3rd Battalion, led a group to the third exit which it seized unopposed before moving on the fourth, where a force under the 502nd's commander, Colonel John H. Michaelis, and the commanding officer of his 2nd Battalion, Lieutenant Colonel Patrick F. Cassidy, had encountered stiff opposition. Another group under Lieutenant Colonel Steve A. Chappuis, the commanding officer of the

2nd Battalion, meanwhile captured the coastal artillery battery position, which was found to be unoccupied.

The 101st Airborne Division thus succeeded in its initial mission of capturing and securing the exit points through which the 4th Infantry Division would begin to advance inland. Its secondary mission, of destroying the main rail and road bridges over the Douve and holding the line of the river and the Carentan Canal to protect the southern flank of the US VII Corps, proved less successful due to the scattered drop of the 501st Parachute Infantry Regiment and the 3rd Battalion of the 506th, and the swift reactions of the enemy whose flak took its toll. Nevertheless, elements of the 501st under the regiment's commander, Colonel Howard R. Johnson, crossed the Douve at La Barquette and established roadblocks at the bridges near Le Port and Brevands. The 2nd Battalion, under Lieutenant Colonel Robert A. Ballard, failed to take the bridges that carried the main road linking Carentan and Sainte Mère Église over the Douve, enabling the Germans to despatch two battalions of the 6th Parachute Regiment northwards along the road to Saint Côme-du-Mont and Sainte Marie-du-Mont.

The 82nd Airborne Division had been attempting meantime to regroup after the disastrous drop which had seen it scattered over a very wide area. Hampered by an almost total absence of communications as the majority of the division's radios had been lost during the drop and glider landings, and with most of his headquarters staff missing, Major General Ridgway had no information as to the state of the division or the progress it was making in achieving its objectives. Located in an orchard just over 1,000 yards to the west of Sainte Mère Église, however, he could do little but concentrate his attention in those first few hours on the capture of the town which was the objective of the 3rd Battalion 505th Parachute Infantry Regiment. By 3.00 a.m. only 150 men had appeared at the battalion's RV. Fortunately, information was obtained from a local Frenchman that the German garrison in the town at that juncture was only approximately fifty strong, the rest having withdrawn to some woods to the south earlier in the night. Without further ado, the commanding officer, Lieutenant Colonel Edward C. Krause, and his small force launched an immediate attack and captured the town after a brief skirmish in which ten enemy were killed, the remainder surrendering. There they found a number of dead and wounded members of the 505th and 506th Parachute Infantry Regiments who had been dropped accidentally into the town itself. One of these men had snagged his parachute on the spire of the town's church and he had hung there pretending to be dead as enemy troops fired at him from below, fortunately only hitting the heel of one of his boots.

The 2nd Battalion meanwhile was making its way to a point two miles north of Sainte Mère Église on the main road between Cherbourg and Carentan which it was to interdict. Concerned that Krause's force would be unable to resist a German counter-attack, Ridgway despatched a radio message to the commanding officer, Lieutenant Colonel Benjamin H. Vandervoort, who had sustained a broken ankle in the drop, ordering him to halt and be ready if necessary to reinforce the 3rd Battalion in the town. At 7.00 a.m. the commander of the 505th Parachute Infantry Regiment, Colonel William E. Ekman, who was heading south after being dropped well to the north of the DZ, appeared and held a brief conference with Vandervoort before continuing on to his command post, located by the DZ and where he arrived about an hour later. Unable to make radio contact with the 3rd Battalion and becoming increasingly anxious that it was vulnerable to a counter-attack, Ekman ordered Vandervoort to abandon his original mission and head for Sainte Mère Église. The latter complied with all haste but took the precaution of despatching a platoon under Lieutenant Turner B. Turnbull to establish a roadblock at the village of Neuville-au-Plain.

Ridgway's and Ekman's anxiety about a German counter-attack was well-founded, as a force of 200 enemy, comprising those who had withdrawn from the town earlier that night, attacked from the woods to the south. Shortly afterwards, however, Vandervoort and the 2nd Battalion appeared and the enemy withdrew once again to the woods where they remained for the time being.

The late morning of 6 June saw the Germans despatch a battle group from Montbourg to recapture the town, this comprising elements of a regiment of the 91st Infantry Division and other units, the whole force amounting to between three and four battalions. At around 1.00 p.m. they encountered Lieutenant Turnbull and his platoon of the 2nd Battalion of the 505th at Neuville-sur-Plain. Turnbull and his men, supported by a 57mm anti-tank gun, put up a stiff fight for three hours, inflicting serious casualties on the Germans but suffering heavily themselves. At around 4.30 p.m. help arrived in the form of another platoon sent by Vandervoort to assist Turnbull's platoon to withdraw and rejoin the 2nd Battalion which by this time had established defensive positions on the northern edge of Sainte Mère Église. Both platoons reached the battalion, which was soon heavily engaged by the German battle group in a battle which lasted throughout the rest of the day and into the evening. At this point naval gunfire support from the 14-inch guns of the USS *Nevada* came to the assistance of the 2nd Battalion, enabling Vandervoort and his men to stand their ground and beat off the enemy.

Elsewhere in the 82nd Airborne Division's area, however, the situation was somewhat grimmer as the 507th and 508th Parachute Infantry Regiments, badly scattered during the drop, had not been able to seize the bridges over the River Merderet at La Fière and Chef-du-Pont. The 507th was to have been dropped on DZ 'T' to the west of La Fière, after which it was to send a detachment to Cauquigny, a hamlet situated on the western end of the raised causeway that ran west from the La Fière bridge across 500 yards of low-lying open terrain to high ground. Having taken Cauquigny, this force was then to seize the bridge. Meanwhile A Company of the 1st Battalion of the 505th was to move west from DZ 'O' to La Fière, clear it of any enemy and prevent it from being blown, thereafter linking up with the detachment of the 507th Parachute Infantry Regiment at the bridge. At the same time, the 505th was to despatch a fighting patrol to the Chef-du-Pont bridge where it would link up with a detachment of the 508th, the latter having been dropped on DZ 'N'.

Following the drop, the only unit to the west of the Merderet capable of carrying out any part of the mission to capture the bridges was a group of the 2nd Battalion of the 507th which had assembled near the western end of the La Fière causeway under the commanding officer, Lieutenant Colonel Charles J. Timmes. The Germans, however, reacted swiftly and deployed infantry and armour of the 91st Infantry Division from Saint Sauveur-le-Vicomte to La Fière and Timmes and his group soon found themselves heavily engaged. He did manage, however, to despatch a patrol to Cauquigny, where it encountered another from the 507th Parachute Infantry Regiment and joined forces. Unable to see any sign of men of the 1st Battalion of the 505th at the bridge 500 yards away, both patrols decided to remain in Cauquigny. This was just as well, for unknown to them, a thirty-strong German platoon equipped with three machine guns had taken up well-concealed positions at a farm, named Le Manoir La Fière, on the east bank of the river near the bridge. Two of the machine guns were sited on the causeway with good fields of fire while the third was located close to the buildings and covering the approach to the bridge from Sainte Mère Église.

A Company of the 1st Battalion of the 505th, commanded by Major John J. Dolan, was one of the few sub-units in the division to have been dropped accurately and was soon heading for La Fière bridge. Shortly after reaching it, however, Dolan and his men came under fire from the enemy platoon at the farm and suffered five men killed. Next to arrive was a company of the 2nd Battalion of the 507th, under Major Ben Schwarzwalder, followed by another led by the commander of the 508th, Colonel Roy E. Lindquist. Shortly afterwards C Company of the 1st Battalion of the 505th and a group of sappers also appeared, the latter bringing with them a 57mm anti-tank gun. Finally, Brigadier General James Gavin, Ridgway's ADC and second-in-command of the division, arrived on the scene with a group of men of the 507th Parachute Infantry Regiment, bringing the size of the force at La Fière to between 600 and 700.

An attack was launched on the farm by Major Dolan's company, while Major Schwarzwalder and his men tackled the machine-gun position covering the approach from Sainte Mère Église, casualties being incurred on both sides before the remaining Germans were overrun and surrendered. Schwarzwalder's company then began to advance along the causeway but came under fire at close range from one of the two machine-gun positions sited on it. Both were swiftly rushed without further loss, the company pushing on along the causeway to Cauquigny where it linked up with the two 507th patrols dug in there. Instead of remaining and reinforcing the bridgehead, Schwarzwalder decided to press on and link up with Lieutenant Colonel Timmes and his group of the 2nd Battalion of the 507th. Shortly afterwards, the two patrols in Cauquigny were reinforced by some fifty men of the 508th sent across from Le Manoir La Fière by Colonel Lindquist who by this time had established his command post in the farm.

In the meantime, Brigadier General James Gavin had set off for Chef-du-Pont with two 100-strong groups of the 507th headed respectively by the regiment's executive officer, Lieutenant Colonel Arthur A. Maloney, and the commanding officer of the 1st Battalion, Lieutenant Colonel Edwin J. Ostberg. The two groups marched separately, following the east bank of the Merderet until they reached Chef-du-Pont, which they found to be held by a force of Germans equipped with machine guns. During the ensuing action, the two groups cleared the enemy from their positions in and around the hamlet but the Germans withdrew to the causeway leading west where they set up positions covering the bridge itself. Unable to advance any further, Gavin's force had to remain on the east bank.

By this time, almost the entire 1st Battalion 505th Parachute Infantry Regiment had assembled in the area of the La Fière bridge. Uneasy at the lull in the battle, the commanding officer, Lieutenant Colonel Francis C. Kellam, sent out a small reconnaissance patrol which moved through Cauquigny until it heard the sound of armoured vehicles approaching in the distance. Withdrawing, the patrol alerted the small bridgehead force in the hamlet before returning to inform Kellam, who immediately deployed his battalion around the bridge, placing A Company forward with the battalion's single 57mm anti-tank gun. Not long afterwards, an enemy force comprising a large contingent of infantry spearheaded by two light tanks appeared and overran the bridgehead force in Cauquigny before pushing on to the bridge. Advancing along the causeway, the leading tank knocked out Kellam's anti-tank gun but within seconds had been set ablaze and its companion disabled by well-aimed bazooka rockets. At the same time, the enemy infantry following the tanks were subjected to a murderous hail of fire, causing heavy casualties. By this time, however, the Germans were bringing down supporting artillery fire, killing Lieutenant Colonel Kellam and two members of his battalion headquarters.

News of the battle at La Fière reached Gavin at Chef-du-Pont. Leaving a group of thirty-five of his men there, he and the rest of his force rushed back up the east bank of the Merderet to reinforce the 1st Battalion of the 505th, command of which had been assumed by the 505th's Executive Officer, Lieutenant Colonel Mark Alexander. On reaching the scene, however, Gavin found that the battalion had beaten off the enemy and had a firm hold on the bridge.

By the evening of 6 June, the 82nd Airborne Division found itself contained in a triangle each of whose sides were some two miles long and whose three points were Sainte Mère Église, La Fière and Chef-du-Pont. The situation was critical as the force holding the triangle was only some 2,500 strong, consisting mainly of the 505th Parachute Infantry Regiment augmented by a small number of the 507th and 508th, supported by only six anti-tank guns and with very limited supplies of ammunition. Further supplies, however, were scheduled to arrive at 9.00 p.m. and 11.00 p.m. with the arrival of two glider lifts which would also bring in the division's artillery, more anti-tank guns and vehicles. Lacking any form of rear-link radio communications, Major General Ridgway had no way of discovering the progress of the seaborne landings and thus how soon he could expect the arrival of the armoured task force, comprising a company of twenty-one Sherman tanks led by Colonel Edson Raff, whose task it was to break through to the division at Sainte Mère Église and to ensure that LZ'W' was clear and secure for the glider landings that night. In fact, Raff and the task force had landed at 1.30 p.m., thereafter heading with all speed for Sainte Mère Église and making good progress until they reached a point two miles south of the town, on the Carentan–Cherbourg road; here they encountered an enemy force in the woods on either side of the road, the leading three Shermans being swiftly knocked out by 88mm guns. Not only unable to break through to Ridgway and his division, Raff was also powerless to clear and secure LZ 'W' which, along with LZ 'E', was overlooked by the woods and thus dominated by the enemy.

The glider lift that night comprised three elements, with the first and smallest, consisting of thirty-two Horsas, carrying supplies for the 101st Airborne Division on to LZ 'E'. The other two, comprising 177 Horsas and thirty-seven Wacos, would bring in the sorely needed 319th and 320th Glider Field Artillery Battalions together with their 75mm pack and M-3 105mm howitzers, along with the 57mm anti-tank guns of the 80th Airborne Anti-Aircraft Artillery Battalion. In England, the tugs of the 434th Troop Carrier Group took off at 6.30 p.m. and, following a flight without mishap, made their final approach to LZ 'E' at 8.53 p.m. Most of the Horsas were cast off prematurely, landing two or three miles to the north-east of the LZ and thus beyond the range of the enemy forces in the woods. Five gliders landed on the LZ and were immediately subjected to heavy fire, fourteen of the 157 troops aboard being killed and thirty wounded.

Half an hour later, the 82nd Airborne Division's leading lift of seventy-five Horsas approached LZ 'W'. By this time it had become apparent that the enemy was dominating the area of the LZ, so an alternative LZ had been established on DZ 'O', on which a Eureka had been positioned next to a green 'T' formed from green smoke grenades. Unfortunately, the tug and glider crews did not observe the new LZ, the Horsas encountering heavy fire as they arrived over LZ 'W'. A few landed on the LZ but the majority crashed in neighbouring fields too small to accommodate such large aircraft landing at speeds of up to 100 mph. Others crash-landed on nearby roads and ended up in hedgerows or ditches.

The second lift of 100 tug-glider combinations detected the signal of the Eureka on DZ 'O' and responded accordingly, but the new course took it over the enemy-held areas to the north and north-east of Sainte Mère Église from which it encountered a heavy barrage of ground fire. Having cast off at 11.05 p.m., just as dusk was falling, the gliders suffered heavy casualties from enemy fire and the poor visibility which made landing in the small fields, divided by banks and thick hedgerows, very difficult.

Of the 175 gliders that arrived in Normandy (one Horsa and one Waco having aborted after take-off), only eight Horsas survived their landings undamaged. Of the troops in the other 139 gliders, 142 were casualties. The thirty-six Wacos survived the landings better, with only fifteen troop casualties. The total number of casualties in the 82nd Airborne Division lift was thirty-three killed and 124 wounded or injured.

That night, Ridgway despatched a patrol under Lieutenant Colonel Walter F. Winton to make contact with the commander of the US 4th Infantry Division, Major General Raymond O. Barton, whose head-quarters, he had learned, was near Beuzevilleau-Plain, only two miles north-east of Sainte Mère Église. Winton succeeded in getting through and arrived at Barton's headquarters around midnight, to reveal the very serious situation facing the 82nd Airborne Division. This was the first sound information that Barton had received concerning Ridgway and his men, and he undertook immediately to send assistance to Sainte Mère Église at first light. In the early hours of 7 June, however, the commander of the US VII Corps, Lieutenant General J. Lawton 'Joe' Collins, arrived at Barton's headquarters and, on learning of the 82nd Airborne Division's predicament, ordered that the 746th Tank Battalion, at that point at Reuzeville, be despatched immediately to Sainte Mère Église to break through to the paratroops.

The early morning of 7 June found Colonel James A. Van Fleet's 8th Infantry Regiment, which had advanced inland on the previous day and reached Les Forges, where it linked up with Colonel Raff's armoured task force, on the move northwards once more. During the night much of the enemy force in that area, consisting mainly of elements of the 1057th Infantry Regiment, had withdrawn north through the woods to link up with the 1058th Infantry Regiment, located to the north of Sainte Mère Église. Nevertheless, the remaining enemy, now deployed in pockets, put up sufficient opposition to slow down Van Fleet's three battalions and delay their reaching the beleaguered 82nd Airborne Division.

Once again, with no immediate hope of assistance from the advancing ground forces, Ridgway had to pin his hopes of reinforcement and resupply on the next glider lift, the first element of which took off from England at 4.30 a.m. Towed by aircraft of the 434th and 437th Troop Carrier Groups, it comprised 100 Horsa and Waco gliders carrying the 1st Battalion 325th Glider Infantry Regiment, commanded by Lieutenant Colonel Klemm Boyd, along with some gunners and sappers. Arriving over the Cotentin Peninsula at 7.00 a.m., it flew towards LZ 'E' and came under heavy fire from the ground. All the gliders were cast off prematurely and at too low an altitude, so that they landed over a wide area, none on the LZ. Seventeen men were killed and ninety-eight injured, the latter including Lieutenant Colonel Boyd whose place was taken by his executive officer, Major Teddy H. Sanford.

The second lift also comprised 100 gliders carrying the 2nd Battalion and 3rd Battalions of the 325th commanded by Lieutenant Colonels John H. Swenson and Charles A. Carrell respectively. Cast off at just after 9.00 a.m., the gliders headed for LZ 'W' which by this time was just one mile to the north of Colonel Raff's task force and on the line of advance of the 8th Infantry Regiment. Once again, the landings were haphazard with gliders crash-landing over the entire area, those coming down on the northern part of the LZ encountering enemy fire.

Casualties sustained during the landings amounted to sixteen killed and seventy-four injured.

Despite the casualties, the landing was considered to have been successful in that it brought in 2,000 sorely needed men. By 11.00 a.m. the 325th had regrouped and, with its commander, Colonel Harry Lewis, adhering to his original orders as he had received none to head instead for Sainte Mère Église, its three battalions moved off west from Les Forges towards the Merderet, subsequently taking up a position near Chef-du-Pont where the regiment remained as divisional reserve for the time being.

Colonel Raff's task force followed the 325th Glider Infantry Regiment to Chef-du-Pont, from where it swung north-west and headed for Sainte Mère Église, where the situation remained grim. The enemy to the immediate north of the town, consisting of the 1058th Infantry Regiment, reinforced by two motorised battalions of heavy artillery and an anti-tank battalion equipped with self-propelled guns, had stepped up their attacks on the town but their advance was blocked by Lieutenant Colonel Vandervoort's 2nd Battalion 505th Parachute Infantry Regiment reinforced by a number of men of the 507th and 508th.

The enemy began by bombarding the town with shellfire before sending in the infantry, supported by self-propelled guns. The 2nd Battalion of the 505th nevertheless stood firm, inflicting heavy casualties. One member of the battalion, Lieutenant Waverly W. Wray, succeeded in infiltrating through the German positions and made his way to the command post of the 1st Battalion 1058th Infantry Regiment which he attacked single-handed, killing the commanding officer and nine members of his headquarters before calling in mortar fire on the area. The effect of the removal of the command element was devastating and resulted in the rout of the complete battalion, which withdrew northwards in confusion. Lieutenant Wray, who was killed in action three months later, was subsequently recommended for the Congressional Medal of Honor for this feat of arms but was awarded the Distinguished Service Cross instead.

Eventually, reinforcements arrived from the south in the form of the 8th Infantry Regiment, while the 746th Tank Battalion, despatched to Sainte Mère Église that morning by 4th Infantry Division on the direct orders of Lieutenant General Collins, appeared from the east. Shortly afterwards, Raff and his task force also appeared, followed by Collins himself and the commander of the 8th Infantry Regiment, Colonel Van Fleet. Almost immediately, Major General Ridgway launched a counter-attack with the 2nd Battalion of the 505th supported by the 746th Tank Battalion and the armoured task force which had accompanied Raff. This had the desired effect of driving back the Germans who, having suffered heavy casualties, withdrew from Sainte Mère Église to north of Neuville-au-Plain where they established new positions.

Meanwhile, at La Fière around 9.00 a.m. on the morning of D+1, the 1057th Infantry Regiment had launched an assault from the west against Lieutenant Colonel Alexander's 1st Battalion of the 505th rein-forced by men of the 507th and 508th. Four light tanks, followed by lorried infantry, led the advance along the raised road which Alexander's men had mined and partly blocked with wrecked vehicles. Covering the approaching force was a 57mm anti-tank gun and two bazooka teams which opened fire, disabling the leading tank which slewed to a halt, blocking the road. The other three withdrew as the enemy infantry advanced, using the wrecked vehicles as cover. Enemy artillery and mortars then opened fire, bringing down a hail of shells and bombs on the paratroops who nevertheless stood firm and eventually beat off the enemy, who had advanced to within twenty-five yards of the battalion's forward positions before being forced to withdraw. Shortly afterwards, the artillery and mortar barrage ceased as the Germans came forward under a flag of truce to recover their dead and wounded; no sooner had they finished doing so than the guns and mortars opened fire again. This was the last attempt by the enemy, however, to recapture the bridge at La Fière. In capturing and holding it, the 1st Battalion of the 505th had incurred serious casualties, with its original commanding officer and five other officers killed. Company A, which had held the forwardmost position at the bridge itself, had suffered sixty-six men (almost half of its strength) killed or seriously wounded, and a further twenty-three men wounded but still capable of fighting.

With Sainte Mère Église secure and La Fière in his hands, Ridgway turned his attention to occupying and holding the area west of the Merderet to the Douve and south in the direction of Pont-l'Abbé, the division having been unable to fulfil this task due to the 507th and 508th Parachute Infantry Regiments being badly scattered during their respective drops. Furthermore, a number of groups from both regiments were trapped in locations west of the Merderet and it was essential that these should be rescued at the earliest opportunity. In addition, the commander of US VII Corps, General Joe Collins, had requested that the 505th Parachute Infantry Regiment take part in the advance by the 4th Infantry Division northwards against the 1058th Infantry Regiment now dug in north of Neuville-au-Plain. Ridgway agreed, and the 505th, reinforced by the 2nd Battalion 325th Glider Infantry Regiment, was ordered to move forward on the left (western) flank of the 8th Infantry Regiment as it advanced along the east bank of the Merderet to Le Ham and subsequently Montebourg station.

The attack across the Merderet would be carried out primarily by Lieutenant Colonel Teddy H. Sanford's 1st Battalion of the 325th. The river would be crossed at a ford to the north of La Fière where the 1st Battalion would link up with an isolated group of the 2nd Battalion of the 507th led by the commanding officer, Lieutenant Colonel Charles J. Timmes. Simultaneously, another group under the 507th's commander, Colonel George V. Millett, would move eastwards to link up with Sanford and Timmes who would establish a bridgehead at Cauquigny. In the meantime, Lieutenant Colonel Charles Carrell's 3rd Battalion of the 325th would be in the area of La Fière, ready to move to Cauquigny and reinforce the bridgehead.

The operation began at 8.00 a.m. on 8 June with the 4th Infantry Division spearheading the US VII Corps advance north. On the left flank, the 505th Parachute Infantry Regiment sustained heavy casualties but nevertheless continued its advance with the 2nd and 3rd Battalions forward and the 1st Battalion in reserve, the 2nd Battalion of the 325th moving up behind. The enemy, comprising the 1058th Infantry Regiment, reinforced heavily by artillery and elements of the 77th and 243rd Infantry Divisions, put up very stiff resistance which eventually forced the other three formations in 4th Infantry Division, the 8th, 12th and 22nd Infantry Regiments, to grind to a halt; but eventually, after some hard fighting, Le Ham was taken.

The attack over the Merderet had begun as planned under the watchful eye of Brigadier General Gavin. During the initial phase, the causeway at Chef-du-Pont was to be secured while at the same time an isolated group of the 1st and 2nd Battalions 508th Parachute Infantry Regiment, led by the commanding officer of the 2nd Battalion, Lieutenant Colonel Thomas J. Shanley, was to clear the road leading southwest from the causeway to Pont-l'Abbé. Once that had been achieved, a convoy would be despatched by the commander of the 508th, Colonel Roy Lindquist, across the causeway to rescue Shanley and his men who were under continual heavy fire in their positions on a feature known as Hill 30 just to the west of the Merderet.

Shanley sent a twenty-three-strong patrol under two officers, Lieutenants Lloyd Pollette and Woodrow W. Millsaps, which cleared the road and subsequently fought its way across the causeway to Chef du Pont and Lindquist's headquarters. The Germans, however, brought down heavy artillery fire on the causeway, preventing the convoy being sent across and forcing Shanley and his men to remain beleaguered on Hill 30.

The operation to take the La Fière causeway was launched on the night of 8 June when at 11.00 p.m. the 1st Battalion 325th Glider Infantry Regiment crossed the Merderet via the ford farther north, shortly afterwards linking up with Lieutenant Colonel Timmes and his group of the 2nd Battalion of the 507th. Meanwhile, Colonel Millett and his 250-strong group were moving east to link up with Sanford, but in the darkness his force became split. He and his leading 100 men now encountered enemy troops, and in the ensuing action Millett was captured and most of his men killed or taken prisoner. The other half of the group, led by Major Paul F. Smith and comprising 150 men of the 507th Parachute Infantry Regiment and ninety German prisoners, continued to head east for the Merderet. Following orders given over the radio by Colonel Arthur Maloney, who assumed command of the 507th immediately following Millett's capture, Smith and his men started towards the ford to join up with the 1st Battalion 325th Glider Infantry Regiment. Shortly afterwards, however, they met Lieutenant Colonel Harry J. Harrison, the executive officer of the 508th, who had been with Millett's group but had avoided capture. Harrison took command and ordered Smith and his men to head instead across the marshes of the Merderet to the east bank of the river. This was in contravention to Maloney's orders and Smith registered a protest. Nevertheless Harrison insisted and eventually the group reached La Fière. An official investigation into this contravention was subsequently ordered by Major General Ridgway, with adverse results for Harrison.

Later that night the 1st Battalion 325th Glider Infantry Regiment, reinforced by Lieutenant Colonel Timmes's force, advanced on Cauquigny, by now held in strength by the enemy who were well dug in. Heavy casualties were inflicted on the battalion and Timmes's men, who were forced to withdraw and take up positions to deal with the counter-attack that duly took place.

In view of the failures of these operations on 8 June, Ridgway decided on the following morning to launch an all-out assault on the La Fière causeway and cross it in force. The only unit available to carry out the operation was the 3rd Battalion 325th Glider Infantry Regiment, which would be required to advance along the 500 yards of open road above the level of the marshy terrain on either side, thus exposing it to enemy fire from in front and both flanks. As reinforcement for the battalion, Brigadier General Gavin ordered Colonel Maloney to provide a company-sized force of the 507th Parachute Infantry Regiment which would follow immediately behind the glider infantrymen and, if necessary, advance through them to the west bank.

Ridgway appreciated that the operation would require heavy supporting firepower from artillery to have any chance of success. Within the 82nd Airborne Division, organic artillery support now comprised the 319th and 320th Glider Field Artillery Battalions with their seven 75mm pack howitzers and eight M-3 105mm howitzers respectively. The firepower of these two battalions, however, would not be sufficient and the division's third artillery unit, the 456th Parachute Field Artillery Battalion, with its ten 75mm pack howitzers, was not due to land until that afternoon, 9 June. Ridgway therefore turned for further artillery support to the 90th Infantry Division which allotted the task to the 344th and 345th Field Artillery Battalions, these being equipped with twelve 75mm and twelve 155mm howitzers respectively. In addition, the 746th Tank Battalion was brought up to provide additional support with its M4 Sherman tanks.

The artillery barrage began at 10.30 a.m. on 9 June, the howitzers of the 344th and 345th Field Artillery Battalions being joined by the 75mm guns of the 746th Tank Battalion's Shermans as well as the mortars and machine guns of the parachute and glider infantry battalions. The Germans responded swiftly with their own artillery and machine guns, and soon the entire area from La Fière across the 500 yards to the river and its west bank beyond was subjected to a maelstrom of fire. Ridgway's plan had stipulated that the artillery should also lay down smoke to cover the advance across the causeway but for some unknown reason this was not forthcoming. At this juncture, Lieutenant Colonel Carrell expressed his reluctance to lead the 3rd Battalion 325th Glider Infantry Regiment forward and was immediately relieved of his command by Brigadier General Gavin, being replaced by Major Arthur W. Gardner who led the battalion forward on to the causeway. Such was the intense fire that casualties were suffered instantly, with men continuing to fall as the battalion pressed on along the road which was littered with bodies and the debris of wrecked or disabled vehicles.

Seeing that the impetus of the advance was being lost, Gavin ordered Maloney to send his company of the 507th Parachute Infantry Regiment forward immediately. With Maloney and its commander, Major Robert D. Rae, at its head, the company advanced across the causeway until it reached the cover of a disabled Sherman from which Major Rae led a charge which took him and his men across to the west bank, suffering a number of casualties before they reached it. He and his men were followed by others and at this point, Major General Ridgway himself appeared on the causeway, assisting in the clearing of bodies and wreckage to allow the Shermans of the 746th Tank Battalion to move across in support of the bitter hand-to-hand fighting which was now taking place on the west bank as paratroops and glider infantrymen assaulted the enemy's positions.

During the late afternoon, however, the Germans launched a fierce counter-attack against the 325th Glider Infantry Regiment, which began to fall back until the situation was stabilised by Brigadier General Gavin who in turn organised a counter-attack on the German assembly area in the area of the town of Le Motey. Supported by the 155mm howitzers of the 345th Field Artillery Battalion, this ultimately proved successful and Le Motey and Cauquigny were taken and occupied by the 325th. Shortly afterwards, the 508th Parachute Infantry Regiment moved north from Chef-du-Pont to La Fière, advancing over the causeway and then heading south towards Guettevile. That evening saw the regiment break through to Lieutenant Colonel Shanley's group of the 508th at Hill 30 where Colonel Roy Lindquist proceeded to site his headquarters.

While the 82nd had been defending its enclave around Sainte Mère Église and striving to cross to the west of the Merderet, the 101st Airborne Division had been primarily concerned with achieving its major objective of capturing Carentan. The city should have been taken on D+1 by the 501st Parachute Infantry Regiment and the 327th Glider Infantry Regiment, the latter being scheduled to land by sea on D-Day. The operation was delayed, however, by a number of factors. Firstly, the 501st was badly scattered during its drop, as was the 377th Parachute

Field Artillery Battalion, whose gunners and pack howitzers were scattered up to twenty miles from their DZ. Secondly, the 1st Battalion 327th Glider Infantry Regiment landed by sea on Utah Beach on schedule but the regiment's other two battalions did not come ashore until the afternoon of 7 June. Thirdly, the rest of the 101st's artillery, namely the 321st and 907th Glider Field Artillery Battalions, had also been transported by sea in two ships; one of these was sunk by a mine while the other, carrying the majority of the two regiments' guns and ammunition, remained off Utah for two days. Furthermore, it was learned that the Germans had moved two battalions of the 6th Parachute Regiment into the 101st's area of operations. Thus it was that by D+3, they still held Carentan.

Major General Maxwell Taylor was forced to make extensive changes to his plan which now called for the 502nd Parachute Infantry Regiment to advance south-eastwards down the main road linking Carentan and Cherbourg, crossing the River Douve and negotiating its marshes, which could only be traversed via a series of bridges and causeways, before beginning its attack on the city itself. Meantime, the 327th Glider Infantry Regiment would cross the Douve via the bridgehead at Brevands and attack from the east.

The operation began in the early hours of 10 June with Lieutenant Robert Coles' 3rd Battalion 502nd Parachute Infantry Regiment leading the way. From the very start, the Germans put up a stiff resistance, particularly in the areas of the exposed causeways and bridges, several of the latter having been demolished or blocked. Despite heroic efforts on its part, the battalion, already weak in numbers, was unable to penetrate through the maze of waterways and marshes; thus the commander of the 502nd, Colonel John H. Michaelis, sent forward Lieutenant Colonel Patrick Cassidy's 1st Battalion to support the 3rd Battalion. This measure did not prove sufficient and that afternoon Michaelis was forced to commit his 2nd Battalion as well. Eventually, with heavy artillery support, the 502nd reached the outskirts of Carentan, at which point it was relieved by the 506th Parachute Infantry Regiment.

The 327th Glider Infantry Regiment, meanwhile, had crossed the Douve successfully. One of its battalions then advanced to the east to Auville-sur-le-Vey where it linked up with a unit of the 29th Infantry Division while the remainder of the regiment advanced on Carentan. Unfortunately, however, the commander of the 327th, Colonel George Wear, who had already incurred the wrath of Major General Maxwell Taylor by his somewhat dilatory performance since coming ashore, mishandled the operation badly. He was relieved of his command, being replaced by Colonel Joseph H. Harper, previously the commander of the 401st Glider Infantry Regiment.

Next day saw the 501st Parachute Infantry Regiment also committed to the operation in support of the 327th Glider Infantry Regiment which attacked from the north-east while the 501st, having crossed the Douve at Brevands, did likewise from the east. Meanwhile, the 506th Parachute Infantry Regiment attacked from the north-west, effectively completing the encirclement of Carentan which was also being subjected to a heavy volume of artillery fire. This proved too much for the Germans and in particular for the 6th Parachute Regiment, which abandoned the city. In the early hours of 12 June, after two days of heavy fighting, Carentan finally fell to the 101st Airborne Division. The Germans, however, were not prepared to give up the city without a further fight and launched a counter-attack on the following day. Fortunately, warning of this had come via Ultra, the highly secret Allied code-breaking operation which intercepted and deciphered enemy signals traffic and which now provided vital intelligence that the 17th SS Panzer Grenadier Division had joined forces with the 6th Parachute Regiment for a counter-attack. On learning of this, the commander of the US First Army, General Omar Bradley, responded immediately by moving up the 2nd Armoured Division and some heavy artillery in support of the 101st Airborne Division. These proved sufficient to beat off the enemy and by the following day the city was firmly in Allied hands.

The 101st Airborne Division had achieved its objectives in seizing the four causeways and capturing the city of Carentan. The price, however, had been very heavy, the division suffering 4,670 casualties in the first seven days of the Normandy campaign.

Following the 82nd Airborne Division's successful crossing of the Merderet and the establishment of a bridgehead, the leading elements of the US VII Corps had meanwhile begun advancing west on 10 June with the aim of cutting off the Cotentin Peninsula. They soon encountered stiff resistance from the Germans. Spearheaded by the 90th Infantry Division whose troops had little, if any, combat experience, the advance quickly ground to a halt and the corps commander, Lieutenant General Collins, was forced to commit his reserve, the 9th Infantry Division. In view of the heavy German resistance, he requested General Bradley that the 82nd Airborne Division, despite its heavy losses incurred during the previous four days, be placed under command and join the advance westwards across the Cotentin.

At this juncture the 82nd was widely dispersed with the 505th Parachute Infantry Regiment in the process of withdrawing from Le Ham into divisional reserve while the 507th was regrouping in the bridgehead area. The 508th, supported by the 319th Glider Field Artillery Battalion, meanwhile was attacking southwards across the lower Douve from Picauville in the direction of Beuzeville-la-Bastille with the aim of establishing a bridgehead and linking up with units of the 101st Airborne Division moving west from Carentan. This it did, with some of its leading elements reaching as far south as Baupte before halting and digging in. Shortly afterwards, however, the regiment was ordered to withdraw and regroup with the rest of the division.

On 14 June the 82nd Airborne Division began its advance westwards, the 507th Parachute Infantry Regiment and 325th Glider Infantry Regiment in the lead as they moved through the 90th Infantry Division and then swung north. In reserve at Pont-l'Abbé were the 505th and 508th Parachute Infantry Regiments. On the right of the 82nd, but lagging behind, was the 9th Infantry Division. Despite its sorely depleted strength, the 507th set a fierce pace, soon outstripping the 325th and the supporting artillery which at one point brought down heavy shellfire on the 2nd Battalion of the 507th which was spearheading the advance. On the following day the 507th, which had suffered a further 192 casualties in two days of fighting, went into reserve. At this point Lieutenant Colonel Arthur Maloney, who had been temporarily commanding the regiment, was replaced by Colonel Edson Raff and immediately took over command of the 3rd Battalion whose previous commanding officer, Lieutenant Colonel William Kuhn, had been evacuated after being injured in the drop on the night of 5/6 June.

The afternoon of 15 June saw the advance resumed with the 505th Parachute Infantry Regiment taking over the lead as the division headed for its objective, the town of Saint Sauveur-le-Vicomte. Midday on 16 June found the 82nd Airborne Division on the east bank of the Douve from which the enemy could be observed withdrawing from the town, which had been heavily bombed by Allied aircraft. Without further ado, the 505th led the way across the river and by that evening, along with the 508th, had established defensive positions extending south to the Prairies Marécageuses, an extensive area of marshland spanned by the main road that led south to La Haye du Puits.

The capture of Saint Sauveur le Vicomte facilitated the final phase of the advance west across the Cotentin and the cutting off of the peninsula, trapping those enemy forces north of the line established by the US VII Corps. This was carried out by elements of the 9th Infantry Division, which arrived at Barneville on the west coast in the early hours of 18 June. On the following day, having been reinforced by the 79th Infantry Division, VII Corps attacked northwards towards Cherbourg.

The 82nd Airborne Division meantime had been tasked with reinforcing and enlarging the bridgehead over the lower Douve to the south of Pont l'Abbé, in the area of Baupte, where elements of the 507th and 508th Parachute Infantry Regiments had linked up with units of the 101st Airborne Division. The 325th Glider Infantry Regiment, reinforced by the 3rd Battalion 508th Parachute Infantry Regiment and sappers of the 307th Airborne Engineer Battalion, would cross to the southern bank of the Douve via the Pont l'Abbé bridge on the night of 18 June. The bridge itself had been blown by the Germans and would need to be repaired by the sappers before it could be negotiated.

By last light, however, the Germans had moved some units into the area on the south bank and the 325th had to prepare itself for an opposed crossing that night. The bridge was under artillery fire but sappers of the 307th Airborne Engineer Battalion nevertheless continued their efforts to repair it. Initially, the leading elements of the 325th Glider Infantry Regiment were hesitant to cross the bridge, even though Ridgway personally urged them forward; but eventually they crossed the bridge and advanced south to Pretot, where they dug in after encountering stiff opposition from the enemy. At that point, elements of the 507th Parachute Infantry Regiment came forward to relieve the 3rd Battalion of the 508th which withdrew and rejoined the regiment. The bridgehead was then extended eastwards, where further links were established with units of the 101st Airborne Division, and to the south-west in the direction of La Haye du Puits.

It was at this juncture that the 82nd and 101st Airborne Divisions were transferred from VII Corps to VIII Corps, the latter commanded by Major General Troy Middleton. Together with V, VII and XIX Corps which formed Bradley's US First Army, VIII Corps would now attack southwards, it own axis of advance being from Saint Sauveur le Vicomte via La Haye du Puits to Coutances.

The 101st Airborne Division was moved to Cherbourg, where it assumed responsibility for the occupation of the city and port. The 82nd, however, was to advance in the centre of the corps with the 79th Infantry Division on its right flank and the 90th on its left. Following in reserve was the 8th Infantry Division, which would take over from the 82nd after the initial phase of the operation, the latter then being withdrawn from acton and transferred back to England for rest and refit.

At 6.30 a.m. on 3 July, the 82nd Airborne Division broke out from the bridgehead to the south of Pont l'Abbé and began its advance with the 505th Parachute Infantry Regiment in the lead, followed by the 508th, 325th Glider Infantry Regiment and the 2nd Battalion of the 507th, the remainder of the battalion due to be committed on the following day. The 505th's advance was swift and by last light on 3 July it had reached the outskirts of La Haye du Puits, having captured La Poterie Ridge before dusk. Next morning, 4 July, the 505th and 508th Parachute Infantry Regiments stormed and captured Hill 95, a feature of high ground dominating the city.

Fierce fighting continued during the following three days, the 82nd Airborne Division being withdrawn from operations on 8 July. By this time it had been in combat for thirty-three days, having established a fighting reputation second to none. Despite the disastrous drop on the night of 5/6 June and subsequently being surrounded in its enclave at Sainte Mère Église, it had fought against overwhelming odds and held off vastly superior forces before being relieved. Thereafter, it had taken part in the VII Corps advance northwards on Le Ham and Montebourg while at the same time attacking westwards and eventually crossing to the west bank of the Merderet in the teeth of heavy enemy opposition. After its establishment of a bridgehead to the south of the lower Douve, the division had then participated in the advance west across the Cotentin to seal off the peninsula, subsequently regrouping and leading the way during the attack south by VIII Corps.

Like the 101st Airborne Division, however, the 82nd had paid dearly for its successes. Of its original strength of almost 12,000 men, 5,245 were casualties with 1,282 listed as killed and 2,373 as seriously wounded. When it left Normandy, embarking at Utah Beach for England on 13 July, it numbered only 6,545 all ranks.

CHAPTER ELEVEN

ALLIED AIRBORNE OPERATIONS IN ITALY, SOUTHERN FRANCE AND GREECE 1943-5

When 1st Airborne Division returned from Italy to Britain in November 1943, it left behind 2nd Parachute Brigade at the behest of General Sir Harold Alexander, the commander of 15th Army Group, who felt strongly that he needed to retain an airborne capability. Still commanded by Brigadier Charles Pritchard, it was redesignated 2nd Independent Parachute Brigade Group and incorporated 4th, 5th and 6th Parachute Battalions, 2nd Parachute Squadron RE, 127th Parachute Field Ambulance, a REME light aid detachment and a Corps of Military Police provost unit.

The brigade was transferred south to Gioia to carry out airborne training. This had only just been completed, however, when it received orders on 30 November from Headquarters Eighth Army to move within forty-eight hours to an area in the British line north of Sangro for deployment in the infantry role. The evening of 2 December 1943 found it under command of Lieutenant General Sir Bernard Freyberg's 2nd New Zealand Division and travelling north by road and rail. Eventually, in driving rain, it advanced along a narrow and muddy mountain track to take up its new positions, en route encountering some opposition south of Guardiagrele, which was overcome without difficulty.

By 6 December, the brigade was holding a twenty-five-mile wide front north of the River Sangro and south of Castelfrentano. The Germans held the town of Torricella and the high ground to the south of Orsogna which overlooked the Sangro. On 8 December, 2nd New Zealand Division mounted an attack but this failed. This was followed by a successful second attack, launched from the east on 13 December, and during which the brigade's three battalions operated against the enemy from the south.

Weather conditions during this period were appalling and the brigade was ill-equipped to cope with the blizzards that lashed its positions on New Year's Eve and the following day, 1 January 1944, the snow lying six feet deep in some areas. Worst affected were those members of 6th Parachute Battalion who had lost their clothing and personal equipment when, as recounted in Chapter 7, the minelayer HMS *Abdiel* was blown up and sunk in Taranto harbour. The weather caused problems with resupply, even by jeep, and ammunition and rations frequently had to be manpacked up to forward positions on mountain ridges. In some instances these were overlooked by the enemy, making movement by day very difficult.

The brigade was deployed in a series of strongpoints. On observing any enemy movement within its area, it could call for support from the guns of the divisional and corps artillery. The Germans adopted similar tactics and there was a considerable amount of shelling and mortar fire brought to bear by both sides. The brigade's operations during this period consisted predominantly of patrolling. Intelligence concerning the enemy's order of battle was of a high priority and all three battalions had been ordered to take prisoners wherever possible. Much was learned from those captured, one individual being so obliging as to assist an artillery forward observation officer (FOO) to bring down fire on positions occupied by his former comrades.

Clad in white sheets to provide camouflage in the snow-covered terrain, patrols sallied forth to lay ambushes and raid enemy positions.

The commander of one such patrol, Lieutenant Mike Shepherd, the intelligence officer of 5th Parachute Battalion, calmly entered a house occupied by a number of Germans and helped himself to a cooked chicken waiting to be eaten. On another occasion a C Company 4th Parachute Battalion patrol under Lieutenant Geoff Mortimer made its way into Orsogna and returned with a number of prisoners.

On 16 January 1944, 2nd Independent Parachute Brigade Group came under command of 8th Indian Division, which relieved the New Zealanders. On 16 February, having been relieved by 17th Indian Infantry Brigade, it was withdrawn into reserve in the area of Castel-frentano. A week later, however, it returned to the area of Casoli to resume patrolling and harassing the enemy at every opportunity.

At the end of March, by which time it had been in action for four months and suffered a considerable number of casualties, the brigade pulled back to Guardia, near Naples, for a rest. 5th Parachute Battalion, which had been in very exposed positions overlooked by the enemy, had lost a number of men in the Salorola sector facing the main German defensive line that ran along a ridgeline between Orsogna and Guardi-grela. They could not be replaced easily because no reinforcements were forthcoming from England and the only source of replacements was volunteers from British forces in the Mediterranean theatre. These were trained at the Airborne Base commanded by the brigade's deputy commander, Colonel Tom Pearson, whose staff comprised a staff captain, an officer in charge of parachute training, a number of Army Physical Training Corps parachute jumping instructors, and No. 2 Mobile Parachute Servicing Unit RAF. In addition to recruiting and training volunteers, the Airborne Base was responsible for organising resupply drops for 15th Army Group and for the running of a convalescent depot for rehabilitation of wounded or injured paratroops. This latter establishment proved very successful in reducing the loss of trained parachutists who, if sent elsewhere, might not have been posted back to the brigade.

On 4 April, 2nd Independent Parachute Brigade Group was transferred west to the Cassino sector where, with the 10th Battalion The Rifle Brigade under command, it relieved 1st Guards Brigade and a number of New Zealand units. From its positions, overlooked by the famous monastery, it patrolled the line of the River Rapido with cover being provided to a certain extent during the day by a constant barrage of smokeshells fired by divisional artillery. At some points throughout the sector, Allied and German positions were within short distances of each other and when B Company 4th Parachute Battalion occupied the railway station in Cassino itself, it found that enemy troops were established in a hotel across the town square.

Shortly after the brigade's arrival, 6th Parachute Battalion, commanded by Lieutenant Colonel Bill Barlow, carried out a number of reconnaissance patrols on the far side of the River Garigliano in order to obtain information on the dispositions of enemy minefields. One such patrol, commanded by Lieutenant Gerry Pearson, was provided by C Company, its task being to find a path through a minefield in front of the enemy positions facing those of the battalion. Accompanied by a party of sappers equipped with mine detectors, Pearson and his men were making their way through the field when a mine was set off, wounding four of their number. The patrol attempted to retrace its steps, Pearson leading the way on all fours. Tragically, he knelt on a mine which blew off both his legs below the knees. Despite his terrible wounds, he ordered his men to evacuate the other wounded first and to leave him behind. This they refused to do and carried their young officer out of the minefield. Eventually, he was evacuated on the back of a mule, the journey taking several hours.

On 16 April, the brigade handed over to 21st Indian Infantry Brigade and withdrew for two days' rest. On 20 April, it relieved 6th New Zealand Infantry Brigade in another sector to the north-east of Cassino, once more coming under command of 2nd New Zealand Division. It was then joined by 300th Airlanding Anti-Tank Battery RA, deployed in the infantry role. During this period, the three parachute battalions patrolled intensively, often beset by heavy rain and severe cold which, combined with the constant enemy shelling, made life very unpleasant. On 21 May, 6th Parachute Battalion was withdrawn, being followed a week later by the rest of the brigade which went into reserve at Portecagnano and Filignano, near Salerno.

By this time, the Germans were pulling back to a line between Pisa and Rimini, pursued by the US Fifth and British Eighth Armies, the latter now commanded by General Sir Oliver Leese. As they retreated along a route from Sora to Avezzano, the enemy blew up roads and bridges to delay the Allied advance. In an attempt to deter them, Headquarters Eighth Army ordered 2nd Parachute Brigade to detail one of its battalions to harass the Germans at every opportunity, this task to be initiated on the night of 1/2 June. Brigadier Charles Pritchard, however, did not consider that the operation, codenamed Hasty, justified the use of a complete battalion and it was agreed that a smaller force would be sufficient. 6th Parachute Battalion was given the task and a group of sixty men, including signallers and a detachment of 127th Parachute Field Ambulance, was assembled under the command of Captain L. A. 'Fitz' Fitzroy-Smith.

At 7.00 p.m. on 1 June, the group took off in three aircraft, followed by eight more carrying dummy parachutists which would be dropped at the same time to give the impression of a larger force. An hour and half later, Fitzroy-Smith and his men were dropped successfully near Torricella and by 9.00 p.m. had rallied at their RV. There had been only one casualty during the drop, one man suffering a broken rib. Shortly afterwards, radio contact was established with 2nd New Zealand Division and Fitzroy-Smith requested that a prearranged resupply drop should proceed as planned.

Having established a firm base, Fitzroy-Smith split his force into three groups under himself and Lieutenants Fred Ashby and J. Evans. During the following weeks, these harassed the Germans whenever and wherever possible, and with a certain amount of success. In doing so, however, they incurred casualties, including a detachment of signallers who were taken prisoner. Moreover, contact with 2nd

New Zealand Division was lost when the sole remaining radio became inoperable and the force's carrier pigeons failed to reach their home destination.

By 7 June it had been decided to withdraw Fitzroy-Smith and his men but there was no way of communicating with them until Brigadier Pritchard conceived the idea of dropping leaflets, bearing the cryptic message 'Proceed Awdry forthwith', over the area. While this puzzled the enemy, Fitzroy-Smith was well aware that Captain John Awdry, an officer of 6th Parachute Battalion, was acting as a liaison officer with 2nd New Zealand Division. Accordingly, he and his men made their way back to Allied lines in small groups. Although almost two-thirds of Fitzroy-Smith's force had been lost and little damage caused to the enemy in terms of casualties, Operation Hasty had achieved some success in that it led the enemy to believe a much larger body of paratroops had been dropped and so forced them to deploy forces to counter it. The use of dummies proved highly effective, increasing concern among the Germans of possible airborne operations in their rear areas.

During the remainder of June 1944, 2nd Independent Parachute Brigade Group conducted airborne training in the Salerno area. Meanwhile, the Allied invasion of Normandy having begun, the Supreme Allied Commander Europe, General Eisenhower, had produced a plan for the invasion of southern France. Codenamed Operation Dragoon, it would see the US Seventh Army landing between Fréjus and St Raphael, thereafter advancing north up the Rhône valley and linking up with other US forces following the breakout from Normandy.

Southern France was occupied by the 250,000-strong German Nineteenth Army, which was responsible for the entire 300-mile-long Mediterranean coastline between Spain and Italy. Commanded by General Frederick Wiese, it comprised three corps incorporating seven divisions. Located in the area of the estuary of the Rhône was the 338th Infantry Division, elements of which had been transferred to the north, leaving it with three-quarters of its strength. To the west of the Rhône were the 189th, 198th and 716th Infantry Divisions while to the east, along the Côte d'Azur, was the 244th Infantry Division, under Major General Hans Schaefer, whose artillery comprised several batteries of field artillery and eighty-eight coastal guns. Defending the coast from Toulon eastwards to Agay was Major General Johannes Baessler's 242nd Infantry Division which possessed 106 coastal guns, some of which could fire a 700-pound shell at ranges of up to twenty miles, and therefore posed a major threat to any seaborne invasion force. The final stretch of coastline, from Agay to the Maritime Alps on the border with Italy, was defended by the understrength 148th Infantry Division, commanded by Major General Otto Fretter-Pico, which comprised two brigades instead of three.

The only reserves available to the Nineteenth Army were those under command of Army Group G, which was responsible for the defence of all France south of the River Loire. The first of these comprised the 11th Panzer Division, commanded by Major General Wend von Wietersheim, located in the Bordeaux area and only at half-strength, having seen extensive service in Russia on the Eastern Front. Nevertheless, its remaining armour, consisting of 26 Mk. IV tanks and 49 Mk. Vs, posed a considerable threat to any Allied invasion force. The second reserve formation, the 157th Infantry Division, was located a considerable distance to the north of the Côte d'Azur and was heavily embroiled in operations against resistance fighters in the mountains.

In mid-May, Nineteenth Army had received a visit from Field Marshal Erwin Rommel. Ordered by Hitler to 'Smash the Allied invasion effort!', Rommel had inspected the coastal defences along the whole coast of France and found little to please him. Immediately after the field marshal's departure, the commander of Army Group G, General Johannes Blaskowitz, had given orders for the strengthening of coastal defences throughout the length of coastline within Nineteenth Army's area of responsibility. Minefields and barbed-wire defences, covered by machine-gun positions, were laid on all beaches, and buildings turned into blockhouses. Likely landing points for seaborne invasion forces were blocked with pointed steel posts sunk into the seabed and designed to tear open the hulls of landing craft. Anti-personnel minefields were planted in areas likely to be used by infantry once ashore, while networks of trenches were dug along the entire coastline.

Inland, the Germans also took measures against the threat of airborne landings. Orders were given for thousands of long, sharpened stakes, designed so that paratroops would impale themselves upon them, to be erected in areas deemed suitable for use as DZs. Similarly, areas of terrain considered likely LZs for gliders were to be sown with thick poles with wires stretched between them.

The Allied plan for Dragoon called for a massive amphibious assault along a forty-five-mile stretch of the coast to the east of Toulon, between Cavalaire-sur-Mer and Agay. Just after midnight on 15/16 August, the 2nd and 3rd Regiments of the 1st Special Service Force, a 2,000-strong American/Canadian commando-type formation, would carry out a night landing on the Îles d'Hyères, two small islands situated off the coast at the western flank of the assault area. Positioned on the Île du Levant, the more easterly of the two, was a battery of three 6.5 inch guns which had to be knocked out before the arrival of the fleet carrying the invasion force that comprised the three divisions of the US VI Corps commanded by General Lucian Truscott. Meanwhile the 1st Special Service Force's 1st Regiment would land on the nearby Île du Port Cros, while a Free French commando unit, the Groupe des Commandos d'Afrique commanded by Lieutenant Colonel Georges Regis-Bouvet and codenamed Romeo Force, did likewise on the mainland, just north of the two islands on a beach between Rayaol and Cavalaire, with the initial mission of knocking out another gun battery on Cap Nègre. It was then to block the coastal road at Cavalaire and halt the move of any enemy reinforcements along the coastal road from Toulon. Farther to the north, Rosie Force, a sixty-seven-strong team of the Groupe Navale d'Assaut de Corse – a Free French naval commando unit under Captain Sériot – would land at Pointe de l'Esquillon, just to

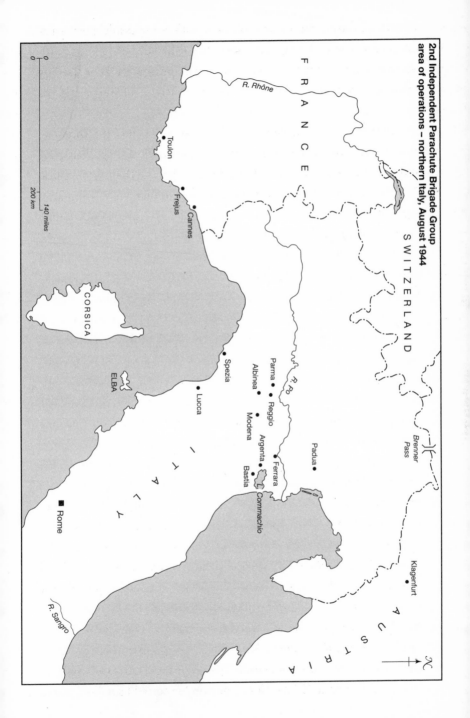

2nd Independent Parachute Brigade Group
area of operations – northern Italy, August 1944

FRANCE

R. Rhône

SWITZERLAND

Toulon

Fréjus

Cannes

CORSICA

ELBA

Spezia

Lucca

Parma

Albinea

Reggio

Modena

Argenta

Ferrara

Bastia

Commachio

Padua

Brenner Pass

R. Po

ITALY

Rome

R. Sangro

AUSTRIA

Klagenfurt

0

140 miles

200 km

411

the west of Cannes. Its mission was to blow up a number of key bridges along the Corniche road and on Route 7 further inland, thereby blocking the movement of enemy troops heading west from the city towards the invasion beaches.

H-Hour on 15 August was to be 8.00 a.m., when enemy defences along the entire invasion sector would be subjected to a massive bombardment by Allied warships and bombers, after which the US VI Corps would be landed. On its left, Major General John W. Daniels' 3rd Infantry Division would land on two beaches thirteen miles apart at Cavalaire and Pampelonne. In the centre, the 45th Infantry Division, commanded by Major General William W. Eagles, was to come ashore at Baie de Bougnon and La Nartelle, while Major General John E. Dahlquist's 36th Infantry Division would do likewise at Saint Raphael. Once all three divisions had landed in sufficient strength, the French II Corps, commanded by General Jean-Marie de Lattre de Tassigny, would also come ashore and then push along the coast to the south-west to take two major objectives: the cities and ports of Toulon and Marseilles.

The Germans were correct in assuming that the Allies would use their airborne forces in an invasion of southern France. In February 1944, initial planning had begun for an airborne operation to drop and land a force of paratroops and gliderborne infantry to block any move by Army Group G to counter the seaborne landings with Major General Wend von Wietersheim's 11th Panzer Division. The plan, however, had been restricted by the availability of airborne units, which were still at a low state of readiness, and by the lack of transport aircraft. The USAAF's 51st Troop Carrier Wing, consisting of three troop carrier groups, had remained in the Mediterranean theatre following the deactivation of the 12th Troop Carrier Command, but only a part of the wing was available for an airborne mission due to heavy requirements for transport aircraft for special operations, medical evacuation and general air transport tasks.

The US War Department had been requested to provide a full airborne division for Operation Dragoon but had declined to do so.

Instead, a number of units were transferred to the theatre from the United States, these comprising the 517th Parachute Regimental Combat Team; the 551st Parachute Infantry Battalion and the 550th Glider Infantry Battalion. On its arrival, the 517th was attached to the US Fifth Army for ten days in order to obtain some combat experience, while the 509th Parachute Infantry Battalion was transferred from its base in North Africa to Italy. Shortly afterwards, the decision was taken to add 2nd Independent Parachute Brigade Group and a Free French unit, the 1er Regiment de Chasseurs Parachutistes commanded by Lieutenant Colonel Faure. By the end of June 1944 a composite airborne formation, designated the Provisional Airborne Division, had been formed under Brigadier General Robert T. Frederick who was supported by a thirty-six-strong headquarters staff transferred from the United States, the majority being from the US 13th Airborne Division which had been activated on 13 August 1943. It comprised the following:

US TROOPS

517th Parachute Regimental Combat Team: 1st, 2nd and 3rd Battalions 517th Parachute Infantry Regiment, 463rd Parachute Field Artillery Battalion, 596th Parachute Engineer Company, 512th Airborne Signal Company.

509th Parachute Infantry Battalion
551st Parachute Infantry Battalion
550th Glider Infantry Battalion
602nd Pack Field Artillery Battalion
Anti-tank company of 442nd Infantry Regiment
887th Airborne Engineer Company – its three platoons attached to
    the 509th and 551st Parachute Infantry Battalions and 550th
    Glider Infantry Battalion respectively
Company A 2nd Chemical Mortar Battalion – attached to 2nd
    Independent Parachute Brigade Group
Company D 83rd Chemical Mortar Battalion
676th Medical Collecting Company

1st and 2nd Provisional Pathfinder Platoons
1st Military Police Platoon

BRITISH TROOPS

2nd Independent Parachute Brigade Group – 4th, 5th and 6th Parachute Battalions, 1st Independent Parachute Platoon, 64th Light Battery RA, 300th Airlanding Anti-Tank Battery RA, 2nd Parachute Squadron RE, 127th Parachute Field Ambulance.

FREE FRENCH TROOPS

1er Régiment de Chasseurs Parachutistes – attached to 517th
    Parachute Regimental Combat Team

The initial outline plan for the airborne element of Dragoon, code-named Rugby and produced by Headquarters Seventh US Army, had called for the Provisional Airborne Division to be dropped in small detachments prior to the seaborne landings. This, however, was rejected by Brigadier General Frederick who, with the commanding officer of the 509th Parachute Infantry Battalion, Lieutenant Colonel William P. Yarborough, drew up an alternative whereby the division would seize the town of Le Muy situated some fifteen miles inland from Fréjus. All roads approaching from the north, east and west passed through the town and hence its capture would block any move by the enemy reinforcements to move up, in particular the 11th Panzer Division, which posed the greatest threat.

The operation would be led by the 509th which would drop to the south and south-east of Le Muy at 4.15 a.m. on D-Day, 16 August, and take the high ground dominating the town. The 517th Parachute Regimental Combat Team, commanded by Colonel Rupert D. Graves, would follow fifteen minutes later and take the high ground to the north and west of the town, thereafter covering the main routes leading west to Toulon and Draguignan, the latter being the location of a German corps headquarters. At 4.45 a.m. 2nd Independent Parachute Brigade Group would drop and seize the area around Le Muy and the village of La Motte, but exclusive of Le Muy itself, holding it for further landings that day. During the first phase of the operation 4th Parachute Battalion, commanded by Lieutenant Colonel H. B. 'Vic' Coxen, was to dominate Le Muy, which was held by a strong force of enemy, while Lieutenant Colonel Bill Barlow's 6th Parachute Battalion was to occupy an area of high ground to the north-east of La Motte, ready to support the 2nd Battalion 517th Parachute Regimental Combat Team. 5th Parachute Battalion, commanded by Lieutenant Colonel David Hunter, meanwhile would be in reserve in the area of La Mitan. The gliders carrying 64th Light Battery RA and 300th Airlanding Anti-Tank Battery RA would land later at 8.15 a.m., the rest of the Provisional Airborne Division's artillery and mortars arriving in another lift at 9.00 a.m. The rest of the division, consisting of the 551st Parachute Infantry Battalion and 550th Glider Infantry Battalion, commanded by Lieutenant Colonels Wood G. Joerg and Edward Sachs respectively, would drop and land at 6.00 p.m. that evening.

On 12 July 2nd Independent Parachute Brigade Group moved from Salerno to Rome, where it joined the other elements of the Provisional Airborne Division to undergo four weeks of intensive joint training at the US Fifth Army's Airborne Training Centre which had moved from Sicily to two airfields at Ciampino and Lido de Roma, in the area of the Italian capital. Of all the elements in the force, only the parachute units within 2nd Independent Parachute Brigade Group and the 509th Parachute Infantry Battalion had undergone combined airborne training with the troop carrier units that would transport them. The remainder needed to carry out such training as a matter of priority, the task of converting the non-airborne units to the gliderborne role being of particular urgency. A glider school was swiftly established at the Airborne Training Centre and instruction given in the loading and lashing down of heavy weapons and equipment, this being followed by training flights and one tactical landing as part of an exercise.

At this stage there was still a shortage of aircraft for Dragoon with only two of the 51st Troop Carrier Wing's groups available, the third still being deployed in support of special operations. In order to provide sufficient lift, for which a total of 450 C-47s were required, the 50th and 53rd Troop Carrier Wings of the 4th Troop Carrier Command were transferred temporarily from Britain to Italy during July, each comprising four groups of three squadrons each. Accompanying these was the 9th Troop Carrier Pathfinder Unit, bringing the total number of aircraft transferred from Britain for Dragoon to 413. In addition, 375 glider pilots, the 819th Medical Air Evacuation Squadron and a number of signals detachments also arrived via Gibraltar and Marrakesh. The entire USAAF element taking part in Dragoon was grouped under an ad hoc formation designated the Provisional Troop Carrier Air Division, led by Brigadier General Paul L. Williams, the commander of the 9th Troop Carrier Command. By 20 July, the entire air division had arrived in Italy.

One of the problems facing the planners was the lack of gliders, as only some 130 Wacos and 30 Horsas were available for the operation. Fortunately, however, a requisition had already been placed in the United States for a quantity of 350 Wacos and this was now expedited, the gliders arriving in Italy and being ready for operational use shortly afterwards. At the same time, a further 350 glider pilots were also transferred from Britain to augment those who had arrived earlier.

On 21 July the Provisional Airborne Division had been redesignated the 1st Airborne Task Force. This was proposed by Brigadier General Fredrick, who considered the term 'division' to be a misnomer, his request being granted by the commander of the US Seventh Army, Major General Alexander M. Patch .

It was about then that the 1er Régiment de Chasseurs Parachutistes was withdrawn from the task force. This was apparently at the insistence of the Free French leader, General Charles de Gaulle, who intended to use the regiment in an operation in central France, in the Massif Central, to rally resistance units throughout that area. Later, however, that plan was vetoed by the Supreme Headquarters Allied Expeditionary Force (SHAEF).

With the 1st Airborne Task Force and Provisional Troop Carrier

Air Division complete and ready for operations, final detailed planning for Operation Rugby began around 2 July. Fourteen mounting airfields had already been selected, these being located at Ciampino, Calera, Marcigliano, Fabrisi, Viterbo, Tarquinia, Voltone, Montalto, Canino, Orbetello, Ombrone, Grosseto, Fallonica and Piombino. The Provisional Troop Carrier Air Division now undertook the flight planning, including coordination, timings, routes, corridors, rendezvous points and traffic patterns. Flight routes were based on a number of criteria, including: shortest feasible distance; prominent terrain features; traffic control for ten carrier groups; naval convoy routes; locations of assault beaches; primary assault beaches; primary aerial targets; enemy radar installations; avoidance of excessive dog-legs; prominent landfalls and positions of charted enemy flak installations. The route followed the Italian coast from the Rome area to the island of Elba, the latter being the first waypoint with a Eureka homing transmitter and an MF beacon (radio compass homing device) positioned on its northern tip. Other Eurekas were placed on the island of Giroglia and, together with an MF beacon, on the northern tip of Corsica from which the aircraft would continue on an azimuth course over three Eureka-equipped naval vessels (the centre boat also being fitted with an MF beacon) positioned thirty miles apart, to a landfall at Agay just north of Fréjus.

Meanwhile the troop carrier units and Headquarters 1st Airborne Task Force, the latter by this time located at Lido de Roma, drew up the composition of lifts for which detailed planning was complete by 25 July. In essence, these were as follows. At 3.23 a.m. on 15 August, pathfinder teams would be dropped to mark the DZs for the main drop by 396 aircraft which would begin at 4.12 a.m. and be complete by 5.09 a.m., being followed at 8.14 a.m. by the main glider landing by 103 Wacos and thirty Horsas. Later that same day a drop of forty-two sticks of paratroops would take place, this being followed by a landing by 374 Waco gliders beginning at 6.10 p.m. and ending at 6.59 p.m. On D+1, a resupply drop would take place with 112 planeloads being delivered on call.

Due to the expanses of high terrain within the operational area, the decision was taken to drop the paratroops and release gliders from exceptionally high altitudes of between 1,500 and 2,000 feet, with dropping and release speeds being set at 104 and 95 knots respectively. The paratroop aircraft would fly in formations of universal 'V of Vs', each of nine C-47s, in serials of forty-five aircraft with five-minute intervals between serials. Glider and tug combinations meanwhile would fly in a 'pair of pairs' formation echeloned to the right rear with 1,000 feet between pairs in column. Serials would comprise forty-eight aircraft with eight minutes between them.

The accuracy of the drops and landings would depend heavily on the marking of DZs and LZs by the 1st and 2nd Provisional Pathfinder Platoons and the 1st Independent Parachute Platoon, 2nd Independent Parachute Brigade Group's pathfinder sub-unit, commanded by Captain Peter Baker. Joint training was carried out by all three platoons with the Provisional Troop Carrier Air Division's pathfinder unit, which also tested their Eurekas; these would transmit to the Rebecca receivers fitted in the transport and tug aircraft, as well as other items of equipment, such as holophane lights, to be used in the operation. All the pathfinder teams underwent thorough refresher training and carried out exercises in all possible conditions, with small groups of troops being dropped on to marked DZs to test the accuracy of the equipment.

Lack of time, together with difficulties over repacking of parachutes, precluded the staging of a full-scale final exercise as a rehearsal for Rugby. Units did, however, conduct drops with two or three men representing a full stick of eighteen while the remainder waited on the DZ to rehearse rallying procedures. The Provisional Troop Carrier Air Division meanwhile conducted joint exercises with naval forces acting in support of Rugby, flying a token force of three aircraft per serial at the exact timing schedules and altitudes over the three Eureka-equipped naval vessels, the latter being placed in the same relative positions they would occupy during the operation. Thereafter two serials, each of thirty-six C-47s, flew along the route in daylight in order to familiarise the naval forces further with the appearance of troop carrier aircraft in formation. Other practice flights were also carried out in conjunction with the USAAF's 31st and 325th Fighter Groups to work out the details for fighter cover and air-sea rescue.

From early August onwards, the officers and men of the 1st Airborne Task Force were briefed on the forthcoming operation. Despite efforts to maintain maximum secrecy, however, it soon became all too apparent that the enemy were expecting an airborne landing as part of the awaited invasion of southern France. German propaganda radio featured 'Axis Sally', a female presenter who on one occasion informed members of the 517th Parachute Regimental Combat Team listening to one of her broadcasts of the reception they would meet when arriving over southern France, startling them when she announced that she was aware of where they were going to land. On another, she told listeners of the 509th Parachute Infantry Battalion that her masters were fully familiar with the 1st Airborne Task Force and its commander, Brigadier General Robert T. Frederick.

By D-2, all units of the entire task force had been moved from their concentration areas to the mounting airfields where the troop carrier squadrons had already assembled and all gliders had been marshalled. As with all airborne operations, the weather was the major factor and on D-1, 14 August, the whole of Western Europe was covered by a large area of high pressure centred over the North Sea. A part of this had broken off and now lay settled exactly above the operational area, preventing the likelihood of storms or high winds but raising the possibility of cloud or fog. The meteorological forecast was for clear weather conditions for the flight up to the island of Elba, visibility thereafter decreasing to two or three miles during the final stage to the DZs and LZs.

In the early hours of 15 August, six C-47s took off from the Italian peninsula and headed for southern France. As they crossed the coast, they began dropping 'window', strips of aluminium foil that created the impression of a large number of aircraft on enemy radar screens.

The 'window' was followed by 600 dummy parachutists dropped on to DZs to the north and west of Toulon, each being fitted with rifle simulators and other pyrotechnics which were activated on landing and simulated small arms fire.

Operation Rugby itself began just after midnight on 14/15 August with troops emplaning, engines being warmed up and aircraft marshalled into positions for take-off. At 3.30 a.m. a total of 396 C-47s carrying 1st Airborne Task Force's main lift took off from ten airfields. Some three hours beforehand, nine aircraft, carrying the 1st Independent Parachute Platoon and the 1st and 2nd Provisional Pathfinder Platoons, had also flown from Italy. As predicted, weather conditions were good during the flight but on reaching the French coast the aircraft encountered thick fog, which obscured all landmarks below, and shortly afterwards they were subjected to enemy anti-aircraft fire. The C-47 carrying the pathfinder team tasked with guiding in the aircraft transporting the 509th Parachute Infantry Battalion circled twice in an attempt to locate the battalion's designated DZ, but without success. On the third pass the team, commanded by Lieutenant Dan A. DeLeo, jumped blind into the mist, DeLeo soon afterwards being wounded in the head by shrapnel from an anti-aircraft shell exploding near by during his descent. Unconscious, he landed in some trees and awoke to find himself hanging twelve feet from the ground. He was soon found by a member of his team, but of the remainder of his men there was no sign.

Lieutenant Russell Fuller's pathfinder team, which had been allotted to the 551st Parachute Infantry Battalion, also found itself in trouble when some of its number became scattered during the drop, one of them carrying the Eureka beacon to guide in the 551st's main body. On landing, some encountered enemy troops but escaped capture.

Captain Peter Baker's forty-five-strong 1st Independent Parachute Platoon had been dropped meanwhile without mishap and by 3.23 a.m. had marked the DZs for 2nd Independent Parachute Brigade Group. DZs 'A' and 'O', on to which the 517th Parachute Regimental Combat

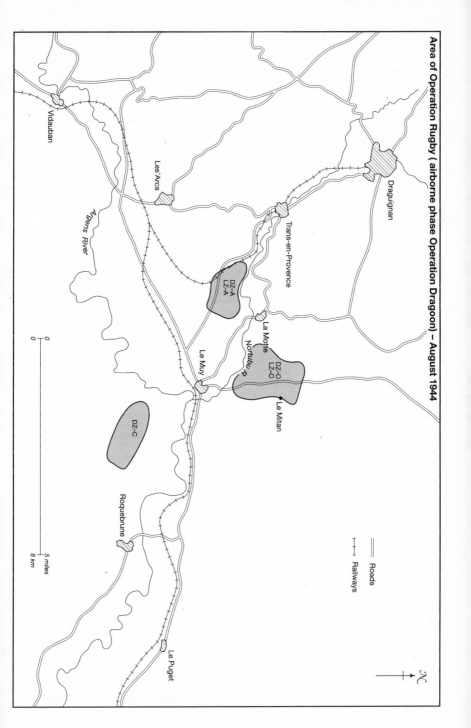

Area of Operation Rugby (airborne phase Operation Dragoon) – August 1944

Roads

Railways

0 ___ 5 miles
0 ___ 8 km

Vidauban

Les Arcs

Argens River

Draguignan

Trans-en-Provence

DZ-A
LZ-A

La Motte

Le Muy

DZ-O
LZ-O

Nartuby R.

Le Mitan

DZ-C

Roquebrune

Le Puget

Team and 2nd Independent Parachute Brigade Group respectively would drop, were situated on cultivated terrain consisting mainly of small vineyards and orchards with very few large buildings, tall trees, telephone wires or other obstacles that might pose a threat to parachutists. DZ 'C', on to which the 509th Parachute Infantry Battalion would drop, comprised a hill feature with somewhat rugged terrain. Those anti-airborne defences which had been put in place on the DZs by the Germans generally proved ineffective as the stakes had not been sharpened, nor had they been erected in sufficient density to pose any real threat.

2nd Independent Parachute Brigade Group arrived over DZ 'O' on time at 4.45 a.m. During the flight, several pilots had experienced problems with the signals from the Eurekas, which had tended to drift off frequency despite constant checking of the Rebecca receiver fitted in each aircraft. Fortunately, the MF beacons, whose signals could be received at ranges of up to thirty miles, had proved more reliable and enabled the aircraft to remain on-beam. The DZ, however, was shrouded from the air by thick haze and ground mist and this, combined with some of 1st Independent Parachute Platoon's Eurekas suddenly becoming faulty, resulted in fifty-three of the 126 aircraft carrying the brigade dropping their sticks well away from the DZ. The remaining planes dropped theirs accurately, but once the brigade had rallied on the ground it was discovered that only its headquarters was complete, with 4th Parachute Battalion numbering only between thirty to forty per cent of its strength and 6th Parachute Battalion sixty per cent. By 6.15 a.m. the brigade headquarters had been established at Le Mitan and within ten minutes had established radio contact with the headquarters of the US 36th Infantry Division, which was still at sea.

As both battalions moved off towards their respective objectives, 2nd Parachute Squadron RE, assisted by 1st Independent Parachute Platoon, had been clearing the LZs of anti-glider obstacles. This did not prove an onerous task as the twelve-foot long poles, planted some 30-40 feet apart, had been driven only two feet into the ground and required relatively little effort to uproot them. The Wacos carrying 64th Light Battery RA landed at 9.20 a.m., but the Horsas transporting 300th Airlanding Anti-Tank Battery RA had been forced to return to Italy because of the poor visibility. After the tug aircraft had been refuelled, however, they and their gliders headed back for southern France.

Despite its very low strength, 4th Parachute Battalion succeeded by 7.30 a.m. in taking its initial objective: Point 113, a feature of high ground dominating Le Muy from the north. Later that morning, it captured Les Serres, which it held against a series of small counter-attacks launched by the Germans. A small group of houses at Les Serres, dominating the bridge over the River Naturby and the road leading to Le Muy, remained in enemy hands, however, and the task of clearing them and securing the bridge was given to C Company. Their attack was successful but the company suffered casualties of seven killed and nine wounded, the enemy suffering sixteen killed and twenty-nine taken prisoner.

The commanding officer, Lieutenant Colonel Vic Coxen, and some eighty members of the battalion had been dropped meantime in the area of Fayence, some fifteen miles to the north of Le Muy. After joining up with a group from the 3rd Battalion 517th Parachute Regimental Combat Team, Coxen and his men set off across country to rejoin the battalion. Major Dan Calvert, commanding A Company, landed some twenty miles away from the DZ and hitched a lift on a bus, concealing himself under a pile of cabbages and being shielded by local people as the vehicle passed through a number of enemy roadblocks.

With the exception of B Company, commanded by Major Douglas McCall, 5th Parachute Battalion was badly scattered during the drop, landing in three groups in the area of Feyence. The first of these comprised the commanding officer, Lieutenant Colonel David Hunter, half of his battalion headquarters and the majority of C Company, while the second consisted of D Company. The third group comprised the battalion's intelligence officer and a group of twenty men.

Hunter and two of his men set off for the brigade headquarters, heading south without encountering any opposition and reaching their destination at 3.30 p.m. The rest of the first group split into two under the adjutant, Captain Jimmy Holden, and C Company's commander, Major David West-Russell, arriving at the brigade headquarters between 8.30 p.m. and 10.30 p.m. that night.

The second group, under D Company's commander, Major Bill Blackwood, approached Tourettes where, having reconnoitred the village and found it clear of enemy, it took up defensive positions. Shortly afterwards, a convoy of fifteen enemy vehicles was observed about two miles away approaching from the west. D Company swiftly took up ambush positions but before the convoy could approach the killing area it came under fire from a mixed force of some twenty-five British and American paratroops further down the road. The latter then came under attack from a seventy-strong enemy force but were saved by D Company, which moved up and engaged the enemy, inflicting heavy casualties and severely damaging several of the vehicles. Not long after this action, five Americans appeared from a farmhouse nearby, one of them the Chief of Staff of 1st Airborne Task Force, and joined forces with D Company. Later that day, contact was made with a large group of the 3rd Battalion 517th Parachute Regimental Combat Team and the combined force then headed south towards Le Muy.

In the darkness one senior NCO, Sergeant Bert Tucker of 5th Parachute Battalion's Anti-Tank Platoon, landed on a building housing enemy troops. On coming under fire from its occupants, he replied with his Sten gun, killing two Germans and wounding another, and continued to put up a stout resistance until forced to surrender by the threat of grenades being thrown on to the roof where he was concealed. Taken prisoner, he attempted to convince his captors that they were surrounded by two divisions of airborne troops but failed to do so. At around 8.15 a.m., however, the second lift of C-47s appeared overhead, dropping their sticks, along with a number of gliders. Without further ado the enemy troops, who numbered over eighty, surrendered to Sergeant Tucker, who then marched them to the battalion's RV.

One member of B Company, Lieutenant George Christie, the commander of No. 10 Platoon, found himself landing in the deep waters of the River Argens, some four miles from 5th Parachute Battalion's RV. Releasing himself from his equipment container and having been forced to relinquish his Sten gun, he swam to the nearest bank. There he encountered a small group of resistance fighters, led by a young woman, who issued him with a new Sten gun and remained with him until he had assembled a group of eight British and American paratroopers. Shortly after setting off towards the RV, Christie and his men were ambushed by a group of ten Germans. Seven of the enemy died in the ensuing firefight, while the remaining three managed to escape, though wounded. One of Christie's men was also wounded, but the group pushed on and shortly afterwards ambushed a motor-cycle combination being ridden by two SS officers and two women, all of whom were killed.

Lieutenant Christie then continued towards the RV where he rejoined B Company, which subsequently set off north towards Draguignan, en route ambushing an enemy convoy of five trucks and killing twelve Germans. Shortly afterwards, however, it came under fire from a large chateau. B Company mounted an attack and in the ensuing battle killed over thirty Germans before the remaining fifty or so surrendered and lay down their arms. This action was followed by an unpleasant incident when a German officer pulled a small pistol from his pocket and shot dead a member of B Company, Corporal 'Doc' Davies, before dropping the weapon and holding up his hands. Only the swift intervention of Major Douglas McCall prevented the German from being shot immediately by other members of the company.

6th Parachute Battalion's drop proceeded relatively well, with only a small number landing wide of the DZ. A few men came under enemy fire as they landed, being killed before they could release themselves from their parachute harnesses, while others found themselves in action as they left the DZ. Most of the battalion, however, succeeded in rallying and reaching the RV, its companies then heading off to their respective objectives, one of them subsequently being deployed into Clastron following the surrender of the enemy garrison there. B Company took La Motte, which became the first village in southern France to be liberated, and by midday all companies had secured their objectives, suffering minimal casualties and taking over 100 prisoners. C Company was particularly fortunate in capturing a supply depot along with sixty enemy troops, a considerable amount of transport and stores that included a large quantity of wine and brandy.

2nd Independent Parachute Brigade Group experienced very light casualties during the drop and in subsequent actions. Furthermore, its initial glider landing was unopposed and thus a success. Despite the numbers missing from its ranks, with only seventy-three out of 126 sticks having been dropped on the DZ, it achieved all of its initial objectives without difficulty by 10.15 a.m., encountering only light enemy opposition. Throughout the day, missing men reappeared after making their way back from where they had been dropped.

By early evening of 15 August, all was quiet in most of 2nd Independent Parachute Brigade Group's area. 4th Parachute Battalion by then comprised almost two complete rifle companies, but with little in the way of support weapons, with Lieutenant Colonel Coxen and his eighty-strong group still on their way south from Fayence. 6th Parachute Battalion numbered seventeen officers and 300 other ranks. C Company was despatched to a location on the road between Le Muy and Le Luc to conduct a standing patrol and ambush any enemy withdrawing west from Le Muy. Other patrols were sent into Le Muy to ascertain the strength of the enemy in the town. 5th Parachute Battalion was by this time of sufficient strength to be deployed to positions around the road leading to the brigade's LZ from the north.

The American elements of 1st Airborne Task Force had meantime encountered similar problems. The pilots of the 442nd Troop Carrier Group, carrying Lieutenant Colonel William P. Yarborough's 509th

Parachute Infantry Battalion, received no signals from Lieutenant Dan DeLeo's pathfinder team's Eureka beacon and were prevented by the thick fog from locating the battalion's DZ visually. In the distance, however, they observed the dim silhouettes of hills they knew to be on the perimeter of the DZ and, roughly calculating their position, decided to drop their sticks. At around 4.20 a.m. the leading elements of the 509th jumped from their C-47s. Two sticks, however, were despatched prematurely and dropped over the Mediterranean, being lost without trace. Meanwhile the whole of Company C, commanded by Captain Jess H. Walls, found itself landing near Saint Tropez, some twelve miles to the south of the DZ, along with nineteen members of Company B and elements of the 463rd Parachute Field Artillery Battalion. Soon after he landed, Lieutenant Colonel Yarborough met a small group of his men with whom he headed to a nearby hill from where he flashed a blue torch, successfully drawing in other members of the unit.

Meanwhile Company A of the 509th , commanded by Captain Ernest T. Siegel, had been dropped accurately and rallied within thirty minutes. By first light, it had taken a bridge on the road leading to Le Muy and Siegel sent a patrol to reconnoitre the town itself. In due course, having been joined by Lieutenant Colonel Yarborough, he learned that a column of German infantry and a number of vehicles were heading north out of Le Muy towards his positions. He quickly moved his platoons into ambush positions in some woods near by, deploying his mortars and machine guns so that they could cover the entire length of road along which the enemy were approaching. The latter, however, were fully alert and, on nearing the ambush area, halted to open fire on the woods where Siegel's men were concealed. The response was immediate and a fierce battle developed, lasting two hours before the enemy pulled back, leaving behind a large number killed or wounded and sixty taken prisoner.

Following close behind the 509th came Colonel Rupert D. Graves' 517th Parachute Regimental Combat Team which dropped at 4.30 a.m. On landing, Graves found himself alone but duly came across two of his men with whom he set off towards Le Muy. At first light, he could hear firing from the direction of the wooded hills to the north of the town which he decided to bypass and head for La Motte, collecting other members of the 517th as he went.

The 1st Battalion of the 517th, commanded by Major William J. Boyle, had been scattered during the drop with one group landing close to an enemy position manned by eighty-five Germans, less than a mile to the north-east of Le Muy. As dawn broke, it launched an attack and a fierce action ensued during which twenty-nine Germans were killed, twenty-one wounded and thirty-two taken prisoner. The majority of Lieutenant Colonel Richard Seitz's 2nd Battalion had similarly been dispersed over a wide area.

Lieutenant Colonel Melvin Zais and his 3rd Battalion of the 517th landed in the area of the villages of Callian, Fayence and Seillans, almost twenty-five miles from their DZ. Zais swiftly rounded up some eighty-five of his men and made for the village of Sainte Clariers, en route for Le Muy, only to be attacked by USAAF fighter bombers which mistook the paratroopers for enemy reinforcements heading for the coast. Two hours later, while moving through a heavily wooded area, Zais' group met another from 2nd Independent Parachute Brigade Group, this being led by Lieutenant Colonel Vic Coxen of 4th Parachute Battalion. Joining forces, the two groups continued to head for Le Muy. As they neared the DZs they encountered an enemy convoy making its way to the landing beaches. A fierce battle ensued with the convoy being destroyed and all the enemy being killed or captured. Elsewhere in the area around the 517th's DZs, engagements took place as small groups of paratroops or individuals came under fire as they landed. One stick came down in an enemy bivouac area and after a sharp clash the surviving eight members of the stick were overrun and taken prisoner.

Despite the inaccuracy of the drops and the scattering of units, the 1st Airborne Task Force succeeded in sowing confusion and panic among the enemy during the dark hours before dawn on 15 August. The headquarters of General Ferdinand Neuling's German LXII Corps was deluged with terrified and exaggerated reports of Allied airborne troops of many times their actual strength. Several indications of a large airborne force that had been dropped to the north and west of Toulon proved the 600 dummy parachutists and their pyrotechnics to have been highly effective. Small groups of paratroops attacked enemy positions, ambushed German patrols and despatch riders, blew up bridges, cut telephone wires and generally created mayhem throughout the area.

Having been warned by members of a local resistance unit that the Germans intended to blow up the port installations in Saint Tropez, Captain Jess Walls, the commander of Company C 509th Parachute Infantry Battalion, assembled a force of 250 and at 7.45 a.m. headed for the city, taking 250 prisoners and two coastal gun batteries en route. On reaching the city centre, Walls and his men, by now reinforced by some fifty resistance fighters, encountered a large enemy force which had taken refuge in the old citadel where it was making a stand. Throughout the morning, Walls and his men rained harassing fire on the enemy until joined at 3.00 p.m. by a company of the US 45th Infantry Division, which brought up bazookas and heavy machine guns. Half an hour later, the enemy in the citadel surrendered, by which time they had suffered some 130 casualties. Nevertheless, it took several hours of street-fighting before all resistance was overcome.

Yet the airborne troops did not have things all their own way. While Captain Walls and his men besieged the enemy in Saint Tropez, Major William J. Boyle and a fifty-strong group of his 1st Battalion 517th Parachute Regimental Combat Team found themselves surrounded and pinned down in the town of Les Arcs. Following the earlier successful attack on a strongly held enemy position, one of Boyle's platoons had ventured into the town where it had been engaged by the enemy garrison. Boyle and others subsequently joined the platoon and shortly after first light came under very heavy fire as large numbers of enemy troops appeared and began working their way round through side streets to attack the paratroops on both flanks. Boyle had no alternative but to conduct a fighting withdrawal, which he and his men proceeded to do, carrying their wounded with them. Leaving the town, they headed down a road, only to fall into an enemy ambush. Despite being surrounded on all sides and pinned down by heavy fire, Boyle and his men broke through the German net and after a mile or so reached an abandoned farm, where they established a defensive position. Here, with the enemy advancing on them, they prepared to sell their lives dearly.

The evening of 15 August saw Lieutenant Colonel Wood G. Joerg's 842-strong 551st Parachute Infantry Battalion taking off from an airfield at Montalto, some 100 miles to the north of Rome, in C-47s of the 437th Troop Carrier Group and heading for southern France where it was due to drop at 6.00 p.m.. Weather conditions were good and the flight proved uneventful, the leading flight crossing the Côte d'Azur exactly on schedule. Although accurate, the drop itself was not without incident. The commander of Company A, Captain Marshall Dalton, found his parachute canopy collapsing after a mid-air collision with a parachute carrying an equipment container. Reacting swiftly, Dalton grabbed the container, held on tight as it descended, and came down safely. Several members of the battalion landed in trees near the DZ, encountering enemy troops who were swiftly killed or captured. Within minutes, the 551st was rallying prior to moving off towards its objectives.

The gods of war had not smiled so kindly on the 550th Glider Infantry Battalion which had taken off from an airfield at Onbrone, just outside Rome, at 4.10 p.m. that afternoon. The battalion was being transported in 337 Waco gliders towed by C-47s and escorted by large numbers of USAAF fighters and fighter-bombers. Flying with them were the thirty Horsa gliders, carrying 300th Airlanding Anti-Tank Battery RA, which had been forced to return to Italy earlier that day because of poor visibility over the LZ. The flight proceeded smoothly but as the aircraft approached the French coast the pilots observed ahead of them a huge pall of smog and cloud lying over the invasion area and the two LZs designated for the 550th Glider Infantry Battalion. Minutes later, tugs and gliders flew into it and visibility deteriorated sharply. Pandemonium now broke out in mid-air as the leading element of one column of C-47s and gliders, realising that it had flown too far because of the bad visibility, turned 180 degrees and began flying back towards the LZs and the rest of the formation which by this time was casting off its gliders. Faced with the oncoming aircraft, the pilots of the cast-off Wacos took violent evasive action, weaving their way through them to avoid collision. Some gliders crashed head-on, others became entangled in towropes dangling from the C-47s flying in their direction. Some of the ropes became entangled, wrenching off wings and pulling fuselages apart, men and vehicles spilling out of the stricken Wacos as they plunged earthwards.

Miraculously, a number of gliders landed safely, some hurtling in among the paratroops of the 551st Parachute Infantry Battalion dashing across the area to the battalion's RV. The scene was one of chaos as the Wacos swept in, some hitting 'Rommel's Asparagus' – the name given to the poles erected by the Germans as anti-glider defences – while others collided with houses, trees and boulders. All around the LZ the scene was one of carnage, with injured and dying men lying trapped in the wreckage of the gliders. One of the 551st's two medical officers, Captain Jud Chalkley, and his team of medical orderlies, who were on the LZ at the time, immediately began giving morphine and emergency first aid. Eleven of the glider pilots were killed in the landings, others suffering terrible injuries to their legs as the flimsy nose sections of their aircraft collapsed on impact.

By last light on 15 August, reports arriving at Brigadier General Robert Frederick's command post situated in a farmhouse just outside Le Mitan, a short distance north of Le Muy, indicated that the 517th Parachute Regimental Combat Team had achieved its immediate objectives, having taken the area of high ground to the south and west of La Motte, and blocked the road leading from it to Draguignan. The village of Les Arcs was still held by the enemy but the 517th was in control of the roads to the south of it. Initial reports indicated that enemy casualties had been high with hundreds killed and over a thousand taken prisoner. However, casualties suffered by the 1st Airborne Task Force in the first day of the operation had also been considerable with 450 men killed, captured or reported as missing, while a further 290 casualties had been incurred during the parachute drops and glider landings, the majority among the 550th Glider Infantry Battalion and the glider pilots.

At this stage, Le Muy itself was still in enemy hands. As is clearly shown in the operation order, which has been studied in detail by the author of this book, 2nd Independent Parachute Brigade Group's task in the second phase of the operation was to be prepared to attack and seize the town, any such assault to be carried out by 4th Parachute Battalion with 5th Parachute Battalion in support. Thereafter, the brigade was to operate against enemy forces to the north and east. During the period leading up to Dragoon, however, the commander of 15th Army Group, General Sir Harold Alexander, had instructed Brigadier Charles Pritchard that he was to make every effort to minimise casualties. The reasons for this were twofold. Firstly, after nearly five years of war, Britain was suffering a manpower shortage and could ill afford to sustain major losses, in particular among the specialist elements of her forces such as airborne troops. Secondly, Pritchard was informed that the brigade was to be deployed to Greece immediately after Operation Rugby was completed and therefore it could not afford to incur heavy casualties.

Pritchard had communicated Alexander's orders to Brigadier General Frederick shortly after receiving them. In view of this, and bearing in mind the fact that Le Muy was held by a strong enemy force, Frederick gave the task of taking the town to Lieutenant Colonel Edward Sachs's 550th Glider Infantry Battalion. Sachs was ordered to mount an attack on the following morning and thus at 2.15 a.m. on 16 August, artillery fire was brought down by a battery of 105mm howitzers as the battalion began its advance, moving through the positions of 2nd Independent Parachute Brigade Group as it did so. As its two leading companies approached the edge of the town, however, they came under heavy fire from machine guns, which caught them in open ground that afforded no cover, forcing the battalion to pull back and regroup. But during the withdrawal, confusion reigned when a number of enemy, who had infiltrated behind the battalion, were spotted and shot. In the darkness, a company from another unit moving along a road assumed it was under attack and responded accordingly. The 550th returned the fire and a 'blue on blue' engagement took place, lasting for several minutes before order was restored.

The battalion launched its second assault on Le Muy at 11.40 a.m., the leading companies encountering an enemy outpost 300 yards south of the River Naturby and wiping it out before fording the river itself and advancing across the open fields towards the town. As they reached the outskirts, they came under fire and the battle commenced in earnest, the fighting lasting until mid-afternoon by which time the town was in the hands of the 550th Glider Infantry Battalion. Some 300 enemy were killed or wounded during the battle, and over 700 taken prisoner.

The two missing groups from 5th Parachute Battalion were meantime still making their way south from Fayence. The small group led by the battalion's intelligence officer, Captain Mike Shepherd, observed a convoy of enemy vehicles heading south along a road in the direction of Le Muy. Swiftly taking up ambush positions, it opened fire, knocking out the leading four vehicles before turning its attention on the rest. At that moment, enemy infantry appeared and Shepherd and his men were forced to withdraw to some hills near by but not before they had destroyed more vehicles that had been abandoned by the enemy. Having taken seven prisoners, they commandeered three enemy vehicles and drove to the village of Bagnols, where they handed over their prisoners to members of a local resistance unit.

Meanwhile, at his command post in the Château Sainte-Rosseline, the commander of the 517th Parachute Regimental Combat Team, Colonel Rupert D. Graves, was becoming increasingly concerned that the key village of Les Arcs was still held by the enemy who were opposed only by the small group of the 1st Battalion headed by the commanding officer, Major William J. Boyle. Accordingly, he ordered Lieutenant Colonel Richard J. Seitz, whose 2nd Battalion was in positions to the north of Les Arcs, to go to Boyle's assistance. Seitz had his unit on the march within minutes of receiving Graves' order and soon reached the northern outskirts of the town, where it dug in while reconnaissance patrols were sent forward. One of these came under fire from machine guns as it approached a vineyard and Graves was quick to call down mortar fire on the German positions, soon silencing them.

Seitz planned to launch his attack on the town at 6.00 a.m. the next morning, 17 August. During the afternoon, Graves decided to use his 3rd Battalion, which had just arrived at 4.00 p.m. at an assembly area in woods close to the Château Sainte-Rosseline after completing an exhausting twenty-five-mile march. At 6.00 p.m. the 3rd Battalion moved off, heading for the high ground to the south of Les Arcs with Company H, commanded by Captain Marvin D. Morris, in the lead. At the same time, Company D 83rd Chemical Mortar Battalion, which had landed by glider on the previous day, opened fire with its 4.2-inch heavy mortars, laying down a bombardment of white phosphorus bombs whose smoke initially covered the movement of the 3rd Battalion. No sooner had the mortars fallen quiet than Morris and his men came under fire from machine guns, which killed two men. Nevertheless, despite occasional opposition, the battalion continued its advance and by last light had reached its objective where it dug in.

At 9.00 p.m. on the night of 16 August, meanwhile, the 551st Parachute Infantry Battalion had received intelligence that the enemy troops who had withdrawn earlier from Draguignan were now returning. This information was passed to Headquarters 1st Airborne Task Force and Brigadier General Frederick responded by ordering the 551st to attack and take the town without delay. Two hours later, the battalion was marching through the darkness, led by Company C whose role during the attack would be that of reserve. As they moved down a track in single file, the leading elements of the company came under fire from a machine gun in a farmhouse and a firefight ensued before the battalion resumed its march towards Draguignan.

On reaching the outskirts of the town, Companies A and B, commanded by Captains Marshall Dalton and James Evans respectively, formed up for the attack and began their advance towards the buildings silhouetted in the darkness before them. Company B, led by three resistance fighters acting as guides, soon came under fire and began fighting its way into the town. Company A also moved forward cautiously through the outskirts, unaware that it was making for the headquarters of Major General Ludwig Bieringer, the commander of the German military district in which Draguignan was situated. On reaching the town centre, however, the leading platoon spotted a large building with a Nazi flag hanging outside. Storming the main entrance, the platoon burst into a large room where Bieringer was in conference with several members of his staff. It was duly joined by other members of Company A, who frogmarched the luckless district commander and his staff away to join other Germans being taken prisoner.

The battle for the town continued to rage as the 551st Parachute Infantry Battalion cleared pockets of resistance street by street. Casualties mounted on both sides and soon the town's hospital was crowded with American and German casualties. In the early hours of 17 August, one of the 551st's medical officers, Captain John Y. Battenfield, and his team of orderlies, arrived in the town and in error were led by a French guide to the enemy military hospital. Realising the situation, the quick-witted doctor swiftly convinced the German lieutenant colonel in charge that the building was surrounded, and sent out a medical orderly for help. This arrived in the form of a squad of the 551st, who rounded up a number of fully armed German troops skulking among the enemy wounded.

By first light, the 551st Parachute Infantry Battalion held approximately half of the town and were having to clear out pockets of

resistance bypassed during the night. In the morning, an enemy lieutenant approached the positions of Company B under a white flag and
told Captain James Evans that the Germans wished to propose a truce
and the surrender of all their troops in Draguignan and the surrounding area. Accompanied by the lieutenant, Evans drove in a jeep to a
heavily fortified headquarters located on a mountainside two miles
from the town. Evans waited outside the defensive perimeter while the
German disappeared inside, reappearing a short while later with a
message informing him that surrender was out of the question and
that he should return to the American lines immediately. Evans complied,
unaware that the headquarters was that of General Ferdinand Neuling,
commander of the German XII Corps. Apparently the idea of a truce
and surrender had been conceived by the lieutenant himself, this being
rejected violently by a furious Neuling when it was put to him.

Fighting in Draguignan continued throughout the day until the
noise of firing began to slacken, petering out around 5.00 p.m. At 5.15
p.m. the commanding officer of the 551st Parachute Infantry Battalion,
Lieutenant Colonel Wood Joerg, reported by radio to Brigadier General
Frederick that the town finally had been taken.

While the 551st had been fighting its way into Draguignan during
the early hours of 17 August, the 2nd Battalion 517th Parachute Regimental Combat Team had launched its attack on the town of Les Arcs
from the east. Leading the way was Company D, commanded by Lieutenant Loren S. James, which advanced through vineyards and across
open ground without seeing any sign of the enemy. But as the two
leading platoons reached the town outskirts, they came under very
heavy fire from automatic weapons and shellfire, forcing them to take
cover in some houses approximately 200 yards from the railway station.
Shortly afterwards, a large body of enemy were observed forming up in
the area of the station prior to launching an attack, but this was broken
up by Company D's machine guns and mortar fire.

An hour later, the enemy were observed regrouping in the same
area and this time they were subjected to bombing and strafing by a

flight of P-51 Mustang fighter-bombers called in by the battalion head-quarters. No sooner had the Mustangs completed their attacks than the Germans could be seen once again forming up near the railway station. This time it was the turn of Company D 83rd Chemical Mortar Battalion, which opened fire with its 4.2-inch heavy mortars, firing several salvoes of bombs which showered the enemy with white phosphorus, setting them alight. The mortars then switched to high explosive and bombarded the entire enemy assembly area. Having suffered heavy casualties, the Germans now settled for a stand-off firefight.

Lieutenant Colonel Melvin Zais' 3rd Battalion 517th Parachute Regimental Combat Team was meantime advancing into the town from the south. Faced with the threat of being caught between the two parachute battalions, the enemy began to pull back and shortly afterwards withdrew completely from the town.

The morning of 17 August witnessed the arrival at Le Muy of the 142nd Regimental Combat Team, the leading element of the US 36th Infantry Division. Later that day, the 1st Airborne Task Force and the 36th Division advanced towards Draguignan and Toulon. Until Draguignan had been captured by the US 45th Infantry Division, however, the right flank of US Seventh Army was exposed and during this period B and C Companies of 5th Parachute Battalion were in contact with the enemy around a crossroads at Quatre Chemins.

At 6.30 p.m. Headquarters 2nd Independent Parachute Brigade Group learned that the two companies had been counter-attacked and forced to withdraw from the crossroads to an adjacent area of high ground. At dawn on the morning of 18 August, B Company observed movement as a group of enemy began withdrawing to the north; it despatched a party to interdict the Germans' line of retreat. This proved successful and all ninety-seven of the enemy were taken prisoner.

On the following day, the brigade went into reserve but was then ordered to take over at short notice a sector on the Allied right flank between Grasse and Cannes. It possessed little in the way of its own transport but within twenty-four hours had commandeered a number of buses, trucks, tractors and even horse-drawn wagons to lift it to its new area. It remained there for only a few days, however, as on 25 August it received orders for embarkation for Italy.

Thus ended Operation Rugby, which saw the 1st Airborne Task Force achieving all its objectives within the first forty-eight hours of Dragoon by interdicting enemy lines of communication and blocking the movement of German reinforcements. Despite the successful achievement of the task force, however, the airborne phase of the operation can only be regarded as a fiasco. Apart from that of the 551st Parachute Infantry Battalion, the parachute drops in the main were inaccurate and led to units being scattered over a wide area. Moreover, the landings of the 550th Glider Infantry Battalion and other gliderborne elements of the task force during the afternoon of 15 August were nothing short of disastrous, resulting as they did in heavy casualties.

Bearing in mind the serious losses sustained by the 82nd and 101st Airborne Divisions in Normandy, Rugby was a matter of keen interest to Major General Matthew Ridgway and other senior commanders in XVIII Airborne Corps and First Allied Airborne Army. Had the truth about the drops and the landing been publicised, it might well have had an adverse effect, particularly at high level, on approval for other airborne operations already being planned for the latter part of 1944 and the following year. It was in fact concealed in the USAAF's post-operation official report written by the commander of the 9th Troop Carrier Command and Provisional Troop Carrier Air Division, Brigadier General Paul L. Williams, who stated that the parachute drops were '85 to 90 per cent accurate'. The report also stated that the main body of aircraft 'effectively overcame the adverse weather conditions' and 'only 20 aircraft missed their DZs by an appreciable distance', this resulting in a 'well executed' operation. It also contained the comment, 'Airborne operations had come a long way since those unhappy days on Sicily.' The true details of Rugby did not emerge until months later, by which time it was too late for them to have any negative effect on plans for further airborne operations in the European theatre.

The end of Operations Dragoon and Rugby saw the US Seventh Army pushing through southern France in pursuit of the retreating Germans while the US elements of 1st Airborne Task Force were redeployed to occupy the French Riviera and establish a defensive line in the mountains behind Monaco to block any attacks by German forces in Italy.

On 26 August, 2nd Independent Parachute Brigade Group returned to Italy and was warned to prepare for deployment to Greece where, as the Russians advanced through the Balkans, the Germans were preparing to withdraw before the end of September. Greece was a country divided into royalist (EDES) and communist (ELAS) factions which had been warring with one another for some time, even under enemy occupation. It had become apparent to the British that a German withdrawal would produce a political vacuum which the communists would seek to fill, while requesting support from Russian forces following their entry into Yugoslavia and Bulgaria.

Accordingly, the decision was taken to forestall any such intentions by sending in forces to support the pro-Western factions in Greece. 2nd Independent Parachute Brigade Group, together with 23rd Armoured Brigade, which was to be deployed initially in the infantry role, was given the task of accelerating the Germans' withdrawal by harassing them. In an operation codenamed Manna, leading elements of the brigade would be inserted into Greece by parachute, the remainder being flown in or landing from the sea after an airfield and port had been secured. 23rd Armoured Brigade would carry out a seaborne landing on the following day.

The Germans, however, did not commence their withdrawal from Greece until October, by which time 4th Parachute Battalion had been detailed to secure the airfield on which elements of the rest of the brigade would land. Initially, it was intended to use an airfield at Kalamaki, on the eastern outskirts of Athens, but on the evening of 11 October, while briefing his officers on the forthcoming operation, Lieutenant Colonel Vic Coxen was informed that the battalion was to drop on another airfield at Megara, situated some forty miles west of the Greek capital.

At 1200 hours on 12 October, Major James Gourlay's C Company, accompanied by Lieutenant Colonel Coxen, the 1st Independent Parachute Platoon, a detachment of 2nd Parachute Squadron RE, detachments of the Mortar Platoon and some signallers, dropped on Megara airfield. The wind speed was thirty-five knots, far in excess of the maximum permitted for operational parachuting, and the company suffered several casualties on landing. Lieutenant Donald Marsh and two other men were killed and forty others injured – men being dragged for considerable distances by their parachute before they could release themselves from their harnesses. Nevertheless, the airfield was taken and swiftly secured, but weather conditions deteriorated and the landing of the rest of the brigade had to be postponed until they improved. Two days later 6th Parachute Battalion dropped on the airfield, high winds once again taking their toll and resulting in several casualties.

On leaving Megara, Brigadier Charles Pritchard and the advance elements of the brigade discovered that the road to Athens had been blown by the retreating Germans. Quickly commandeering a flotilla of caiques (schooners) and other fishing craft, they sailed from Megara to Piraeus, subsequently making their way to Athens in similarly commandeered local transport. Two days later, 5th Parachute Battalion was also dropped at Megara, rejoining the brigade in Athens.

During the following month, 2nd Independent Parachute Brigade Group took part in operations with other British and Indian forces to restore order in Greece, where civil war broke out in November. By the end of that month, the brigade was preparing to return to Italy, where it was required for airborne operations being planned by Eighth Army, but instead was redeployed to Athens on which an ELAS force of several thousand was advancing. Fierce fighting in the city ensued and the British forces there found themselves hard pressed until 8 December and the arrival of 4th Infantry Division, following which offensive operations against the communists commenced, continuing for the next four weeks or so.

On 16 January, the brigade handed over its areas of responsibility to Greek troops and by mid-February had returned to Italy where for the next three months it remained in a constant state of preparedness to carry out airborne operations in support of Eighth Army. More than 30 operations were planned but subsequently cancelled, five of them being aborted after the brigade had emplaned and was waiting for take-off. Finally, in May 1945, 2nd Independent Parachute Brigade Group returned to Britain, its achievements being best summed up in the words of General Sir Harold Alexander, in a letter to Brigadier Charles Pritchard: 'You have a wonderful record of successes and in every battle that you have fought you have shown all the true qualities of good soldiers – high morale, dash and fighting efficiency.'

CHAPTER TWELVE

ARNHEM, SEPTEMBER 1944

By mid-September 1944, following the hard-fought campaign in Normandy and having crossed the River Seine, some forty Allied divisions advanced north-east through France towards Belgium. On the left was the British 21st Army Group, under General Sir Bernard Montgomery, comprising the First Canadian and Second British Armies commanded by Lieutenant Generals Henry Crerar and Miles Dempsey respectively. On the right was the US 12th Army Group, under Lieutenant General Omar Bradley, which incorporated the US First and Third Armies led by Lieutenant Generals Courtney Hodge and George Patton.

The British Second Army, comprising VIII, XII and XXX Corps, was drawn up on a line roughly following that of the Meuse–Escaut Canal. To the west, the First Canadian Army had advanced to a line stretching between Zeebrugge and Ghent, while to the south-east the US First Army had reached the German border where it had encountered the Siegfried Line. Farther south, the US Third Army had established bridgeheads over the Moselle.

During the Allied advance, the question of the future conduct of the campaign in north-west Europe had been the cause of considerable discord among senior commanders, each of whom pressed his case with the Supreme Allied Commander, General Dwight D.

Eisenhower. The most vociferous was Montgomery who, alarmed at the lack of any firm plan emanating from Eisenhower's Supreme Headquarters Allied Expeditionary Forces (SHAEF), drew up his own.

On 20 August a conference to discuss ideas had been held at Eisenhower's advance headquarters in Normandy. It had been attended by Montgomery's Chief of Staff, Major General Francis de Guingand, who reported on his return that Eisenhower had taken the decision to assume personal command of both Army Groups on 1 September. Furthermore, he had also decided that Bradley's US 12th Army Group would advance on Metz and the Saar, where it would link up with the US 6th Army Group, which had landed on the Côte d'Azur on 15 August and was moving north up the Rhône Valley. Eisenhower's intention was to push forward, presenting the Germans with a broad front and forcing them to cope simultaneously with more than one threat. Priority would be given to his left, liberating the Channel ports, and in particular Antwerp; these were vital to the supply of the Allied forces which, advancing into northern Holland, subsequently would swing east to threaten the Ruhr.

Montgomery was unhappy with both of Eisenhower's decisions. Three days earlier, on 17 August, he had submitted his own plan to Bradley, proposing that both Army Groups advance north-east in a single concentrated thrust, his own 21st Army Group pushing forward on the western flank to clear the Channel coast, the Pas de Calais and western Flanders before taking Antwerp and southern Holland. Bradley's US 12th Army Group would meanwhile advance on the eastern flank, with the Ardennes on its right, to take Aachen and Cologne. Thereafter, bridgeheads would be established for an advance into the Ruhr.

According to Montgomery, Bradley was entirely in agreement with this proposal. In his memoirs, *A Soldier's Story*, Bradley states that he and Montgomery agreed on a plan which, following the advance into Belgium and the capture of Brussels, would consist of a thrust by three corps, one British and two American, eastwards across the plains of

Cologne between Düsseldorf and Bonn. Meanwhile, the left-hand corps of Dempsey's Second British Army would advance north-eastwards of this thrust. On its left flank, First Canadian Army would move north up the coast, seizing the Channel ports, capturing the sites from which the Germans were launching their V-weapons against Britain, and clearing the Scheldt, the area of inland waterways leading to Antwerp.

On 23 August, Eisenhower attended a meeting with Montgomery at the latter's tactical headquarters. By this time Bradley had changed his mind and was now supporting Eisenhower's plan for a thrust eastwards on a broad front. Montgomery, however, made it abundantly clear that a broad-front strategy would result in the Allied advance losing momentum and eventually grinding to a halt, giving the Germans the opportunity to recover and regroup, and ultimately resulting in the war continuing into 1945. Once again he put forward his own plan, pointing out the advantages of a single bold thrust and the necessity of concentrating all available logistical resources behind it. He stressed that there were insufficient resources to support fully both Army Groups at full stretch and thus priority would have to be given to one, the other meanwhile being halted.

Of the two possible axes of advance for a single thrust, Montgomery had selected the northern route on the grounds that the plains of Germany in the north would facilitate better deployment of armoured formations than the heavily forested mountainous areas of the south. The major obstacle facing such a thrust, however, was the Rhine. Montgomery was of the opinion that the establishment of bridgeheads on the far side was of paramount importance and therefore it was essential that the Germans be kept under pressure all the way to the river, being given no opportunity to regroup. Such bridgeheads would be launching platforms for a subsequent advance into the industrial heartland of the Ruhr and then onwards into the plains of northern Germany. Montgomery believed that the capture of the Ruhr would reduce Germany's capability to wage war by six months, so it was likely that the Germans would deploy all their available forces to defend it and thus be drawn into an area which would favour the superior mobility of the Allied armoured formations.

Montgomery's plan was bold and imaginative. However, even if Eisenhower had been convinced of its strategic soundness, which he was not, it contained one requirement that was politically impossible for him to accept: the halting of Patton's US Third Army on the right flank of the US 12th Army Group. American public opinion would not stand for 'Old Blood n' Guts', whose charismatic pistol-toting image and reputation as a thrusting commander had endeared him to the nation, being halted in his tracks in favour of the British.

Nevertheless, Eisenhower appreciated fully the urgent need for the capture of the Channel ports and Antwerp at the earliest opportunity in order to expedite delivery of supplies to the front. Until then, his forces would continue to be supplied from rear maintenance areas in Normandy, the lines of supply becoming increasingly extended as the Allied advance continued through France and Belgium.

Following a lengthy discussion, Eisenhower accepted that 21st Army Group was unable to advance north on its own and agreed not only that American support would be forthcoming but that Montgomery should coordinate and direct the thrust. Montgomery then pressed his case further, requesting that one of US 12th Army Group's two armies should advance on his right flank. Eisenhower refused, but then compromised by agreeing that the US First Army would support 21st Army Group's advance to Antwerp while Patton's US Third Army continued moving east as far as Rheims and Châlons-sur-Marne. He made it clear to Montgomery, however, that once the V-weapon launch sites had been captured and Antwerp seized, Patton would be permitted to continue his advance east to the Saar.

Two days after the meeting, Dempsey's Second British Army had begun crossing the Seine on the evening of 25 August. On the 27th, the leading elements of the First Canadian Army also crossed and began to expand the bridgehead. On 29 August, Paris was liberated by elements of the US First Army which had crossed the river between

Melun and Mantes-Gassicourt on the 26th, subsequently advancing to a line between Péronne and Laon. On the right of the US 12th Army Group, meanwhile, the US Third Army, which had crossed the Seine on 21 August, advanced swiftly to Troyes, Châlons-sur-Marne and Rheims.

In 21st Army Group, the advance was rapid. On 29 August, 11th Armoured Division broke out of XXX Corps's bridgehead on two axes and reached Manneville by the end of that day. On 3 September, the Belgian frontier was crossed by the 2nd Household Cavalry Regiment, the divisional reconnaissance unit of the Guards Armoured Division, and by nightfall Brussels had been liberated. On the next day, Antwerp and its vital port fell to the 4th Armoured Division. Two days later, XII Corps relieved XXX Corps in Antwerp an Alost, enabling the latter to swing north-east for the next stage of the advance.

Second British Army had advanced 250 miles in six days. On its right flank, US First Army had reached a line between Namur and Tirlemont while on its left First Canadian Army's II Corps had crossed the Somme on 3 September and advanced rapidly northwards. In the south-east, meanwhile, the US Third Army had reached Commercy and Verdun on the River Meuse, while in the south the US 6th Army Group was advancing steadily up the Rhône Valley.

The rapid rate of advance, however, inevitably had placed great strain on logistical resources which were already overstretched. Now that Second British Army had reached Antwerp, lines of supply were some 300 miles long. It had been assumed previously that the end of the Normandy campaign would see a pause prior to the start of operations in Belgium, this being used to establish forward supply and maintenance areas. No such pause was forthcoming, however, and the abundant supplies in 21st Army Group's rear maintenance area at Bayeux in Normandy had to be transported by road to XII and XXX Corps, which were advancing at the rate of forty miles per day.

The formations of Bradley's US 12th Army Group faced even greater problems as their supply lines extended even further, almost 400 miles back to the Cotentin Peninsula via Paris. Le Havre was still held by the Germans and thus the nearest port available to the Allies was Cherbourg. Although Dieppe was captured by the Canadians on 1 September, its port would not be operational for another seven days. In an attempt to overcome this problem, US 12th Army Group established a one-way traffic system between its rear maintenance area and Paris on which only supply transport was permitted to travel. This operated for twenty-four hours per day and delivered 7,000 tons of supplies daily. In accordance with Eisenhower's directives concerning the advance into Belgium, US First Army received 5,000 tons per day and Second British Army 2,000 tons.

Lieutenant General George Patton, however, was unhappy about the quota of supplies allotted to US Third Army and complained vociferously to both Bradley and Eisenhower during a meeting of the three commanders on 2 September. His reconnaissance units had reached Metz but lack of fuel had forced him to halt the remainder of his forces on the line of the Meuse. Indeed, his fuel reserves were almost exhausted by 30 August, when he received only 32,000 gallons instead of the 400,000 requested. Moreover, Bradley had informed him that no more fuel would be forthcoming until 3 September.

Supported by Bradley, Patton urged Eisenhower to supply him with more fuel so that he could advance to the Rhine as swiftly as possible. At the same time, Bradley pressed Eisenhower to allow him to turn US First Army eastwards. Eventually, Eisenhower gave in and compromised by agreeing that Patton should attack the Siegfried Line as soon as the Calais area had been stabilised, and by giving permission for crossings over the Moselle to be established as soon as fuel became available. He also acceded in part to Bradley's request by agreeing that US First Army's XV Corps should join US Third Army in attacking the Siegfried Line.

By giving in to Bradley and Patton, however, Eisenhower had compromised the plan for the advance through Belgium and Holland to which he had previously given priority. Any advance eastwards beyond the Moselle would inevitably incur a greater demand for supplies which would have to be diverted from US First Army. Moreover, intelligence reports had indicated that fresh enemy forces, comprising the 3rd and 15th Panzer Divisions and two Waffen SS brigades, had recently been moved up to the far banks of the Moselle to confront US Third Army. It was important therefore that any moves against them should be carried out rapidly before they could establish themselves firmly. The quantity of additional fuel allocated to Patton was sufficient for him to engage the enemy but not enough for him to win the battle.

Montgomery, who had been promoted to the rank of Field Marshal on 1 September, was meanwhile becoming increasingly unhappy, as he had received reports from his liaison officer at Headquarters US 12th Army Group that the US First Army formations on 21st Army Group's right flank were no longer receiving priority of resupply. He decide to attempt once again to persuade Eisenhower to adopt his plan for a single thrust northwards and on 4 September sent a signal to which he received a response on the following day. Eisenhower, while agreeing with the idea of a strong thrust to Berlin, could not accept that it should be carried out at the expense of all other operations. It was his belief that the German forces in the west had been destroyed and that this should be exploited by an attack on the Siegfried Line, followed by a crossing of the Rhine over a wide front and an advance to capture the Saar and the Ruhr. This would secure two of Germany's main industrial areas and destroy much of its capability to continue waging war. Eisenhower continued by stating his belief that reallocation of available resources would be insufficient to support a single thrust to Berlin, and concluded his signal by declaring that it was his intention to capture the Saar and Ruhr, by which time Le Havre and Antwerp would be able to support either or both of the thrusts advocated by Montgomery.

That same day, Eisenhower issued a new directive ordering 21st Army Group and US 12th Army Group to secure Antwerp, advance across the Rhine and seize the Ruhr. US Third Army was to take and hold the sector of the Siegfried Line covering the Saar and then capture

Frankfurt. The directive also stated that Patton was to launch his offensive as soon as possible but clearly added the proviso that those elements of US 12th Army Group tasked with taking the Ruhr 'must first be adequately supported'. This implied that priority of resupply within US 12th Army Group was to be given to US First Army but on the following day Eisenhower issued a memorandum referring to his broad-front policy, stating that he saw no reason to change it and that US Third Army's operations should begin as soon as possible. Bradley saw this as the signal to unleash Patton and increase US Third Army's share of the available supply tonnage from 2,000 to 3,500 tons per day. Patton's forces had already been reinforced by the transfer of XV Corps from the centre of US First Army to its right so as to cover US Third Army's northern flank during its advance eastwards; they would now be strengthened further on their southern flank by XV Corps.

Inevitably, these transfers of resources resulted in US First Army being unable to advance alongside 21st Army Group at the same rate. It required a minimum daily supply of 4,500 tons but its allocation had been reduced to 3,500 tons. Moreover, its strength had been reduced by the transfer of the 79th Infantry Division from its left flank, alongside 21st Army Group, to XV Corps on the right flank of US Third Army. Hitherto, the 79th had been part of XIX Corps which was now immobilised on the Belgian border for lack of fuel.

It was under these circumstances that Montgomery sent a further signal to Eisenhower on 7 September, pointing out that his logistical resources were strained to the limit. His daily requirement was for 1,000 tons but during the previous two days he had received only 375 tons per day. Moreover, with his rear maintenance area still at Bayeux and with his lines of supply now 300 miles long, he did not have the resources to capture the Ruhr. Once again, he restated his conviction that a reallocation of available resources would be adequate to support a single strong thrust to Berlin and ended by asking Eisenhower to visit him to discuss matters further. Eisenhower agreed to do so and a date was set for 10 September.

Prior to his conference with Eisenhower, Montgomery had a meeting with Lieutenant General Sir Miles Dempsey at Headquarters Second British Army. The purpose of this was to discuss plans for the use of airborne forces in an operation to be carried out as the spearhead of 21st Army Group's northward thrust. Also present at the headquarters, but not in attendance at the meeting, was Lieutenant General Sir Frederick 'Boy' Browning, the commander of I Airborne Corps, who had received a summons but was unaware of the reason for it.

Since the Normandy campaign, the Allied airborne forces in Britain had been grouped together as the newly formed First Allied Airborne Army under Lieutenant General Louis Brereton, hitherto commander of the US Ninth Air Force. This formation consisted of the recently established US XVIII Airborne Corps, commanded by Major General Matthew Ridgway and comprising the 17th, 82nd and 101st Airborne Divisions, and the British I Airborne Corps incorporating 1st and 6th Airborne Divisions, 1st Special Air Service Brigade and 1st Polish Independent Parachute Brigade Group. In addition, Brereton's command also embraced the 9th Troop Carrier Command USAAF, 38 and 46 Groups RAF and the 1st and 2nd Regiments of The Glider Pilot Regiment.

First Allied Airborne Army formed Eisenhower's only strategic reserve and on 4 September he had allocated it to 21st Army Group for use in its northward thrust. Plans had been drawn up for an operation codenamed Comet, to be carried out by 1st Airborne Division and 1st Polish Independent Parachute Brigade Group. This involved night landings with the use of gliderborne *coup de main* forces to capture the bridges over the Maas, Waal and Lower Rhine at Grave, Nijmegen and Arnhem respectively, coordinated with an advance by Second British Army. The operation had been planned for 8 September but had been postponed for seventy-two hours.

During his meeting with Dempsey, Montgomery revealed that he proposed to use three airborne divisions and 1st Polish Independent Parachute Brigade Group in an enlarged version of Comet. Codenamed

Market Garden – Market for the airborne phase and Garden for the advance by Second British Army – the operation would see the four airborne formations, under command of Browning's I Airborne Corps, seizing the bridges over the three rivers and two canals, the Wilhelmina and Zuid Willems Vaart, to establish a corridor along which Second British Army would advance rapidly into northern Holland before crossing into Germany and heading south-eastwards for the Ruhr.

Montgomery met Eisenhower that afternoon in the latter's aircraft and lost little time in not only criticising the broad-front policy but also putting forward his own plan for a single thrust, which once again was rejected by Eisenhower. At that juncture, Montgomery produced information, received from London the previous day, concerning V-2 missile attacks on England which were being launched from western Holland, posing a far greater threat than the V-1, and emphasised the importance of the early capture of the launch sites.

Eisenhower responded by saying that he had allotted priority to the northern advance and that this had been observed. Montgomery argued that this was not the case and eventually Eisenhower admitted that he had not given it 'absolute priority' but insisted that he could not reduce support for the advance to the Saar. Montgomery then advised Eisenhower that enemy resistance along the Albert Canal was stiffening and emphasised that because he would be unable to launch a strong thrust northwards as soon as he had hoped, the enemy would be given more opportunity to regroup.

It was at this point that Montgomery unveiled Market Garden. Despite being annoyed at his subordinate's somewhat high-handed manner, Eisenhower was impressed with the plan. Although he appreciated that it would mean the diversion of resources from US Third Army, he realised that Montgomery's proposal would inject renewed momentum into the slowing Allied advance and carry it into Germany itself. He was aware, however, of Montgomery's ambitions for an advance into the Ruhr and ultimately to Berlin. Agreeing to Market Garden in principle, he placed certain limitations on it, emphasising that the operation was 'merely an extension of the northern advance to the Rhine and the Ruhr'.

Following the meeting, Montgomery notified Dempsey that Eisenhower had given approval for Market Garden. Dempsey in turn briefed Browning who learned that, in addition to seizing and holding five major bridges and a series of crossings, I Airborne Corps would also have to hold the corridor that would stretch sixty-four miles from the Dutch border to Arnhem. All in all this was a massive undertaking and Browning was uneasy that his corps was being over-committed. Furthermore, prior to his return to England that same day, he was informed by Dempsey that the operation was to be mounted within a matter of days. On being pressed for a date by which he could be ready, he proposed 15 or 16 September.

Despite Eisenhower's agreement, the problem of inadequate logistical resources continued to plague Montgomery, who despatched a signal to SHAEF on 11 September stating that Market Garden could not be mounted before 23 September because of the failure to accord the northern advance priority over other operations. Eisenhower responded by sending his Chief of Staff, Major General Walter Bedell Smith, who arrived at Headquarters 21st Army Group on the following day and informed Montgomery that Eisenhower had now reversed his decision and that Patton's advance eastwards would be halted, as would that of three other US formations whose transport resources were to be diverted to move supplies for 21st Army Group. Within US 12th Army Group, US First Army would be allotted priority for support. In other words, complete priority was now to be given to the northern thrust. On this basis, Montgomery agreed that Market Garden would be launched on 17 September.

On the following day, however, Montgomery received a signal indicating that the extra logistical support allotted to him would not be of the level agreed with Bedell Smith, being limited to 1,000 tons. As the daily requirement for a division engaged on operations was 450 tons, this extra tonnage would only permit 21st Army Group to retain two extra divisions in action. Moreover, the signal stated that US First Army would receive a level of supply deemed 'adequate' to enable it to carry out its tasks.

When Bradley learned of Eisenhower's support for Market Garden, he objected vociferously but Eisenhower refused to listen, maintaining that Montgomery's plan might enable the Siegfried Line to be out-flanked and a bridgehead established over the Rhine. Angered by his objections being overridden, Bradley decided to ignore Eisenhower's change in strategy and to permit the US Third Army to become so heavily engaged beyond the Moselle that it would be impossible to reduce support for Patton or to halt his advance to the Saar.

On 4 September, as the British 11th Armoured Division entered Antwerp, Field Marshal Gerd von Runstedt, who had been dismissed as Commander-in-Chief West only two months previously, was reappointed by Hitler to the same post, now relinquished by Field Marshal Walther Model who assumed command of Army Group B. The situation for the Germans was grim, their shattered divisions retreating in disorder as the Allies advanced relentlessly through France and Belgium. Responsible for stemming the Allied advance, von Runstedt faced an almost impossible task. In the west, from Calais to just south of the Scheldt estuary in the low-lying areas of Flanders, General Gustav von Zangen's Fifteenth Army was trapped between the sea and the British Second Army to the east. The only possible escape route lay northwards by sea across the estuary to the island of Walcheren, and then by road east to the mainland. In the east, the surviving elements of the Seventh Army, commanded by General Paul Hauser, which had been badly mauled during the fighting in Normandy, were retreating in disorder to the north and north-east in the direction of Maastricht, Aachen, the Meuse and the Ardennes, being harassed by forces of US 12th Army Group. Between von Zangen's and Hausser's armies was a fifty-mile gap stretching from Antwerp to Maastricht.

When Model assumed command of Army Group B on 4 September, it was little more than a formation in name only, comprising mainly the 719th Division, commanded by Lieutenant General Karl Sievers, which as part of LXXXVIII Corps had been deployed for the previous four years along the Dutch coast where it had seen no action. Model immediately ordered LXXXVIII Corps to despatch the 719th southwards to the line of the Albert Canal as an initial move to block the gap in the path of the advancing Second British Army. At the same time, he requested reinforcements from Germany, stating that his requirements for holding a line stretching from Antwerp via Maastricht to south of Metz, along the line of the Albert Canal, the Meuse and the Siegfried Line, would be twenty-five infantry divisions supported by six armoured divisions. There was, however, no hope of such reinforcements being forthcoming as all available forces had already been despatched in late August to the area west of the Saar to counter the threat of Patton's US Third Army. Throughout Germany, new formations and units were being created but these were made up of men from training regiments, officer cadet schools, logistic support units, and convalescent depots. Even Luftwaffe and Kriegsmarine personnel, along with members of the Todt labour organisation, found themselves being pressed into service. Numbering 135,000 in total, they were sent to the Siegfried Line and Metz to man the defences there.

On the afternoon of 4 September, the newly promoted Colonel General Kurt Student received a telephone call from Berlin ordering him to form 'First Parachute Army' immediately. Since the Crete campaign of 1941, when Student's XI Air Corps had suffered over 6,700 casualties, Hitler had vetoed further large-scale airborne operations and Student had found himself commanding an airborne training establishment while his parachute regiments were deployed as infantry in different theatres.

Student's new command, which at this stage did not exist even on paper, was to plug the gap from Antwerp to Maastricht along the line of the north bank of the Albert Canal. The forces immediately available to him comprised six Luftwaffe parachute regiments under training, with two more which could be raised from paratroops convalescing in depots. These numbered 20,000 men in total and could be augmented by a further 10,000 Luftwaffe air and ground crew personnel made redundant because of the shortage of aviation fuel.

In addition, Student was allotted the 719th and 176th Divisions, the latter consisting of men from convalescent units and commanded by Colonel Christian Landau. Neither of these formations possessed any artillery or armour and, when querying the availability of the latter, Student was informed that he had been allocated twenty-five tanks. Indeed, the total number of tanks in the whole of Army Group B was approximately 100, consisting mainly of heavy Tigers and Panthers which, although armed respectively with 88mm and high velocity 75mm guns that could knock out any Allied tank, did not possess the mobility and speed of the M4 Sherman tank with which the British and American armoured formations were equipped. This was because Hitler had allocated all available production of the faster and more agile Mark IV to the Eastern Front.

Other forces allotted to Student included the 347th Division, a number of Waffen-SS training units and garrison troops from Holland, ten battalions of Luftwaffe infantry and flak troops from the 6th Military District which were to be equipped with heavy anti-tank guns and short range anti-tank weapons. Moreover, additional armour was on the way as Hitler had promised Field Marshal Model 200 new Panther tanks while ordering all available Tiger tanks, Jagdpanther self-propelled anti-tank guns and 88mm guns in Germany to be sent to the west.

On the afternoon of 5 September, Lieutenant General Willi Bittrich, commander of II SS Panzer Corps, arrived at Model's headquarters near Liège. His corps, comprising the 9th Hohenstaufen and 10th Frundsberg SS Panzer Divisions, had been badly mauled during and since the campaign in Normandy, suffering heavy losses in men and vehicles. On his arrival, Bittrich received orders from Model which were brief and to the point, as is summarised in the text of Luftwaffe radio intercepted and decoded in Britain by the Government Code & Cipher School's Station X at Bletchley Park in Buckinghamshire. Reproduced in Ultra Intercept No. XL9245 of 6 September 1944, Model's orders were as follows:

Army Group B Order quoted by FLIVO [Luftwaffe liaison officer] 1730 hrs 5th. (1) Stab Panzer Army Five with subordinated head-quarters 58th Panzer Corps to transfer beginning 6th to area Koblenz for rest and refit by C-in-C West. (2) Headquarters 2nd SS Panzer Corps subordinated Army Group B, to transfer to Eindhoven to rest and refit in cooperation with General of Panzer Troops West and direct rest and refit of 2nd and 116th Panzer Divisions, 9th SS Panzer Division and 217th Heavy Assault Gun Abteilung. (COMMENT: Elements these divisions and 10th SS Panzer Division ordered 4th to area Venlo-Arnhem-Hertogenbosch for refit in XL9188.)

The scene on the northern bank of the Albert Canal on 5 September was one of frenetic activity. The first of the fallschirmjäger units had arrived and were digging in while engineers busied themselves placing demolitions charges on the bridges over the canal. In the meantime, 719th Division was arriving at in its allotted area north of Antwerp.

While First Parachute Army was hastily establishing its line of defence, other German formations were streaming north in retreat, among them elements of the 84th, 85th and 89th Infantry Divisions that had seen hard fighting in Normandy. The commander of the 85th was Lieutenant General Kurt Chill who, following his arrival in northern Belgium on 4 September, succeeded in slowing the retreat and, in con-travention of orders to move his troops to the Rhineland to rest and refit, deployed them along the northern bank of the Albert Canal. Shortly afterwards, the commander of LXXXVIII Corps, Lieutenant General Hans Rheinhard, allocated Chill responsibility for the area of the front between Antwerp and Herenthals and reinforced him with a regiment from 719th Division. Two days later, on 7 September, the 176th Division arrived and established its positions between Hasselt and Maastricht.

To the west, meanwhile, half of the Fifteenth Army was being evacuated via Walcheren across the Scheldt estuary prior to marching eastwards to link up with First Parachute Army. Designated elements were remaining behind to man positions on the northern and southern shores of the estuary as well as the fortresses at Le Havre, Boulogne, Calais and Dunkirk, their task being to deny the four Channel ports and Antwerp to the Allies. The evacuation was carried out using two Dutch freighters, three large rafts and sixteen small assorted craft. The hour-long crossings to Walcheren and South Beveland were conducted at night and despite Allied air attacks the entire force was evacuated in sixteen days. Consisting of 65,000 men, 225 artillery pieces, 750 vehicles and 1,000 horses, this comprised the remnants of nine infantry formations – the 59th, 70th, 245th, 331st, 344th, 346th, 711th and 712th Infantry Divisions and the 17th Luftwaffe Field Division. On 16 and 17 September the 59th and 245th Infantry Divisions, both understrength and badly equipped, took up positions in depth, the 245th to the west of Eindhoven and the 59th south-west of s'Hertogenbosch near Headquarters First Parachute Army.

Despite the efforts of the Germans to stem its advance, Dempsey's Second British Army succeeded in establishing a bridgehead across the Albert Canal at Beeringen and pressed on northwards. Its leading element, Lieutenant General Sir Brian Horrocks's XXX Corps, however, encountered increasingly stiff resistance and it took four days of hard fighting to reach its next objective, the Meuse–Escaut Canal. On 10 September, bridgeheads were established at Neerpelt and Gheel and by mid-September the area north of the Albert Canal was clear of all enemy and the front had stabilised along the line of the Meuse–Escaut Canal.

By this time, the German analysis of Allied intentions pointed to a thrust north to cut off all German forces in Holland, this being illustrated in the text of Ultra Intercept No. HP242 of 15 September:

> Allies in German reports: (A) addressed to unspecified on evening 9th. 30 British Corps (2nd Br Army) between Antwerp and Hasselt. Bringing up further corps possible. Eleven to fourteen divisions with

eight to nine hundred tanks. Photo recce tasks (COENT: presumably known from intercepts) indicate probable intention is thrust mainly from Wilhelmina Canal on both sides Eindhoven into Arnhem (COMMENT: further specification of area incomplete but includes 'west of Nijmegen' and 'Wesel') to cut off and surround German forces in Netherlands.

The Germans apparently also believed that the Allies' ultimate objective was the Ruhr and that they would use their airborne forces in a drop and landing to the rear of the Siegfried Line, in an area between Düsseldorf and Duisburg, in a two-pronged operation to seize it. Evidence of this exists in an intelligence report from Army Group B:

> 2nd British Army will assemble its units at the Maas-Scheldt [Meuse-Escaut] and Albert Canals. On its right wing it will concentrate an attack force mainly of armoured units, and, after forcing a Maas crossng, will launch operations to break through to the Rhenish-Westphalian Industrial Area [Ruhr] with the main effort via Roermond. To cover the northern flank of this drive the left wing of the 2nd British Army will close the Waal at Nijmegen and thus create the basic conditions necessary to cut off the German forces committed in the Dutch coastal areas. In conjunction with these operations a large-scale airborne landing by 1st Allied Airborne Army north of the Lippe River in the area south of Münster is planned for an as yet indefinite date.

The Germans thus incorrectly anticipated airborne landings to the east and made their dispositions accordingly. As part of these, responsibility for the area to the north of Arnhem was allotted to Lieutenant General Willi Bittrich's II SS Panzer Corps. Located in the area between Arnhem and Apeldoorn, where it had arrived on 7 September, was the 9th Hohenstaufen SS Panzer Division, commanded by SS-Obersturmbannführer Walter Harzer, with its headquarters at Beekbergen. The 10th Frundsberg SS Panzer Division, under SS-Brigadeführer Heinz Harmel, was based in the area stretching eastwards from Zutphen to Ruurloi, on the Dutch-German border.

Following its heavy losses during the fighting in Normandy and throughout the withdrawal through northern France, the 9th SS Panzer Division's strength stood at approximately 3,500 men (out of its established strength of 18,000) comprising one armoured infantry regiment, the divisional reconnaissance battalion, a company of armour equipped with Panther Mark V tanks, an artillery battalion, two batteries of self-propelled guns, and remnants of its anti-aircraft and engineer battalions. Although it possessed only twenty tanks (as opposed to its full complement of 170), it did possess a number of armoured vehicles, namely armoured cars and troop carriers, in addition to its self-propelled guns. The 10th SS Panzer Division had suffered more heavily, losing most of its divisional signals regiment and communications equipment in Normandy. Its strength stood at less than 3,000 men comprising an armoured infantry regiment, divisional reconnaissance battalion, two artillery battalions and an engineer battalion, all these units being only partially motorised due to heavy losses of vehicles in Normandy.

During this period, a steady stream of intelligence on German dispositions and movements was being provided by Station X at Bletchley Park, but this was passed down as far as army headquarters level and no further. Examination of the Ultra intercepts during the period 1–17 September 1944 reveals that very detailed information was available to senior Allied commanders, this including the movement of II SS Panzer Corps as it moved to the area around Eindhoven and Arnhem. It appears, however, that intelligence staff at SHAEF were paying little heed to Ultra as it was not until 16 September that the presence of II S Panzer Corps in the Arnhem area was acknowledged in Intelligence Summary No. 26 of that date as follows:

> 9th SS Panzer Division and presumably the 10th, has been reported withdrawing to the Arnhem area in Holland; there they will probably collect new tanks from a depot reported in the area of Cleves.

Among the recipients of Ultra intelligence was 21st Army Group whose chief of intelligence, Brigadier Bill Williams, was sufficiently concerned about the presence of II Panzer Corps, and in particular that of the 9th SS Panzer Division to the north of Arnhem, that he drew it to the attention of Field Marshal Montgomery on 10 September after the latter's meetings with Eisenhower and Dempsey that day. Montgomery, however, refused to alter his plans for the landing of 1st Airborne Division at Arnhem. Undaunted, Williams tried again two days later with the support of Brigadier David Belchem, the Brigadier General Staff (Operations) who was standing in as Chief of Staff in the absence of Major General Francis de Guingand who was absent on sick leave. Unfortunately, their warnings fell on deaf ears.

Three days later, a further attempt was made to warn Montgomery. Eisenhower's Chief of Staff, Major General Walter Bedell Smith, received a report from SHAEF's head of intelligence, Major General Kenneth Strong, concerning the presence of the two German divisions to the north and east of Arnhem. Bedell Smith immediately brought the matter to the attention of Eisenhower himself and advised that a second airborne division be landed in the Arnhem area. Eisenhower, however, was nervous of incurring Montgomery's wrath and decided that any alteration could only be made by Montgomery himself and accordingly despatched Bedell Smith and Strong to Headquarters 21st Army Group at Brussels. At a meeting alone with Montgomery, Bedell Smith voiced his fears about the German armour in the area of Arnhem but Montgomery waved these aside, making light of the information and dismissing the very idea of any alteration to his plans.

Another visitor to 21st Army Group was His Royal Highness Prince Bernhard of the Netherlands who arrived there on 6 September with copious information concerning the enemy's deployments around Arnhem and elsewhere in Holland. Montgomery, however, gave him a cold welcome and dismissed the intelligence offered to him, his attitude no doubt coloured by the fact that the source of the information was the Dutch Resistance. Towards the end of 1941, elements of the Resistance had been penetrated by the Abwehr, the German military intelligence service, in an operation codenamed North Pole. This had been extremely successful, resulting in sixty Dutch agents of the Special Operations Executive, 500,000 guilders in cash and large quantities of weapons, explosives and equipment falling into German hands from early 1942 until early 1944. In addition, twelve aircraft and eighty-three aircrew of the RAF's special duties squadrons were shot down by Luftwaffe night fighters after dropping the agents and supplies.

Once details of this debacle became known in Britain, steps had been taken to repair the damage to the Resistance but suspicion lingered towards it and the information it provided thereafter.

At Headquarters Second British Army, however, the Resistance reports about the enemy formations in the areas of Nijmegen and Eindhoven were taken seriously, for they supported other evidence that the Germans would do all in their power to impede any further Allied advance. Lieutenant General Sir Miles Dempsey harboured serious doubts about the wisdom of a thrust northwards and committed them to paper when making an entry in his diary on 9 September:

> It is clear that the enemy is bringing up all the reinforcements he can lay hands on for the defence of the Albert Canal, and that he appreciates the importance of the area of Arnhem–Nijmegen. It looks as though he is going to do all he can to hold it. This being the case, any question of a rapid advance to the north-east seems unlikely. Owing to our maintenance situation, we will not be in a position to fight a real battle for perhaps ten days to a fortnight. Are we right to direct Second Army to Arnhem, or would it be better to hold a left flank along the Albert Canal, and strike due east towards Cologne in conjunction with First Army?

Indeed, such was the strength of Dempsey's doubts that he decided to propose an alternative direction of attack farther east, parallel to that of Bradley's US 12th Army Group, towards the town of Wesel on the Rhine, intending to do so at his meeting with Montgomery at the latter's headquarters on 10 September. He was forestalled on his arrival, however, when Montgomery showed him a signal from London announcing the first attack by V-2 missiles on the city. This appeared to reinforce Montgomery's case for the thrust north and Dempsey decided not to reveal his misgivings.

Within the British 1st Airborne Division there was overriding enthusiasm combined with mounting frustration. As the strategic reserve during and after the campaign in Normandy, the division had seen fifteen planned airborne operations cancelled at the last minute during the period June to September. This had been due to the speed of the Allied advance or other reasons which either had negated the requirements for such operations or prevented them from taking place.

The first of these was Tuxedo, which called for 4th Parachute Brigade to be dropped into Normandy in the event of difficulties arising during the landings. This was followed by Wastage, which would have seen the whole of 1st Airborne Division being dropped and landed in Normandy in the event of bad weather delaying the seaborne landings. Next came a third, unnamed, operation in which the division would have been dropped between D+1 and D+4 in support of the US 82nd Airborne Division. The fourth operation, Wild Oats, called for the division to be landed west of Caen to block a German withdrawal to the south-west, while the fifth, Beneficiary, would have taken place at the end of June with the division being landed in Brittany along with 1st Polish Independent Parachute Brigade Group, a squadron of 1st Special Air Service Regiment and a number of American airborne units, with the task of taking the port of Saint Malo in conjunction with the US XX Corps.

The seventh operation, Sword Hilt, at the end of July, would have required 1st Airborne Division to destroy a viaduct at Morlaix, east of Brest, in order to cut the enemy line of communication with the city. During the first half of August, the eighth, Hands Up, involved the capture of an airfield at Vannes on the Brittany coast, south-east of Brest, by the division, 1st Polish Independent Parachute Brigade Group and 52nd Lowland Division (the last a formation equipped and trained for air-portable operations) in support of Third US Army. Next was Transfigure in mid-August, which was designed to cut the German withdrawal route by landing 1st Airborne Division, the 101st Airborne Division, other American airborne units and 52nd Lowland Division between Paris and Orléans.

The tenth cancelled operation was Boxer, using the same force as Transfigure and planned for the second half of August, this involving an assault on Boulogne near which were V-1 launching sites. Following this in late August was Axehead, which would have seen 1st Airborne division and 1st Polish Independent Parachute Brigade Group establishing bridgeheads along the Seine to assist 21st Army Group to cross the river in its advance northwards through France. This was followed by Linnet I which was also planned for late August and involved a force under I Airborne Corps comprising 1st, 82nd and 101st Airborne Divisions, 52nd Lowland Division, 1st Polish Independent Parachute Brigade Group, 878th Aviation Engineer Battalion and 2nd Airlanding Light Anti-Aircraft Battery RA. Its task would have been to seize and secure a bridgehead over the River Escaut near Tournai, in Belgium, cutting the roads to the west and thus severing the German line of withdrawal.

Linnet II, the thirteenth operation, involved the use of the same force as Linnet I, which would have been dropped and landed to block the gap between Maastricht in Holland and Aaachen, in Germany, to the east. This was followed by Infatuate, which was designed to place pressure on the German Fifteenth Army and expedite its retreat northwards over the Scheldt estuary.

The fifteenth and final operation to be cancelled was Comet, planned for 10 September and, as mentioned earlier, calling for the capture of the bridges over the Maas, Waal and Lower Rhine at Grave, Nijmegen and Arnhem.

The same enthusiasm to see action was felt at Headquarters I Airborne Corps, with the exception of one man, Major Brian Urquhart, the GSO 2 (Intelligence) who received his intelligence for Market Garden from 21st Army Group as opposed to I Airborne Corps' parent formation, First Allied Airborne Army. Although ignorant of Ultra, due to the strict limitations placed on the dissemination of its information, Urquhart did have access to the Dutch Resistance communications. Disturbed by the reports of the presence of enemy armour in the area of Arnhem, he requested low-level photographic reconnaissance flights to be flown over the Arnhem area on 12 September. Three days later he received a number of photographs clearly showing armoured vehicles in areas close to the planned DZs and LZs. He immediately brought this information to the attention of I Airborne Corps' commander, Lieutenant General 'Boy' Browning, who made light of it. Major Urquhart was undeterred, however, and persisted in warning about this potential threat to Market Garden. He was rewarded for his efforts by being removed from his post and sent on sick leave.

At Headquarters First Allied Airborne Army, meanwhile, an RAF air intelligence officer, Wing Commander Asher Lee, was becoming increasingly concerned while studying the amount of enemy activity in the Arnhem area. He had previously been a member of Section A13b of the Air Staff, a department which received a large amount of Ultra intelligence. Subsequently posted to First Allied Airborne Army, Lee nevertheless had succeeded in retaining access to another Ultra source which now confirmed the presence of German armour in the vicinity of Arnhem. On bringing this to the notice of Lieutenant General Lewis Brereton, Lee was ordered to raise the matter with 21st Army Group. When he visited Montgomery's headquarters, however, Lee could find no one who would listen to him.

Thus it was, against a background of disregard for sound detailed intelligence about enemy dispositions in northern Holland, that planning and preparations for Market Garden went ahead.

Following his meeting with Dempsey, Lieutenant General 'Boy' Browning returned to his headquarters on the afternoon of 10 September before travelling to Headquarters First Allied Airborne Army. There he met Lieutenant General Lewis Brereton before holding a briefing for the commanders of the formations and units due to take part in Market Garden.

The forces allotted to the operation comprised 1st, 82nd and 101st Airborne Divisions, 52nd Lowland Division and 1st Polish Independent Parachute Brigade Group. In outline, these formations were allocated the following tasks in chronological order:

101st Airborne Division – to seize the bridges and crossings between Eindhoven and Grave.

82nd Airborne Division – to capture the two major bridges at Nijmegen and Grave, and to take and hold the high ground between Nijmegen and Groesbeek.

1st Airborne Division, with 1st Polish Independent Parachute Brigade Group – to seize the road and rail bridges at Arnhem and establish a bridgehead in preparation for a further advance northwards by Second British Army.

52nd Lowland Division would be held in reserve, ready to be flown into landing strips established north of Arnhem as and when the situation permitted. These would be constructed by the 878th Aviation Engineer Battalion which would be landed by glider with 2nd Air-landing Light Anti-Aircraft Battery RA, the latter being charged with the defence of the airstrips. Operation of the strips would be the responsibility of the Airborne Forward Delivery Airfield Group, a joint Army-RAF unit.

While I Airborne Corps was carrying out its task of laying a 'carpet' of airborne troops from Eindoven to Arnhem, Second British Army, spearheaded by XXX Corps with VIII and XII Corps advancing in echelon on its right and left flanks respectively, would break out of its bridgehead on the Meuse–Escaut Canal and advance along the road leading through Valkenswaard to Eindhoven. Thereafter, it would push on through Zon, Saint Oedenrode, Veghel, Uden, Grave, Nijmegen and Elst to Arnhem, linking up with the three airborne divisions along the way. Protection of the line of communication along the corridor would be the responsibility of VII Corps, which was to take the towns of Weert and Soerondonk, and subsequently secure as far north as Helmond. XII Corps was to capture Rethy, Arendonck and Turnhout before pressing on to the River Maas.

Having reached Arnhem, Dempsey's forces were to secure and dominate the country northwards to the Zuider Zee, severing the lines of communications between Germany and her forces in the Low Countries. Ultimately, Dempsey was to take up a line facing eastwards from Arnhem through Deventer to Zwolle, with bridgeheads established over the River Ijssel. Thereafter, 21st Army Group would advance eastwards to the area of Rheine–Osnabruck–Hamm–Münster prior to a major thrust being mounted from Hamm along the eastern face of the Ruhr.

Montgomery's plan for a thrust into Germany via Arnhem was based on three factors: firstly, an advance from the north towards the Ruhr would outflank the northern end of the Siegfried Line; secondly, any thrust via Wesel, as favoured by Dempsey, would risk the airborne landings being exposed to a strong threat from the Luftwaffe and the flak defences in the area of the Ruhr; thirdly, England had just experienced the first attacks by V-2 missiles, far more devastating than the V-1, and thus the launch sites had to be seized and put out of action as swiftly as possible. The last factor had settled in Montgomery's mind the decision to advance north via Arnhem as his forces would be better placed to neutralise this latest threat swiftly than would be the case if they were to advance north-eastwards towards Wesel.

Those present at Browning's briefing were taken aback not only by the size of the operation and the boldness of the plan but also by the very limited time available to plan and execute it. Whereas the planning for Neptune, the airborne element of Overlord, had taken months, the time allowed for Market Garden was just seven days. The problems attendant on such hasty preparation were immense, and the consequent shortcomings in planning would later become apparent during the operation.

On the following day, a conference was held at Headquarters 9th

Troop Carrier Command USAAF to begin the planning of the air side of the operation. The absence of a moon during the week commencing 17 September meant that a large-scale landing at night had to be discounted; in any case, memories of major airborne operations at night, notably in Normandy, in which brigades and battalions had been dispersed over wide areas, were fresh in the planners' minds. The decision to opt for daylight landings was taken by Lieutenant General Brereton himself.

The most pressing problem was that of allocation of aircraft. A total of 35,000 paratroops and gliderborne forces would have to be dropped and landed in the three areas covered by Market Garden, but there were only sufficient aircraft to carry 16,500 men. Airborne Corps' requirement was for 3,790: 2,495 to carry paratroops and 1,295 to tow gliders. The combined resources of 9th Troop Carrier Command and those of 38 and 46 Groups RAF, however, were insufficient to meet this requirement. Moreover, in order to ensure that the southernmost objectives were seized successfully, the greater proportion of aircraft had to be allotted on the first day to the 101st and 82nd Airborne Divisions which were both larger than 1st Airborne Division and whose landings would take place in the areas of Eindhoven–Grave and Grave–Nijmegen respectively.

Consequently, allocation of aircraft was made as follows:

Headquarters I Airborne Corps	38 glider tugs (RAF)
101st Airborne Division	424 paratroop aircraft (USAAF)
	70 glider tugs (USAAF)
82nd Airborne Division	482 paratroop aircraft (USAAF)
	50 glider tugs (USAAF)
1st Airborne Division	161 paratroop aircraft (USAAF)
	320 glider tugs (RAF)

In order that the greater part of I Airborne Corps could be dropped or landed on the first day, it was suggested that two lifts should be made. Air Vice Marshal Leslie Hollingsworth, who commanded 38 Group

RAF and was responsible for coordinating its operations with those of its sister formation 46 Group RAF, was prepared to allow his aircraft to make two sorties, the first taking off before dawn. Major General Paul Williams, the commander of 9th Troop Carrier Command, however, would not agree on the grounds of aircrew fatigue and aircraft maintenance. His reasoning was also based on the fact that while the number of aircraft and aircrew in his command had just been doubled, he had not received any reinforcements in ground crew. Furthermore, his aircrews were not as experienced in night flying as their RAF counterparts. Williams was supported in his decision, which would ultimately prove fatal for Market Garden, by Brereton who, although an airman, had no previous experience of airborne operations.

A strong objection to this decision should have been made by Browning as it meant that, like the 101st and 82nd, 1st Airborne Division would have to be flown in three lifts over three days, which should have been regarded as unacceptable given that the division was to be dropped and landed at the furthermost point from Second British Army, the vital element of surprise having been lost on the first day. Browning's relations with Brereton, however, were fragile as the two men had already crossed swords over one of the cancelled operations, Linnet II. The dispute had been resolved but the relationship between the two men had deteriorated further and Browning obviously felt that he was not in a position to become involved in another confrontation with his superior.

Montgomery, however, did object on reading the copy of the I Airborne Corps plan sent to him, and despatched his Acting Chief of Staff, Brigadier David Belchem, to Headquarters First Allied Airborne Army to take up the matter with Brereton, who refused to alter his decision. Another very unhappy man was the commander of 1st Airborne Division, Major General Roy Urquhart, who was dissatisfied with the number of aircraft allotted to him and approached Browning with a request for forty more. Browning explained that the allocation had been made on the basis that priority had to be given primarily to the 101st Airborne Division and then the 82nd, as it was essential that the southernmost objectives were secured to ensure that XXX Corps could begin its advance on breaking out of its bridgehead.

During a conference next day, 11 September, at which the selection of DZs and LZs was discussed, Urquhart's problems were compounded when Air Vice Marshal Hollingsworth objected to the locations proposed by Urquhart, who wished to land his division on both sides of the Lower Rhine and as close as possible to the Arnhem bridge. Hollingsworth maintained that there were heavy anti-aircraft defences in the area of Arnhem and around the bridge itself, claiming that these had been encountered previously by RAF bombers en route to the Ruhr. In addition, he stated that RAF tug aircraft, turning north after casting off their gliders, would meet heavy flak over the Luftwaffe base at Deelen, seven miles north of Arnhem; if they turned south there was a danger of their becoming mixed up with aircraft dropping the 82nd Airborne Division over the Nijmegen area.

Hollingsworth, however, was incorrect with regard to the flak defences around Arnhem and at Deelen. There were none in the area of the town and on 3 September RAF bombers had carried out a raid on the air base, rendering it temporarily unusable; all aircraft had been evacuated and anti-aircraft guns removed shortly afterwards. This was confirmed by air photographic reconnaissance three days after the raid but this information had not been passed to Headquarters 38 Group.

Urquhart thus was forced to select an area located west of Arnhem and approximately eight miles from its bridges. Two LZs, 'L' and 'S', were to the north of the railway line running between Arnhem and Utrecht, while DZ 'Y' was situated on Ginkels Heath. DZ and LZ 'X', along with LZ 'Z', were on Renkum Heath, to the south of the railway line. The area was far from ideal as the distance between the zones and the division's objectives was such that the vital element of surprise would be lost and there was the risk that the second lift would be prevented from linking up with the rest of the division. Furthermore, elements of 1st Airlanding Brigade would have to remain on the DZs and LZs to hold them until the remainder of the division had landed, thus reducing the number of troops available to take and hold the bridge and other objectives on the first day. In addition to the five main DZs and LZs, a sixth, DZ 'K', was selected south of the town for 1st Polish Independent Polish Parachute Brigade Group which would be dropped on the morning of the third day by which time it was expected that the threat from the enemy flak defences in the area would have been neutralised.

One of Urquhart's major concerns was the lack of intelligence concerning enemy forces in the area. His intelligence staff were, in his own words, 'scratching around for morsels of information'. The little that existed filtered down from Headquarters Second British Army and Headquarters I Airborne Corps. In the light of the information now known to have been available to Headquarters 21st Army Group, First Allied Airborne Army and I Airborne Corps from Ultra, Dutch Resistance sources and RAF air photographic reconnaissance, the lack of intelligence passed on to 1st Airborne Division seems scarcely credible.

Urquhart decided to land 1st Parachute Brigade, the greater part of 1st Airlanding Brigade, some divisional troops and his own tactical headquarters on the first day. 4th Parachute Brigade, along with the remainder of 1st Airlanding Brigade, the gliderborne element of 1st Polish Independent Parachute Brigade Group and remaining divisional troops would be dropped and landed on the second day. The main element of 1st Polish Independent Parachute Brigade Group would be dropped south of the river on DZ 'K' on the third day.

Meanwhile, farther south, Major General Maxwell Taylor's 101st Airborne Division would be dropped and landed to capture the bridges and crossings between Eindhoven and Veghel. Its objectives consisted of nine road and rail bridges, and two canal crossings, along the fifteen-mile stretch of its sector of the 'corridor'. Taylor's plan called for the 502nd and 506th Parachute Infantry Regiments to land in the centre between Eindhoven and Veghel while the 501st would be dropped on two DZs a few hundred yards to the north and west of Veghel. Its task would be to seize four of the bridges and one of the crossings, at Veghel itself, which spanned the River Aa and the Zuid Willems Vaart Canal.

The 82nd Airborne Division, under Brigadier General James Gavin, faced an equally onerous task. Having been dropped four miles from its objectives, and having seized the bridge over the Maas at Grave, as well as at least one of the railway bridges over the Maas-Waal Canal, the division was to take the bridge over the Waal at Nijmegen and thereafter hold and secure the Groesbeek Heights – the feature of high ground between Nijmegen and Groesbeek dominating the area. The 505th and 508th Parachute Infantry Regiments, along with Gavin's tactical headquarters, would be delivered in two drops a mile and a half from the Groesbeek Heights and some four miles to the south-west of Nijmegen. The 504th Parachute Infantry Regiment, which had rejoined the division following its return from Normandy, replacing the 507th which was transferred to the 17th Airborne Division, would be dropped on the western side of the heights between the Maas and the Maas–Waal Canal, a mile from the eastern end of the bridge at Grave and two miles from the canal bridges. A company of the 504th would also be dropped a mile from the western end of the Grave bridge, enabling the regiment to attack it from both sides of the river.

In view of the number of objectives to be taken and held, both Taylor and Gavin decided that all their parachute infantry would be dropped on the first day. This, however, would limit the supporting arm elements which could accompany the infantry in the first lift. Following the Normandy campaign and the disastrous drops and glider landings which had resulted in little of either division's artillery being of assistance in the early days of the campaign, the artillery in both had undergone intensive training while at the same time changes had been made to their order of battle. The 376th Parachute Field Artillery Battalion had been incorporated into the 82nd Airborne Division which now possessed four artillery units, the others being the 456th Parachute

Field Artillery Battalion and the 319th and 320th Glider Field Artillery Battalions. The 101st Airborne Division's artillery would still comprise three units: the 377th Parachute Field Artillery Battalion and the 321st and 907th Glider Field Artillery Battalions.

Taylor, whose division would be dropped and landed the nearest to the advancing British XXX Corps, decided that his need for artillery would not be paramount. This was reflected in his decision to deploy Headquarters Battery and Batteries A and C of the 377th Parachute Field Artillery Battalion by glider on the first day of Market Garden, with Battery B being dropped on the following day, D+1, along with two companies of the 326th Airborne Engineer Battalion and Battery A of the 80th Airborne Anti-Aircraft Battalion. The 321st and 907th Glider Field Artillery Battalions would be landed on D+2.

Gavin, whose parachute infantry regiments would almost certainly require artillery support immediately following their drop, opted to drop his 376th Parachute Field Artillery Battalion on the first day with the 456th Parachute Field Artillery Battalion being landed by glider on D+1 along with the 319th and 320th Glider Field Artillery Battalions. Both divisions' glider infantry regiments would arrive with the anti-tank, engineer and other supporting arm elements on D+2 and D+3.

The success of Market Garden depended totally on the ability of XXX Corps to punch through the German defences and thrust north up the main road to Arnhem in order to link up with 1st Airborne Division before the enemy had time to react and launch a counter-attack. The essential factor was speed, and Montgomery emphasised this more than once to XXX Corps' commander, Lieutenant General Sir Brian Horrocks, during a briefing at Headquarters 21st Army Group on 12 September.

The main problem facing XXX Corps, however, was the terrain over which it would have to advance. Flat and low-lying, it was heavily wooded and very marshy, being intersected by dykes, canals and large rivers which would restrict movement by armour to the few roads that traversed the area. The combination of adverse terrain and the ever-increasing strength of the enemy meant that the breakout from the bridgehead, which was small and was served by only two bridges, would not be easy. Horrocks realised that a successful breakout would rely greatly on heavy artillery and air support.

The route for the advance was the main road stretching from the Meuse–Escaut Canal via Valkenswaard to Eindhoven, and then on to Zon, Saint Oedenrode, Uden, Grave, Nijmegen and Arnhem. Varying in width between twenty and thirty feet, widening to forty feet near Arnhem, it was of tarmac or concrete construction except on stretches between Nijmegen and Arnhem where it was composed of rolled cinders. The stretch between Eindhoven and Grave was in very poor condition but the final stretch to Arnhem was new, as was the road bridge by which it crossed the Lower Rhine, and part of it was still under construction. It was considered passable to armoured vehicles although somehow those would have to bypass two fly-over bridges.

In several areas, including the initial stage, the road was embanked between four and six feet above the level of the surrounding terrain, so that vehicles on it would be clearly silhouetted and easy targets for anti-tank guns, and was flanked on either side by deep ditches that would make movement off it impossible. Moreover, almost the entire stretch between Grave and Nijmegen was dominated by the Groesbeek Heights south and east of Nijmegen.

Horrocks's plan was for the Guards Armoured Division, commanded by Major General Sir Allan Adair, to lead the breakout, advancing behind a rolling artillery barrage laid down by six field and three medium regiments. Further support would come from three more field regiments, a heavy battery, a heavy anti-aircraft regiment firing airburst shells, and from Dutch and Belgian artillery firing concentrations at specified times during the breakout.

Close air support would be provided by rocket-firing Typhoon fighter-bombers of 83 Group RAF. One squadron would strafe the road and rocket areas of likely enemy positions on either side of the road in the path of the advance every five minutes for a period of thirty-five minutes. This would be followed by a 'cab rank' of Typhoons flying above the leading squadrons of tanks, controlled from the ground by an RAF forward air controller travelling in a vehicle equipped with VHF radios, thus ensuring that close air support would be rapidly available when required. Another RAF vehicle would travel alongside that of Horrocks, to supply him with information from RAF tactical reconnaissance aircraft covering the area, while further air support would be provided by 83 Group RAF in the form of fighter cover tasked with engaging any enemy aircraft that might make an appearance.

Thus the stage was set for the largest airborne operation yet to be carried out by the Allies. Among many in 1st Airborne Division there was an overwhelming desire to see action before the war ended. Those with previous experience of fighting the Germans, however, had few illusions about the difficulties they would face after landing. Brigadier John Hackett, the commander of 4th Parachute Brigade, who had seen a considerable amount of action in the Middle East and Italy, having given his final orders to the commanding officers of his three battalions and the members of his staff, ended by saying: 'You can now forget all that. Your hardest and worst casualties will not be in defending the northern sector of the Arnhem perimeter, but in trying to get there!'

Sunday 17 September dawned with fog over southern England but it had lifted by 9.00 a.m., giving way to a perfect autumn day. Three-quarters of an hour later the first aircraft, carrying the leading elements of all three airborne divisions, took off from eight RAF and fourteen USAF airfields in Oxfordshire, Gloucestershire, Dorset and Lincolnshire, and headed for Holland.

The aircraft flew in two large groups, following separate routes via RVs and turning points marked by Eurekas and signalling lamps flashing coded signals. Those aircraft carrying the 1st and 82nd Airborne Divisions and Headquarters I Airborne Corps flew to initial RVs over the towns of March in Cambridgeshire and Hatfield in Hertfordshire before heading on to a second RV over Aldeburgh, on the Suffolk coast. There-

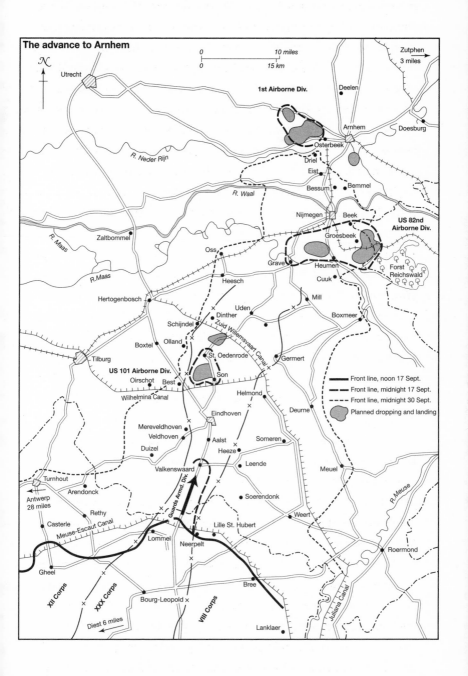

The advance to Arnhem

N

| 0 | 10 miles |
| 0 | 15 km |

Utrecht

Zutphen
3 miles

1st Airborne Div.

Deelen

Arnhem

Doesburg

R. Neder Rijn

Osterbeek

Driel

Eist

Bemmel

Bessum

R. Waal

Nijmegen

Beek

**US 82nd
Airborne Div.**

Zaltbommel

Groesbeek

R. Maas

Oss

Grave

Heumen

Forst
Reichswald

Heesch

Cuuk

R. Maas

Hertogenbosch

Dinther

Uden

Mill

Boxmeer

Schijndel

Zuid Willemsvaart Canal

Boxtel

Olland

St. Oedenrode

Germert

Tilburg

US 101 Airborne Div.

Son

Oirschot

Best

Helmond

Wilhelmina Canal

Deurne

Mereveldhoven

Eindhoven

Veldhoven

Aalst

Someren

Duizel

Heeze

Valkenswaard

Leende

Meuel

Turnhout

Soerendonk

R. Meuse

Antwerp
28 miles

Arendonck

Rethy

Guards Armd. Div.

Weert

Casterle

Lille St. Hubert

Meuse-Escaut Canal

Lommel

Neerpelt

Roermond

Gheel

Bree

Juliana Canal

XII Corps

XXX Corps

Bourg-Leopold

VIII Corps

Diest 6 miles

Lanklaer

▬▬▬	Front line, noon 17 Sept.
▬ ▬ ▬	Front line, midnight 17 Sept.
- - - -	Front line, midnight 30 Sept.
⬤	Planned dropping and landing

475

after, they flew on over the North Sea, guided by Eurekas installed on warships, via the Dutch island of Schouwen and then on to an interception point over the town of Boxtel. There the aircraft transporting the 82nd Airborne Division turned in the direction of the DZs and LZs near Nijmegen while 1st Airborne Division headed on towards Arnhem.

Meanwhile, the aircraft carrying the 101st Airborne Division were flying a more southern route. The initial RV was over Hatfield, followed by two more over North Fenland and North Foreland, after which the route took the division east over the Channel to Gheel in Belgium, before turning north-east towards Eindhoven.

As the vast armada of transport aircraft, tugs and gliders formed up over their respective RVs, the pathfinders of the three airborne divisions were already en route for Holland. Twelve Stirling bombers carried 1st Airborne Division's 21st Independent Parachute Company, while six C-47s bore its counterparts of the two American divisions. These would jump twenty minutes before the arrival of their respective formations, each setting up their Eurekas, laying out DZ marker panels and setting off smoke signals to guide in the approaching aircraft.

On both routes, the flight from England over the North Sea passed without mishap, visibility being good and winds light. Of the total of 320 gliders in 1st Airborne Division, only two failed to take off, but before the coast had been reached, twenty-four had come adrift, half of these experiencing problems with cloud: one glider crashed and the remaining twenty-three force-landed, the loads of all but one being recovered for transfer to the second lift. Over the Channel, four gliders were forced to ditch – two because of broken towropes and two due to their tugs experiencing engine trouble.

On crossing the Dutch coast, the leading aircraft encountered flak, some of it heavy. One C-47 carrying pathfinders of the 101st Airborne Division was shot down while one tug and glider combination of the 82nd was hit over Schouwen Island, the glider breaking up in mid-air and the tug crashing with the loss of all its crew. Another C-47, also carrying a stick of the 82nd, was also hit and set ablaze; the entire stick

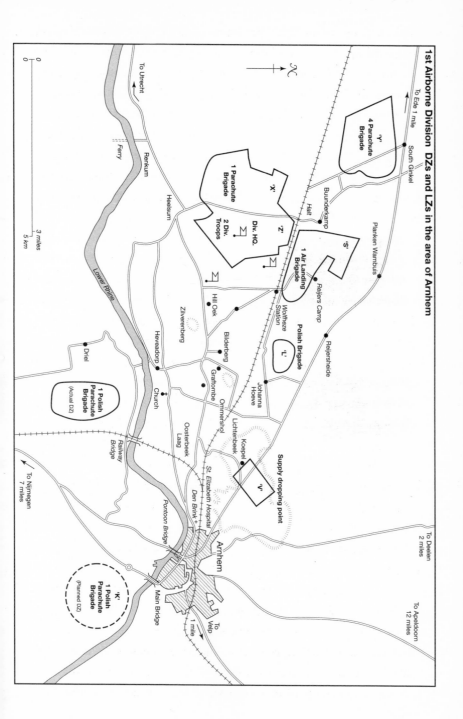

1st Airborne Division DZs and LZs in the area of Arnhem

To Ede 1 mile
South Ginkel
'Y' 4 Parachute Brigade
Buunderkamp Halt
Planken Wambuis
'X' 1 Parachute Brigade
2 Div. Troops
'Z' Div. HQ.
'S' 1 Air Landing Brigade
Reijers Camp
Reijersheide
Polish Brigade
Wolfheze Station
'L'
Johanna Hoeve
Supply dropping point
'V'
Koepel
Lichtenbeek
Ommershof
Oosterbeek Laag
St. Elizabeth Hospital
Den Brink
Arnhem
To Velp
To Deelen 2 miles
To Apeldoorn 12 miles
Gratfombe
Church
Blilderberg
Zilverenberg
Hill Oek
Heelsum
Heveadorp
Renkum
Ferry
To Utrecht
Lower Rhine
Driel
1 Polish Parachute Brigade (Actual DZ)
Railway Bridge
Pontoon Bridge
Main Bridge
'K' 1 Polish Parachute Brigade (Planned DZ)
To Nijmegen 7 miles
1 mile

0
0
3 miles
5 km

N

477

and the jumpmaster succeeded in jumping clear but the crew perished when the aircraft crashed.

There was then little flak until the aircraft approached their respective target areas. On the approach to Nijmegen, the 82nd Airborne Division encountered light flak from the areas of Groesbeek and Cuijk, inflicting only slight damage. One glider suffered a broken towrope and was forced to land a few miles from its designated LZ. On the Arnhem route, eight more gliders were lost due to problems caused by turbulent slipstreams from aircraft in front of them. Heavy, medium and light flak was encountered near the target areas but only one pathfinder aircraft and six tugs were hit and damaged.

At approximately 1.00 p.m., the pathfinders of 21st Independent Parachute Company, commanded by Major 'Boy' Wilson, dropped on to Dutch soil. As they did so, they came under fire from a small group of enemy in a position on the DZ, two being wounded before they landed. The enemy surrendered almost immediately afterwards and the company busied itself with setting up its Eurekas and laying out coloured DZ marker panels to guide in the approaching aircraft.

At 1.30 p.m. 147 Horsa gliders, carrying 1st Airlanding Brigade less two companies of the 2nd Battalion The South Staffordshire Regiment, arrived on LZ 'S'. Ten minutes later another 150 gliders, including eighteen Hamilcars, carrying Major General Roy Urquhart's tactical headquarters, 1st Airborne Reconnaissance Squadron, 1st Airlanding Light Regiment RA (less one battery), two airlanding anti-tank batteries and half of 1st Parachute Brigade's transport, landed on LZ 'Z'. These were followed at 2.00 p.m. by 161 aircraft carrying Brigadier Gerald Lathbury's 1st Parachute Brigade and the advance party of 4th Parachute Brigade.

The landings were unopposed, the small groups of enemy in the areas of the DZs and LZs putting up no resistance. The majority of casualties were among the gliders, some of which, landing downwind and overshooting the LZs, crash-landed in the woods near by. Two Hamilcars, carrying 17-pounder guns of 1st Airlanding Anti-Tank

Battery RA, overturned when landing on soft ground, both pilots and co-pilots being killed and the guns lost. Elsewhere, only a few loads were lost and casualties were minimal.

Shortly after 3.00 p.m., 2nd and 3rd Parachute Battalions, commanded by Lieutenant Colonels Johnny Frost and Tony Fitch, set off for Arnhem. Lieutenant Colonel David Dobie's 1st Parachute Battalion, which was in reserve, followed at 3.30 p.m.

The 82nd Airborne Division had arrived meanwhile over its DZs and LZs some four miles to the south-east and south-west of Nijmegen. Brigadier General James Gavin had decided to drop the 505th and 508th Parachute Infantry Regiments, together with the 376th Parachute Field Artillery Battalion, to the north-east and south-east of Groesbeek, between the Groesbeek Heights and the forests of the Reichswald. The 504th Parachute Infantry Regiment, tasked with seizing the bridge at Grave, was to be dropped north of the Maas, to the north of the village of Overasselt, with one company being dropped south of the river so that the bridge could be attacked from both directions. The gliderborne element of the division, transported in fifty Waco gliders, was to land on an LZ to the east of Groesbeek, followed by thirty-eight gliders carrying Headquarters I Airborne Corps.

First to appear were the divisional pathfinders, one of whose sticks had been lost when its C-47 had been shot down en route. Half an hour later, 479 C-47s of the 50th and 52nd Troop Carrier Wings USAAF arrived over the DZs and LZs and at 1.00 p.m. the 505th Parachute Infantry Regiment, commanded by Colonel William Ekman, led the jump with Lieutenant Colonel Edwin Bedell's 307th Airborne Engineer Battalion following close behind. Next came the 504th, under Colonel Reuben Tucker, trailed by Colonel Roy Lindquist's 508th. Last to jump were the gunners of 376th Parachute Field Artillery Battalion, under Lieutenant Colonel Wilbur Griffith, who were dropped with their twelve 75mm pack howitzers and 544 rounds of ammunition.

Following behind the paratroops came forty-six Waco gliders, bringing in Lieutenant Colonel Raymond Singleton's 80th Airborne

Anti-Aircraft Battalion, with eight 57mm anti-tank guns, members of the divisional staff and other personnel. After them came twenty-nine Horsas and six Wacos carrying the tactical forward element of Lieutenant General 'Boy' Browning's Headquarters I Airborne Corps. Three of the 82nd's original fifty Wacos had aborted after take-off and a fourth had its tug shot down over Schouwen Island; the glider landed successfully and its passengers succeeded in evading capture for three days before being taken prisoner. Of the thirty-two Horsas that had taken off from England, two aborted shortly afterwards and a third went astray.

The gliders approached LZ 'N', south-east of Groesbeek, at around 1.45 p.m. The majority of the Wacos cast off too soon, however, and only six succeeded in landing on the LZ itself. The other forty landed a mile away to the west, two being destroyed and fourteen damaged on landing. Casualties were light, with only seven men being injured, and all the anti-tank guns surviving intact. Twenty-eight Horsas landed safely on the LZ and shortly afterwards Browning established his headquarters in the woods on the northern edge of the LZ, while Gavin located his 1,000 yards west of Groesbeek.

The 1st and 3rd Battalions 505th Parachute Infantry Regiment dropped on DZ 'N', south-east of Groesbeek, landing almost on top of some enemy flak batteries, which were swiftly overrun. Regimental Headquarters and the 2nd Battalion, however, were dropped on DZ 'T', which had been allotted to the 508th Parachute Infantry Regiment, but nevertheless rallied quickly and seized Groesbeek as it moved south. Having cleared the town of any enemy, it took up defensive positions in reserve on the high ground west of the town, extending south to Mook which had been taken by detachments of the 1st Battalion.

The 508th, having dropped on DZ 'T' to the north-east of Groesbeek, established itself in positions on the northern part of the Groesbeek Heights. Having received reports from local inhabitants that both were only lightly held by the Germans, Brigadier General Gavin ordered Colonel Lindquist to despatch one battalion without delay to Nijmegen to seize the road bridge over the Waal.

The 1st Battalion, commanded by Lieutenant Colonel Shields Warren, moved off immediately. At 8.00 p.m. that evening it encountered stiff opposition some 400 yards from the bridge. Taking up positions due east of the Maas–Waal Canal, the battalion established roadblocks to cut off any enemy moving south and sent a company to clear any Germans from the LZ north-east of Groesbeek, but this met considerable resistance. Lieutenant Colonel Otho E. Holmes' 2nd Battalion established positions on the vital high ground in the area of Berg en Dal, encountering little resistance.

The 504th Parachute Infantry Regiment, meanwhile, dropped on to three DZs west of the Maas–Waal Canal, two to the north and one to the south of the Maas. The 1st Battalion, commanded by Lieutenant Colonel Willard Harrison, was dropped north-east of Overasselt and, having encountered strong opposition, took the Maas–Waal Canal bridge at 4.00 p.m. The canal bridges near Blankenburg and Hatert, however, were blown by the Germans, as the battalion approached them, but after nightfall both sites were subsequently captured and the southernmost canal bridge at Heumon captured intact.

Lieutenant Colonel Edward N. Wellems's 2nd Battalion dropped on DZ 'O', west of Overasselt, and half an hour after landing headed for its objective, the bridge over the Maas at Grave. Coming under fire from 20mm anti-aircraft cannon emplaced at the bridge, Company E worked its way to within attacking distance of the objective. A squad of eight men duly seized a flak tower at the northern end of the bridge and turned its cannon against the remaining defenders. At 4.30 p.m. the company overcame any remaining resistance and took control of the bridge. Thereafter, the 2nd Battalion captured Grave itself and established a bridgehead to the south while the 3rd Battalion established defensive positions to the north.

The 376th Parachute Field Artillery Battalion, meanwhile, had carried out a successful drop on to DZ 'N' south of Groesbeek and moved its ten 75mm pack howitzers some 1,000 yards to establish its first gun line. At 6.00 p.m. that evening it carried out its fire mission in support of the 505th Parachute Infantry Regiment.

Companies B, C and D of the 307th Airborne Engineer Battalion also dropped south of Groesbeek, B and D covering the move of the divisional headquarters to its initial location and thereafter providing local protection for it. Company C meanwhile linked up with the 504th Parachute Infantry Regiment to the west of the Maas–Waal Canal.

Anti-tank support also arrived in the form of Battery A 80th Airborne Anti-Aircraft Battalion and its eight 57mm anti-tank guns, two of which were deployed to each parachute infantry regimental group, with two being held in reserve at the divisional headquarters' location.

To the south, the 101st Airborne Division had been having a much tougher time. Transported in 434 C-47s of the 53rd Troop Carrier Wing, it had encountered heavy flak as it flew over Holland to its DZs and LZs with several aircraft sustaining hits. Sixteen were shot down although all their sticks succeeded in jumping clear, the pilots of four heroically keeping their blazing aircraft aloft long enough for their sticks to do so.

First to jump were the 2nd and 3rd Battalions of Colonel Howard R. Johnson's 501st Parachute Infantry Regiment, commanded by Lieutenant Colonels Robert A. Ballard and Julian J. Ewell respectively. Along with two platoons of the 326th Airborne Engineer Battalion attached, they dropped on DZ 'A' two miles west of Veghel where they encountered little resistance. Within an hour both battalions had moved off towards the town and by 3.00 p.m. had seized all their initial objectives, namely the bridges over the Aa and the Zuid Willems Vaart Canal. Lieutenant Colonel Harry Kinnard's 1st Battalion meanwhile had dropped on DZ 'A-1', near Kasteel, some three miles to the north-west of Veghel, where it encountered some resistance from small groups of enemy lines-of-communication troops near the DZ. The battalion reached Veghel at 5.00 p.m., encountering scattered groups of enemy en route, and linked up with the rest of the regiment.

The 502nd Parachute Infantry Regiment, commanded by Colonel John H. Michaelis, was the next to jump with its two attached platoons of 326th Airborne Engineer Battalion, landing on DZ 'B' where it encountered no opposition. By 3.00 p.m. the regiment had regrouped and the 1st Battalion, under Lieutenant Colonel Patrick F. Cassidy, set off for Saint Oedenrode, which it captured after a skirmish, thereafter taking intact its objective, the bridge over the Dommel, before assuming defensive positions around it and digging in.

Company H of the 3rd Battalion, meanwhile, had headed four miles to the west, to the road bridge at Best which it was to secure as an alternative crossing over the canal. En route, however, it had lost its way and only one platoon arrived at the bridge where it encountered an enemy roadblock manned by troops of the 59th Infantry Division, supported by an anti-aircraft battalion using its 20mm guns in the ground defence role. Eventually, the remainder of the company arrived and a fierce battle ensued before the company was forced to withdraw. On hearing of the situation there, Colonel Michaelis despatched the rest of the 3rd Battalion, commanded by Lieutenant Colonel Robert G. Cole, with the task of seizing the bridge on the following morning.

The last to jump, the 506th Parachute Infantry Regiment, commanded by Colonel Robert F. Sink, was dropped on DZ 'C' where it encountered no opposition. The 1st Battalion immediately set off for its three objectives, the three bridges over the Wilhelmina Canal. Only slight resistance was met from scattered groups of enemy and the leading elements of the battalion were only 100 yards from the main bridge at Zon when it was blown by troops of the Hermann Göring Training Regiment as they withdrew. Shortly afterwards, the battalion discovered that the other two bridges had also been blown; in fact, they had been destroyed two days earlier.

Major General Maxwell Taylor's tactical headquarters had dropped with the 502nd Parachute Infantry Regiment and he subsequently set up his command post in Zon. An hour saw the arrival of fifty-three tug and glider combinations bringing in Lieutenant Colonel Harry W. Elkins's 377th Parachute Field Artillery Battalion, headquarters personnel, the division's reconnaissance platoon, its signals and medical companies, together with equipment. A total of seventy had taken off from England but six had aborted en route. The remainder had encountered heavy flak during the rest of the flight, six tugs being shot down and forty-six severely damaged, some being forced to cut their gliders adrift. Of the fifty-six that arrived over the LZ, three crash-landed but the remainder landed safely, one being flown by a soldier who had taken over from the badly-wounded pilot.

To the west of Arnhem, meanwhile, all was not well with 1st Airborne Division. The spearhead for the move to the bridge was the 1st Airborne Reconnaissance Squadron, commanded by Major Freddie Gough, whose task was to make a dash for the bridge, and to seize and hold it until the arrival of 1st Parachute Brigade. Having landed, the squadron's parachute element had assembled at the rallying point where it awaited the arrival of the squadron's armed jeeps being brought in by glider. Following the landings, however, it was found that the glider carrying one of Headquarters Troop's jeeps had been forced to turn back after take-off while A Troop's vehicles were either missing or trapped inside their gliders: two gliders carrying No. 2 Section's jeeps had not arrived and the four vehicles of Nos. 1 and 3 Sections could not be extricated, as was the case with one of the troop's headquarters vehicles. Moreover, two of D Troop's vehicles were also trapped inside their gliders and it would take some time for them to be extracted.

Other than these losses, the squadron was nearly complete and still capable of carrying out its *coup de main* task of seizing the bridge. At 3.40 p.m., less A Troop and comprising twenty-eight jeeps, it set off towards a level crossing at Wolheze from which it would advance down a track running parallel to the railway line to Wolfheze station, move through the northern edge of Oosterbeek towards Arnhem, and then head straight for the bridge.

On reaching the level crossing, the squadron had travelled some

600 yards when the leading section of C Troop came under fire from troops of the 16th SS Panzer Grenadier Depot & Reserve Battalion in positions on a railway embankment and on a wooded ridgeline to the north. Commanded by SS-Sturmbannführer Sepp Krafft and numbering 306 all ranks, the battalion was a reserve unit of an ad hoc formation of Wehrmacht, Luftwaffe and Kreigsmarine personnel organised in seven battalion-sized units. It had been tasked with countering any airborne landings in its area as well as defending, and preparing for demolition, the bridges and ferries over the Lower Rhine in the area of Arnhem.

On learning of the landings, Krafft had guessed that the airborne troops' objectives were the Arnhem road and rail bridges, and the establishment of a bridgehead. Well aware that the most effective response to an airborne landing is an immediate counter-attack while enemy troops are still on their DZs and LZs, he ordered one of his two rifle companies and his heavy machine-gun platoon to mount an immediate attack. At the same time, he moved his headquarters and his other rifle company to the Hotel Wolfheze while summoning one of the independent quick-reaction units garrisoned in Arnhem to join him as quickly as possible.

Krafft established a defensive line west of Oosterbeek to block any advance by the British into the town. At 2.00 p.m. his No. 2 Company began moving towards the DZs and LZs but did so without reconnoitring the exact locations of the zones, which were concealed from it by the wooded terrain. Emerging unexpectedly on to LZ 'Z', it came under fire and withdrew after a brief engagement. Its heavy machine-gun section, however, deployed to the north to protect the company's right flank, brought fire to bear on four gliders, killing all those in them. After about twenty minutes, however, it was forced to move back to avoid being outflanked and cut off, rejoining the company as it withdrew to take up positions on the left of No. 4 Company along the eastern side of the Wolfhezeweg.

It was No. 4 Company, the second of Krafft's two rifle companies, which engaged the leading elements of 1st Airborne Reconnaissance Squadron as they headed east along the track running parallel to the railway line. Heavy machine guns raked the jeeps of No. 8 Section and pinned down its crews, the survivors eventually being forced to surrender. The other two sections of C Troop, under its commander, Captain John Hay, tried to work their way forward to assist No. 8 Section but came under fire from the railway embankment to their right.

2nd Parachute Battalion, meantime, was pressing on with A Company, under Major Digby Tatham-Warter, leading the way. En route, it ambushed a number of enemy vehicles, taking some prisoners. As they entered the village of Heelsum, Lieutenant Colonel Johnny Frost and his men were greeted with open arms by the local inhabitants who came pouring out of their homes; it was with difficulty that the battalion continued on its way through the throngs of excited people. On reaching the next village of Heveadorp, however, A Company came under fire, suffering light casualties, but pressed on towards Oosterbeek.

Leaving Oosterbeek, Major Victor Dover and C Company headed for the river and the railway bridge but no sooner had they reached it, and started to cross under cover of smoke and covering fire from some of the company's Bren LMGs, than the enemy blew the bridge, leaving the southernmost span lying semi-immersed in the river. With the bridge rendered useless, C Company was ordered to head for its second objective, a house reported as accommodating an enemy headquarters.

A Company meanwhile had reached the western outskirts of Arnhem near the railway line where it had encountered armoured cars which were preventing any movement along the roads. At the same time, any movement across the railway line drew machine-gun fire from a force of enemy positioned on a feature known as Den Brink. B Company, commanded by Major Douglas Crawley, was despatched to deal with the enemy there while Major Digby Tatham-Warter called up a 6-pounder anti-tank gun to cope with the armoured cars.

As last light fell, A Company pushed on into Arnhem via the back gardens of houses. Meanwhile, Battalion Headquarters and elements of Headquarter Company were pressing on through the town to a pontoon bridge, the centre section of which was found to be missing. Shortly afterwards, Lieutenant Colonel Frost and his group caught up with A Company which by 9.00 p.m. had taken up positions on an embankment near the northern end of the bridge from which it watched traffic crossing to and fro.

A Company prepared to send a platoon forward to take the southern end of the bridge, while Battalion Headquarters occupied a house overlooking the bridge and Headquarter Company moved into one next door. Shortly afterwards, a fifteen-strong group of A Company, led by Lieutenant A. J. McDermont, ran up the embankment and started across the bridge. It had not advanced very far before it came under machine-gun fire from a pillbox. At the same time, a troop of armoured cars appeared at the southern end and, on being engaged by A Company, opened fire on the battalion's positions. McDermont and his men were forced to withdraw but a second attempt to cross the bridge was mounted shortly afterwards by a platoon under Lieutenant Jack Grayburn. This, too, was unsuccessful, the platoon suffering heavy casualties.

Almost immediately, an enemy battalion, later identified as being part of the 10th SS Panzer Division heading for Nijmegen, approached the northern end of the bridge and was engaged by 2nd Parachute Battalion. Just after last light, a company of the 21st SS Panzer Grenadier Regiment also arrived and joined the battle.

A short time later, part of Headquarters 1st Parachute Brigade, led by Major Tony Hibbert, the brigade major, appeared with its defence platoon. These welcome reinforcements were followed by a troop of 1st Parachute Squadron RE under Captain Eric McKay, Major Freddie Gough and a small element of 1st Airborne Reconnaissance Squadron, a platoon of divisional RASC troops with a captured truck filled with ammunition collected from the DZ, and a troop of 6-pounder anti-tank guns accompanied by some glider pilots. At 8.00 p.m. the commander of 3rd Airlanding Light Battery RA, Major Denis Munford, arrived with one of his troop commanders and an FOO and signallers from 1st Forward Observation Unit RA. Later a platoon of 9th Field Company RE also arrived and during the night further reinforcements appeared in the form of C Company 3rd Parachute Battalion whose headquarters and one platoon took up positions on the eastern side of the bridge.

A Company meanwhile was attempting to dislodge the enemy from the bridge. A platoon led by Lieutenant Robin Vlasto, accompanied by a small group of sappers equipped with a flamethrower, moved off to mount an attack from a flank. While doing so, however, the enemy put in an attack supported by mortars, but this was beaten off. Shortly afterwards, Vlasto and his men attacked the pillbox on the bridge with PIATs and the flamethrower, this resulting in a number of large detonations and the sound of ammunition exploding. Just as A Company was preparing to cross the bridge, a convoy of four enemy trucks filled with infantry approached it from the south and were swiftly engaged, a few survivors quickly surrendering.

One of the main predicaments facing the force at the bridge was that radio communications appeared to have broken down completely. All efforts to establish contact with the divisional headquarters proved fruitless, this being a problem that would plague the division throughout the following days of the battle. Indeed, Lieutenant Colonel Frost was unable to establish contact with B and C Companies, the latter being pinned down near its objective, the enemy headquarters building, and unable to break through to rejoin the battalion. Similarly, B Company, which had been despatched earlier to take the den Brink feature, was unable to respond to a message from Frost, carried by a runner, ordering it to move to the area of the pontoon bridge because of heavy enemy activity.

3rd Parachute Battalion, having rallied with ninety-five per cent of its strength, had set off shortly after Frost and his men, following the middle road to Arnhem. At 4.00 p.m. No. 5 Platoon, under Lieutenant

James Cleminson, which was leading the battalion, reached a cross-roads west of Oosterbeek when an enemy staff car was observed approaching at high speed. The vehicle was ambushed and all its occupants killed, among them the German Commandant of Arnhem, Major General Friedrich Kussin, who had been visiting the 16th SS Panzer Grenadier Depot & Reserve Battalion and was returning to his headquarters.

As the battalion pressed on, the Germans brought down mortar fire on the crossroads, the bombs bursting in the trees overhead and inflicting casualties among those who took cover in the undergrowth below – others who had taken shelter in some old German trenches near by were more fortunate. Shortly afterwards, Brigadier Gerald Lathbury ordered Lieutenant Colonel Tony Fitch to resume his advance. Radio communications were poor and Lathbury, who was becoming increasingly concerned at the lack of information as to his brigade's progress, was unable to establish contact with 1st Parachute Battalion and only intermittently with the force at the bridge.

At this juncture, a mortar bomb hit the jeep of Major General Roy Urquhart, who had appeared on the scene as 3rd Parachute Battalion was being mortared, wounding his his signaller and rendering the radio inoperable, thus severing Urquhart's sole link with his tactical head-quarters. Deciding to remain with Lathbury, he followed 3rd Parachute Battalion as it resumed its cautious advance towards Arnhem.

Just before last light B Company, commanded by Major Peter Waddy, came under fire from a self-propelled gun at close range. Waddy and his men were about to engage it when a 6-pounder anti-tank detach-ment appeared and proceeded to bring its gun to bear. It was too slow, however, and the self-propelled gun quickly put the 6-pounder out of action. Its crew then draped one of the wounded gunners across the front of the vehicle, which reversed towards the German lines. No sooner had it disappeared and 3rd Parachute Battalion resumed its march, than other self-propelled guns and armoured cars appeared and prevented any further move forward.

While the battalion was dealing with this new threat, C Company, commanded by Major Peter Lewis, was despatched in a flanking move to the north. Advancing along a road leading to the railway, it encountered a number of enemy vehicles near Oosterbeek station. These were destroyed before the company resumed its advance along the railway line to Arnhem station. Thereafter, moving through the town via side streets, Lewis and his men succeeded in reaching 2nd Parachute Battalion, bringing the total of Lieutenant Colonel Frost's force to between 600 and 700 men.

The remainder of 3rd Parachute Battalion meanwhile had encountered enemy units supported by patrols from a battle group of the 9th SS Panzer Division, and was being held up by them on the outskirts of Oosterbeek, near the Park Hotel at Hartenstein. By then, last light was falling and Brigadier Lathbury suggested that the battalion halt for a few hours.

1st Parachute Battalion had made a perfect drop and, having rallied, set off for the DZ towards the high ground to the north of Arnhem, encountering en route crowds of jubilant Dutch people. At about 4.30 p.m., as R Company, which was in the lead, approached a crossroads north of Wolfheze, it came under fire from enemy armour, mortars and machine guns. Failing light and the onset of heavy rain made it difficult to engage the enemy as the company took cover in the nearby woods. Armoured vehicles were prowling about the area of the crossroads and shortly afterwards the company was attacked by enemy infantry. The battle, fought at close range, was bitter, and heavy casualties were suffered on both sides. By the time R Company managed to extricate itself and fight its way to the northern outskirts of Arnhem, its strength had been reduced by fifty per cent.

The commanding officer, Lieutenant Colonel David Dobie, meanwhile had decided to bypass the opposition and the battalion, leaving R Company heavily engaged, moved east along a track by the edge of the woods before striking north once more towards the main road. On reaching it, however, the battalion encountered tanks and other armour advancing from the south-east and observed enemy infantry taking up positions in the woods farther to the east. At midnight, having waited for some time for R Company to rejoin it, the battalion pressed on southwards once more, leaving behind guides for R Company. Having heard over the radio that 2nd Parachute Battalion was in dire straits at the bridge, Dobie decided that he must go to its aid. His attempts to contact Brigadier Lathbury by radio were unsuccessful and so he issued orders for his battalion to head for the bridge later that night.

While 1st Parachute Brigade's three battalions were fighting their way towards Arnhem, 1st Airlanding Brigade, commanded by Brigadier Philip 'Pip' Hicks, was holding the DZs and LZs in preparation for the arrival of 4th Parachute Brigade on the morning of D+1, 18 September. The brigade itself would drop on DZs 'X' and 'Y' while its gliderborne element and remaining divisional troops would land on LZs 'S' and 'Z'. The gliderborne element of 1st Polish Independent Parachute Brigade Group meanwhile would land on LZ 'L'.

The 7th Battalion The King's Own Scottish Borderers was in positions in the woods bordering the edge of Ginkels Heath covering DZ 'Y', while the 2nd Battalion The South Staffordshire Regiment protected LZ 'S' at Reyerscamp. LZs 'X' and 'Z', situated immediately north of Heelsum and Renkum, were held by the 1st Battalion The Border Regiment. The brigade headquarters was located just to the east of DZ 'Y'.

To the east of LZs 'X' and 'Z', and to the south of Wolfheze, were the gun lines of 1st Airlanding Light Regiment RA, commanded by Lieutenant Colonel W. F. K. 'Sheriff' Thompson, whose 1st and 3rd Airlanding Light Batteries RA, led by Majors Arthur Norman-Walker and Denis Munford respectively, had landed in the first lift. Major Jeffrey Linton's 2nd Airlanding Light Battery RA would arrive with 4th Parachute Brigade on D+1.

1st Airlanding Anti-Tank Battery RA, under Major Bill Arnold, had also arrived with the first lift and a troop of its 6-pounder guns had

accompanied 2nd Parachute Battalion to the bridge while the rest of
the battery remained with 1st Airlanding Brigade. Some of the Hamilcar
gliders bringing in the battery's 17-pounder guns had come to grief
when landing on unexpectedly soft ground, but the majority of the
guns and their tractors were retrieved intact and in working order. 1st
Airborne Division's other anti-tank unit, 2nd Airlanding Anti-Tank
Battery RA, commanded by Major A. F. Haynes, would arrive in the
second lift.

There was little activity for 1st Airlanding Brigade during the
afternoon of 17 September until the appearance at 5.00 p.m. of a detachment of the 3rd Dutch SS Landsturm Niederland Battalion in trucks
on the road bordering Ginkels Heath. The Dutchmen began reconnoitring the woods on the western edge of DZ 'Y' but were ambushed
at close range by a platoon of the King's Own Scottish Borderers. The
detachment commander was killed and the remainder fled.

Nothing further occurred until 9.00 p.m. that night when a company
of the Dutch SS battalion appeared again, moving eastwards along the
Ede–Arnhem road and subsequently through the woods on the eastern
side of Ginkels Heath in order to probe 1st Airlanding Brigade's positions. Once again, the Dutchmen encountered the King's Own Scottish
Borderers, who opened fire at close range, inflicting severe casualties.

News of the landings near Nijmegen and Arnhem had been com-
municated to Headquarters II SS Panzer Corps by the Luftwaffe. Lieu-
tenant General Willi Bittrich reacted swiftly by ordering the 9th SS
Panzer Division to seize the Arnhem road bridge and occupy the town.
The 10th SS Panzer Division was ordered to head south, cross the Lower
Rhine by ferry at Pannerden and assist in the defence of Nijmegen and
hold the bridges over the Waal. At the same time, the 9th SS Panzer
Division's reconnaissance battalion was despatched south towards the
Lower Rhine, via the road bridge at Arnhem, to join other units in preventing any advance by the 82nd Airborne Division from Nijmegen
and any link-up between Second British Army and the airborne troops
in Arnhem.

It soon became apparent, however, that the 10th SS Panzer Division and its heavy Tiger and Panther tanks would be unable to cross at Pannerden without the use of a heavy ferry. Construction of one would take time as the work would have to be done at night to avoid detection by Allied aircraft. Bittrich therefore decided that the immediate priority was to remove the presence of the British paratroops in Arnhem while also containing and destroying the rest of the airborne division heading for the town. This task was given to SS-Obersturmbannführer Walter Harzer and his 9th SS Panzer Division.

At first light on 18 September, a convoy of trucks filled with enemy troops drove through the streets dominated by 2nd Parachute Battalion and other elements of 1st Parachute Brigade who opened fire, killing most of the occupants. Shortly afterwards, a column of fourteen armoured cars and half-tracks of the 9th SS Panzer Division's reconnaissance battalion began crossing the bridge from the south, heading north to rejoin the rest of the division after being relieved at Nijmegen by a unit of the 10th SS Panzer Division. Driving at high speed, the first four vehicles succeeded in reaching the northern end of the bridge and disappeared. The other ten, however, were not so fortunate and were destroyed by a 6-pounder anti-tank gun and PIATs.

Shortly afterwards, SS panzer grenadiers attacked 2nd Parachute Battalion in force and a fierce battle ensued at close range, lasting for two hours, during which buildings were set ablaze as shells and mortar bombs rained down into the area. Casualties among 2nd Parachute Battalion, however, were light and morale remained extremely high. The enemy, on the other hand, suffered heavily, losing four more armoured vehicles and a considerable number of men killed or wounded. During the battle, the pack howitzers of 1st and 3rd Air-landing Light Batteries RA, directed by Major Denis Munford, who had succeeded in establishing radio contact with the gun line, provided excellent support with their accurate fire helping to break up the enemy attacks.

At this point radio contact was established with B Company, which had succeeded in making its way to the area of the pontoon bridge. After fighting their way through the streets, Major Douglas and most of the company arrived to rejoin the battalion. There was still, however, no word of C Company.

Meanwhile, the sound of battle could be heard from the west of Arnhem where 1st and 3rd Parachute Battalions were continuing their attempts to break through to the bridge.

First light on 18 September had found 3rd Parachute Battalion resuming its advance after spending most of the night near the Harten-stein Hotel in Oosterbeek. Having set off at 4.30 a.m., it moved along the southernmost road running alongside the river, accompanied by Major General Roy Urquhart and Brigadier Gerald Lathbury. B Company was in the lead, passing under the railway bridge at 5.30 a.m., but the pace was so fast that in the darkness B Company, Headquarter Company, the Mortar and Machine gun Platoons and some anti-tank guns became separated and cut off.

On reaching the outskirts of Arnhem, near the Saint Elizabeth Hospital, the battalion was held up at the junction where the southern road joined the central route. There it encountered tanks and self-propelled guns of a battle group of the 9th SS Panzer Division; these brought heavy fire to bear on the battalion which was also subjected to sniping and machine-gun fire from the upper storeys of buildings around it. Lieuetanant Colonel Fitch and his men soon found them-selves surrounded as enemy troops closed in around them.

1st Parachute Battalion, meanwhile, had moved off at 1.00 a.m. for the Arnhem bridge and, having crossed the railway at Oosterbeek station, joined the main road. At 4.30 a.m., however, S Company, which was in the lead, came under heavy fire from mortars, machine guns and armoured cars sited on high ground above a railway bridge to its front. Putting in a left-flanking attack, the company cleared the enemy position but suffered some thirty casualties while doing so.

By 6.30 a.m. the battalion was pressing on again, heading for the railway bridge on the southernmost road into Arnhem along which

3rd Parachute Battalion had passed earlier. Some thirty minutes later, it encountered 3rd Parachute Battalion's Headquarter Company, together with detachments of the Mortar Platoon and some anti-tank guns, which Lieutenant Colonel David Dobie added to his own depleted strength.

By this time it was dawn and the Germans brought mortar fire to bear on the area around the railway bridge. T Company, commanded by Major Christopher Perrin-Brown, encountered the enemy in strength in houses and a factory some 400 yards beyond the bridge. At the same time, a number of armoured vehicles were observed on the den Brink feature. Supported by fire from 1st Airlanding Light Regiment RA and the battalion's mortars, the latter being augmented by those of 3rd Parachute Battalion, T Company put in an attack on some houses on the crossroads near by but was held up by a 20mm cannon which opened fire from the factory.

A Company 3rd Parachute Battalion, commanded by Major Mervyn Dennison, now appeared on the scene and another assault was mounted with A Company on the left of the road and T Company on the right, once again with artillery and mortar-fire support. The action lasted for approximately an hour during which the enemy launched a counter-attack on 1st Parachute Battalion's left flank. Nevertheless, the battalion fought its way through to the road junction, reaching it at about 3.00 p.m. By this time its strength was down to some 100 men.

The situation in Arnhem and Osterbeek by the morning of 18 September was grim. 2nd Parachute Battalion was holding on at the bridge but had suffered casualties and was running very low on ammunition. 1st and 3rd Parachute Battalions were held up in heavy fighting on the outskirts of Arnhem, unable to reinforce Lieutenant Colonel Frost and his men. To make matters worse, Major General Urquhart and Brigadier Lathbury were both still separated from their headquarters and thus were out of contact from their respective formations. Both had taken shelter in a house with the headquarters element of 3rd Parachute Battalion, but at 3.00 p.m., when the battalion set off in a further attempt to reach the bridge by heading north and approaching it via the railway, they decided to make their own way to the bridge. As they were moving down a street, however, accompanied by Lieutenant James Cleminson and men of No. 5 Platoon of B Company 3rd Parachute Battalion, Lathbury was hit in the back by fire from a machine gun. Dragging him into a nearby house, and shooting dead an enemy soldier who attempted to follow them, Urquhart left Lathbury in the care of a Dutch couple before pressing on with two men, but they were soon forced to take refuge in a house to avoid capture by enemy troops approaching in the opposite direction.

At the DZs and LZs to the west of Arnhem, meanwhile, 1st Airlanding Brigade was under attack from German forces approaching from the west. At 5.00 a.m., the 1st Battalion The Border Regiment was engaged by an ad hoc battalion-sized force comprising an SS battalion formed from an officer cadet school, a unit of Kriegsmarine personnel and members of a Luftwaffe ground-crew battalion. Farther north, on Ginkels Heath, the 7th Battalion The King's Own Scottish Borderers was attacked by the Dutch SS battalion while an SS depot battalion advanced north-eastwards, between the Dutch and Luftwaffe units, in an attempt to drive a wedge between the two airlanding battalions defending the LZs and DZs.

By 7.00 a.m. the SS officer cadet battalion had cleared Renkum but an attack by the Kriegsmarine unit was beaten off with the sailors suffering heavy casualties. By early afternoon, the Germans had reached Heelsum, on the southern edge of DZ 'X' and LZ 'Z'. The Dutch SS battalion was meanwhile still attempting to dislodge the King's Own Scottish Borderers from their positions in the woods on the eastern side of Ginkels Heath covering DZ 'X' and LZ 'Z'. The Luftwaffe battalion had been halted in its advance by the Borderers but had been reinforced by two companies of the SS officer cadet battalion and six Renault tanks. The Germans launched an attack, but this ground to a halt after all six tanks had been knocked out. A second assault proved successful and the Borderers were forced to withdraw east towards Oosterbeek.

At Headquarters 1st Airborne Division, located in the Hartenstein Hotel, Brigadier 'Pip' Hicks, the commander of 1st Airlanding Brigade, had temporarily assumed command of the division in the absence of Major General Urquhart. Aware of 2nd Parachute Battalion's perilous situation, he despatched B and D Companies of the 2nd Battalion The South Staffordshire Regiment (whose other two rifle companies were due to arrive with the second lift) as reinforcements for Lieutenant Colonel Frost and his hard-pressed force. Unfortunately they became held up as they attempted to make their way towards the bridge. The division's only hope now lay with Brigadier John Hackett's 4th Parachute Brigade, due to arrive at 10.00 a.m.

Back in England, all the mounting airfields were covered in low-lying mist and it was not until late morning that conditions improved sufficiently for aircraft to take off. Thus, it was not until 3.00 p.m. that the second lift arrived over DZ 'Y' and LZ 'L' where the pathfinders of 21st Independent Parachute Company had set up their Eurekas and laid out their marker panels. Unlike the drops and landings on the previous day, the approaching aircraft had encountered flak during the final twenty minutes of the approach. 4th Parachute Brigade's drop was accurate but it encountered considerable opposition on the DZ, Lieutenant Colonel Ken Smyth's 10th Parachute Battalion in particular suffering casualties from heavy fire from the Dutch SS battalion. In due course, however, the latter was counter-attacked by the King's Own Scottish Borderers who virtually annihilated it.

Despite their casualties, the three parachute battalions rallied quickly and headed for their respective RVs. Two hours after the drop, the brigade was advancing towards Arnhem, with 10th and 156th Parachute Battalions, the latter commanded by Lieutenant Colonel Sir Richard des Voeux, making for the high ground north of Arnhem which they were to take and hold. 11th Parachute Battalion, commanded by Lieutenant Colonel George Lea, was to head for the bridge with the two companies of the South Staffordshires who had just landed by glider.

As last light approached on 18 September, the two South Stafford-shire companies were heading towards Arnhem with 11th Parachute Battalion following up. Just after darkness fell, they met Lieutenant Colonel David Dobie and the remnants of 1st Parachute Battalion. It was decided that the advance would be continued at 4.00 a.m. on the following morning, 19 September, with 1st Parachute Battalion and its attached elements of 3rd Parachute Battalion heading south to the river and then approaching 2nd Parachute Battalion's positions along the northern bank. 11th Parachute Battalion and the two South Stafford-shire companies meanwhile would move along the main road.

By this time, however, the Germans had created a 'box' to hem in those elements of 1st Airborne Division in Oosterbeek. The eastern side was firmly established by a battle group of the 9th SS Panzer Division while to the north of the Arnhem–Ede road, forming the box's 'lid', was SS-Sturmbannführer Sepp Krafft's 16th SS Panzer Grenadier Depot & Reserve Battalion (less one company) reinforced by elements of the 9th SS Panzerjäger Battalion, an army infantry battalion, 642nd Marine Regiment, 1st Marine Cadre Regiment and No. 10 Company of 3rd Police Regiment. On Krafft's left was an army battle group while in the centre, covering the Arnhem-Utrecht road, was another formation comprising elements of 9th SS Panzer Division's anti-aircraft battalion, its engineer battalion and the detached company of the 16th SS Panzer Grenadier Depot & Reserve Battalion. Manning the line in the southern sector, covering the area of the Arnhem–Utrecht road to the Lower Rhine, were elements of the 19th and 20th SS Panzer Grenadier Regiments. In all, the line was held by seven battalions supported by self-propelled guns, half-tracks and armoured cars. To the rear was a second blocking line, stretching from the station to the river, manned by another battle group consisting of two infantry companies formed from elements of 9th SS Panzer Regiment and a third from Kriegsma-rine personnel.

The situation facing 1st Parachute Battalion was grim. In the early hours of 19 September, after heading for the river, Lieutenant Colonel

Dobie and his men encountered troops of the 20th SS Panzer Grenadier Regiment and some fierce close-quarter fighting took place near the area of the pontoon bridge. Major John Timothy led R Company in a bayonet charge, as did Major Chris Perrin-Brown and T Company, but these achieved only limited success in driving the enemy back.

At first light the battalion, together with the remaining elements of 3rd Parachute Battalion, also came under fire from 9th SS Panzer Division's reconnaissance battalion which had moved into positions in a brickworks on the southern bank of the river, its half-tracks and armoured cars bringing fire to bear with their 20mm and 37mm cannons. By 6.00 a.m. both battalions numbered fewer than forty men each and the arrival of more enemy armour made the situation all the more impossible.

As Lieutenant Colonel Dobie and the other survivors attempted to take cover in houses near by, enemy troops appeared inside the buildings and opened fire, Dobie himself being wounded by a grenade. Eventually he and six others found shelter in a cellar occupied by Dutch civilians but an hour later were discovered by enemy troops who took them prisoner.

At 5.00 a.m., 156th Parachute Battalion had begun its attack through the woods of Johanna Hoeve, heading for the Lichtenbeek feature. By 10.00 a.m. it had failed and the battalion had suffered heavy losses with A Company losing all of its officers. In the meantime, 10th Parachute Battalion had fared little better, having come under fire from 88mm anti-aircraft guns being used in the ground target role as well as from tanks and self-propelled guns on the main Arnhem–Ede road. The battalion had been tasked with establishing a firm base 1,000 yards from a small farm at Johanna Hoeve but Lieutenant Colonel Ken Smyth ordered his men instead to dig in where they were, astride the Arnhem–Ede road, as he planned to attack and seize his objective that night. Throughout the day the battalion was subjected to heavy fire, but stood its ground.

It was during the morning of 19 September that Major General

Urquhart eventually succeeded in reaching his headquarters at the Hartenstein Hotel in Oosterbeek where he was briefed on the situation by Brigadier 'Pip' Hicks. Appalled at what he learned, he decided to see the situation for himself and drove to Headquarters 4th Parachute Brigade near Wolfheze where he found Brigadier John Hackett and his brigade heavily committed against troops of the 9th SS Panzerjäger Battalion supported by armour. During the night, the brigade had advanced on its objective, the high ground to the north of Arnhem, with 10th and 156th Parachute Battalions gaining ground. Unfortunately, enemy reinforcements had arrived in the form of an SS unit of self-propelled anti-aircraft guns and an army anti-aircraft battalion equipped with twin and quadruple-barrelled 20mm cannon mounted on half-tracks. Two companies of 156th Parachute Battalion had fallen victim to the very heavy firepower of these two units and had been forced to retreat.

Urquhart decided to withdraw the brigade south to the centre road leading into Arnhem but ordered Hackett not to pull back until ordered to do so. Shortly after he left for his own headquarters, the 1st Battalion The Border Regiment, which was behind 4th Parachute Brigade on the western outskirts of Oosterbeek, was attacked from the west. At the same time, two enemy battle groups began advancing southwards to close the lid on the German 'box' while others began advancing west towards Oosterbeek. 4th Parachute Brigade was in danger of being cut off, particularly if the Germans took Wolfheze, whose level crossing was the only point for the brigade's vehicles to cross the railway, elsewhere lined by steep embankments. 10th Parachute Battalion was despatched to secure the crossing and almost immediately the order to withdraw was received from 1st Airborne Division.

The withdrawal was carried out in contact with the enemy harassing the brigade as it pulled back. Meanwhile, on approaching Wolfheze, 10th Parachute Battalion had encountered an enemy battle group and fierce fighting took place. Captain Lionel Queripel, commanding a composite company of men from two other battalions as well his own, was hit as he carried a wounded NCO to shelter. Disregarding his own wound, he then led an attack on an enemy strongpoint, killing the crews of two machine guns and a 6-pounder gun captured and pressed into service by the enemy. At this point, the enemy counter-attacked and Queripel was wounded again in the face and both arms. Together with several men, he stood his ground against the enemy who showered him with grenades. Despite his injuries, Queripel succeeded in throwing several back at his attackers, ordering his men to withdraw while he covered them. Shortly afterwards, however, the enemy closed in and killed him. His great gallantry was later recognised by the posthumous award of the Victoria Cross.

By the time 10th Parachute Battalion withdrew across the railway line, it numbered only some 250 men. 156th Parachute Battalion had also suffered badly, now numbering approximately 270 all ranks and having lost almost all its transport. Nevertheless, as it drew back, 4th Parachute Brigade made the enemy pay a very heavy price for every yard gained.

At 4.00 a.m., meanwhile, some of the gliderborne element of 1st Polish Independent Parachute Brigade began approaching and landing on LZ 'L' over which 10th Parachute Battalion was currently withdrawing in full view of the enemy. The Poles immediately came under very heavy fire from the enemy on the ground and from a number of Messchersmitt Bf 109 fighters which appeared at the same time. A number of gliders were set ablaze in mid-air while others exploded on landing. Tragically, in the confusion and poor visibility caused by smoke, some of the Poles opened fire on 10th Parachute Battalion and other elements of 4th Parachute Brigade, and their fire was returned.

The South Staffordshires, advancing east from Saint Elizabeth's Hospital, had meantime been held up in the main street of Arnhem. Having run out of PIAT ammunition, they were soon overrun by enemy armour and forced to withdraw westwards. After regrouping, they attacked the den Brink feature in order to allow 11th Parachute Battalion to reach the road running north of it. No sooner had they taken it than they were subjected to heavy mortar fire and were driven off the feature by enemy armour which then turned its attention on 11th Parachute Battalion, inflicting heavy casualties.

The surviving South Staffordshires, along with those of 11th Parachute Battalion, withdrew to Oosterbeek station. Together with remnants of 1st and 3rd Parachute Battalions, they were formed into a composite unit, dubbed 'Lonsdale Force', under the command of Major Dickie Lonsdale, the second-in-command of 11th Parachute Battalion.

During that day, the RAF dropped supplies to the beleaguered division. Unfortunately, however, radio messages transmitted by Headquarters 1st Airborne Division to England giving details of the necessary changes to DZ locations had not been received, and consequently Dakotas and Stirlings ran into a heavy barrage of flak as they flew in and dropped their containers accurately on Supply DZ 'V' which by now was behind enemy lines. A new DZ had been marked out near the divisional headquarters and a Eureka set up near by, but the coloured marker panels only served to attract the attention of enemy fighters which strafed the area.

One of the aircraft was a Dakota of No 217 Squadron RAF, flown by Flight Lieutenant David Lord, which was hit and set ablaze as it made its run-in over the DZ. The crew nevertheless dropped six panniers of ammunition before Lord turned his aircraft for a second approach. As the last two panniers were being despatched, the flames took hold of the plane but Lord remained at the controls and ordered the rest of the crew to bale out. Unfortunately, all but one, Flying Officer Henry King, had taken off their parachutes. As they were donning them, there was an explosion and the starboard wing broke off. King, who was standing by the door, was flung clear and succeeded in pulling the ripcord of his parachute. Along with the remainder of his crew, Flight Lieutenant Lord was killed when the aircraft crashed. He was subsequently awarded a posthumous Victoria Cross for his great gallantry.

Other aircraft crash-landed in the area, some landing south of the

Lower Rhine. Of the 390 tons of supplies dropped, only a tiny proportion fell into 1st Airborne Division's hands. During the RAF's efforts to
resupply the division, its aircraft and crews suffered heavily: thirteen
aircraft were shot down and ninety-seven damaged.

Meanwhile, at the bridge in Arnhem, 2nd Parachute Battalion was
under constant fire from two battle groups supported by artillery and
eight tanks of 6th Panzer Regiment; the latter included two Tiger tanks
which were impervious to 2nd Parachute Battalion's 6-pounder anti-
tank guns and PIATs, and their 88mm guns rapidly reduced buildings to
rubble. In turn, the two battle groups were supported by two 88mm
guns positioned at the southern end of the bridge and a battery of
Nebelwerfer multi-barrelled rocket launchers.

By the afternoon of 19 September, most of the buildings in which
Lieutenant Colonel Frost and his men had installed themselves had
been set on fire by phosphorus shells. Each artillery barrage was
followed by infantry attacks but these were beaten off by counter-
attacks with the bayonet. Morale was still very high despite the appalling
conditions and Frost's men frequently left their positions with PIATs
and gammon bombs to hunt enemy tanks which crawled through the
streets blasting houses on either side.

In Oosterbeek, meanwhile, by the evening of 19 September the
remnants of 1st Airborne Division were being pushed back on all sides,
the majority being in an area between Heveadorp and Wolfheze to the
west and from Oosterbeek to Johanna Hoeve to the east. Major General
Urquhart decided that the only chance of conserving his remaining
forces until the arrival of XXX Corps lay in withdrawing and consoli-
dating them inside a defensive box which would also form a bridgehead on the northern bank of the river for any crossing from the south.
Although it meant abandoning 2nd Parachute Battalion and the other
units at the bridge, Urquhart knew it was the only course open to him.
That evening, therefore, orders were issued for the troops to withdraw
into the perimeter around Oosterbeek.

While 1st Airborne Division was fighting desperately for survival, farther to the south its two American counterparts were engaged in establishing and holding the corridor along which XXX Corps was to advance. On the morning of 18 September, in the 101st Airborne Division's sector, the 501st Parachute Infantry Regiment was continuing its defence of Veghel, beating off several small-scale attacks, while at Saint Oedenrode the 1st Battalion of the 502nd held on to the town, repelling several half-hearted assaults. At Best, however, the 502nd's 3rd Battalion suffered heavy casualties when it mounted an attack at first light on the road bridge; among them was the commanding officer, Lieutenant Colonel Robert G. Cole, who had won the Congressional Medal of Honor during the Normandy campaign. Colonel John Michaelis sent in his 2nd Battalion to assist. Carrying out a flanking move, and supported by its own mortars, the battalion advanced across open ground but was forced to withdraw after coming under heavy artillery, mortar and small-arms fire. At 11.00 a.m., while the battle was still in progress, the enemy blew the bridge. The 2nd Battalion subsequently moved up on the left of the 3rd Battalion and by last light the whole of the 502nd had taken up defensive positions to the east of the road.

At first light on 18 September, the 506th Parachute Infantry Regiment, with its 3rd Battalion in the lead, commenced its advance on Eindhoven. One mile from the city, however, it met stiff opposition at Woensel but the 2nd Battalion circled round to the east, outflanked the enemy positions and at 1.00 p.m. took the city. A British reconnaissance patrol had been encountered just north of Eindhoven soon after midday and at 7.15 p.m. that evening contact was established with the Guards Armoured Division, the leading element of XXX Corps, just south of the city.

At 3.30 p.m., other elements of the 101st Airborne Division had landed by glider. First to arrive was the 3rd Battalion 327th Glider Infantry Regiment, followed by Lieutenant Colonel John C. Pappus' 326th Airborne Engineer Battalion, Battery B 377th Parachute Field Artillery Battalion, the division's signals, quartermaster and medical companies along with some of its logistics and administrative transport. The gliderborne infantrymen were given the task of securing the LZ and the divisional administrative area.

Dawn on 19 September witnessed another attack on the bridge at Best by the 2nd Battalion 502nd Parachute Infantry Regiment, but this was also beaten off by the enemy who had been reinforced by two battalions and three companies of infantry. During the afternoon, a further attack was mounted, this time by the 2nd and 3rd Battalions along with elements of the 327th Glider Infantry Regiment. Support was provided by XXX Corps which provided a squadron of the 15th/19th King's Royal Hussars and artillery support, its guns now being in range. This final attack proved successful, resulting in over 300 enemy killed, 1, 056 prisoners taken and fifteen 88mm guns knocked out.

That afternoon saw the take-off from England of the division's third glider lift which brought in the 1st and 2nd Battalions 327th Glider Infantry Regiment, 81st Airborne Anti-Aircraft Battalion, 377th Parachute Field Artillery Battalion (less B Battery), and the 321st and 907th Glider Field Artillery Battalions. Unfortunately, due to bad weather, a large number of gliders failed to arrive at the LZs. Some tug-glider combinations were forced to turn back while several tugs cast off their gliders early, the latter being forced to land wherever possible in enemy-held territory. Flak also took its toll, shooting down several gliders. Those troops that arrived safely deployed to their allotted areas, elements of the two glider infantry units joining the 3rd Battalion in protecting the LZs with some being sent to assist the 502nd Parachute Infantry Regiment in its attack on the bridge at Best.

At around 5.00 p.m. approximately forty enemy tanks appeared and approached to within a few hundred yards of the bridge at Zon, opening fire on the town and Major General Maxwell Taylor's divisional command post. Little damage was inflicted, however, before the tanks withdrew on the appearance of detachments of the 81st Airborne Anti-Aircraft Battalion whose 57mm anti-tank guns knocked out two of them.

Farther north, meanwhile, the morning of 18 September in the 82nd Airborne Division's sector found the 504th Parachute Infantry Regiment still holding the bridges over the Maas at Grave and over the Maas–Waal Canal at Heuman, while carrying out extensive patrolling to the west and north-west along the Grave–Nijmegen road. At midday, it despatched a platoon northwards along the west bank of the canal to assist a platoon of the 505th in taking a bridge near Honinghutie. As the two platoons neared the bridge, however, it was blown by the enemy. Although not destroyed, it was sufficiently weakened as to render it unusable by vehicles, which had to be diverted eastwards to the bridge at Heuman.

Within the 505th Parachute Infantry Regiment's area, meanwhile, the Germans mounted a counter-attack at 6.30 a.m. with four battalion-sized battle groups, supported by five armoured cars and three half-tracks armed with 20mm anti-aircraft cannons. Advancing north-west from the northern Reichswald, these took the 82nd Airborne Division by surprise. For a time the division was under pressure as it was already overstretched, but eventually attacks at Horst, Grafwegen and Riethorst were beaten off.

The main problem facing the division was that its DZs and LZs had been overrun by the enemy and the second lift was due to arrive at 1.00 p.m. Clearance of the zones thus became a matter of priority and the 505th commenced the task at 12.40 a.m. The battle was still in progress when the first gliders began landing twenty minutes later, the 1st Battalion attacking downhill across the northernmost LZ under heavy fire from 20mm cannons and small arms, but eventually forcing the enemy to withdraw. Fortunately, casualties in the battalion were light, numbering eleven in all, but the enemy had suffered heavily: fifty killed, 150 taken prisoner and sixteen 20mm cannons captured.

The 450 gliders which landed brought in the 319th and 320th Glider Field Artillery Battalions, 456th Parachute Field Artillery Battalion, 80th Airborne Anti-Aircraft Battalion (less Battery A) and the 307th Airborne Medical Company. Losses among the gliders were light and most of their loads, including thirty 75mm pack howitzers and eight 57mm anti-tank guns, were unloaded intact. Having rallied, the 319th Glider and 456th Parachute Field Artillery Battalions were placed in direct support of the 508th and 505th Parachute Infantry Regiments respectively while the 320th Glider Field Artillery Battalion was tasked with providing support for the rest of the division.

At Nijmegen, meanwhile, the 508th Parachute Infantry Regiment had withdrawn its 1st Battalion from the town but at 9.00 a.m. Company G re-entered it and worked its way forward to the same location reached on the previous day. A strong force of enemy was encountered and fighting lasted until 3.00 p.m. when the company was withdrawn to the area of Berg en Dal. At 1.10 p.m. other elements of the regiment carried out an attack to clear the enemy from the area of the glider LZ to the north and north-east of Groesbeek in preparation for the arrival of the second lift. The enemy were taken completely by surprise and by 2.00 p.m. the area was clear, the enemy having lost fifty killed, 149 wounded and sixteen anti-aircraft guns captured. Throughout the rest of 8 September, the regiment continued to hold the high ground in the area of Berg en Dal, suffering sporadic shelling and probing attacks by the enemy.

From the very start of its advance at 2.35 p.m. on 17 September, the Guards Armoured Division, commanded by Major General Allan Adair and comprising 5th Guards Armoured Brigade and 32nd Guards Brigade, had been forced to fight every step of the way along the road towards Arnhem. It had encountered stiff opposition from enemy paratroops and SS units supported by self-propelled guns and tanks which had caused heavy casualties to men and tanks as the division advanced to Eindhoven, where it linked up with the 506th Parachute Infantry Regiment during the evening of 18 September. There it was forced to wait while the bridge over the Wilhelmina Canal was replaced by a Bailey bridge which was completed in time for the division to resume its advance by 6.00 a.m. the following morning.

Now thirty hours behind schedule, the division had sped rapidly along the corridor cleared and secured by the 101st Airborne Division; by 7.00 a.m. on 19 September the Grenadier Guards Group, comprising the 1st (Motor) and 2nd (Armoured) Battalions, had passed through Veghel, crossing over the Maas at Grave at 8.30 a.m., closely followed by the remainder of 5th Guards Armoured Brigade. At 8.20 a.m. the Grenadiers linked up with the 504th Parachute Infantry Regiment. Detaching a company to guard the bridge at Grave, along with two other companies to protect the Maas–Waal Canal bridges at Heumen and Honinghutie, as well as another to patrol and guard the road between Grave and the Honinghutie bridge, the 504th moved east of the canal where it relieved the 2nd Battalion of the 505th and occupied the Jonker Bosch woods. The 3rd Battalion of the 505th meanwhile moved into the 82nd Airborne Division reserve in the area of Malden.

The latter part of the day on the 19th saw 32nd Guards Brigade arriving at a concentration area between Grave and the Maas-Waal Canal. Its Coldstream Guards Group, comprising the 1st (Armoured) and 5th (Motorised) Battalions, was placed under command of 82nd Airborne Division and moved to Dekkerswald in divisional reserve, ready to protect the division's right flank against any threat from enemy armour emanating from the Reichswald.

The remainder of the Guards Armoured Division, meanwhile, had halted after receiving a message from Headquarters I Airborne Corps that Lieutenant General Browning wished to see the two command-ing officers of the Grenadier Guards Group, Lieutenant Colonels Edward Goulburn and Rodney Moore. At the meeting, Browning informed them that the bridge over the Maas–Waal, three miles south-west of Nijmegen, was damaged and unusable by tanks but that an alternative route lay to the east via Overasselt and Heumen. Following this diversion, the Grenadiers pressed on and by midday had halted and regrouped at Marienboom, just south of Nijmegen.

By this time Major General Allan Adair and the commander of XXX Corps, Lieutenant General Sir Brian Horrocks, had arrived at Head-quarters I Airborne Corps where they met Browning and Brigadier

General James Gavin who told them that the 82nd Airborne Division had achieved all of its objectives except the capture of Nijmegen and its two bridges. They also learned from Gavin that his division was over-stretched as bad weather had delayed the arrival of his second lift, while the constant threat to his LZs had forced him to withdraw units from Nijmegen to protect them. Of 1st Airborne Division, Browning could tell them little more than the landings had been successful.

On being relieved by the 504th, the 2nd Battalion 505th Parachute Infantry Regiment was placed under command of the Guards Armoured Division and at 4.00 p.m. on the afternoon of 19 September moved north to take part in an attack on the two Nijmegen bridges with the Grenadier Guards Group. The assault would be carried out in three columns with the right-hand one, comprising Companies E and F of the 2nd Battalion of the 505th, most of No. 2 Company of the Grenadiers' 1st Battalion and elements of No. 3 Squadron of the 2nd Battalion, heading for the main bridge. The centre column, consisting of a troop of tanks and a platoon of infantry, would make its way to the town's post office where, it was reported, demolition apparatus for blowing the bridge was located. The left-hand column, comprising a platoon of No. 2 Company, the remainder of No. 3 Squadron and Company D of the 2nd Battalion of the 505th, would meanwhile head for the town centre and then north-west to the railway bridge.

The road and railway bridges at Nijmegen lie respectively to the north and north-west of the town and are the only crossings of the Waal for some twenty miles. The road bridge, situated on high ground, is some 2,000 feet long with a centre span of 800 feet.

The approaches to both bridges favoured the defenders, a battle group of the 10th SS Panzer Division. Those at the road bridge were defended by an infantry battalion, which previously had belonged to the 9th SS Panzer Division, while the force at the railway bridge and the area to the south of it comprised four companies of the 6th Ersatz Battalion. North of the river was a panzer battalion fighting in the infantry role. Both bridges were being prepared for demolition by a company of the 10th SS Panzer Division's engineer battalion which had also been tasked with improving defences at the southern end of the road bridge.

At 4.00 p.m. the three columns of guardsmen and paratroops set off, encountering artillery fire as they moved through the outskirts of the city. The centre column occupied the post office, having encountered little resistance, while the right-hand column headed for the road bridge, guided by members of the Dutch Resistance riding on the leading tanks. On approaching a large roundabout some 400 yards short of the bridge, however, the column came under very heavy fire from enemy troops in houses converted into strongpoints. The leading tank was knocked out by anti-tank guns as soon as it appeared, as were the following two which came under fire from a large force of infantry, supported by two 88mm guns, manning a large barricade that blocked the road. A platoon of Grenadiers was despatched on a flanking move but was unable to make much headway. By this time dusk was approaching and, as little progress was being made, the column took up positions for the night.

The left-hand column meanwhile had headed for the railway bridge but as it approached came under very heavy artillery and machine-gun fire which knocked out the leading tank. The railway line itself proved an obstacle for the tanks while the combined force of the parachute company and Grenadier platoon was insufficient to take the objective without armoured support. The column thus withdrew and regrouped in the area of a crossroads to the north of the railway station. There it remained, cut off by enemy troops who infiltrated past it back into the city during the night.

The fighting had been fierce and the 2nd Battalion of the 505th had suffered heavy losses, which since the drop now amounted to 150 killed and 600 wounded, with an unspecified number missing. The enemy, however, were in strength; their numbers at the southern end of the road bridge alone being estimated at approximately 500.

At Headquarters I Airborne Corps during the night of 19 September, a plan for a second attack was produced by Browning, Horrocks, Gavin and Adair. The first phase, the clearing of the city, would begin at first light, to be followed later in the day by the second phase: an attack with artillery support on the road bridge. An additional element of the operation, proposed by Gavin, would comprise an assault river-crossing west of Nijmegen; once across, the troops would head east and attack the bridge from the north.

At 8.00 a.m. on 20 September the Grenadier Guards Group, supported by elements of the 2nd Battalion 505th Parachute Infantry Regiment, began the arduous task of clearing Nijmegen of the enemy. Despite encountering stiff opposition, with the streets having to be cleared building by building, it was achieved by the early afternoon, at which point Lieutenant Colonel Edward Goulburn decided that his troops were in a position to attack the bridge. On the left and in the centre the Grenadiers began pushing forward, clearing the enemy from houses as they advanced towards the bridge while on the right the para-troops did likewise in the area east of the bridge.

Meanwhile the 3rd Battalion 504th Parachute Infantry Regiment, commanded by Major Julian Cook, was preparing for the assault river-crossing and awaiting the arrival of the convoy carrying the assault boats in which the battalion would paddle across the Waal under cover of a smokescreen. At 2.30 p.m. squadrons of RAF Typhoon fighter-bombers appeared and began to strafe and rocket the enemy positions on the northern bank. Shortly afterwards, the Sherman tanks of the 2nd (Armoured) Battalion Irish Guards lined up on the south bank. Waiting alongside them was Lieutenant Colonel Edward N. Wellems, the commanding officer of the 504th's 2nd Battalion which would also cross the river if necessary. Minutes later, the convoy carrying the assault boats appeared. Engineers rapidly assembled the canvas, flat-bottomed craft which were immediately hauled away to the river's edge. Meanwhile, the Irish Guards' tanks had begun firing smokeshells while to the rear artillery began to bring down supporting fire. On a signal from Major Cook, Companies H and I dragged their boats into the river and began paddling towards the northern bank 400 yards away.

Before long, however, the smokescreen began to be dispersed by wind, and despite the heavy amount of suppressive fire brought down on them during the previous thirty minutes, the enemy opened fire on the two companies as they paddled frantically across the Waal. Shells and mortar bombs began to rain down on the 3rd Battalion, some boats receiving direct hits while others were swamped and capsized. Several, caught by the current, spun round as their occupants tried desperately to bring them under control.

About half of the boats succeeded in reaching the far bank, the troops disembarking swiftly and clearing the foremost enemy positions with fixed bayonets during the following half-hour. Major Cook and his men then regrouped, providing covering fire for the second wave paddling across in the thirteen boats that had survived the first crossing. Despite continuing enemy artillery fire, all but two boats succeeded in reaching the north bank; the remaining eleven then made five more crossings to bring across the rest of the battalion.

Such was the ferocity of the 3rd Battalion's assault that the surviving enemy broke and fled, pursued by Cook and his men. While the main body of the battalion headed east for the bridge, one company was detached to attack and seize the strongly defended van Holland fort. Swimming the moat that surrounded it, the paratroops succeeded in scaling the walls and set about the fort's defenders, who quickly surrendered.

At around 5.00 p.m. Companies H and I reached the northern end of the road and railway bridges and launched attacks against the defenders, who put up a stout resistance. The Grenadier Guards and the 2nd Battalion of the 505th, however, were by now also pushing forward. Suddenly the pressure proved too great and the enemy at the southern end of the railway bridge broke and retreated across the bridge in disorder, only to encounter Company H, which opened fire. Within the space of a few minutes, almost 500 enemy lay dead or wounded, or had been taken prisoner.

The enemy at the southern end of the road bridge had suffered a similar fate. The King's Company of the Grenadiers had stormed the Valkhof, the ancient fort on the edge of the river dominating the approaches to the bridge, and a short fierce battle ensued before the fort fell to the guardsmen, who then brought fire to bear on the enemy at the southern end of the bridge. Meanwhile, No. 4 Company had pushed forward, clearing the enemy from houses in the area. The successes of the two Grenadier companies enabled the 2nd Battalion of the 505th also to press on and by 6.30 p.m. the paratroops and guardsmen had reached the embankment leading to the bridge.

Meantime, No. 1 Squadron of the 2nd (Armoured) Battalion Grenadier Guards had moved up. Shortly before 7.00 p.m. it received a report that the Stars and Stripes had been seen at the far end of the bridge. The leading troop, under Sergeant Robinson, had already been ordered by the squadron leader, Major John Trotter, to be prepared to rush the bridge. Sergeant Robinson immediately ordered his troop forward and the four Shermans, led by Sergeant Pacey with Robinson following behind, thundered across the bridge with the latter's gunner engaging an 88mm gun on the far side and knocking it out with his second round. Despite heavy enemy fire, Pacey and Robinson crossed unscathed, but the third and fourth tanks in the troop were both hit and their crews baled out. The crew of the third, however, realising that their Sherman had not caught fire, remounted and followed the rest of the troop, which took up covering positions where they were joined shortly afterwards by Companies H and I of the 3rd Battalion 504th Parachute Infantry Regiment.

The remainder of No. 1 Squadron now arrived and pushed forward to the northern edge of the village of Lent, immediately north of the road bridge, where it overran the survivors of a company of the 10th SS Panzer Division's engineer battalion making a last stand. Thereafter, it took up positions to form a bridgehead, where it was reinforced an hour later by Nos. 1 and 3 Companies of the 3rd Battalion Irish Guards.

The railway bridge had also fallen by this time and so XXX Corps was able to establish its bridgehead over the Waal before making its final push towards Arnhem to relieve 1st Airborne Division. Unknown to Horrocks and the other senior Allied commanders at Nijmegen, a major factor in both bridges being captured intact was the order issued previously by Field Marshal Walter Model that the bridges at Nijmegen and Arnhem must not be blown in case they were required for counter-attacks. It was only at the very last minute, as Sergeant Robinson's troop was crossing the bridge, that the commander of the 10th SS Panzer Division, SS-Brigadeführer Heinz Harmel, who was observing the battle from a forward divisional command post which was also the location of the demolition firing box connected to the charges on the road bridge, gave the order to blow the bridge. Nothing happened, despite the frantic efforts of the sapper beside him, and the charges failed to explode. The reason for the failure has never been determined and thus must be put down to the fortunes of war.

The two days spent taking Nijmegen and its bridges meant that XXX Corps was now severely behind schedule, and the junior commanders, who had spearheaded the advance and were fully aware of the urgency to reach Arnhem and 1st Airborne Division, were anxious to continue immediately. Colonel Reuben Tucker, commander of the 504th Parachute Infantry Regiment which had suffered particularly heavy casualties, the 3rd Battalion having lost 134 men killed or wounded, therefore could scarcely contain his fury when he heard that the Grenadier and Irish Guards Groups had been ordered to halt for the night instead of pushing on over the last eleven miles to Arnhem.

The main problem facing the commander of the Guards Armoured Division, Major General Adair, was that his division was already fully committed. The majority of the infantry of the Grenadier and Irish Guards Groups were still clearing pockets of enemy in Nijmegen. Moreover, both infantry battalions had taken very heavy casualties. The 3rd Battalion Irish Guards had previously lost many men during the fighting in the Meuse–Escaut Canal bridgehead and had not received any replacements. More losses were incurred during the advance to

Nijmegen and by the time it crossed the bridge, the battalion's rifle companies were only five platoons strong, with only one surviving subaltern officer. Moreover, both the Grenadier and Irish Guards Groups were very low on ammunition and fuel, and due to frequent interdiction by the enemy of the sole route along which XXX Corps could resupply the division, it was taking time for the supply echelons to come forward to replenish the squadrons and companies.

At this stage, Adair had no reserve which could take over the advance. The Coldstream Guards Group of 32 Guards Brigade was deployed to the east, protecting the 82nd Airborne Division's right flank from counter-attacks from the Reichswald and continually moving to where the threat was greatest. The afternoon of 20 September saw the heaviest of these attacks, a main assault on Groesbeek, and two others thrusting north-west through Mook and south-west via Beek. The Welsh Guards Group meanwhile was still defending the vital bridge at Grave which, if recaptured by the Germans, would have caused severe disruption to XXX Corps' line of communications and supply, already under pressure from both flanks, and would have jeopardised the entire operation.

The requirement for the next stage of the advance was, in any case, for infantry and not for armour. The last eleven miles would continue to be along a single embanked road on both sides of which were woods and orchards providing excellent cover for enemy infantry and anti-tank guns. More infantry could have been provided by the formation following the Guards Armoured Division: the 43rd (Wessex) Infantry Division, commanded by Major General Ivo Thomas. Indeed, Lieutenant General Sir Brian Horrocks had decided already that it should move through and mount a divisional attack on Arnhem. Once again, however, the problems of using a single road were making themselves all too apparent: overcrowded, with stretches under constant enemy fire, it would take time for the 43rd's troops to make their way forward. One element of the division, however, was only a relatively short distance from Nijmegen. Although it had been delayed by enemy action at Zon, 130th Infantry Brigade had arrived just south of Grave by last light on 20 September. Instead of being ordered forward to relieve the Welsh Guards Group, or indeed to move on through Nijmegen to spearhead the advance to Arnhem, it was permitted to rest for the night.

Thus, while 1st Airborne Division was fighting for its life in Arnhem and Oosterbeek, XXX Corps' advance came to a halt.

In Arnhem, first light on 20 September had witnessed the resumption of heavy shelling of the positions held by 2nd Parachute Battalion. By this time most of the buildings occupied by the battalion had been destroyed, and thus Lieutenant Colonel Frost and his men had been forced to evacuate them and dig in around those that sheltered Headquarters 1st Parachute Brigade. Below ground, the cellars of the ruined buildings were crammed with the wounded who were tended by medical officers and orderlies working under virtually impossible conditions.

That afternoon, Frost was wounded in both legs by splinters from a mortar bomb and was evacuated to the battalion's Regimental Aid Post. Major Digby Tatham-Warter assumed command of 2nd Parachute Battalion while Major Freddie Gough took over command of the force at the bridge.

During the day, several attacks were launched by enemy infantry, supported by tanks and self-propelled guns, against a keypoint in the battalion's perimeter held by a platoon of A Company under Lieutenant Jack Grayburn. These had been beaten off despite the platoon suffering casualties. Although wounded in the shoulder, Grayburn had subsequently led a number of fighting patrols, one of which removed fuses from demolition charges which German sappers had been observed placing. Wounded again, Grayburn refused to leave his men or to desist from carrying the fight to the enemy. That evening, however, he was killed by fire from a tank at close range while standing in full view of the enemy, directing the withdrawal of the remnants of his platoon to the battalion's main defensive position. His great gallantry was later recognised by the award of a posthumous Victoria Cross.

During the evening the sole remaining undamaged building that housed the brigade headquarters was set ablaze several times, although the flames were extinguished on each occasion. The greatest concern was for the 200 or so wounded crammed into its cellars. Captain Jimmy Logan, 2nd Parachute Battalion's Regimental Medical Officer, told Lieutenant Colonel Frost that they would have to be evacuated and surrendered to the enemy, or they would perish. Having discussed the situation with Major Freddie Gough, and with the building catching fire again, Frost ordered him to move those troops still capable of fighting to new positions. The wounded remained behind in the cellars and just after last light were carried out and removed from the area by SS troops under a flag of truce.

During the two hours of the truce, further enemy reinforcements arrived in the form of troops of the 21st SS Panzer Grenadier Regiment. More were en route to Arnhem, including a battalion of heavy tanks. Meantime, orders had been given that the British paratroops at the bridge were to be annihilated by the following morning.

The battle was duly resumed as tanks, some Tigers among them, blasted the battalion's positions. By now the northern end of the bridge was no longer held and each man was down to only a few rounds of ammunition. At this point the brigade major, Major Tony Hibbert, issued orders that the remaining force was to break up into small groups and, at first light on the next day, infiltrate back to the buildings in the area of the bridge. In the event, this proved impossible and, to the best of his ability, Hibbert ordered those whom he could contact to withdraw westwards to Oosterbeek and divisional headquarters. Most of those who attempted to do so, however, were killed or wounded, the rest being taken prisoner.

By dawn on 22 September, only 150 men of 2nd Parachute Battalion were left. They fought back tenaciously as SS panzer grenadiers advanced once again to clear the area, which they only succeeded in doing when all the paratroops had been killed or wounded. By 9.00

a.m. the surviving members of the battalion and elements of other units of 1st Parachute Brigade had been overrun. Ordered to hold the bridge for two days, they had done so against overwhelming odds for three days and three nights.

Meantime, 4th Parachute Brigade had almost ceased to exist. At around 6.00 a.m. on 20 September, Brigadier John Hackett marched his heavily depleted battalions towards the divisional perimeter, led by the remnants of 156th Parachute Battalion. A Company, now only twenty-five-strong, came under fire from machine guns and self-propelled guns as it moved through the woods at Wolfheze. C Company, commanded by Major Geoffrey Powell, attempted a flanking attack but this failed and the company suffered heavy losses.

Realising that he must avoid any further major contact with the enemy, Hackett ordered 10th Parachute Battalion to take an alternative route to the east in an attempt to bypass the enemy while 156th Parachute Battalion acted as a rearguard, covering the brigade's rear as it withdrew. 10th Parachute Battalion, however, found itself having to fight its way through the woods. Eventually, having been ordered over the radio by Brigadier Hackett to 'pull the plug out', Lieutenant Colonel Ken Smyth and his men fixed bayonets and charged, battling their way through to the divisional perimeter which they reached at 1.00 p.m.. By then numbering only sixty all ranks, the remnants of 10th Parachute Battalion took up defensive positions in buildings by the crossroads in Oosterbeek.

The situation facing the remnants of Brigadier Hackett's 156th Parachute Battalion and the brigade headquarters was equally grim. Although hard pressed by enemy infantry and tanks, they launched counter-attacks on several occasions, driving the enemy back but suffering more casualties in the process. Taking cover in a hollow, they were attacked again but the enemy were driven off by Major Geoffrey Powell and the remnants of C Company who charged with the bayonet. By late afternoon, ammunition was running very low and further casualties had been sustained; 156th Parachute Battalion now numbered less than thirty men, and the brigade headquarters, including Hackett, only twelve. Among those killed that day was the commanding officer of the battalion, Lieutenant Colonel Sir Richard des Voeux.

Faced with increasingly overwhelming odds, Hackett realised that, rather than stay and be overrun, he and his men would have to break through the enemy to reach the divisional perimeter which lay approximately half a mile away. At 6.00 p.m., charging with fixed bayonets, they swept their German opponents aside and ran the few hundred yards to join the remainder of 1st Airborne Division.

The perimeter enclosed a horseshoe-shaped area centred on the Hartenstein Hotel, sheltering the divisional headquarters. Major General Roy Urquhart now divided it into eastern and western sectors, commanded by Brigadiers Hackett and Hicks respectively. The northern curved end was held by men of the 21st Independent Parachute Company and the 7th Battalion King's Own Scottish Borderers, while the eastern side was defended by the surviving members of 10th and 156th Parachute Battalions reinforced by some glider pilots and gunners of 1st Airlanding Light Regiment A. On the western side was the 1st Battalion The Border Regiment augmented by glider pilots, sappers, men of 1st Polish Independent Parachute Brigade's gliderborne element and members of other units. The southern end of the area was held by Lonsdale Force, comprising men of 1st, 3rd and 11th Parachute Battalions, 1st Battalion The Border Regiment, 2nd Battalion The South Staffordshire Regiment and divisional troops. Positioned at the base of this area was the gun line of 1st Airlanding Light Regiment RA.

As the battle continued, German reinforcements continued to pour into the area, among them an anti-aircraft artillery brigade of five battalions, the 171st Light Artillery and 191st Artillery Regiments, two SS batteries equipped with 320mm nebelwerfer multi-barrelled rocket launchers and the 9th Pioner-Lehr Battalion, an assault engineer unit equipped with flamethrowers and specially trained for fighting in urban areas. Others included a panzer grenadier battalion and several companies of Luftwaffe ground crew reformed as infantry.

The perimeter was kept under constant bombardment by mortars which at times reached a rate of fire of fifty bombs per minute. Added to this was the threat of snipers, although many of these themselves fell victim to the airborne troops who became adept at picking them off. On 21 September, the Germans attempted to break through the perimeter but were driven back by a bayonet charge by the 1st Battalion The Border Regiment. Much of the fighting took place at close quarters and in the weaker sectors enemy tanks and infantry, sometimes equipped with flamethrowers, infiltrated between individual positions where they inflicted casualties.

Conditions within the area were appalling, with water scarce and little or no food. All the buildings had been damaged, many having been demolished or burnt down. Slit trenches were dug in once-immaculate gardens and the local inhabitants crowded into cellars with the wounded whom they nursed to the best of their ability. Throughout the area, some of the dead lay unburied among shell craters, burned-out vehicles and the general flotsam of battle. In the Hotels Schoonoord, Vreewyck and Tafelberg, medical officers and orderlies worked tirelessly on an ever-increasing stream of wounded who at one point numbered almost 1,200.

Urquhart's hopes for reinforcement and resupply rested on the Heveadorp ferry, a cable-operated craft capable of carrying vehicles and personnel. On the night of 20 September, a patrol was despatched from the perimeter to secure the northern end of the ferry which was to be used to bring across men of 1st Polish Independent Parachute Brigade, due to drop south of the river at Driel, a village just south of the Lower Rhine, on the afternoon of 21 September. The patrol, however, was unable to locate the ferry in the darkness despite searching for a quarter of a mile up and downstream of the landing stage. It was assumed that the ferry had been sunk by artillery fire but it was eventually discovered by Dutch civilians washed up intact downstream near the Arnhem railway bridge. Its loss was a bitter blow as it removed the only effective means of bringing vehicles across the Lower Rhine.

The early afternoon of 21 September saw Major General Stanislaw Sosabowski's 1st Polish Independent Parachute Brigade Group taking off from England, having been delayed by heavy fog. Unfortunately, forty-one aircraft, carrying one of the brigade's 500-strong battalions, were forced to turn back because of bad weather. In addition, the Luftwaffe and flak units had been alerted to the columns of aircraft as they crossed the French coast near Dunkirk.

At 5.00 p.m. the aircraft approached the DZ at Driel but were attacked by two squadrons of Messchersmitt Bf 109s. At the same time, they encountered heavy flak which, together with the fighters, shot down thirteen C-47s. Sosabowski and his men jumped into a barrage of fire from the ground, suffering relatively light casualties on landing even though the DZ was under heavy fire from machine guns, mortars, rocket launchers, artillery and tanks. The 9th SS Panzer Division's reconnaissance battalion, which by this time had deployed near the village of Elden, also joined the fray with its half-track-mounted 20mm cannons. By the time Sosabowski and his men had fought their way to cover in the dykes and nearby embankments, before regrouping by last light, they numbered only some 750, including the wounded.

The appearance of Sosabowski's brigade heightened German fears of the road south of Arnhem being interdicted and the risk of the 10th SS Panzer Division, by this time heavily committed in Nijmegen, being cut off. The commander of II SS Panzer Corps, Lieutenant General Willi Bittrich, was so concerned at this new threat that he deployed an ad hoc battle group of five battalion-sized units under Obersturmbann-nführer Walter Harzer, commander of the 9th SS Panzer Division, to block any attempt by the Polish paratroops to advance east towards the road. Reinforced by Bittrich's reserve, comprising the 10th SS Panzer Division's reconnaissance battalion and an army panzer grenadier training and replacement battalion, Harzer deployed his force along the embankment running north from Nijmegen through the village of Elst across the river to Oosterbeek. That afternoon, he ordered one of his battalions to carry out a counter-attack through Elst against some of the leading elements of XXX Corps which by this time were beginning to appear from the south. On reaching the area south of the village, however, the battalion found the flat featureless terrain afforded no cover for further advance and withdrew into Elst itself.

At 9.00 p.m. on the night of 21 September, Captain Zwolanski, the Polish liaison officer attached to Headquarters 1st Airborne Division, succeeded in swimming the Lower Rhine and making his way to Sosabowski's headquarters, bringing news that rafts would be sent across the river later that night to ferry the brigade across. The Poles moved up to the southern bank of the river and awaited the rafts but none appeared. At 3.00 a.m. on 22 September, Sosabowski withdrew his men.

That morning, the GSO 1 Headquarters 1st Airborne Division, Lieutenant Colonel Charles McKenzie, and the Commander Royal Engineers, Lieutenant Colonel Eddie Myers, appeared at Sosabowski's headquarters, after crossing the river in an inflatable dinghy. Having arranged with him for some of his men to be ferried across that night in small rubber boats, they sent a signal to Headquarters XXX Corps asking for reinforcements and supplies.

To the south, 43rd (Wessex) Infantry Division was attempting to push on towards Arnhem, hindered by traffic jams in Nijmegen which it reached on the morning of 21 September and where it had been misrouted over the wrong bridge. So it was not until 9.30 a.m. that morning that it reached the village of Oosterhout, some seven miles south of Arnhem. That same day, however, the Germans captured a patrol and vehicle belonging to the division's reconnaissance unit and realised that an infantry, rather than an armoured, formation was now spearheading the British advance. Well aware that the terrain favoured infantry rather than armour, both Model and Bittrich agreed that 1st Airborne Division must be overrun before 43rd Infantry Division could link up with it. At the same time, every effort had to be made to halt the advance of XXX Corps.

That night, Colonel General Kurt Student, the commander of the First Parachute Army, acting on orders from Model, launched an attack on XXX Corps' line of communications at Veghel in a pincer movement by two battle groups from the east and west. Bittrich meanwhile received news that his II SS Panzer Corps would receive further reinforcements in the form of forty-five Tiger tanks of the 506th Panzer Battalion which would reach Arnhem on the morning of 24 September.

In Oosterbeek, 22 September witnessed further acts of immense gallantry as the battle continued with the defenders of the perimeter being subjected to an endless bombardment of mortar and shellfire. Sergeant Calloway of 3rd Parachute Battalion single-handedly charged a Tiger tank, immobilising it with a PIAT before it gunned him down. Major Robert Cain of the 2nd Battalion The South Staffordshire Regiment personally hunted down and knocked out six tanks and a number of self-propelled guns with a PIAT, later being awarded the Victoria Cross for this feat. Sergeant Baskeyfield, also of the South Staffordshires, engaged three tanks with his 6-pounder anti-tank gun. Having knocked out the leading vehicle with his first round, he badly damaged the second and was about to take on the third when his gun was hit and disabled. Moving to another gun, whose crew were dead, he continued to engage the remaining tank until he too was killed. He was subsequently awarded a posthumous Victoria Cross for his gallantry and self-sacrifice.

At 9.00 p.m. that night, men of 1st Polish Independent Parachute Brigade Group moved up to the southern bank of the Lower Rhine. Sappers on both banks had set up a hawser on pulleys with which to pull four inflatable dinghies and a number of improvised rafts back and forth across the river, ferrying across six men and a quantity of supplies at a time. All went well for a while until the sky was suddenly illuminated by parachute illuminating flares. Almost immediately, the crossing point came under heavy mortar fire which destroyed two of the dinghies. No sooner had the flares burned out than the crossing was resumed, Sosabowski's men suffering heavy casualties as the desperate attempt to ferry men across the river continued. Only fifty men and a limited quantity of supplies reached the northern bank.

Throughout Saturday 23 September, the hell in Oosterbeek persisted as the enemy launched a series of attacks at different points along the perimeter and bombarded the defenders with mortar and artillery fire. Overhead, the RAF continued its desperate attempts to drop supplies, some aircraft being shot down at almost point-blank range by flak. As they fought on against increasingly overwhelming odds, the surviving members of 1st Airborne Division hoped against hope that relief from XXX Corps would soon be forthcoming.

XXX Corps had meanwhile resumed its advance towards Arnhem at 12.30 p.m. on 21 September, the Guards Armoured Division once again leading the way with the Irish Guards Group as its spearhead. The forward squadron of the 2nd (Armoured) Battalion had travelled less than a mile, however, when all three Shermans of its leading troop were knocked out on rounding a bend in the road. Unable to move off the road, which ran along the top of an embankment flanked by deep ditches, the rest of the battalion was forced to a halt as the infantry of the 3rd Battalion dismounted and deployed to positions in the ditches, coming under mortar and shellfire which inflicted heavy casualties. Artillery support came from a medium battery but this proved inadequate, the situation being exacerbated by the inability of the RAF forward air controller to establish radio contact with the cab-rank of Typhoons on call.

The Welsh Guards Group, having been relieved at Grave and moved up to replace the Grenadier Guards Group, now advanced on another road to the east, the companies of the 1st Battalion riding on the tanks of the 2nd (Armoured) Battalion. No. 1 Squadron led the way and was soon heavily engaged, its leading troop knocking out three enemy tanks. Meanwhile, the Irish Guards Group had pushed forward to within striking distance of the station at Bemmel where it was joined twenty-four hours later by 69th Infantry Brigade which had been detached from 50th (Northumbrian) Infantry Division and sent forward.

43rd (Wessex) Infantry Division was advancing meantime to take over the lead from the Guards Armoured Division which would remain in its positions and protect the 43rd's right flank as it moved up to the west. Unfortunately, it was making slow progress and it was not until the early hours of 21 September that its leading element, 214th Infantry Brigade, commanded by Brigadier Hubert Essame, concentrated to the south of Nijmegen. On its arrival, the brigade received orders to press on immediately through the city and proceed west of the Guards Armoured Division via Oosterhout. It encountered difficulty in making its way through the city and thus its advance did not begin until 8.30 a.m. on 22 September.

Shortly after leaving the Nijmegen bridgehead and heading west, the leading unit of the brigade, the 7th Battalion Somerset Light Infantry, encountered stiff opposition from the area of Oosterhout which was held by an enemy battle group supported by tanks and self-propelled guns. Three attacks were mounted by the brigade, the last with all of 43rd Infantry Division's artillery in support, before it succeeded in punching a hole through the enemy line at 5.00 p.m. Thereafter, a mobile column, formed earlier in preparation for such an eventuality, was despatched by Brigadier Essame with orders to advance northwards with all speed to Driel to link up with 1st Polish Independent Parachute Brigade Group. It comprised the 5th Battalion Duke of Cornwall's Light Infantry, commanded by Lieutenant Colonel George Taylor, a machine-gun platoon of the 8th Battalion The Middlesex Regiment, a squadron of the 4th/7th Royal Dragoon Guards and two DUKW amphibious vehicles heavily laden with ammunition, medical stores and other supplies for 1st Airborne Division.

To the south, meanwhile, on the morning of 22 September, the Germans struck again at XXX Corps' line of communications which was still very exposed owing to the lack of progress by VIII and XII Corps whose leading elements had advanced no further than Eindhoven due to the difficult terrain and heavy fighting in their respective sectors.

At 9.00 a.m. an enemy battle group advanced through Erp and by 11.00 a.m. was in sight of Veghel and the village of Uden on the road to the north-east. As the tanks and panzer grenadiers of the 107th Panzer Brigade reached the road and headed left for Veghel, they encountered the leading company of the 506th Parachute Infantry Regiment as it arrived in Uden, the regiment having been despatched with all haste by Major General Maxwell Taylor on being alerted by the Dutch Resistance to this new threat. On the eastern outskirts of Veghel, meanwhile, the 2nd Battalion 501st Parachute Infantry Regiment was under pressure as it fought to halt the enemy advance from the direction of Erp.

To the west, another enemy battle group had reached Eerde, a short distance south-west of Veghel, at 11.00 a.m. and at 2.00 p.m. began shelling the bridge over the canal while continuing to advance up the road. At that juncture, a company of the 506th Parachute Infantry Regiment, supported by a squadron of the 44th Royal Tank Regiment, appeared and beat off the enemy. The Germans attempted to interdict the road farther south but were again thwarted, this time by two battalions of the 327th Glider Infantry Regiment. Meanwhile, the 2nd and 3rd Battalions 501st Parachute Infantry Regiment were heading for Veghel from Schijndel to reinforce the 1st Battalion. Heading south, they encountered the first enemy battle group, which soon found itself cut off.

The fighting around Veghel grew fierce during the day as the defenders beat off attacks on all sides. The town was held by six parachute and glider battalions of the 101st Airborne Division under Brigadier General Tony McAuliffe, commander of the division's artillery. In support were two squadrons of the 44th Royal Tank Regiment which formed part of an armoured brigade detached from 7th Armoured Division and sent forward to assist in countering the threat to XXX Corps' line of communications.

On hearing of the attack, Lieutenant General Horrocks despatched 32nd Guards Brigade to the 101st Airborne Division's assistance. The Grenadier Guards Group, which had swapped places with the Welsh Guards who now were part of 5th Guards Armoured Brigade following the taking of Nijmegen, led the advance south and reached Uden during mid-afternoon. Two miles south of the town a troop of the 2nd (Armoured) Battalion, sent forward to reconnoitre with a platoon of the 1st (Motor) Battalion, came under fire and its leading tank was knocked out.

Next morning, 23 September, an attack was launched on the enemy battle group astride the road. This was preceded by a heavy artillery concentration which proved so effective that the Germans withdrew to the east and at 3.00 p.m. the Grenadiers linked up with the 44th Royal Tank Regiment squadrons at Veghel.

The Coldstream Guards Group had followed the Grenadiers, its objectives being to clear Volkel, to the south-east of Uden, and an airfield there, then to head south to clear Erp and the surrounding area of any threat to the main road. During the morning of 23 September, the Coldstreamers attacked Volkel and a short but fierce battle ensued during which several tanks on both sides were knocked out and casualties inflicted. By early afternoon, Volkel and the surrounding area had been cleared of enemy.

That morning also saw Colonel Freiherr Friedrich von der Heydte's 6th Parachute Regiment advancing east towards the road south of Veghel with the aim of seizing the canal bridge and cutting the road. But his three battalions of ill-trained and inexperienced troops, very different to the fallschirmjäger who had taken part in the airborne actions at Eben Emael and Crete, soon came under fire from two battalions of the 501st Parachute Infantry Regiment. As the fighting escalated, casualties mounted on both sides, but by 1.00 p.m. the attack had failed and von der Heydte's men began to dig in.

An enemy battle group similarly failed in another attack on Veghel, breaking off contact at midday and withdrawing to an area just east of Gemert. During the afternoon, some of its units encountered the Coldstream Guards Group and one of the 44th Royal Tank Regiment squadrons north-east of Veghel. By this time, the enemy were facing a threat from the leading elements of VIII Corps which had crossed the Zuid Willems Vaart Canal on the previous day and were heading north towards Helmond. To the west, meanwhile, XII Corps' leading troops were advancing north-east of Eindhoven.

By 1.00 p.m. it had become apparent that the enemy's attempts to cut the road had lost momentum, and two battalions of the 506th Parachute Infantry Regiment were ordered to link up with the Grenadier Guards Group which by now was advancing south from Uden to Veghel. By 3.30 p.m. the road had been opened and vehicles were once more heading north towards Nijmegen in convoys of ten every half an hour. The enemy still posed a threat, however, occasionally shelling the road and firing on the convoys with panzerfausts and small arms.

On the morning of 24 September the Germans struck again, launching a strong attack at the small village of Koevering, on the road just north of Saint Oedenrode, and at Eerde. This was carried out by a battle group of four understrength units, comprising the three battalions of von der Heydte's 6th Parachute Regiment and a fourth ad hoc battalion, commanded by a veteran fallschirmjäger officer, Major Hans Jungwirth, supported by the Jagdpanther tank destroyers of a company of the 559th Panzerjäger Battalion.

The attack began at 9.00 a.m. and about an hour later von der Heydte's three battalions, supported by artillery, overran the 1st Battalion 501st Parachute Infantry Regiment's positions in Eerde. One of the 44th Royal Tank Regiment's squadrons appeared at that point and was engaged by the Jagdpanthers which knocked out three of its tanks. The 501st then counter-attacked and fierce fighting ensued at close quarters. Meanwhile, two of the Jagdpanthers made their way on to the road where they caused mayhem; soft-skinned vehicles and a troop of tanks fell victim to their 88mm guns, bursting into flames and blocking the road as they were abandoned by their crews. Traffic came to a halt for miles to the rear, causing chaos.

At Koevering, meanwhile, Major Jungwirth's battalion had destroyed fifty vehicles that it found parked on the outskirts of the village. Its advance was halted, however, by two companies of the 502nd

Parachute Infantry Regiment which established blocking positions astride the road. Despite heavy artillery fire, one of von der Heydte's battalions reinforced Jungwirth's force during the night but American counter-attacks were not long in coming. The 506th Parachute Infantry Regiment, supported by a squadron of tanks, attacked from the north-east while a battalion of the 502nd, supported by a brigade of the 50th (Northumbrian) Infantry Division, attacked from the direction of Saint Oedenrode. Although almost surrounded, Jungwirth maintained his grip on the road, and it was not until the evening of 25 September, by which time he was at risk of being overrun, that he was ordered to withdraw. Under cover of darkness, his battalion moved off north-west under heavy fire from artillery and tanks, and by mid-morning on 26 September had reached an area south of Schijndel, having suffered severe casualties en route.

The enemy attacks blocked XXX Corps' line of communications for two days, causing severe congestion frther south, preventing sorely needed supplies from being transported forward and forcing troops intended to link up with 1st Airborne Division to be diverted south to counter the attacks on the road.

The leading elements of XXX Corps, meanwhile, were still battling their way forward against very stiff opposition. The Guards Armoured Division's Irish and Welsh Guards Groups, supported by 69th Infantry Brigade, were still trying to clear the enemy from the village of Bemmel while 129th and 214th Infantry Brigades were having a very tough fight at Elst where elements of an enemy battle group were resisting all attempts to dislodge them. By now, 130th Infantry Brigade had succeeded in reaching Driel and linking up with 1st Polish Independent Parachute Brigade Group.

In Oosterbeek the remnants of 1st Airborne Division were still putting up a fierce resistance while German artillery, comprising over 100 guns plus heavy and medium mortars, kept up an unceasing bombardment. At the same time, further reinforcements continued to pour into Arnhem and Oosterbeek as Field Marshal Model's orders to crush the British paratroops were put into effect. Among them was a company of the 506th Panzer Battalion whose fifteen Tiger tanks arrived on the morning of 24 September, the rest of the battalion having been sent to Elst to reinforce 10th SS Panzer Division in its attempts to stem the advance of the Guards Armoured and 43rd Infantry Divisions.

By now, however, artillery support from XXX Corps was helping to alleviate the pressure on the perimeter. On the morning of 21 September, radio contact had been established between the Commander Royal Artillery 1st Airborne Division, Lieutenant Colonel Robert Loder-Symonds, and 64th Medium Regiment RA which was now within range to provide support with its 5.5 inch and 7.2 inch howitzers. Thereafter, assistance had become available from two of 43rd Infantry Division's field regiments and a battery of 7th Medium Regiment RA. Throughout the battle, too, the three batteries of 1st Airlanding Light Regiment RA never failed to answer calls for support while, in the best traditions of the Royal Artillery, the regiment's FOO parties were located with the forwardmost elements of the division. Moreover, improvement in the weather ensured that close air support, notably absent so far, was also available, with RAF Typhoons now attacking enemy armour as well as artillery and mortar positions.

Nevertheless, the never-ending bombardment of the perimeter was claiming an increasing number of casualties. At 9.30 a.m. on Sunday 24 September, Colonel Graeme Warrack, the Assistant Director Medical Services 1st Airborne Division, informed Major General Roy Urquhart that he wished to arrange a cease-fire with the Germans to evacuate all the wounded. Urquhart agreed and the truce was arranged via the senior German medical officer at the dressing station in the Hotel Schoonoord, which was now manned by British and German medical staff.

The truce came into effect at 3.00 p.m. that afternoon and the evacuation began. An unearthly hush settled over the area as all firing ceased and during the following two hours 250 wounded were evacuated in convoys of vehicles while a further 200 walking wounded were led out of the area to the Saint Elisabeth's Hospital in Arnhem. The ceasefire ended at 5 p.m. and the battle was resumed in earnest with the divisional area once again being subjected to a constant bombardment by artillery and mortars.

On the afternoon of the following day, 25 September, the enemy mounted a strong attack on the eastern perimeter and managed to break through the line held by the 2nd Battalion The South Staffordshire Regiment and Lonsdale Force, subsequently reaching the gun line of 1st Airlanding Light Regiment RA whose gunners were engaging the enemy over open sights at a range of fifty yards. Indeed, the divisional area was almost cut in two as the enemy reached a point some 500 yards to the rear of the positions in the western sector. Fortunately, help was at hand in the form of artillery support from XXX Corps which broke up the attack and forced the enemy to retreat.

So dire was 1st Airborne Division's predicament that consideration was now being given to its withdrawal. Accounts differ as to when and by whom the decision to withdraw was taken. During the afternoon of 24 September, a conference was held at Saint Oedenrode, attended by the commander of Second British Army, Lieutenant General Sir Miles Dempsey, Lieutenant General 'Boy' Browning and Lieutenant General Sir Brian Horrocks. The latter had already given orders for a crossing of the Lower Rhine opposite 1st Airborne Division's perimeter by a battalion of 130th Infantry Brigade and elements of 1st Polish Independent Parachute Brigade Group, taking with them the maximum possible amount of ammunition and other stores. 43rd Infantry Division would meanwhile cross farther to the west and carry out a flanking attack into the rear of the enemy forces forming the western side of the 'box'. Browning, however, was of the opinion that 1st Airborne Division should be pulled out and had expressed doubts to Dempsey about Horrocks's plan.

Whatever the truth about the decision to withdraw, in the early hours of 25 September some 400 men of the 4th Battalion The Dorset Regiment, commanded by Lieutenant Colonel Gerald Tilly, prepared to

1st Airborne Division perimeter, Oosterbeek, 25 September 1944

Limits of perimeter

Divisional Headquarters

1st Airlanding Brigade H.Q.

4th Parachute Brigade H.Q.

Hotel Vreek

Hotel Schoonord

Hotel Tafelberg

Oosterbeek Laag Church

Gas works

LOWER RHINE

0 ———————— 1 mile
0 ———————— 1.5 km

Approximate locations of troops

1 + 2.	B & D Companies 1st Border	14.	21 Ind Para Coy and 10th Para Bn
3.	2nd S. Staffs	15.	Glider pilots
4.	Glider pilots	16.	Div troops
5.	Poles	17.	4th Bde HQ Troops
6.	C Coy 1st Border	18.	RASC
7.	A Coy 1st Border	19.	1st Aldg Light Regt RA, HQ
8.	Glider pilots	20.	2nd S. Staffs
9 +10.	7th KOSB	21.	Lonsdale Force
11.	Royal Engineers	22.	Glider pilots
12.	1st Abn Recce Sqn	23.	2nd S. Staffs
13.	Poles, glider pilots and 156th Para Bn		

cross the Lower Rhine in assault boats. Setting off at just after 2.00 a.m., under covering fire from the 5th Battalion and supporting artillery, the Dorsets encountered heavy machine-gun and mortar fire from an alert enemy. Several boats were hit while others were swept away downstream by the strong current. Despite these setbacks the operation continued and by first light 239 men had reached the far bank. Most of them, however, landed in small groups out of contact with one another, many subsequently being killed, wounded or captured outside the base line of 1st Airborne Division's perimeter. Only a small number succeeded in reaching the hard-pressed airborne troops; 140 of the 400 or so who crossed the river were captured, among them the commanding officer, Lieutenant Colonel Tilly.

As the Dorsets were struggling to gain a foothold on the far bank, Lieutenant Colonel Eddie Myers, the Commander Royal Engineers 1st Airborne Division, crossed farther upstream and made his way back to the divisional headquarters. He was carrying two letters addressed to Urquhart from Browning and Major General Ivo Thomas, the commander of 43rd Infantry Division. Thomas' letter informed him that plans to establish a bridgehead at Arnhem had been abandoned and that 1st Airborne Division would be withdrawn. Shortly afterwards, Urquhart made contact with Thomas by radio and informed him that the withdrawal had to take place that night.

It began at 9.45 p.m. Three-quarters of an hour earlier, XXX Corps' artillery had opened fire, bringing down a massive barrage which rained on the enemy positions and would continue to do so until 8.00 a.m. the following morning. To the west of the perimeter, units of 130th Infantry Brigade were carrying out a diversionary operation while Second British Army's artillery was firing a barrage as part of another diversion.

As part of a plan to deceive the enemy that nothing untoward was taking place, groups of men, including those wounded who could still use their weapons, kept up a show of force by firing from different positions while the main body of the division began to withdraw under cover of darkness. At the same time, radio transmissions were maintained as normal while the guns of 1st Airlanding Light Regiment RA continued firing. Medical officers and orderlies remained with the seriously wounded while the withdrawal took place, those in the north of the perimeter moving down the eastern and western flanks towards the river where glider pilots acted as a human chain along the escape route which was marked at intervals by strips of white tape. The night was dark and the weather bad, the strong winds and heavy rain all helping to conceal the survivors of 1st Airborne Division as they made their way to the river and embarked in assault boats manned by sappers. The first boats headed south across the Lower Rhine at 10.00 p.m.

At this point the enemy were wholly unaware that a withdrawal was in progress. Those airborne troops encountered in the darkness were presumed to be members of patrols or taking part in counter-attacks, and even when the boats were spotted it was assumed that further attempts were being made to reinforce 1st Airborne Division. Artillery and mortar fire was brought to bear and within an hour fifty per cent of the boats had been sunk. Nevertheless, the operation continued and by 5.50 a.m. on 26 September, when it ceased, 2,398 men had been evacuated – these comprising 1,741 officers and men of 1st Airborne Division, 160 of 1st Polish Independent Parachute Brigade Group, 420 glider pilots and seventy-five officers and men of the 4th Battalion The Dorset Regiment. Others had swum across but 300 men were left on the northern side of the river.

First light saw the enemy advancing on all three sides but it was not until mid-morning that they approached the now-abandoned perimeter where, even then, they encountered small pockets of resistance. On reaching the Hartenstein Hotel they found the positions deserted except for corpses. On the hotel's tennis courts, they discovered some of their number who had been taken prisoner earlier and thereafter guarded by men of the 1st Airborne Division Provost Company until these slipped away at 2.30 a.m. with the last of those withdrawing to the river.

It was only at this stage that the Germans realised their quarry had flown. There was considerable relief that the fighting was over at last as their own losses had been very heavy during the ten days of the battle. The majority of German units involved in the battle of Arnhem and Oosterbeek had lost on average fifty per cent of their strengths; in one or two instances, losses were as high as eighty or ninety per cent, with one unit numbering only seven men by the end of the battle. The cost of victory had been very high indeed.

By midday on 26 September the exhausted but still unbowed survivors of 1st Airborne Division had been moved to Nijmegen, where they met the division's administrative 'tail' which had landed by sea and travelled overland. Four days later, Major General Roy Urquhart and his men returned to England, leaving behind them 7,212 of their number killed, wounded, captured or missing.

The reasons for the failure of Market Garden are manifold, but there is insufficient space available here to provide anything more than a summary of the principal causes. Firstly, the plan itself was flawed, depending for success on the ability of the ground forces, namely XXX Corps, to link up with 1st Airborne Division. These, however, were expected to advance along a single axis consisting of a road running through terrain that favoured the enemy, was unsuitable for armour and featured major water obstacles. Moreover, that same road was XXX Corps' sole line of communications and was highly vulnerable to interdiction by the enemy – as proved the case. The plan also was highly inflexible due to its very tight time schedule; when problems arose in the early stages and XXX Corps' advance fell behind schedule, the entire operation was thrown into jeopardy.

Disregard of available intelligence about enemy forces in the area of Arnhem played a major part in causing the debacle that all but annihilated 1st Airborne Division. Information was available from Ultra and other sources but was ignored, particularly by Montgomery and Browning, who were dismissive of it. It is true that the 9th and 10th SS Panzer Divisions had suffered heavily during the fighting in Normandy and thereafter during the withdrawal through northern France and Belgium, but their remaining troops were well trained, very experienced and still possessed sufficient firepower to cause major problems for 1st Airborne Division. Moreover, Allied intelligence assessments during the build-up to Market Garden concentrated on those enemy forces in Holland, yet apparently neglected to consider the fact that Germans possessed resources in Germany which they were able to despatch rapidly as reinforcements. Prior to the start of its advance, XXX Corps was given no intelligence about the enemy assembling to its front. This was later questioned by Lieutenant General Sir Brian Horrocks who believed that it was due to determination at high level to commit First Allied Airborne Army to battle in an operation intended to finish the war before the end of 1944.

Another factor was the serious underestimation of the Germans and their fighting state; this stemmed from the degree of success following the breakout from Normandy and the advance through France which may have led to a feeling of overconfidence at senior levels. The commanders of the enemy forces in Holland were some of Germany's most able officers, many of them veterans of campaigns in Europe, Russia and North Africa: Model, Student, Bittrich and von der Heydte to name just four. They were served at corps, divisional and regimental level by staffs who were well trained and experienced and, when required, capable of responding swiftly to a crisis.

Inaccurate air intelligence about enemy flak defences in the area of Arnhem and south of the Lower Rhine also played its part, resulting in the RAF's refusal to allow Major General Roy Urquhart to site his DZs and LZs nearer his main objectives, thus giving the Germans time to react and establish a line to block the advance of the leading elements of the division. This information, proved incorrect by air photographic reconnaissance on 19 September, led to Urquhart discarding his idea for a gliderborne *coup de main* attack on the bridge at the start of the operation along the lines of that carried out successfully on the Orne bridge in Normandy.

The decision by the commander of the 9th Troop Carrier Command, Major General Paul Williams, that his crews would not fly more than one sortie on the first day of Market Garden also proved fatal for the operation, the critical element of surprise being lost when a large part of 1st Airborne Division had yet to arrive.

The problems caused by delivery in three lifts were compounded for all three airborne divisions by the bad weather that delayed the arrival of the second and third lifts. 1st Polish Independent Parachute Brigade Group was not dropped until the fifth day of the operation while the 82nd Airborne Division had to wait until the seventh for its sorely needed 325th Glider Infantry Regiment and remaining elements of its supporting arms. The 101st Airborne Division was similarly affected, the final elements of the 327th Glider Infantry Regiment and 907th Glider Field Artillery Battalion not arriving until the seventh day.

Bad weather was also a major factor in preventing close air support being available. It had been laid down by Headquarters First Allied Airborne Army that all close air support operations by 2nd Allied Tactical Air Force would be suspended while transport aircraft were dropping troops or carrying out resupply missions. When combined with the arrival of bad weather over airfields in England and target areas in Holland, the effect of the First Allied Airborne Army directive was such that there were many occasions when Typhoon fighter-bombers of 83 Group RAF could not take off to support the three airborne divisions.

The crucial problem facing 1st Airborne Division almost immediately after it landed was the almost total failure of radio communications. Generally speaking, the radios with which the division was equipped were unsuitable for use by airborne forces, possessing inadequate power to provide any degree of reliability. This had been known beforehand and vociferous complaints made by the commanding officer of 1st Airborne Divisional Signals, Lieutenant Colonel Tom Stephenson. Despite assurances that suitable sets would be forthcoming, nothing had been produced.

In the past, the finger of blame has been pointed at XXX Corps which was accused of displaying a lack of urgency. In fact, the leading element in particular, the Guards Armoured Division, was only too well aware of the importance of reaching Arnhem in two days but, as recounted in this chapter, it was hindered from the very start by unsuitable terrain and a single axis of advance, a determined enemy who put up a very stiff resistance and inflicted heavy casualties, and a shortage of fuel and ammunition.

In the final analysis, Market Garden failed due to a combination of flawed planning, errors, oversights and shortcomings, all at a very heavy cost: the destruction of Arnhem and Oosterbeek with heavy casualties among the local population, the near-annihilation of 1st Airborne Division and a total of over 16,000 casualties sustained by the four corps that took part. In spite of all the factors that militated against it, however, those who participated in the operation very nearly achieved success, and thus it was with great pride that the survivors were able to say 'I fought at Arnhem'.

CHAPTER THIRTEEN

THE ARDENNES AND THE RHINE CROSSING, 1944–5

Following the debacle at Arnhem, the Allies continued their advance through Holland, encountering continued stiff opposition from the German First Parachute Army, now commanded by General Alfred Schlemm, a veteran of Crete, the Eastern Front, Italy and bitter combat in the Reichswald, and the Twenty Fifth Army. Along with XXX Corps, the First Canadian Army was opposed by the 2nd, 6th, 7th and 8th Parachute Divisions which inflicted 13,000 casualties on the Canadians alone during fighting that lasted until 8 November. Meanwhile, Field Marshal Sir Bernard Montgomery's 21st Army Group was having to turn its attention to clearing the remaining enemy forces from the area of the Scheldt in order to open up the sorely needed port of Antwerp.

Early November saw Lieutenant General Omar Bradley's US 12th Army Group launch an attack by the US First, Third and Ninth Armies in an attempt to thrust into Germany via Cologne and Mainz. Lieutenant General George S. Patton's US Third Army led the way on 8 November and advanced forty miles in three weeks, but encountered increasingly stubborn opposition from the Germans, who inflicted 27,000 casualties, before it was halted by the Siegfried Line.

The US First and Ninth Armies, commanded by Lieutenant

Generals Courtney H. Hodges and William H. Simpson respectively, began their advances on 16 November and also met very stiff resistance. Although both succeeded in penetrating the Siegfried Line and advancing to the River Roer, they suffered 35,000 losses. The total casualties incurred by the US 12th Army Group amounted to 62,000 as the result of enemy action while a further 70,000 men fell victim to exposure, disease and illness caused by the extreme cold and heavy rain.

Mid-December found the front in an apparent state of stalemate with the Allies drawn up north to south; 21st Army Group, still comprising First Canadian and Second British Armies, was on the left, and US 12th Army Group, consisting of the US First, Third and Ninth Armies, on the right. One particular sector, seventy-five miles in width and held by Major General Troy H. Middleton's US VIII Corps, ran through the heavily forested and mountainous terrain of the Ardennes. And it was here on 16 December that the Germans launched a strong counter-attack in the form of Operation Autumn Mist.

Before first light, fourteen German infantry divisions moved stealthily through the Eifel forests, the sounds of their advance blanketed by the roar of V-1 pilotless aircraft launched against the Belgian cities of Liège and Antwerp. At 5.30 a.m., 2,000 guns opened fire on American positions between Monschau and Echternach, laying down a creeping barrage behind which infantry advanced with the support of five panzer divisions.

The German forces comprised the Fifth Panzer Army under General Hasso von Manteuffel; the Sixth Panzer Army commanded by SS-Oberstgruppenführer Josef 'Sepp' Dietrich; and the Seventh Army under General Erich Brandenberger. The plan was for the Sixth Panzer Army, which consisted of four SS panzer, one parachute and four infantry divisions, to advance westwards and head via Bütgenbach and Malmédy for the River Meuse, crossing it at Liège and Huy before swinging north-west and encircling Antwerp.

Preceding the Sixth Panzer Army would be a 1,200-strong airborne

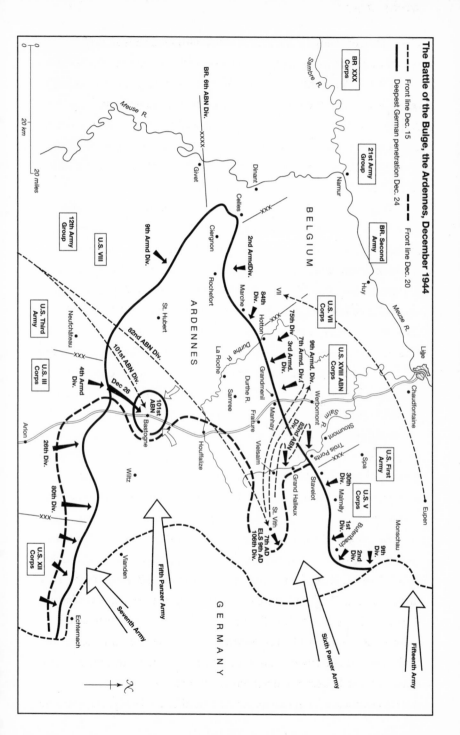

The Battle of the Bulge, the Ardennes, December 1944

- - - - Front line Dec. 15
- - - - Deepest German penetration Dec. 24
────── Front line Dec. 20

battle group under Lieutenant Colonel Freiherr Friedrich von der Heydte, the former commanding officer of the 1st Battalion 3rd Parachute Regiment and the 6th Parachute Regiment, now commanding the First Parachute Army's training centre at Aalten. Comprising a 1,200-strong composite battalion made up of 100-strong detachments drawn from each of the parachute battalions in First Parachute Army, it would be dropped in the area of Monschau ahead of Dietrich's force.

The Fifth Panzer Army, consisting of three panzer divisions, a parachute division and an infantry division, meanwhile would advance on Dietrich's left and, by way of Saint Vith, Houffalize and Bastogne, cross the Meuse at Namur before heading north-west for Brussels. The flanks of this assault would be protected by the Fifteenth Army on the right and Seventh Army on the left, the latter to cross the Meuse between Vianden and Echternach, thereafter providing a flank guard to the north of Luxembourg and Arlon. The Germans' aim was to disrupt the build-up of Allied forces in preparation for the invasion of Germany and at the same time allow themselves a breathing space to regroup and re-equip their own forces for the defence of the Fatherland.

Once again, the Germans' capability to recover had taken the Allies completely by surprise. In the US VIII Corps area the 28th Infantry Division, holding a front some thirty miles wide, was attacked and rapidly overrun by five enemy divisions while two regiments of the 106th Infantry Division were swiftly outflanked.

Operation Stösser, the airborne drop in advance of Sixth Panzer Army, took place on the night of 16 December. General Kurt Student, hitherto the commander of the First Parachute Army and now commanding Army Group H, had instructed the commanding officers of all battalions in the First Parachute Army to send a hundred of their best men to von der Heydte who was forming his new composite unit into four rifle companies, a heavy weapons' support company, an intelligence platoon and a pioneer platoon. With the exception of von der Heydte's old unit, the 6th Parachute Regiment, the majority, however, failed to comply, sending men of poor quality, some 150 of whom he rejected and returned to their units. At this late stage in the war, there were only a small number of men in the fallschirmjäger units who had undergone parachute training and fewer still who were veterans of airborne operations.

Under command of the Sixth Panzer Army and reporting direct to SS-Oberstgruppenführer Dietrich himself, Colonel von der Heydte and his men were to drop ahead of the Sixth Panzer Army and secure a key road junction from which roads led to Verviers, Eupen and Malmédy and through which American reinforcements would move up en route to the front. They were then to hold it until such time as the leading element of Dietrich's forces, the SS Division Hitler Jugend, linked up with them. If, for whatever reason, the operation was delayed, von der Heydte's secondary mission was to seize the bridges across the River Amblève and hold them until the leading elements of the Sixth Panzer Army arrived. Artillery support would be available and an FOO from the 12th SS Panzer Division would accompany von der Heydte. He himself felt little enthusiasm for the operation; indeed, his private opinion was that a night drop by a largely inexperienced unit, in bad weather over enemy-held terrain, was insane.

The drop was due to take place at 4.30 a.m. on the morning of 16 December but the battle group was delayed in reaching its mounting airfields at Lippspringe and Padeborn, and the operation had to be postponed until the following night. With German radio intercepts confirming that American reinforcements were being despatched rapidly to the front, von der Heydte's mission was still to take the road junction and prevent US forces from passing through.

At just after midnight on the night of 16/17 December, he and his men took off from the two airfields in 112 Ju-52 transports. From the start the flight was difficult, as the aircraft encountered strong headwinds with which the inexperienced pilots, all the Luftwaffe could produce for the operation, could hardly cope. Pathfinder aircraft were due to drop incendiary bombs one mile apart as markers on the DZ which was situated approximately seven miles to the north of Malmédy in the Monte Rigi area of the Eifel mountains. These, however, joined the formation late, causing confusion among the other aircraft.

Shortly after crossing the Allied front line, the formations of Ju-52s came under anti-aircraft fire which dispersed some of them, causing their pilots to stray several miles off course and resulting in several sticks being dropped considerable distances from the DZ, some even finding themselves landing in Holland. Only thirty-five aircraft reached the DZ and dropped their sticks accurately, von der Heydte and his men jumping into winds of over thirty knots which scattered them over a wide area around the DZ.

Von der Heydte, who had jumped with a badly wounded arm and was using a Russian parachute equipped with a triangular canopy, was knocked unconscious on landing. Having recovered his senses, he set about assembling his force which by first light on 17 December numbered only 125 men, several of whom were injured. The radios dropped with the force had been damaged and were inoperable, thus cutting the force off from the Sixth Panzer Army and its supporting artillery, and most of the heavy weapons containers had been lost.

Von der Heydte despatched patrols to make contact with the Sixth Panzer Army but most of these never returned; those that did so had failed to get through the Allied lines. During the morning of 17 December, he moved his small force to a position in the area of the road junction from which he and his men watched an apparently unending stream of US reinforcements moving up to the front. It was only too evident that any attempt to take the junction was out of the question and von der Heydte therefore led his men away back into the forests. That afternoon, they met another 150 men of the battalion under one of the rifle company commanders, Lieutenant Bruno von Kayser.

By this time, the Allies had become aware that the Germans had dropped a force behind their lines. Reports indicated that this could be up to a division in strength and thus caused a considerable amount of concern, resulting in units being diverted from the front to provide security in rear areas rather than being committed to combat.

Attempts were made by the Luftwaffe to resupply von der Heydte and his men but only a few containers were recovered. With a large number of his men injured and approaching exhaustion, with little hope of achieving either of his missions, and with American troops rapidly closing in on all sides, von der Heydte decided to evacuate his injured and sick men by sending them in a group back towards the German lines while he and the rest tried to break out. The attempt failed, however, and he and his men incurred heavy casualties.

On 21 December, von der Heydte broke his remaining force up into small groups of two to three men, sending them off towards the German lines in the hope that they would have a better chance of getting through. Accompanied by his adjutant and orderly, he himself set off towards Monschau, one of the Sixth Panzer Army's initial objectives, in the belief that it would be in German hands. By this time, he was in considerable pain from his broken left forearm and the injury to his right arm. On 23 December, having ordered his two companions to leave him, he approached the outskirts of the town alone and took shelter in a house where he surrendered to members of a US engineer battalion on the following day. Thus ended ignominiously the last German airborne operation of the Second World War.

Meanwhile, the Allies had been rushing forward reinforcements in haste. Among these was XVIII Corps, which, in addition to the 82nd and 101st Airborne Divisions, hitherto having formed the SHAEF reserve, had the 517th Parachute Infantry Regiment available to it, along with the 509th and 551st Parachute Infantry Battalions and the 460th and 463rd Parachute Field Artillery Battalions. In addition, Major General William 'Bud' Miley's 17th Airborne Division, which in late August had arrived in Britain from the United States to join XVIII Airborne Corps, was flown to Belgium and then moved up to the front with haste.

Two days later, the 82nd Airborne Division launched a counter-attack in the area of Vielsalm and Saint Vith, the 504th Parachute Infantry Regiment successfully taking Monceau, forcing the Germans to draw back across the River Amblève on the following day. On 22 December, however, the 505th Parachute Infantry Regiment came under heavy attack in the Trois Ponts area and by 24 December the 82nd had lost Manhay. Christmas Day found the division retreating from the Vielsalm salient prior to attacking north-east of Bra three days later and reaching Salm by 4 January 1945. On 7 January, the 504th and 508th Parachute Infantry Regiments mounted an attack in the area of Thier du Mont, the latter suffering heavy casualties before being withdrawn into reserve until 21 January, when it relieved elements of the 2nd Infantry Division. On 7 February, the 82nd Airborne Division attacked the town of Bergstein, on the River Roer, crossing it on 17 February.

The 101st Airborne Division, temporarily commanded by Brigadier Anthony C. McAuliffe in the absence on leave of Major General Maxwell Taylor, had meanwhile been deployed to Bastogne. Situated at the centre of the main highways traversing the southern sector of the Ardennes, the city was vital to the Germans in their advance west. It was also the location of the sorely pressed US VIII Corps, commanded by Major General Troy Middleton, which had been hit hard by the Germans and was unable to stem their advance. Reinforcements had been requested from SHAEF by the commander of the US First Army, Lieutenant General Courtney H. Hodges, but the only ones in reserve were the 82nd and 101st Airborne Divisions, both of which were released to him, the 101st being despatched to Bastogne.

Travelling by road, the division arrived in the city on 18 December where it was augmented by units of the 9th and 10th Armoured Divisions, both of which had suffered heavily during the German offensive, a tank destroyer battalion, two battalions of field artillery and a number of other miscellaneous units. On the morning of the following day, the 501st Parachute Infantry Regiment advanced eastwards in an attempt to link up with other US forces protecting the approaches to the city but was halted by stiff opposition in the area of Neffe. The Germans thereafter mounted a number of strong attacks to the east of Bastogne and by 20 December all US units had pulled back to a defensive perimeter outside the city, Brigadier General McAuliffe reinforcing his defences to the north and east as the Germans continued their advance west. The 502nd Parachute Infantry Regiment took up positions in the north, in the area of Longchamps, while the 506th did likewise between Foy and the Bourcy–Bastogne railway line. The 501st established itself on the 506th's right, facing east, with its southern flank around Neffe, while the 2nd Battalion 327th Glider Infantry Regiment dug in at Marvie.

The first of the German assaults on Bastogne fell on elements of the 501st Parachute Infantry Regiment at Neffe but they stood firm, beating off a number of attacks before the enemy switched to another sector to the south. On 21 December the enemy probed the 327th Glider Infantry Regiment's defences and launched an attack which succeeded in penetrating them before being beaten back by a counterattack. On the following day, the Germans issued an ultimatum, demanding the city's surrender within two hours or it would face annihilation. Brigadier General McAuliffe's response was one word, 'Nuts!', thereafter recorded for posterity in the annals of military history.

The weather, which hitherto had been appalling, improved considerably on 23 December, and with it came much needed air support. That same day, however, witnessed the enemy attacking the western area of the defensive perimeter and on Christmas Day penetrating the line around Hemroulle. Having broken through, the Germans split into two columns, the first turning right towards Hemroulle, which was defended by elements of the 10th Armoured Division and the tank destroyer battalion, and the second swinging left for Champs, which was held by the 502nd Parachute Infantry Regiment. Both columns, however, were halted and virtually annihilated shortly afterwards.

On 26 December, the Germans mounted a final attack to overrun

Bastogne and its defenders but this was broken up by heavy artillery support. That afternoon, the US 4th Armoured Division succeeded in breaking through from the south to reach the beleaguered city. The enemy attempted to close the breach in their lines but it was too late, the siege had been broken.

The defence of Bastogne and its denial to the enemy had played a considerable part in slowing down the German offensive, while also forcing the enemy to divert resources badly needed elsewhere. During the following weeks, the 101st Airborne Division helped to clear remaining enemy forces from the area of the city before moving on 18 January to the region of Alsace where, as part of US Seventh Army, it was employed in the defensive role until late February. It then reverted to under command of First Allied Airborne Army and returned to its base at Mourmelon in Belgium.

The 17th Airborne Division meanwhile had arrived in France from Britain, being landed at Rheims and thereafter travelling by road to Mourmelon. On 25 December, having assumed responsibility for the defence of the sector along the Meuse from Givet to Verdun, the division moved to Neufchâteau in Belgium before marching through deep snow to Morhet where it relieved the 28th Infantry Division on 3 January 1945.

The division received its baptism of fire during the following six days, 4–9 January, in what became known as the Battle of Dead Man's Ridge. It captured several small towns before entering Flamierge on 7 January, but was forced to withdraw in the face of enemy counter-attacks. Heavy pressure exerted by the division, combined with aggressive patrolling, resulted in the enemy subsequently withdrawing to the River Our.

On 18 January, the 17th Airborne Division relieved the 11th Armoured Division at Houffalize, thereafter taking part in an operation to push remaining enemy forces back from the area dubbed the 'Bulge' before taking the towns of Wattermal and Espeler on 26 January. Under command of US III Corps, the division then swung in the direction of

Luxembourg, capturing Eschweiler and Clervaux before clearing enemy forces from the west bank of the Our. Patrols were despatched across the river to probe the Siegfried Line prior to the division establishing a small bridgehead just south of Clervaux, in Luxembourg.

On 6 February, the division received a warning order indicating the likelihood of its being committed to a major operation, around the end of March or beginning of April, to force a crossing of the Rhine. Four days later, it was relieved by 11th Armoured Division and began moving by road and rail to the area of Châlons-sur-Marne, in France.

Meanwhile, 22 December had seen the deployment of the British 6th Airborne Division, now commanded by Major General Eric Bols, which was moved by sea and road from Britain to the Ardennes, concentrating between Dinant and Namur on 26 December. Three days later, it advanced against the tip of the German salient with 3rd Parachute Brigade occupying the area of Rochefort while 5th Parachute Brigade, on the right of the division, advanced towards Grupont.

On 3 January 1945, an attack was mounted on the strongly held village of Bure by 13th Parachute Battalion which advanced over open ground under very heavy machine-gun fire. The battalion nevertheless succeeded in reaching the town and bitter fighting at close quarters ensued, the battle lasting until 9.00 p.m. on the night of 5 January, by which time the battalion had suffered 189 casualties, 68 of them fatal.

By the end of January, 6th Airborne Division had been withdrawn to Holland where it took up positions along the River Maas in the area of Venlo and Roermond. All three of its brigades conducted vigorous patrolling, although such operations were made hazardous by the necessity of having to cross the river, which was wide and in flood. The small assault boats used by patrols were frequently swept away by the strong current, and landfall at any predetermined point on the far bank became difficult to achieve.

By mid-February, conditions on the front were relatively quiet. Having crossed the Maas, First Canadian Army had cleared the Reichswald by 13 February and was only a day's march from the town of

Emmerich on the banks of the Rhine. The failure of the Ardennes offensive had cost the Germans very dear. They had incurred casualties amounting to some 40,000 killed and 50,000 taken prisoner by the time they withdrew over the Rhine.

During the third week of the month 6th Airborne Division, less its seaborne 'tail' which remained in Belgium, was withdrawn to England to prepare for its role in a forthcoming major operation scheduled to take place in the latter part of March. Codenamed Plunder, it was the crossing of the Rhine and the initial phase of the invasion of Germany.

The plan for Plunder called for the crossing to be made north of the Ruhr, between the towns of Wesel and Emmerich, by ten corps whose total strength would be over 1,250,000 men. It would be carried out on a two-arm front with Lieutenant General William H. Simpson's US Ninth Army on the right, spearheaded by XVI Corps, and Lieutenant General Sir Miles Dempsey's Second British Army on the left, led by XII and XXX Corps. A bridgehead would be established from which the Allied forces would break out, thereafter advancing northwards and eastwards into Germany. It would extend from Emmerich in the north to Wesel in the south and would be of sufficient depth to enable divisions to form up prior to the breakout.

The task of establishing the bridgehead was given to XVIII Airborne Corps, commanded by Major General Matthew Ridgway and comprising for this operation, codenamed Varsity, the 6th and 17th Airborne Divisions. Numbering in all some 17,000 men, it was allotted a number of objectives in the XII Corps sector. Its orders were to seize and hold a feature called the Diesfordterwald, an area of dense forest north-west of Wesel, and the ground north of Wesel up to the line of the River Ijssel; seize a number of bridges over the Ijssel and the town of Hamminkeln situated to the east of the Diersfordterwald; and defend the bridgehead against all enemy counter-attacks.

Initially, Headquarters First Allied Airborne Army had decided that three divisions would take part in the operation, the third being the 13th Airborne Division commanded by Major General Elbridge G.

Chapman; but there were insufficient transport aircraft to lift three such formations and thus the 13th, which had not seen any action since its activation in August 1943, was stood down.

Unlike at Arnhem, from which several bitter lessons had been learned, the entire airborne force would be flown in one lift and dropped or landed during daylight on its objectives, all of which were in range of supporting artillery on the west bank of the Rhine. Moreover, link-ups with ground troops would take place on the first day of the operation.

D-Day for Operation Plunder was to be 23 March 1945. From D-2 intensive bombing would be carried out on all known enemy artillery and flak positions and fifteen Luftwaffe airfields in the area. During the evening of D-Day, a massive artillery barrage would be brought down on the enemy positions to the east of the Rhine while Allied aircraft would also attack selected targets. That night, Second British Army's crossing was to begin with 51st (Highland) Division, the spearhead of XXX Corps, crossing the river at Rees and Speldrop. To the south, the leading element of XII Corps, 1st Commando Brigade, in an operation codenamed Widgeon, would cross an hour later two miles north of Wesel to take and hold the town, including a large factory on the northern edge. The commandos' task was to deny the enemy the use of routes through the town and thus disrupt any counter-attacks made through it against the bridgehead. Meanwhile, the remainder of XII Corps would cross the Rhine near Xanten.

Varsity would begin at 10.00 a.m. on 24 March with both airborne formations being dropped and landed simultaneously. The 17th Airborne Division was to drop and secure the southern half of the operational area, giving priority to the high ground to the east of the Diesfordterwald and to the bridges over the Ijssel. It was also to protect the right flank of XVIII Airborne Corps while linking up with 1st Commando Brigade. The 507th Parachute Regimental Combat Team, along with elements of the divisional headquarters, would drop first on DZ 'W', followed by the 513th Parachute Regimental Combat Team on DZ ''E' and the 194th Glider Regimental Combat Team on LZ 'S'.

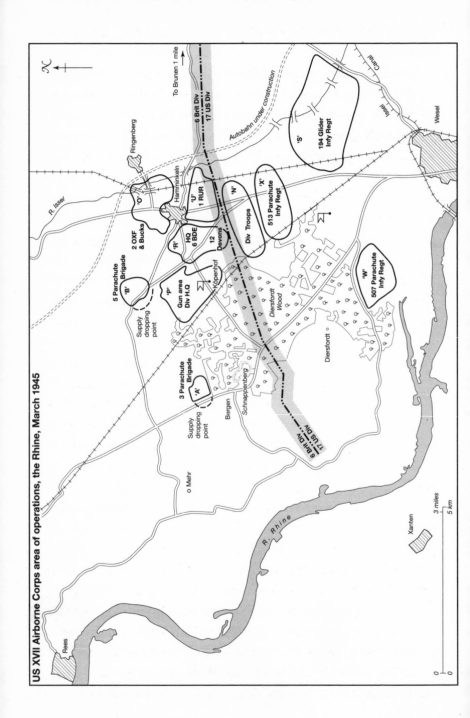

US XVII Airborne Corps area of operations, the Rhine, March 1945

N

To Brunen 1 mile →

6 Brit Div
17 US Div

Autobahn under construction

Issel

Canal

Wesel

'S'
194 Glider
Infy Regt

Ringenberg

R. Issel

Hamminkeln

'O'

'U'
1 RUR

'N'

'X'
513 Parachute
Infy Regt

2 OXF
& Bucks

'R'

HQ
6 BDE

12
Devons

Div Troops

'W'
507 Parachute
Infy Regt

5 Parachute
Brigade

'B'

'P'

Gun area
Div H.Q

Köpenhof

Diersfordt
Wood

Supply
dropping
point

Diersfordt

3 Parachute
Brigade

'A'

Bergen

Schnappenberg

6 Brit Div
17 US Div

Supply
dropping
point

o Mehr

R. Rhine

Xanten

Rees

3 miles
5 km

0
0

552

The remainder of the divisional headquarters and other units would land on LZ 'N'.

Meantime, 6th Airborne Division would drop and land on the northern half of the area. Its objectives were the high ground east of Bergen, the town of Hamminkeln and certain bridges over the Ijssel. 3rd Parachute Brigade would drop on DZ 'A', at the north-west corner of the Diersfordterwald, seize a feature called the Schneppenberg and thereafter clear and hold the western side of the forest, secure the road junction at Bergen, and patrol out to the area of the railway line running north-east through the forest – holding it if necessary. 5th Parachute Brigade would meanwhile drop on DZ 'B' north-west of Hamminkeln, thereafter patrolling westwards. It was also to hold the area to the east of the railway line and link up with 3rd Parachute Brigade. 6th Air-landing Brigade had been allotted a series of objectives and would land as close as possible to them in company groups. Each battalion had been allocated its own LZ within which there was a carefully planned location for each company. The 12th Battalion The Devonshire Regiment, which was tasked with capturing Hamminkeln, would land on LZ 'R' to the south-west of the town while the 2nd Battalion The Oxfordshire & Buckinghamshire Light Infantry would land to the north on LZ 'O' with the objective of taking the road and rail bridges over the Ijssel between Hamminkeln and Ringenberg. The 1st Battalion The Royal Ulster Rifles meanwhile would land on LZ 'U' to the south of Hamminkeln and seize the bridge over the Ijssel on the main road to Brunen.

6th Airborne Division was also to protect the northern flank of XVIII Airborne Corps, link up with the 17th Airborne Division on its right and with XII Corps which, following the completion of its crossing, would move up from the rear on to the division's left flank. Armoured support would be provided by 6th Guards Tank Brigade as soon as it crossed the river: a squadron of the 3rd Tank Battalion Scots Guards would link up with the division on the second day, being joined by the remainder of the battalion as soon as possible. The division would be backed by a large amount of artillery comprising three field and two medium regiments in direct support and two further medium regiments on call. In addition, a battery of American long-range guns would be available for harassing fire tasks.

The enemy forces opposing the crossing comprised the First Parachute Army, still under the command of General Alfred Schlemm and now consisting of: II Parachute Corps; LXIII Corps and LXXXVI Infantry Corps, with XLVII Panzer Corps in reserve. II Parachute Corps comprised the 6th, 7th and 8th Parachute Divisions, each of which consisted of only 3,000-4,000 men but nevertheless were still effective as fighting formations. LXXXVI Infantry Corps consisted mainly of the 84th Infantry Division, which numbered only 1,500 men, while XLVII Panzer Corps comprised the 116th Panzer and 15th Panzer Grenadier Divisions. Enemy armour consisted of some 100–150 vehicles while artillery was reported as comprising only some fifty field or medium guns. Anti-aircraft artillery, however, had originally been reported as being in strength in the form of 153 light and 103 heavy guns. By the third week of March, these had increased considerably to 712 light and 114 heavy guns, indicating clearly that the Germans were anticipating that the Allies would employ airborne forces during the crossing.

A massive bombardment of the German positions throughout the area began on 21 March; during the following two days 5,561 Allied bombers dropped 15,100 tons of bombs on defensive positions, headquarters locations, barracks, roads, railways and airfields. At the same time, fighter-bombers attacked convoys, anti-aircraft artillery batteries and the headquarters of the First Parachute Army. The attack on the latter resulted in General Schlemm being wounded and evacuated, command of the First Parachute Army being assumed in his absence by General Günther Blummentritt.

At 5.30 p.m. on 23 March, RAF Boston medium bombers carried out a raid on Wesel. Half an hour later 5,500 guns opened fire along the twenty-two-mile-wide front, being followed by another raid on

Wesel during which 250 Lancaster heavy bombers dropped more than 2,000 tons of bombs.

At 9.00 p.m. XXX Corps' leading element, 51st (Highland) Division, crossed the Rhine just north of Rees. At the same time 1st Commando Brigade, under covering fire from XII Corps' artillery, crossed the Rhine in assault craft and Buffalo amphibious vehicles. By 1.00 a.m. on 24 March, the entire brigade was across the Rhine and had taken Wesel, where it dug in.

By 4.00 a.m., the US Ninth Army had begun crossing south of Wesel and by first light on 24 March a number of bridgeheads had been established on the east bank of the river.

The first enemy counter-attacks came at 9.00 a.m. when a large force of infantry, supported by armour and self-propelled guns, attacked 1st Commando Brigade which, as planned, was blocking the routes to the bridgeheads. Several attacks were launched against the commandos who beat them off before the enemy eventually withdrew.

In England, meanwhile, weather conditions were good at 6th Airborne Division's mounting airfields as the parachute and airlanding troops waited beside their aircraft to emplane. 3rd and 5th Parachute Brigades, a total of 3,837 men, would be transported in 242 C-47s of the 9th Troop Carrier Command's 61st, 315th and 316th Troop Carrier Wings, while 6th Airlanding Brigade and the other gliderborne elements of the division, comprising 3,383 men, sixty-six guns and 846 vehicles, would be towed in 392 Horsas and fourteen Hamilcars by aircraft of 38 and 46 Groups RAF.

At 7.30 a.m., the tugs and gliders carrying 6th Airlanding Brigade were the first to take off and before long a vast armada of aircraft was airborne and heading for Germany and the Rhine, en route meeting bombers returning from softening up targets on the ground. Over Belgium, it swung north-east and shortly afterwards found itself flying alongside aircraft of the 9th Troop Carrier Command carrying the 17th Airborne Division, which had taken off from twelve airfields in France.

West of the Rhine, meanwhile, one hour and forty minutes before the scheduled parachute drops and glider landings (P-100), the Allied artillery opened fire. Nine field regiments, eleven medium regiments, one heavy regiment, four heavy batteries, one heavy anti-aircraft regiment, one super heavy battery and three 155mm battalions opened fire on the areas on which both airborne divisions were due to land. An hour later (P-40), they ceased fire. Ten minutes later (P-30), another massive barrage was brought to bear on the enemy anti-aircraft defences. At P-Hour, as the leading aircraft of both divisions flew over the gun lines, the artillery ceased fire to avoid any risk of inadvertently hitting any aircraft.

3rd Parachute Brigade jumped nine minutes late on to DZ 'A' at the north-west corner of the Diesfordterwald. 8th Parachute Battalion, commanded by Lieutenant Colonel George Hewetson, was the first to land. It was followed by Brigadier James Hill and his headquarters, 1st Canadian and then 9th Parachute Battalions under Lieutenant Colonels Jeff Nicklin and Napier Crookenden respectively, a troop of 3rd Parachute Squadron RE and 224th Parachute Field Ambulance.

While the drop continued, the flak grew thicker as the enemy anti-aircraft gunners recovered from the effects of the artillery barrages. 8th Parachute Battalion had been allowed only four minutes to secure the DZ and clear the enemy from the woods to the south and from two copses which dominated the DZ. As they landed, its companies immediately went into action. A Company, commanded by Major Bob Flood, took a wood in the north-eastern corner of the DZ while Major John Shappee's C Company, together with Battalion Head-quarters and the Mortar Platoon, occupied another in the south-eastern corner.

B Company and the Machine Gun Platoon meanwhile encountered stiff opposition from two platoons of enemy paratroops when attempting to take their objective, a wood on the southern side of the DZ. Unfortunately, the company had become disorganised on landing, and came under fire on the DZ. The company commander, Major John Kippen, eventually assembled a force of about platoon strength with which he assaulted the enemy positions. His attack, however, was beaten off and Kippen, together with one of his platoon commanders, was killed. Shortly afterwards, another platoon of B Company succeeded in taking the objective under covering fire from the first platoon.

1st Canadian Parachute Battalion encountered heavy ground fire as it jumped from its aircraft, several men being killed as they dropped or when they landed in some trees. Among these was the commanding officer, Lieutenant Colonel Jeff Nicklin, who landed in a tree above a machine-gun position and was shot dead as he hung in his parachute harness. On his death, the second-in-command, Major Fraser Eadie, assumed command of the battalion.

C Company was the first to land, coming under heavy machine-gun fire as it did so. The company commander, Major John Hanson, broke his collarbone on landing while the aircraft carrying his second-in-command, Captain John Clancy, was hit by flak over the DZ. Along with two other members of his stick, Clancy managed to jump clear of the stricken aircraft but landed in an enemy-held area and was captured. One of his two companions was carrying the company headquarters' radio set. As he descended, a burst of machine-gun fire severed the suspension cord from which his equipment container hung below him, the radio being destroyed on hitting the ground. Despite the absence of both its commander and second-in-command, the company rallied quickly, clearing the enemy from its objective and knocking out several enemy gun crews.

A Company, commanded by Major Peter Griffin, landed at the eastern end of the DZ, putting in an immediate attack on the buildings designated for use by Battalion Headquarters. An assault was also mounted on a group of houses which were part of the company's objective, but this encountered stiff opposition and faltered. The situation was resolved by Company Sergeant Major Green, who led a group of men to the first house and cleared it after fierce close-quarter fighting. The remaining houses were subsequently cleared until the entire objective had been taken.

B Company, under Captain Sam McGowan, attacked a group of farm buildings and an area of woodland from which it had come under fire. Supported by its own Bren LMGs, the company mounted an assault on the enemy positions, clearing bunkers and trenches with grenades. Under heavy fire, Company Sergeant Major Kemp then led an attack on the farmhouse itself and within thirty minutes the objective had been taken. One of the company's three platoons, however, had suffered heavy casualties on the DZ, among them its commander, Lieutenant Jack Brunnette, who had been killed.

The terrain on which 6th Airborne Division dropped and landed was open grassland offering little or no cover. Consequently, heavy casualties were incurred on the DZs. In one instance, a wounded man was lying in the open and two members of 224th Parachute Field Ambulance were killed while trying to rescue him. Corporal Topham, a medical orderly in 1st Canadian Parachute Battalion, went forward under heavy fire and rendered first aid to the wounded man. While doing so, he was shot through the nose but, in spite of being in severe pain and bleeding profusely, he continued with his task. Having completed giving first aid, he then carried the man to safety.

During the following two hours, Corporal Topham continued to bring in and treat wounded men, refusing treatment for his own wound until all the casualties had been cleared from the DZ. Subsequently, while returning to his company, he came across a Bren carrier which had received a direct hit. The area was under heavy fire from enemy mortars and the carrier, which contained mortar bombs, had been set ablaze. Disregarding the enemy fire and the orders of an officer not to approach the vehicle, Corporal Topham went forward and rescued the vehicle's three crew, all of whom were wounded, carrying them to safety and giving them first aid. His gallantry and disregard for his own life that day was subsequently recognised by the award of the Victoria Cross.

The last unit of 3rd Parachute Brigade to drop was 9th Parachute

Battalion and forty-five minutes after landing it was assembled in its RV area. As it advanced towards the Schneppenberg feature, it encountered only light resistance which was dealt with by A Company, commanded by Major Alan Parry. B Company attacked and silenced a battery of 76mm guns sited along the western edge of the woods and by 1.00 p.m. the battalion had taken and secured its objective. A Company took up positions on the Schneppenberg itself, while B Company was deployed astride the main road to the south-east. C Company meanwhile occupied positions in the wood south of the road.

5th Parachute Brigade had received a rougher reception, as the enemy anti-aircraft gunners had recovered from the anti-flak bombardment by the time the brigade's aircraft arrived over DZ 'A' to the north-west of Hamminkeln. Jumping with the three battalions were a detachment of 2nd Forward Observation Unit RA, a troop of 591st Parachute Squadron RE and 225th Parachute Field Ambulance. As the drop took place, the DZ itself came under heavy fire and the three battalion RV areas were subjected to artillery and mortar barrages.

Lieutenant Colonel Geoffrey Pine Coffin's 7th Parachute Battalion suffered a number of casualties from artillery firing airburst shells which exploded among the sticks of paratroops as they descended. By the time he and his men landed on the DZ, they were under fire from artillery and mortars. A Company, together with the Mortar and Machine Gun Platoons, sustained very heavy casualties from a troop of 88mm guns sited in a small wood some 700 yards away. These were also bringing fire to bear on 12th Parachute Battalion and Brigadier Nigel Poett's brigade headquarters, and continued to inflict considerable damage until silenced.

The battalion's initial task was to establish itself in positions on the northern edge of the DZ, and thereafter to engage any enemy while 12th and 13th Parachute Battalions took the brigade's objective, namely the ground astride the road leading from the DZ to Hamminkeln, thus preventing any enemy movement through the area. In addition, it was to take and hold a key road junction situated in a clearing in a big wood between 3rd and 5th Parachute Brigades. Lieutenant Colonel Pine Coffin despatched a platoon, under Lieutenant Patterson, which reached the clearing after narrowly avoiding several encounters with enemy troops. Subsequently, the platoon was subjected to a number of attacks, all of which were beaten off in a somewhat unorthodox but highly successful fashion. If the attack was a weak one, the platoon would remain in its positions but if the enemy appeared to be approaching in force, Patterson would withdraw his men to a flank and wait. As the enemy assaulted the deserted position, the platoon would attack. This tactic was used on a number of occasions and inflicted heavy casualties on the enemy.

12th Parachute Battalion moved off rapidly after landing. The commanding officer, Lieutenant Colonel Ken Darling, had appreciated fully that speed would be of the essence in the initial phase of the operation, and had organised his battalion so that it could go straight into the attack on landing. The jumping order of each company and platoon had been rearranged so that individuals dropped in relation to where they were required to be on the DZ. In addition, weight of equipment was reduced to the barest minimum, items such as spare clothing, entrenching tools and grenades being discarded.

Unfortunately, due to the poor visibility caused by the pall of smoke and dust covering the area, most of the battalion made its way to the wrong location while seeking the RV, but the error was soon discovered and the second-in-command, Major Frank Bucher, led it to the correct spot. As it moved across the DZ, however, the battalion came under heavy small arms fire and was shelled by the troop of 88mm guns that had also caused casualties among 7th Parachute Battalion. Nevertheless, it regrouped and A Company, commanded by Major Gerald Ritchie, proceeded to take its objective. No. 1 Platoon, under Lieutenant Phil Burkinshaw, then attacked and silenced the 88mm guns while Lieutenant C. E. Crook's No. 2 Platoon cleared some enemy from a nearby farm.

C Company, under Major Steve Stephens, meanwhile was attacking its target, led by a group headed by Lieutenant T. Reed which cleared a number of buildings while the remainder of the company followed up and secured the rest of the area.

Major E. J. O'B 'Rip' Croker's B Company was having a tough time taking its objective, a group of farm buildings held by a large number of enemy who were putting up a stiff fight. Lieutenant Peter Cattell, leading the assault, was wounded while clearing a building, as shortly afterwards was Lieutenant Ginger Delaney. At that point No. 4 Platoon appeared and took the rest of the objective, by which time the company had incurred several casualties among its officers and senior NCOs, including the commander of No. 6 Platoon, Lieutenant M. Mustoe, who had been captured after landing some distance from the DZ, and Company Sergeant Major Warcup, who had been wounded.

By the time the aircraft carrying 13th Parachute Battalion arrived over DZ 'B', a thick pall of dust and smoke covered the entire area. Nevertheless, the battalion landed virtually intact and rallied swiftly to the sounds of the company commanders' hunting horns blowing in morse code the respective identification letters of their companies. A Company, led by Major Jack Watson, went straight into action, one of its platoons capturing an enemy machine-gun position. Soon, the battalion had secured all of its objectives and had taken a large number of prisoners.

As the day wore on, the intensity of the fighting diminished. By 3.00 p.m. 5th Parachute Brigade had taken all of its objectives and at 3.45 p.m. 7th Parachute Battalion was ordered to begin withdrawing. This was carried out with some difficulty, however, as B and C Companies were still in contact with the enemy, but the withdrawal was eventually achieved without loss and the battalion moved into reserve. It had suffered heavy casualties, amounting to ninety-two out of its strength of just over 500 men who had dropped that morning, these mainly caused by anti-aircraft fire during the drop and by mortar and artillery fire on its positions during the day.

Headquarters 5th Parachute Brigade had also incurred losses. Brigadier Nigel Poett, who had followed his usual custom of jumping with the leading elements of the brigade, had lost his brigade major, Major Mike Brennan, his signals officer, Lieutenant Crawford, and his DAA & QMG, Major Ted Lough, who had been badly wounded while flying in by glider. Consequently, Poett was forced to reorganise his headquarters after reaching its RV.

The heaviest casualties in 6th Airborne Division, however, were suffered by 6th Airborne Brigade and the gliderborne elements of the parachute brigades and divisional troops. The flight from England had been uneventful but as the armada of gliders and tugs approached the Rhine, a vast pall of smoke could be seen rising from the area of the battle ahead. As the combinations approached the LZs, they came under heavy flak and several gliders were hit in mid-air or as they landed, sustaining heavy losses. Moreover, the poor visibility on the ground made landing difficult and there were several collisions. In some instances, pilots were unable to find their bearings and landed their gliders in the wrong locations. One outcome of this was that only a small proportion of the vehicles, anti-tank guns, mortars and ammunition reached the parachute battalions. Of the twenty-four pack howitzers of 53rd Airlanding Light Regiment RA, only eleven could be brought into action after landing, the remainder having been destroyed or reported missing. 2nd Airlanding Anti-Tank Battery RA suffered similarly, with only half of its guns being brought into action, while only four of 6th Airborne Armoured Reconnaissance Regiment's eight Locust light tanks, flown in by Hamilcar gliders, survived the landings and reached the regiment's RV. Of those, only two were fit for action. Among the glider pilots themselves, losses were high with over 100 being killed, wounded or subsequently listed as missing.

Despite the chaos on the LZs, all three battalions of 6th Airlanding Brigade were landed in the correct locations and succeeded in taking their objectives, although not without losses. The 2nd Battalion The Oxfordshire Buckinghamshire Light Infantry, commanded by Lieu-

THE ARDENNES AND THE RHINE CROSSING, 1944–5

tenant Colonel Mark Darell-Brown, landed on LZ 'O' but lost almost half its strength during the landing, which lasted ten minutes. On the approach to the LS, Darell-Brown's glider came under fire from a 20mm anti-aircraft battery in the area of Hamminkeln and was hit. The pilot immediately put the aircraft into a nosedive and, as he did so, the co-pilot opened fire at the battery with his Sten gun through the windshield. The Horsa landed beside the battery and Darell-Brown and his men disembarked at speed, attacking the enemy gunners and swiftly overpowering them.

Throughout the battalion's area all was confusion. Individual actions were taking place on and around each of the company objectives while in the background the continual noise of ammunition exploding in burning gliders added to the din. As the battalion stormed and overran the enemy anti-aircraft batteries, it came under fire from machine guns and mortars in the area of the LZ near Ringenberg.

Despite the severe setbacks it encountered, the battalion succeeded in taking all of its objectives and by 11.00 a.m. B Company, commanded by Major Gilbert Rahr, took up positions around the road bridge over the Ijssel while C Company, under Major James Molloy, established itself in defence of the rail bridge. Major Harry Styles's A Company meanwhile occupied the area of the road junction to the west while D Company, under Major John Tillett, was in reserve to the west of the railway station which was occupied by the Reconnaissance Platoon.

The action during the landings had cost the battalion dear. It now numbered only 226 all ranks and possessed only four of its twelve mortars and a few of its anti-tank guns. One hundred and three officers and men had been killed, mostly in the gliders, while there were more than a hundred wounded, with several in a very serious condition.

There was little disturbance during the rest of the day but that evening C Company came under fire from a machine gun which was eventually silenced by a patrol despatched for the purpose. Shortly afterwards, B Company detected enemy tanks moving up from

Ringenberg, this being followed by ineffective artillery fire directed at the company's positions.

At midnight enemy infantry, supported by tanks, attacked B Company. The company's anti-tank detachments scored several hits but their 6-pounder guns were ineffectual against the tanks' heavy armour. The fighting continued in the dark and one of the company's positions at the eastern end of the road bridge was overrun but then retaken by a counter-attack led by Lieutenant Hugh Clark. Two hours later, another strong attack, also supported by armour, was launched against the bridge and it soon became evident that B Company would not be able to beat it off. On orders from the brigade commander, Brigadier Hugh Bellamy, the bridge was therefore blown.

The 12th Battalion The Devonshire Regiment landed on LZ 'R' with the task of taking and holding Hamminkeln after first isolating it by preventing any enemy movement in or out of it west of the main road running north and south. In support, the battalion had 3rd Air-landing Anti-Tank Battery RA less three of its 17-pounder guns.

All did not go to plan, however, and the battalion's landing proved as chaotic as those of other units dropped around it. The glider carrying the commanding officer, Lieutenant Colonel Paul Gleadell, landed under fire between the positions of C Company of the Oxfordshire & Buckinghamshire Light Infantry, holding the Ijssel railway bridge, and the enemy holding Ringenberg. Gleadell and his men headed south, avoiding groups of enemy and a number of tanks, self-propelled guns, armoured cars and half-tracks cruising around the LZ and engaging troops disembarking from their gliders. Eventually linking up with D Company, Gleadell made his way to a road junction where he made radio contact with Battalion Headquarters and B Company. At 11.35 a.m., he gave the order for the second phase of the operation, the assault on Hamminkeln itself, to begin and all four rifle companies launched their assaults on the town, which was taken by midday. Thereafter, the battalion regrouped with Gleadell establishing his headquarters in the town's school. During the afternoon, enemy activity was light, consisting mainly of shelling the town sporadically with two 88mm guns and mortars. By the end of the day, the Devons had suffered casualties totalling 110 killed and thirty wounded.

The 1st Battalion The Royal Ulster Rifles was also greeted by heavy anti-aircraft fire as it approached LZ 'U'. As its gliders touched down, enemy armoured cars and self-propelled guns brought fire to bear, causing a number of casualties.

D Company, commanded by Major Tony Dyball, landed on LZ 'U1' which was astride the Ijssel, his own glider touching down in the lead about 150 yards from the bridge which was his objective. As it landed, it came under fire from a machine gun some seventy-five yards away, this being silenced shortly afterwards by one of Dyball's men using a Bren LMG. Two of D Company's four platoons, along with some gliders, some anti-tank gunners without their guns and a small group of men of the Oxfordshire & Buckinghamshire Light Infantry, took the bridge after clearing a number of houses nearby. Shortly afterwards, five self-propelled guns approached along the road and the leading vehicle was engaged at close range with a PIAT which scored a direct hit but failed to knock out the vehicle. The enemy showed little willingness to fight and the guns withdrew as quickly as possible, some twenty Germans having been killed and fifty captured during this engagement.

A Company, which was tasked with taking Ringenberg railway station and the area of the level crossing near by, should have landed on LZ 'U2'. Only two of its gliders succeeded in doing so, however, bringing in two platoons, under Lieutenants Fred Laird and John Stewart; these moved off immediately for their objectives where they encountered little or no opposition although the area was under fire from 20mm guns near Hamminkeln. They met, however, a platoon of the Devons, in a position some 100 yards west of the railway, which had captured some fifty enemy found in a barn waiting to be taken prisoner.

Lieutenant Laird organised a defence of the level crossing area and shortly afterwards Support Company, commanded by Major Paddy

Liddell, arrived with two Vickers MMGs. There was no sign, however, of the rest of A Company or the remainder of the battalion.

The expected enemy counter-attack against the force holding the level crossing did not materialise. Shortly after the two platoons had taken up their positions there, three self-propelled guns approached from the direction of Hamminkeln and passed over the level crossing and the river bridge before heading off eastwards. A PIAT was fired at one of them, damaging but not knocking it out. All three were obviously intent on withdrawing as rapidly as possible as none of them engaged either of the platoons whose positions were only a few feet from them by the road.

By this time, the rest of the battalion was landing on LZ 'U3', coming under a very heavy volume of fire from houses in the area where the battalion was due to assemble prior to moving off to join A and D Companies. The glider carrying the commanding officer, Lieutenant Colonel Jack Carson, broke in half on landing and he was injured. Battalion Headquarters was established in a wood south-west of the level crossing while B and C Companies moved to their respective areas and dug in. The glider pilot squadron, in whose Horsas the battalion had flown, took over the defence of the station and level crossing from A Company, which moved to a new position covering the exits from Hamminkeln.

By early afternoon, the fighting had died down and the battalion had secured all of its objectives. Missing elements rejoined during the day, having landed some distance away and fought their way to the battalion's area. Among them was the second-in-command, Major Gerald Rickord, who assumed command in the absence of Lieutenant Colonel Carson who was by then with the other wounded in a house near the railway, awaiting evacuation to 195th Airlanding Field Ambulance's main dressing station. The battalion had suffered heavy casualties, totalling sixteen officers and 243 other ranks. It had taken and held all of its objectives, however, and was in firm control of its area.

During the rest of the day, there was little enemy activity except for the appearance of three self-propelled guns which were seen off with the assistance of some RAF Typhoon fighter-bombers. The Germans, however, were still occupying some buildings to the east of the bridge and armoured vehicles were detected moving near Ringenberg and the wooded areas around it.

The night of 24/25 March was a busy one for the Oxfordshire & Buckinghamshire Light Infantry. The bridge held by B Company had been blown at 2.30 a.m. to prevent the enemy from crossing and the attack on it petered out some thirty minutes later. At 4.00 a.m. a small force of enemy infantry succeeded in infiltrating itself between A and C Companies and at 4.45 a.m. attacked the latter, overrunning one of its platoon positions and capturing a 6-pounder anti-tank gun and its crew. Emergency DF artillery fire was called down immediately and A Company put in a counter-attack while a company of the Devons moved up and took over A Company's positions at the road junction. The enemy withdrew and the battalion's perimeter was restored.

At 5.30 a.m., enemy armour was detected moving in the area of Ringenberg and two medium tanks were spotted. Air support was requested via the brigade headquarters and at 7.00 a.m. two flights of Typhoons arrived overhead. Several tanks were knocked out but one heavy tank, in a hull-down position, escaped destruction and continued to trouble the battalion throughout the day.

Just after first light, meanwhile, an attack was launched against 1st Canadian Parachute Battalion by infantry supported by tanks, but this was beaten off.

At 7.30 a.m., in 6th Airlanding Brigade's area, two Panther tanks with infantry aboard them attempted to retake the bridge over the Ijssel held by the Royal Ulster Rifles. As they approached at speed along the road, however, the leading tank was knocked out by one of the battalion's 6-pounders while the other was damaged by a 17-pounder positioned near by. Later that morning, the battalion was reinforced by a battery of self-propelled guns, a troop being positioned to protect each of the bridges. Meanwhile, a squadron of tanks was sent forward to the area occupied by the brigade headquarters to provide armoured support if required.

During the afternoon, D Company 2nd Battalion Oxfordshire & Buckinghamshire Light Infantry attacked and cleared some buildings to the north and north-west of its positions where movement had been observed earlier. At 8.40 p.m. A Company mounted an attack on a building to the north and engaged several groups of enemy. At midnight, a battalion of The Cameronians (Scottish Rifles) arrived to relieve the 2nd Battalion which withdrew and by 2.00 a.m. on 26 March was concentrated in a farm on the western outskirts of Hamminkeln.

Major General Eric Bols had set up his forward divisional head-quarters by 11.00 a.m. in a farm at Kopenhof, his glider having landed him and members of his staff to within 100 yards of their intended location. Ten minutes after arriving, radio contact had been made with 3rd and 5th Parachute Brigades. Half an hour later, radio communication with 6th Airlanding Brigade was also established. Contact with the 17th Airborne Division, however, was not made until 4.00 p.m.

Half a mile away, the rear element of the divisional headquarters had encountered problems from enemy snipers and mortars at its location in a farm to the west of the railway. That evening, it moved and joined the forward element as there was insufficient manpower and resources to defend both separately.

During the night of 24 March the commander of XVIII Airborne Corps, Major General Matthew Ridgway, accompanied by Major General 'Bud' Miley, commander of the 17th Airborne Division, arrived at Headquarters 6th Airborne Division. In his orders to Major General Bols, Ridgway stated that 6th Airborne Division would remain in its positions, with the exception of 6th Airlanding Brigade, which would be relieved by 157th Infantry Brigade of 52nd (Lowland) Division during the night of 25/26 March. 6th Airborne Division was to be ready to break out and advance east at dawn on 26 March.

The 17th Airborne Division had received a similar reception to that of its British counterpart when it landed on the morning of 24 March. Mounting from twelve airfields in the area of Châlons-sur-Marne in France, its leading element took off at 7.30 a.m. This consisted of the 2,479-strong 507th Parachute Regimental Combat Team, commanded by Colonel Edson Raff and comprising the 507th Parachute Infantry Regiment and 464th Parachute Field Artillery Battalion, being flown in 181 C-47s of the 53rd Troop Carrier Wing. Leading the 507th was Lieutenant Colonel Paul F. Smith's 1st Battalion, followed by the 2nd and 3rd Battalions commanded respectively by Lieutenant Colonels Charles Timmes and Allen W. Taylor. Bringing up the rear were Lieutenant Colonel Edward S. Branigan's gunners of the 464th Parachute Field Artillery Battalion who were accompanied by the divisional commander, Major General William 'Bud' Miley, and members of his forward tactical headquarters staff.

Following the 507th was the 513th Parachute Regimental Combat Team, commanded by Colonel James Coutts. Its three infantry battalions were being carried in seventy-two C-46s of the 313th Troop Carrier Group while the regiment's artillery component, the 466th Parachute Field Artillery Battalion, travelled in forty-five C-47s of the 434th.

Last to take off was Colonel James R. Pierce's 194th Glider Regimental Combat Team, comprising the 194th Glider Infantry Regiment and the 681st Glider Field Artillery Battalion, as well as other gliderborne elements of the division. The last included the 680th Glider Field Artillery Battalion and the 155th Airborne Anti-Aircraft Battalion, commanded by Lieutenant Colonels Paul F. Oswald and John W. Paddock, and the 139th Airborne Engineer Battalion under Lieutenant Colonel Stanley T. Johnson. These were being transported in a total of 906 Waco gliders, 600 of which were double-towed by 300 C-47s of the 53rd Troop Carrier Wing, the remaining 306 gliders being towed by C-47s of the 50th and 52nd.

The flight was not a comfortable one for the gliderborne force. Severe turbulence was experienced en route, causing a number of casualties. The wings of one Waco, carrying a howitzer and its crew, suddenly broke off at an altitude of some 300 feet, the fuselage plunging to the ground. Three pairs of the double-towed gliders became entangled: two crashed, all aboard being killed; three cast off and landed without further mishap; and the sixth continued the flight alone. Approximately 880 gliders survived to complete the flight, transporting 4,813 men, 439 vehicles and trailers, and ninety-eight howitzers and mortars.

The paratroops of the 507th and 513th Parachute Regimental Combat Teams experienced a relatively more enjoyable flight until the moment when their aircraft flew over the Allied ground forces drawn up west of the Rhine and began to cross the Rhine. As the aircraft approached from the south-west at an altitude of 1,500 feet, they encountered heavy flak and the thick pall of smoke and dust which made location of the DZs and LZs difficult and disorientated a number of crews. As a result, a large proportion of the 1st Battalion 507th Parachute Infantry Regiment, accompanied by Colonel Edson Raff and members of his staff, were dropped over two miles to the north-west of DZ 'W' where they landed near the Schloss Diesfordter. The commanding officer, Lieutenant Colonel Paul Smith, and some 200 of his men were dropped approximately a mile to the north-west of the DZ while elements of the 464th Parachute Field Artillery Battalion landed near by. The remainder of the 464th, along with Major General 'Bud' Miley and those members of his staff accompanying him, were dropped accurately on the DZ along with the 2nd and 3rd Battalions of the 507th.

Following close behind came the 513th Parachute Regimental Combat Team which, as mentioned earlier, was being flown in C-46 Curtiss Commandos. The C-46 had only recently entered service with the USAAF and, unlike the C-47, was not equipped with self-sealing fuel tanks; moreover, the design of the wing tanks was such that if punctured, fuel leaked down the wing to the fuselage, with disastrous results. Fifty-seven of the seventy-two C-46s carrying the 513th were hit by flak, nineteen bursting into flames and fourteen crashing. The majority of sticks aboard these jumped clear but five aircraft crashed with their sticks still aboard. The other aircraft which had been hit were seriously damaged but managed to return to their bases in France.

The 513th's drop was a disaster as many men, including Colonel James W. Coutts and members of his staff, were scattered over an area some two to three miles to the north-east of the DZ within 6th Airborne Division's sector. The grassland on which they landed afforded little or no cover from the heavy fire directed at them and they had either to remain hugging the earth or take their lives in their hands and sprint across open ground to reach the cover of woods.

The sole element of the 513th to be dropped accurately on DZ 'X' was the 466th Parachute Field Artillery Battalion, commanded by Lieutenant Colonel Ken Booth, which was flown in 45 C-47s. Like the three infantry battalions, however, it encountered heavy fire on landing. While half of the battalion returned the enemy fire, the remainder assembled the battalion's 75mm pack howitzers and brought them into action. Meanwhile Brigadier General Josiah T. Dalbey, the commander of the Airborne Training Centre who was accompanying the 507th Parachute Regimental Combat Team as an observer, assembled a small force and led an attack on an enemy 20mm battery which was swiftly silenced.

Next came the 194th Glider Regimental Combat Team and the gliderborne elements of the division, led by the 578 Wacos being towed in pairs. The tug aircraft suffered badly during the approach, twelve being shot down and fourteen being forced to crashland. A further 126 were also hit and suffered damage but subsequently returned to base. The majority of the gliders cast off at altitudes of between 400 and 800 feet, with more than half hit by flak but only six being shot down. Eighty-three landed well to the north of the LZ, in 6th Airborne Division's sector, but the remainder landed on or close to it, encountering heavy fire.

Two hours after the initial landings by the 507th and 513th Parachute Regimental Combat Teams, the 300 single-towed Wacos appeared, heading for LZ 'N' which lay to the north of DZ 'X'. Forty-four tug aircraft were hit by flak, but only three were shot down, while some seventy-five gliders were hit by small arms fire, as by this time the intensity of the flak had lessened, but only one was shot down. The majority of the Wacos landed on the LZ; only a small number of men were wounded and there were no fatalities. Half the gliders were destroyed in crash-landings but their passengers and cargoes survived intact.

Despite being dropped to the north-west of its DZ, Colonel Edson Raff and 500 men of the 1st Battalion of the 507th rallied quickly and launched an attack east into the Diersfordterwald during which they captured a battery of howitzers, killing over fifty enemy and capturing 300. To the south, meanwhile, Lieutenant Colonel Paul Smith and the remainder of the 1st Battalion attacked the Schloss Diefordterwald, the 3rd Battalion's initial objective, being joined an hour later by Colonel Raff and the rest of the battalion. Shortly afterwards, Lieutenant Colonel Allen Taylor and the 3rd Battalion arrived and the 1st Battalion handed over to them. Taylor and his men subsequently stormed the castle, clearing it room by room and taking 500 prisoners. Meanwhile, Colonel Raff and the 1st Battalion headed for the DZ where the 2nd Battalion was busy clearing enemy from the area and where the 466th Parachute Field Artillery Battalion had established its gun line. By the end of the day, the 507th had knocked out five tanks, captured or destroyed several artillery batteries and taken 1,000 prisoners. Its own casualties numbered approximately 150 men killed or wounded.

The 513th Parachute Regimental Combat Team, meanwhile, was having a far more difficult time following its disastrous drop. On landing, Colonel James Coutts rapidly assembled the major part of his three battalions and headed south for DZ 'X'; here the hard-pressed 466th Parachute Field Artillery Battalion was attempting to establish its gunline while also returning the enemy's fire. En route he encountered stiff opposition but overcame it with supporting fire from the 466th which engaged the enemy over open sights. It was not until 3.30 p.m., however, that the three battalions reached the DZ and proceeded towards their respective initial objectives. By the end of the day, despite suffering heavy casualties, the 513th had taken and secured all of its objectives, having destroyed two batteries of 88mm guns and some armour, and taken 1,100 prisoners.

The 194th Glider Regimental Combat Team, despite encountering very heavy fire on LZ 'S' which inflicted heavy casualties on the 3rd Battalion, had assembled rapidly and moved off with some seventy-five per cent of its strength. The 1st Battalion, commanded by Lieutenant Colonel Frank L. Barnett, duly cleared all enemy from its objective, while the 2nd Battalion, under Lieutenant Colonel William S. Stewart, resisted repeated attempts by the Germans to infiltrate into the area and beat off two counter-attacks. The 3rd Battalion, commanded by Lieutenant Colonel Robert Ashworth, likewise cleared the enemy from all of its objectives, thereafter filling gaps in the 194th's perimeter. By 2.00 p.m. it had achieved total success except for the capture of several bridges over the Ijssel to the east, and the canal to the south, and the clearing of enemy from the area of the Diersfordterwald between DZs 'X' and 'W'. Although it suffered heavy casualties, the 194th Glider Regimental Combat Team captured or knocked out six tanks and self-propelled guns, along with some fifty artillery pieces, and took 1,150 prisoners. During the late afternoon, having linked up with the 513th Parachute Regimental Combat Team on its left and 1st Commando Brigade on its right, the 194th dug in on the east bank of the Ijssel and prepared to beat off any enemy counter-attacks.

The commander of XVIII Airborne Corps, Major General Matthew Ridgway, crossed the Rhine during the afternoon of 24 March, arriving at Major General 'Bud' Miley's headquarters just before 3.30 p.m. By this time the 17th Airborne Division had achieved most of its objectives and remaining enemy resistance was light. Later that afternoon, Ridgway moved on, he and those accompanying him heading in a small convoy of jeeps east of the Diesfordterwald through the sectors held by the 194th Glider and the 513th Parachute Regimental Combat Teams, visiting the headquarters of each to confer with their commanders. That night, accompanied by Major General Miley, he visited Headquarters 6th Airborne Division where he briefed Major General Eric Bols on the forthcoming breakout.

Thus ended Operation Varsity, the last major airborne operation of the Second World War. A force of 1,545 aircraft and 1,305 gliders had delivered 17,000 paratroops and gliderborne troops, along with their heavy weapons and equipment, within the space of two hours. While success had been achieved, there had been a heavy price to pay for it. The number of casualties incurred by both divisions during Varsity was similar. 6th Airborne Division suffered approximately 1,200 in total while the 17th Airborne Division's losses amounted to 1,300. Seventy-seven Allied aircraft, including fifteen heavy bombers, were shot down and 475 others were damaged, several seriously. Most of the 1,305 gliders were also damaged, only 148 Wacos and twenty-four Horsas being salvaged after the operation.

CHAPTER FOURTEEN

ASIA AND THE PACIFIC, 1941–5

During 1941 it became apparent that there would be a role for airborne forces in India and Burma, and in October of that year 50th Indian Parachute Brigade was formed under Brigadier Bill Gough at Delhi, comprising: a British unit, 151st Parachute Battalion, commanded by Lieutenant Colonel Martin Lindsay; two Indian Army units: 152nd Indian and 153rd Gurkha Parachute Battalions, under Lieutenant Colonels B. E. 'Abbo' Abbott and Freddy Loftus-Tottenham; and 411th (Royal Bombay) Parachute Section Indian Engineers, commanded by Captain Mike Rolt. The Airlanding School was established at New Delhi under the command of Wing Commander J. H. D. Chapple with five elderly Vickers Valencia biplanes being allocated for parachute training. Despite a drastic shortage of parachutes, of which there were only fourteen in India at that time, training commenced in mid-October.

In February 1942, the brigade carried out its first exercise, albeit the airborne phase consisted merely of a stick of ten men from 151st Parachute Battalion being dropped while the remainder of the brigade was transported to its DZs in trucks. Shortly afterwards, the five Valencias were withdrawn from service and although six Hudson bombers had been earmarked to replace them, these had not materialised. The shortage of parachutes was, however, overcome by Leslie Irvin, the American manufacturer, who established a factory at Kanpur which by June was producing 300 parachutes per month, the eventual monthly target rate being 1,750.

Thereafter, a number of changes took place. The Paratroops Training Centre was established at Delhi and in October 50th Indian Parachute Brigade moved to a new base at Campbellpur in the Punjab. Soon afterwards, the Airlanding School moved to Chaklala, near Rawalpindi. During this period, 151st Parachute Battalion left the brigade and sailed for the Middle East where it joined 4th Parachute Brigade, being redesignated 156th Parachute Battalion.

In 1942 two small airborne operations were carried out by 50th Indian Parachute Brigade. The first took place in July when a company of 152nd Indian Parachute Battalion was dropped from Valencias in an action against the Hurs, a tribe in Sind province who were terrorising the region. Despite a successful drop, however, the tribesmen avoided contact with the paratroops. The second operation, codenamed Puddle, was an intelligence-gathering mission behind Japanese lines to determine whether the enemy were constructing airfields in the area of Myitkina. A patrol of eleven officers and men from 153rd Gurkha Parachute Battalion, under the command of Captain Jimmy Roberts, was dropped on 3 July from a Lockheed Lodestar over the Ningchan-gyang Valley in the Kachin Hills of Burma. Attempts to gather intelligence proved unsuccessful and the patrol's problems were compounded when its radio became unserviceable. Roberts thus led his men on a long march to Fort Hertz, a base with an airstrip, which lay 150 miles away through very thick jungle. Despite heavy monsoon rains, which made the going very difficult and with six of its members stricken by malaria, the patrol eventually arrived at Fort Hertz from which it was evacuated on 20 August.

December 1942 saw 50th Indian Parachute Brigade receiving a new battalion to replace 151st Parachute Battalion. This was the 3rd Battalion 7th Gurkha Rifles which was redesignated 154th Gurkha Parachute Battalion. By this time parachute training in India had progressed and the Airlanding School had been redesignated No.3 Parachute Training

School (No.3 PTS). Parachute training was now being carried out from modified Wellington bombers of No. 99 Squadron RAF, as well as from Valencias and Hudsons, but in May 1943, the Wellingtons were replaced by Hudsons of No. 62 Squadon. June 1943, however, saw the appearance at No. 3 PTS of the first C-47 which was in use by the end of July. More followed later in the year, replacing the Hudsons.

The Japanese, meantime, had also formed their own airborne forces, establishing four parachute training centres at Shimonoseki, Shizuoka, Hiroshima and Himeji in early 1940. The duration of the parachute course at each was initially six months but this was condensed and reduced to two months on the advice of a small group of Luftwaffe parachute jumping instructors who arrived from Germany during the summer. A total of 100 Luftwaffe instructors had arrived by the autumn, by which time there were nine parachute training centres in operation and some 15,000 men undergoing training.

During this period, the Imperial Japanese Army (IJA), the Imperial Japanese Air Army Force (IJAAF) and the Imperial Japanese Navy (IJN) set up parachute formations and units within their respective orders of battle. The IJA formed the 1st Parachute Brigade, comprising three regiments, while the IJAAF raised the approximately 6,000-strong Raiding Group, commanded by a major general and consisting of a group headquarters, a parachute brigade, two glider infantry regiments, supporting arms units made up of machine-gun, signals and engineer companies, and an aviation brigade. The 1,500-strong parachute brigade was commanded by a lieutenant colonel and consisted of two 700-strong parachute battalions, while the strength of each of the two gliderborne infantry regiments was just under 900. The aviation brigade comprised two transport regiments, a glider-towing regiment and a brigade signals unit. Each of the three regiments had a strength of some 500 all ranks and was equipped with thirty-five transport aircraft for dropping paratroops and towing gliders.

The size of sticks dropped from these aircraft depended on the type of aircraft which included the Kawasaki Ki-56, a Japanese-built Lockheed

Lodestar, and the Mitsubishi Ki-57, the latter resembling a smaller version of the Douglas DC-3.

Many different types of glider were developed and flown by the IJAAF but the only model to enter operational service was the Ku-8-11, a large high-wing glider fitted with an undercarriage consisting of two small wheels and two skids. Flown by two pilots and capable of carrying twenty fully equipped troops, it comprised a tubular steel frame with a fabric skin and featured a nose section which swung open sideways to facilitate loading and unloading. With a maximum towing speed of 120 knots and normally towed by a Mitsubishi Ki-21-11 twin-engined bomber, it was only used in the transport role and never as an assault glider.

The IJN's airborne force comprised some 2,000 paratroops organised into three units: the 1st, 2nd and 3rd Yokosuka Special Naval Landing Forces (SNLF), so-named because all SNLF units bore the name of an IJN base although they were attached to various fleet headquarters as required. The 1st Yokosuka SNLF was formed on 20 September 1941 under Commander Horiuchi Toyoaki, comprising 849 all ranks of whom 750 were trained parachutists. On 15 October, the 2nd Yokosuka SNLF was formed under Commander Tomonari Kiyoshi with a strength of 746 all ranks, all of whom were trained parachutists. The first training parachute drops by these two units were carried out on 16 November. Four days later, the 1st Yokosuka SNLF was split, with half forming the 3rd Yokosuka SNLF under Lieutenant Commander Fukumi Koichi.

The 1st and 3rd Yokosuka SNLF were grouped under the 1001st Butai together with the 1001st Naval Air Group which provided air transport support. Commanded by Captain Araki Keikichi, the latter was equipped with LB3Y converted bombers, G6M1-L2 Betty converted heavy escorts and G3M1-L transports. The 1001st Butai was under command of the 11th Naval Air Fleet which in turn assigned it to the 21st Naval Air Flotilla based at Chiai on Formosa. Meanwhile, the 2nd Yokosuka SNLF was detached, being placed under command of the IJN's Southern Fleet.

SNLF units played an important role in Japanese amphibious operations, particularly in the Dutch East Indies and the Philippines, where they acted as spearheads and established beachheads during the initial assaults. On the morning of 8 December 1941, the 3rd Yokosuka SNLF carried out an amphibious landing on Calayan Island, in the Philippines, where it set up an airstrip before being withdrawn to its base on Formosa.

The first operation carried out by the IJN's airborne units took place on 11 January 1942 – the day Japan declared war on the Netherlands – when three companies of the 1st Yokosuka SNLF, totalling 334 men, were dropped from G3M1-L transports on an airfield at Menado, situated on the north-eastern end of the Celebes Islands in the Dutch East Indies. Four hours previously, an amphibious unit, the 1st Kure SNLF, had carried out an amphibious landing farther north on the island which was held by a small force of Dutch troops and local irregulars.

Preceded by squadrons of Zero fighters, the three companies jumped from an altitude of 900 feet. The local irregulars fled as soon as the drop took place but the Dutch stood firm, all but thirty of them being killed during the ensuing action that lasted five hours, the remainder being taken prisoner. On the following day, a further 185 men were dropped. Thereafter, the airfield at Menado was used to extend the range of air cover provided for the IJN as Japanese forces advanced through the region.

At the start of the campaign to seize Java and Sumatra, the Japanese realised that their highest priority was to capture the oil refineries near Palembang, on Sumatra, before they were destroyed by the Dutch and British, and that the only way they could do so swiftly was to mount an airborne operation. Each of the refineries, at Pladjoe and Soengei Gerong, were defended by troops supported by four 3.7 inch and four Bofors 40mm anti-aircraft guns, while those at Palembang's airfield, which was also a Japanese objective, were equipped with eight 3.7 inch and seven Bofors guns.

On 14 February, IJAAF medium bombers attacked the airfield from high altitude and at 6.30 p.m. a 360-strong force of the 2nd Parachute Regiment of the IJA's 1st Parachute Brigade, commanded by Colonel Seiichi Kume, was parachuted on to the airfield from Ki-56 and Ki-57 transports; these flew over Palembang in two waves, dropping the paratroops in an area astride the Moestri river, some five miles from the airfield. Such was the effectiveness of the Allied anti-aircraft fire, however, that the transports were forced to fly too high and thus the ten-man sticks were scattered over a wide area. Consequently, the battalion had difficulty in rallying rapidly and in locating its equipment containers. Having done so, it assembled into three groups, one setting off for the airfield while the others headed for the two refineries. On arrival at the airfield, the first group split into three sections, two attacking the airfield itself while the third attempted to cut the road leading to Palembang.

Fierce fighting ensued, the battle lasting through the following day when another drop, bringing in 100 reinforcements, took place before the airfield was captured. Meanwhile, the attacks on the two refineries had both failed, with the anti-aircraft guns shooting down sixteen aircraft. The Allies thus were able to complete their demolitions and by the time an amphibious enemy force landed on 15 February, both refineries had been seriously damaged.

Six days later, the Japanese used airborne troops in an operation against the island of Timor. On 20 February, five G3M1-L transports dropped a small force of the IJN's 3rd Yokosuka SNLF over the southernmost tip of the island to seize the airfield there and to act as a feint in diverting attention from a seaborne attack on Koepang which was intended to cut the Allies' line of communications. That same day, following a low-level heavy bombing and strafing raid by the IJAAF, 308 men of the same unit were dropped on to a DZ some one and a half miles in front of the Allied positions. This was followed on the next day by another bombing raid and a drop of a further 323 men. Both drops were successful, with the paratroops taking a large number of Dutch and Australian troops prisoner, and Koepang itself fell after a landing by the 18,000-strong Sasebo Combined Special Naval Landing Force. During this action, however, which was the last to be carried out by the three IJN airborne units, the 3rd Yokosuka SNLF suffered heavy casualties.

Early 1943 saw the first Allied airlanding operation on the island of New Guinea, this taking place after an attack on 28 January by the Japanese on Wau, a strategically important Australian outpost that overlooked Japanese bases at Lae and Salamaua and also possessed an airstrip from which attacks could be launched on them.

Wau was garrisoned by 'Kanga Force', comprising the 2/5th and 2/7th Australian Independent Companies and a detachment of a locally recruited unit, the New Guinea Volunteer Rifles, whose primary task was to locate and reconnoitre trails leading through the jungle to the two enemy bases. Although they found two of these, the Australians failed to locate a third, familiar to the Japanese who, sending a group along both known trails as feints, despatched their principal assault along that route.

Reacting to the two feints, the Australians remained unaware of the main enemy force which infiltrated to within 800 yards of the Wau airstrip before it was detected. Reinforcements waiting at Port Moresby were immediately requested but bad weather prevented them from being flown in until the morning of the following day when 57 USAAF C-47s brought in 1,400 troops of the 2/5th and 2/7th Australian Infantry Battalions.

Next day, 30 January, the Japanese mounted a strong attack on the airstrip but this was eventually beaten off by a counter-attack. That day witnessed a further airlift of fifty-four aircraft bringing in the 2/1st Field Regiment Royal Australian Artillery (RAA); its 25-pounder guns, more troops with heavy weapons and equipment were landed on the next day. Both airlifts came under small arms and mortar fire with troops moving to defensive positions immediately after deplaning, in some instances opening fire as they left the aircraft.

The effect of these landings was to discourage further attacks by the Japanese, who not only suffered heavy casualties but also were unable to mount any subsequent offensive. They also marked the beginning of a major offensive by Australian forces against the Japanese in New Guinea with the aim of seizing the enemy airfields in the areas of the coastal town of Lae and the Markham Valley, and with the overall objective of advancing along the northern coast of the island. An initial phase in this was the capture of the coastal town of Lae which was to provide a forward base from which airfields could be established in the Markham Valley. From here, Allied fighters would provide protection for medium bombers from Dobadura attacking the Japanese main bases at Rabaul, Wewak and Madang and their airfields in western New Britain.

The combined operation to capture Lae entailed an amphibious landing to the east of Lae by the 9th Australian Division, an advance overland by Australian pioneer, signals and medical units, and a parachute drop at Nadzab by the US 503rd Parachute Infantry Regiment, supported by a troop of the 2/4th Australian Field Regiment RAA equipped with two short-barrelled Q.F. Light (Australian) Mk. I 25-pounder guns. Following the 503rd's drop, the 7th Australian Division would be flown into Nadzab, some nineteen miles to the west of Lae.

The 9th Division, commanded by Major General George Wootten, was to capture Lae while the 7th, under Major General George Vasey, advanced from Nadzab. With Lae captured and a firm foothold established, the two divisions were then to surround the Huon Peninsula whose heavily forested mountains and foothills, intersected by fast-flowing rivers, were occupied by the Japanese, whose strength was unknown. The 7th Division would advance down the Markham-Ramu Valley to the west until it eventually linked up with the 9th which meanwhile would move along the Finschhafen coast.

Before the offensive could begin, however, measures were taken to deceive the Japanese into believing that the main Allied effort in the Huon Peninsula was being concentrated in the area of Salamaua. These comprised a series of attacks on enemy outposts which had the desired effect of persuading the Japanese to transfer troops to Salamaua, reducing the strength of their force at Lae.

Preparations for the operation took place in mainland Australia. The 503rd Parachute Infantry Regiment, consisting of three battalions, had arrived in Australia from the United States on 2 December 1942, disembarking at Cairns in northern Queensland. In mid-August 1943 it moved to the Port Moresby area to prepare for the forthcoming operation but the artillery troop was not informed of its part in the mission until one week beforehand. The latter was a composite troop drawn from all batteries of the 2/4th Field Regiment RAA, made up of four officers, Lieutenants Johnnie Pearson, Frank Ross, Frank Faulkner, 'Puck' Evans, and thirty other ranks; none were trained parachutists and therefore would be required to undergo a short crash course entailing ground training and one jump. In total ignorance of their forthcoming role, other than being told it was classified as top secret, they underwent a week of tough physical training following which they were loaded aboard two trucks and driven to the camp of the 503rd. It was only at that point, as they entered the paratroops' lines, that they began to have an inkling of what was in store for them.

The commander of the 503rd Parachute Infantry Regiment, Colonel Kenneth H. Kinsler, was dumbfounded on learning from the troop's commander, Lieutenant Pearson, that the gunners were not trained parachutists and that they had no knowledge of their mission. When addressing them, he offered them the opportunity to withdraw but not one man did so. Twenty-four hours later, having undergone a day's ground training, the troop carried out its first jump from an altitude of 1,200 feet over an airstrip outside Port Moresby. Three men, including Lieutenant Evans, were injured; another officer, Lieutenant Alan Clayton, volunteered to replace him and drop into action with the troop on his first jump.

The 503rd's tasks were firstly: to take the area bounded by the villages of Nadzab, Gabmatzung and Gabsonkek, thereafter providing protection for the Australian 2/2nd Pioneer Battalion which was to construct an emergency landing airfield at Nadzab; secondly, to establish a roadblock interdicting the Markham Valley road and prevent any enemy movement towards Nadzab; and finally, to commence the initial preparatory work for the construction of the airfield prior to the arrival of the pioneer unit.

D-Day for the 503rd Parachute Infantry Regiment was 5 September. At 6.30 a.m. on D-1, Allied warships laid down a brief bombardment on 9th Division's landing beaches east of Lae. 20th Australia Infantry Brigade was the first to land, being followed by 26th Australian Infantry Brigade. Immediately after the landing, the 2/17th Infantry Battalion of 20th Infantry Brigade, and the 2/23rd and 2/24th Infantry Battalions of 26th Infantry Brigade, began the advance towards Lae. The remaining element of the 9th Division, 24th Australian Infantry Brigade, was due to land that night.

The following morning dawned with good weather and the leading aircraft of the formation of ninety-six C-47s subsequently took off from Port Moresby on schedule at 8.00 a.m. The flight proved uneventful, with the aircraft flying low-level in Vs of six before climbing to the jump height of 500 feet as they approached the DZ which they reached by 10.30 a.m. By this time, six squadrons of B-25 Mitchell medium bombers had bombed and strafed the areas of the three villages, followed by six A-20 Havoc medium bombers which delivered smoke bombs to screen the drop of the 1,720-strong 503rd Parachute Infantry Regiment and its attached artillery troop.

The landing was unopposed except for the presence of a number of small Japanese patrols encountered while the 503rd was assembling. Within two hours, all units had taken up their respective positions and the preparatory work of burning off the eight-foot-high grass, which covered the entire area, was being carried out with flamethrowers. Meanwhile, as soon as the drop had been carried out, the 2/2nd Australian Pioneer Battalion, along with the 2/6th Pioneer Company, signals and medical detachments, had crossed the River Markham by way of a footbridge constructed earlier by the 2/6th Pioneer Company and headed for the airfield where they set to work, continuing through the night. By 10.00 a.m. next morning the first aircraft landed, bringing in US sappers and heavy plant. Work then commenced on two more airstrips and on the morning of 7 September Headquarters 7th Australian Division, and elements of the 25th Australian Infantry Brigade Group, were flown in, the remainder of the division arriving during the following days in a total of 250 aircraft loads. The entire operation, which employed in all 303 C-47s, had been a total success.

March 1944 witnessed a major airlanding operation carried out by the Allies in Burma. During the previous year, in an operation code-named Longcloth, Chindits of 77th Infantry Brigade, commanded by Brigadier Orde Wingate, had infiltrated deep into Japanese-occupied territory in seven columns which fought some minor actions with the enemy before splitting up into groups and exfiltrating back to India. The tactical effects of the operation were small and losses were high, numbering 883 out of a total strength of 3,000, this arousing considerable criticism. Nevertheless, it had demonstrated the ability of long-range deep penetration units to operate behind enemy lines, a point not lost on the Japanese High Command.

Despite the lack of success of Longcloth, Wingate was able to persuade his superiors that the Chindit concept was viable if he was given the necessary resources. He was promoted to the rank of major general and given permission to set up a new formation designated Special Force but given the cover name of 3rd Indian Division for security purposes. It comprised fifteen British, four Gurkha and three West African battalions, two artillery regiments converted to the infantry role, a battalion of The Burma Rifles, a battery of 25-pounder guns and a battery of Bofors 40mm anti-aircraft guns.

These units were organised into five brigades, each given a codename and its battalions divided into columns, and two smaller forces as follows:

3rd West African Brigade (Thunder) – Brigadier A. H. Gillmore
6th Bn The Nigerian Regiment – Nos 39 & 66 Columns
7th Bn The Nigerian Regiment – Nos 29 & 35 Columns
12th Bn The Nigerian Regiment – Nos 12 & 43 Columns

14th Infantry Brigade (Javelin) – Brigadier T. Brodie
2nd Bn The Black Watch – Nos 42 & 73 Columns
1st Bn Bedfordshire & Hertfordshire Regiment – Nos 16 & 61 Columns
2nd Bn The York & Lancaster Regiment – Nos 65 & 84 Columns
7th Bn The Leicestershire Regiment – Nos 47 & 74 Columns

16th Infantry Brigade (Enterprise) – Brigadier B. E. Fergusson
1st Bn The Queen's Regiment – Nos 21 & 22 Columns
2nd Bn The Leicestershire Regiment – Nos 17 and 71 Columns
51/69 Regiment Royal Artillery – Nos 51 & 69 Columns
45th Reconnaissance Regiment – Nos 45 and 54 Columns

77th Indian Infantry Brigade (Emphasis) – Brigadier M. Calvert
3rd Bn 6th Gurkha Rifles – Nos 36 & 63 Columns
1st Bn The King's Regiment – Nos 81 & 82 Columns
1st Bn The Lancashire Fusiliers – Nos 20 & 50 Columns
1st Bn The South Staffordshire Regiment – Nos 38 & 80 Columns
3rd Bn 9th Gurkha Rifles – Nos 57 & 93 Columns

111th Indian Infantry Brigade (Profound) – Brigadier W. D. A. Lentaigne
1st Bn The Cameronians (Scottish Rifles) – Nos 26 & 90 Columns
2nd Bn The King's Own Royal Regiment – Nos 41 & 46 Columns
3rd Bn 4th Gurkha Rifles – No. 30 Column

Morris Force – Brigadier J. T. Morris
4th Bn 9th Gurkha Rifles – Nos 49 & 94 Columns
3rd Bn 4th Gurkha Rifles – No. 40 Column

Dah Force – Lieutenant Colonel D. C. Herring

Kachin Levies

Bladet (Blain's Detachment) – Major Blain
Gliderborne commando engineers

R, S & U Troops 160th Field Regiment RA
W, X, Y & Z Troops 69th Light Anti-Aircraft Regiment RA

*1st Air Commando Group USAAF – Colonel P. G. Cochrane
20 B-25 Mitchell medium bombers
30 P-51A fighter-bombers
20 C-47 transports
12 UC-64 transports
100 L-5 & L-1 STOL light aircraft
100 CG-4A gliders
25 TG-5 training gliders (for use on remote LZs)

The beginning of 1944 in Burma witnessed two major Japanese offensives carried out a month apart. The first, mounted in February in the Arakan region, was aimed at drawing in the reserves of General Sir William ' Bill' Slim's Fourteenth Army, while the following month saw the Japanese Fifteenth Army launch another against Fourteenth Army's IC Corps. Both of these offensives were soundly defeated.

Meanwhile, on 4 February 1944, Wingate received orders from Fourteenth Army to carry out the following tasks:

1 To interdict the flow of supplies and reinforcements heading northwards to the Japanese 18th 'Chrysanthemum' Division opposing the First Chinese Army under General Joseph W. Stilwell and divert the enemy's reserves against Special Force.

2 To create a favourable situation for the First Chinese Army in Yunnan to advance westwards across the Salween river.

---

* Not under command but exclusively in support of Special Force, this unit was initially designated Project 9 and subsequently the 5318th Provisional Unit (Air). On 29 March 1944, it was redesignated again as 1st Air Commando Group.

3 To inflict the maximum confusion, damage and loss on the enemy forces in Burma.

Wingate's plan was to compel the Japanese to withdraw from all areas in Burma north of the 24th parallel by carrying out a long-range infiltration. This would be conducted in three phases, the first being an approach march by Brigadier Bernard Fergusson's 16th Infantry Brigade from Ledo to Indaw. Situated on the railway line between Myitkina in the north to Mandalay in the south, Indaw, together with a road linking Bhamo and Myitkina, was the principal line of communication and supply for the 18th Chrysanthemum Division, commanded by Lieutenant General Shinichi Tanaka. En route to Indaw, the brigade was to assist the First Chinese Army by detaching two columns to take and secure Lonkin, which was held by an enemy force guarding the left flank of the 18th Chrysanthemum Division.

Thereafter, Fergusson was to establish a stronghold near Indaw. Codenamed Aberdeen, it would be situated near a small village called Taungle, some twenty-three miles to the north-east of Indaw in a deep valley, closed at its northern end by a high ridge. Lying at the headwaters of the River Meza, the site was remote with difficult access, and easy to defend. Moreover, the local inhabitants were pro-British and would give early warning of any approach by Japanese forces. Aberdeen would be garrisoned by the 6th Battalion The Nigeria Regiment following the subsequent arrival of 3rd West African Brigade.

A month later, 77th and 111th Indian Infantry Brigades would be flown from three airfields at Hailekandi, Lalaghat and Tulihal in Assam to three LZs in Burma codenamed Broadway, Piccadilly and Chowringhee respectively. The 77th was to be landed east of the railway at Broadway where a stronghold would be established and garrisoned by the 3rd Battalion 9th Gurkha Rifles. The 111th would also land east of the railway at Piccadilly and head for the area to the south of Indaw. En route, it was to interdict the railway with demolitions, ambushes and roadblocks to prevent any interference with 16th Infantry Brigade's operations by enemy forces coming up from the south. It would be assisted in its demolitions tasks by Bladet's commando engineers who would be tasked with blowing bridges on the line.

Morris Force, meanwhile, would be landed at Chowringhee, to the east of the River Irrawaddy, from where it would head for the mountains flanking the road from Bhamo to Myitkina, subsequently establishing a base from which it would mount raiding operations.

The third phase of Operation Thursday would see a follow-up airlift of 3rd West African and 14th Infantry Brigades into the operational area.

D-Day for the airborne element of Thursday was 5 March. At Lailaghat, eighty CG-4A Waco gliders were lined up behind their C-47 tugs, waiting for the signal to take off at H-Hour, 5.00 p.m. Half an hour beforehand, however, a light aircraft of 1st Air Commando Group landed with aerial photographs of the three LZs. These clearly showed that, while Broadway and Chowringhee were clear, Piccadilly had been blocked with felled trees. (Wingate had banned photo-reconnaissance flights over the operational area for fear of alerting the Japanese to the forthcoming mission. This, however, was an unnecessary precaution as high-level reconnaissance flights were flown almost daily at altitudes of up to 20,000 feet and could have monitored any enemy activity in the areas of the three LZs without arousing suspicion. The commander of 1st Air Commando Group, Colonel Philip G. Cochrane, was unhappy about the absence of any form of surveillance on the LZs during the period leading up to D-Day and thus despatched a B-25 to reconnoitre and photograph all three on the morning of 5 March.)

The immediate reaction to the photographs showing Piccadilly strewn with tree trunks was that the enemy had discovered details of Thursday, and it raised the question as to whether they would be waiting in ambush at the other two LZs. It later transpired, however, that the trees had been felled as part of routine forestry work in the area.

After due discussion between Major General Wingate, Brigadier Calvert, whose 77th Indian Infantry Brigade was to have been flown

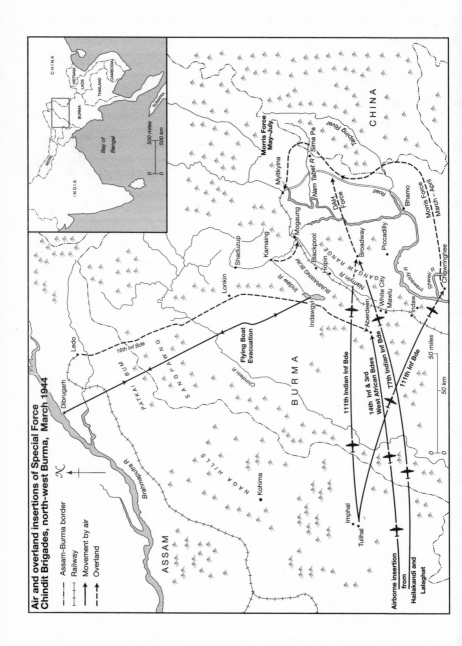

Air and overland insertions of Special Force
Chindit Brigades, north-west Burma, March 1944

- - - Assam–Burma border
⊢⊢⊢ Railway
→ Movement by air
⇢ Overland

500 miles
500 km

CHINA
VIETNAM
LAOS
(CAMBODIA)
THAILAND
SUMATRA
BURMA
INDIA
Bay of Bengal

Morris Force May–July
Myitkyina
Nam Tabet R
Sima Pa
Taiping River
CHINA
Mogaung
Kamaing
Shaduzup
Blackpool
Hopin
Broadway
Piccadilly
Bhamo
Road
DAH Force
Morris Force March–April
Lonkin
BUMRAWNG BUM
Namyin R
NGANGAW RANGE
White City
Mawlu
Chowringhee
Irrawaddy R
Shweli R
Indaw
Indawgyi
Aberdeen
Ledo
Dibrugarh
16th Inf Bde
PATKAI BUM
SANGPAING
Chindwin R
Flying Boat Evacuation
BURMA
Indaw R
111th Indian Inf Bde
14th Inf & 3rd West African Bdes
77th Indian Inf Bde
111th Inf Bde
50 miles
50 km
NAGA HILLS
Kohima
Brahmaputra R
ASSAM
Imphal
Tulihal
Airborne insertion from Hailakandi and Lalaghat
N

into Piccadilly, and General Slim, who was present to see the take-off, the decision was taken that Calvert and his men would fly into Broadway instead.

At 6.12 p.m., the leading pair of double-towed Wacos took off behind their C-47 tug. A total of eighty-three transport aircraft were involved in the airlift, these comprising forty-four C-47s of Nos 31, 62, 117 and 194 Squadrons RAF and a further thirty-nine of the 27th and 315th Troop Carrier Squadrons USAAF and 1st Air Commando Group. The delay had cost just over an hour of moonlight and thus the number of gliders flying in had been reduced from eighty to sixty-one. Due to the possibility of the threat of ambush on the gliders touching down, the initial element comprised eight Wacos whose passengers included a 1st Air Commando Group pathfinding team, under Colonel John R. Alison, and a ground protection group. The latter was provided by the 1st Battalion The King's Regiment and led by the commanding officer, Lieutenant Colonel Walter Scott.

After a flight lasting two and a half hours, the leading eight gliders touched down on Broadway without mishap and fifteen minutes later were joined by those bringing in the advance element of Headquarters 77th Indian Infantry Brigade. The method used for the approach to the LZ was for the tug C-47s to fly low towards the line of the LZ lights and for the gliders to cast off at a point marked by a pilot light half a mile short of the LZ. This was adopted to minimise the risk of tug aircraft being exposed to enemy small arms fire in the event that the landing was opposed.

Meanwhile, the pathfinding team was laying out the lights to mark the LZ for the main body which arrived shortly afterwards. The first two Wacos landed safely but the next three pairs fell foul of deep ruts in the ground, caused earlier by logging in the area, which knocked off the gliders' undercarriages, causing them to swing round and block the LZ. Before the landing lights could be moved to realign the runway, another pair of Wacos landed, one of them crashing into the wrecked gliders. The following gliders succeeded in avoiding the obstacle in front of them, one pair by taking off again over it and landing beyond and the remainder by landing on the re-marked LZ.

Following the arrival of the first wave of gliders, the decision was taken that no more would be accepted that night; the codewords Soya Link, cancelling all further flights, were transmitted to Lalaghat. They were not received until 2.27 a.m. on 6 March by which time nine gliders of the second wave were already en route to Broadway. Eight were recalled successfully but the ninth, carrying a bulldozer, flew on and arrived at the LZ. Landing at too great a speed, it overshot the strip and came to a sudden halt jammed between two trees. Its load careered forward, causing the nose section to be raised and fortunately taking the two pilots with it, lifting them clear as the bulldozer hurtled out of the aircraft into the jungle beyond where it was destroyed.

The flights that night had proved to be difficult for both gliders and tugs. While some of the pilots were sufficiently experienced to cope with a double tow, many others had received insufficient practice prior to the operation. Moreover, the flight path took them over the River Chindwin where conditions were somewhat bumpy and the aircraft were required to climb to an altitude of 10,000 feet to clear the mountains bordering the river. An added difficulty was that most of the Wacos, which normally were loaded to a maximum of 3,500 lbs, were carrying consignments weighing 4,500 lbs. In addition, the tables governing the loading of the aircraft had sometimes been ignored, with troops stowing additional equipment, so that those aircraft pitched and yawed on encountering any degree of turbulence. In some cases, tow-ropes snapped or pilots were forced to cast off, the gliders subsequently disappearing into the thick jungle along the route.

In the first wave of gliders, four broke their towropes shortly after taking off from Lalaghat. Two combinations were forced to return to base after the tugs developed electrical problems while two more landed at Imphal as a result of engine trouble. Eight Wacos landed in Japanese-held territory east of the Chindwin. Of these, the passengers of two returned to the river, crossed it and returned to Lalaghat safely while those of two others continued on to Broadway on foot. Troops travelling in another two were captured by the enemy while those of the last pair disappeared without trace. Two more gliders were cast off prematurely near Broadway and crashed half a mile from the LZ, all but two of the troops aboard being killed. Out of sixty-one Wacos despatched from Lalaghat only thirty-four arrived at Broadway.

By first light on 6 March, the LZ at Broadway had been cleared and the codewords Pork Sausage were transmitted at 6.30 a.m. to Lalaghat to resume the fly-in. The casualties incurred during the landings on the LZ numbered two men killed and thirty-four injured, a large number of them being sappers of the US Army airfield construction party, but despite these losses there were sufficient personnel to proceed with the construction work. During the day, a number of light aircraft of 1st Air Commando Group, headed by an L-5 flown by Major Andy Rebori, arrived to evacuate the dead and wounded, and that evening sixty-one C-47s from Hailakandi, led by an aircraft flown by Brigadier General Donald Old USAAF, landed at 8.00 p.m. at Broadway.

The night of 6 March also witnessed the advance party of Brigadier W. D. A. 'Joe' Lentaigne's 111th Indian Infantry Brigade landing in twelve gliders at Chowringhee, some forty miles from Broadway. One glider overshot the strip, its three-man crew being killed and its load of a tractor being damaged beyond repair, the latter being replaced by another despatched from Broadway with other engineer stores. By 11.15 p.m. on the following day, the codeword Roorkee was transmitted to signal that the strip was ready to accept aircraft. Twenty C-47s were despatched but for some reason doubts arose among those controlling the movement of aircraft and a signal was sent to Chowringhee, asking for verification that the strip was sufficient in length to accept fully loaded C-47s. Aghast when advised that it was only 2,700 feet long, the air controllers immediately recalled all the aircraft but only thirteen responded and turned back. The remaining seven, however, managed to land safely at Broadway and unloaded before taking off and returning to Hailakandi.

On D+4, 9 March, Major General Wingate decided to land only four columns of 111th Indian Infantry Brigade at Chowringhee, and to fly the remainder into Broadway. His reasoning was that it had served its purpose of drawing the enemy's attention from Broadway but it lay only fifteen miles from an enemy airfield at Katha and was near a major road, which would allow the Japanese to move forces swiftly into the area. On being advised of Wingate's change of plan, Brigadier Lentaigne prepared to evacuate the LZ and by 11.00 a.m. on 10 March Chowringhee was deserted except for a number of damaged gliders. Wingate's judgment was proved sound as two hours later Japanese fighters and bombers bombed and strafed the LZ, attacking again at 6.00 a.m. on the following day.

By 11 March, the first phase of the airborne landings of Special Force had been completed. During that night, four gliders landed on the banks of the Irrawaddy bringing in equipment for 111th Indian Infantry Brigade to cross the river as it headed west for Whuntho on the Myitkina–Mandalay railway. Two of these aircraft were recovered by 'snatching', a process by which a C-47 trailing a hook flew in at low level and 'snatched' the towrope of a glider suspended in mid-air between two poles, but the other two were abandoned and destroyed.

Next day, 12 March, saw 16th Infantry Brigade complete its approach march and arrive in the Meza Valley where it was to establish Aberdeen. Meanwhile, Morris Force was en route to cut the Bhamo–Myitkina road while 111th Indian Infantry Brigade was crossing the Irrawaddy to mount an attack on the base area and supply dumps of the Japanese 31st Division. On 17 March, a patrol of Bladet, commanded by Major Blain himself, was landed in five gliders with the task of carrying out demolition operations against the enemy line of communications in the area of Kawlin and Wuntho, and subsequently to direct Allied bombers on to selected targets.

Wingate now had three of his brigades behind Japanese lines, in an area more or less at the centre of four enemy divisions. Broadway was by this time firmly established and 77th Indian Infantry Brigade was within two days' march of Henu where it was to establish a strong-hold, codenamed White City, and cut the main lines of communication of the 18th Chrysanthemum Division facing General Joseph W. Stilwell's First Chinese Army in the Hukawng Valley. Nine thousand men, 1,300 mules and 223 tons of weapons and equipment had been landed, with casualties amounting to only 120 men, none of them caused by enemy action. This in itself was a remarkable achievement.

The third phase of Thursday now began with the flying in of 14th Infantry Brigade and 3rd West African Brigade into the Meza Valley where they would join 16th Infantry Brigade in establishing Aberdeen. Wingate himself arrived first on 21 March in a light aircraft to conduct a reconnaissance of the area designated for the stronghold. First light next day saw the arrival of six Wacos bringing in US Army engineers and equipment and the strip was ready to receive C-47s by the following evening.

It had been planned to complete the airlift of both brigades in a total of 360 sorties over six nights but during this period Fourteenth Army was experiencing difficulty in stemming an offensive launched against IV Corps by the Japanese and required all of its aircraft for resupply missions. Consequently only twenty-five C-47s, including ten from 1st Air Commando Group, could be spared for Special Force. Thus the airlift of the two brigades, hampered by bad weather and the threat of enemy fighters, lasted twenty days. The Japanese mounted several air attacks on Aberdeen, and on one occasion enemy aircraft were only just leaving the area when twelve C-47s began making their approach to the airstrip.

On 24 March, Special Force suffered a major blow when a B-25H bomber of 1st Air Commando Group, in which Major General Orde Wingate was returning to his headquarters at Lalaghat, crashed near the village of Pabram, between Imphal and Silchar, during a storm. A ground rescue party was despatched from Headquarters Special Force and reached the area of the crash site on 27 March. There it discovered that the aircraft had exploded on crashing and that identification of the bodies was impossible. Documents and Wingate's Wolsey topee, which he always wore, were however found among the debris and thus confirmed that he had lost his life. Command of Special Force was assumed by Brigadier 'Joe' Lentaigne, who in turn handed over 111th Indian Infantry Brigade to Lieutenant Colonel John Masters.

The beginning of April found 77th Indian Infantry Brigade established in White City, a stronghold astride the Irrawaddy and the road and railway line linking Indaw with Mogaung and Myitkina. Its main supply route cut, the 18th Chrysanthemum Division mounted several attempts to dislodge Calvert and his men but these all failed, the Japanese suffering heavy losses. Realising, however, that General Tanaka had no choice but to increase his efforts to reopen the line of communications that was so vital to his division, the now-promoted Major General Lentaigne decided to close Aberdeen and reinforce White City, strengthening its defences with 25-pounders, 2-pounder anti-tank guns and Bofors 40mm anti-aircraft guns. This required the construction of an airstrip and thus on 3 April, five gliders landed a group of US Army engineers and equipment to carry out the work.

The night of 5 April saw the arrival of the first C-47s at White City, although heavy rain waterlogged the newly constructed airstrip. Twenty-six aircraft landed during the night, bringing in 250 troops, four 25-pounder guns, six Bofors and two 2-pounder anti-tank guns. Despite the presence of an enemy force known to be in the area, the landings took place successfully.

The enemy attacked White City in strength on the following day, using infantry supported by artillery, mortars and tanks. The battle lasted for several days until 15 April by which time the Japanese had failed to overrun the stronghold and its garrison, incurring heavy casualties estimated at between 1,500 and 2,000. Thereafter, they mounted no further serious efforts to dislodge Brigadier Michael Calvert and his men.

Phase 3 of Operation Thursday was complete by 27 April, by which time Special Force dominated the entire area within a radius of forty miles of Indaw. The road and rail links forming the 18th Chrysanthe-mum Division's line of communications remained cut as did the Bhamo–Myitkina road dominated by Morris Force, which had blown all bridges and roads and was vigorously attacking enemy forces attempt-ing to use that route. Meanwhile, Dah Force had deployed to the Kachin country to the east of the Irrawaddy and was actively engaged in prepa-rations to lead a revolt by the tribes when required to do so. Finally, supply dumps in the base area of the Japanese 31st Division had been attacked and destroyed by 111th Indian Infantry Brigade, and enemy lines of communication via Banmauk and Humalin blocked.

Special Force had achieved all of its objectives but others were unable to take due advantage as originally planned. Indeed, its success was proving to be an embarrassment to Fourteenth Army which failed to exploit it. Consequently, it was decided that Special Force would now operate in support of General Joseph Stilwell's First Chinese Army.

The new plan called for the evacuation of 16th Infantry Brigade to Broadway which would be followed by the closure of all the strong-holds. 111th Indian Infantry Brigade would establish a new stronghold, codenamed Blackpool, between Pinbaw and Hopin in the Mogaung Valley where it would be nearer to the First Chinese Army. It would be protected by 14th Infantry Brigade and 77th Indian Infantry Brigade operating as floating formations.

On 2 May, Major General 'Joe' Lentaigne had moved his tactical headquarters to Shadazup where it was co-located with the headquar-ters of the First Chinese Army. At the same time, Special Force's logistic support base began moving from Sylhet in eastern Bengal to Dinjan in Assam, where it became operational on 27 May.

On 5/6 May, Aberdeen was evacuated as 16th Infantry Brigade, exhausted after three months of operations, withdrew, all the strong-hold's guns and heavy equipment being flown out to Special Force's base at the airfield at Sylhet. The evacuation of White City by 77th Infantry Brigade occurred on 9 May, although the stronghold was almost surrounded by enemy forces, its guns and equipment also being flown out at night. On that same day four gliders, carrying US Army engineers and plant, were towed to Blackpool where they came under fire on landing. One glider stalled and crashed, its crew being killed and its load destroyed. On the following day, five C-47s landed but the airstrip was too rough, resulting in two aircraft being damaged and one over-shooting the strip and bursting into flames. Thereafter, several sorties were flown to Blackpool, all landing successfully. By this time the evac-uation of Broadway was in progress with 16th Infantry Brigade being flown out to Sylhet and the light anti-aircraft artillery troop being ferried across to Blackpool. It ended on 13 May, having taken two nights to complete.

The new deployment of Special Force proved far from successful, disregarding as it did the principles of long-range penetration opera-tions as evolved and developed by Major General Orde Wingate. Unlike Operation Thursday, it failed to interdict enemy lines of communication effectively, albeit it succeeded in goading the enemy into attacking Blackpool and thereafter building up their forces in the area, diverting them from those facing the First Chinese Army. By now, however, the monsoon rains had arrived, making aerial resupply by night impossi-ble. Swiftly appreciating this, the Japanese moved anti-aircraft artillery into the area, rendering supply by daylight equally impracticable. The monsoon also prevented direct air support from Lalaghat and Hailekandi, and furthermore, 1st Air Commando Group, which had provided such invaluable support since the beginning of Thursday, had to be withdrawn for rest and refitting and thus ceased operations in support of Special Force on 20 May.

The absence of air supply and support had the inevitable conse-quences. On 25 May, following twenty days of heavy fighting during which its stocks of ammunition and supplies were almost exhausted, the airstrip lost and its perimeter breached, Blackpool was evacuated. Although almost surrounded by troops of the Japanese 53rd Division, the garrison began to withdraw on foot at 5.50 a.m., taking its sick and wounded with it as it headed off over the hills towards Mokso Sakkan, blocking and booby trapping the route it had taken. The Japanese, however, did not follow. On arrival at Mokso Sakkan three days later, 130 sick and wounded were flown out in a series of sorties by light aircraft and Sunderland flying boats.

The final operations of Special Force saw 14th Infantry and 3rd West African Brigades, and the 2,000 survivors of 111th Indian Infantry Brigade, operating west of Mogaung. 111th Indian Infantry Brigade attacked a hill feature known as Point 2171, the battle lasting for over two weeks before the remnants of the brigade were ordered to withdraw. Meanwhile, 77th Indian Infantry Brigade had been ordered to attack Mogaung, the battle beginning on 6 June and ending when the town was taken on 27 June. Casualties were heavy, reducing the brigade's strength from 2,355 to 806.

By this time, the ranks of the Chindits were heavily depleted with further losses continuing through exhaustion and illness. This came to the attention of the Supreme Allied Commander South East Asia, Admiral Lord Louis Mountbatten, who ordered an investigation. On learning that only 100 men of the 111th Indian Infantry Brigade were fit for duty, he ordered General Joseph Stilwell to evacuate immediately all injured and wounded. Shortly afterwards, it was agreed that the remaining Special Force brigades would be withdrawn. The last Chindits left Burma on 27 August 1944, half of their strength having to be admitted to hospital on their return to India.

In the Dutch East Indies, meanwhile, the 503rd Parachute Infantry Regiment, commanded by Colonel George Jones, who had taken over from Colonel Kenneth H. Kinsler in October 1943, took part in Operation Table Top during July 1944. Off the north-west coast of New Guinea lay the strategically important island of Noemfoor, situated halfway between the island of Biak, the larger of two main islands comprising the Schouten Group, and the western end of New Guinea. Located on the island at Kamiri was an enemy airfield whose capture would enable the Allies to position their own advance airstrips there and impose a blockade on Japanese shipping from the air.

During May, Noemfoor Island became indirectly involved in the advance westwards through New Guinea by US forces, under General Douglas MacArthur. At that time, troops of the 41st Infantry Division were engaged in heavy fighting on Biak which, with its three enemy airfields, was another important stepping-stone in MacArthur's advance. Despite being outnumbered, the island's Japanese garrison, reinforced by troops ferried from Noemfoor, a distance of seventy-five miles, by barge under cover of darkness, counter-attacked and forced the 41st Division back to the shoreline. Once the source of reinforcements was discovered by the Americans, General MacArthur ordered that Noemfoor be taken.

Approximately fifteen miles in length, Noemfoor was very flat, with only a small area above 400 feet in elevation, and almost entirely covered in jungle except for small plots of land cleared by the local inhabitants. Employing slave labour, the Japanese had constructed two airfields: the first and larger one at Kamiri, in the north-west corner of the island, and the second, little more than a strip for occasional use, in the south-west of the island at Namber. A third airfield was under construction at Kornasoren, at the northern end of the island.

The US Navy's Task Force 77, commanded by Rear Admiral William M. Fechteler and comprising one heavy cruiser, two light cruisers, twenty-five destroyers, seven fast patrol boats and more than sixty landing craft, was allotted the landing operation, with air support being provided by the US Thirteenth Air Force. The amphibious landing element was supplied by a US Army formation, the 158th Regimental Combat Team (RCT) commanded by Brigadier General Hanford MacNider.

Japanese forces on Noemfoor were believed to comprise 1,200 IJAAF personnel commanded by a colonel and well armed with automatic weapons and mortars. Elements of this force had withdrawn from the airfields at Kamiri and Konrasoren and made their way to the island's only feature of high ground, dubbed Hill 670 and located between six and seven miles from the northern end of the island. Access to it was difficult as it was surrounded by thick jungle through which there were no roads and few tracks. The feature could not be observed from the air and accurate bombardment of it by naval gunfire, artillery or mortars would be a matter of pure guesswork. The only way to attack it would be to locate and assault it from the ground.

At 6.40 a.m. on 2 July, the warships of Task Force 77 began bombarding known enemy positions on the island as the landing force headed towards the northern shore near Konrasoren in eight landing ships tank (LST), subsequently transferring into smaller and shallow-draught landing craft infantry (LCI) at the edge of the reef guarding the approaches to the beaches.

Having landed and secured a beachhead, the 158th Regimental Combat Team thereafter encountered strong opposition and therefore the operational reserve, the 503rd Parachute Infantry Regiment was committed. At 10.30 a.m., Colonel Jones's Regimental Headquarters and the 1st Battalion dropped on to the airstrip at Konrasoren. Since the DZ was long and narrow, the aircraft were forced to fly in line astern. Unfortunately, some pilots omitted to adjust their altimeters and hence did not adhere to the specified drop height of 300 feet, subsequently dropping their sticks from as low as 150 feet. This error, combined with the fact that the airfield was littered with equipment and vehicles, resulted in several casualties who sustained broken legs and ankles when landing on the airstrip, which was constructed from crushed coral.

Next day saw a drop on the same DZ by the 3rd Battalion along with elements of the 503rd's headquarter and quartermaster companies. Further casualties were sustained, although not as many as on the previous day; consequently the third drop by the 2nd Battalion was cancelled, the battalion subsequently being landed by sea.

During the following six weeks, all three battalions of the 503rd Parachute Infantry Regiment took part in heavy fighting against the enemy force on the island until all resistance ceased on 22 August.

Two months earlier, the 503rd had been joined in New Guinea by the US 11th Airborne Division, commanded by Major General Joseph M. Swing. Activated at Camp Mackall, North Carolina, on 25 February 1943, the division comprised: the 511th Parachute Infantry Regiment, 187th and 188th Glider Infantry Regiments, 457th Parachute Field Artillery Battalion, 674th and 675th Glider Field Artillery Battalions, 127th Airborne Engineer Battalion, 152nd Airborne Anti-Aircraft Battalion, together with headquarters, signals, medical, quartermaster and ordnance maintenance companies, and a military police platoon.

The division left the United States in early May and arrived twenty-eight days later in New Guinea, disembarking at Oro Bay; from there it was transported to the US base area at Dobadura where it spent the month of June becoming acclimatised and preparing for operations. Divisional parachute and glider schools were established in August, in conjunction with the USAAF's 54th Troop Carrier Wing, to train and qualify the majority of the division's gliderborne troops as parachutists and a major proportion of its paratroops in gliderborne skills. The division was unique among US airborne formations in pursuing such a policy, Major General Swing's belief being that his men should be able to enter battle by parachute or glider. At one point, approximately three-quarters of the division's gliderborne personnel were also qualified parachutists.

During August and September, amphibious warfare training was conducted in Oro Bay while elements of the division attended courses held at schools established by the US Sixth Army. Among these was a long-range patrol course attended by the division's reconnaissance platoon at a school run by the Alamo Scouts, the Sixth Army's long-range reconnaissance and intelligence-gathering unit.

On 12 October, Major General Swing received orders to move the division to Leyte. On 7 November, the division left Oro Bay in nine transports escorted by a flotilla of warships and began its voyage to the Philippines.

Almost three years previously, in December 1941, the Philippines had been invaded by the Japanese Fourteenth Army, commanded by

General Masaharu Homma. Fierce fighting ensued, during which General Douglas MacArthur, commander of the United States Army Forces in the Far East (USAFFE) withdrew all his forces in the Philippines to the Bataan Peninsula. On 9 April 1942, following three months of bitter fighting, by which time his exhausted and starving 73,000 American and Filipino troops were no longer in any condition to fight, the commander of the forces on the peninsula, Major General Edward P. King, surrendered to the Japanese. The fortified island of Corregidor, on which General MacArthur's headquarters was located, fell on 8 May with all organised resistance in the Philippines ending a few weeks later.

By that time, however, acting on an order from President Roosevelt, General Macarthur had left Corregidor on 11 March, handing over command of all US forces in the Philippines to Lieutenant General Jonathan M. Wainwright, and travelling in a motor torpedo boat to the island of Mindanao. From here he flew to Australia at just after midnight on 17 March 1942. As he departed, he made his famous vow to the Philippines: 'I shall return.'

Two years and seven months later, MacArthur kept his word when he waded ashore on Leyte after the landing on the morning 20 October 1944 of 100,000 US troops on the east coast of the island near the town of Tacloban. The following three months would witness fierce fighting, with the 80,000-strong Japanese garrison putting up a stiff resistance.

The 11th Airborne Division arrived off Leyte around 18 November, disembarking at Bito soon afterwards and completing the unloading of its equipment by the 23rd. Meanwhile, the 503rd Parachute Infantry Regiment had also arrived and, like the 11th Airborne Division, was ordered to prepare itself for immediate operations. The 511th Parachute Infantry Regiment, commanded by Colonel Orin D. Haugen, was the first element of the division to see action. During the following three months, the division was involved in bitter fighting as it carried out its task of clearing the mountain pass from Burauen to Omoc, killing more than 5,700 Japanese in the process.

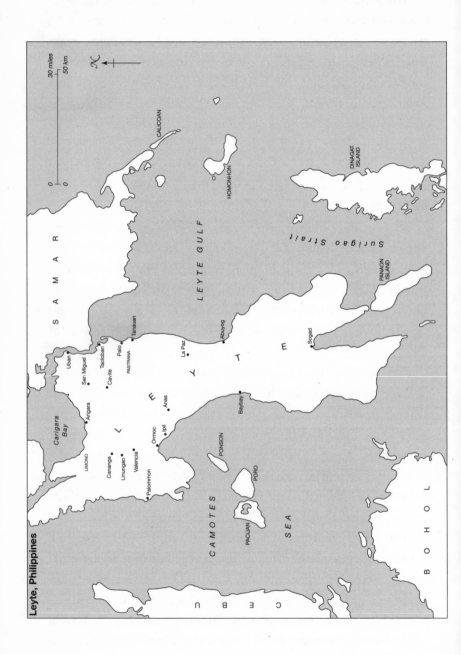

Leyte, Philippines

The 503rd Parachute Regimental Combat Team, as the regiment had now become, was being deployed elsewhere. On 15 December it carried out an amphibious landing on the island of Mindoro, in the central Philippines, with the purpose of securing sites for airstrips to provide forward base facilities for USAAF aircraft supporting subsequent landings. It had initially been intended that the regiment would be dropped on to the island but because the airstrip on Leyte was inadequate for use by C-47s, it soon became apparent that an airborne operation would be impossible. Following its landing, the 503rd found itself under heavy attack by Japanese aircraft and warships, the latter bombarding the regiment's positions for almost half an hour.

During this period, Leyte itself witnessed the first of two airborne operations carried out by the Japanese. The first took place on the night of 26 /27 November when three Ki-57 transports flew at low level north over the Leyte Gulf and along the coast of the island at around midnight, carrying paratroops whose mission was to carry out sabotage attacks on US aircraft based on the island, to prevent them from attacking a Japanese convoy due to enter Ormoc Bay on 28 November.

One aircraft crash-landed in the sea, approximately twenty-five yards offshore near the base area of an American unit, the 728th Amphibian Tractor Battalion, one of whose men, under the impression that the aircraft was a USAAF C-47, ran over to render assistance but was met by a grenade thrown in his direction. Alerted by the explosion, men of the 728th opened fire, killing two of the enemy, the rest of whom escaped into a nearby area of swamp. A search of the aircraft revealed a large quantity of explosive charges.

The second aircraft crash-landed on the airstrip at Buri, killing all its occupants, while the third landed on the beach at Bito, on the opposite side of the river running along the northern edge of 11th Airborne Division's rear base area. In the dark, believing it to be a C-47 forced down by mechanical trouble, the members of a nearby detachment of 152nd Airborne Anti-Aircraft Battalion merely called across to enquire if all was well, receiving an acknowledgment in English. It was only after first light that they saw the rising sun roundels on the aircraft's wings and fuselage, by which time all those aboard the aircraft had succeeded in escaping westwards.

The second operation was mounted in the first week of December, in a further effort to prevent US aircraft from attacking convoys in the area off Ormoc and from interfering with Japanese air operations based on Luzon. The first phase would comprise a parachute drop on the airfield at San Pablo on the evening of 6 December by elements of the IJA's 3rd Parachute Regiment, commanded by Lieutenant Colonel Tsunehiro Shirai, which had been tasked with capturing three USAAF airstrips at Buri, San Pablo and Bayug on Leyte. Initially, the entire 1st Parachute Brigade had been allocated to the task but insufficient transport aircraft were available and the force was cut to one regiment. This was further reduced to a force of approximately 500, again due to the lack of transport aircraft, obliging the men to be flown in three lifts over three days.

The second phase of the operation would consist of an amphibious landing in Ormoc Bay on 7 December while troops of the Japanese 26th Infantry Division attacked from the west of Burauen to link up with the paratroops. Smaller attacks were to be launched against airfields at Buri, Dulag and Tacloban which were to be held until midnight on 7 December, destroying as many enemy aircraft as possible.

Preceded by bombers which carried out a preliminary raid on the San Pablo airfield, dropping incendiary bombs which hit a light aircraft and an aviation fuel dump, thirty-nine IJAAF Ki-57 transports arrived over the objectives at just before 6.00 p.m. on 6 December and dropped their sticks, some of which jumped from directly above the adjacent headquarters and administrative base area of 11th Airborne Division. In fact, the division had received advance warning of the raid from intelligence channels. Major Henry J. Muller, the G-2 Headquarters 11th Airborne Division, had included it in his intelligence estimate to the divisional commander, Major General Swing, but the latter had apparently chosen to disregard the threat as he considered that the Japanese

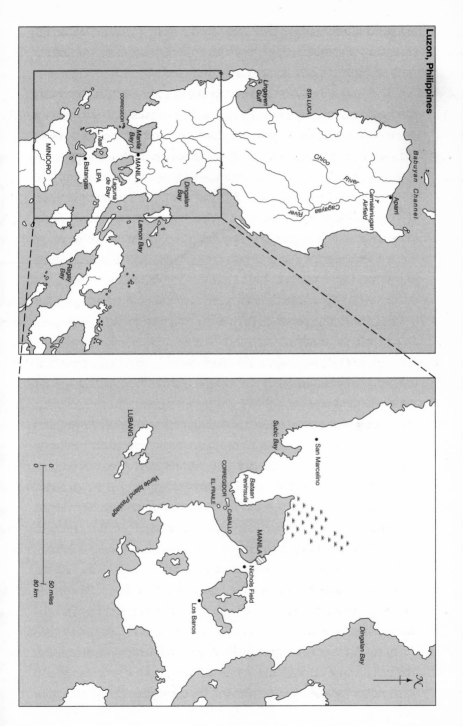

Luzon, Philippines

STA LUCA

Lingayen
Gulf

Babuyan Channel

Chico

River

Cagayan

River

Camalaniugan
Airfield

Aparri

CORREGIDOR

MINDORO

Manila
Bay

MANILA

L. Taal

LIPA

Batangas

Laguna
de Bay

Dingalan
Bay

Lamon Bay

Ragay
Bay

LUBANG

Verde Island Passage

Subic Bay

San Marcelino

Bataan
Peninsula

CORREGIDOR

EL FRAILE

CABALLO

MANILA

Nichols Field

Los Banos

Dingalan Bay

N

0

50 miles

80 km

607

did not possess sufficient air transport assets to launch such an operation.

Some 250–300 paratroops were dropped around the San Pablo airfield area. During that night a platoon of the 127th Airborne Engineer Battalion, led by Lieutenant Paul J. Pergamo, encountered a number and routed them before digging in on the south-west corner of the airfield. The enemy regrouped, however, and attacked the platoon's position three times, at one point advancing to within a few feet, before being beaten off with heavy losses. To the west of the airfield, a member of Company B 1st Battalion 187th Glider Infantry Regiment died in a hand-to-hand fight with two paratroops whom he killed with his fighting knife, he himself being killed by a grenade held to his back by one of his opponents.

Other paratroops had landed to the west of the airfield, thereafter heading for an airstrip at Bayug where they destroyed more light aircraft used by the division for aerial resupply of its forward units. There they encountered seventy-five members of the 11th Airborne Division's resupply unit who manned their trenches on the southern side of the airstrip and fought back until the enemy withdrew.

A further sixty paratroops, including the commanding officer of the 3rd Parachute Regiment, dropped on the airstrip at Buri, landing just after an L-4 light aircraft touched down bringing in radio equipment for the 1st Battalion 187th Glider Infantry Regiment. The pilot was killed when the enemy opened fire but his co-pilot escaped.

Meanwhile, the two aircraft carrying the detachment to drop at Tacloban approached the airstrip with their undercarriages lowered as if about to land; one was shot down and the other crashed. Two Ki-57s appeared over Dulag, one dropping a stick of five paratroops before crash-landing while the other crashed without dropping any troops, killing all those aboard.

At first light, to the west of the San Pablo airfield, the 1st Battalion 187th Glider Infantry Regiment came under increasing fire from snipers, three of whom were located and killed in the area of the battalion's command post. By this time, an ad hoc battalion had been formed from the 11th Airborne Division's quartermaster and ordnance maintenance companies. Shortly after first light, led by Lieutenant Colonel Douglas C. Davis, the commanding officer of the 127th Airborne Engineer Battalion, it began a counter-attack to clear the airfield of the enemy who had destroyed a number of light aircraft, a jeep, some tents and a fuel dump. Just then, Lieutenant Colonel Lukas E. Hoska's 674th Glider Field Artillery Battalion, minus its pack howitzers, arrived in DUKW amphibious vehicles from its base area at Bito Beach. The two battalions, with Major General Swing in the centre, then advanced across the airfield, clearing pockets of the enemy as they went.

During the afternoon of 7 December, reinforcements arrived at San Pablo in the form of the 1st and 2nd Battalions 149th Infantry Regiment. The 1st Battalion was tasked by Major General Swing with clearing the enemy paratroops from the area between the airfield and the Buri airstrip. Setting off at 2.30 p.m., it began moving through an area of swamp where it encountered the enemy in greater numbers than had been expected. Its companies did not reach the south side of the airstrip until late afternoon.

That same morning of 7 December witnessed the 1st Battalion 187th Glider Infantry Regiment attempting to recapture the Buri airstrip. The battalion had come under fire from a platoon of enemy to the west of the Dagami–Burauen road, engaging it while the 1st Battalion 382nd Infantry Regiment, which arrived on the scene at 9.30 a.m., immediately moved up to join it, the two units thereafter mounting an attack on the airstrip at 9.45 a.m. The enemy paratroops put a stiff fight, beating off several attacks before both battalions were withdrawn to the north to regroup.

Another attack was mounted at 2.00 p.m. that afternoon but this also proved unsuccessful. Led by Lieutenant Colonel George O. Pearson, commanding officer of the 1st Battalion of the 187th, the two battalions regrouped to the west of Buri before mounting yet another assault under heavy fire, this time gaining a foothold at the south-west corner of the airstrip. Shortly afterwards, the 1st Battalion of the 187th linked up with the 1st Battalion 149th Infantry Regiment at the western end of the airstrip. That night saw further heavy fighting during which Private Ova A. Kelly of Company A 1st Battalion 382nd Infantry Regiment charged an enemy machine-gun position single-handed, killing eight paratroops before he was shot dead, an act of gallantry subsequently recognised by the award of the Congressional Medal of Honor.

Although there were now three infantry battalions, Lieutenant Colonel Pearson was still unable to dislodge the enemy from the area of the Buri airstrip. During the late afternoon of 7 December, he was relieved of the task and ordered to move his battalion to the location of Headquarters Fifth Air Force, situated not far from the San Pablo airfield, and defend it.

On 8 December, Colonel Harry D. Hildebrand, commander of the 187th Glider Infantry Regiment, assumed command of all units now involved in clearing the enemy paratroop force from the area of Burauen. On the morning of the following day, the 1st Battalion 149th Infantry Regiment attacked north towards Buri but came under heavy fire from some 200 enemy dug in on a feature to the north of the airstrip. The battalion eventually withdrew, having killed some fifty men. At midnight on 9/10 December, the 1st Battalion 382nd Infantry Regiment was attacked by approximately 150 Japanese. The battalion's defensive perimeter was being held by its headquarter company and logistic support element as the rifle companies were on patrol tasks. Nevertheless, the attack was beaten off with the enemy suffering fifty killed and the defenders seven casualties.

Next morning found the 1st Battalion 149th Infantry Regiment launching yet another attack on the airstrip, this time with artillery support. By 5.00 p.m., the area had been cleared and the strip secured.

That evening, however, a battalion of the Japanese 26th Division appeared from the hills to the west of Burauen in an attempt to link up with the enemy paratroops. It was four days late in arriving, however, having encountered the 511th Parachute Regimental Combat Team using the same tracks through the jungle as it headed west. By the time the enemy battalion arrived in the area, the greater part of the paratroop force had been eliminated. Nevertheless, it proceeded to mount an attack on Headquarters Fifth Air Force which lasted for much of the night of 10 December.

This assault heralded the final gasp of the Japanese operation to seize the airfield and airstrips in the Burauen area. The last remaining elements of the 3rd Parachute Regiment force were mopped up by 12 December, by which time the remnants of the 26th Division battalion had straggled back into the hills where they suffered further losses at the hands of the 511th Parachute Regimental Combat Team. Meanwhile, the convoy which was to put into Ormoc Bay had been attacked and destroyed on 7 December by US aircraft operating from Tacloban.

Whereas the operation, which was the last use of airborne troops by the Japanese in the Second World War, had failed in its objective, it had succeeded in destroying a number of light aircraft sorely needed by the division for its resupply operations in the mountains, had inflicted a number of casualties and generally had caused four days of mayhem in the 11th Airborne Division's rear base area.

The campaign on Leyte was effectively over by the end of December 1944. By 15 January 1945, the 11th Airborne Division had been withdrawn to its rear base area at Bito Beach for rest, reorganisation and refitting. A week later, however, Major General Swing received a warning order alerting him to the division's participation in the forthcoming invasion of the island of Luzon, the principal island of the Philippines archipelago. Shortly afterwards, he received an operational order from Headquarters US Eighth Army, under whose command the division would be, giving him the details of the impending operation.

Codenamed Mike VI, the operation was to be a combined amphibious and airborne landing by the 11th Airborne Division in the south of Luzon on 31 January. The amphibious element, comprising the division less the 511th Parachute Regimental Combat Team, would land in the area of Nasugbu, a town on the coast to the south of Manila Bay, establishing a beachhead. Once the division was ashore and ready to break out, the 511th would carry out a drop on 2 February on to Tagaytay Ridge, a key feature some thirty miles from Nasugbu which formed the northern edge of Lake Taal, the latter situated in the crater of an extinct volcano. Thereafter, the division would advance along Highway 17, heading east over foothills and a number of rivers to a range of mountains through which it would make its way up to Tagaytay Ridge, linking up with the 511th within twenty-four hours. From there it would continue to follow the highway, turning north towards Manila Bay and the capital of Manila, a distance of another thirty-seven miles.

Some time prior to the American invasion, the commander of the Japanese forces in the Philippines, General Tomoyuki Yamashita, divided his forces on Luzon into three groups, each centred around a region of the island. The largest of these, under the direct command of Yamashita himself, was the 152,000-strong Shobu Group, based in the north of the island. The smaller Kembu Group, commanded by Major General Rikichi Tsukada and numbering approximately 30,000 men, occupied the Clark Air Field complex as well as the Bataan Peninsula. Yamashita's third force, the Shimbu Group commanded by Lieutenant General Shizuo Yokoyam, comprised some 80,000 troops and occupied the southern region of Luzon.

The enemy in the area where the 11th Airborne Division's landing would take place comprised an 8,500-strong formation designated the Fuji Force and commanded by a Colonel Fujishige. Under command of the Shimbu Group, Fujishige's force consisted of three battalions from two regiments of the 8th Infantry Division supported by the division's artillery and engineer battalions as well as logistic support troops. In addition, Fujishige had under command approximately 500 men of the 2nd Raiding Force, a special forces unit made up of six raiding squadrons, each of a hundred men equipped with explosive-packed suicide boats. The unit had suffered heavily during actions against Allied naval units during the previous weeks, losing all of its boats, and its remaining men had been assigned to reinforce the Fuji Force.

Fujishige ruled by fear, instilling terror in the local civilian population, all of whom he regarded as being guerrillas; it was estimated that in Batangas Province alone some 25,000 Filipinos were executed on his orders. With a large area to defend but with only limited resources at his disposal, he had deployed his troops to defend it from an invasion from the south as opposed to the west. A battalion group supported by artillery held the area to be converted in the forthcoming landing and advance inland by the 11th Airborne Division. Some 600 men manned a position just to the west of Tagaytay Ridge, while a further 400 occupied another in the south-western area of the ridge itself. The area of coast around Nasugbu was very lightly defended, with only a company-sized group around the town.

On the afternoon of 27 January, the 11th Airborne Division sailed from Leyte in a large flotilla of vessels carrying the invasion force to Luzon. En route, the 511th Parachute Regimental Combat Team disembarked on the island of Mindoro, where it began its preparations for its drop on Tagaytay Ridge.

At first light on 31 January, the vessels transporting the amphibious landing force arrived off Nasugbu. Shortly afterwards, warships began their bombardment of the landing beaches which were also bombed and strafed by US aircraft. At around 8.30 a.m., the leading element of the 11th Airborne Division, the 1st Battalion 188th Glider Infantry Regiment, commanded by Lieutenant Colonel Ernest Laflamme, landed and immediately headed for Nasugbu itself which, situated just under a mile away, was the battalion's initial objective. Scant opposition, in the form of light machine-gun fire from the area of Nasugbu Point to the north and San Diego Point to the south, along with some sporadic shelling, was encountered. The 2nd Battalion of the 188th, commanded by Lieutenant Colonel Thomas Mann, was the next to land, one of its companies being despatched south to deal with the enemy at San Diego Point and thereafter protect the right flank of the landing, while a company of the 1st Battalion set off northwards for Nasugbu Point with a similar mission.

The 1st Battalion then advanced inland with orders to press on as fast as possible up Highway 17 to prevent the Japanese from establishing any defences along it. Meanwhile, the 2nd Battalion advanced to the south across the River Lian to attack an enemy position at San Diego Point and protect the right flank of the division during the rest of the landing and the initial stage of its move inland.

By 10.30 a.m., the 188th Glider Infantry Regiment had advanced through Nasugbu and Wawa; the remainder of the division, led by the 1st Battalion of the 187th under Lieutenant Colonel Arthur H. Wilson, began coming ashore with the 2nd Battalion of the 187th subsequently assuming responsibility for the defence of Nasugbu and relieving the two companies of the 188th of their flank protection tasks.

The rest of the division meanwhile landed, though not without encountering problems caused by surf, sandbars and some enemy machine-gun and artillery fire from the area of Wawa; this was countered by Battery D 457th Parachute Field Artillery Battalion which established a gun line on the beach.

Such was the swift pace set by the 188th Glider Infantry Regiment that by 2.30 p.m. it had reached the River Palico and the bridge which spanned a deep gorge some 250 feet wide. It was guarded by a detachment of Japanese who were taken completely by surprise by the leading elements of the regiment who arrived just in time to prevent a squad of sappers from blowing the bridge. Six enemy were killed in the ensuing action, the remainder fleeing to the east.

The 188th now followed Highway 17 as it continued eastwards to Tumalin, which the regiment reached at around 6.00 p.m. that evening. By this time, the 674th (less one battery) and 675th Glider Field Artillery Battalions had moved up to Palico and established their 75mm pack howitzer gun lines, while Battery D 457th Parachute Field Artillery Battalion, commanded by Captain Lou Burris, had deployed forward with the 188th Glider Infantry Regiment to provide immediate direct support. Meanwhile, Major General Joseph Swing had established his command post in a barracks at Palico.

Having passed through Tumalin, the 188th had to exercise more caution as it followed Highway 17 through areas where the road was bordered on either side by steep, thickly wooded banks which offered ideal ambush positions for the enemy. On reaching the intersection with the road from Nasugbu, the leading elements of the regiment came under fire from enemy on the high ground to the right of the highway.

Despite the onset of darkness, the division maintained its advance in order to keep the enemy off-balance. At midnight, the 1st Battalion 187th Glider Infantry Regiment took over the lead and continued marching until 4.00 a.m. on 1 February when it halted for two hours' rest before resuming the advance at 6.00 a.m.

At first light, the enemy opened fire from forward positions on mountains overlooking the highway against the leading elements of the 1st Battalion of the 187th as they came into view. Positions to the north and south of the road were engaged and knocked out by Battery D 457th Parachute Field Artillery Battalion as the battalion pushed on under fire from artillery, mortars and machine guns.

Despite increasing resistance, the division continued its advance but soon ran into heavy fire from the Japanese main line of defence, based on a series of positions on Mounts Aiming, Cariliao and Batuilao, and comprising a network of trenches that linked a large number of bunkers and fortified caves manned by 400 infantry. To the north and east of Mount Aiming were the gun lines of Colonel Fujishige's artillery battalions, equipped with six 75mm, seven 105mm and 15mm howitzers. Deployed further forward were a number of 37mm anti-tank guns being used in the anti-personnel role.

At 9.00 a.m. the 188th Glider Infantry Regiment launched an attack on the Japanese line, support being provided by the 674th and 675th Glider Field Artillery Battalions which shelled the main enemy defences while USAAF and US Navy aircraft attacked other positions on the mountains. At midday Company A 1st Battalion of the 188th, commanded by Captain Raymond Lee, broke through the enemy line on Mount Aiming and occupied a number of positions in caves; here, although cut off from the battalion, it held firm and beat off several counter-attacks that afternoon until joined by the rest of the battalion at 4.00 p.m.

Having split the enemy positions in two, the 188th Glider Infantry Regiment continued its attack, the 2nd Battalion moving south of Highway 17 on the regiment's right flank and attacking enemy positions located between Mount Batulao and the highway. The 1st Battalion of the 187th also joined in, moving up between the 188th's two battalions in the centre.

The morning of 2 February found the 1st Battalion of the 187th and 2nd Battalion of the 188th mounting an attack to the east with air support while aircraft and the two glider field artillery battalions pounded enemy positions in the area of Aga which lay between Mounts Aiming and Batulao, eventually knocking out an enemy gun position at Kaytitinga. The 1st Battalion of the 188th meanwhile remained on Mount Aiming to protect the left flank.

Unable to withstand such fierce pressure, the enemy broke and retreated. At 1.00 p.m., the 188th Glider Infantry Regiment took Aga where it discovered Colonel Fujishige's command post and large quantities of ammunition, supplies and equipment. Pausing only briefly, the 1st Battalion of the 188th set off northwards in pursuit of the enemy, the 2nd Battalion meanwhile continuing to attack Japanese positions on the foothills north of Mount Batulao.

By last light on 2 February, the division had encountered the enemy's third line of defences which lay astride Highway 17. Advancing east, however, it bypassed several enemy positions which were left to the Filipino guerrilla units who, numbering over 5.000 men, operated with the division under the control of the commander of the 187th Glider Infantry Regiment, Colonel Harry D. Hildebrand.

The divisional reconnaissance platoon, meantime, commanded by Lieutenant George Skau, was heading towards Tagaytay Ridge via a route which led to the north of Mount Cariliao. In addition to gathering intelligence on the strength and dispositions of the enemy, the platoon had also been tasked with guiding a group of the demolitions platoon of Headquarters Company 511th Parachute Regimental Combat Team, under Lieutenant David L. Hover, to the ridge. Hover and his men were the pathfinders for the 511th's drop due to take place next morning.

On Mindoro, the 511th had been busy preparing for its operation. The drop had originally been scheduled to take place on 2 February, but continuing stiff enemy resistance around Mounts Aiming and Cariliao had resulted in its being postponed until the following day. It would only take place once it was certain that the rest of the division would be able to link up with the 511th within twenty-four hours.

A major problem was the shortage of transport aircraft. Only forty-eight C-47s of the 317th Troop Carrier Group were available and thus the 511th would have to be transported in three lifts. Lieutenant Colonel Frank S. Holcombe's 2nd Battalion, half of the 3rd Battalion and Colonel Orin D. Haugen's Regimental Headquarters were flown in first, with the 1st and 3rd Battalions, commanded respectively by Lieutenant Colonels Henry Burgess and Edward H. Lahti, following in the second lift. The 457th Parachute Field Artillery Battalion (less Battery D), commanded by Lieutenant Colonel Nicholas Stadtherr, would be dropped in the third lift on the following day, 4 February.

At 7.00 a.m. on 3 February, the leading C-47 took off from Mindoro and fifteen minutes later the entire formation was heading for Luzon where it would make landfall at Batangas Bay. At around 8.15 a.m., the leading wave of eighteen aircraft approached Tagaytay, guided in by green smoke grenades marking the DZ. Shortly afterwards, Colonel Orin D. Haugen led the jump as he made his exit from the leading aircraft, he and the 344 other men in the first wave landing on the DZ without mishap.

The second wave of 30 C-47s, however, travelling three minutes behind the first, were despatched too early, with the result that 570 men landed 8,000 yards to the east of the DZ, fortunately without mishap as the terrain was open and the area had been cleared of enemy by guerrilla units.

At just after midday the second lift, bringing in the rest of the 1st and 3rd Battalions, made its approach. By this time thick cloud had descended to between 300 and 500 feet above Tagaytay Ridge, considerably reducing visibility. Many of the pilots had little experience of dropping paratroops and, fearful of crashing into other craft, a number split from the formation with the result that some sticks were dropped wide of the DZ. Although 425 men landed on the zone, 1,325 more were dropped between four and six miles to the north and north-east. Despite these problems, the three battalions of the 511th Parachute Regimental Combat Team had assembled within five hours, having sustained very few casualties during the drop.

The 2nd Battalion swiftly set out on its tasks: Company D despatched patrols in the direction of Alfonso while taking up positions to the south of the DZ, Company F doing likewise to the north of it. Meantime, Company E established defensive positions at the junction of Highways 17 and 25B. Once the 3rd Battalion had rallied and assembled, it took over the task of securing the DZ from the 2nd Battalion which moved off to assume positions around the junction of Highways 17 and 25B.

The early hours of the following morning, 4 February, found the 511th heading north for the capital of Manila. On reaching the town of Imus the 2nd Battalion, which was in the lead, found that the main bridge spanning the River Imus had been blown. A second bridge was intact but the approach to it was dominated by an old barracks occupied by the enemy. Shortly afterwards, Company D launched an attack but its mortars and the two 75mm pack howitzers of a detachment of the 674th Glider Field Artillery Battalion made little effect on the building's thick stone walls. The situation was resolved by a senior NCO who clambered up on to the roof, smashed a hole with a pickaxe, poured in a jerrycan of patrol and then tossed in a white phosphorus grenade. The result was almost instantaneous: the enemy rushed out of the building only to be annihilated by heavy fire from Company D.

With the bridge taken and secured, the 2nd Battalion pressed on towards Las Pinas, some three miles north of Imus. There it surprised the Japanese who had prepared the Las Pinas bridge spanning the Zapote river for demolition. Although they prevented it from being blown, Lieutenant Colonel Holcombe and his men had to fight fiercely for the bridge.

A convoy of trucks from the beachhead now ferried the 3rd Battalion forward. Meanwhile, the 1st Battalion was following up on foot and was ordered by Colonel Haugen to bypass Las Pinas and the 2nd Battalion and continue heading north as fast as possible. On reaching the town of Paranaque, some two miles beyond Las Pinas, the battalion ran into increasingly stiff opposition, coming under heavy machine-gun and small-arms fire. The town's bridge across the River Paranaque had been blown and badly damaged, and was covered by enemy positions on the north side supported by artillery and mortars sited at Nichols Field, an airfield a mile and a half to the north-east.

The 1st Battalion was now only about four and a half miles from Manila. Darkness was gathering by the time the 2nd Battalion also arrived at Paranaque and was ordered to halt for the night. Next morning they were to cross the river and lead the advance on Manila.

The 457th Parachute Field Artillery Battalion had dropped on to Tagaytay Ridge at 8.15 a.m. on the morning of 4 February. Rallying and assembling quickly, the battalion established a gun line on the ridge from which it was ready to provide fire support against any attempt to interdict the 11th Airborne Division's line of communications and supply; this now stretched for some sixty miles along Highway 17 from the beachhead at Nasugbu to the forward units on the south bank of the Paranaque.

The Japanese forces holding Manila comprised 16,000 troops of the IJN's Manila Naval Defence Force, commanded by Rear Admiral Sanji

Iwabuchi, and 4,000 men of the IJA who were remnants of the Shimbu Group. This formation, commanded by Lieutenant General Shizuo Yokoyama, was responsible for Manila and the southern area of Luzon. The general had been ordered by the commander of the Fourteenth Area Army, General Tomoyuki Yamashita, to withdraw his troops from Manila, and had complied, apart from the 4,000 men whom he had left to bolster Iwabuchi's force.

Iwabuchi was convinced that the main American assault would come from the south and had deployed 12,500 of the 20,000 men under his command to block the threat from that direction, constructing a formidable series of defences called the Genko Line. This consisted of a chain of concrete pillboxes, bunkers and emplacements, the last being equipped with 5-inch and 6-inch naval guns, forty-four artillery pieces, 164 anti-aircraft guns deployed in the ground target role, and 150mm heavy mortars. Infantry well armed with automatic weapons occupied the 1,200 pillboxes and bunkers. All these defences, which extended to a depth of 6,000 yards, were sited so as to be mutually supporting, many being heavily camouflaged and virtually undetectable up to a few yards away.

At 5.00 a.m. on 5 February, the 2nd Battalion 511th Parachute Regimental Combat Team launched its attack across the Paranaque bridge, advancing along Route 1 through a narrow strip between the river on its right and Manila Bay to the left, with the 3rd Battalion following up behind. During the next two days, the 511th advanced north some 2,000 yards in the teeth of very fierce opposition from an enemy who had to be cleared from every fortified house and defensive position. Casualties were surprisingly light, with only six men killed and thirty-five wounded, while the enemy suffered 200 killed.

Next day, 6 February, the 511th halted and went into reserve as the 188th Glider Infantry Regiment, reinforced by the 2nd Battalion of the 187th under Lieutenant Colonel Norman E. Tipton, moved through and took up the role of spearhead. The 188th continued the advance on the morning of 7 February but soon encountered very heavy artillery, mortar and machine-gun fire. To the west, meanwhile, the 511th Parachute Regimental Combat Team also met stiff opposition as it advanced north through the city. On the night of 7 February, the enemy mounted a counter-attack on the 3rd Battalion but this was beaten off by its machine-gun platoon which inflicted heavy casualties. At the same time, they attempted to infiltrate the regiment's positions by drifting in boats down the Paranaque; this ploy was spotted by members of the local population who warned the nearest unit which opened fire at point-blank range, killing all in the boats.

By 11 February, the 11th Airborne Division had reached Nichols Field, which formed the centre of the Genko Line, and had established positions in a line stretching from the north-west corner of the airfield to the south-east corner, having cleared all enemy on the western side. The Japanese were still bringing a heavy volume of fire to bear from the large number of 5-inch naval guns, anti-aircraft guns and machine guns sited in the complex of concrete bunkers and emplacements.

The attack on Nichols Field began on 12 February with an artillery bombardment, after which the 2nd Battalion 187th Glider Infantry Regiment attacked eastwards from the north-west corner of the airfield while the 188th and the 1st Battalion of the 187th did likewise from the south and south-east respectively. During the afternoon, the enemy counter-attacked but were beaten off, and by last light most of the airfield had been cleared.

The following day saw the division continuing its advance across Nichols Field and on towards Fort McKinley to which Rear Admiral Iwabuchi had transferred his headquarters on the morning of 9 February. Until the Japanese invasion, the fort had been the headquarters location of the Philippine Division, a 10,500-strong formation comprising the US Army's 31st Infantry Regiment and a locally recruited force called the Phillipine Scouts. That same day, Iwabuchi was ordered by General Yokoyama to withdraw his remaining forces from Manila but refused to do so. By this time, the US XIV Corps was attacking the city from the north while the 11th Airborne Division, having captured the whole of Nichols Field, was now preparing for an all-out assault on the last remaining elements of the Genko Line still in the hands of the enemy. Fort McKinley and Mabato Point, the latter an area of high ground overlooking Laguna de Bay, a large freshwater lake, some 2,000 yards to the south of the fort.

On 17 February, the 188th Glider Infantry Regiment, with the 2nd Battalion of the 187th attached, and the 511th Parachute Regimental Combat Team, now commanded by Colonel Edward H. Lahti following the wounding in action and subsequent death of Colonel Orin D. Haugen, launched their assault on Fort McKinley. The 1st Battalion of the 511th led the way and soon encountered the fort's outer defences comprising a large number of concrete bunkers and emplacements from which artillery pieces and 120mm anti-aircraft guns brought heavy fire to bear. During the advance along the road from Nichols Field, Company A of the 1st Battalion knocked out eleven emplacements but was held up by a twelfth from which two heavy machine guns were preventing any further progress. Private First Class Manuel Perez of No. 3 Platoon proceeded to outflank the enemy position and, having killed four enemy as he did so, worked his way to within grenade-throwing distance to the rear of the emplacement and shot dead eight more Japanese attempting to withdraw via a tunnel. He then killed five more with the bayonet or clubbed them to death with the butt of his rifle before entering the emplacement and killing the one surviving Japanese with his bayonet. He was later awarded a posthumous Congressional Medal of Honor for this feat of arms, having been killed later in the battle for the fort.

Enemy resistance intensified as the 511th and 188th drew closer to the fort which dominated the surrounding area where the approaches were open, affording little or no cover. The assault over the last stage was led by the 2nd Battalion of the 187th, commanded by Lieutenant Colonel Norman E. Tipton, and as the gliderborne troops covered the final approaches, the enemy detonated a quantity of naval depth charges buried under an area of the smooth grass lawns leading to the

fort's wide paved streets. The explosions caused a large number of casualties, among them Colonel Edward Lahti who was wounded in the
arm by shrapnel while standing some distance away conferring with
Lieutenant Colonels Henry Burgess and Frank S. Holcombe, the
commanding officers of the 1st and 2nd Battalions of the 511th.

A fierce battle raged as the 188th Glider Infantry Regiment fought
its way through the streets of the fort, clearing them building by
building. By next day, however, the regiment had gained control of the
fort and, together with the 511th Parachute Regimental Combat Team
and units of the 1st Cavalry Division, spent the following days clearing
the last few pockets of resistance. By that time, however, the remnants
of the enemy garrison, comprising 300 men of the 3rd Naval Battalion
and approximately 1,000 of the 4th, whose casualties amounted to 961
men killed in the battle, had retreated east. The remnants of the force
holding Nichols Field, meanwhile had withdrawn eastwards on the
night of 17/18 February and linked up with General Yokoyama's
Shimbu Group.

On 15 February, the 11th Airborne Division had also launched its
attack on Mabato Point with a task force under Brigadier General Albert
Pierson, the assistant divisional commander; it consisted of the 1st
Battalion 187th Glider Infantry Regiment, the 3rd Battalion 19th Infantry
Regiment, Company A 44th Tank Battalion, and platoons of the 121st
Engineer Battalion and 221st Airborne Medical Company. Providing
direct support was the 457th Parachute Field Artillery Battalion.

The Japanese had burrowed deep into Mabato Point which,
occupied by a force known as the 'Abe Battalion', was now a warren of
interconnecting tunnels, barracks, communications centres, hospitals
and storage chambers. All approaches were covered by bunkers with
interlocking arcs of fire, and weapons pits containing mortars and
artillery pieces.

Prior to the attack, the entire area was bombarded by artillery,
mortars and napalm air strikes after it was found that conventional
bombs were causing little damage. Thereafter, the 1st Battalion 187th

Glider Infantry Regiment attacked from the west while the 3rd Battalion 19th Infantry Regiment assaulted from the north. The 3rd Battalion 511th Parachute Regimental Combat Team, now commanded by Lieutenant Colonel John L. Strong, and a force of Filipino guerrillas meanwhile formed a line across the road to the south.

It took six days of hard fighting before the task force managed to surround Mabato Point and cut off all possible escape routes. In Laguna de Bay itself, US Navy warships patrolled offshore to intercept any enemy attempting to escape by sea. At just after midday on 21 February, the task force launched its final assault with air strikes and heavy fire from tanks as Company C of the 1st Battalion of the 187th led the way. Despite coming under heavy fire from 150mm heavy mortars, the battalion closed on the enemy positions and stormed them. Vicious close-quarter fighting ensued which resulted in 750 enemy being killed, the task force's casualties amounting to fewer than ten killed and fifty wounded.

Sporadic combat continued throughout the area of Manila until 3 March by which time all organised enemy resistance had ceased. The city bore the scars of the fierce fighting that had raged during the weeks of the battle, while the civilian population had suffered grievously from the atrocities perpetrated on them by Rear Admiral Iwabuchi's forces during the final weeks of the Japanese occupation of the capital.

While the 11th Airborne Division had been fighting hard at Fort McKinley and Mabato Point, attention had turned to the task of capturing the key objective of Corregidor, which commanded the entrance to Manila Bay. When attempting to take the island in 1942 by amphibious assault, the Japanese had suffered heavy losses and thus it was decided to mount a combined airborne and amphibious assault on the island. Intelligence on the enemy force that held it was negligible, however, as the Japanese had barred any Filipinos from the island since its occupation; but it was estimated as having a minimum strength of 850. In fact, the island's garrison numbered some 6,000 men under the command of an IJN officer, Captain Ijn Itagaki, who had been warned by his superiors of the likelihood of a full-scale attack by the Americans and the strong possibility that airborne troops would be used.

Taking this seriously, Itagaki conducted a reconnaissance of the island which was a honeycomb of tunnels, barracks, storage areas and underground fortifications designed and constructed by the Americans to withstand heavy shelling and bombing. Its western end consisted of a massive rocky headland some 2,500 yards across, with almost vertical cliffs rising precipitously from the sea to a height of 500 feet. From there the island sloped and tapered away to a low-lying area where an airstrip was located. Itagaki considered that the headland, with its steep cliffs, would not provide an ideal DZ for paratroops who would be more likely to drop on the area of the airstrip. However, since this was dominated by the high ground to the west, he eventually ruled out the possibility of an airborne attack. He gave orders, nevertheless, that the airstrip was to be mined and the area covered by machine-gun positions. Thereafter, he concentrated on the far more likely threat of an amphibious landing.

Captain Itagaki would therefore have been surprised if he had been privy to the plan conceived by the commander of the 503rd Parachute Regimental Combat Team, Colonel George Jones, who decided that the airstrip was unsuitable as a DZ and chose to concentrate upon the flat-topped western end of the island which was known as 'Topside'. Jones was of the opinion that there were two possible DZs in that area: a disused golf course, covered with bomb craters and debris, measuring some 300 yards by 150 yards, and an even smaller parade ground. Given their limited size, plus the almost constant wind that blew across the island at a speed of some 15–20 knots, his force would be restricted to sticks of six men dropped at each pass by aircraft flying in line astern in two columns, one for each DZ. Each aircraft would have to carry out three passes, turning away after dropping its first stick and circling round to rejoin the queue to drop its second and third.

Only sixty C-47s were available to transport a force of approximately 3,000 men and thus only one battalion group could be dropped at a time, the first at 8.30 a.m. on 16 February, the second at 12.30 p.m. and the third at 8.30 a.m. on the following morning. No weapon containers would be dropped and support weapons such as mortars and medium machine guns would therefore have to be dismantled and their component parts carried by the members of their platoons. The 75mm pack howitzers of the 462nd Parachute Field Artillery Battalion, however, would be dropped as normal.

On the morning of 16 February, Captain Itagaki and his men woke to the sounds of heavy bombing as US aircraft pounded Corregidor. At 7.15 a.m., fifty-one C-47s of the 317th Troop Carrier Group took off from Mindoro carrying the leading element of the 503rd Parachute Regimental Combat Team which comprised: the 3rd Battalion; a detachment of Regimental Headquarters; Company C 161st Airborne Engineer Battalion; and Battery A, a platoon of Battery D (equipped with .50 calibre heavy machine guns) and a detachment of Headquarters Battery of the 462nd Parachute Field Artillery Battalion. The planes then headed for Corregidor where a thick pall of smoke and dust hung over the island from the bombing. Fortunately, this had cleared by the time the aircraft approached the island on schedule at 8.30 a.m.

Flying into a wind of 18 knots at an altitude of 600 feet, the green light in each C-47 was switched on as the aircraft reached its release point, each jumpmaster counting three seconds after the green light before releasing his stick in order to allow for drift. This proved insufficient, however, and the leading sticks were carried by the wind back off the DZ, some men landing on the slopes and others in the sea. Colonel Jones, flying in a command aircraft over the area, immediately ordered the ensuing drops to be made from 500 feet, with jumpmasters increasing the delay factor to six seconds. This had the desired effect and the majority of sticks landed accurately on the DZs. Nevertheless the 3rd Battalion, commanded by Lieutenant Colonel John Erickson, suffered twenty-five per cent casualties during the drop, mainly due to broken ankles and more serious injuries incurred while landing.

It was during this early stage of the operation that Captain Itagaki, with several members of his staff, was unwise enough to venture out to an observation post on the lower slopes where some troops of the 3rd Battalion had been blown by the wind. They spotted him and opened fire, killing him and all but one of his companions.

The 3rd Battalion rallied and assembled for action, swiftly taking the predesignated positions from which its support weapons and the 462nd Parachute Field Artillery Battalion were to provide supporting fire for the amphibious landing which began at 10.40 a.m. By 11.00 a.m., the 34th Infantry Regiment had taken Malinta Hill, near the centre of the island, with fire support being provided by the 503rd. At 12.44 p.m. the second lift of fifty-one aircraft arrived, bringing in the 2nd Battalion and further elements of the regimental headquarters along with Battery B and another platoon of Battery D of the 462nd Parachute Field Artillery Battalion, and the 503rd's Service Company. The drop was successful with fewer casualties being suffered even though the wind had strengthened to 20 knots, causing the delay factor to be increased from six to ten seconds.

By last light on 16 February, the 503rd Parachute Regimental Combat Team had linked up with the 34th Infantry Regiment and a secure foothold had been established on Corregidor. At this stage in the operation, due to the fact that some 280 men had been injured in the two drops, it was decided to cancel the drop on the following morning. Instead, the 1st Battalion, together with Battery C and the remaining platoon of Battery D of the 462nd Parachute Field Artillery Battalion, were flown from Mindoro to Corregidor, where equipment containers were dropped at 8.30 a.m. on 17 February; the troops then flew on to an airstrip at San Marcellino at Subic Bay, in Bataan, from where they subsequently travelled by sea to Corregidor, arriving at 4.30 p.m.

The island's garrison, meanwhile, was continuing to put up a fanatical resistance; on one occasion, a strongly fortified position was only overcome after petrol, oil and other highly inflammable material had been poured down its ventilating shaft and ignited with grenades. In the early hours of 19 February, the Japanese responded by attempting to blow up the southern part of the American perimeter, detonating explosives stored in vaults below it. In other instances, they resorted to blowing up their own positions, killing themselves and in several cases members of the 503rd Parachute Regimental Combat Team or 34th Infantry Regiment as well. Two days later, at 9.30 p.m., they let off a vast quantity of explosives in a tunnel under Malinta Hill, which was occupied by the 34th Infantry Regiment. The shock-wave was enormous, being felt as far away as the Bataan Peninsula, with flames shooting out of tunnel entrances and air vents, and causing a landslide on the southern side of the hill which buried some of the 34th's men. A large number of enemy died in this explosion.

On 26 February, the 1st Battalion of the 503rd, with Battery A of the 462nd Parachute Field Artillery Battalion in support, attacked a feature called Monkey Hill where it encountered stiff resistance from a force of Japanese positioned at the entrance to a tunnel. Two Sherman tanks moved up to support the battalion, one advancing to a point near the entrance and firing into it with its main armament. It is not clear whether the resulting massive explosion was initiated by the Japanese themselves or whether it was caused by the shell from the Sherman's 75mm gun hitting an explosives and ammunition dump inside the tunnel. The blast was such, however, that it blew the leading tank fifty feet into the air and the other some thirty-five to forty feet back down the hillside. Large rocks and boulders rained down on the battalion, killing fifty-four men and injuring a further 145. It was estimated that over 150 Japanese died in the explosion. All that was left of Monkey Hill was a huge crater.

That same day saw all enemy resistance on the island overcome. By then, the 503rd Parachute Regimental Combat Team had sustained 163 killed and 620 injured or wounded in action. Known Japanese casualties amounted to a total of 4,509 killed and twenty captured, not to mention those who died sealed up in the island's tunnels and caves.

Despite the relatively heavy casualties incurred by the 503rd, the operation had been entirely successful and the Japanese no longer controlled the approaches to Manila Bay.

Many men performed feats of great bravery during the battle for Corregidor but one man in particular distinguished himself from the first day onwards. Shortly after the 1st Battalion's drop, one of its scouts, Private Lloyd G. McCarter, crossed thirty yards of open ground under heavy fire and knocked out an enemy machine-gun position with grenades. Two days later, on 18 February, he killed six enemy snipers and on the evening of the 18th, when a large force of Japanese attempted to outflank his company, he moved to an exposed position and opened fire, standing his ground in the face of repeated attacks and continuing to do so even after all the other members of his company in his area had been wounded. At first light on the 19th the Japanese launched another attack, but Private McCarter, despite being seriously wounded, succeeded in halting and breaking up the assault, following which the enemy withdrew. It was later stated that his action had contributed greatly to the ultimate success of the operation and the capture of Corregidor. Private McCarter's great courage and feat of arms was duly recognised by the award of the Congressional Medal of Honor.

While the battle raged on Corregidor, another airborne operation was taking place on Luzon. On 18 February the commanding officer of the 1st Battalion 511th Parachute Regimental Combat Team, Lieutenant Colonel Henry Burgess, received an order from Major General Swing to withdraw his unit and, having handed over command to his executive officer, to report immediately to the divisional headquarters. There, Burgess was met by Colonel Douglass P. Quandt, the divisional G-3, who informed him that he was to lead an airborne operation twenty-five miles behind Japanese lines to rescue a large number of Allied prisoners-of-war and civilian prisoners from an internment camp near Los Baños, some forty miles south of Manila on the southern shore of Laguna de Bay.

Initial preparation for the operation had begun on 5 February following orders received by Major General Swing from Lieutenant General Robert L. Eichelberger, the commander of the US Eighth Army, to mount the rescue. Responsibility for planning was delegated to Lieutenant Colonel Quandt who immediately began to accumulate intelligence on the camp and the Japanese guarding it, as well as the dispositions of enemy forces in the area. One of his sources was an NCO of the 511th Airborne Signal Company, Sergeant John Fulton, who on 11 February was landed by boat with two guides on the eastern shore of Laguna de Bay, from where he headed south to a rendezvous with a group of guerrillas. During the following days, he gathered intelligence, transmitting it back to Headquarters 11th Airborne Division. Another source was a small group of the prisoners themselves who were in the habit of slipping out of the camp at night to obtain food from the local inhabitants. One of these, an American engineer named Peter Miles, who had worked for the US Army in the Philippines before being interned by the Japanese, escaped from the camp and, escorted by a party of guerrillas, was taken across Laguna de Bay to Paranaque and Headquarters 11th Airborne Division. There he provided full details of the camp, its layout, the dispositions of the guards and their routine.

The guard force consisted of some 250 troops. Two miles to the east of the camp was an infantry company of about 200 men supported by an artillery section of two 105mm guns and four medium machine guns. In addition, a twenty-strong platoon was based at Mayondon Point, situated two miles to the north of the camp, while on Los Baños Wharf itself were sited two 3-inch guns. Other troops in the area comprised a company of eighty men located west of Calamba, just to the south of the San Juan river. A far more serious threat, however, was posed by the 9,000-strong 8th 'Tiger' Division, based about an hour and a half's march away just to the south of the area of San Pablo.

Having obtained as much intelligence as possible, Lieutenant Colonel Quandt drew up a plan which called initially for the divisional reconnaissance platoon to deploy two days prior to the operation, crossing Laguna de Bay and linking up with a force of guerrillas with whom it would infiltrate into the area of the camp, surrounding it at first light on D-Day, 23 February. At 7.00 a.m. a company of the 1st Battalion of the 511th would drop on to a DZ, marked beforehand by the reconnaissance platoon, 200 yards to the north-east of the camp. As the company dropped, the reconnaissance platoon and guerrillas were to dispose of the camp's guards who, according to their normal routine, would be engaged in physical training at that time. Having landed, the parachute company would move to the camp and begin organising the prisoners for evacuation.

The remainder of the 1st Battalion of the 511th and Battery D 457th Parachute Field Artillery Battalion would meantime cross the Laguna de Bay in Amtrac amphibious armoured personnel carriers of the 672nd Amphibious Tractor Battalion, moving on to the camp as rapidly as possible. At the same time, a task force commanded by Colonel Robert H. Soule, the commander of the 188th Glider Infantry Regiment and comprising the regiment's 1st Battalion, Company B 637th Tank Destroyer Battalion and elements of the 472nd and 675th Field Artillery Battalions, would move south from Manila towards Mamatid on the northern side of the River San Juan. From there it was to mount a diversionary attack across the river in the area of Calamba against the Japanese 8th Division.

On the night of 20 February, the commander of the divisional reconnaissance platoon, Lieutenant George Skau, accompanied by Lieutenant Ben Haggerty of the 127th Airborne Engineer Battalion, crossed the Laguna de Bay and made their way to Nanhaya where they met two prisoners who had escaped from the camp and would now guide them to it. Accompanied by a group of guerrillas, and led by the two prisoners, Skau and Haggerty made their way to Los Baños where they reconnoitred the DZ area before reaching the camp; there they carried out a close reconnaissance of the entire perimeter and its guard posts before withdrawing to the beach on which the 511th Parachute

Regimental Combat Team would land in its Amtracs. Thereafter, Skau and Haggerty returned across the Laguna de Bay to Paranaque and the divisional headquarters.

On the afternoon of 22 February, Company B of the 1st Battalion 511th Parachute Regimental Combat Team, commanded by Captain John Ringler, moved to Nichols Field, the rest of the battalion meanwhile having been transported from Manila to Mamatid where it rendezvoused at last light with the Amtracs of the 672nd Amphibious Tractor Battalion. That evening also saw Colonel Soule's task force moving up to the north bank of the San Juan river.

Next morning, Company B took off from Nichols Field in ten C-47s and precisely on schedule at 7.00 a.m. arrived over the DZ which was marked with green smoke by members of the divisional reconnaissance platoon. No sooner had Captain Ringler and his men begun leaving their aircraft than the reconnaissance platoon and the guerrillas launched their attack on the prison camp. Members of the platoon came under fire from a machine gun which wounded one man before it was put out of action by a well-aimed salvo of bombs from one of the company's 60mm light mortars. Meanwhile, a bunker at the main gate was knocked out by Lieutenant Skau and several of his men. They then turned their attention to some of the guards who, having been engaged in physical training when the attack began and hence being unarmed, were either killed or managed to find cover. The battle lasted about twenty minutes before all resistance was overcome, a number of guards being killed by Company B as they attempted to escape. Captain Ringler and his men then entered the camp and, together with the reconnaissance platoon, proceeded to locate and kill the remainder.

The 1st Battalion 511th Parachute Regimental Combat Team had landed on the south shore of the Laguna de Bay at 7.00 a.m., Captain Lou Burris's battery of four 75mm pack howitzers establishing its gun line on the beach which had been secured prior to the landing by a guerrilla company. Company C headed for Mayondon Point to deal with the enemy platoon there before establishing a roadblock on the road leading to the town of Los Baños. Meanwhile Company A took up positions to block any advance by the enemy from the east.

Lieutenant Colonel Henry Burgess and the rest of the battalion pushed on towards the camp in their fifty-four Amtracs, encountering some sporadic fire from the direction of Mayondon Point en route. Having arrived at the camp, where it received a tumultuous welcome from the prisoners, the battalion set about evacuating the latter as swiftly as possible, since the threat of the Japanese 8th Division was foremost in Burgess's mind.

Colonel Soule and his task force had attacked south across the San Juan river in the early hours, encountering some light resistance in the area of the Lecheria Hills, and by mid-morning had cleared the area of all enemy. By that time, Burgess and his men had completed the evacuation of the camp and were withdrawing to the beach from where the prisoners were already being ferried in the Amtracs across the Laguna de Bay. At 3.00 p.m. that afternoon, the last six Amtracs carrying the battalion's rearguard left the beach and headed north across the lake under fire from enemy artillery. Arriving safely at Mamatid, they joined the remainder of the unit and the prisoners, the latter thereafter being ferried to Mutinlupa where they were to be accommodated before being evacuated to the United States.

The operation, mounted twenty-five miles behind Japanese lines, had been entirely successful with 2,122 prisoners rescued, the prison camp destroyed and at least seventy enemy killed. Casualties among the troops taking part had been light, amounting to five men killed, with one female prisoner receiving a graze from a bullet.

Four months later, in June 1945, the 11th Airborne Division mounted its last airborne operation of the Second World War. Despite the hard fighting which had taken place in Manila, on the Bataan Peninsula and southern Luzon, the main Japanese force, comprising General Tomoyuki Yamashita's 152,000-strong Shobu Group, was still intact in the northern part of the island. It occupied a large area shaped like an inverted triangle, in the east of which lay the Sierra Madre mountains with the hills of the Cordillera Central to the west and the Babuyan Channel to the north. In the centre of the triangle was the Cagayan Valley, stretching from Aparri on the north coast of Luzon to Bambang in the south, which was an important supply area for the Japanese. Yamashita had assembled a force made up of the 19th and 23rd Divisions and elements of the 10th and 1093rd Divisions and the 2nd Tank Division. His intention was to harass the Americans, whose main attack he expected to come from the direction of Manila along the roads that wound north through Bambang and Baguio to the Cagayan Valley, and tie up their forces for as long as possible by fighting a delaying action.

In February, Lieutenant General Walter Krueger, the commander of the US Sixth Army, had allotted the task of pursuing the Shobu Group to I Corps, commanded by Lieutenant General Ennis Swift, whose 33rd Infantry Division, under Major General Percy W. Clarkson, began to probe northwards by the end of February. Early March found part of the division heading north-east along Route 11, which wound through the mountains towards Bambang, running into stiff opposition which made progress difficult. Other elements, however, were advancing along the coast north of the Lingayane Gulf and encountered little resistance. Having taken some minor towns farther up the coast and having turned inland, Clarkson decided to advance swiftly along Route 9 and take Baguio from the north-east.

To assist Clarkson, Lieutenant General Krueger reinforced I Corps with the 37th Infantry Division, commanded by Major General Robert S. Beightler, which joined the fray and by 17 June was advancing along Route 5 up the Cagayan Valley towards Aparri. Two days later, the division met an enemy force attempting to head south on the same route; during the ensuing battle, which took place along a fifteen-mile stretch of the highway and lasted four days, the Japanese lost more than 600 men killed and 285 taken prisoner, while fifteen tanks were destroyed. The remnants of the enemy fled east towards the Sierra Madre.

At this juncture, Lieutenant General Krueger decided that the 37th Infantry Division needed the assistance of an airborne force which would be dropped near Aparri and, advancing south, seal off the northern end of the Cagayan Valley. He ordered the 11th Airborne Division to mount such an operation on 25 June.

Meantime, an 800-strong task force under Major Robert Connolly, comprising a reinforced company of the 33rd Infantry Division, a company of rangers and an artillery battery, reached Aparri from the west. Next day Connolly and his men, together with the 2nd Battalion 11th Infantry Regiment, secured the airfield at Camalaniugan, approximately three miles south of Aparri.

In view of the unexpectedly swift advance of the 37th Infantry Division, the airborne operation was brought forward by two days to 23 June. The operation had been allotted to the 1st Battalion 511th Parachute Regimental Combat Team and would be under the overall command of Lieutenant Colonel Henry Burgess who by this time was the executive officer of the regiment. His 1,030-strong force would comprise: the 1st Battalion reinforced by Companies G and I of the 3rd Battalion; Battery C of the 457th Parachute Field Artillery Battalion; a platoon of Company C 127th Airborne Engineer Battalion; a platoon of the 221st Airborne Medical Company; and detachments of the 511th Airborne Signal Company and other specialist units. The operation would be mounted from an airfield at Lipa and the aircraft transporting Burgess' force would comprise fifty-four C-47s and thirteen C-46s of the 317th Troop Carrier Group, along with six CG-4A Wacos and one CG-13 glider which would be used to land six jeeps, one trailer, ammunition, medical supplies and radios.

On 21 June, pathfinders of the 511th Parachute Regimental Combat Team were flown to the area and made contact with the 2nd Battalion 11th Regiment of the Philippine Army which had taken up positions on the west side of the River Cagayan. On the night of 22 June, they crossed the river and moved to the DZ.

At 4.30 a.m. on 23 June, Lieutenant Colonel Burgess and his men emplaned and at 6.00 a.m. the first aircraft took off and headed for Camalaniugan, followed by the other fifty-three aircraft which soon took up formation with escorting fighters cruising overhead. Bombers of the Fifth Air Force carried out diversionary attacks and dropped smokebombs to screen the drop from Japanese forces in the hills to the east.

At 9.00 a.m., the pathfinders marked the DZ with green smoke and shortly afterwards the leading wave of nine aircraft dropped their sticks. Although the drop was accurate and the entire force landed on the DZ, casualties were high with two men killed by parachute malfunction and seventy injured due to the high wind of some 17-22 knots and the rough terrain of rice paddies interspersed with bomb craters and areas of tall grass. Nevertheless, the force rallied, assembled quickly, and headed south along the River Cagayan and Route 5 to link up with the 37th Infantry Division, encountering light resistance which in some instances was cleared with the help of flamethrowers. On 26 June, Burgess and his men met the leading elements of the 37th Infantry Division and two days later were flown from a nearby airstrip at Tuguegaro to Lipa.

Despite the success of Operation Gypsy, the battle for northern Luzon was not over, and until the end of hostilities in the Philippines the US Sixth Army continued to pursue the Shobu Group farther into the mountains, taking heavy casualties in the process. By the end of the war the Japanese, whose ranks had been thinned considerably by disease and starvation, were still holding out in the Asin Valley of the Sierra Madre in north central Luzon. It was only after the cessation of hostilities on 15 August 1945 that General Yamashita and some 50,000 surviving members of the Shobu Group surrendered.

Meanwhile in Asia, as the 11th Airborne Division and the 503rd Parachute Regimental Combat Team played their respective parts in the final stages of the recapture of the Philippines, May 1945 witnessed an element of India's newly formed airborne forces, The Indian Parachute Regiment, about to take part in its first major airborne operation.

By early 1945, the Indian Army's airborne forces had expanded considerably from its original single formation, 50th Indian Parachute Brigade, which had seen a considerable amount of action in Burma in the infantry role, particularly during the fierce battle at Sangshak in March 1944 and during the following months of fighting in the area of Imphal.

9th Indian Airborne Division was formed in November 1944 under the command of Major General Eric Down, but shortly afterwards its numerical designation was changed to 44th. 50th Indian Parachute Brigade was joined in the division by 14th (Long Range Penetration) Brigade which as 14th Infantry Brigade had taken part in Special Force's Operation Thursday, as recounted earlier in this chapter. On joining the division under the command of Brigadier Tom Brodie, it was redesignated 14th Airlanding Brigade and comprised: the 2nd Battalion The Black Watch; 4th Battalion (Outram's) 6th Rajputana Rifles; and the 6th Battalion 16th Punjab Regiment.

Divisional troops comprised: the 44th Independent Pathfinder Company (formed from the Special Force parachute company); 44th Indian Airborne Divisional Reconnaissance Squadron (Governor General's Bodyguard); 159th Parachute Light Regiment RA; and 23rd Light Anti-Aircraft/Anti-Tank Regiment RA. Sapper units in the division consisted of: 12th Parachute Squadron RE; 33rd Parachute Squadron IE; 411th (Royal Bombay) Parachute Squadron IE; and 40th Indian Airborne Field Park Squadron IE.

A second parachute brigade was still required for the new division and in January 1945, following the disbandment of Special Force, 77th Indian Infantry Brigade was converted to the parachute role and redesignated 77th Indian Parachute Brigade, being commanded by Brigadier Charles Wilkinson.

This period saw a considerable amount of reorganisation among the division's parachute battalions and it was decided that both parachute brigades would contain a British unit. Accordingly, two were raised by converting two battalions of the by then disbanded Special

Force, the 1st Battalion The King's Regiment and the 1st Battalion The South Staffordshire Regiment, to the parachute role and redesignating them the 15th and 16th Parachute Battalions respectively. Both were initially reduced to cadre strength and their ranks subsequently filled by volunteers from England and from British units in India. They were commanded respectively by Lieutenant Colonels Terence Otway (who had commanded the 9th Parachute Battalion in Normandy) and A. W. E. 'Danny' Daniell.

On 18 December 1944, authorisation had been given for the formation of The Indian Parachute Regiment, this taking place on 1 March 1945. Thereafter, the individual battalions were redesignated as follows: 153rd and 154th Gurkha Parachute Battalions became the 2nd and 3rd Gurkha Parachute Battalions, while 152nd Indian Parachute Battalion was divided to form two new units designated the 1st and 4th Indian Parachute Battalions. In addition, four independent parachute companies, the 44th, 14th, 50th and 77th, were formed as defence units for the divisional and brigade headquarters. 1st Indian, 3rd Gurkha and 16th Parachute Battalions were allotted to 50th Indian Parachute Brigade, while 2nd Gurkha, 4th Indian and 15th Parachute Battalions went to 77th Indian Parachute Brigade.

While the expansion and reorganisation of India's airborne forces was under way in early 1945, the campaign in Burma was continuing apace. Originally, two airborne operations had been planned as part of Fourteenth Army's operations for the recapture of Burma: the first to seize the Yeu-Shwebo Plain and the other to capture the capital of Rangoon.

Consideration had also been given to a third operation to capture Kalewa and Kalemyo. The commander of Fourteenth Army, General Sir William Slim, had, however, been unwilling to divert much-needed transport aircraft from the task of supplying his forward formations, which depended heavily on air resupply. Fourteenth Army, in fact, had advanced south rapidly and taken both Kalewa and Kalewmyo, Slim's intention being to thrust swiftly into Burma and defeat the Japanese before they could recover from their defeat at Imphal. The Yeu-Shwebo Plain had been seized a month ahead of schedule but an unexpected enemy counter-attack had slowed the advance on Rangoon, which had to be taken before the arrival of the monsoon and the inevitable accompanying problems.

An amphibious operation, codenamed Dracula, had been planned for the capture of Rangoon and at the end of March the decision was taken to proceed with it in a modified form. Meteorological forecasts predicted that 2 May would be the most suitable date from the point of view of the weather, which meant that there was only a month to prepare for it.

Dracula consisted of a landing by 26th Indian Division, with naval and air support, on both banks of the River Rangoon to the south of the city and halfway between Elephant Point and the Bassein Creek. The river itself had been mined by the Japanese, as well as by Allied aircraft, and therefore minesweepers would have to precede the vessels carrying the landing force. Coastal defences were sited on the west bank of the river and these would have to be neutralised before the minesweepers could enter the river mouth. This task would be given to a parachute battalion dropped on 1 May, the day before the amphibious landing.

When details of the operation were passed to 44th Indian Airborne Division, it was in the midst of reorganisation. Moreover, many of its officers were in England on leave as were the men of the two Gurkha units stationed in Nepal or, as in the case of 3rd Gurkha Parachute Battalion, in the process of transferring to 77th Indian Parachute Brigade.

Consequently, a composite battalion was formed from elements of the two Gurkha battalions under the command of Major Jack Newland. It consisted of: battalion headquarters and Headquarter Company comprising men of 2nd and 3rd Gurkha Parachute Battalions; A and B Companies supplied by the 2nd Battalion; C and D Companies formed from the 3rd Battalion; mortar platoon comprising men of both units; and machine gun platoon, supplied by the 2nd Battalion.

On moving to Chaklala, the battalion was augmented by two teams of pathfinders, a section of 411th (Royal Bombay) Parachute Squadron IE, a section of 80th Parachute Field Ambulance, and detachments from the signals and intelligence sections of Headquarters 50th Indian Parachute Brigade. After completion of training at Chaklala, the battalion moved to Midnapore where it remained for the following ten days while assembling its equipment and conducting a rehearsal of the operation. On 29 April, it flew to Akyab on the coast of Burma and 200 miles north of Rangoon. There it was joined by a 200-strong reserve force comprising men of both Gurkha battalions and the old 152nd Indian Parachute Battalion under Major Maurice Fry.

At 2.30 a.m. on 1 May, two C-47s took off from Akyab carrying two pathfinder teams, forward air controllers, a small number of agents of Force 136 (the Asian and Far Eastern arm of the Special Operations Executive) and a platoon to provide initial defence of the DZ. At 3.00 a.m., the main force took off in thirty-eight C-47s and at 5.45 a.m. jumped over Tawhai. It was raining, with only a light wind, and there were few casualties during the drop, one of them a medical officer accompanying the force.

The battalion rallied quickly in the pouring rain and headed for its objectives, covering the first two and a half miles well ahead of schedule. At that point it was forced to halt and wait for Liberator bombers of the USAAF to carry out a raid on Elephant Point. Although it was some 3,000 yards from the nearest of the bombers' targets, and despite the fact that officers and men were wearing yellow recognition panels on their backs and carried orange umbrellas, C Company was bombed and strafed from the air, losing fifteen men killed and thirty wounded. Consequently, one of the forward air controller detachments called a halt to any further bombing except when ordered.

Despite the continuing heavy downpour, the battalion pushed on through flooded terrain and at 4.00 p.m. came under fire from an enemy bunker and some craft on the river. Air support was called in and the craft destroyed, after which the bunker was attacked by a company supported by flamethrowers which killed all but one of its thirty-seven occupants. The battalion suffered forty-one casualties during this action.

The reserve force, accompanied by a field surgical team, dropped on Thaungang at 3.30 p.m., and thirty minutes later a supply drop was also carried out. Having linked up with some of the medical personnel who had arrived earlier, the field surgical team moved off after last light to join the battalion. Unfortunately, it was mistaken for an enemy force and was fired upon, losing four wounded.

The rain continued unabated and the spring tides that night were so high that the battalion's positions were submerged under three feet of water, men being forced to evacuate them and seek refuge on a spot of dry ground. Next morning, as it cleared and searched a number of bunkers in the area, the battalion observed the convoys of vessels carrying 26th Indian Division upriver.

On the following day, 3 May, the battalion moved to Sadainghmut as 36th Indian Infantry Brigade occupied Rangoon without firing a shot. Two days later, leaving a company at Sadainghmut, it marched to Rangoon where it was deployed in anti-looting operations and searching for enemy stragglers. On 16 May, it left by ship for India and ten days later rejoined 44th Indian Airborne Division. There was naturally some pride that The Indian Parachute Regiment had successfully completed its first major airborne operation.

In July 1945, the advance headquarters of I Airborne Corps, now commanded by Lieutenant General Sir Richard Gale, arrived at Gwalior in central India. The war in Europe had ended and Allied attention was now focused on defeating the Japanese. 6th Airborne Division would form part of the corps, joining it in India in due course.

Headquarters Fourteenth Army had meanwhile moved to Secunderabad to prepare for operations to retake Malaya; and 44th Indian Airborne Division was therefore moved to Bilaspur, selected as it was close to five airfields, had good DZs and excellent facilities for jungle warfare training. Otherwise it had little to recommend it, being in an area where malaria, elephantiasis, cholera and other equally deadly diseases were commonplace.

On 11 August 1945, the war with Japan ended. A week later, thirty teams from 44th Indian Airborne Division, each comprising two medical personnel and two escorts, were dropped into Japanese prisoner-of-war camps in Malaya, Java, French Indo-China and Hong Kong. On 30 August, another group of six dropped into Singapore. All these teams found Allied prisoners-of-war in the most appalling physical shape after years of imprisonment under conditions which beggared description. This was the final airborne operation carried out by 44th Indian Airborne Division and indeed was the last carried out during the Second World War.

Over the three and a half years from January 1942 to August 1945, the Asian and Pacific theatres witnessed a total of eighteen airborne operations carried out by the Allies and Japanese. The drop of the 503rd Parachute Infantry Regiment at Nadzab in September 1943 was an outstanding success and the airlanding of a large number of troops behind enemy lines by Major General Orde Wingate's Special Force, during Operation Thursday in March 1944, also proved successful, albeit Fourteenth Army subsequently failed to make use of them. Furthermore, whereas none were on the vast scale of those conducted in Europe, the operations launched in the Pacific by the 11th Airborne Division and 503rd Parachute Regimental Combat Team played a significant part in the operations of the US Sixth and Eighth Armies to recapture the Philippines.

SELECT BIBLIOGRAPHY

Ailsby, Christopher, *Hitler's Sky Warriors – German Paratroopers in Action 1939–1945*.Spellmount, Staplehurst, 2001

Barley, Eric and Fohlen, Yves, *Para Memories – The 12th Yorkshire Parachute Battalion*. ParaPress, Tunbridge Wells, 1996

Bauer, Cornelis, *The Battle of Arnhem*. Hodder & Stoughton, London, 1966

Baynes, John, *Urquhart of Arnhem*. Brassey's, London, 1993

Beevor, Antony, *Crete – The Battle and The Resistance*, John Murray, London, 1991

Bidwell, Shelford, *The Chindit War – The Campaign in Burma 1944*. Hodder & Stoughton, London, 1979

Blair, Clay. *Ridgway's Paratroopers – The American Airborne in World War II*. Dial Press, 1985

Bowen, Robert M., *Fighting With The Screaming Eagles – With the 101st Airborne From Normandy to Bastogne*. Greenhill Books, London, 2001

Breuer, William B., *Operation Dragoon – The Allied Invasion of the South of France*. Airlife, Shrewsbury, 1988

Chatterton, Brigadier George, *The Wings of Pegasus – The Story of The Glider Pilot Regiment*. Macdonald, London, 1962

Cox, Geoffrey, *A Tale of Two Battles – A Personal Memoir of Crete and the Western Desert 1941*. William Kimber, London, 1987

Crookenden, Napier, *Dropzone Normandy – The Story of the American and British Airborne Assault on D-Day 1944*. Purnell Book Services, Abingdon, 1976

Davin, D. M., *Official History of New Zealand in The Second World War – Crete*. Oxford University Press, London, 1953

Edwards, Roger, *German Airborne Troops*. Macdonald & Jane's, London, 1974

Fairley, John, *Remember Arnhem – The Story of the 1st Airborne Reconnaissance Squadron*. Peaton Press, Bearsden, 1978

Fergusson, Bernard, *Beyond The Chindwin*. St James's Library, London, 1951

— *The Wild Green Earth*. Collins, London, 1946

Flanagan, Lt Gen. E. M., *The Angels – History of The 11th Airborne Division*. Presidio Press, Novato, 1989

— *The Rakkasans – The Combat History of The 187th Airborne Infantry*, Presidio Press, Novato, 1997

Freyberg, Paul, *Bernard Freyberg VC – A Soldier of Two Nations*. Hodder & Stoughton, London, 1991

Frost, Major General John, *A Drop Too Many*. Cassell, London, 1980

— *Nearly There – The Memoirs of John Frost of Arnhem Bridge*. Leo Cooper, London, 1991

Glantz, David M., *A History of Soviet Airborne Forces*. Frank Cass, Ilford, 1994

Golden, Lewis, *Echoes From Arnhem*. William Kimber, London, 1984

Gregory, Barry, *British Airborne Troops*. Purnell Book Services, Abingdon, 1974

Hackett, General Sir John, *I Was A Stranger*. Chatto & Windus, London, 1977

Hagen, Louis, *Arnhem Lift*. Hammond, London, 1955

Harclerode, Peter, *Go To It! The Illustrated History of the 6th Airborne Division*. Bloomsbury, London, 1990

— *PARA! Fifty Years of The Parachute Regiment*. Arms & Armour, London, 1992

— *Arnhem – A Tragedy of Errors*. Arms & Armour, London, 1994

Henniker, Mark, *An Image of War*. Leo Cooper, London, 1987

Hibbert, Christopher, *The Battle of Arnhem*. Batsford, London, 1962

Hickey, Michael, *Out of The Sky – A History of Airborne Warfare*. Mills & Boon, London, 1979

Hoyt, Edwin P., *Airborne – The History of American Parachute Forces*. Stein & Day, London, 1979

Huston, James, *Out of The Blue – US Army Airborne Operations in World War II*. Purdue University Press, West Lafayette, 1972

Kershaw, Robert J., *It Never Snows in September*. The Crowood Press, London, 1990

Kuhn, Volkmar, *German Paratroopers in World War II*. Ian Allan, London, 1978

Lucas, John, *The Silken Canopy – A History of The Parachute*. Airlife, Shrewsbury, 1997

Macdonald, Callum, *The Lost Battle – Crete 1941*. Macmillan, London, 1993

Millar, George, *The Bruneval Raid*. Bodley Head, London, 1974

Montgomery of Alamein, Field Marshal The Viscount, *Normandy to The Baltic*. Hutchinson, London, 1946

Morrison, Will, *Horsa Squadron*. William Kimber, London, 1988

Otway, Lieutenant Colonel T. B. H., *Airborne Forces*. Imperial War Museum, London, 1990

Pöppel, Martin, *Heaven & Hell – The War Diary of a German Paratrooper*. Spellmount, Staplehurst, 2000

Powell, Geoffrey, *The Devil's Birthday*. Buchan & Enright, London, 1984

— *Men At Arnhem*. Buchan & Enright, London, 1986

Praval, K. C., *India's Paratroopers – A History of The Parachute Regiment of India*. Leo Cooper, London, 1975

Ryan, Cornelius, *A Bridge Too Far*, Book Club Associates, London, 1964

Saunders, Hilary St George, *The Red Beret – The Story of The Parachute Regiment At War 1940–1945*. Michael Joseph, London, 1950

Shapiro, Milton, *The Screaming Eagles – The 101st Airborne Division in World War II*. Julian Messner, New York, 1976

Stewart, I. McD. G., *The Struggle For Crete – A Story of Lost Opportunity 20 May–1 June 1941*. Oxford University Press, London, 1966

Tugwell, Maurice, *Airborne to Battle – A History of Airborne Warfare 1918–1971*. William Kimber, London, 1971

Urquhart, Brian, *A Life in Peace and War*. Weidenfeld & Nicolson, London, 1987

Weeks, John, *The Airborne Soldier*. Blandford, Poole, 1982

Wiggan, Richard, *Operation Freshman – The Rjukan Heavy Water Raid 1942*. William Kimber, London, 1986

Wilmot, Chester, *The Struggle For Europe*. Collins, London, 1952

Wood, Alan, *History of the World's Glider Forces*. Patrick Stephens, Wellingborough, 1990

INDEX